Loserville

How Professional Sports
Remade Atlanta—and
How Atlanta Remade
Professional Sports

CLAYTON TRUTOR

University of Nebraska Press

LINCOLN

Library of Congress Cataloging-in-Publication Data
Names: Trutor, Clayton, author.
Title: Loserville: how professional sports remade Atlanta—and
how Atlanta remade professional sports / Clayton Trutor.
Description: Lincoln: University of Nebraska Press, 2021. |
Includes bibliographical references and index.
Identifiers: LCCN 2021015300
ISBN 9781496225047 (hardback)
ISBN 9781496230089 (epub)
ISBN 9781496230096 (pdf)
Subjects: LCSH: Professional sports—Georgia—Atlanta—
History—20th century. | Sports franchises—Georgia—
Atlanta—History—20th century. | BISAC: Sports & Recreation /
History | History / United States / State &
Local / South (AL, AR, FL, GA, KY, LA, MS, NC, SC, TN, VA, WV)
Classification: LCC GV584.5.A85 T78 2021 | DDC
796.04/409758231—dc23
LC record available at https://lccn.loc.gov/2021015300

Set in Questa by Laura Buis.

For my family, for a lifetime of love and support

Games lose part of their charm when they are pressed into the service of education, social improvement, and character development.

—CHRISTOPHER LASCH

Contents

....

Illustrations

....

Acknowledgments

....

I HAVE CHALKED UP INNUMERABLE DEBTS TO FRIENDS,
family members, and colleagues as I completed this book. My
first thanks are to my literary agent, John Rudolph, at Dystel,
Goderich, and Bourret, who helped me find the right home
for this book. I couldn't ask for a better advocate or advisor.
I'd also like to thank the University of Nebraska Press for taking a chance on this project, in particular my editor, Rob Taylor. Just as instrumental in the making of this book are the
writers who offered me guidance as I tried to figure out how
to even pursue a book deal: Dan Epstein, Michael MacCambridge, Andy McCue, Mike Stadler, and Jack Gilden. Foremost among these writers is Greg Renoff, who didn't know
me from Adam but spent many hours of his time helping me
figure out how to put together a book proposal.

I owe particular thanks to my colleagues at Boston College,
especially my graduate school advisor, Lynn Johnson, whose
guidance and patience has made this project possible. Without
Lynn's stewardship, these chapters would still be boxes full
of photocopies sitting in my storage locker. I would also like
to thank Patrick Maney and Bruce Schulman for their time
and insights into my book. I also owe thanks to Ginny Rein-
burg, Jim O'Toole, Dana Sajdi, Seth Jacobs, David Northrup,
Stephen Schloesser sj, Kevin Kenny, Pete Cajka, David Quig-
ley, Jeff Dyer, Rebecca Rea, John Spiers, Lynn Lyerly, and Mike
Bailey in particular for their support during my time at BC.
I would also like to thank Vlad Perju and the Clough Center

for Constitutional Democracy for its generous support of my research expenses.

Among my Boston College peers, I must single out Seth Meehan and Ian Delahanty for their friendship throughout my tenure in the graduate program. An evening of all-you-can-eat riblets at the dearly departed Cleveland Circle Applebee's with Ian and Seth was the best professional development that money could buy. My first roommate in Boston, Jonathan Koefoed, became one of my best friends and intellectual compatriots. My life is far richer having him for a friend. Furthermore, I must thank Ted Miller for his singular friendship and generosity over the past decade. I found myself on many occasions during this process aspiring to be as good of a scholar and teacher as my dear friend Ted. My brother, best friend, and favorite historian, Johnny Trutor, has always been my foremost peer and mentor. My mother, Kathy Trutor, is my most-trusted copyeditor.

Before I came to Boston College, I was already indebted to a host of teachers and professors at Rice Memorial High School and the University of Vermont who encouraged me to pursue my intellectual interests. At Rice, I am especially grateful for the guidance of Lloyd Hulburd, Andrea Torello, Coach Tremblay, Judith Miles, Mari Miller, the late Coach Pearo, the late Brother Adrian, the late Sister Elizabeth, and, especially, the late Manfred Hummel, the finest teacher I ever had. At the University of Vermont I incurred just as great debts to Bogac Ergene, Patrick Hutton, Denise Youngblood, Melanie Gustafson, Kathy Purnell, Jan Feldman, Amani Whitfield, Gregory Gause, Robert Kaufman, Paul Searls, Kathy Morris, and the late Jerry Felt. In particular I offer thanks to Paul Searls, who convinced me that sports history is a legitimate area of scholarly inquiry. Recently my colleagues at Norwich University have been highly supportive of my work, particularly John "Doc" Broom and David Ulbrich.

The researching of this project brought me to archives across the country. I would like to thank the staffs at the Library of

Congress, the New York Public Library, the Georgia Tech Athletic Department, the University of Georgia Athletic Department, the Baseball Hall of Fame Archives, the Professional Football Hall of Fame Archives, Boston College Libraries, Harvard University Libraries, the University of Rochester Libraries, and the Kenan Research Library at the Atlanta History Center for their ceaseless energy in helping me track down research materials. On several occasions my father, Barry Trutor, traveled with me and helped me scan or copy research documents. I certainly hit the lottery when it came to a father. He's a phenomenal researcher and an even better dad. I would also like to thank the more than thirty interviewees who added texture and nuance to this story. The people of the American Southeast have been extraordinarily generous to me with their time and their recollections. The greatest resource I consulted in my research was the late Marshall Solomon, the quintessential Atlantan. On a daylong tour Marshall showed me his city, both past and present. The wisdom he imparted is the architecture of this project.

Finally, and foremost, I thank my friends and family for their love and support over the past few years. Friends, including Ian and Cam Boyd, Jonathan and Suzanne Koefoed, Reggie, Jared Kitchen, Tucker Wells, Greg Fulchino, Mike Abelson, and Phil Neuffer, have been great sounding boards as I've written this book. In recent years my colleagues at the Society for American Baseball Research (SABR) and SB Nation have provided me with a fantastic series of diversions. I would also like to thank my family friend Dennis Sullivan for selling the Trutors the multivolume *World Book Encyclopedia* back in 1989. These green-and-white volumes played no small role in transforming my brother and me into little historians.

No one will take as great pleasure in the completion of this book as my beloved family. As I complete this project I reflect on the memory of my grandmothers, Anna Champine and Genevieve Trutor, as well as my great-uncle Herman Champine, all of whom helped make me a historian and a writer. I am genuinely grateful for the love and support of my many dear relatives across Vermont and "across the lake" in New York's North Country. I offer my most profound thanks to Barry, Kathy, Johnny, Heather, and Eleanor. This book is dedicated to all of them. They are the most wonderful people I know. They have always been on my side.

Introduction

....

IN JULY 1975 THE EDITORS OF THE *ATLANTA CONSTITUTION*
ran a two-part front-page series entitled "Loserville, U.S.A."
Lewis Grizzard, the morning newspaper's special assignments
editor, who later made a name for himself as an up-market
Southern humorist, authored both pieces.[1] The provocatively
titled series detailed the futility of Atlanta's four professional
sports teams in the decade since the 1966 arrival of its first two
major league franchises: the Atlanta Braves of Major League
Baseball (MLB)'s National League (NL) and the Atlanta Falcons
of the National Football League (NFL). Two years later, in 1968,
the Hawks of the National Basketball Association (NBA) relocated to Atlanta from St. Louis, becoming the city's third major
professional sports franchise. In 1972 the Atlanta Flames, an
expansion team in the National Hockey League (NHL), began
play, making Atlanta one of only nine North American cities
with franchises in all four major professional sports leagues
and the first southern city to achieve this distinction. The
excitement surrounding the arrival of professional sports in
Atlanta soon gave way to widespread frustration and, eventually, widespread apathy toward its home teams. All four of
Atlanta's franchises struggled in the standings and struggled
to draw fans to their games. "Atlanta's decade long involvement with major-league sports," Grizzard wrote in the first
of his two philippics, "has been a major-league flop."[2]

The *Constitution* published the "Loserville" series during
the post-Watergate heyday of newspaper exposés of all vari-

ety of social and institutional corruption. By the mid-1970s, uncovering the shortcomings of Atlanta's major institutions had become as fashionable among the city's press corps as boosting the city's pursuit of professional sports franchises had been in the same circles a decade earlier. "We wanted to shake up the city, wake them up," Jim Minter, the editor of the *Constitution* at the time, said, reflecting on the "Loserville, U.S.A." series in 2013.[3] Despite the confrontational tone of Grizzard's pieces and his analytical dissection of the local franchises' failures on the field and at the box office, the "Loserville" stories exposed remarkably little to metropolitan Atlantans with even a passing interest in professional sports.

The year 1975 proved to be the nadir of a decade marked by the unmet expectations of the region's big league franchises. That July the Braves were in the midst of the franchise's worst season in nearly a quarter century, eventually falling forty and a half games behind the Cincinnati Reds in the NL West. The Braves had the league's second-worst attendance that season, averaging just 6,600 fans per game at Atlanta Stadium, a venue that could accommodate nearly 53,000 for baseball.[4] In fall 1974 the perennially hapless Falcons broke single-game and season-long NFL records for no-shows: fans who purchased tickets to a game but chose not to attend. A total of 143,488 tickets, or 35.1 percent of those sold by the Atlanta Falcons for the 1974 season, were purchased but went unused in their seven home dates.[5] During their 1974–75 season the Hawks drew slightly more than half of the NBA's per-game average attendance, while finishing twenty-nine games out of first place. The 1974–75 Flames finished last in their division and drew the second-worst average home attendance in their conference.

Professional sports in Atlanta had been, in the words of the *Chicago Tribune*'s Anthony Monahan, a "disappointing success."[6] Monahan, in an August 1966 profile of Atlanta for the *Tribune*'s Sunday magazine, described the Braves' first season in Georgia in those terms, citing the less-than-half-filled home stadium the team played to almost every night. That designation proved to be an apt description not only of the Braves' first campaign in the city but also more broadly of the metropolitan area's relationship to professional sports during its first decade. That reputation, decades later, continues to shape the national perception and local image of Atlanta's sporting culture. As recently as 2012, Rob Parker of espn.com characterized Atlanta as the "worst sports town in America," a sentiment that many other sports writers have echoed in the decades since Atlanta's own sportswriters took to calling their community "Loserville, U.S.A."[7]

This book examines the pursuit, advent, and popular response to professional sports in Atlanta during its first decade as a major league city. It explores the origins of what has become business-as-usual for moving professional sports franchises, acquiring expansion teams, and financing stadiums and arenas. Atlanta's concerted civic effort to build and buy its way into the big leagues became the model that all subsequent aspiring cities have adopted as they tried to lure teams to their communities. All too often the local response to these luxurious amenities has been as lukewarm as Atlanta's was in the 1960s and 1970s.

Loserville begins with the concerted effort by Atlanta's municipal elite to acquire professional sports franchises for their city, its burgeoning suburbs, and the southeastern United States as a whole. Mayor Ivan Allen Jr. (1962–70), who inherited the biracial governing coalition of William B. Hartsfield (1937–41, 1942–62), looked to build on Atlanta's reputation as a racially moderate, economically booming "City Too Busy to Hate." Allen, who oversaw the end of legal segregation during his first year in office, turned much of his attention to transforming Atlanta into a "Major League City." He popularized the phrase as a descriptor for the national stature he envisioned for Atlanta once it acquired the most prestigious of late-twentieth-century American institutions: professional sports franchises. Allen and his successor, Sam Massell (1970–74), worked closely with the "Big Mules," a term used in the local media to describe the core of Atlanta's corporate leadership, to secure generous public and private investments in professional sports between the mid-1960s and the early 1970s.[8]

Municipal leaders succeeded at luring four major professional sports franchises to Atlanta in a six-year period (1966–72) by securing significant public and private investments in two playing facilities in the city's Central Business District (CBD). Atlanta Stadium, which opened in 1965, served as the home field for MLB's Atlanta Braves and the NFL's Atlanta Falcons. The Omni Coliseum, which opened in 1972, became the home arena for the NHL's Atlanta Flames and the NBA's Atlanta Hawks.

Allen campaigned successfully for municipal financing of a multipurpose stadium, which was co-owned by the city of Atlanta and surrounding Fulton County. He revived the dormant Atlanta–Fulton County Stadium Authority, which facilitated the construction of $18 million Atlanta Stadium and lured the Milwaukee Braves baseball club to Georgia with a highly favorable lease. In addition, the completion of Atlanta Stadium convinced the NFL to award the city an expansion franchise, which became the Falcons. Several years later Massell negotiated a financing deal for a downtown coliseum with developer Tom Cousins, who had acquired NBA and NHL franchises to serve as the drawing cards to his prospective mixed-use development (MXD). The Stadium Authority floated $17 million in revenue bonds for construction of the 16,000-seat Omni Coliseum, which opened in 1972 and housed both of Cousins's franchises. In return, Cousins agreed to municipal ownership of the arena, pay for the building's upkeep, and an annual repayment plan which would reimburse the city in full for the construction bond.

Atlanta's successful pursuit of Major League teams, which was unprecedented among southern cities, took place in an increasingly competitive national marketplace for professional sports. Scholars who research the economic history of professional sports describe the expansion of the Major Leagues and the increasing geographic mobility of teams in the decades after World War II as "franchise free agency."[9] Atlanta took advantage of the newly flexible national sports market by making generous civic investments in two playing venues as a means of attracting franchises. *Loserville* uses both a local and a national lens to analyze how the emerging metropolis's negotiation of franchise free agency reshaped the culture, public policy, and urban planning of Atlanta, which was one of the first American cities to make the pursuit of professional sports a matter of government business. It will also show how Atlanta provided a model for other Sunbelt cities, such as San Diego, Tampa, and Phoenix, to pursue their own Major League teams, often luring clubs from economically struggling Rust Belt cities with lucrative offers of public support.

While the fate of most relocated and expansion franchises proved just as frustrating as those of Atlanta's teams, cities continued to pursue professional sports franchises as a matter of public policy. Many civic leaders believed the mere acquisition of a team was a prestigious civic end in itself, a sign of the noblesse oblige of an emergent ruling class in a rising Sunbelt city. Many of the entrepreneurs who invested in teams believed, often mistakenly, that they could manage a franchise better than other newcomers who had tried before them, underestimating the extent to which past experience in this highly specialized industry was indicative of future success.

Atlanta's civic elite, exemplified by the Big Mules, assumed that residents would embrace the newly acquired teams and transform their state-of-the-art playing facilities into the region's twin focal points of leisure and communal pride. Instead, Atlantans from all of the region's racial, socioeconomic, and residential clusters responded apathetically to the teams. The collective shrug with which Atlantans reacted to their new professional sports franchises demonstrated the growing cultural divergence that characterized life in the booming Sunbelt center over the course of the 1960s and 1970s.

Metropolitan Atlantans' shared indifference to their big league teams took place amid the social and political fracturing of the city's postwar, biracial governing regime. Professional sports proved an insufficient tie to bind the region's divergent communities together. During Atlanta's first Major League decade, the city's professional franchises provided neither a catalyst for national prestige nor the source of social cohesion that the civic elite had envisioned. Instead, the City Too Busy to Hate turned "Major League City" had become the divided metropolis known pejoratively as "Loserville, U.S.A." By casting their city as "Loserville," the local sports media contributed to this shift. Initially the most fervent boosters of the city's professional sports teams, they soon became the architects of the still-prevailing narrative that ignoring Atlanta's typically hapless teams was just part of being an Atlantan. Ironically, the emergence of the Loserville narrative served the purposes of civic leaders in other Sunbelt cities eager to invest in professional sports. These cities could employ the methods Atlanta used to acquire professional sports while believing simultaneously that the failure of Atlanta's teams to earn durable local support was reflective of circumstances specific to Atlanta.

Atlanta was not the first city whose leadership played an instrumental role in drawing a professional sports franchise to its community. Beginning in the early 1950s, municipalities offered the owners of professional sports franchises financial incentives to relocate their teams, mirroring efforts by local governments dating back to the nineteenth century to influence the movement of capital by granting public subsidies to corporations such as railroads and shipping lines. The earliest known example of a municipality offering public subsidies to lure a far-away professional sports franchise came in 1953. Baltimore convinced the owners of the St. Louis Browns baseball team to move to Maryland by building a second seating deck on their municipally owned stadium. This was the first of a dozen such ad hoc efforts by cities during the 1950s and early 1960s to entice a specific franchise or convince a professional sports league to grant them an expansion franchise through municipal largesse.[10]

The push by Atlanta's Big Mules to make their hometown a Major League City was something quite different. Never before had the leaders of an American city pursued professional sports franchises with the same concerted civic energy they employed when trying to lure corporate investment. Atlanta made the pursuit of professional sports franchises one of the foremost enterprises of its political and corporate leadership during the 1960s and early 1970s. Atlanta's coordinated civic boosting campaign to become a Major League City was the first such effort that aimed explicitly to bring all of the major professional sports leagues to one municipality. Atlanta's pioneering path to big league status transformed the acquisition of professional sports franchises into a grand civic enterprise.

Following in Atlanta's footsteps, political and corporate leaders in many southern and western cities partnered in the late twentieth century to procure major professional sports franchises by offering individual clubs and professional leagues tens of millions of dollars in public subsidies. More often than not, residents of Sunbelt cities responded apathetically to the teams that resulted from these civic investments. Rarely did these second-wave Sunbelt franchises become community pillars any more so than their predecessors in Georgia.

The ability of civic boosters in emerging cities like Atlanta to attract franchises with promises of public subsidies perpetuated the increasing movement of capital in postwar America away from the urban North and toward the business-friendly Sunbelt.[11] In the decades after World War II, the population growth experienced in the up-and-coming metropolitan areas of the South and West, improvements in the nation's transportation infrastructure, and the rapidly rising standard of living in many Sunbelt cities made boomtowns like Atlanta seem like desirable locations for professional sports franchises.[12] The willingness of Atlanta and its imitators to make massive public and private investments in professional sports jump-started the phenomenon of franchise free agency.[13]

At the end of World War II, major professional sports in America existed almost exclusively in center cities in the urban north. Over the course of the next five decades, new southern and western metropolises accumulated dozens of professional sports teams, either through the relocation of existing franchises or decisions by the professional leagues to grant them expansion franchises. Nearly two-thirds of the fifty professional sports franchise relocations and sixty-three expansions approved by major professional leagues between 1946 and 1999 placed teams south of the Mason-Dixon Line or west of the Mississippi River. Three-quarters of these franchise relocations and league expansions to the Sunbelt have taken place since 1966, the year that Atlanta secured its first two professional sports franchises.[14] The decentralization of American professional sports in the late twentieth century both shaped and reflected the shifting of the nation's political, economic, and cultural center of gravity to the suburbs and to the emerging Sunbelt.[15] Atlanta stood at the vanguard of this transformation of mass leisure in late-twentieth-century America by pioneering the kinds of corporatized civic boosting campaigns that other Sunbelt cities later used to lure professional sports franchises.

The divergence in Atlanta between the civic leadership's vision for professional sports and the residents' anemic response foreshadowed social divisions that would soon emerge in many Sunbelt cities. Beyond their private enthusiasms for spectator sports, Atlanta's civic leaders wanted to bring professional teams to their community for two primary reasons: to enhance the city's national prestige and to foster bonds of social cohesion. Despite its reputation as the City Too Busy to Hate, the Atlanta of the 1960s and 1970s was increasingly characterized by metropolitan divergence and regional fragmentation, its impoverished inner-city Black majority cut off from its sprawling, politically autonomous white suburbs.[16]

Civic leaders in Atlanta and every Sunbelt city that followed it into the Major Leagues desired the "arch-cachet of American cityhood" that came with the acquisition of professional sports franchises.[17] Specific to Atlanta's situation was the local leadership's belief that professional sports would constitute a self-perpetuating source of regional and metropolitan consensus. Sources of transmetropolitan communalism were sorely needed in a city abandoned by white residents unwilling to acquiesce to legally proscribed integration and avoided by the region's white-collar newcomers. Professional sports failed to live up to the city fathers' grand expectations that they would serve as a lasting source of civic pride and social cohesion. Rather than alleviating Atlanta's social divisions, professional sports made them more evident, both locally and nationally, as a result of the intense media focus cast on the new Major League City. Atlanta's elite anticipated that the city's professional teams would receive widespread and durable support from a grateful public, but metropolitan-area residents were not given to sacrificing their leisure time to acts of civic devotion. Metropolitan Atlantans' relationship to their new Major League teams was more that of consumers of a new leisure amenity than that of devotees to a long-tenured civic institution.[18]

Residents from diverse racial, social, and cultural backgrounds forged what would become the quintessential Sunbelt response to the acquisition of these leisure amenities. Atlantans proved to be discerning consumers, unwilling to simply support teams as an act of civic fealty. By and large, local consumers regarded the city's teams as mismanaged. They regarded attending a game at the city's downtown playing facilities as inconvenient and potentially unsafe. Relatively few Atlantans, whether natives or transplants, made the city's teams a focus of their leisure time. It was largely the investment of cable television entrepreneur Ted Turner, who became the owner of two of his primary sources of broadcasting, the Braves (1976) and Hawks (1977), that kept Atlanta a

Major League City beyond the mid-1970s. Locals remained indifferent to the franchises, while Turner lost millions of dollars operating them for the next two decades.

Within the marketplace of Metropolitan Atlanta, suburbanites displayed a definite preference for locally controlled social experiences situated in communities of their choosing while shunning the kind of social mixing that outings in downtown Atlanta entailed. Metropolitan Atlantans' fondness for intentional and ordered social experiences pointed toward an emerging set of cultural preferences in late-twentieth-century America. As the United States became a majority suburban nation, citizens of different racial and socioeconomic backgrounds shared less and less common physical space, especially during their leisure time. They also started to consume in progressively more dissimilar ways. This market segmentation came with a series of trade-offs. It legitimized the place in the consumer market for traditionally disempowered groups while simultaneously strengthening the cultural boundaries between social groups, which in turn further fragmented the society.[19]

Rather than embracing the cultural institutions with which the Big Mules adorned their city, residents engaged in leisure of their own making. For the mass of suburban whites, the desire to live, shop, and enjoy their free time within self-selecting communities proved paramount among their lifestyle choices. They displayed a strong desire for political and cultural independence from the city and its institutions, including its professional sports franchises and the facilities in which they played. Atlanta's new Black majority also demonstrated a cultural autonomy inextricably intertwined with its political autonomy. For African American residents of the city and its inner-ring suburbs, desegregation in its social and cultural forms proved to be less a matter of desiring spatial integration than being able to reside, work, and seek services where they wished and to come and go as they desired. Spaces like Atlanta Stadium and the Omni, which were neither fully public nor privatized, nor fully inside the hub of Black or white

Atlanta, made for unsuccessful civic centers of gravity. The agency that Atlantans displayed when they decided how to spend their leisure time helped to foster a local political culture characterized by regional fragmentation and metropolitan divergence.

During the early 1960s, Atlanta's elites convinced the region's disparate groups that they collectively needed professional sports to endow their city with prestige and to create a civic "center of gravity," as the editorialists at the *Atlanta Journal* described Atlanta Stadium on its opening weekend in 1965.[20] Initially, Atlantans embraced the idea of being Major League and provided each franchise with an ever-shorter honeymoon of enthusiasm. Once the novelty of each franchise wore off, Atlantans, by and large, withdrew their support from these new prestige institutions, preferring familiar leisure activities or those situated within controlled environments to those being offered in the center city. The lifestyle clusters that emerged in Atlanta and its expansive suburbs refused to acquiesce to the longstanding civic elite's visions of mass leisure for their region.

Atlantans, it turned out, preferred free agency in their leisure pursuits to an elite-driven metropolitan communalism built around their new home teams. The response of Atlantans to the arrival of professional sports in their city proved to be the archetypal response of Sunbelt residents to the Major Leagues' arrival in their respective communities. In city after city, a consensus emerged within the municipal leadership that the presence of the Major Leagues would serve social and cultural purposes beyond mere entertainment, including downtown development, civic pride, and the fostering of a sense of communal identity. Invariably, sports fans in these Sunbelt boomtowns—as they had in Atlanta—proved more aloof than local leaders had anticipated. By putting professional sports in the service of lofty civic goals, elites in Atlanta and numerous other Sunbelt cities set themselves up for disappointments as grand as the enterprises they undertook on behalf of their communities.

Loserville

1

Forward Atlanta

....

ON SEPTEMBER 22, 1961, ATLANTANS ELECTED IVAN ALLEN
Jr. as their fifty-second mayor. Allen won in a landslide, garnering 64 percent of the vote in a runoff against Lester Maddox. Neither candidate had ever held elective office, but the
city's standing political alliances coalesced around them rapidly, selecting the novices over three esteemed local legislators
also running in the primary. Despite their lack of experience,
both Allen and Maddox were well-known figures in Atlanta
with well-known political views. Allen, the president of the
Atlanta Chamber of Commerce and scion of the region's largest office-supply business, favored steady progress on civil
rights, winning him the support of virtually every African
American voter in the city. Atlanta's white business leaders
and professionals supported Allen with similar fervor. Not
only was Allen one of their own—a handsome, white-haired,
fifty-year-old, Georgia Tech graduate who belonged to the
city's best clubs and personified the modern southern patri-
cian. Allen also understood that Atlanta's postwar economic
boom was the product of investments by northern firms. To
keep the investments coming, Atlanta needed to maintain a
reputation for racial moderation relative to other southern
cities with similarly business-friendly climates.

In the eyes of Atlanta's professional classes, Lester Maddox
embodied that threat to Atlanta's reputation. The diminutive
and quick-tempered owner of a diner near the Georgia Tech
campus, Maddox gained notoriety in the 1950s by incorporating segregationist screeds into his weekly newspaper adver-

tisements for the restaurant. Maddox ran for mayor in 1957, losing a thoroughly uncompetitive race to William Hartsfield, the city's longtime mayor and the architect of the political coalition that went on to support Allen, whom Hartsfield had selected as his successor. Maddox's support came primarily from middle- and working-class whites who feared the integration of their neighborhoods and schools.

Some of the most virulent opposition to Maddox came from the very newspapers in which he advertised his restaurant. The editorial pages of Atlanta's three largest papers, the morning *Constitution*, the afternoon *Journal*, and the *Daily World*, the nation's longest-running Black-owned newspaper, were unanimous in their support for Allen. In the two weeks between the primary and runoff, each newspaper made its preferences known on an almost daily basis. The election of Allen, all three papers argued, would keep Atlanta on the path of peace and economic progress fostered by the Hartsfield administration, which had transformed Atlanta from a second-tier regional center into the economic hub of the Southeast.[1] The Atlanta media presented Allen as a force for social cohesion engaged in a righteous struggle against a regressive, bigoted tempter who encouraged citizens to embrace their worst impulses. If Maddox won the election, he would follow the course of *massive resistance*, undermining Atlanta's ability to lure northern capital and threatening its status as a "citadel of reason."[2]

Despite the ease with which Allen defeated Maddox in the runoff, the 1961 mayoral race had been Atlanta's most contentious in recent memory. Allen accused Maddox of being a reactionary race baiter with strong ties to the Ku Klux Klan. Maddox accused Allen of being a puppet of the Atlanta newspapers, a mouthpiece for the Chamber of Commerce, a Communist sympathizer, and a tool of "Auburn Avenue Bankers," a code word for the city's Black business community.[3] The contentiousness of the 1961 mayoral race was a product of more than the inflammatory accusations the candidates made about one another. It demonstrated the profound racial and class divisions that existed within the City Too Busy to Hate, a nickname for Atlanta popularized by Hartsfield. These divisions shaped the troubled context in which Metropolitan Atlanta would pursue, secure, and possess professional sports franchises.

Allen viewed professional sports as a potential counter to these divisions. He ran for mayor on a platform that explicitly tied Atlanta's Major League aspirations to its pursuit of civic unity. His Six Point Forward Atlanta Plan called for the construction of a municipal stadium suitable for baseball and football as well as an auditorium suitable for indoor professional sports, such as basketball. Allen envisioned professional sports as a means of promoting and unifying the rapidly decentralizing metropolitan region. His other proposals in the Six Point Plan, as it was commonly referred to, were focused on highway construction, mass transit, school desegregation, affordable housing, and a municipally orchestrated promotional campaign for the city. Each one of these planks was crafted with the same civic goals in mind. Allen wanted to cultivate unprecedented national prestige for Atlanta by fostering continued economic growth and endowing the city with amenities both necessary and befitting a city its size.

TO UNDERSTAND ALLEN'S IMPERATIVES, NAMELY HIS DESIRE to promote the city's continued economic development while cultivating a sense of civic unity, one need examine the political culture of Atlanta in the years before it became a Major League City, a nickname Allen fastened to the emerging metropolis during his campaign. The new mayor's pursuit of professional sports would not have been possible without the support of the durable political coalition cultivated by his predecessor at city hall. The alliance between Atlanta's business establishment and African American voters was an invention of William Hartsfield's political imagination. From the time he took office in 1937, Hartsfield put considerable energy into earning the trust of Atlanta's business establishment. The most pow-

erful of Atlanta's corporate leaders came to be known as the
Big Mules, a cluster of executives in the banking, manufacturing, retail, and real estate industries with close ties to the city's
political leadership. Among the Big Mules, Hartsfield counted
Coca-Cola's Robert Woodruff and Mills B. Lane Sr. of the Citizens and Southern National Bank (c&s) among his closest advi-
sors.[4] During his early years in office, Hartsfield won over voters
outside of Atlanta's boardrooms by developing a reputation as a
reformer of the city's old ward-based political patronage system
and presenting himself as a civic booster. The changing legal,
demographic, and political circumstances of post–World War
II Atlanta forced Hartsfield to change his strategy.

The invalidation by the Fifth Circuit Court of Appeals of
Georgia's white-only primary system in the 1946 *Chapman
v. King* decision opened the door to wider Black participation
in Atlanta's electoral politics. A voter-registration drive led
by the Atlanta Negro Voters League in the aftermath of the
Chapman decision made African Americans an immediate
political force in the city. In 1940 approximately 3,000 African Americans out of a population of 105,000 were registered
to vote. Thus, one-third of Atlanta's population accounted
for less than five percent of its voters. By the time of the 1949
mayoral race, African Americans constituted 27.2 percent of
the city's electorate with more than 21,000 registered voters.[5]
Hartsfield adapted quickly to the demographic transformation of the Atlanta electorate. He won the endorsement of the
Atlanta Negro Voters League and the *Daily World* for the 1949
mayoral race by agreeing to hire more Black police officers,
increasing the number of Black city employees, and expanding the amount of land available in the still-segregated city
for both publicly and privately owned Black housing. Hartsfield won 82.5 percent of the African American vote in the 1949
mayoral primary, enabling him to earn a majority of the votes
and avoid a runoff election.[6]

For the remainder of Hartsfield's tenure, African Americans comprised a substantial part of his political base and

governing coalition. In the 1953 and 1957 mayoral elections,
Blacks continued their bloc voting for Hartsfield. In return,
he accepted the demands of African American leaders for
the gradual though often symbolic desegregation of Atlanta's public spaces and facilities, as well as improvements to
the quality of life in Black neighborhoods, especially in the
form of public-works projects. Paved roads, street lights, and
modern sanitation came to many of the Black neighborhoods
west of downtown for the first time during the 1950s.[7] When
Atlanta annexed eighty-two unincorporated square miles of
Fulton County in 1952, Hartsfield facilitated the efforts of
Black entrepreneurs to build dozens of self-contained Black
housing subdivisions and apartment complexes on the new
western periphery of the city.[8]

Hartsfield did not simply seek out the counsel of Black leaders in the weeks before an election. He worked closely with
Atlanta's powerful Black leadership, a long-established and
widely accepted group of prosperous businessmen, professionals, and religious leaders, in a continuous, behind-the-scenes
renegotiation of their covenant. Atlanta's most influential Black
leaders were the cofounders of the Atlanta Negro Voters League,
civil rights attorney Austin Thomas "A. T." Walden and longtime political activist John Wesley Dobbs. Walden and Dobbs
had the most direct contact with Hartsfield among the figures
in Atlanta's Black leadership. They had taken the lead in organizing Black voter registration during the 1940s and cemented
the relationship between Black leaders and Hartsfield in the
run-up to the 1949 election. Walden and Dobbs's Atlanta Negro
Voters League kept its base informed about the candidates in
citywide and statewide races. They made sure that incum-
bents knew Black voters would hold them accountable for legislative actions that conflicted with their group interests. In
the days before an election, the Atlanta Negro Voters League
directed highly effective get-out-the-vote drives.[9]

The political power exercised by Walden and Dobbs was a
product not only of the vastly increased number of Black vot-

ers in Atlanta but also of the institutional strength of the city's African American community, which predated the formation of the Hartsfield coalition by decades. Beginning in the 1920s, Atlanta earned a reputation as the American city that provided African Americans with the greatest number of economic and educational opportunities. The 1929 formation of the Atlanta University Center, a consortium of the city's Black colleges and universities located southwest of downtown, made Atlanta the hub of American Black higher education. Opened in the late 1930s, the Fountain Heights subdivision near Atlanta University was one of the nation's first privately-financed housing developments designed explicitly for Black middle-class homebuyers. The bungalows in Fountain Heights afforded Black professionals the same large yards and modern utilities that white middle-class homebuyers had come to expect in their suburban developments.[10]

To the east of downtown, Auburn Avenue, dubbed "Sweet Auburn" by Dobbs, became the commercial center of Black Atlanta. Retail outlets, professional offices, theaters, and hotels lined Auburn Avenue, which *Fortune* in 1956 called "the richest negro street in the world."[11] Sweet Auburn housed several of the largest Black-owned businesses in the United States, including the Atlanta Life Insurance Company and the Citizens Trust Bank. Alongside the accumulated Black-owned capital on Auburn Avenue were some of Black America's most revered institutions, including the *Daily World* and churches that housed some of the most esteemed pastors in the nation. The names of the Ebenezer Baptist Church, Wheat Street Baptist Church, and Big Bethel African Methodist Episcopal Churches were well known in Black communities across the country. The core of Atlanta's Black leadership emerged from the institutions of the Atlanta University Center and Sweet Auburn. The leaders included Citizens Trust Bank President Lorimer D. Milton, Morehouse College President Benjamin Mays, Rev. Martin Luther "Daddy" King Sr. of the Ebenezer Baptist Church, Atlanta Life Insurance executive Jesse Hill Jr., *Daily World* publisher Cornelius Adolphus "C. A." Scott, Atlanta University President Rufus E. Clement, and Rev. William Holmes Borders of the Wheat Street Baptist Church.

Sweet Auburn, the Big Mules, and the mayor formed a tripartite system of civic negotiation that local political observers referred to as the "Atlanta Way."[12] All sides in this arrangement drove a hard bargain. Hartsfield adopted an explicitly gradualist approach to the negotiation of matters related to desegregation, which he described as "go-slow, go-easy, but go."[13] Leaders in the Atlanta Chamber held divergent views on the proper speed and scale of integration. Similarly, there was disagreement among the city's Black leadership on the extent to which they should accommodate the pace of reform favored by Hartsfield and the Big Mules. Collectively, this top-down system of civic readjustment created a flexible social consensus whose boundaries corresponded to the recognized contours of their community.

Ivan Allen Jr. was an ideal candidate to replace Hartsfield as the leader of Atlanta's biracial governing coalition. For one thing, he had at least as much name recognition as any other mayoral candidate. Atlantans had been familiar with the name "Ivan Allen" for decades, not only from the office-supply business that bore his name but also from the candidate's father, Ivan Allen Sr., the founder and namesake of the company. In addition to his success in business, Ivan Allen Sr. had been one of the city's most vocal boosters since the 1920s. He spearheaded that decade's original Forward Atlanta promotional campaign, which touted the city's first-rate transportation infrastructure, its abundant supply of nonunion labor, its welcoming business community, and its short winters in national publications. The work of Ivan Allen Sr. and his contemporaries in the Atlanta Chamber attracted millions of dollars in capital investment from the urban North. In the four years after the launch of the 1926 media campaign, Atlanta lured 679 new branch offices, manufacturing facilities, and warehouses to the city, adding more than seventeen thousand jobs to the local economy.[14]

The Forward Atlanta campaign of the 1920s transformed Atlanta into the Southeast's economic hub. When Ivan Allen Sr. started raising funds for the campaign, the list of Atlanta's corporate giants began and ended with Coca-Cola. By the time his son ran for mayor in 1961, Atlanta had one of the nation's most diversified economic bases. The reputation Atlanta had earned as a business-friendly city served it well in the intervening decades. Following the economic stagnation of the 1930s, Atlanta flourished during World War II as a distribution and defense-manufacturing center, particularly of airplanes. The influx of federal spending to Atlanta during the war undergirded further development of its aeronautical industry during the 1940s and 1950s. Atlanta Municipal Airport grew into the nation's fourth-busiest airport by 1960 as a result of extensive federal and municipal investments and its early adoption of numerous aviation-related technologies. At the same time, four of the Southeast's ten largest banks were based in Atlanta. Between 1940 and 1960, the size of Atlanta's manufacturing workforce doubled to more than eighty thousand. Thousands of hourly workers earned their livings at Ford's and General Motors's Atlanta assembly plants, which opened soon after World War II. Atlanta also retained its historic status as a ground-transportation hub by expanding its rail and trucking services. At the time of the 1961 race, Atlanta was home to branches of more than 350 of the Fortune 500 companies and led all American cities in annual job growth.[15]

The younger Allen came of age in the Atlanta that his father's generation of corporate and political leaders had transformed into an economic powerhouse through a combination of cooperative boosting and municipal consensus-building. Deal-making and the accommodation of differing interests were the foundations of Allen's political common sense. He was self-consciously a product of Atlanta's civic establishment and proud of all it had accomplished for the city. Allen became a leading figure in the new generation of politically savvy, racially moderate businessmen who came to power in the Atlanta Chamber after the cementing of the Hartsfield political coalition. Through personal experience, Allen and his peers understood the contours of the city's biracial electoral coalition. They participated directly in the negotiating of Atlanta's governing consensus during the last years of the Hartsfield administration. This group included future Chamber president Opie Shelton, Coca-Cola bottler Arthur Montgomery, and c&s Bank scion Mills Lane Jr., all of whom would play prominent roles in the making of Major League Atlanta during Allen's two terms as mayor. This new generation of Big Mules proved adept at working with Mayor Hartsfield to balance Atlanta's different interest groups: African American civic leaders pushing for more opportunities, economic security, and tangible quality-of-life improvements for their community; corporate leaders who wanted to ensure the continued growth of the region's economy; working-class whites in search of plant and warehouse jobs; and white homeowners who wanted to maintain residential segregation in the city and its expanding suburbs. The Atlanta Chamber's pragmatic approach to civic affairs provided much of the economic clout and political influence behind Hartsfield's vision of a City Too Busy to Hate. They tied the rapid economic growth of Atlanta not only to its favorable business climate but also to its image as a progressive oasis in the segregated South.[16]

Ivan Allen cemented his status as the candidate of choice for Atlanta's African American leadership during his 1961 tenure as Atlanta Chamber president. Despite his familiarity with the Atlanta Way, many Black leaders were suspicious of Allen the politician based on his one previous foray into office-seeking. In 1954 Allen ran unsuccessfully for governor on a segregationist platform. He was not alone in this stance. Every candidate in the 1954 Georgia gubernatorial contest favored segregation and expressed their opposition to the *Brown v. Board of Education* decision handed down by the U.S. Supreme Court earlier that year. Allen, though, was the only one of them seeking the office of mayor of Atlanta in 1961. By his actions and his words, though, Allen changed many minds among the city's Black leadership in the months before the September 1961 mayoral primary. Over the opposition of many merchants in the Atlanta Chamber, Allen negotiated the desegregation of downtown stores and lunch counters with the city's Black leadership in March 1961, ending two years of sit-ins and demonstrations by young civil rights activists at Rich's department store. Many white customers cancelled their accounts at Rich's to protest the agreement.[17]

In the weeks before the September primary, the Atlanta Negro Voters League interviewed every mayoral candidate except Lester Maddox to determine their endorsement. Allen excelled in his interview, expressing his support for the complete desegregation of public facilities, an expedited schedule for school integration, nondiscrimination clauses in city contracts, and the expansion of municipal employment opportunities for African Americans. The Atlanta Chamber president also campaigned more openly and vigorously for Black votes than any previous candidate for mayor. He held campaign events in a dozen different Black churches in the lead-up to the primary to demonstrate his commitment to racial progress in the city. Allen won the endorsement of Black Atlanta's traditional institutional power bases: the Atlanta Negro Voters League, the local branch of the National Association for the Advancement of Colored People (NAACP), and the *Daily World*. He swept the endorsements of Atlanta's longest-tenured Black leaders, including A. T. Walden, John Wesley Dobbs, Martin Luther King Sr., and Atlanta Life's Jesse Hill Jr. State Representative Milton M. "Muggsy" Smith presented the only major challenge to Allen for Black votes in the primary. Smith won the primary endorsement of youth-oriented civil rights organizations such as the Student Nonviolent Coordinating Committee (SNCC) and the Southern Christian Leadership Conference (SCLC) on the strength of his legislative record of racial progressivism and his attacks on Allen's segregationist past. Despite the challenge presented by Smith, Allen's standing with Black Atlanta's long-established power base enabled him to win more than two-thirds of the African American vote. The SCLC and SNCC offered Allen their unequivocal endorsements for the runoff election against Maddox.[18]

"IF YOU LOVE YOUR FAMILY, CHURCH, HOME, SCHOOL AND Your City," read one of Lester Maddox's campaign advertisements, "Vote for Lester Maddox! His Stand Is the Same as Yours."[19] The arch-segregationist Maddox ran for mayor in 1961 with the same approach he used in 1957. He ran not to balance the city's disparate racial and socioeconomic groups but as the advocate of a constellation of frequently overlapping identities in Atlanta. The vast majority of Maddox's supporters were white, middle- and working-class homeowners in south and west Atlanta who opposed the integration of their neighborhoods and the institutions they patronized. Most of them belonged to conservative Protestant denominations, and many of them supported strong restrictions on the sale and consumption of alcohol. A majority of them were migrants from rural Georgia or the descendants of migrants from earlier in the twentieth century. Displaced by the mechanization of southern agriculture or discouraged by the hardscrabble life of a tenant farmer, they came to Atlanta to work in its textile mills or its industrial plants or distribution centers. The growth of Atlanta proper from a city of sixty-five thousand in 1890 to one of nearly a half million residents by 1960 was due in large part to the migration of rural white Georgians to the city.[20]

"The Question is," Maddox wrote in one of his wordy 1961 campaign advertisements, "will we move Backward to Honor, Decency and Government by the People in Atlanta . . . or will we move Forward to forced racial integration and amalgamation of the races as supported by the Atlanta papers and my opponent (the people's opponent) in this race?"[21] Maddox won over "the little people," as he nicknamed his voter base with more than a hint of irony, through his stinging attacks on the alleged hypocrisies and efforts at social engineering by Atlanta's elites in government, the media, and big business. Quick-witted and adept in the theatrical, Maddox practiced a brand of southern populism that dated back to the late nineteenth century in Georgia. Like the founding father of Georgia populism, Tom Watson, Maddox appealed to white nationalism and a producerist ethic that he steeped in the eschatological language of his Baptist upbringing.[22] When explaining his political views, Maddox made use of a set of insights and an idiom that made sense to many blue-collar Atlantans. He spoke from their perspective because he had led a life much like theirs.

The 1954 *Brown v. Board* decision, which declared segregated education unconstitutional, politicized Maddox. Soon thereafter, he began politicking for massive resistance to either federally or locally initiated efforts at desegregating public institutions or places of public accommodation. Maddox made his views on desegregation widely known in the regular "Pickrick Says" advertisements he placed in the city's newspapers. Half a column in length, the advertisements predated Maddox's politicization. In their earlier form, they were the promotional equivalent of a vanity license plate. They included a headshot of Maddox, positive comments from customers to which the restaurateur responded, and the prices of his weekly two- and three-piece fried-chicken dinner specials. By the mid-1950s, Pickrick Says columns consisted primarily of commentary on federal efforts to enforce *Brown v. Board*, "racial amalgamation," alleged corruption in local politics, and the domestic threat posed by communism. The *Journal* and the *Constitution* tired of Maddox's antics and threatened to increase the advertising rates they charged him. Both papers backed down when Maddox threatened to expose their decision.[23] Maddox and the Atlanta papers had an adversarial relationship for the remainder of his public life. During the 1961 campaign, *Constitution* editor Eugene Patterson went so far as to tip off Allen's campaign to a controversial Maddox advertisement before it ran so that the Allen camp had more time to plan its response.[24]

Maddox found his way into more formal politics by founding the pro-segregation organization GUTS (Georgians Unwilling to Surrender), which focused much of its energy on preventing school desegregation. In 1957 Maddox ran for mayor for the first time, challenging Hartsfield in the primary on an anti-desegregation and anti-cronyism platform. Hartsfield responded to Maddox's pointed attacks by emphasizing the political pragmatism of his racially moderate stances. Cities with militantly segregationist reputations, like Little Rock, Birmingham, and Montgomery, were not luring outside investments like racially moderate Atlanta. Racial peace in Atlanta, Hartsfield argued, would ensure its continued economic progress.[25] Atlantans reelected the longtime mayor by a wide margin, but Maddox tapped sufficiently into populist resentments against the status quo to earn 37 percent of the vote. Rather than discouraging Maddox, the result encouraged him to concentrate more of his efforts on politics. The growing popularity of his Saturday Pickrick Says advertisements boosted weekend newspaper sales. His pro-segregation activism with GUTS also kept him in the public eye. In many respects, Maddox never stopped campaigning for mayor. He kept his one-man show going full force until it was time to file paperwork for his 1961 campaign.

"ATLANTA," THE AFTERNOON *JOURNAL* EDITORIALIZED, "voted for peace and progress" in its 1961 mayoral election, endorsing Ivan Allen and continuity with William Hartsfield's governing coalition by a nearly two-to-one margin.[26] Allen described the victory as a "mandate for me to move Atlanta forward."[27] The Atlanta media seconded the mayor-elect's interpretation of the result, regarding it as a renunciation of the kind of divisive racial politics that "could have greatly hampered our city." "Atlanta," the *Journal*'s editors went on the say, "declared herself too progressive to become sidetracked from its trip to the top, too wise to become ensnared in trouble and hatred."[28] The leaders of Atlanta's governing coalition were well represented at Allen's election celebration. William Hartsfield and A. T. Walden, among others, attended the gathering and praised the result as proof of Atlanta's civic unity.

The civic establishment's understandably optimistic assessments of the results of the mayoral race overlooked the divisiveness that the vote reflected in the city. Allen won 64 percent of the vote, a slightly higher percentage than Hartsfield in 1957, but twelve thousand more Atlantans voted for Maddox and against the city's governing coalition in 1961 than in 1957. More than one hundred thousand Atlantans voted in the 1961 runoff, a record turnout that surpassed the 1957 mark by nearly a third. Ivan Allen won as a result of the near unanimous support he received from the Black community. He received 99.4 percent of the vote in the city's predominately Black wards. Maddox won a slight majority of the white vote, a feat he had not accomplished in 1957. Allen received more than 80 percent of the vote in upper-income white neighborhoods, but less than 30 percent of the vote in lower-income white areas. Maddox won two of the city's eight wards, both located in working class South Atlanta.[29]

Ivan Allen inherited the Atlanta that came into being during the Hartsfield administration. He came to power as the representative of a governing coalition that would fracture over the course of the next fifteen years as the demographics of Atlanta proper and its expanding metropolitan area changed. White flight, the suburbanization of middle-class Blacks, and the continued influx of outsiders to the counties surrounding the city reconfigured Metropolitan Atlanta into an expansive region in which the vast majority of citizens chose to distance themselves from the experiences of its urban core. By 1960, fewer than half of the residents and fewer than half of the jobs in the metropolitan area were located in the city of Atlanta.

Over the course of the next decade, these trends accelerated to the point that less than a third of the people and jobs in the metropolitan area resided in Atlanta proper.

To combat the decentralization and fragmentation of Metropolitan Atlanta, Mayor Allen pursued a set of policies aimed at securing Atlanta's continued prosperity by further boosting its national reputation while streamlining the relationship between the city and its suburbs. In keeping with the Six Point Plan, he incorporated his desire to bring professional sports to Atlanta into his larger vision for the city. Major League status would not only serve as a source of prestige and cohesion but also draw suburbanites into the city, ensuring that the center city, the traditional anchor of the region's social and commercial life, was not left behind amid the suburban boom. Allen relied on a like-minded civic establishment to help bring his vision to life. Atlanta's leadership pursued a set of policies in the 1960s and 1970s that sought to retain the city's status as the center of gravity in the booming metropolitan area. They endorsed a number of expensive civic investments aimed at making downtown the focal point of leisure and commerce in the region. The vision Atlanta's establishment articulated came straight from the reform program Allen proposed first as Chamber president and then as a mayoral candidate.

IN THE YEAR BEFORE HE BECAME CHAMBER PRESIDENT, Ivan Allen researched and wrote a broad plan for metropolitan development entitled the Six Point Forward Atlanta Plan. Allen borrowed the well-known "Forward Atlanta" catchphrase from the highly successful civic boosting campaign his father spearheaded during the 1920s. The Chamber approved Allen's plan unanimously in December 1960 as the organization's platform for the coming decade. It published the plan as a white paper in early 1961, months before Hartsfield's decision not to seek another term. In a move orchestrated by the outgoing mayor and his closest confidants in the Atlanta Chamber, Allen declared his candidacy within days of Hartsfield's announcement. The Six Point Plan served as a ready-made platform for Allen's immediately high-profile campaign.[30]

Allen and his contemporaries believed the 1960s would be the decade that Atlanta became a "National City." In the white paper, he defined National City as an urban center that exerts "a powerful economic force far beyond its normal regional functions."[31] The Chamber regarded Atlanta's climb to National City status as the economic foundation for its ascension to Major League City prestige. The policies endorsed in the Six Point Plan were aimed at helping the city cement its economic position as a National City and attain the cultural stature of a Major League City. The Six Point Plan called for the timely completion of all approved expressway projects; large scale rapid transit accessible throughout the metropolitan area; the gradual desegregation of Atlanta schools; further federal and local investment in urban renewal, with a particular focus on providing housing for the city's growing African American population; the construction of an auditorium-coliseum and a stadium suitable for large-scale public gatherings, particularly sporting events; and a new Forward Atlanta national advertising campaign financed by local businesses.[32]

In many respects, Allen's platform offered voters a continuation of the policies of Mayor Hartsfield. Allen regarded continued economic growth as the driving force behind all progress in the city. He argued that Atlanta's economic growth in the 1960s was predicated on its national image as a racially tolerant city, the upgrading of its infrastructure and amenities to the standards of other major cities, and the coordination of economic and political activity across the metropolitan area. Collectively, these elements would guarantee Atlanta's continued reputation as a business-friendly city, which in turn would lure more investment to the area. He promised to redouble the city's already extensive efforts to pursue outside capital and federal dollars.[33] "I am willing to personally go anywhere and talk to anybody about the superiority of Atlanta and the practical advantages of moving plants, offices, services, and people to our city," Allen told the audience in his 1962 inaugural address.[34] Allen's description of Atlanta's pursuit of outside capital was a more refined rendition of the same idea that Hartsfield expressed to *Newsweek*'s William Emerson in 1959. "We roll out the red carpet for every damn Yankee who comes in here with two strong hands and some money," Hartsfield told the reporter.[35]

The expressway-building and rapid-transit programs endorsed in Allen's Six Point Plan aimed to alleviate the evident inefficiencies in the region's transportation system. By 1960 suburban commuters encountered daily traffic jams on the city's already outmoded Northeast and South Expressways. Traffic came to a standstill every morning and evening when the roads merged into the I-75/I-85 Downtown Connector. Several major expressway construction programs had been approved by state and local bodies, including a proposed highway perimeter around the city, known as I-285, but the financing and political will to execute these plans had yet to materialize. Atlanta's mass-transit situation was even more problematic. The city and its inner-ring suburbs relied on the privately owned, recently desegregated Atlanta Transit Company (ATC), a bus and trolleybus service, for its mass transit. Less than half of the metropolitan area's population had access to the service. By 1960 Blacks constituted nearly 60 percent of the ATC's ridership, leading some white passengers to abandon mass transit.[36] The formation of an alternative, metropolitan-wide system would take some time. Creating a multicounty metropolitan transit authority required the approval of the State General Assembly, a first step that Allen endorsed in the Six Point Plan as a prelude to future battles over financing and voter approval for the system.[37]

Allen's plan also called for immediate action by city agencies on urban-renewal programs. Atlanta began its federally subsidized urban renewal during the 1950s. Federal and local agencies excelled at slum clearance in Atlanta during the Hartsfield era, removing more than nine hundred acres worth of blighted homes and commercial properties, much of it on lots adjacent to the city's CBD. As in many cities, urban renewal in Atlanta was characterized as "negro removal" by its critics, since few new units of affordable housing were being built to replace homes destroyed in the name of slum clearance. Collectively, 1950s and 1960s urban-renewal programs in Atlanta displaced sixty-seven thousand residents, mainly African Americans. At the time of Ivan Allen's election, Atlanta's Black population, which constituted 39 percent of the city's total, lived on 17 percent of the city's land, in effect forcing Black residents displaced by urban renewal to seek out housing in already densely packed neighborhoods or to leave the city. During the 1950s, there had been a boom in home-building in designated "negro expansion areas" in newly annexed land on the far western side of the city. The homes in these subdivisions were aimed at middle- and upper-middle-class Black homebuyers, not the primarily lower-income African Americans displaced by slum clearance from the neighborhoods that ringed downtown Atlanta. New home prices in Collier Heights Estates, the most exclusive of these far west side neighborhoods, averaged $18,500, nearly five times the average annual income of a Black family in the city. Allen's plan for urban renewal focused on the opportunities it provided for two prongs of his electoral base: African Americans and the city's business class. When candidate Allen described his plans for urban renewal, he prioritized the construction of additional low-income housing for African American residents. He also made it clear that he considered recently cleared urban renewal land to be a legitimate space for large scale public or private developments that would be an obvious benefit to the community. The definition of an obvious community benefit would soon be stretched to include municipal stadiums.[38]

By the time Ivan Allen took over in City Hall, Atlanta had succeeded at keeping its public schools open while others in the South were closing to avoid court-mandated desegregation. Atlanta, unlike its peer cities in the region, actually began the process of desegregating its schools, ever so gradually. The 1959 *Calhoun v. Latimer* decision required Atlanta, which had resisted federal court mandates along with the rest of the state, to submit a desegregation plan within one year. The Georgia General Assembly intervened in the matter, forming the Sibley Commission to study the opinions of Georgians on the matter of school desegregation. The commission held a series of highly contentious hearings around the state. Within the city of Atlanta, formal organizations on all sides of the issue lobbied the commission. Lester Maddox's GUTS and the more sedate Metropolitan Association for Segregated Education (MASE) pushed for Atlanta to close its public schools rather than desegregate them, which would have been in keeping with the state's long-term policy of massive resistance to federal intervention on civil rights issues. An umbrella group known as OASIS (Organizations Assisting Schools in September) lobbied the commission to follow the mandates and to keep the schools open. The Atlanta Chamber played a major role in persuading many policy makers, including a majority of the Sibley Commission, to support open schools. In January 1961, the General Assembly adopted the commission's recommendation to keep the state's schools open.[39]

Atlanta's public schools were officially desegregated less than two weeks before the September 1961 mayoral primary. On August 30, 1961, nine Black students attended their first day of classes at four previously all-white Atlanta high schools as part of a highly orchestrated, covertly executed operation that took place without any serious incidents that day or in any of the succeeding days.[40] The success of Atlanta's fall 1961 school desegregation plan was a public-relations coup for the city, for its outgoing mayor, and for the Atlanta Chamber.

The Six Point Forward Atlanta Plan led to a renewal of the storied civic-boosting campaign that served as its namesake. In 1961 the Atlanta Chamber initiated a new three-year promotional effort, a "program of education, advertising, and research to carry the Atlanta story all over the nation."[41] Allen kicked off the fundraising drive for the new Forward Atlanta campaign that brought in more than $1.6 million in donations from the city's business community. He hired a full-time professional staff to conduct research for the campaign and recruited several Big Mules to work with him behind the scenes at convincing corporate leaders from other parts of the country to open branches in Atlanta. Like its 1920s predecessor, the Forward Atlanta campaign of the 1960s placed numerous advertisements in national publications touting the benefits of doing business in their economically vibrant and now racially progressive city.[42]

The agenda Ivan Allen and the Atlanta Chamber pursued during the early 1960s built onto the framework of urban development crafted by William Hartsfield's generation of city leaders. But Allen's vision deviated from Hartsfield's when it came to the issue of civic luxuries. The new mayor believed that the city government and the corporate community should strongly support the construction of a stadium and an auditorium-coliseum that would soon be anchored by the professional sports teams they would inevitably lure to Atlanta. Like the leadership in many New South cities, Atlanta's 1960s political and economic establishment invested large-scale construction projects, such as Atlanta Stadium, with deep social and psychological meaning, transfiguring the work of planners and contractors into referendums on the merit of their community. Allen regarded the luring of professional sports teams to Atlanta as a political imperative. The public, Allen wrote in the Six Point Plan, desired the entertainment and cultural offerings of a first-tier American city. Moreover, Allen, affirming the long-held sentiments of many of the Big Mules, considered professional sports teams to be an amenity befitting a city of Atlanta's economic stature. The Big Mules believed that professional sports provided cities with an unparalleled showpiece and source of civic unity. They also believed that the arrival of professional sports in a community demonstrated that city's momentum and helped to spur further investment in the area.[43]

Many of Atlanta's most prominent civic boosters had long been calling for the construction of a large-scale municipal stadium. For years, columnists on the sports pages of the *Constitution* and the *Journal* had editorialized on behalf of building a stadium and attracting Major League teams to the city. All the nation's professional sports leagues coveted Atlanta. Many Big Mules reported that sports executives had told them Atlanta would get its share of teams once it built playing facilities with modern amenities and sufficiently large seating capacities. The Georgia General Assembly even intervened to help Atlanta build a stadium, creating the Atlanta–Fulton County Stadium Authority in March 1960, a public corporation charged with financing, planning, and building a stadium if representatives of Atlanta and surrounding Fulton County chose to do so. The primary person holding up Atlanta's pursuit of professional sports was Hartsfield. The mayor manufactured a series of delays that prevented the Stadium Authority from convening during the final twenty months of his tenure.[44]

Mayor Hartsfield, in fact, stymied every attempt to involve the city in the planning, financing, or construction of a large stadium or arena. Hartsfield regarded sports and leisure as a private matter beyond the scope of municipal government. He was not opposed to private entities pursuing professional teams or making their own financial arrangements to build a stadium, though he feared that big league sports would bring organized crime to the city, namely bookmakers working with the Dixie Mafia. Hartsfield wanted his city government to avoid the nuisances that entanglements in stadium politics would cause for the administration.[45]

In a more general sense, Hartsfield preferred pothole politics to grand projects. He believed tax dollars should be spent on tangible civic needs or spent delivering targeted benefits to specific constituencies. He thought municipal capital expenditures should be focused on infrastructural improvements to the city's public and economic functions, not on civic luxuries, no matter how much the project's boosters touted its economic benefits. From the outset of his political career, Hartsfield's pet project had been the city's airport, which would eventually be renamed in his honor. Public investments in forward-looking aviation technology, continuous improvements to its terminal, and an aggressive expansion of its capacity made Atlanta Municipal Airport an engine for the city's growing prosperity. Spending millions of dollars to build stadiums for nonexistent teams struck Hartsfield as an impractical public expenditure.[46]

IN THE SUMMER OF 1963, ALLEN WAS THE ONLY SOUTHERN politician to testify before the U.S. Senate on behalf of the legislation that became the Civil Rights Act of 1964. He displayed striking courage in speaking on behalf of the measure, which was wildly unpopular throughout the South and in many sections of his city. Atlanta's mayor, though, did not present his efforts or those of the city's leaders to desegregate their community as heroic. Instead, Allen portrayed the gradual desegregation of Atlanta as the product of pragmatic decisions by men whose primary business was business, not the policing of the archaic social boundaries of the Jim Crow South. This was partially a rhetorical device on Allen's part, one that had been employed by civic leaders in Atlanta for decades to convince undecided residents of the wisdom of desegregation. More broadly, though, the practicality of racial moderation in public affairs had become the common sense of Atlanta's postwar governing consensus. "Having embraced realism in general, we set out to solve specific problems by local cooperation between people of good will and good sense representing both races," Allen said before listing Atlanta's civil rights successes during his year and a half in city government as well as those accomplished during Hartsfield's administration.[47] Allen spoke of Hartsfield's successful desegregation of public transportation, public schools, city libraries, and municipal golf courses.[48] Allen then ticked off his own list of accomplishments as mayor, which included a January 1962 executive order banning discrimination in all of Atlanta's public facilities, a March 1962 ban on discrimination in downtown theaters, and, in the month before his testimony before the Senate, a June 1963 agreement to desegregate the hotels, restaurants, and shops of downtown Atlanta, which extended a voluntary desegregation of downtown lunch counters put in place during the last months of the Hartsfield administration.[49]

Atlanta's civic leaders fostered a political culture during the 1950s and 1960s that linked racial progressivism to pragmatism and economic self-interest. Their community was a more economically vibrant place, one that was more attractive to outside investors, because it had eschewed the confrontational racial politics of its historical peer southern cities. As Atlanta entered the 1960s, the Big Mules envisioned something new for their city, a grand civic enterprise that required the old cooperative spirit but also a new desire to endow their community with something grandiose, an amenity exclusive to the first tier of American cities. The pursuit of professional sports by Atlanta's elites during the 1960s and early 1970s was the pursuit of an exceptional civic luxury for the city. The language of pragmatism in which Atlanta's leaders steeped their civil rights accomplishments was absent from their discourse on professional sports. Instead, the pursuit of the Major Leagues was an idealistic "assault on the impossible," as Big Mule and Allen confidant Mills B. Lane once described it.[50] The Big Mules spoke of the city's push for professional sports in reverential tones akin to those used to describe the then-contemporary space program. When Ivan Allen ran for mayor in 1961, he, like many of his peers, saw a city whose sporting culture was in keeping with regional traditions. Allen wanted mass leisure in Metropolitan Atlanta to resemble that of America's other major cities. His professed idealism with regard to professional sports and professed pragmatism with regard to civil rights both aimed at achieving the same end. He wanted Atlanta to become a major city among major cities. It could still be a southern city, but it had to be one on national terms, not simply regional ones. In less than a decade, this governing and cultural consensus would unravel in Atlanta, just as the city's professional sports franchises were struggling to build broad local constituencies of their own.

2

America's Virgin Sports Territory

IVAN ALLEN AND THE BIG MULES REGARDED ATLANTA'S sports scene as moribund. Outside of the city's leadership class, this view was not widely shared in the early 1960s. Atlantans, in fact, had a long tradition of supporting and participating in a diverse range of athletic pursuits, many of which were popular throughout the South but had yet to develop large audiences in other parts of the country. Sporting events patronized by Atlanta's social elite flourished as did those embraced by the working class. Historically, Black and white Atlantans had separately supported a number of sports at different levels of competition. By the early 1960s, they were watching them in increasingly integrated settings. Atlanta desegregated seating at all major sporting events in the summer of 1962, several years ahead of the other cities in the Southeast.[1]

In 1964 *Journal* sports editor Furman Bisher characterized Atlanta as "America's Virgin Territory," its most significant cultural and economic center without Major League teams.[2] As Bisher well knew, Atlanta had a vibrant sporting culture decades in advance of the Braves and Falcons' 1966 arrival. The region's local sporting culture would offer an ongoing challenge to the hegemony of the big leagues in Metropolitan Atlanta's competitive marketplace for leisure time and discretionary income. Atlanta, like many cities subsequently, found out that grandiose public investments in stadiums and arenas did little to ensure that metropolitan-area residents would embrace their new teams. The local sporting culture not only survived but also thrived in the face of its new municipally subsidized, Major League competition, anticipating the persistence of local sporting cultures across the Sunbelt, even as the region welcomed the lion's share of professional sports relocations and expansions.

Football, both at the college and high school levels, was unquestionably the most popular spectator sport in Metropolitan Atlanta. It enjoyed a wide following across the color line and the socioeconomic spectrum. Every Friday night in the fall, the Atlanta area played host to several high school football games that drew more than ten thousand spectators. "We had a lot of competition with the NBA, NFL, MLB, University of Georgia and Georgia Tech, but our biggest competition was Friday nights in the early part of the hockey season when the local high school football games would draw, combined, about 250,000 people," Atlanta Flames general manager (GM) Cliff Fletcher said.[3]

Atlanta was one of the South's earliest hotbeds of college football. The *Journal* and the *Constitution* sent reporters to eight states across Dixie to cover Southeastern Conference (SEC) and Atlantic Coast Conference (ACC) football games every fall weekend. Many alumni from SEC and ACC schools who relocated to Atlanta after graduation relied on the *Journal*'s and *Constitution*'s extensive coverage to follow their alma maters' teams. The Touchdown Club of Atlanta, one of the nation's most-well known football organizations, handed out awards to the country's outstanding collegiate and high school players at an annual dinner that began in 1938. Statewide radio coverage of major college football originated at Atlanta radio stations. WGST, a station owned by Georgia Tech, served as the radio flagship for coverage of the school's football games. WSB, Atlanta's oldest radio station, served as the flagship for radio coverage of University of Georgia football. In addition, Atlanta's Black colleges, especially Clark College, Atlanta University, and Morehouse College, developed heated local football rivalries and followings that well exceeded their alumni bases.[4]

"College football was king," *Journal-Constitution* editor

and longtime sportswriter Jim Minter said of the metropolitan area's sporting culture, even when Atlanta became the home of several professional sports teams.[5] The intense loyalty of local fans to Georgia Tech, Georgia, or another southern football program proved to be a liability for the NFL's Falcons. Georgia Tech had been one of the nation's premier college football programs for more than half a century. "Most of the city's present population," wrote Furman Bisher in 1965, "grew up with 'Ramblin Wreck,'" the school's fight song, "ringing in their ears." John Heisman, the namesake of college football's most prestigious award, the Heisman Trophy, transformed Georgia Tech into a national power in the early twentieth century, leading the Yellow Jackets to the first of their four national championships in 1917. Football Saturdays at Tech's Grant Field had long been the centerpiece of the autumn social calendar for the city's elite, many of them alumni of the Atlanta school. Throughout the 1950s and early 1960s, capacity crowds of more than 44,000 (later, following a 1962 expansion, crowds of 53,300) filled Grant Field to watch nationally ranked Georgia Tech teams compete annually for the SEC and national championships. More than thirty thousand Tech fans held season tickets, a remarkable number considering the school's graduate and undergraduate population was just seven thousand. In 1965 the waiting list for season tickets had more than five thousand names on it. The popularity of Georgia Tech football was so great that segregationist politicians, including Governor Marvin Griffin, wavered on their massive-resistance positions when Tech students and fans pressured them to allow the Yellow Jackets to play road games against integrated teams, several years before the 1961 desegregation of the prestigious engineering school.[6]

Seventy miles east of Atlanta in Athens, the University of Georgia (UGA) Bulldogs began to challenge Tech's reputation as the state's most successful and popular college team during the late 1950s. Following a long run of Georgia Tech victories in "Clean, Old-Fashioned Hate," the nickname given to the

Thanksgiving weekend Georgia–Georgia Tech football game, Georgia won four consecutive meetings from 1957 to 1960, the final years of Wally Butts's long tenure as the Bulldogs' coach. Following a brief interlude of mediocre seasons and Tech victories in the early 1960s, new coach Vince Dooley took over the program in 1964. Dooley reasserted Georgia's supremacy in the rivalry while UGA emerged as the most formidable SEC contender to Bear Bryant and the University of Alabama's football juggernaut, the nation's top program during the 1960s and 1970s. The transformation of the Georgia Bulldogs into a football power corresponded with the university's rapid growth. UGA more than tripled its enrollment from roughly six thousand students in 1950 to more than twenty thousand students in the mid-1960s. Seating capacity at the Bulldogs' Sanford Stadium grew accordingly, from thirty-six thousand to nearly sixty thousand in the same period. UGA alumni traveling from Atlanta to Athens caused Saturday traffic backups along I-20 every time the Bulldogs played at home. At the time of the Falcons' arrival in Atlanta, 101 chapters of the Bulldog Club, the University of Georgia's football booster organization, operated across the state.[7]

Though not as popular as football, Minor League baseball dated back to the nineteenth century in Atlanta, making it the city's longest-tenured spectator sport. The number of people playing baseball still outpaced the number of people playing football in Atlanta in 1960, but football had long ago displaced baseball as the city's most attended sporting event. Support for Minor League baseball in Atlanta waned in the decades after World War II, mirroring the struggles it faced nationwide. The rise of television as a rival entertainment and expanding number of cities with MLB teams, as well as the streamlining of the Minors into a formalized farm system that focused more on player development than capturing the interest of local fans, hurt all Minor League baseball franchises, including Atlanta's AA Southern Association affiliate, the Crackers. Despite this, Atlanta fans continued to support the franchise throughout the 1950s far better than fans of many of their rivals did. The continuity of local support for the Crackers in Atlanta took place not only as Minor League baseball struggled in general but also, more specifically, while the remnants of the Southern Association tried to continue playing as a segregated league within integrated baseball.[8]

The Atlanta Crackers joined the Southern League, the precursor to the Southern Association, in 1901. Atlanta had been home to several short-lived minor league baseball teams since the 1880s, including a team named the Firecrackers, which played in the 1892 season. The exact origin of the Crackers name is unknown. Some historians have speculated that it was a takeoff on the Firecrackers name, while others think it came directly from the well-known epithet for rural white southerners. The Atlanta Crackers' sixty-five-year history (1901–65) corresponded roughly with the period during which the majority of Atlanta's population were rural white migrants or their immediate descendants. The team enjoyed enthusiastic support from the very people who would have been described as crackers, making this a possible early example of a socially maligned group appropriating a term of disparagement and turning it into a source of communal pride and identity.[9]

Sportswriters took to calling the Crackers the "Yankees of the South" in recognition of their dominance of the Southern Association. Like the Yankees of the North, the Atlanta Crackers were regarded by both their enthusiasts and detractors as the premier organization in their league. Over the course of the team's history it won seventeen league championships. The club's popularity peaked along with the rest of the Southern Association in the immediate aftermath of World War II. The Crackers drew a league-record 404,584 fans in 1947. Beginning in 1950, the formerly independent Crackers began affiliating with MLB teams, as control over the farm systems in professional baseball became more centralized. Between 1950 and 1965, the Crackers served as the affiliate of the Boston/ Milwaukee Braves (1950–59), the Los Angeles Dodgers (1960–

61), the St. Louis Cardinals (1962–63), the Minnesota Twins (1964), and, once again, the Milwaukee Braves (1965). Crackers fans did not necessarily embrace the big league team with whom Atlanta was affiliated at the moment. "Although the Crackers had been the Braves farm team in the 1950s," Karl Green, a longtime Atlanta baseball fan recalled, "most fans' allegiance was to the Crackers, who played home games at Ponce de Leon Park."[10]

Located in East Atlanta along Ponce de Leon Avenue, "Poncey" was built across the street from an amusement park and situated amid the yards of the Southern Railway. The original wood-framed park burned down in 1923 and was replaced the next season by a more permanent concrete and steel structure. Around the same time, Sears, Roebuck and Company's southeastern distribution center replaced the amusement park, giving the surrounding neighborhood more the character of an urban industrial area than a space for mass leisure. Rell Jackson Spiller, the local businessman who owned the stadium, made up for his ballpark's less than bucolic surroundings by incorporating some southern idiosyncrasy into its design. Spiller planted a magnolia tree in centerfield rather than build a fence that went all the way around the outfield. Balls that hit the tree or passed on either side of it remained in play. White blossoms often littered the outfield during its spring bloom.

Poncey served primarily as the home of the Crackers, but the team's ownership also rented out the park for high school and small-college football games. The primary subtenant for the Crackers was the Atlanta Black Crackers, a professional Negro League baseball team that played from 1920 until 1952. For the vast majority of its history, the Black Crackers played either as a Minor League team in the Negro Southern League or as an independent Black professional baseball team. The Black Crackers team was originally made up of former college baseball players from the Atlanta area before the team broadened its player-recruiting efforts. It drew small crowds to Poncey unless it had scheduled exhibition games against the nation's most popular Black barnstorming teams, such as the Indianapolis Clowns or the Zulu Giants.[11]

Sunday doubleheaders at Poncey punctuated the summer calendar of many families living in and around Atlanta. "People came from long distances to see the Crackers play two games for the price of one on those hot, dusty, and frequently bombastic days," wrote Furman Bisher, conjuring Poncey's atmosphere as the park approached its 1965 demise.[12] As the Crackers' status in organized baseball became more tenuous during the early 1960s, fans started to take greater notice of Poncey's faults. Its lack of surrounding amenities and dearth of available parking became a greater issue for fans in an increasingly suburban and car-dependent metropolitan area. Mounting safety concerns about the surrounding residential areas, particularly the deteriorating Virginia-Highland neighborhood just north of the ballpark, discouraged some fans from attending, though not the most stalwart baseball fanatics.[13] "I didn't live close to Ponce de Leon, but it was close enough that I could walk there," recalled Joel Gross, whose family relocated from Jersey City to the suburban outskirts east of Atlanta in Fulton County in 1959. On several occasions, the baseball-mad eleven-year-old walked with friends to Sunday doubleheaders. "From North Highland and Ponce de Leon down to the ballpark wasn't particularly a great neighborhood," he recalled, "but it wasn't something my parents said, 'Don't walk through it.'"[14]

The Southern Association suffered from the same problems as the other minor leagues during the 1950s. The addition of segregationist politics to the equation put the Southern Association in an untenable position. The unwillingness of several Southern Association franchises to desegregate or play desegregated teams led to the AA league's demise in 1961. MLB teams, all of whom had fielded Black players by the end of the 1959 season, refused to further accommodate the laws and customs of southern states to the detriment of their farm systems. Several teams in the Southern Association were unable to secure working agreements with MLB franchises, making it impossible for them to field competitive teams any longer. MLB's unmistakably progressive stand on desegregation effectively led to the Southern Association's demise.[15]

The Crackers had tread lightly around the issues of desegregation on the field and in the stands for years. In April 1949 Atlanta hosted its first desegregated professional baseball game, an exhibition between the Crackers and the Brooklyn Dodgers, the team that had broken baseball's color line two seasons earlier with the addition of Jackie Robinson to its roster. Dodgers executive Branch Rickey, one of the most successful champions of desegregation in American history, had scheduled a series of exhibition games across the segregated South that spring in front of integrated audiences. The three-game series between the Dodgers and the Crackers would be no different. More than fifty thousand Black and white fans sat in integrated seating at Ponce de Leon Park for three of what were then the most attended baseball games in Atlanta history. They watched a Dodgers team that counted two African Americans, Robinson and catcher Roy Campanella, among their most popular players. Black fans had previously sat in a segregated leftfield bleacher section at Poncey, but never before in the grandstand or box seats as they did in large numbers that weekend.[16]

Following the 1949 exhibition games against the Dodgers, seating arrangements at Poncey returned to their traditionally segregated designations, and the Crackers continued to play segregated baseball against their Southern Association rivals. Much like their home city, though, the Crackers began to desegregate aspects of their operation. Beginning in 1952, the Crackers reserved a section of grandstand seats for Black fans. In 1954 the Crackers added Nat Peeples to their roster, the only Black player in the history of the Southern Association. Peeples's tenure with the Crackers proved short-lived. He excelled in the exhibition season for the Crackers but only played in two regular-season games for the team, going hitless in four at bats on the road in Mobile, Alabama. Peeples was soon demoted to the Braves' A Minor League affiliate in Jacksonville, Florida, a decision that likely had more to do with Jim Crow than his on-field performance. Despite the Crackers' Hartsfield-like approach to desegregation, the end of segregated Minor League baseball came quickly in Atlanta. Following the demise of the Southern Association, the Crackers became the AAA affiliate of the St. Louis Cardinals in the International League. As dictated by league rules, they fielded an integrated team and integrated the stands of Poncey in 1962, a decision that proceeded with little public notice amid more contentious issues related to desegregation in the city.[17]

Desegregation posed even fewer problems in the sport of golf. In 1960 the Greater Atlanta area was arguably the sport's most enthusiastic market, both as an activity and a spectator sport. Atlanta was the home of Bobby Jones, America's first golfer to achieve celebrity status. Born into a prominent Atlanta family, Jones spent his entire career as an amateur, although he later made a great deal of money endorsing golf clubs for Spalding and starring in short instructional films. Few athletes have dominated their sport as Jones did in the 1920s, winning thirteen major championships between 1923 and 1930. In 1930 Jones became the only golfer in history to win the Grand Slam, golf's four major tournaments, all in one season. Subsequently, Jones retired from competition and pursued a number of other golf-related ventures, including cofounding the Augusta National Golf Club and helping to design its famed golf course, which opened in 1933. The following spring, the Augusta National Golf Club held the inaugural Masters Tournament, which was soon recognized by the Professional Golf Association (PGA) as one of its four major tournaments. By the early 1960s, more than 150,000 spectators attended the four rounds of the nationally televised Masters Tournament in Augusta, located 150 miles east of Atlanta.

The free-to-attend practice round the day before the annual tournament drew as many as twenty thousand spectators.[18]

Atlanta's continued reputation as a golf hotbed relied not only on the reputation of Bobby Jones and the city's proximity to Augusta but also on the large number of metropolitan-area residents who took personal pleasure in the sport. Participation in golf extended beyond the local elite into the white and Black middle classes. In 1965 an estimated seventy thousand golfers kept the more than three-dozen public and private courses in the Atlanta area busy throughout Georgia's nine-month playing season. The range of golf courses available to players in Metropolitan Atlanta reflected the racial and social barriers of the region. Bobby Jones's home course, East Lake Golf Club, was the city's most exclusive. Owned and operated by the Atlanta Athletic Club, the course became an enclave of segregated white affluence in close proximity to the increasingly Black neighborhoods of East Atlanta. The Black-owned Lincoln Country Club, a nine-hole course known for its rough conditions, long served as the primary playing venue for Atlanta's Black business and professional classes. In December 1955 the U.S. Supreme Court ordered the city of Atlanta to desegregate its five public golf courses. Three years earlier, four African American golfers had filed suit against the city of Atlanta, arguing that a city ordinance banning them from playing on the municipally owned courses was unconstitutional. The plaintiffs in *Holmes v. Atlanta* challenged the city's policy in part because the board of directors at Lincoln Country Club refused to upgrade the conditions at the course. In spring 1956 African American golfers, including the four plaintiffs in the *Holmes* case, began patronizing Atlanta's well-maintained public courses without major incident.[19]

Other leisure pursuits also proved popular in Greater Atlanta. While boating on the region's many lakes became a favorite pastime in the city's affluent northern suburbs during the 1950s and 1960s, a different motor sport reached unprecedented levels of popularity among working-class Atlantans.

Stock car racing drew hundreds of thousands of fans annually to raceways and dirt tracks around the region, more than any other sporting event in Greater Atlanta. From March through October, legions of predominately white working-class fans attended Saturday-night and Sunday-afternoon races. In November 1959 the $1.8 million Atlanta International Raceway (AIR) opened twenty miles south of the city in Hampton, Georgia. The modern high-banked course in Hampton replaced Lakewood Park, a dirt track just south of Atlanta, as the top raceway in the region. Unlike the notoriously cramped parking facilities at Lakewood Park, AIR had an eight-lane entrance and enough parking for thirty-two thousand vehicles. The benefits of AIR's improved parking facilities were tempered by the massive traffic backups that race days caused on Route 41 South to Hampton. The twenty-mile drive down the South Expressway to AIR could take Atlanta race fans as long as four hours. Despite the hassle of getting to Hampton in time for a two o'clock Sunday event, stock car racing provided many blue-collar Atlantans with an affordable, day-long form of entertainment. Racing fans could purchase a $35 grandstand season pass for 22 races in 1964, less than one-fifth the price of the most inexpensive Braves' season ticket two years later. To showcase the state-of-the art facility, NASCAR (National Association for Stock Car Auto Racing) granted AIR two brand-new events in 1960: the Dixie 300 in July and the Atlanta 500 in October. By the mid-1960s, both events drew crowds in excess of sixty thousand spectators.[20]

Stock car racing drew an undoubtedly rowdy crowd, both at Lakewood Park and at AIR. As racing at Lakewood Park grew in popularity in the years after World War II, reform-minded Atlantans raised questions in the local press about the safety of the activity and the behavior of the crowds that attended these events. During the 1950 racing season alone, three separate incidents led the *Journal* to call for an end to racing at Lakewood. A driver named Skimp Hersey died in June from burns he sustained in a crash. Later that season, a spectator standing close to the track was killed by a multi-car crash that jumped Lakewood's modest barrier. That same weekend, Atlanta Police were pelted with rocks by approximately fifty spectators when they tried to arrest a fan for public drunkenness.[21]

There is no indication that the relocation of Atlanta's major raceway to Hampton in 1959 was a product of its organizers' desire to distance their event from the gaze of Atlanta-based custodians of public safety and mores. Building a raceway twenty miles from the city of Atlanta, though, minimized the potential for surveillance by disapproving civic guardians interested in preserving the well-being and reputation of Atlanta. The cultural autonomy provided to race organizers and fans by locating AIR in Hampton came with an overlapping political autonomy. It enabled AIR to avoid complying with Atlanta's legal and customary desegregation during the early 1960s. As late as April 1964, three months before the Civil Rights Act of 1964 went into effect, Marion E. Jackson of the *Daily World* complained that many facilities at AIR, including toilets and water fountains, remained segregated and almost no Black fans were at the event. "Henry County isn't Atlanta," Jackson wrote, referring to the rural location of the Hampton raceway. Several months later, AIR would be forced by law to fully integrate its accommodations.[22]

While the Atlanta newspapers covered stock car racing alongside athletics on their sports pages, they all but ignored professional wrestling, which also had a loyal local audience. Despite its lack of mainstream media coverage, pro wrestling drew large live and televised audiences. Standing-room-only crowds filled the 5,500-seat City Armory (later renamed the City Auditorium) every Friday night to watch professional wrestling. Frequent Saturday-night wrestling cards filled in other open dates at the air-conditioned, downtown venue. By the mid-1960s, audiences for wrestling at the City Armory included a noticeable Black minority while the performers in the ring included wrestlers from a variety of racial and ethnic backgrounds. The proximity of the City Armory to predominately African American east side neighborhoods and the affordable $1.50 price of admission likely aided in the decisions of many Black wrestling fans to attend the Friday-night events. Although wrestlers, to the delight of the audience, often portrayed the racial or ethnic group they belonged to (or were depicting) in an exaggerated or stereotypical manner, Friday-night wrestling at Atlanta's City Armory was undoubtedly the most thoroughly integrated sporting event in pre–Major League Atlanta.

Promoter Paul Jones began staging weekly Atlanta wrestling cards in 1944 at the cramped Warren Arena east of downtown, a stuffy, dusty dirt-floored venue that uncomfortably hosted as many as three thousand spectators. Jones ran a regional wrestling promotion known as ABC Booking that put on events in Georgia's smaller cities. He moved his Friday-night wrestling cards to the City Armory in the late 1940s, around the same time that Atlanta radio station WQXI began airing weekly broadcasts of his shows. In 1954 ABC affiliate WLWA (later, WAII) began airing *Live Atlanta Wrestling* on Saturday afternoons, a one-hour television program featuring matches between wrestlers from Paul Jones's promotion. Immediately, wrestling became one of WAII's highest-rated programs. To ensure the visual and sound quality of the program, WAII filmed the matches in front of a small audience in its television studio rather than trying to broadcast from the raucous, poorly lit City Armory. Tickets to the weekly television taping were given away by a drawing to fans who purchased the twenty-five cent *Ringsider* program on Friday night at the City Armory. Moreover, the distinction between televised studio wrestling, which featured mostly uncompetitive matches that highlighted the strengths of the promotion's new talent, and live events, which featured competitive matches between the promotion's top stars, helped Jones ensure that fans continued to patronize his City Armory shows. The television program was, in essence, an advertisement for the live events. Saturday-afternoon wrestling developed into a fixture of Atlanta television, anchoring the early evening weekend programming of affiliates across the Southeast for the next half century. While the management, ownership, and television rights to professional wrestling in Atlanta, specifically, and the Southeast, more broadly, changed on several occasions during the 1970s and 1980s, never did a Saturday afternoon pass in Atlanta without a wrestling broadcast emanating from one of the city's television studios.[23]

Competition for time and discretionary income between the new major professional sports franchises and existing local spectator and participatory athletic events became a hallmark of the Atlanta marketplace in the late twentieth century. The national context that enabled Atlanta's civic leadership to buy its way into the big leagues during the 1960s and 1970s was in conflict with Atlanta's long-tenured sporting culture, which thrived for decades before the arrival of major professional teams. The mere fact that cities chose to invest public money in professional sports franchises did not ensure that area residents would embrace these teams. Quite to the contrary, Atlanta's continued embrace of its local sporting traditions and apathy toward its new big league amenities anticipated the response of many Sunbelt cities to the teams they acquired in the late twentieth century.

3

Franchise Free Agency

....

ATLANTA'S PURSUIT OF THE MAJOR LEAGUES WAS MADE possible by a phenomenon known as *franchise free agency*, a term that economic historians use to describe the expansion and increasing mobility of professional sports teams and leagues in the decades after World War II.[1] Between 1945 and 2000, fifty franchises in the four major North American professional sports leagues moved from one metropolitan area to another. Major professional sports leagues granted an additional sixty-three expansion franchises to cities during this period.[2] Nearly two-thirds of the fifty franchise relocations and sixty-three expansions approved by major professional leagues between 1945 and 2000 were south of the Mason-Dixon Line or west of the Mississippi River. Three-quarters of these relocations and expansions to the Sunbelt took place after 1966, the year that Atlanta secured its first two professional sports franchises.[3]

For Sunbelt cities like Atlanta, the acquisition of professional sports franchises was a rite of passage on the path to national prominence. In the 1950s and 1960s the likes of Los Angeles, Houston, and Atlanta achieved this status. In subsequent decades cities like San Diego, Tampa, and Phoenix gained a larger national profile in part because of their inclusion in major professional sports.[4] As the number of cities willing and able to support franchises has grown, expansion has proven the path of least resistance for professional leagues. Expansion teams allow a league to offer its product in previously underserved markets while avoiding the legal battles and public-relations headaches of relocations.[5]

The NFL was the first major professional league to move a franchise west of the Mississippi. Professional football's once-per-week schedule made cross-country road trips feasible for teams before jet travel became commonplace in the late 1950s. In 1946 the financially struggling Cleveland Rams relocated to Los Angeles. A decade before the other Major Leagues moved into California, the Rams proved a huge success, averaging a league-leading 38,700 fans per game at the Los Angeles Memorial Coliseum in their first season. The Rams went on to become one of the NFL's most popular and glamorous franchises. The 1958 relocation of two of MLB's most high-profile teams, the Brooklyn Dodgers and New York Giants to Los Angeles and San Francisco, respectively, was the milestone that made the expansion of professional sports to the West Coast seem plausible to the other leagues. In the jet age, clubs on the East Coast could reach California in a matter of hours.

The peak period for expansion took place between 1960 and 1976, as the demand for teams in emerging Sunbelt markets grew considerably. Other major contributing factors to expansion included the political pressure put on the Major Leagues, especially MLB, to replace relocated teams in cities such as New York, Milwaukee, and Washington DC. On several occasions, influential members of Congress threatened to push for an end to the special antitrust exemptions enjoyed by professional sports leagues if certain relocated franchises were not replaced. Moreover, the creation of rival professional hockey, basketball, and football leagues in addition to a proposed rival baseball league forced all four of the major professional sports cartels to expand to avoid losing out on up-and-coming sports markets. Between the merger and direct expansion, the NFL grew from a thirteen-team league in 1960 to a twenty-eight-team league by 1976. During the same period, the NHL expanded from six to eighteen teams, and the

NBA grew from eight to twenty-three teams. MLB grew from sixteen to twenty-six teams between 1960 and 1976 simply through direct expansion.[6]

Mergers between major professional leagues and competitor professional leagues played a major role in the expansion of franchises into a larger number of markets across the North American continent, providing cities with new opportunities to acquire a team. During the 1960s and 1970s, the NFL, NHL, and NBA all faced existential threats from well-financed rival organizations. Formed in 1967, the American Basketball Association (ABA) challenged the NBA for nine seasons before agreeing to a partial merger in 1976. Four of its seven remaining teams paid a $3.2 million expansion fee to join the NBA, while the other ABA franchise owners agreed to buyout plans from the league. The NHL faced a serious challenge from the World Hockey Association (WHA) for seven seasons (1972–79) before agreeing to a partial merger with the rival league. Four of the WHA's six remaining teams paid a $6 million franchise fee to join the NHL for the 1979–80 season.[7]

Well before the formation of the rival American Football League (AFL) in 1960, the NFL faced off with another legitimate rival. In the late 1940s, the All-America Football Conference (AAFC) attempted to expand professional football beyond its small cluster of established NFL markets in the urban north, placing teams in southern and western cities like Miami, Los Angeles, and San Francisco. The starting point of franchise free agency, the NFL's 1946 decision to allow the Cleveland Rams to relocate to Los Angeles, was prompted in large part by the league's desire to keep the AAFC from monopolizing the lucrative Southern California market. After four years of play, the AAFC dissolved, and its top three teams, Cleveland, San Francisco, and Baltimore, were absorbed into the NFL.

The most high-profile and successful competition faced by the NFL, though, came from the American Football League (AFL) of the 1960s. It served as the model that rival leagues in all professional sports adopted when they challenged an existing Major League. The AFL proved capable of competing with the NFL because of the personal wealth of the AFL's owners, most of whom were the scions of incredibly affluent families. Most NFL owners had a fraction of the wealth. Their teams were their family businesses. The AFL placed franchises in several large, unoccupied Sunbelt markets that the NFL had wanted to keep open for expansion at an indeterminate future date. Additionally, the AFL cut into the NFL's talent pool by luring dozens of elite college players onto its rosters with lucrative, long-term contracts, which were historically a rarity in as injury-prone a sport as professional football. Eventually, the AFL forced the NFL to accept a complete merger of its ten teams into their league for the 1970 season, doubling the size and geographic scope of professional football.

A NUMBER OF SOCIAL, POLITICAL, AND ECONOMIC FACTORS contributed to the expansion of major professional sports into a continent-wide phenomenon in the postwar era. The three most significant factors in this shift were the economic expansion and population growth of the nation's south and west; the improvement and expansion of the country's transportation infrastructure, which made transcontinental travel more efficient and affordable; and the increasing amount of discretionary income afforded Americans by the nation's postwar affluence, especially in suburban areas and the nation's emerging Sunbelt.

The United States grew from a country of 132.1 million people in 1940 to one of 284.1 million in 2000. The regional distribution of the nation's growth skewed markedly to the cities and states of the south and west, endowing many of its emerging urban areas with a sufficient number of inhabitants to support professional sports franchises. In 1940 eight of the nation's ten most populous states were either in the Northeast or Midwest. By 2000, three of the nation's four most populous states and six of the top twelve were located in the Sunbelt. In the 1940 Census, twenty-two of the nation's one hundred largest metropolitan areas were located in the South or West. By 2000 a majority were located in these regions.

Accompanying the population growth in the Sunbelt were significant improvements to the country's transportation infrastructure, which made the expansion of professional sports into all regions of the United States a logistical possibility. Rail travel and the often-inefficient pre–World War II national highway system made travel from one city to another, especially those far from the nation's northern urban centers, a cumbersome, time-consuming process. The emergence of commercial jet travel during the late 1950s and the construction of the Interstate Highway System following the passage of the Federal-Aid Highway Act of 1956 expedited transcontinental travel considerably. For the purposes of professional sports, it made feasible the expansion of the Major Leagues into the far-flung cities of the South and West.[8]

The expansion of the American middle class in the decades after World War II created a larger potential customer base for professional sports in all parts of the country. In 1940 the median household income in the United States was $956 (approximately $17,664.01 in 2020). By 1970 the median household income in the United States was $7,592, or $50,615.55 in 2020. The Sunbelt states showed a marked increase in their household income relative to the rest of the nation during the postwar era. In 1950 the South and West lagged behind the national average median income by more than 25 percent. By 1975 the median household income gap between both regions and the rest of the nation had been cut in half, and the purchasing-power parity of southerners and westerners equaled the national average. During the 1970s, the first golden age for professional sports expansion into the South and West, every Sunbelt state increased its per capita income more rapidly than the national average.[9]

"PROFESSIONAL SPORTS," ARTHUR T. JOHNSON WROTE IN 1983, "could not exist as we know them without local subsidies and federal antitrust exemptions."[10] Franchise free agency was facilitated by the new willingness of cities like Atlanta to subsidize professional sports, most significantly through the investment of public money into professional sports venues. The local subsidies that individual franchise owners have been able to secure from cities since the 1950s are a product of the legally proscribed monopoly status enjoyed by the four major professional leagues. Cities that wanted professional sports franchises had no other option than to buy into these exclusive clubs. Federal antitrust laws, dating back to the Sherman Antitrust Act of 1890, prohibit corporate combinations and contracts that harm consumers and workers by limiting competition for their business and services, leading to a "restraint of trade." Yet courts have shown a reluctance to intervene in the uniquely internally competitive cartel business model of professional sports. This both explicit and tacit acceptance of the monopoly status of professional sports allows the leagues to decide how many teams will exist, where they will play, and how revenue and talent will be divided among member teams.[11]

It enabled individual franchises and entire leagues to negotiate aggressively with cities when coming to terms on the financing, leasing, and revenue distribution of publicly financed playing facilities.[12] The artificial scarcity of the commodity that professional leagues possess enabled them to use their monopoly status to restrict the supply of teams. By limiting the supply of franchises, the Major Leagues have been able to pressure dozens of cities into building stadiums at taxpayer expense.[13] For decades, team owners have not borne the true costs of relocations because they have almost always forced taxpayers in their new city to subsidize a large percentage of their move.[14] A 1995 *New York Times*–commissioned study concluded that forty-seven North American cities could support MLB teams.[15] None of the four Major Leagues had more than thirty franchises in 1995, providing each one with plenty of options if a city decided not to accede to its demands.

All four major professional sports leagues are protected by explicit statutory federal antitrust exemptions stemming from the Sports Broadcasting Act of 1961. This legislation enabled the franchises that constitute a professional league to pool their national broadcasting rights to sell to networks. The upshot of the Sports Broadcasting Act has been an unwillingness by courts to intervene in the organization of professional leagues. Subsequent legislative action by Congress has only strengthened the antitrust exemptions enjoyed by the big four.[16]

Long before the Sports Broadcasting Act of 1961, federal courts afforded MLB an exemption from antitrust laws, enabling it to become an explicitly sanctioned legal monopoly. In the 1922 Supreme Court case *Federal Baseball Club v. National League*, the court ruled that the Sherman Antitrust Act did not apply to MLB. Writing the unanimous opinion on behalf of the defendants, Justice Oliver Wendell Holmes reasoned that baseball games are purely state affairs not beholden to regulations on interstate commerce. Holmes's decision was written before modern legal notions of interstate commerce were broadened by the court during the 1930s. In spite of the court's changing interpretations of the nature of interstate commerce, it has held up baseball's antitrust exemption every time it has been brought before the court.[17]

The antitrust exemptions enjoyed by the professional Major Leagues have created a situation in which most municipalities that want to retain or lure a franchise must offer it competitive local subsidies in support of stadium development to keep it from seeking out a new home either inside or outside of its present metropolitan area. Before franchise free agency, team relocations were usually the result of the club's financial collapse and lack of local support. Moving to another city was typically the last-ditch effort of an owner who wanted to keep his team from folding. Between 1876 and 1950, thirty-five major professional sports franchises relocated from one city to another, while approximately fifty others simply went out of business.[18]

By the late 1950s, major professional sports franchises became too lucrative a commodity to simply go out of business. Just three major professional sports franchises have folded in the last seventy years. The growing demand for teams and the lucrative new national television contracts signed by the major sports leagues were the primary contributors to the rapid increase in their value. From 1962 to 1972, the gross revenues of professional sports franchises increased 201 percent, while the gross national product increased only 88 percent. Simultaneously, the price of a professional sports franchise grew considerably, particularly when it came to NFL teams, whose television deal paid them geometrically more than teams in the other professional leagues. In 1964 automobile heir William Clay Ford paid $5 million for the Detroit Lions. Eight years later, Robert Irsay paid three times as much for the Baltimore Colts. By the mid-1980s, the going rate for an NFL franchise was $70 million.[19]

In the age of franchise free agency, financial enticements offered by other cities have prompted relocations as often as the financial failures of clubs in their home markets. Beginning in the 1950s, political and corporate leaders in cities sought to maintain or attract professional sports teams by building them expensive playing facilities and promising the teams financial incentives, including attractive stadium and arena leases.[20] By the end of the 1950s, most stadium deals involved more public money than private. Simultaneously, professional leagues in all four major sports were moving rapidly into the South and West in response to financial incentives offered by local governments in the region's rapidly growing cities.[21] In 1950 fewer than half of the NBA and NFL's playing facilities were publicly owned. Only two MLB stadiums were then publicly owned. No NHL arenas were publicly owned in 1950. By 1970, nearly 70 percent of the venues that hosted professional franchises were publicly owned, a figure that grew to more than 80 percent by the early 1990s.[22] In the second half of the twentieth century, only three major professional sports facilities were built primarily with private money: Dodger Stadium in Los Angeles, Foxboro Stadium in Massachusetts, and Joe Robbie Stadium in Miami.[23]

Atlanta Stadium and the Omni Coliseum were built amid the first nationwide boom in stadium construction, which took place between the late 1950s and the mid-1970s. The confluence of franchise free agency, the local bargaining leverage that antitrust exemptions provided team owners, and the new willingness of municipalities to subsidize professional sports made this boom possible. Between 1956 and 1976, fifty new venues that served as the homes of major North American professional sports franchises were built at a cost of nearly $12 billion in 2020 dollars. Three quarters of the funding for these facilities came from the public. In the previous forty-seven years (1908–55), only twenty-seven such venues were built in North America. Collectively, those stadiums cost $1.2 billion in 2020 dollars with 47 percent of the funding coming from public sources.[24]

In an effort to contain public spending on their professional sports venues, many municipalities chose in the 1960s and 1970s to build multipurpose stadiums. These facilities were the home for at least two local professional sports franchises as well as a venue for other large civic gatherings and events. Between 1960 and 1971, twelve publicly financed multipurpose stadiums were built in North America. These projects ranged in price from the $18 million Atlanta Stadium (approximately $147 million in 2020 dollars) to the $45 million Houston Astrodome (approximately $369 million in 2018 dollars).

Following a slowdown in stadium building during the 1980s, the 1990s and 2000s witnessed a new, unprecedented boom. Between 1990 and 2007, seventy-eight stadiums were built for professional sports franchises in forty-three metropolitan areas at a cost of nearly $29 billion in 2020 dollars. Public sources provided 61 percent of the money for these projects.[25] The confluence of economic factors that inaugurated the first stadium building boom remained in place in the 1990s. Yet several new factors specific to the late twentieth century helped to reinvigorate the market for stadium building.

First, the further expansion of professional sports created an immediate need for stadiums in the Sunbelt cities that followed Atlanta into the Major Leagues.

Second, stadium projects came to be seen by political and corporate leaders in many cities during the 1990s as they were by Atlanta's Big Mules during the 1960s: as a magic bullet for revitalizing their downtowns, despite the clear academic consensus that had concluded otherwise. Rust Belt cities like Baltimore, Cleveland, and Detroit made similarly massive civic investments in professional sports venues during the 1990s, both as a means of keeping away poachers from the Sunbelt and as a mechanism for revitalizing their downtowns. Many of these projects succeeded at bringing suburban visitors by the millions back downtown for a game and some pre- or post-event refreshments, but none of them transformed the economy or residential patterns in their respective communities.

Third, many of the stadiums built during the 1990s and 2000s replaced multipurpose facilities constructed during the 1960s and 1970s, virtually all of which have now been torn down. In some instances, hastily constructed multipurpose venues like the Omni in Atlanta decayed rapidly and required immediate replacement. In most cases, franchise owners whose teams played in multipurpose venues wanted stadiums of their own. The scheduling inconveniences of sharing a facility with another team had been multidecade annoyances for dozens of owners. Furthermore, multipurpose stadiums chafed the aesthetic sensibilities of many owners whose teams were forced to play on often unsightly fields designed to accommodate two sports. When negotiating with their local civic leaders, though, franchise owners employed primarily economic arguments, telling municipal officials that their teams could not compete financially without additional revenue-generating features in their stadiums such as luxury boxes and club seats. Unlike the revenue that teams derived from normal ticket sales, the revenue generated by these specialty seats did not have to be shared with visiting teams.[26]

To finance the tens of billions of dollars in subsidies they have promised to professional franchises, cities and municipalities have employed a number of creative revenue-generating mechanisms. Until the mid-1960s, most public financing for stadiums came through general obligation bonds secured by cities, counties, or states. Typically, they were repaid through the taxing entity's general revenue from property, income, and sales taxes. Reliance on general obligation bonds to build stadiums became increasingly unfeasible. Exponential increases in the price of stadium building during the 1960s and 1970s made it financially impossible for many municipalities to simply dip into their general revenues to pay for such expensive projects. Competing demands for other, more pressing capital projects in cities were increasingly given preferred access to funding from general revenue streams.

As stadium financing came to be dominated by governments during the 1960s, alternate public funding mechanisms such as special tax bonds and revenue bonds became more common. These bonds were typically project-specific or came from specifically pledged sources of revenue. New municipal authorities created to facilitate the financing of stadium projects were usually the issuers of these securities. In an effort to limit the financial risk of such projects to a municipality, repayment of these bonds has typically been secured by revenue that derives from the project, such as ticket taxes, event fees, or an agreed-upon percentage of the gate, parking revenues, or concessions. Since the 1990s, repayment of these bonds has often been secured through levies presented to the voters as sin taxes on lottery tickets, cigarettes, or alcohol or taxes on out-of-towners, such as room and meal taxes or rental-car fees. Regardless of the mechanism, funding for professional sports stadiums has fallen largely on local taxpayers. Atlanta, too, adopted similar funding mechanisms as it continued to play the stadium game in the early twenty-first century, evolving away from the residentially based taxation model that Ivan Allen and his allies employed in the city's initial efforts to make their community Major League.[27]

Civic leaders representing the public and corporate sectors, including those pioneering elites in 1960s Atlanta, have long made the argument that spending tax dollars to build stadiums to either lure or keep a professional sports franchise is an economic boon to their cities. They make the argument that publicly financed stadium projects generate temporary, high paying construction jobs as well as permanent employment opportunities at the stadium. They assert that stadiums generate enough revenue through taxes and lease payments over the life of a facility to make up for the initial expenditures. They claim that stadiums provide further indirect economic benefits to the community by channeling further discretionary expenditures to nearby dining, retail, and lodging establishments. They argue that professional sports bring new money into the community by attracting tourists. Beyond its economic benefit, civic leaders in cities across North America have argued that sports provide their communities with unique cultural benefits, endowing cities with an enduring engine of civic unity and pride. Civic leaders in Atlanta were among the first to successfully articulate to their public both the economic and cultural arguments on behalf of building a stadium for a professional sports franchise.[28]

Atlanta became a Major League City decades before a multidisciplinary academic consensus emerged on the question of whether providing public subsidies to build stadiums for professional sports teams was a good public-policy decision. Over the past forty years, economists, historians, and political scientists have produced an extensive literature on the economics of professional sports focused on that question.[29]

Scholars who study the economics of professional sports are almost universal in discrediting the economic arguments on behalf of publicly financed stadiums. Public investment in professional sports venues, whether aimed at luring a new team to a city or keeping an existing team from leaving a city, create few long-term jobs and concentrate financial benefits in the hands of ultrawealthy franchise owners. Moreover, sports franchises are too small a part of a metropolitan area's economy to have a significant impact on the economic growth of a region. They attract a far smaller number of tourists from outside of the metropolitan area to center cities than booster-financed impact studies almost always project. The out-of-towners that do come to center cities to watch downtown sporting events spend far less money than anticipated by the hypothetical multiplier effects posited in virtually all booster-financed impact studies. The foot traffic generated in downtowns by stadiums benefit a handful of businesses near playing facilities, but the economic impact of a stadium's presence downtown is not transformative. It merely redistributes an insignificant amount of spending within a metropolitan area.[30]

According to the extensive scholarship on the topic, the primary benefits of cities investing in professional sports facilities come from the cultural prestige and source of common identity they lend to a metropolitan area. Atlanta's civic leaders were the first to assert that professional sports would endow these cultural benefits on their city. Yet, in the case of Atlanta, civic leaders were strikingly disappointed by the limited cultural benefits. Many subsequent Sunbelt cities that have reached the Major Leagues experienced similar disappointments.[31]

THE FOUR MAJOR NORTH AMERICAN PROFESSIONAL SPORTS leagues have all been transformed by franchise free agency, both the more historically stable MLB and NHL and the more institutionally chaotic NFL and NBA. Economist John Vrooman describes the history of league expansions and franchise mobility in Major League Baseball as characterized by "punctuated equilibrium." Between 1903 and 1953, there were no franchise moves or expansions in the American or National Leagues.

The same sixteen teams played in the same ten cities.[32] Boston, St. Louis, Philadelphia, and Chicago all had two teams. New York had three teams. The southernmost and westernmost city in the Major Leagues was St. Louis.[33]

The 1953 move of the Boston Braves to Milwaukee was the first franchise shift in MLB in fifty years. Following years of box-office struggles, the Braves were allowed by the National League to relocate to Milwaukee and its brand-new, municipally built stadium. The Braves proved an immediate success in Wisconsin, drawing an NL record of more than 1.8 million fans in the team's inaugural season. The Braves' success led other struggling franchises to seek greener pastures in new cities. By the end of the 1950s, MLB's sixteen teams were located in fifteen cities. The relocations of the 1950s did not dilute MLB's product. Instead, it redistributed teams in a manner more reflective of the nation's changing regional demographics.[34]

The most culturally and economically significant relocations of any professional sports franchise, MLB or otherwise, took place in 1958 when the NL's Brooklyn Dodgers and New York Giants, two of the sports' most successful franchises both on the field and at the box office, left the nation's largest city for California. Culturally, no professional sports franchise was as closely identified with its host city as the Dodgers were with Brooklyn. "Dem Bums," as they were nicknamed lovingly by the local press, served as a national symbol of the culture and personality of Brooklyn, a borough whose population was greater than all but four American cities.[35] If the Dodgers could leave Brooklyn, then any franchise was apt to leave its hometown for a city that made it a better offer. Both the Giants and Dodgers were unhappy with their stadium situations. The Giants played at the Polo Grounds in upper Manhattan, a stadium that had been constructed during Benjamin Harrison's administration. Ebbetts Field, the Dodgers' home since 1913, suffered from deteriorating conditions, a lack of parking, and the demographic transformation of its surrounding Flatbush neighborhood into a predominately Black area, which made the location of the stadium undesirable to many of Brooklyn's fans.

Ten MLB franchises relocated during the second half of the twentieth century, each of which occurred between 1953 and 1972. Eight of the ten relocations placed franchises in metropolitan areas significantly west or south of their city of origin. The 1972 relocation of the Washington Senators to Arlington, Texas, was the last move by a Major League franchise for more than thirty years until the Montreal Expos left for Washington DC in 2004.[36] After 1972 MLB moved into the metropolitan areas of the Sunbelt through periodic expansions rather than relocations. After adding eight expansion teams during the 1960s, MLB approved the addition of two expansion franchises in 1977, 1993, and 1998 respectively. By 2000, fifteen of the league's thirty teams were located south or west of St. Louis. The geographic stability among MLB's existing teams that has held since the 1970s has come at a steep price to taxpayers. In a number of cities, franchise owners threatened to move their clubs, convincing local political leaders to support massive public expenditures for stadiums.[37] Between 1989 and 2001, sixteen baseball stadiums were built at taxpayer expense in North America at a cost of $4.9 billion; $3.27 billion of that money, or slightly more than two-thirds, came from public sources.[38]

The NHL has approved eight franchise relocations since World War II. Half of these moves took place during the 1990s. In each instance during the 1990s, the team moved from a traditional northern or Canadian hockey market (Minneapolis, Quebec City, Winnipeg, and Hartford) into an unproven hockey market in the southern or western United States (Dallas, Denver, Phoenix, and Raleigh). These shifts to the Sunbelt corresponded with the NHL's efforts during that era to remake itself into a continent-wide league like the other three major sports. During that same decade, the NHL approved the addition of nine expansion teams, seven of which were located in Sunbelt metropolitan areas. A construction boom in the NHL accompanied the disruptive expansions and relocations of the 1990s. Twenty-four of the NHL's thirty teams play in arenas built between 1991 and 2003, which cost a combined $3.6 billion.[39]

The geographic instability of the NHL during the 1990s was contrary to the league's historic steadiness. Before the league's first expansion in 1967, the NHL had a long history as a small but stable organization. From 1939 until 1967, the NHL consisted of six franchises, all located in major media markets in the urban north or in eastern Canada: Toronto, Montreal, Boston, New York, Chicago, and Detroit. In 1967 the league doubled in size, expanding its membership to twelve teams in response to the growing demand for new franchises of the suddenly fashionable sport. During the 1960s, following the emergence of professional football as the nation's most popular spectator and televised sport, sports-minded entrepreneurs were on the lookout for the "next football." Basketball and hockey were the two primary beneficiaries of this new desire to invest capital in professional sports. The NHL placed its 1967 expansion franchises in both hockey hotbeds, like Minneapolis, and West Coast cities with no hockey tradition whatsoever, like Los Angeles and Oakland. The league continued to add members soon after its dramatic expansion in 1967.

During the 1970s, the NHL added four more expansion franchises, placing teams in established hockey towns like Vancouver and fledgling ones like Atlanta. The league's continued expansion was prompted by the aggressive expansion of the rival WHA into open North American markets. During its seven-year history (1972–79), the WHA placed teams in twenty-seven different North American markets, often for only a season or two and often in improbable hockey markets, including Houston, Phoenix, and San Diego. On the brink of financial collapse, the WHA agreed to a partial merger with the NHL in 1979 that added four new franchises to the league. While every single WHA Sunbelt franchise failed, the rival league's efforts to expand professional hockey to the South and West set the precedent for the NHL's expansion model during the 1990s. By 2000, only six of the NHL's thirty teams were located in Canada, hockey's most fervent heartland and its place of origin.[40]

The NBA has been the most unstable of the major North American leagues and also the most prone to franchise relocations. Twenty of the fifty franchise shifts between World War II and the end of the twentieth century involved NBA clubs. Half of those moves took place between 1950 and 1963, when the league actively tried to place teams in larger markets, replacing many of the medium-sized Midwestern cities that served as the original bases for professional basketball. Like the NFL, the NBA was characterized in its early years by unstable membership. Until World War II, professional basketball existed primarily in the Midwest. The National Basketball League (NBL), which was one of the two predecessor leagues that merged to form the NBA, started as an industrial league supported by the recreation departments at large manufacturing firms, such as Goodyear and Firestone. The Basketball Association of America (BAA), the NBA's other ancestor, was organized in 1946 by the businessmen who owned the top arenas in the Midwest and Northeast. Typically, these men owned hockey clubs and wanted to add a basketball team to fill the open dates on their winter calendar. The NBL and BAA merged in 1949 to form the NBA. Numerous franchises failed in the early years of the league, leaving the NBA with eight teams for the 1954–55 season. As late as 1956, more than half of the NBA's teams were based in metropolitan areas with fewer than one million residents, including Rochester (NY), Fort Wayne, and Syracuse. The league spent much of the early 1960s as an eight-team league before solidifying into a ten-team league with two five-team divisions for the 1966–67 season. Slowly but surely, the NBA moved into larger Midwestern markets, such as St. Louis and Detroit. It followed the other professional leagues to the West Coast in the early 1960s, adding franchises in Los Angeles and San Francisco. During the

1960s and 1970s, the NBA expanded more cautiously than other leagues, adding ten expansion teams and four teams through mergers between 1960 and 1976. Their caution was understandable. Before 1985, the league had never gone more than five years without a relocation. As the NBA's popularity grew during the 1980s, it became more aggressive in its expansion plans, adding seven new franchises between 1988 and 2000.[41]

The NFL experienced eleven franchise relocations between 1945 and 2000. Six of these moves took place between 1982 and 1997 in the aftermath of Oakland Raiders owner Al Davis's successful antitrust suit against the NFL, which voided the league's 1982 vote to prevent Davis from moving his franchise to Los Angeles. NFL owners, fearful of losing future antitrust suits, approved most proposed moves by their fellow owners during the 1980s and 1990s. Allowing other owners to move their franchises as they wished helped the league avoid further legal entanglements. More significant to most NFL cities was the increased bargaining leverage that the Davis decision gave to NFL owners in stadium negotiations. The very real threat of relocation provided all NFL owners with a free hand in negotiating new stadium deals with their home cities. In the twenty years after the Raiders' move to Los Angeles, eighteen of the league's current thirty-two teams signed leases to play in new, predominately publicly financed facilities.[42] Prior to the Davis decision, NFL relocations had been rare events. Before the Raiders' move, the NFL's most recent franchise shift was the Chicago Cardinals' 1960 relocation to St. Louis.

4

The Greatest Location in the World

....

THE ATLANTA—FULTON COUNTY STADIUM AUTHORITY
broke ground on a multipurpose, municipal stadium on April
15, 1964. Ivan Allen, Georgia Governor Carl Sanders, and Stadium Authority chairman Arthur Montgomery turned ceremonial shovels of sand at the Washington-Rawson urban
renewal site. After lending a brief hand to the physical construction of the stadium, Allen told reporters that the project had swept Atlanta up in a "romance of accomplishment,"
a belief that the city could achieve any grand enterprise if it
made a concerted civic effort to reach that goal.[1]

The location for Atlanta's municipally owned stadium had
not been driven by civic elites like Allen or the Big Mules.
Instead, it was the result of local leaders indulging the whims
of an eccentric baseball franchise owner whose team did not
even end up moving to the city. A desire by local doyens to
please the first MLB owner who considered moving to Atlanta
brought about dramatic changes in the city's urban planning
and housing policy.

Despite the relatively quick turnaround between Allen's
January 1962 inauguration and the April 1964 groundbreaking on a new stadium, the mayor spent little time on the issue
during his first year in office. Other aspects of his Six Point
Plan, especially executing the backlog of approved highway-
construction projects and managing the continued desegregation of Atlanta's public life, occupied much of his time. Allen
spent many of his waking hours in 1962 monitoring work on
the Downtown Connector between Interstates 75 and 85 and

ensuring that his executive order desegregating the city's public facilities was being enforced. Moreover, there was no indication that the arrival of a professional sports franchise in Atlanta was imminent, so the need to break ground on an outdoor stadium lost some of the imperative that Allen afforded it during the campaign.[2]

Allen was more interested in a multipurpose municipal auditorium, suitable for conventions, public performances, and indoor sporting events, especially basketball games. The auditorium-coliseum became the centerpiece of an $80 million municipal-bond package he submitted for public approval. Allen's bond initiatives faced heavy opposition from working- and middle-class white voters, many of whom regarded the plans for new investments in recreational facilities and urban renewal projects around the city as the mayor's repayment to Black voters for their support in the recent election. Conversely, the city's predominately Black neighborhoods supported all of the bond initiatives by at least a two to one margin. High voter turnout in predominately white neighborhoods in South and West Atlanta swung the vote tallies strongly against Allen's proposals. Voters turned down every one of the proposed municipal bonds in August 1962, forcing Allen to pursue a smaller $55 million package the following year with a more modest plan for an auditorium. The revised 1963 version of the auditorium-coliseum plan excluded accommodations for spectator sports. The pared-down plan won voter approval in May 1963, facilitating the construction of the Atlanta Civic Center on urban renewal land east of the CBD in the predominately African American Buttermilk Bottom neighborhood.[3]

The Atlanta Civic Center opened in 1967, several years later than initially anticipated. Black voters, prompted by enthusiastic support from the Black business community for the proposed large-scale construction project in a predominately African American neighborhood, voted heavily for the 1963 bond initiative. But when details of the Civic Center plan became public, many Blacks in the surrounding districts opposed the project because the proposed site required the destruction of a public school, one of their neighborhood's principal institutions. Opposition to the plan eased when Allen promised expedited residential construction on the remaining acres of the Buttermilk Bottom urban renewal site, reiterating his campaign pledge to build more new housing targeted at African American residents. When the Civic Center finally opened, it never achieved the prominent position in civic life its boosters envisioned. The 4,500-seat theater was soon overshadowed by the 1968 opening of the privately supported Memorial Arts Center (later renamed the Woodruff Arts Center), home to the Atlanta Symphony Orchestra, the Alliance Theatre, and the High Museum of Art. The Civic Center's convention hall was also displaced as the city's top publicly owned exhibition space within a decade by the state-run Georgia World Congress Center, which opened on the southern edge of the CBD in 1976. Following the approval of his more modest municipal-bond package, Allen declared that the outdoor stadium would be the next major project on the city's agenda.[4]

Despite Allen's declaration, it was actually *Journal* sports editor Furman Bisher who instigated the stadium building process. For years, Bisher had boosted the idea of bringing the big leagues to Atlanta in his columns. More importantly, the well-connected journalist worked behind the scenes to pitch Atlanta as a future site to insiders in all the major sports leagues. Bisher's connections put him in the right place at the right time to be a sympathetic ear for Charlie Finley, the mercurial owner of the Kansas City Athletics (A's). The A's owner and Bisher became acquainted through their charity work in the Easter Seals campaign.

Finley wore out his welcome in Kansas City soon after he purchased the team in December 1960. Within weeks of buying the A's, he threatened to move his franchise unless the city agreed to build him a new stadium. During a 1962 dinner meeting on Easter Seals business, Finley complained to Bisher about the treatment he received from the media and politicians in Kansas City. Bisher told the A's owner that if he was considering moving his franchise, Atlanta's mayor had campaigned on building a stadium and bringing MLB to town, and he should keep Atlanta in mind. Several months after their initial conversation, Finley called Bisher to tell him he was considering moving his franchise to Atlanta. Earlier that day, the newly elected Kansas City Board of Alderman terminated a contract for a new municipal stadium that Finley had negotiated with the previous administration. Finley accepted Bisher's offer and soon traveled to Atlanta for a look at potential stadium sites.[5]

Finley and Bisher looked at three locations around Atlanta, all of which were either too small or too far from the CBD for Finley's liking. In 1962 Allen expressed his preference for building the stadium at the recently abandoned Lakewood Park race track, but the A's owner, who surveyed the site on his tour, considered the out-of-the-way location the least desirable of the three. Finley wanted his A's to play in a showpiece, downtown stadium. Bisher consulted with Allen after the unsuccessful tour while the Alabama-born Finley indulged in Atlanta's array of barbeque restaurants. If Finley wanted a center-city location, Allen suggested Bisher take him to the vacant Washington-Rawson urban renewal site, located just south of the state capitol and the CBD. Days earlier, Allen said in his memoir, the idea of building the stadium at Washington-Rawson occurred to him while gazing at the city map on the wall in his office.[6]

"I've got the greatest location in the world," Allen told Bisher.[7] The City of Atlanta cleared Washington-Rawson during its first round of urban renewal slum clearance in the late 1950s, demolishing the homes of more than 5,500 predominately poor and working-class Black residents of the neighborhood. Over the first half of the twentieth century, Washington-Rawson deteriorated from a stable, middle-class neighborhood into one of the city's worst slums, populated primarily by economically imperiled Black migrants from rural Georgia. Atlanta's

Black leadership supported the "slum clearance" program in Washington-Rawson, believing the land would soon be filled with affordable housing. Instead, the strategically situated lot sat vacant for years as the city's expressway system started to encircle it.

The Atlanta Housing Authority (AHA), the agency that owned Washington-Rawson, wanted the 598-acre site to be a buffer between the CBD and the impoverished, predominately African American neighborhoods to its south, namely Summerhill, Mechanicsville, and Peoplestown. In its 1957 plan for Washington-Rawson, the AHA envisioned the new neighborhood as having a mix of recreational, commercial, and light-industrial uses, anchored by a residential area populated by single family homes. In subsequent years, the AHA encouraged private investors to finance the construction of middle-income housing on the site, but no developers expressed interest. By the time Finley toured the land in April 1963, three interstate highways (I-20, I-75, and I-85) and a thirty-two-lane interchange, the largest in the South, encircled the then desolate Washington-Rawson site.[8]

Allen visited the site with Bisher and Finley. As Finley looked over Washington-Rawson, Allen described the ongoing expressway development around the site. He explained that the interstates converging on the site would enable three-quarters of Georgia's population to drive to the prospective stadium within ninety minutes. Nearly twenty million people in the southeastern United States, none of whom lived in a city with an MLB team, resided within three hundred miles of Washington-Rawson. Allen pointed out the landmarks of downtown Atlanta and described how close each one of them was to the prospective stadium. The Five Points, the historic core of the CBD, stood less than a mile away. Finley offered effusive praise for the site, agreeing with Allen that it was the best location in the nation for a municipal stadium.[9]

"Mr. Mayor," Bisher and Allen recalled Finley saying, "build a stadium here, and you will have a Major League team." Finley went so far as to promise to move the A's to Atlanta once the city completed the stadium.[10] Allen and Finley started discussing what dimensions the A's owner wanted for the prospective stadium when Bisher interjected, asking if Finley could win league approval for the move. Finley said he would inquire with AL owners when he returned to Missouri. Before leaving town, Finley met with a group of Big Mules, including bank executive Mills Lane Jr., one of Allen's closest confidants and a tireless civic booster, to describe his enthusiasm for Atlanta and the potential stadium site.[11]

The prospect of luring an MLB team set Allen, Lane, and the rest of the civic establishment to work on the stadium project immediately. Allen later described the effort as building a stadium "on land we didn't own, with money we didn't have, and for teams we had not signed."[12] After the Big Mules meeting with the A's suddenly bubbly owner, Lane advised Allen on how to proceed with the stadium project. The bank executive was known to the public as an eccentric, flamboyant-dressing gadabout, but he was arguably the most influential member of the Big Mules. Lane asked Allen to recreate the moribund Atlanta–Fulton County Recreation Authority, typically referred to as the Stadium Authority, with Atlanta Coca-Cola bottler Arthur Montgomery as its chairman and Lane as its treasurer.

The Stadium Authority for Atlanta and surrounding Fulton County was established by the Georgia General Assembly in 1960, endowing the public corporation with the power to facilitate the financing, planning, and construction of a municipal stadium. The legislation that created the Authority had enabled the body to issue revenue certificates to finance the building of a stadium, which would later be retired by stadium income. William Hartsfield's opposition to public involvement in stadium construction kept the organization dormant during the final years of his administration, but now it would open for business with a clear mandate from the civic elite.[13]

In exchange for recreating the Stadium Authority, Lane

pledged the full credit of his C&S Bank behind the project. Additionally, he agreed to invest $600,000 of his own money in a feasibility study for building the stadium at the Washington-Rawson site. Allen agreed to Lane's terms for reactivating the nine-member Authority. He made appointments for the six city positions on the Stadium Authority based on Lane's recommendations. The Fulton County Board of Commissioners made its three appointments to the Authority based on recommendations by Lane as well. This approach was business as usual for the Big Mules, who had shaped a governing consensus in Atlanta that blurred the lines between municipal and corporate power, all in the name of pushing the city forward.[14]

By June 1963, Atlanta had an activist Stadium Authority in place. Allen and Stadium Authority chairman Montgomery continued secret talks with Finley over the details of the stadium plan, negotiating everything from the prospective seating capacity to the dimensions of the field to the number of available parking spaces in the area. Finley haggled over even the most asinine aspects of the stadium's design, demanding that the ballpark be tailor-made in every respect. Montgomery and Allen were inclined to indulge Finley's impulses since he was the only baseball owner who had shown genuine interest in moving his franchise to Atlanta. As negotiations continued through the early summer of 1963, rumors that Finley would not win AL approval for the move reached the Stadium Authority. Finley had floated the idea of relocating his franchise and received uniformly negative responses from his peers. In his brief tenure as owner, Finley had already made a number of enemies. His tacky stadium gimmicks, his tendency to quarrel with other owners, and the crass and decidedly public way in which he engaged in stadium negotiations with Kansas City put him at odds with the rest of the league. Additionally, many AL owners did not like the idea of wasting a prime market like Atlanta on a retread franchise like the A's with an off-kilter owner like Finley. Others disapproved of Atlanta because of the additional travel expenses that trips to the Southeast would force them to incur. The Big Mules remained open to the idea of the A's coming to town, but, as their doubts about Finley grew, they decided to broaden their campaign to bring MLB to Atlanta.[15]

Ivan Allen led a booster expedition to Cleveland to meet with other potentially interested team owners during the festivities surrounding the 1963 All-Star Game. Accompanying Allen were Montgomery, Lane, Bisher, *Constitution* sports editor Jesse Outlar, and Crackers owner Earl Mann. Over the three-day All-Star break, they pitched Atlanta as a Major League City and described their campaign to build a new stadium. Allen advised Montgomery to offer flexible stadium leasing terms to interested teams. The mayor encouraged Montgomery to focus more on luring a franchise than driving a hard bargain in these early stages of discussion. While Finley scuttled his plans to move his club to Georgia during the All-Star break, the Atlanta delegation held formal meetings with two other franchises during the visit. Montgomery admitted to the media that he was discussing the stadium with organizations other than Kansas City, but he refused to divulge their names. The Atlanta party met first with officials from the hometown Cleveland Indians, whose struggles on the field were matched by their consistently poor attendance and unstable ownership situation. Discussions with the Indians' owners about moving to Atlanta proved short-lived. Representatives of Seattle, Oakland, and Arlington, Texas, were already in negotiations with the Cleveland owners. Atlanta's leaders decided to stay out of the crowded field of cities vying for the Indians, which ended up staying put in Cleveland.[16]

The following spring, the Stadium Authority received a consulting firm's feasibility study that described the impact it foresaw a municipal stadium and professional sports having on Metropolitan Atlanta. The report said that building a stadium would serve as "a symbol to the nation of Atlanta's growth in spirit . . . this special quality of Atlanta—this spirit—it is the spirit of progressive action that the rest of the nation has come to expect of Atlanta and which will be enhanced when the Stadium is built and major league contests are held."[17] Atlanta's leadership had long regarded their city as unique among its regional peers, both for its economic dynamism and racial moderation. Their decision to try to make their community a Major League City reflected a desire on their part to assert Atlanta's distinctiveness from the rest of the South while simultaneously becoming its primary point of reference, both for the region and the nation.

To achieve this grand civic enterprise, Atlanta's leaders, both Black and white, prioritized stadium building above many other municipal ventures, especially the city's commitment to building affordable housing to replace the thousands of units destroyed during the city's slum-clearance campaign of the 1950s. The stadium was not the first nor the last civic enterprise prioritized ahead of housing construction. Both highway construction and the building of the Atlanta Civic Center proceeded on land adjacent to the CBD that had been cleared during the 1950s as part of urban renewal, but the city's political and economic leadership invested neither of those developments with the kind of social and cultural meaning that they did Atlanta Stadium. The Stadium, in the words of Ivan Allen, had "sprung from a previously blighted area, like the mythological Phoenix from the ashes." It would transform Atlanta from a regional center into a "truly cosmopolitan city."[18]

THE ATLANTA JUNKET'S MOST PROMISING DISCUSSIONS in Cleveland took place with some of the co-owners of the Milwaukee Braves. In June 1963 Braves co-owner Delbert Coleman met with Montgomery to discuss his team's problems in Milwaukee and learn more about Atlanta's plans for a stadium. A larger party from the LaSalle Corporation, the Braves' ownership group, came to Cleveland that July to listen to Atlanta's pitch. Atlanta's representatives described their plans for the stadium and the city's prospects for continued economic growth, and they concluded by offering the Braves generous stadium leasing terms, which included a flexible annual rental fee and control over parking and concession revenues. Additionally, Atlanta officials promised that any team that moved to their city would benefit from its lucrative radio and television market that spanned seven southern states, none of whom had their own Major League franchise.[19]

Rumors of the meeting in Cleveland circulated in the press throughout the summer of 1963. The Braves owners denied the rumors vehemently, but, privately, they told the other NL owners about the lucrative deal Atlanta offered them to relocate. Local support for the Milwaukee Braves had declined in recent years. In the five seasons since the Braves won the World Series in 1957, their attendance dropped every single year. The Braves continued to post winning records every season but kept falling further out of contention for the NL pennant. In 1957 the Braves had drawn an NL record 2,215,404 fans to Milwaukee County Stadium. In 1962 the Braves finished eighth out of ten NL teams in attendance, drawing 766,921 fans to watch a team that fell out of contention by Memorial Day. The Braves' anemic broadcasting revenue proved insufficient to make up for the team's poor gate. The franchise lost money in Milwaukee for the first time that season.[20]

The Braves' economic problems stemmed from more than their declining fortunes on the diamond. Team ownership had become decidedly stingier with its promotions. A 1961 Milwaukee County statute banning fans from carrying in their own beverages dissuaded many fans from attending. Historically, Braves fans came to games with ice chests filled with six packs of beer. Suddenly, fans were expected to purchase twelve-ounce draft beers for thirty cents from stadium vendors. Milwaukee County overturned the unpopular statute after the 1961 season, but the damage to the stadium's reputation as a fan-friendly environment had been done.

The 1961 relocation of the AL's Washington Senators to Minneapolis–Saint Paul put the rechristened Minnesota Twins franchise into direct competition with the Braves for the loyalties of fans in the Upper Midwest. The Twins poached a number of the Braves' radio affiliates in Minnesota, Iowa, and northern Wisconsin, cutting the Milwaukee franchise off from this revenue stream and circumscribing the Braves' regional appeal. The emergence of the Green Bay Packers as a professional football power in the early 1960s also diverted a great deal of fan and media interest away from the Braves. The opening of the Packers' summer training camp often coincided with the Braves' fading from pennant contention, making the seasonal transition to football easier for frustrated Wisconsin sports fans. Moreover, the Packers scheduled home and exhibition dates in Milwaukee every season, competing directly with the Braves for the discretionary income of Southeastern Wisconsinites.[21]

Longtime Braves owner Lou Perini decided to sell the franchise after the 1962 season. Unable to find a local buyer, Perini sold eighty-five percent of the team for $6.2 million to the LaSalle Corporation, a syndicate of young Chicago corporate leaders led by thirty-four-year-old insurance executive Bill Bartholomay. The Braves new ownership group consisted primarily of the sons of wealthy industrialists. The group included heirs to the Johnson's Floor Wax, Searle Pharmaceuticals, and Palmer House fortunes and current executives at Sara Lee and Johnson & Johnson. *Milwaukee Journal* sports editor Oliver Kuechle nicknamed them the "Rover Boys" after the series of children's books about a mischievous group of young lads. The Rover Boys started complaining about their treatment in the local press as soon as they purchased the team. Kuechle was the group's most vociferous critic. He accused them of sabotaging Milwaukee as a baseball market. The new owners disputed Kuechle's assertion, pointing to a comment he made in a column two years earlier, referring to baseball as a "moribund" sport quickly losing its hold on the American public to professional football. It was hard for Wisconsin sports fans, who witnessed the simultaneous decline of the

Braves and ascension of Vince Lombardi's Green Bay Packers in the early 1960s, not to agree with Kuechle's assessment.[22]

Soon after the Rover Boys purchased the Braves, they offered 115,000 shares of common stock in the team for sale to Wisconsin residents at ten dollars per share. The idea of the public buying stock in a professional sports franchise was a familiar one to Wisconsinites. Since their founding in 1923, the Green Bay Packers football team had been owned by small, local stockholders, none of whom were allowed to control more than four percent of the team's stock. The Packers were the only nonprofit and community-owned team in professional sports, an organizational model that has since been prohibited for future ownership groups by all four major professional sports leagues. When the Rover Boys sold stock in the Braves in the early 1960s, they were not trying to expand the Packers' community ownership model to the state's other professional sports franchise. Primarily, the Rover Boys were interested in using the money to repay the millions of dollars in personal debt they collectively took on when they bought the team. To finance the purchase of the Braves, the Rover Boys borrowed $3 million in the team's name from the First Wisconsin National Bank and an additional $900,000 from the Marshall & Ilsley Bank of Milwaukee. The Braves promoted the sale of approximately one-third of the team's stock extensively in the local media, but fewer than one thousand investors purchased a total of thirteen thousand shares. Few Milwaukeeans wanted to help the Chicago "carpetbaggers," as they were often referred to in the local press, pay off the debts they incurred purchasing the team. Shortly thereafter, the Rover Boys began looking for a more agreeable home for their franchise.[23]

When rumors surfaced that the Braves were considering relocation, it was greeted locally and nationally with disbelief. Over the course of their first decade in Milwaukee, the Braves drew more fans than any other franchise in MLB. The Braves had moved to Milwaukee in 1953 after more than eighty seasons in Boston, where they spent decades as the Red Sox's poor relation. Between 1917 and 1946, the Boston Braves never finished higher than fourth place in the NL. Even when the Braves put together their best season in decades, winning the 1948 NL Pennant, the Red Sox outdrew them by more than one hundred thousand fans. By the early 1950s, Braves attendance had fallen dramatically as the team returned to its typical mediocrity. The 1952 Braves drew 281,278 fans in seventy-seven home dates, the second worst attendance by any team since World War II. In March 1953 the NL voted to give Braves owner Lou Perini the right to move his franchise to Milwaukee, the first such franchise relocation in MLB in fifty years.[24]

Milwaukee greeted the Braves with unprecedented civic enthusiasm. More than sixty thousand people welcomed the team to the city at a chilly, early April parade.[25] "The Braves couldn't spend a dime in this town or pay for a meal," sportswriter Frank Deford said, recalling Milwaukee's infatuation with the team during the 1950s.[26] The players were showered with free cars, groceries, and clothing. "Dry cleaners clamored for the honor of doing their laundry," later Braves manager Bobby Bragan recalled.[27] Fans from a dozen states across the Upper Midwest and the Great Plains filled the parking lot of the Braves' new $5 million municipally financed ballpark, Milwaukee County Stadium. In their first season in Milwaukee, the Braves drew more than 1.8 million fans, a new NL attendance record. On the way to their first pennant in Milwaukee, the 1957 Braves broke their own attendance mark, drawing more than 2.2 million fans to County Stadium. Milwaukee faced the heavily favored New York Yankees in the World Series. Before the first game, Yankees manager Casey Stengel referred to Milwaukee as "Bushville" in an offhand comment to a reporter. Milwaukeeans embraced the patronizing moniker, filling County Stadium with Bushville banners during the seven-game series. When the Braves clinched the deciding seventh game in the Bronx, more than four hun-

dred thousand people gathered in downtown Milwaukee to
celebrate the city's first professional sports championship.[28]

The idea that the Braves would consider moving from
Milwaukee, then the nation's seventeenth largest market, to
Atlanta, then the nation's twenty-fourth largest market, surprised many of the baseball insiders with whom the Braves'
owners discussed the matter. Atlanta offered to build the
Braves a brand-new stadium and provide them with a generous rental agreement. Milwaukee had done the same for the
Braves a decade earlier when it lured the franchise from Boston. Though Milwaukee's stadium was not as new and its leasing arrangement with Milwaukee County did not offer as many
potential revenue streams, Milwaukee was a proven baseball
market. Atlanta, by contrast, struggled to draw enough fans
to support its AAA minor league team. The Rover Boys won
over skeptical NL owners by emphasizing the unique regional
television market available to an Atlanta team. By placing a
club in Atlanta, the media flagship of the Southeast, the NL
would assert its television and radio preeminence in Georgia, Florida, Alabama, Mississippi, and the Carolinas before
the AL moved teams into these growing markets.[29]

NL owners acceded to the Braves' desire for a freehand in
negotiations with Atlanta, even though the other clubs derived
no direct benefit from the Braves' potentially lucrative television contract. MLB teams did not pool their local television money. The Atlanta market provided the Braves with the
opportunity to maximize their total revenues considerably.
Once rumors of the Braves' move to Atlanta went public, Milwaukee boosters tried unsuccessfully to match the television
dollars Atlanta offered the team. The Schlitz Brewery offered
the Milwaukee Braves a lucrative three-year radio and television deal worth $535,000 per season beginning in 1965, a
significant increase over the $400,000 they received in 1964.
The Braves ownership turned down Schlitz's offer. By comparison, Atlanta's WSB-TV had offered the Braves a two-year,
$2.5 million television contract.[30]

WHILE THE BRAVES' OWNERS CONTINUED DENYING THE rumored move, promising the team's return to Milwaukee for the 1964 season, Atlanta officials worked diligently to plan, finance, and prepare to break ground on their new stadium. Two of Atlanta's leading architectural firms, Finch, Alexander, Barnes, Rothschild, and Pascal (FABRAP) and Heery & Heery, collaborated to produce the Lane-financed stadium feasibility study. Rather than building a baseball-specific stadium, the design team advised Atlanta to build a facility capable of accommodating baseball as well as football, since civic boosters were then in the process of pursuing an NFL franchise. Their proposed design was in keeping with virtually all of the major, municipally financed stadiums built during the 1960s and 1970s: DC Stadium (later Robert F. Kennedy Memorial Stadium) in Washington (1961), Shea Stadium in New York (1964), Oakland Coliseum (1966), Busch Memorial Stadium in St. Louis (1966), Jack Murphy Stadium in San Diego (1967), Riverfront Stadium in Cincinnati (1970), Three Rivers Stadium in Pittsburgh (1970), and Veterans Stadium in Philadelphia (1971). These stadiums are now widely criticized for their "flying saucer" structural designs, their insularity from the surrounding urban landscape, and the lack of intimacy afforded spectators as a result of their designers' efforts to fit two profoundly different playing fields into the same space. Yet for municipalities that wanted a stadium, the multipurpose venue proved an economically and spatially convenient development model.[31]

In September 1963 the Stadium Authority, in consultation with the Braves, agreed to the proposed stadium design. The final design expanded the construction site to sixty-two acres, adding land across the Southeast Expressway for additional parking spaces. The size of the construction site was a concern to the housing authority, who expressed concerns that stadium construction could further delay decade-old promises to the area's former residents to build new, affordable housing on the site. Mayor Allen intervened, assuaging the concerns of the AHA by promising city participation in the construction of a thousand new, mixed-income housing units on the western side of the site after the stadium was complete. The Stadium Authority and the AHA agreed to a price of $1.8 million for the sixty-two-acre site, pending a lease agreement between the City of Atlanta and an MLB team to play at the prospective stadium.[32]

On March 5, 1964, Ivan Allen announced he had made a "verbal contract" with an unnamed MLB team to play in Atlanta the following spring. Allen's proclamation was the product of a winter's worth of secret negotiations with the Braves ownership. The mayor announced that he would seek approval from the Board of Aldermen's finance committee for the purchase of the proposed stadium site before seeking the Board's approval of the comprehensive stadium plan. At a public hearing on the stadium at City Hall, dozens of civic leaders and private citizens voiced unequivocal support for the plan, leading Allen to say that the stadium hearings displayed the "greatest unanimity I've ever seen on any issue."[33]

"The Stadium doesn't just represent the city or even the state," former Atlanta Cracker pitcher Bruce Gruber told the assembled Aldermen. "It represents the whole Southeast. Atlanta has efficiency in every area except sports. Now is the opportunity to bring that up to date. Right now, Atlanta is Major League in everything from zoos to auditoriums and bush league in sports."[34] Ivan Allen, during the hearing process, expressed the sentiment that the building of a municipal stadium in Atlanta was a collective responsibility for Atlanta, Fulton County, and the State of Georgia, with mutual benefits for all parties. "The way I see it," Allen said, "this shouldn't be the burden of Atlanta alone, but a joint undertaking of the city, the county, and the state."[35] During the March 1964 approval process, Governor Carl Sanders promised to prioritize the building of dedicated access roads from I-20, I-75, and I-85 once stadium construction began.[36]

Atlanta's Black leadership did not express any public opposition to the proposed new stadium's location, despite the project's tangible impact on the economic and domestic lives of thousands of African Americans. The Washington-Rawson slum-clearance program of the late 1950s had displaced thousands of Black Atlantans living just south of Atlanta's CBD on valuable property in close proximity to countless employment opportunities. The housing needs of thousands of predominately Black Atlantans were secondary to a civic prestige project, despite the mayor's campaign promise to end the housing crisis that affected this core group in his electoral base. Rather than opposing the stadium project, Black political organizations focused instead on ensuring nondiscriminatory hiring practices by stadium contractors and guaranteeing that African Americans received an adequate share of the jobs associated with building and maintaining the facility. During the stadium-approval process, Atlanta's Black leadership prioritized the access of their constituents to jobs associated with the stadium over the impact that stadium construction had on the housing needs of many Black residents.[37]

The approach of the city's Black leaders to the stadium issue demonstrated their commitment to making deals with the city's white leadership on controversial issues so long as their negotiated settlements provided tangible economic benefits to the city's African American community. Specifically, Black leaders' endorsement of the stadium proposal was the product of years of hard work by Ivan Allen and his backers to win African American support for the city's urban renewal projects, dating back to Allen's tenure with the Atlanta Chamber. He built support for urban renewal among the Black business communities south and east of downtown, arguing that the large-scale projects planned for the areas, such as the auditorium-coliseum and the stadium, would provide an engine for economic development in the surrounding neighborhoods.[38]

Moreover, partnering with the white leadership on the stadium issue further cemented the Black leadership's position in the city's governing coalition. Supporting the stadium plan made the Black leadership co-trustees in the creation of a major civic institution and provided many Black Atlantans in the surrounding neighborhoods with access to economic opportunities stemming from the construction of the stadium. Rather than holding out for the perfect, Atlanta's Black leaders grasped successfully for the possible.

Representatives of the city's most prominent Black political organizations expressed unanimous support for the stadium project at the Board of Aldermen's public hearing on the matter. Q. V. Williamson of the Atlanta Negro Voters League challenged the mayor and the Aldermen to live up to their campaign promises and make sure that stadium construction commenced immediately. The Urban League endorsed the stadium building plan and made nonspecific recommendations that housing be built on the remaining acreage of Washington-Rawson, pressing the mayor gently to live up to the promises he made to the AHA when he negotiated a purchase price for the land.[39] Rev. Samuel Williams and Clarence D. Coleman made a joint statement in favor of the stadium plan on behalf of the Atlanta Summit Leadership Conference (ASLC), a coalition of nine civil rights groups, including the SCLC, the Atlanta branch of the NAACP, and Operation Breadbasket. "The Negro community strongly supports the stadium project, providing it is administered so as to protect the interests and rights of all Atlanta and Fulton County citizens." Expressing the consensus of their constituent organizations, the representatives of the ASLC asked for a provision in the contract forbidding discrimination by stadium contractors. They also lobbied for a provision in the stadium lease banning discriminatory hiring practices by future vendors and concessioners. The ASLC conceived of the proposed amendments as part of their broader effort to ensure the de facto desegregation of all public accommodations in the city.[40]

The Board of Alderman rejected 10–4 an amendment aimed at banning racially discriminatory hiring practices by stadium contractors. Despite the widespread support by Black political organizations for the amendment, a clear majority of aldermen considered the amendment unnecessary, demonstrating a chasm between the white and Black leadership's view of the issue. Allen remained silent on the amendment, despite his campaign promise to support nondiscrimination clauses in city contracts. White leaders who spoke publicly against the measure, in particular Stadium Authority chairman Arthur Montgomery, were incredulous at the suggestion that such an amendment was needed in progressive Atlanta.

Montgomery argued that such legislation was unnecessary since all parties to the project already opposed racial discrimination. Moreover, he stated, all of MLB was desegregated, just like Atlanta. Atlanta's leadership had worked out the contours of the city's desegregation through evolution, not through legal mandates of the kind presented in the amendment. Throughout Atlanta's post–World War II history as the City Too Busy to Hate, white civic leaders often responded similarly when their priorities or approach to racially sensitive matters of public policy were questioned. Over the course of the 1960s, virtually every major policy issue in Atlanta seemed to manifest itself as an issue steeped in racial meaning. As Atlanta became a majority-Black city, the city's white leaders could no longer manage major public decisions from above as they did, arguably for the last time, on the stadium question. By the end of the 1960s, the Big Mules lacked the electoral clout to frame such issues on behalf of the city's politically ascendant African American majority. Black Atlantans came increasingly to see their interests as not represented by a civic leadership class that came to expect their support.[41]

LESS THAN A MONTH AFTER ALLEN ANNOUNCED THE ORAL contract he made with an unnamed franchise, the Atlanta–Fulton County Recreation Authority awarded the stadium contract to Thompson & Street Company for approximately $14 million, pending the approval of the stadium funding plan by

the Atlanta Board of Aldermen's finance committee and, subsequently, the entire board. The $14 million for construction
made up the vast majority of the Stadium Authority's proposed $18 million budget. An additional $1.8 million went to
the AHA for the acquisition of the Washington-Rawson site.
The Stadium Authority estimated $893,000 in engineering
and architectural fees for the project, plus an additional $1.32
million in capitalized interest and reserves. Once approved,
the Stadium Authority would put $18 million in thirty-year
municipal bonds up for sale with an estimated $10–13 million
in interest payments over the life of the revenue bond. The
Stadium Authority estimated that annual repayments of the
bond would amount to $1.08 million. An undetermined por-
tion of the annual repayment money would come from their
tenants' gross revenues. Two-thirds of the remaining annual
bill would be paid by the City of Atlanta, while the remaining
third would be paid by Fulton County.[42]

The wait for legislative approval proved short-lived. The
Fulton County Board of Commissioners endorsed the stadium
plan unanimously. In its 1964 session, the Georgia General
Assembly amended the Stadium Authority Bill to allow Fulton
County to finance its portion of the stadium with money from
a previously approved county parks improvement tax. In early
April, the Board of Aldermen's finance committee offered its
unanimous endorsement of the Washington-Rawson site and
the proposed $18 million stadium financing package, referring
the bill to the entire Board of Aldermen, which approved the
plan 13–1. Ed Gilliam, a vocal critic of the administration, cast
the only no vote. Gilliam did not oppose the building of a stadium but opposed the proposed financing mechanism. "We're
pledging the city and the county's money for thirty years for a
total debt of about $31.5 million," Gilliam said before the vote,
reminding the Aldermen of the interest payments the city
would incur as a result of the project. Within a decade of the
stadium's construction, many critics within the city's political leadership class had come around to Gilliam's view. They

regarded the annual debt payments required of the city and the county for Atlanta Stadium as a burden on the community.[43]

At the April 15 groundbreaking, a bulldozer idled behind Allen, Sanders, and Montgomery as they plunged their shovels into the ground. While a parade of construction equipment maneuvered into position for the first day of stadium building, the thousand or so people who gathered for the ceremony— Big Mules in now dust-covered tailored suits, baseball fans who skipped work to attend, and curious children from the surrounding neighborhoods—enjoyed hot dogs and Coca-Cola provided by Montgomery. The contractors didn't have time to wait for lunch to start working. Thompson & Street agreed to a provision penalizing the company $3,000 for every day over twelve months it took to complete the stadium. Atlanta needed the facility ready for Opening Day 1965 for their yet-unnamed new baseball franchise. Most similar stadium projects took at least two years from groundbreaking to grand opening. The stadium contract included a $600,000 premium if the company finished the stadium in less than one year. Thompson & Street finished the stadium in a mere fifty-one weeks.[44]

Furman Bisher dubbed the remarkable speed with which the city planned, approved, and built the stadium the "Miracle in Atlanta," which he later used as the title of his book on the subject. The construction of municipally owned stadiums in northern cities like New York and St. Louis during the 1960s was delayed for years by political and jurisdictional fights over prospective stadium sites, civil rights demonstrations protesting the racial makeup of construction workforces, and ongoing labor disputes. Atlanta had avoided all of this. All bodies relevant to the construction of Atlanta Stadium displayed a single-mindedness in finishing the project on time.[45] At the time, Atlanta Stadium, as city officials decided to name the municipally owned park, was the second-largest construction project in the history of the city behind the Grady Memorial Hospital, which opened in 1959.[46] "Sitting as it did beside a hundred-acre expressway interchange where three major

interstate highways connect, its baby blue seats and gleam-
ing light towers glistening in the sun, the Stadium was visible and literal proof that Atlanta was a big league city," Allen
wrote of the stadium's completion years later in his memoir, reverentially personifying the structure with language
that sounded more like an Italian Futurist manifesto than the
words of a big-city mayor.[47]

5

Wisconsin v. Milwaukee Braves

BRAVES OFFICIALS DENIED REPORTS OF A POSSIBLE MOVE
to Atlanta until the *Sporting News* published an article in July
1964 confirming that the Rover Boys had made an agreement
with Allen and Montgomery back in March to play in the new
stadium in 1965. A month before the *Sporting News* broke
the story, Milwaukee County offered to renegotiate with the
Braves, charging only one dollar in rent for their first million
in attendance each season while offering the team a larger
share of concessions revenue and reduced maintenance fees.
The Rover Boys said they had no problem with the existing
lease, which ran through 1965. Despite the city's efforts, the
new owners said the declining support the Braves received
in Milwaukee made it difficult for the franchise to continue
operating in the city.[1]

At the end of the 1964 season, the Braves announced they
were holding a Board of Directors meeting, fittingly, in Chicago
to discuss the future of the franchise. Up until a week before
the meeting, Braves owners reiterated that they had not purchased the team with plans to move them to another city. On
October 21, 1964, the Braves Board of Directors voted 12–6 to
relocate the franchise to Atlanta. The Rover Boys voted as a
bloc in favor of the move. The no votes all came from minor
Wisconsin-based stockholders. The Braves' majority owners orchestrated the events leading up to the vote to ensure a
smooth transition out of Milwaukee.

Milwaukee County, though, made sure that the Braves'
planned exit did not go as intended. A week before the meet-

ing, Bartholomay met with Allen and Montgomery in Atlanta to finalize a twenty-five-year contract for use of the new stadium. Braves officials consulted with the other nine NL clubs to ensure their unanimous support for the move. The day after the Braves' board voted to move, NL owners met to discuss the franchise's relocation to Atlanta. Before the Braves could make their official relocation request, Wisconsin Circuit Court Judge Ronald Dreschler issued an injunction on behalf of the Milwaukee County Board of Supervisors against the team moving to Atlanta for the 1965 season on the grounds that the Braves' lease required them to play one more season at Milwaukee County Stadium. Rather than fight the injunction, the NL voted unanimously in early November 1964 to require the Braves to play a lame duck 1965 season in Milwaukee while granting them permission to move to Atlanta in 1966.[2]

Once the NL signed off on the Braves' relocation to Atlanta, the Rover Boys went ahead and signed a twenty-five-year lease for the team at Atlanta Stadium beginning in 1966. The contract contained provisions allowing for the lease to begin in 1965 if the Braves could find a way to negotiate their way out of Milwaukee over the off-season. The Braves' lease with the Atlanta–Fulton County Stadium Authority provided them with numerous potential revenue streams in return for a small percentage of their total gate. The team had the right to rent out Atlanta Stadium for any event other than a professional football game. The city retained the right to make a lease with either an NFL or an AFL franchise. The Stadium Authority granted the Braves control over the revenues from six thousand of the eight thousand parking spaces surrounding the stadium. The Braves agreed to pay the Stadium Authority a fixed 7.5 percent of gross proceeds per event date, baseball or otherwise. The 7.5 percent of gross proceeds constituted the Braves' entire responsibility toward paying off the stadium bonds. The city and county guaranteed the rest. The Stadium Authority gave the Braves $500,000 for relocation costs and agreed to pay $280,000 for the minor league territorial rights to Atlanta for the 1965 season. This enabled the AAA Crackers to switch their affiliation from the Twins to the Braves and play in the new stadium during the franchise's lame-duck year.[3]

Never before had a relocating Major League franchise agreed to such generous, multifaceted leasing terms with public officials in its new home city. Decades later, Arthur Montgomery defended the liberal leasing terms he offered the Braves. He acknowledged that "the Braves lease has been called a 'sweetheart deal,'" but, he said, demonstrating the zeal with which Atlanta pursued the Braves franchise, "we had to entice them into coming here."[4] Future Atlanta mayors proved unwilling to offer professional sports franchises such generous leasing terms. In 1970 and 1971, when Sam Massell negotiated with Hawks and Flames owner Tom Cousins on the financing and leasing terms for the Omni, he invoked the Braves' lease at Atlanta Stadium as an experience the city needed to learn from when making deals with private investors. Before agreeing to a plan that empowered the Stadium Authority to sell bonds to finance construction of the arena, Massell won contractual assurances from Cousins that the municipality would not end up paying off the debts of the project like it did on an annual basis for Atlanta Stadium.[5]

The legal impasse and lame-duck 1965 season at Atlanta Stadium tempered the enthusiasm of Georgians' reaction to the news of the Braves' relocation. The Stadium Authority offered Milwaukee County a $500,000 cash settlement to buy out the final year of the Braves' stadium contract, more than twice the amount of revenue the club produced for the county during the 1964 season. The Milwaukee County Board of Supervisors rejected the offer, 24–0. Milwaukeeans were happy to have the Braves sweat out a lame-duck year in town. "Make them conform to the contract," said Milwaukee Mayor Frank Zeidler, supporting Milwaukee County Board of Supervisors chairman Eugene Grobschmidt's hardline approach to the Braves' lease. "Keep them at arm's length. They may learn something about the meaning of responsibility."[6]

Caught in the middle were the players. "It was hard for us to tell the good guys from the bad guys," Hank Aaron, the Braves' All-Star right fielder said, describing the uncomfortable position the Braves players faced throughout the 1965 season in Milwaukee. "Milwaukee was trying to keep us around, but the people there wanted nothing to do with us."[7] By and large, Milwaukee fans boycotted the lame-duck Braves. Local bars and restaurants stopped serving Coca-Cola, Atlanta's best-known export, in protest. Pranksters terrorized the Braves' executives, egging their homes, setting off firecrackers on their lawns, and harassing their children. Attendance at Milwaukee County Stadium plummeted to a new season low of 550,584 for an average of 7,610 per game, less than a quarter as many as the team drew seven seasons earlier.[8] The few fans who showed up "made up for their small numbers with plenty of invective," Braves manager Bobby Bragan wrote of the 1965 season.[9] The Braves lost more than $1.5 million during their lame-duck season in Milwaukee. Coca-Cola softened the financial blow by secretly advancing the franchise money against the team's future television contract, enabling the Braves to operate in Milwaukee that season without taking on any new loans. Atlanta newspapers highlighted the Milwaukee Braves' poor attendance, taking particular glee in the April and May evenings when fewer than a thousand fans attended games at Milwaukee County Stadium.[10]

Despite their lack of local support, the Braves fielded a strong team in 1965, one that remained firmly in the pennant race until the final weeks of the season. As late as August 20, the Braves were in first place in the NL before fading to fifth place in September. When the team started to struggle after the All-Star break, Board of Supervisors chairman Grobschmidt implied that the team was tanking to avoid playing a World Series in Milwaukee, a statement that drew broad derision in both Wisconsin and Georgia. Bragan responded angrily to Grobschmidt's assertion, calling him a "foolish, dimwitted politician." As the Braves faded in the final weeks of the season, Hank Aaron and Eddie Mathews, the two most beloved players in Milwaukee Braves history, broke Lou Gehrig and Babe Ruth's career record for most home runs by teammates. Once the court injunction binding the Braves to Milwaukee ended at the conclusion of the 1965 season, the Braves finally relocated to Atlanta, almost a year after the team moved its administration to the Peach State. A federal judge in Houston empowered the Braves to relocate immediately after the season, providing the Stadium Authority with an injunction that required the team to uphold its new lease in Atlanta the following spring.[11]

The Stadium Authority filled the facility's calendar as best it could during the lame-duck season. The Atlanta Crackers drew sparse crowds all summer, never selling more than seven thousand tickets to a single home game. Local fans were more likely to follow the fifty-five radio and eighteen television broadcasts of the Milwaukee Braves carried that season by WSB than to support the minor league team playing in its new stadium. Atlanta officials had predicted that between three hundred thousand and four hundred thousand spectators would attend Crackers games in 1965. In their seventy-four home dates, the Crackers drew well under two hundred thousand fans, fewer people than attended the Braves' seven exhibition games at the stadium that season. The Braves' exhibition games, which were scattered throughout the calendar, drew roughly 211,000 spectators. Atlanta Stadium also hosted a pair of NFL preseason games in August 1965 that drew a combined eighty-six thousand fans.

BRAVES PLAYERS REACTED TO THE MOVE IN VERY different ways, fostering divisions in a locker room already on edge from the challenges of the lame-duck season. Older players like future Hall of Famers Eddie Mathews and Warren Spahn opposed the move. Their tenures with the Braves dated back to the team's glory years of the 1950s. They had settled their families in Milwaukee and established deep ties with the community. Native white Southerners, including pitcher Billy O'Dell, shortstop Woody Woodward, and manager Bobby Bragan, expressed excitement about returning to their home region.[12] Younger players tended to support the move as well. Many of them looked forward to the opportunity to play in a larger television market in a vibrant, growing city. "I'm ready for Peachtree," Joe Torre, the Braves' twenty-four-year-old catcher, told reporters soon after news of the team's departure went public. "I shed no tears about leaving Milwaukee," Torre wrote in his memoir. "I had great memories in Milwaukee . . . but I liked the idea of going to a more exciting city."[13]

Two of the Braves' African American players expressed a great deal of apprehension about the team's relocation to the South. Alabama natives Lee Maye and Hank Aaron made statements about the possibility of playing in the South that received extensive media coverage. "I hope and pray we don't go," Maye told reporters in October 1964 after the Braves' owners voted to relocate the franchise. "I am positive we will face discrimination, and I have no intention of moving my wife down to Atlanta."[14] Maye never had to make the move from Milwaukee to Atlanta. The Braves traded him early in the 1965 season to Houston, a far less progressive Southern city than Atlanta, in exchange for infielder Jim Beauchamp and veteran starting pitcher Ken Johnson. It is unclear whether the trade was motivated in part by Maye's statements the previous fall. The media portrayed Maye as a locker-room malcontent who came into personal conflict with a number of other players, including Aaron.

While a player of Lee Maye's caliber could be dealt for comparable talent, Atlanta and the Braves regarded it as imperative that a player of Aaron's ability and stature embrace the move, both as a matter of public relations and ensuring the team's on-the-field stability. "I lived in the South, and I don't want to live there again," Aaron told a reporter after the announcement. He never said he would refuse to play in Atlanta. Instead, he emphasized how well he had been treated in Milwaukee. "We can go anywhere in Milwaukee," he said. "I don't know what would happen in Atlanta."[15] Aaron disliked the idea of moving his children out of integrated Milwaukee schools, especially in the middle of the academic year. He feared that his children would have to attend either inferior segregated schools or face hostility in recently desegregated ones. As Aaron biographer Howard Bryant wrote, Aaron feared that his Blackness would become his primary identity, not his personal accomplishments. His wife Barbara also worried that the comforts of home, friendship, and neighborhood their family enjoyed in Milwaukee would disappear amid the racial hostility of Georgia.[16]

Atlanta responded quickly to the star's concerns, lobbying Aaron directly on the merits of the City Too Busy to Hate. With the help of the Rover Boys, Atlanta leaders relayed Aaron backchannel assurances about the integration of Atlanta and its sports facilities. Georgia State Assemblyman Leroy Johnson, who was the only Black state legislator in the South, spoke with Aaron, assuring him that the racial experiences Aaron had growing up in Alabama were not representative of the racial situation in modern Atlanta. Whitney Young of the Urban League and Atlanta NAACP President C. Miles Smith both wrote Aaron, touting Atlanta's racial progressivism and asking him to come to the city for a visit.[17] In response to Aaron's statement, Braves co-owner John McHale met with Allen and Coca-Cola magnate Robert W. Woodruff to discuss race relations in Atlanta. Allen and Woodruff promised McHale that Atlanta Stadium would have no segregated seating and that all public facilities at the ballpark would be desegregated just like they were throughout the city's downtown.[18]

Publicly, representatives of Atlanta's white leadership communicated to both the local and national press how scandalized they were by the suggestion that racial problems persisted in the city. Robert Richardson, attorney for the Stadium Authority, said in an article widely disseminated by the Associated

Press that he was amazed that Black players were concerned about segregation. "All facilities are integrated. It's a friendly place to live . . . a large number of negro athletes, both in pro baseball & pro football, have come to Atlanta to participate in events, and none have had the slightest difficulty in regard to eating or lodging facilities."[19]

In January 1965, Aaron came to Atlanta for a visit that was thoroughly orchestrated by the city's Black leadership. He toured the city with several Black leaders, who insisted that the Braves star would hold just as prominent a social position in Atlanta as he had in Milwaukee. They showed him the city's affluent Black neighborhoods and introduced him to the social life of elite Black Atlanta. They reassured him about the quality of educational opportunities available to African Americans of his economic stature. Aaron toured Atlanta Stadium with teammate Eddie Mathews. Both were impressed by its state-of-the-art features and hitter-friendly dimensions. Convinced of the city's suitability, Aaron soon purchased a home in a wealthy Black neighborhood in Southeast Atlanta, and his family moved into the house the following summer.[20]

In later years, Aaron accused reporters of putting words in players' mouths, including his own, about not wanting to move to Atlanta. He has asserted on a number of occasions that his primary concern was moving his children out of school in the middle of the 1964–65 academic year. Aaron's more recent protestations belie his broader concerns about moving back to the South. While Atlanta won Aaron over as an oasis of racial moderation, the communities surrounding the city and the larger region were far more hostile to the idea of integration. "The Braves were being positioned as a regional team," Howard Bryant wrote in his Aaron biography, "but outside of Atlanta, interracial competition was not a concept being met with great enthusiasm."[21] The demographic transformation of Metropolitan Atlanta—the simultaneous decentralization of population and political and economic power into the surrounding suburban counties and the emergence of a majority Black population in Atlanta proper during the 1960s and 1970s—added new layers of complexity to the public response to Aaron and integrated professional sports in Metropolitan Atlanta.

AS MILWAUKEE'S LEGAL INJUNCTION AGAINST THE BRAVES approached its expiration date, the State of Wisconsin intervened to try to stop the team from moving. In August 1965, State Attorney General Bronson La Follette filed suit against the Braves and the NL in state court, alleging that the defendants had deprived Milwaukee of MLB and were conspiring to keep the city from acquiring a replacement expansion team. The lawsuit charged that the NL had violated state antitrust laws by conspiring to restrain trade in Wisconsin and damage the state's economy by leaving Milwaukee without a franchise. La Follette, the twenty-nine-year-old grandson of Wisconsin progressive icon Robert M. "Fighting Bob" La Follette, offered to drop the antitrust suit if the NL guaranteed Milwaukee an expansion team the following season. NL officials refused the offer, which they considered an attempt by Milwaukee to hold them hostage. If the NL had given in to Milwaukee and granted it a new team, that would have encouraged any city facing a team relocation to try to leverage an expansion team out of the situation, thus creating a permanent threat to the league's sovereignty over its size and membership.[22]

Wisconsin v. The Milwaukee Braves went to trial in Wisconsin State Circuit Court in February 1966, months after the Braves had physically moved the remaining aspects of their operation to Atlanta. Following two months' worth of testimony by officials from the Braves, the NL, and Milwaukee County, Judge Elmer Roller ruled that the Braves and the NL had violated Wisconsin antitrust law by acting as a monopoly in "restraint of trade." The ruling came on April 13, 1966, the same day the Braves played their first regular season home game at Atlanta Stadium. Roller directed the NL to remedy the situation in one of two ways: either return the Braves to

Milwaukee immediately or grant Milwaukee an expansion franchise for the 1967 season. The NL appealed the case to the Wisconsin Supreme Court, which ruled 4–3 on behalf of the league in July. The majority on the Wisconsin Supreme Court reasoned that baseball's unique antitrust exemption stemming from the 1922 US Supreme Court decision in *Federal Baseball Club v. National League* superseded Wisconsin's state antitrust laws. The State of Wisconsin appealed the decision to the US Supreme Court, but the court refused to grant the case a *writ of certiorari*, returning the case to state court and effectively ending the suit.[23]

"Certainly no one, with the possible exception of the citizens of Atlanta (and even they seem to have their doubts), can approve of the carpetbagging tactics of the Braves' owners, nor deny that their callous move to Atlanta was a serious blow to the prestige of Major League Baseball," *Sports Illustrated* editorialized in April 1966, the week after the Braves' first regular-season game in Atlanta and Judge Roller's decision.[24] The largely behind-the-scenes actions that led to the relocation of the Braves and the construction of Atlanta Stadium were an emotionally taxing process for Atlanta's sports fans. "The mood was a combination of excitement, relief, and some civic pride that Atlanta had arrived on the national sports scene," longtime Atlanta baseball fan Karl Green recalled.[25] Atlanta's wait-hurry-wait path to the NL was not the first example of a city muscling its way into the Major Leagues through municipally sanctioned lobbying and municipally subsidized investments in professional sports. In many ways it demonstrated the changing relationship between cities and professional sports franchises, especially in regard to MLB, long considered by fans and informed observers as the steadiest of professional sports leagues. MLB franchises came to be regarded by their home cities as permanent civic institutions over the first half of the twentieth century. During the 1950s and 1960s, though, professional sports franchises took on a social meaning closer to that of mobile capital than of community pillars. Atlanta was one of the first cities to take advantage of the newly flexible national sports market by making generous civic investments in professional sports facilities as a means of attracting existing teams or convincing one of the major sports leagues to grant their community an expansion franchise. As more cities, especially those in the nation's South and West, became sufficiently populous and affluent to support professional sports franchises, the major professional leagues allowed existing franchises to relocate to these burgeoning metropolitan areas or granted them expansion franchises.

In the case of MLB, five teams moved from one city to another between 1953 and 1961. All of these cities had another MLB team in the other league, except for Washington DC, which was awarded a replacement expansion franchise when the Senators left for Minnesota. The relocation of the Braves from Milwaukee to Atlanta was the first move by an MLB franchise that left a city without a big league team. At the time, Milwaukee and Atlanta's struggle over the Braves was one of the most public conflicts to date resulting from franchise free agency, a condition that increasingly came to characterize the relationship between cities and professional sports teams in postwar America. The number of cities that desired big league sports franchises outpaced the number of franchises that monopolistic professional sports leagues were willing to grant, empowering the leagues and their members to largely dictate the terms of franchise relocation or expansion to eager cities.

6

Gravitating toward Atlanta

....

A SERIES OF NEAR MISSES, SHORT-LIVED AND UNDER-
funded investment groups, and half-baked plans for temporary stadiums characterized Atlanta's push for professional
football in the early 1960s. Several Atlanta-based partner-
ships failed between 1959 and 1964 to persuade either the
NFL or the upstart AFL to place an expansion team in the city
or to convince an existing professional franchise to move to
Georgia. Once the city completed Atlanta Stadium, the open
courting of Atlanta in 1965 by the two leagues made a striking
contrast to the studied aloofness that AFL and NFL representatives employed in their discussions with earlier Atlanta-
based groups. In the early summer of 1965, the AFL and NFL
clashed like never before for the privilege of placing a team
in a new stadium in a new market.[1]

Atlanta's push for professional football in the early 1960s
anticipated the soon-to-be standard dynamics of franchise free
agency. Cities unwilling to build new facilities were shut out
of the Major Leagues. Cities that invested in publicly funded
stadiums dramatically improved their bargaining position,
especially during the 1960s and 1970s when rival professional
leagues challenged each one of the big four. Indeed, the 1965
turf war between the AFL and the NFL for Atlanta portended
a decade's worth of conflict between competing professional
sports leagues for control of new markets in the Sunbelt.[2]

Before Atlanta became the most coveted expansion city in
the history of professional football, it spent a half decade trying to get either the NFL or AFL to take one of its numerous

bids seriously. In 1959 Major Sports Inc., an Atlanta-based partnership of local businessmen led by Eaton Chalkley, a used-car salesman turned real estate developer, took its shot at the AFL. Several years earlier, Chalkley had shown his sales acumen by convincing the actress Susan Hayward to marry him soon after introducing himself on a cross-country flight. Chalkley now worked seven days a week pursuing the eighth and final charter franchise in the AFL.[3]

First, the group put together plans to build a seventy-five-thousand-seat stadium at the Lakewood Park racetrack while working out a temporary deal with Atlanta Crackers owner Earl Mann to set up shop with sixteen thousand jerry-rigged bleachers at "Poncey." The seven original AFL owners, a like-minded group of young entrepreneurs and trust-funders, voted to grant Atlanta a franchise but changed their minds when Los Angeles Chargers owner Barron Hilton complained that his club lacked a West Coast rival. The AFL decided instead to grant its final charter franchise to Oakland, which had neither a stable ownership group nor an established playing facility.[4]

Undeterred, Chalkley continued lobbying AFL commissioner Joe Foss. In May 1960 Chalkley finally convinced Foss to award Atlanta a franchise for the 1961 season on the condition that Atlanta obtain a temporary lease at Georgia Tech's Grant Field and demonstrate progress on its plan to build a new football stadium. Major Sports failed on both fronts. Tech refused to lease its stadium out to a professional sports team, in part because the state-supported educational institution and its facilities were still segregated as a matter of state law. Georgia Tech did not desegregate its student body or its facilities until the fall 1961 semester, matching the timetable for desegregation in Atlanta Public Schools (APS). Meanwhile, Mayor Hartsfield refused to activate the Stadium Authority, which stymied Chalkley's plans for Lakewood Park and brought this bid for an AFL franchise to an end.[5]

Despite Hartfield's opposition, Foss encouraged Atlanta to continue its pursuit of an AFL franchise, telling Atlanta's civic leaders that the city would become Major League in all sports once it built a modern stadium with a large seating capacity. Pete Rozelle, the NFL's new commissioner, concurred with Foss's sentiments, stating in 1960 that Atlanta would make a fine NFL city once it had an appropriate stadium.[6]

Considering the less-than-ideal venues that several AFL franchises used in the league's early years, the AFL's firm stance that an Atlanta expansion franchise play its home games at a top-notch venue seems, at first glance, to be either unreasonable or a purely manipulative tactic employed against a frantic investment group. But the AFL's approach to Atlanta's lingering expansion hopes makes more sense when viewed in the context of the league's bid to secure a national television contract.

Major Sports's second effort to persuade the AFL to grant Atlanta an expansion franchise in May 1960 coincided with the league's negotiations with ABC to broadcast AFL games every Sunday from September through early January. On June 9, 1960, ABC agreed to a five-year contract with the AFL that paid each of the eight clubs $2.125 million per season. The AFL's decision to negotiate a television contract that paid all member clubs equally was unprecedented. It served as the model for the NFL's future television contracts, the first of which was negotiated in 1961. This cooperative approach to the distribution of television money provided an engine for the shared prosperity that soon characterized professional football.[7]

At the time the AFL made its initial deal with ABC, though, the mere existence of the new league, let alone its long-term financial stability, remained in question. ABC included a provision in its pact with the AFL stating that the addition of any new franchises during their five-year agreement would not lead to an increase in the size of the league's television contract. Adding a ninth or tenth franchise to the AFL would cut significantly into the original eight's television money, so if the AFL decided to add a new franchise during the five-year span of its first television contract, that franchise's home games had to be a guaranteed moneymaker.

Moreover, for their financial survival, AFL teams depended not only on the revenue they generated at their home games but also on the revenue they earned in their away games. Visiting AFL teams received 40 percent of the home team's total gate. The revenue produced by an undersized, archaic stadium like Poncey would never make up for the television money each franchise would have lost from cutting a new club into the deal. Expanding into Atlanta did not make sense for the AFL as long as its potential gate revenues were so limited.

Less than twelve months after Hartsfield brought Major Sports' push for a football franchise to a halt, Atlanta would have a new mayor in Ivan Allen, whose position on stadium building could not have been more unlike that of his predecessor and political ally. Allen openly campaigned on making Atlanta a Major League City. He expended considerable political capital in his first two years in office convincing civic elites that building a publicly financed stadium and arena to lure Major League franchises was a worthy civic goal.

In the meantime, a series of new local suitors tried their hand at bringing professional football to Atlanta. Jim Clay, a small businessman who worked with Major Sports, continued to pursue a professional football franchise for Atlanta on his own, despite the city's lack of a modern stadium and his lack of a strong financial backer. He convinced the NFL to allow him to schedule two August 1962 preseason games in Atlanta, personally guaranteeing the four franchises that played in the games (Pittsburgh, Chicago, Minnesota, and Dallas) $10,000 each for making the trip.

Scheduling preseason matchups in nonleague cities was common in the 1960s. Hometown fans balked at the idea of paying to watch a glorified scrimmage, leading to consistently sparse exhibition-game crowds. Clay believed that strong turnouts at the games would convince the NFL that Atlanta could support a team. To his credit, both games drew standing-room-only crowds to Grady Stadium, a fifteen-thousand-seat venue owned by APS.

Despite the excellent turnout, NFL leaders remained aloof, reiterating Rozelle's earlier statement that Atlanta would get a team once it built a modern stadium. Privately, league officials came to believe that Clay, who was known to have taken on significant personal debt in his pursuit of professional football, was not personally wealthy enough to support a team. Clay tried again in 1963, organizing a Baltimore Colts–Pittsburgh Steelers exhibition game that drew a sold-out crowd of more than eighteen thousand to Poncey, but the continued lack of interest from NFL officials led Clay to end his pursuit of a franchise shortly thereafter.[8]

Once Clay quit, plenty of other Atlanta-based investors took up the quest during the first half of the 1960s. The most notable and disastrous of these would-be football entrepreneurs was Bill McCane, an Atlanta kitchenware salesman who convinced the AFL to schedule four 1962 exhibition games at American Field, a thirty-thousand-seat stadium he promised to build in less than seven months on the site of a former chicken farm in a remote stretch of DeKalb County.[9]

By the early August evening of the first exhibition game, American Field consisted of portable grandstands and lighting fixtures. The teams did not have dressing rooms. The concession stands looked like "1910 fair booths," according to the *Atlanta Journal*'s Furman Bisher, while the playing surface looked like an "Oklahoma Dust Bowl."[10] Sportswriters dubbed McCane's improvised field "Erector Set Stadium." The out-of-town teams and local spectators alike had difficulty finding the field, located in the unincorporated community of Lithonia, miles off the county's main roads. While McCane claimed that the first two exhibition games at American Field drew a combined 19,500 fans, Bisher quipped that the figure required "double vision." The meager gates and poor conditions at American Field led to the cancellation of the final two games and the quick demise of McCane's career as a football impresario.[11]

Atlanta's bargaining position as a potential AFL or NFL city changed dramatically in April 1964 when construction commenced on Atlanta Stadium. On April 10, 1964, less than a week before breaking ground at Washington-Rawson, the *Journal* reported that an unnamed NFL franchise had made an informal agreement with the Stadium Authority to play at the new facility in 1965. Within days, the local press learned that the St. Louis Cardinals football team, referred to in the media as the "Big Red" to avoid confusion with the St. Louis Cardinals baseball team, was the franchise in question. The Big Red had one year remaining on its stadium lease in St. Louis, and, according to widely published reports, the team would soon seek league approval to move to Atlanta.[12]

The football Cardinals were recent arrivals in St. Louis. Four years earlier, in 1960, the team's owner, Violet Bidwill-Wolfner, moved the franchise to Missouri from its longtime home on the south side of Chicago. The Cardinals had played in Chicago since their origins as a semi-professional rugby team in the late nineteenth century, making them the oldest professional football club still in existence. Bidwill-Wolfner inherited the team in 1947 from her late husband, Charlie "Blue Shirt" Bidwill, a horse-racing magnate with strong ties to Chicago's underworld. During her tenure as owner, she grew tired of the Big Red's perennially second-class status in the city to George Halas' Chicago Bears, one of the NFL's most successful and popular franchises.[13]

Violet Bidwill-Wolfner's second husband, St. Louis businessman Walter Wolfner, convinced her to move the franchise to his hometown, based on an offer they received from Joe Griesedieck, president of the Falstaff Brewing Corporation located in St. Louis. Griesedieck represented the Civic Center Redevelopment Corporation (CCRC), a coalition of St. Louis corporate leaders who were trying to execute a $60 million downtown revitalization plan. The centerpieces of the CCRC's plan for downtown St. Louis were the construction of a multipurpose sports stadium and the construction of the long-anticipated Gateway Arch, a project that had been awaiting financing since the late 1940s.[14]

Griesedieck promised Bidwill-Wolfner a place for the Big Red in the soon-to-be-built stadium, which they would share with August "Gussie" Busch's Cardinals baseball team. While the CCRC built the new downtown stadium, Bidwill-Wolfner agreed to move her team temporarily to Sportsman's Park, a decaying thirty-two-thousand-seat ballpark owned by Gussie Busch that had housed the baseball Cardinals since 1920. When Violet Bidwill-Wolfner died in 1962, her sons William and Charles Bidwill took control of the team, following a prolonged legal struggle with their stepfather. Neither of the Bidwill brothers were enamored of the team's situation in St. Louis. As of April 1964, ground had yet to be broken on the new stadium. The Big Red was stuck as a tenant in a small, decrepit baseball park with virtually nonexistent parking facilities and only twelve thousand seats that provided football spectators with a full, unobstructed view from either side of the playing field. The Big Red was forced to work around the baseball Cardinals' home schedule, preventing the team from playing home games at Sportsman's Park until after the baseball season ended in early October.[15]

Some observers, most notably the *Journal*'s Furman Bisher, suggested that the Bidwill brothers decided to play "footsie" with Atlanta simply to gain leverage in their stadium negotiations in St. Louis. As late as June 1962, five months after their mother's death, the Bidwills submitted a letter of intent to the CCRC, assuring the organization that the Big Red would be a tenant at the new stadium. But despite their relatively recent letter of intent, negotiations between the CCRC and the Bidwills were genuinely strained by the spring of 1964. The CCRC insisted on a thirty-year lease at Busch Stadium, which the Bidwills resisted signing, wary of using a stadium where they would once again be the secondary attraction.[16]

Once the public became aware of the Big Red's potential move to Atlanta, rather than rush to close the deal, the Bidwill brothers moved slowly and aloofly. The Bidwills' tendency to remain silent and draw out negotiations became their trademark bargaining tactic. "Nobody could make a decision," former St. Louis Cardinals All-Pro offensive lineman Tom Banks recalled of the Bidwill organization. "There was always questioning of decisions. It was just a mess."[17]

Atlanta fans responded to the silence by showering the Bidwills with messages encouraging them to relocate their franchise. An Atlanta motel manager named Dave Cowles coordinated a telegram drive aimed at showing the Cardinals' owners the widespread support they would receive from local fans. The Bidwills received more than ten thousand telegrams in April and May 1964 from Atlantans who promised to purchase season tickets. Cowles promised in his personal telegram to sell five hundred season tickets to friends and family if the team agreed to move to Atlanta. By comparison, the Big Red sold a total of twelve thousand season tickets in St. Louis in 1963, little more than a third of the number of season tickets Georgia Tech sold the same year and less than half the number of passes that Griesedieck promised the Bidwills that St. Louis football fans would purchase if they moved to town.[18]

In May 1964 the Bidwills made a public visit to Atlanta to meet with city leaders and tour the stadium construction site. They expressed their pleasure with the plans for the stadium and the speed with which the structure was emerging on Washington-Rawson, a less-than-subtle jab at the grindingly slow planning process for the downtown stadium in St. Louis. Later that month, St. Louis finally broke ground on Busch Stadium. The Bidwills were conveniently out of town that day, one of the most anticipated in St. Louis history.[19]

While in Atlanta that May, the Bidwills met with Allen and Montgomery to discuss the terms of the stadium lease. The Stadium Authority offered the Big Red a ten-year stadium lease with two additional five-year renewal options. Rent for Atlanta Stadium would be a flat ten-percent of gate revenues. Atlanta's offer provided the Big Red with more flexibility and a less onerous rental fee than St. Louis' offer of a thirty-year lease with twelve percent of gate revenues, the median rate paid by NFL franchises in 1964. Additionally, Cardinals football tickets were subject to a 5 percent sales tax in St. Louis, while no such tax existed in Atlanta.

Montgomery later said that the Bidwills told Atlanta representatives that they had already received oral approval for the move from other NFL owners. At the time, though, the Bidwills were not yet ready to sign the contract. They said they needed more time to make an informed decision about the future of their franchise. The Bidwills told the Stadium Authority they were conducting a comparative economic and cultural study of the Atlanta and St. Louis markets. Allen acquiesced to the indefinite timetable the Bidwills afforded themselves, enabling the Cardinals owners to stretch the relocation intrigue from April through late July.[20]

During their May meeting, the Bidwills discussed Atlanta's racial situation with Allen and Montgomery. The mayor and Stadium Authority chairman assured them that Atlanta was a fully desegregated city and that all stadium facilities would be integrated. The Bidwills asked Montgomery if the presence of Black players on the Cardinals would be a problem with Atlanta fans. Montgomery assured them that it would not, stating that "five years ago it would have been, but we've gone about integration gracefully."[21]

When the Bidwills made a return visit in July, they met with a delegation from the ASLC to discuss the status of public accommodations and housing situation in the city. In a private meeting, ASLC leaders made similar assurances to those of Allen and Montgomery about the desegregation of Atlanta. After the meeting, William Bidwill said that they had completed their survey of Atlanta and "were entirely satisfied with everything, including the racial climate." [22]

ON SATURDAY JULY 11, THE *CONSTITUTION* GREETED ITS readers with the headline "Pro Football Cardinals Moving

Here," eight days after the news broke that the Braves were the secret MLB team that had agreed to play in Atlanta Stadium in 1965. Bob Broeg, St. Louis's most respected sportswriter, wrote the previous day in the *Post-Dispatch* that the Bidwills were about to finalize a ten-year lease to play in Atlanta. The Bidwills had surveyed their players on the potential move and encountered no opposition. According to Broeg's sources, the Big Red planned to make the decision public in a press conference the following week.[23]

But the Bidwills and Montgomery denied the reports circulating in Atlanta and St. Louis papers. NFL commissioner Rozelle said the Cardinals had yet to seek formal league approval, but, "I don't think they would have difficulty in getting approval." Rozelle added cryptically that "this office is not pushing the move. But I think it is up to the city of St. Louis to stand up and let the Bidwills know that they really want the team in St. Louis."[24]

Several Cardinals players, in Atlanta at the time to promote an August 15 preseason game the team had previously scheduled at Cheney Stadium, refused to comment on the move, but Cardinals tight end Taz Anderson, formerly of Georgia Tech, said Atlanta was an ideal site for professional football. "I think we could give this town the kind of football that would build up a good following," he told Jan Van Duser of the *Constitution*. Cardinals Assistant Coach Charley Trippi, a Georgia alumnus, told Van Duser he was also "hopeful" that the Cardinals would move to Atlanta.[25]

Other players expressed their opposition to the move in the press, disputing the Bidwill brothers' claim that no players were opposed to the move. Some of the veteran players, understandably, did not want to disrupt the homes they had made for their families in St. Louis. Quarterback Charles Johnson told reporters he wanted to stay to finish his master's degree in engineering at St. Louis University. Running backs Prentice Gautt and Bill Triplett, both African Americans, expressed their concerns about moving to a southern city.[26]

In the end, the reports of the Big Red's departure to Atlanta proved premature. The Bidwills faced intense pressure from St. Louis civic elites and Missouri Senator Stuart Symington to remain in the city. Symington tried to intimidate the Bidwills with talk of legal action, threatening the NFL with an antitrust suit and congressional action on franchise relocations if it permitted the Cardinals to move out of St. Louis, just as Wisconsin Attorney General Bronson La Follette did the following year to save the Braves for Milwaukee. The Missouri Senator had already stymied Charlie Finley's wanderlust by threatening a similar suit in 1963 against the A's, so that when Finley's club finally left Kansas City in 1967, Symington had leveraged the American League into granting the city an expansion team for 1969.[27]

The Bidwills tried to downplay Symington's threat, but they were clearly spooked enough to let Joe Griesedieck, a minority owner of the Big Red, and the baseball Cardinals' owner Gussie Busch attempt to negotiate a settlement to stay in St. Louis. Busch said in an open letter to the brothers that the Big Red was a "great civic asset," and he promised to work with NL executives to create "schedules agreeable to both the baseball and football Cardinals."[28]

Griesedieck came to an agreement with the Bidwills to sell them back the 10 percent stock in the team he purchased in 1960 as a favor to their mother. Busch and Griesedieck's efforts also facilitated a new round of negotiations between the CCRC and the Bidwills. The CCRC worked closely with the Bidwills throughout July and drew up a new lease that matched the Atlanta Stadium Authority's terms, including the enactment of an escape clause that allowed the Big Red to leave Busch Stadium after five years without financial penalty. Additionally, the St. Louis Chamber of Commerce agreed to spearhead a season-ticket sales drive and guarantee $100,000 worth of concessions revenue each season for the Big Red, which was, in essence, an annual subsidy by the local business community for the franchise. The improved leasing terms offered by the CCRC convinced the Bidwills to keep their team in St. Louis.[29]

When news of the Big Red's decision to stay in St. Louis broke late on a Saturday night in July 1964, the Bidwills congratulated Atlanta on its stadium-building effort, pronouncing that the southern city would soon have its own professional football team. They said their decision to stay in St. Louis was a product of the CCRC's improved offer, not anything that Atlanta officials had done incorrectly. Bill Bidwill promised to be an enthusiastic booster of professional football in Atlanta if the matter came up for a league-wide vote.[30]

Following his failed dalliance with the Cardinals, Allen adopted a new approach in his pursuit of professional football. He decided Atlanta needed a well-heeled local investor to buy a professional team and move it to the new stadium. He convinced his close friend J. Leonard Reinsch of Cox Broadcasting, the owner of Atlanta's WSB television and radio stations, to pursue an AFL franchise.

Besides his work for Cox, Reinsch was a powerful operative for the Democratic National Committee. He took a leave of absence every presidential campaign cycle to work on behalf of the party's nominee. In 1960 Reinsch played a particularly prominent role in the Kennedy campaign, coordinating its television and radio operations. Reinsch famously learned of a knee injury Nixon sustained in the days leading up to the candidates' debate. When negotiating with the Nixon camp over the ground rules for the debate, Reinsch asked if the candidates could stand during the debate, a request to which the Nixon camp acceded, forcing the Republican nominee to stand uncomfortably throughout the event. Allen considered Reinsch the ideal man to seek out an AFL franchise not because of his great personal wealth and his work but because Cox and WSB were Atlanta's NBC affiliate. NBC had recently outbid ABC for the AFL's broadcasting rights, beginning in 1965.[31]

Reinsch worked quickly, announcing in February 1965 that he had come to terms with the owners of the Denver Broncos to purchase the team for $4 million and relocate it to Atlanta. The deal for the struggling Broncos franchise fell through within a week, when Gerald and Allan Phipps, brothers who were minority stockholders in the Broncos, organized a coup against Reinsch. But Reinsch continued working behind the scenes, lobbying AFL commissioner Foss and the league's owners in secret to grant him an expansion franchise.[32]

In June 1965, Reinsch announced that the AFL had agreed to award him a team for the 1966 season for the unprecedented price of $7.5 million. The short supply of AFL franchises and intense demand for teams, combined with the value added to each franchise by the league's new $36 million television deal with NBC, increased the price tag considerably in a very short time. By comparison, just two years earlier, Sonny Werblin bought the New York Jets from Harry Wismer for $1 million.[33]

Once news of Reinsch's deal with the AFL went public, Allen expressed his desire to finalize the lease agreement between the new expansion franchise and the Stadium Authority as soon as possible. But the NFL intervened immediately to prevent the Atlanta market and its new stadium from joining up with the rival league. In fact, the day after Reinsch's announcement, NFL commissioner Pete Rozelle flew to Atlanta, taking up a standing invitation from the Stadium Authority to discuss expanding to the city.

"You've come a long way from Grady Stadium," Rozelle told reporters upon his arrival.[34] The NFL's new interest in Atlanta led the Stadium Authority to issue a statement saying that it was not obligated to sign a lease with the first professional football franchise granted to Atlanta. The Stadium Authority also asserted that it could only take on the lease of one professional football team at Atlanta Stadium. Before meeting with Montgomery, Rozelle headed straight to the State Capitol for an impromptu meeting with Governor Carl Sanders. Rozelle asked Sanders to recommend a potential owner for an Atlanta expansion franchise. Sanders suggested his old University of

Georgia fraternity brother, Rankin Smith, scion and vice president of the Life Insurance Company of Georgia.[35]

Initially, the thirty-nine-year-old Smith showed only mild interest in the estimated $4 million investment. Sanders prevailed on his friend for a week until Smith agreed to make an offer for the team. In the meantime, several other wealthy investors expressed interest in bidding on the Atlanta expansion franchise, increasing the NFL's asking price considerably.

The two most serious bidders were Lindsey Hopkins, an Atlanta-based Indy car racing executive who earned millions as an early Coca-Cola investor and built an even larger fortune in Florida real estate, and William Reynolds of Richmond, Virginia, the heir to the Reynolds Wrap fortune. Hopkins and Reynolds both made offers well in excess of the $4 million Rozelle quoted Rankin Smith. By the time Smith agreed to make a bid on the franchise, Rozelle had more than doubled the price to $8.5 million, a record fee, which Smith still agreed to pay.

NFL executives voted 14–0 to approve the Atlanta expansion franchise and its prospective owner Smith, but not before Bears' owner George Halas, the last of the league's founding fathers, cautioned his peers about the potential implications of their war with the AFL for Atlanta. He feared that the AFL would retaliate by placing expansion teams in NFL cities, including Chicago. Halas acquiesced to his fellow owners' desire to scoop up the lucrative Atlanta market, but remained fearful that the upstart AFL and its wealthier group of owners would win future wars for cities and players, forcing a merger between the two leagues.[36]

After five years of struggling to get the attention of either the AFL or the NFL, Atlanta found itself in June 1965 in the enviable position of picking between offers from the competing professional football leagues. To demonstrate the public's preference for their product, the NFL commissioned Lou Harris, the nation's best-known political pollster, to conduct a market research study on the preferences of Atlanta-area sports fans. Harris's survey of Atlanta sports fans confirmed their enthusiasm for professional football and concluded their strong preference for an NFL franchise over an AFL franchise. Harris concluded that Atlanta was "well ahead of the national trend on football," as Atlantans, particularly in the coveted 25–44 demographic, preferred football to baseball, several years before similar surveys found this preference to be common across the country. Harris concluded that Atlanta would have no trouble selling at least thirty thousand season tickets, the median number for an NFL franchise in 1965.[37]

"We of the NFL feel that we are just one segment of the entire industrial, economic, and cultural trend that has been gravitating toward Atlanta and the State of Georgia, particularly during the recent period of leadership by Gov. Carl Sanders," Rozelle said in a press release responding to the positive results of the market research study.[38] Naturally, Reinsch dismissed the NFL commissioned survey, stating that "any league that needs to do research on the Atlanta market and its new stadium should stay up north."[39]

Fans started submitting their names to Rankin Smith's Life Insurance Company of Georgia for season tickets, even though the Stadium Authority had yet to make a formal decision on the competing AFL and NFL bids. Reinsch's chances of securing the lease at Atlanta Stadium became even bleaker when he decided to travel with his wife to New Zealand so that she could undergo an experimental form of heart surgery. He missed the latter stages of the AFL-NFL war for Atlanta, making only occasional contact with Atlanta or AFL officials as the Stadium Authority finalized its decision.[40]

The AFL did not cede Atlanta without putting on a great show. The league sent an all-star junket down to Georgia to persuade, or possibly just charm, the powers that be into selecting Reinsch's franchise. The AFL junket included Commissioner Joe Foss; Kansas City Chiefs owner, AFL founder, and billionaire oil heir Lamar Hunt; New York Jets owner Sonny Werblin; and his prized asset, Joe Namath, the Alabama quarterback whom he had recently signed to the most lucrative deal in the history of professional football. The AFL's ad hoc diplomatic corps shook every hand, smiled for every picture, and told every one of their top-shelf stories over the course of two days in late June 1965, but to no avail. The Stadium Authority, after a few days of deliberation, chose Rankin Smith's franchise from the older, more prestigious NFL as its new tenant at Atlanta Stadium.[41]

Smith agreed to a ten-year stadium lease for 10 percent of the gate. The Stadium Authority stressed that it had chosen not between leagues but between owners. Everyone involved knew this was not the case.[42] "There was no doubt who we'd take since the AFL was the weak sister still," Allen wrote years later in his memoir.[43] Reinsch learned that the Stadium Authority had selected the NFL entry from a radio broadcast in New Zealand, prompting him to return his franchise to the AFL as soon as he got back to the United States. Reinsch had no interest in owning a professional football franchise in a city other than Atlanta. The AFL awarded the returned franchise to Miami for the 1966 season. Meanwhile, losing out on Atlanta cost Joe Foss his job. AFL owners replaced him as commissioner with Al Davis, the Oakland Raiders' ruthless, thirty-six-year-old head coach and general manager.[44]

Davis was the living embodiment of George Halas's fears about an NFL-AFL merger. During Davis's four months as AFL commissioner in the spring of 1966, the league's franchises made a concerted effort to outbid NFL franchises for the services of their star players, a fight that the NFL was sure to lose. The AFL's owners were almost exclusively the sons of industrialists and oil barons, while most NFL owners counted their franchise as their family's primary business. Simultaneously, the AFL's inner circle of owners negotiated a merger with the NFL. The NFL's owners agreed to the merger in large part to prevent AFL teams from poaching players from their rosters, placing new expansion franchises in established NFL markets, and engaging in bidding wars for new markets like they had in 1965 in Atlanta.

On June 8, 1966, less than a year after Atlanta selected the more prestigious NFL over the second-class AFL, the two leagues announced a merger that would become permanent in the 1970 season. Atlanta, it turned out, paid more money to play in the more difficult conference in the league they would have ended up a part of anyway.[45]

7

Not Catching On around Town

....

THE BRAVES LOOKED LIKE SUREFIRE WINNERS WHEN THEY arrived in Atlanta. Baseball writers across the country considered the Braves, which had contended for the pennant in 1965, among the favorites to win the NL in 1966. Atlanta inherited a talented, if aging, Milwaukee Braves roster that included perennial All-Stars Hank Aaron and Eddie Mathews. Aaron, then thirty-two-years-old, was two home runs short of 400 for his career and showed no signs of slowing down, having hit at least 30 home runs in eight of the last nine seasons. Mathews, though two years older, was still in fine fettle himself, having belted 32 home runs and driven in 95 the previous season. Supporting Aaron and Mathews was a nucleus of young emerging stars. Joe Torre, the Braves' Brooklyn-born catcher, earned his third All-Star appearance and won his first Gold Glove in 1965. Outfielder and first baseman Felipe Alou had hit nearly .300 while smacking 23 home runs. 1964 Rookie of the Year runner-up Rico Carty, an outfielder much more adept with his bat than his glove, had followed up the .330 batting average of his inaugural campaign with a .310 average in his second season. While the Braves' pitching staff was certainly not as deep or impressive as its lineup, the club had finished with a team earned run average of 3.52 in 1965, slightly better than the mean mark for the NL. The Braves' rotation was led by Tony Cloninger, a twenty-five-year-old from North Carolina who had won 24 games in 1965, second in the NL to Sandy Koufax.

Braves manager Bobby Bragan told reporters during spring training that he expected his team to win the pennant in 1966. After an up-and-down April, the Braves struggled for the rest of the spring, falling further and further below .500 and building a 13.5 game deficit in the NL standings. The 1966 Braves, like many subsequent Atlanta teams, combined great offensive prowess with poor pitching. The 207 home runs hit by the Braves led the NL, but Atlanta pitchers' inability to prevent their opponents from generating similarly gaudy offensive numbers kept the club mired in mediocrity. Management relieved Bragan of his duties on August 9 with the Braves seven games below .500. Bench coach Billy Hitchcock guided the club for the remainder of the season, jockeying it to a 33–18 finish and a respectable 85–77 record, good enough for fifth place.[1]

The 1966 season proved to be a bellwether of the Braves' performance in their early years in Atlanta. The Braves remained one of the NL's top power-hitting clubs, but its pitching remained suspect, particularly after a series of arm injuries derailed ace Tony Cloninger's career. The club never seriously contended for the pennant in 1967 or 1968, finishing in the middle of the ten-team NL both years. While Atlantans expected it to take a few years for the expansion Falcons to field a quality product, they figured the star-laden Braves would start hoisting championship banners soon after they settled in at Atlanta Stadium. Instead, the club found itself among the NL's also-rans.[2]

Many players and sportswriters blamed the club's struggles on Atlanta's climate and topography, which exaggerated the Braves' offensive strengths and pitching weaknesses. More than one thousand feet above sea level, Atlanta was, at the time, the Major League City situated at the highest elevation. The warm air of a hot and humid Georgia summer caused balls to carry noticeably further at Atlanta Stadium than at other ballparks. Many pitchers claimed the conditions at the stadium prevented their curveballs, sinkers, and sliders from moving properly. *Constitution* sportswriter Wayne Minshew popularized a nickname that Braves pitcher Pat Jarvis coined for the hitter-friendly ballpark: "the launching pad."[3] Minshew quoted Jarvis in a 1967 column about all of the home runs being hit at Atlanta Stadium. "The team bus arrived at the stadium during the wee hours following a road trip," Minshew recalled, "and a sleepy Jarvis came awake to say, 'There she is, boys, the freaking launching pad.'"[4]

Many batters at Atlanta Stadium disregarded conventional offensive wisdom to try to take advantage of its atmosphere. Rather than trying to hit line drives that dropped in among the fielders, players tried to hit the ball high into the air in the hope that the elements would carry their fly balls over the fence. Frequently, Atlanta finished near the top of the NL in both home runs and home runs allowed.[5]

The underachieving Braves were also failing to make a dent at the box office. The 1960s Atlanta Braves drew middling attendance numbers, surprising the team's management and the civic elites who expected professional baseball to be an immediate and durable box-office hit in the city. The Atlanta Braves drew 1,539,801 fans in their first season, sixth in the NL. By 1968, the team's annual attendance had fallen to 1,126,540, a decline of more than 25 percent. The decline was certainly attributable in part to the team's ho-hum performance as well as the declining novelty of big league baseball in Atlanta. But even before the Braves played their first official game in Atlanta, concerns emerged in the press about the team's attendance. The Braves had expected to sell ten thousand season tickets for their 1966 home slate, but in fact sold fewer than three thousand.[6] Team executives downplayed their disappointing sales numbers, noting that baseball clubs always sold far fewer of their eighty-one-date season tickets than football teams, which sold most of their tickets through seven-game season passes. The Falcons, by comparison, sold forty-five thousand season tickets for their 1966 inaugural campaign. Braves officials asserted that wealthy patrons would buy large numbers of season tickets once the stadium club acquired a liquor license, which, the team argued, would make the ballpark a far more attractive place for local corporate leaders to entertain their guests. A lawsuit backed by the state's still-strong temperance lobby held up the issuance of the license until midway through the 1966 season. Contrary to the projections of team management, the privilege of buying cocktails at a members-only stadium bar inspired no uptick in the number of season tickets the team sold to its fans, affluent or otherwise. The Braves never sold more than three thousand season tickets during the team's first decade in Atlanta.[7]

The *Sporting News*'s Barney Kremenko said Atlanta consumers' unwillingness to buy season tickets displayed their "show me" attitude toward the Braves. He quoted an unnamed local source as saying that Atlanta was a football town where fans will only "show up if the team is in the pennant race and to see the likes of Koufax and Mays."[8] The unnamed source proved prophetic, as Atlanta's best drawing game of its first season was a Tuesday-night game against the Los Angeles Dodgers that featured Sandy Koufax's only career start in Atlanta. The 2–1 pitching duel against the Braves' Denny Lemaster drew 52,270 to the Stadium, more fans than had attended the team's previous four home games combined. Atlantans' willingness to turn out in large numbers on a weeknight to see Koufax, but not in any similar fashion for a typical Braves home game, exemplified the relationship that many area residents developed with the city's professional sports teams. Tens of thousands of metropolitan-area residents went to great expense and trouble to be spectators at events they regarded as novel or prestigious, but few chose to become regular patrons of the area's professional teams. Atlanta consumers' response to the Braves in 1966 anticipated the fickleness that area residents would display towards all of the city's franchises over the next decade.[9]

Atlanta sports fans displayed surprising nonchalance toward the Braves even in their first full week in town. A near capacity crowd of 50,671 fans attended the Braves' first official game at Atlanta Stadium on April 12, 1966, the vast majority of whom stayed until well after midnight to see them lose to the Pittsburgh Pirates in thirteen innings. Earlier that day, 150,000 people watched the Braves parade through downtown as the centerpiece of the city's annual Dogwood Festival.[10] The next evening, nearly forty thousand fewer fans attended the Braves second home game.[11] Pittsburgh manager Harry Walker called the poor turnout by Atlanta's "so-called fans one of the most disgusting things I've ever seen. There's no excuse for the way their fans didn't turn out tonight."[12] The *Constitution*'s Furman Bisher agreed, writing that "it cut deeply that only 12,721 people in the South cared enough to come out and sit at the bedside of the Braves."[13]

One week earlier, the Braves had drawn surprisingly small crowds for an exhibition series against the New York Yankees, baseball's most successful and high-profile franchise. As recently as 1958, a survey of Crackers fans indicated that the Yankees were Atlanta's second favorite Major League team. Approximately fifty thousand fans attended the three-game April 1966 series, leaving Atlanta Stadium nearly two-thirds empty for the Friday evening and weekend afternoon games. Two hours west in Augusta, the Masters Tournament drew more than three times as many paying spectators that same weekend. Braves executive John McHale dismissed the sparse crowds at the exhibition games as meaningless, but the small turnout to see Mickey Mantle and Roger Maris play in person portended the box-office struggles the franchise endured even in its early years in Atlanta.[14]

Anthony Monahan of the *Chicago Tribune* characterized the 1966 Braves as a "disappointing success," not only because of its fifth-place finish but also because the team drew nearly three hundred thousand fewer spectators in Atlanta than it had during its first year in Milwaukee.[15] Even when Atlantans turned out in large numbers for the Braves, they were notably passive spectators. "The fans didn't know what to do at a ball game," Braves catcher Joe Torre wrote of Atlanta's fans in his memoir, referring specifically to a late July night in 1966 when fans filled the stadium to see Willie Mays play in person. "At a game against the Giants, there were 45,000 fans in the stands and you could hear a pin drop."[16]

Despite the weekday presence of nearly two hundred thousand workers in downtown Atlanta, relatively few patronized Braves games. By the second half of the 1967 season, fewer than four thousand fans attended many of the seventh-place team's weeknight dates. When the Braves drew little more than twenty thousand fans to their 1968 home opener, the *Constitution*'s Furman Bisher asked his readers why "32,000 people decided they could pass up opening night this year that couldn't pass it up two years ago?" Readers wrote Bisher with numerous explanations, ranging from the game coinciding with Good Friday to the uncertain political situation in Atlanta in the aftermath of Martin Luther King Jr.'s assassination. A self-described "thrifty housekeeper" named H. C. Fargeson explained that she "would be more inclined to go out and watch them lose if they had not upped the admission price."[17] Despite a small price hike in 1968, most Braves tickets remained well below the league's average admission price of $2.50. The Braves' dugout-level tickets, though, were the most expensive in baseball that season at $5 each. Bisher concluded that it wasn't ticket prices keeping fans away but "life in 5th and 7th place," referring to the Braves' finishes the two previous years, that "was not catching on around town," noting that nearly two hundred thousand spectators saw fit to attend the Masters the following weekend.[18]

The Braves' attendance troubles were certainly not for a lack of brand awareness. Hank Aaron, Eddie Mathews, and Joe Torre were all featured frequently in the Atlanta media, having become regular pitchmen for local firms.[19] Moreover, the Braves made civic engagement a centerpiece of their public-relations strategy from the time they arrived in Georgia. Braves representatives made 395 appearances across the Southeast in 1966. During the 1965–66 off-season, a group of Braves players caravanned across the Southeast on a six-state tour. Participating in the multistate junket became an annual rite of passage for young Braves players.[20] During the winter of 1966–67, Braves players, coaches, and executives visited 3,500 patients at hospitals across Georgia, a time-consuming goodwill gesture that became a fixture of the franchise's off-season enterprises.[21]

In 1969 the Atlanta Braves finally lived up to their press, winning the NL West in MLB's first year of divisional play. Manager Lum Harris oversaw the maturation of Atlanta's pitching staff into one worthy of its outstanding lineup. A former big league pitcher, Harris took over in Atlanta in 1968 after brief managerial stints in Baltimore and Houston. Under Harris's tutelage, knuckleballer Phil Niekro had emerged as one of the game's top starting pitchers, winning 23 games in 1969 and eating up 284⅓ innings on the mound. Right-hander Ron Reed became a near-ace himself in his second full season, winning a career-high 18 games. Atlanta's hitters were productive as always in 1969. Thirty-five-year-old Hank Aaron bashed 44 home runs and batted .300, while outfielder Rico Carty (.342 batting average) and first baseman Orlando Cepeda (22 home runs, 88 RBIS) both had strong campaigns.

Despite all of the Braves' strong performances in 1969, the club found itself in fourth place on September 1st, three games behind the Giants, Dodgers, and Reds, who were separated by just one game at the top of the NL West standings. It was the early September acquisition of future Hall of Fame reliever Hoyt Wilhelm that catapulted the Braves from a good team to a great one in the final weeks of the season. Wilhelm allowed just one run in eight appearances for Atlanta, earning 4 saves and 2 wins.

The Braves won 17 of their final 20 games, treating Atlanta to its first pennant race. On September 23, the Braves passed the San Francisco Giants for first place in the NL West, a lead they would never relinquish. On September 30, 46,357 fans erupted in wild celebration at Atlanta Stadium as they watched the Braves defeat the Reds and clinch the NL West championship. Several thousand fans stormed the field and streamed it with toilet paper while the team retreated to the locker room to douse each other and Mayor Allen with champagne. Car horns blared and revelers howled in downtown Atlanta into the early hours of the next morning.[22]

Two-and-a-half weeks earlier, Atlanta's suddenly exuberant fans hadn't been nearly so enthusiastic about the Braves. The fourth-place Braves had drawn as few as 6,317 fans at home as the team seemed well on its way to a fourth straight season of declining attendance.[23] "This division business is a great thing," Braves third baseman Ken Boyer said of their 1969 NL West championship. "The old way, we might have been out here with 2,000 people in the stands booing us tonight. Even if we had the same overall record."[24] Soon after the 1969 season, Braves co-owner Bill Bartholomay became one of the first baseball executives to propose the addition of four wild card teams to the baseball playoffs. Among Bartholomay's explicit motivations for expanding the playoffs was his desire to improve late-season attendance for clubs like the Braves that drew tiny crowds once they fell out of postseason contention.[25]

The Braves hosted the NL East champion New York Mets for games 1 and 2 of the National League Championship Series (NLCS) on Saturday October 4 and Sunday October 5, 1969. Baseball fans filled downtown Atlanta's restaurants and hotels, finally fulfilling civic leaders' predictions that the Braves would draw large numbers of out-of-town visitors into the center city. More than fifty thousand fans attended both of the Braves' postseason games at Atlanta Stadium, but, even amid postseason glory, big league baseball was arguably overshadowed in the metropolitan area that weekend by college football. Three football games in the region, two of which drew larger crowds than either NLCS game, pulled a great deal of attention away from the city's first postseason baseball series. On Saturday, Georgia Tech hosted Clemson at Grant Field for a contest that drew a standing-room-only crowd of 50,224 spectators. On Sunday, Georgia Tech housed the NLCS-displaced Falcons at Grant Field, setting up temporary bleachers around the stadium to accommodate the 57,806 fans who purchased tickets to see Atlanta play the defending NFL champion Baltimore Colts. The state's best-attended sporting event that weekend took place seventy miles west in Athens as the University of Georgia drew a capacity crowd of 59,442 to its home game against South Carolina.[26]

The Braves' postseason proved short-lived. The Mets battered Braves pitching in both games in Atlanta and returned to New York with a 2–0 series advantage. In the waning innings of game 2, Mets fans paraded around the stadium as their team cruised to an 11–6 victory, razzing Atlanta fans in the rapidly emptying stadium. The eventual world champion Mets finished off the Braves in game 3 for a series sweep. The run to the NL West championship helped the Braves boost their attendance in 1969 to 1,458,320, nearly 300,000 more fans than they drew in 1968 but nearly 100,000 fewer than the 1966 club. But Atlanta's improved gate in 1969 proved to be a hiccup on a long-term downward trajectory in their attendance.

The Braves' lackluster attendance in the late 1960s was also starting to take a financial toll on the organization. Legally mandated publication of the profits and losses of the corporation that owned the franchise, Atlanta Braves Inc., a shareholder-owned subsidiary of the Atlanta-LaSalle Corporation created while the club was still in Milwaukee, clarify the Braves' financial situation. Despite the Braves' substantial regional television deal, the franchise was having more trouble each season making it into the black. While Atlanta Braves Inc. turned a profit of nearly $1 million for the Atlanta-LaSalle Company in 1966, profits dropped considerably for 1967 to roughly $480,000. In 1968 the franchise made an impressive looking $2,009,913, enabling Atlanta Braves Inc. to pay its shareholders a one dollar per share dividend, the first in the company's history. Virtually all of the company's profits in 1968 came from the $2

million in expansion fees the club earned from the addition
of franchises in Montreal and San Diego to the NL. Without
the expansion fees, the club would have turned a profit in 1968
of less than $10,000, a steep drop-off from its already rap-
idly declining revenues. The two 1969 NLCS games in Atlanta
earned the Braves nearly $400,000, enabling the team to go
from its first annual loss to a profit of $347,000 for the year.[27]

Contributing further to the financial strains on Atlanta
Braves Inc. was its investment in professional soccer. In 1966
the Braves' parent company bought into the new North American Soccer League (NASL) and formed the Atlanta Chiefs. The
Chiefs began play at Atlanta Stadium in 1967 and lost an average of a quarter of a million dollars annually. Braves executives
Bill Bartholomay and Dick Cecil spearheaded the formation of
the Chiefs. Like millions of other Americans, Bartholomay and
Cecil became soccer fans while watching the 1966 World Cup.
England's championship run on its home soil drew high ratings on American television, leading many wealthy investors
to believe that soccer would become America's next breakout
spectator sport. Bartholomay and Cecil sought to capitalize
on the World Cup's popularity by bringing it to Atlanta, helping the city fill the stadium's empty warm-weather dates with
more revenue-generating events.[28]

The Braves executives joined a number of other well-heeled
sportsmen, including Los Angeles Lakers owner Jack Kent
Cooke, Kansas City Chiefs owner Lamar Hunt, and Detroit
Lions owner William Clay Ford, in bringing professional soccer to the United States. They formed the NASL in 1968, merg-
ing two rival professional leagues formed immediately after
the World Cup. The NASL negotiated a ten-year, multimillion-
dollar television deal with CBS that placed its games in regular weekend spring and summer time slots, similar to the way
that the network presented football in the fall. CBS's hopes for
a ratings bonanza soon evaporated. Dreadful Nielsen numbers
led CBS to cancel its soccer broadcasts after two seasons. No
other network dared broadcast NASL games again until 1974.[29]

In their early years, the Chiefs were among the best-drawing and best-performing teams in American professional soccer. Atlanta Braves Inc. hired Welsh soccer star Phil Woosnam to coach the team and manage its personnel. Woosnam signed up a talented roster made up mostly of European players that asserted itself almost immediately as one of the league's top teams. Woosnam cut a dashing figure as a British gentleman who captained his cosmopolitan band of players from victory to victory. In 1968 he led the Chiefs to an NASL championship, the city's first Major League championship of any kind. After the season, Woosnam went from being the face of the Atlanta franchise to the face of the entire league. He left the Chiefs to become NASL's executive director, a position he held until the league's demise in 1984. Despite continued success, the Chiefs never recovered the public profile they enjoyed during Woosnam's tenure.[30]

While the Chiefs were one of the NASL's winningest teams, the franchise struggled at the box office. In a 1967 letter to their stockholders, Atlanta Braves Inc. estimated that the new soccer club would draw an average of fifteen thousand spectators per home date at Atlanta Stadium. Even at its peak, average attendance at Chiefs games never reached even half as much, peaking at 6,691 per match during their inaugural 1967 campaign. In their 1968 championship season, attendance fell to an average of 5,794. By the 1970 season, the average crowd at a Chiefs' game was barely 3,000.[31] The best crowds the Chiefs ever drew were for exhibition games they played in the 1967 and 1968 seasons against well-known foreign teams, including the British club Manchester City, the German Hertha BSC (Berliner Sports-Club) squad, and Santos, Pelé's Brazilian club. Spectators interested in these novel attractions helped the Chiefs' international exhibitions draw an average of twenty-seven thousand patrons, many of whom likely never saw another NASL game.[32]

Atlanta's major institutions were enthusiastic boosters of the Chiefs. Local broadcast and print media provided the team with ample coverage in its early years. The city's newspaper columnists, always on the lookout for amenities that made Atlanta seem more cosmopolitan, were fervent supporters of the Chiefs. They spoke of professional soccer's arrival in Atlanta as proof of its stature as an international city. The State of Georgia declared April 16–23, 1967, as Soccer Week, during which the Georgia Department of Health sponsored clinics throughout the state with Chiefs players, teaching children how to play the sport. Soccer Week and the press surrounding the arrival of the Chiefs kickstarted the formation of municipal youth soccer leagues throughout the region. The presence of the Chiefs in Atlanta, state government support for youth soccer, and the formation of municipal youth soccer leagues throughout the metropolitan area increased the number of amateur players in the region from fewer than two hundred in 1967 to more than twenty thousand in 1972. Enthusiasm for soccer as a youth participatory sport in suburban Atlanta did not translate into financial success for the Chiefs. During the Chiefs' first five years of play (1967–71), Atlanta Braves Inc. lost more than one million dollars on the club.[33]

8

Losing but Improving

....

WITHIN DAYS OF THE NFL'S JUNE 1965 DECISION TO AWARD Atlanta an expansion franchise, team owner Rankin Smith was swamped with thousands of ticket requests. To satisfy local interest, Smith held a Name the Team contest sponsored by the *Journal* and the *Constitution*. A five-man committee that consisted of Furman Bisher, Jesse Outlar, WSB Public Relations Director Phil Harrison, Georgia football coach Vince Dooley, and Georgia Tech coach Bobby Dodd recommended the name *Falcons* to Smith after reviewing the more than one thousand entries. That August, a prerecorded announcement played during the Colts-Steelers exhibition game at Atlanta Stadium informed fans of Smith's decision. A retired school teacher from McDonough, Georgia, named Julia Elliott had suggested the moniker, describing the bird as "proud and dignified, with great courage and fight. It never drops its prey. It's deadly and has a great sporting tradition" in her entry letter. Smith also revealed the Falcons' red, black, gold, and white uniforms that evening, an homage to the school colors of both Georgia and Georgia Tech, as well as the team's modernistic bird-in-flight insignia emblazoned on a black helmet.[1]

The Falcons began selling season tickets in late October, weeks before the team had any players and months before it had a head coach. The club sold more than forty thousand by Christmas. The team cut off season ticket sales at forty-five thousand, nearly twice as many as any other expansion team in league history. The club left around nine thousand tickets available for each home game for individual sales, allowing

fans who might not be able to afford a season ticket the opportunity to see a game or two in person each year.[2] "We don't
want this to be a rich man's show," Smith said, citing the Falcons' single game ticket prices, which were among the most
affordable in the league. "You take a young fellow who wants to
take his wife and another couple to a game. That's $24 in tick-
ets and maybe he has to spend $6 for a babysitter. He couldn't
afford to do that all season, but he could do it for one or two
games."[3] Nevertheless, the Falcons fanbase had a decidedly
white-collar image in their early years. In 1977 *Sports Illustrated*'s Roy Blount Jr. wrote that, in the 1960s, the Falcons
"sold plenty of season tickets to corporations and to upper
class families who rode buses to the stadium from their private clubs, the wives in the same sort of dressy dresses and
crisp corsages they wore to Tech games."[4]

By Thanksgiving, the Falcons were well on their way to selling through their supply of season tickets. On the Saturday after
the Thanksgiving holiday, the Falcons stimulated even more
local excitement for the team at the 1966 NFL Draft. With the
first pick, they chose University of Texas linebacker Tommy
Nobis, whom the Atlanta press quickly dubbed "Mr. Falcon."
Nobis earned All-American honors twice and played on the
Longhorns' 1963 national championship team. As a senior,
the San Antonio native won the Outland Trophy for best interior lineman and finished his collegiate career as one of the
most decorated defensive players in Southwestern Conference history. The Falcons outbid the Houston Oilers, who had
selected the linebacker in the first round of the final AFL draft,
for Nobis's services. Atlanta signed Nobis to what was then
the richest contract in football history, a five-year deal worth
$600,000, which easily beat out the astonishing four-year,
$427,000 contract that Joe Namath signed with the AFL's New
York Jets the previous season. Nobis would soon show himself
to be worth every penny, anchoring Atlanta's defense for the
next decade and earning numerous league accolades that regularly affirmed his status as one the NFL's best linebackers.[5]

The Atlanta Falcons had a remarkable 1965. In just six months, the Atlanta professional football team went from a civic-minded venture by an initially hesitant investor to an organization that seemed capable of scoring only public-relations victories. Unfortunately, 1966, 1967, and 1968 did not go nearly so well for the organization. The Falcons won six times in their first three seasons, switched head coaches after just thirty-one games, and squandered much of the goodwill they had built up with the Atlanta press and public.

The futility of the Falcons in their early years must be credited in large part to team owner Rankin Smith, who relied on close associates with little or no experience in professional football to manage the operations of the franchise. "I don't know anything about football," Smith was widely quoted as saying when he purchased the Falcons, stating on numerous occasions that he intended "to hire knowledgeable, capable individuals to handle the technical aspects of the game."[6] The aloof Smith did not turn control of the franchise over to experts though. The friends and business associates he empowered in the Falcons organization proved unable to meet the challenges of managing a professional football team. Throughout his ownership, Smith remained behind the scenes, avoiding media scrutiny especially when the team played poorly.[7]

"Right from the get-go, you didn't have football people running the organization and they still haven't let go," former Atlanta Falcon Lou Kirouac said shortly before Rankin Smith's 1997 death.[8] Kirouac's views reflected a broad and durable consensus among the Atlanta media and area football fans. Smith and his associates remained stationary targets for fan outrage for decades. This critique of the Falcons organization had calcified into common sense by the late 1960s and lasted until Smith's family sold the club to Home Depot founder Arthur Blank in 2002.[9]

Insurance executive Frank Wall, a Smith confidante, served as the franchise's first GM, directing team personnel decisions from 1966 until he stepped down in 1970. Wall continued to play an important role in player personnel for years after he dropped the GM title. His failures as a judge of player talent hamstrung the Falcons' coaching staff as they tried to build a competitive team. Most notoriously, Wall was the architect of the Falcons' sixteen-member 1967 draft class, which was arguably the worst in NFL history. None of the sixteen players that Wall drafted played well enough in training camp to earn a spot on the Falcons' roster, which was already one of the weakest in the league.[10]

Wall and Smith mishandled the hiring of their first head coach, settling on a questionable candidate after they spent months pursuing two of the best-known coaches in the country. The Falcons offered their coaching job to both the Green Bay Packers' Vince Lombardi and former Cleveland Browns coach Paul Brown. Smith offered both men contracts that would have given them complete control over team operations and annual salaries that would have made them the highest paid coaches in football, but both turned down the Falcons job.[11] Atlanta settled on Packers assistant Norb Hecker in January 1966, two months after Smith and his associates made the unprecedented move of conducting the team's collegiate draft without a head coach in place. Smith called Lombardi seeking out a reference on Hecker, but the Packers coach refused to recommend his assistant for the job. The Falcons owner decided to hire Hecker anyway, believing that Lombardi was bluffing him in hopes of keeping the thirty-nine-year-old on his staff. Though barely older than many of his players, Hecker had served for six years as defensive backs coach under Lombardi as Green Bay became the league's premier franchise.[12]

Constraining the Falcons even further in their early years was the lack of player talent available to them. The Falcons culled most of their 1966 roster from a league-organized expansion draft. The other fourteen NFL clubs were allowed to protect twenty-nine of their forty roster players from selection, forcing Atlanta to build its team from a collection of marginal professional players. Inevitably, expansion clubs face serious challenges as they try to assemble a competitive roster, but the quality of players available in the 1966 league-sponsored draft was further diminished by the existence of the rival AFL. The four hundred players signed to the AFL's nine teams sapped the pool of available professional football talent even further. Moreover, the AFL and NFL were in the midst of a bidding war for talented players, which drove up the price of competent available players considerably. NFL commissioner Rozelle characterized the expansion draft as being "as liberal as possible," noting that the Falcons had also received an extra selection in each of the first five rounds of the November 1965 NFL collegiate draft.[13] Falcons linebacker and 1966 team captain Bill Jobko characterized the roster that Wall and Smith had assembled for Hecker quite differently, describing it bluntly as "a bunch of old guys nobody wanted anymore."[14]

Hecker tried to transform the Falcons' ragtag roster into something resembling the world champion Packers by running his 1966 training camp in the style of his old boss. The Falcons coach brought his team to a Baptist retreat deep in North Carolina's Blue Ridge Mountains, taught them the Packers' playbook, and put them through a rigorous conditioning program that resembled Marine boot camp.[15] "We were running Green Bay's offense," Falcons tight end Taz Anderson said years later, "but unfortunately, we had Atlanta's personnel."[16]

The 1966 Atlanta Falcons played unequivocally inspired football for Hecker, winning three of their fourteen games, a promising start for an expansion club built from other team's spare parts.[17] The Falcons' defense, led by NFL Rookie of the Year Tommy Nobis, helped the team remain competitive in many games. Middle linebacker Nobis roamed from sideline to sideline, tracking down ball carriers at a level that many NFL experts regarded as comparable to his near-contemporary, Dick Butkus. In his ninth and final NFL season, linebacker Bill Jobko proved a steady, veteran presence alongside Nobis while defensive back Jerry Richardson was among the league leaders in interceptions with five. Unfortunately, the Falcons' offense sputtered all season. Both starting quarterbacks, Randy Johnson, a rookie out of Texas A&I whom Atlanta had selected with their other first round pick, and Dennis Claridge, a third-year pro out of Nebraska who quit football after the season to attend dental school, took a beating behind the Falcons' overmatched offensive line. Atlanta displayed some ability to move the ball on the ground with the backfield tandem of Ernie Wheelwright and Junior Coffey, but that didn't stop the Falcons from finishing last in the league in scoring offense.[18]

Throughout their early seasons, the Falcons were perpetually "losing but improving," a phrase that Hecker used repeatedly in postgame press conferences. "Losing but improving" contented the fans and the media in year one but quickly became a public-relations cliché that aggravated the denizens of the stands and the press box in equal measure.[19] Hecker tried to emphasize how well his team played against top-notch NFL talent, but when his "losing but improving" Falcons failed to remain competitive at home, fans developed the habit of leaving games early in large numbers. Less than a month into the Falcons' inaugural season, the *Constitution*'s Charlie Roberts observed that a majority of fans were responding to large Falcons deficits by heading for the exits, often during the third quarter. A 56–3 drubbing by the Packers in late October 1966 was the most painful instance of this for Hecker, especially after his old boss Vince Lombardi told reporters after the game that the Falcons were "not a tough team."[20]

As the Falcons slipped to 1-12-1 in their second year, Atlanta Stadium fans treated the struggling team to frequent rounds of hometown boos. A combination of the Falcons' fruitless 1967 draft class and the departure of some of the team's veteran leaders, including Jobko, left the team similarly anemic on offense but much weaker on defense. The Falcons were on the wrong side of seven lopsided losses that season, falling by at least 20 points on each occasion. The most embarrassing defeat came in week 11 when the Falcons lost by a field goal to the expansion New Orleans Saints, Atlanta's new southern rival. Hecker found himself in frequent conflict with the Atlanta media in 1967, which helped to cement the Falcons' reputation as antagonistic toward the local press corps. Before the Falcons even played their first official regular season game in 1966, Hecker had a run-in with Atlanta's thoroughly boost-erish press, accusing local sportswriters of "leaking" infor-mation to opposing teams.[21]

"A lot of times people were buying tickets for the show that was going to be there," Tommy Nobis said of the Falcons' season-ticket holders in their early years, patrons who were paying as much to see NFL stars like Johnny Unitas and Paul Hornung in person as they were the new Atlanta team.[22] Like the Braves, the Falcons organization went to great lengths to familiarize the public with their players and present them as good citizens. Falcons players and coaches made an average of 150 appearances per year for local charities with a partic-ular emphasis on hosting football camps for boys in under-privileged sections of metropolitan Atlanta. For a number of years, Falcons players organized an off-season, All-Star bas-ketball team that played games to raise funds for charities throughout the Southeast. Dozens of civic organizations in Georgia hosted viewings of the team's highlight film every offseason. Rich's Department stores held frequent free auto-graph signings with Falcons players both at their downtown location and suburban branch stores. Nevertheless, the Fal-cons' poor performance on the field and deteriorating repu-tation in the press box stymied the team's efforts to win over the public in Metropolitan Atlanta.[23]

Three games into the 1968 season, the Falcons fired Norb Hecker as head coach. The 1968 season was already looking a lot like the 1967 campaign. Atlanta had been outscored by its opponents 103–40. In thirty-one games, Hecker compiled a 4-26-1 record. Smith and Wall replaced Hecker with an even sterner taskmaster, ex-Vikings head coach Norm Van Brock-lin. The legendary former quarterback had been a successful coach with the Vikings, transforming the expansion club into a winner in just four seasons. Despite his success, the irascible Van Brocklin earned the enmity of virtually everyone in that organization and was fired once the team's fortunes headed south. Van Brocklin shared Hecker's boot-camp-like approach to training, but steeped it in his far more antagonistic personality, leading several players to quit soon after he took command. Van Brocklin treated the remainder of the 1968 season as a rebuild, an opportunity to separate the loyalists from the castoffs. Van Brocklin temporarily wrestled control over personnel decisions away from Wall and cleaned house, replacing all but fourteen players from the two-win 1968 roster by the start of the 1969 season.[24]

The continued instability in the Falcons organization and the team's continued futility on the field did nothing for the morale of their fanbase. In the late 1960s, the Falcons' season-ticket base hovered around forty thousand despite the team's poor performance. Fans had moved beyond just leaving blowout losses early. Many season-ticket holders were simply skipping games that seemed either inconsequential or unappealing, a phenomenon NFL executives had started referring to as "no-shows." In 1968 roughly 71,000 of the 405,000 tickets purchased to Falcons games at Atlanta Stadium went unused. At the Falcons' home finale against the 49ers, fewer than twenty-six thousand people bothered to attend despite ticket sales for the game of more than fifty-five thousand.[25] "The people here will come out to see a winner," Rankin Smith said of all the no-shows in the 1968 season. "I think they will give us another couple of years to start winning." Smith believed that new head coach Norm Van Brocklin, with his track record of success as a player and a coach, would be just the man to turn the Falcons into winners.[26]

9

Atlanta Stadium, a Center of Gravity

....

ON APRIL 9, 1965, AN UNSIGNED EDITORIAL IN THE *JOURNAL* commemorated the opening that evening of the city's $18 million multipurpose municipal stadium. Atlanta's investment in the stadium had enabled it to lure the big leagues to the Southeast for the first time. The editorial struck a triumphant tone, describing the opening of Atlanta Stadium as an event that would bind the rapidly growing region together socially, culturally, and economically. In a place where divisions between native and newcomer, Black and white, and city and suburb were striking, the *Journal* predicted that the stadium would serve as a crucible for metropolitan consensus.

"Interest in the stadium certainly indicates a great lift in civic morale and a revival of the famous Atlanta spirit," the editorialist wrote. "It provides a center of gravity for a city which was beginning to need one. Suburban growth was producing a sort of centrifugal force which could make downtown unnecessary in time. But the stadium will be a great center of interest, a meeting place and rallying point for all of us, a source of civic pride and a promoter of civic loyalty," the editorialist wrote, evoking the heady optimism that constituted the common sense of Atlanta's civic elites for much of the 1960s.[1]

That evening, Atlanta hosted its first event at its new municipally financed stadium, a preseason exhibition baseball game between the Milwaukee Braves and the Detroit Tigers. The Friday-night contest was the first in a three-game weekend series, a detour on the Braves' trip back to Wisconsin from spring training in West Palm Beach, Florida. An injunction granted to the Milwaukee Board of Supervisors by a Wisconsin Superior Court in October 1964 prevented the Braves from moving their operations to Georgia until their local stadium lease expired after the 1965 season. The Braves' April 1965 exhibition games with the Tigers, the first of seven the Braves played at Atlanta Stadium that season, were the first opportunity fans in Georgia had to see the team play in person.[2]

The temporary legal setback did little to dampen Atlanta's enthusiasm for its brand-new Major League team. The city celebrated the April 1965 preview in grand fashion, feting the Braves with a downtown parade that drew an estimated sixty thousand people to Peachtree Street, a crowd twice as large as the one that welcomed President Johnson to the city the previous May. Atlanta and Fulton County schools dismissed their students two hours early so that children could secure spots for their families along the parade route.[3] More than six thousand fans, hundreds of whom brought homemade signs, greeted the Braves' chartered flight from Florida. After an hour of signing autographs and posing for pictures with well-wishers, the players, coaches, and executives boarded convertibles and joined a fifty-car motorcade that snaked eleven miles north toward the Five Points along the city's recently expanded freeways.[4] Atlanta's soon-to-be baseball team rolled down Peachtree Street behind a banner that read "Welcome South Braves," waving to fans while the Southern Belles accompanying them in the backseats tossed baseballs to children in the crowds. The clamor of the dozen marching bands positioned throughout the motorcade drowned out the sound of a crowd that looked on with a hushed admiration.[5] "People were rather quiet," Furman Bisher wrote of the parade. "It was an almost reverent atmosphere."[6]

Ivan Allen described the arrival of the Braves and the opening of the new stadium as "the most important occurrence in Atlanta in 100 years" at a post-parade luncheon put on by the Braves 400 Fan Club, a new booster club made up primarily of Big Mules.[7] The Mayor's triumphant statement echoed widespread civic sentiments that April. The day before the Braves' arrival, *Journal* columnist Lee Walburn wrote that the Braves' exhibition game against the Tigers would be the "most significant premiere in Atlanta since *Gone with the Wind* debuted in the city in December 1939 at the Loew's Grand Theatre."[8]

The civic huzzahs continued during a drawn-out stadium dedication ceremony that preceded the Friday-night exhibition game. The 37,232 fans in attendance, the largest crowd to watch a baseball game in Georgia history, applauded at the appropriate times from the baby-blue seats of the three-quarter-filled stadium as an assortment of politicians, city fathers, and Braves representatives gave speeches commemorating the occasion. The patience of the fans was particularly noteworthy, considering that they had just navigated their way into a stadium whose environs looked more like a construction site than a ballpark.[9] Stadium Authority officials warned fans to be cautious on the muddy, largely still-unpaved acres surrounding the facility because "they might stumble over some building materials that were still lying around the premises."[10] "Women in high heels struggled toward the stadium across the raw, soft dirt of a construction site," the *Journal*'s Harry Murphy wrote of the scene outside Atlanta Stadium. As Murphy well knew, the members of Atlanta society whom he was describing had always been willing to endure temporary hardships to be part of a grand event.[11]

Ivan Allen, the most high-profile purveyor of the city fathers' booster ethos, was the featured speaker that night at Atlanta Stadium. The mayor, as he often did, evoked the legacy of Sherman's destruction of Atlanta during the Civil War. He characterized the stadium's completion as the end point in Atlanta's century-long remaking into a major American city. "In eleven months and three weeks, Atlanta has broken the shackles of complacency and the shackles of those who said it couldn't be done and that we must go second-class with a provincial attitude," Allen said before turning the remainder of the evening over to the Detroit and Milwaukee baseball teams.[12]

Atlanta boosters from Henry Grady to Margaret Mitchell to Ivan Allen's own father had evoked the narrative of the city's rise from the ashes of 1864, making its modern triumphs seem all the more magnificent by juxtaposing the agony of its romantic past with the ecstasy of its present. Like his predecessors, Allen transformed the remaking of Atlanta into a sacred duty.[13] As Allen spoke about the cultural significance of the stadium for which he was largely responsible, he stood at the fulcrum of a city that looked to have avoided the most evident pathologies of both the urban north and the urban south. Atlanta had thus far been spared the destructive riots that enveloped Harlem and North Philadelphia the previous summer. Instead, Atlanta's municipal leadership was planning to build thousands of units of affordable housing and reinvest in its residential core by participating in Model Cities, an urban renewal program created as part of President Lyndon Johnson's Great Society. While civic rival Birmingham mired itself in massive resistance, leaders in Atlanta's Black and white communities had negotiated the terms of its desegregation peacefully.[14]

Five months after opening night at Atlanta Stadium, city voters avoided a mayoral runoff. They reelected Ivan Allen with 70 percent of the vote. The mayor faced only token opposition from longtime foe "Muggsy" Smith. Allen, who had been a vocal supporter of the 1964 Civil Rights Act, won 96.4 percent of the Black vote and, unlike in 1961, also won a majority of the white vote. He had earned an electoral mandate in 1965 by overseeing an unprecedented economic boom during his first term and accomplishing many of the policy goals he set forth in his Six Point Plan.[15] During Allen's first term, Atlanta led the nation's metropolitan areas in job expansion, adding an average of more than twenty-five thousand employees to its payrolls per year. The unemployment rate in Metropolitan Atlanta at the time of Ivan Allen's second inauguration in January 1966 was 1.9 percent, the lowest in the country. By 1966, 413 of the Fortune 500 companies had operations in Metropolitan Atlanta.[16]

Atlanta celebrated the fruits of its municipal peace and prosperity at the new stadium's opening night, as an integrated audience (an afterthought in almost every account of the game) watched their Braves in person for the first time. It all seemed like living proof that Atlanta's civic establishment had built a City Too Busy to Hate, largely from the top-down.[17] The crowd that evening seemed like a rejection of the Atlanta envisioned by Ivan Allen's 1961 mayoral rival, Lester Maddox, who had become internationally famous the previous summer for chasing three Black Georgia Tech students away from his Hemphill Avenue restaurant with a pistol and an ax handle. When ordered by a federal judge to integrate the Pickrick, Maddox instead chose to close his establishment. The opening-night crowd at Atlanta Stadium, though predominately white, bore no outward signs of the kind of racial hostility Lester Maddox displayed the previous July outside his restaurant.[18] Atlanta's fans matched the de jure integration of the stands with a willingness to cheer lustily for a home team that fielded five Black and four white starters.[19]

A total of 106,118 fans watched the Milwaukee Braves sweep the Tigers in the three-game exhibition series at Atlanta Stadium that weekend. The Friday night crowd was larger than any that would see the Braves in Milwaukee that season.[20] On opening night 1965, Atlanta's civic elites could rightfully look upon their new stadium as a new metropolitan "center of gravity," as the editorialist in the *Journal* had described it that morning. This center, though, failed to hold, as residents of Metropolitan Atlanta demonstrated a long-term preference for spending their leisure time within the confines of their lifestyle and demographic clusters rather than in a shared civic space. Contrary to the forecasts of civic elites, the prestige and pride that Atlanta Stadium afforded its city dissipated quickly. The city fathers who shepherded Atlanta Stadium into being believed the venue would become one of the region's focal points of mass leisure and entertainment. Much to their collective dismay, neither Atlanta Stadium nor its primary tenants, the Braves and Falcons, proved a durable draw, let alone a wellspring of social cohesion.

Atlantans proved to be discerning consumers of professional sports rather than devotees of the city's franchises, all of which were a long way from becoming tenured civic institutions. Surprisingly few citizens of Metropolitan Atlanta developed an abiding affection for their new teams or the spaces in which they played. The collective shrug with which most area residents came to regard the city's professional sports franchises demonstrated the cultural divergence that increasingly characterized the practice of everyday life in greater Atlanta. Most residents found their leisure within the confines of their geographic, demographic, or lifestyle communities rather than in the public sphere at the center of the city.

Metro-area residents found Atlanta Stadium to be an undesirable focal point for their leisure activities for many reasons. The futility of the Braves and Falcons contributed significantly to the lack of local affection during the 1960s and 1970s, but it was far from the only reason. Events of all kinds at Atlanta Stadium failed to engender any widespread emotional investment in the venue. Special events held at the stadium, including rock concerts, religious meetings, and political rallies, drew frequently underwhelming crowds.

Foremost among the factors was the decentralization of the region's population. Commuting to and from the stadium became an increasingly arduous task, as the vast majority of the region's population settled ever further from the city proper. Metropolitan-area residents living outside the perimeter of I-285 proved unwilling to come back into the city in large numbers on weeknights or weekends to watch the lackluster teams that played downtown. Braves manager Bobby Bragan characterized his 1966 commute into the stadium as a "30 minute ride taken on freeways that more closely resembled the Indianapolis 500."[21] "We're such a suburban city and when they're already out there, they don't like to come into the city. People in the suburbs really don't like to go downtown," former *Constitution* editor Jim Minter said, describing the view of the center city that had calcified quickly into the consensus in the outlying metropolitan counties.[22] Working one's way through Atlanta's freeway traffic to see the Braves or the Falcons was simply too much work for too little payoff for most of the region's consumers. This dynamic had the most profound impact on the Braves, whose marathon 162-game spring and summer schedule required the greatest commitment from spectators and took place outdoors during Georgia's hottest and most humid months.

By opposing the extension of the Metropolitan Area Rapid Transit Authority (MARTA) rail service in the 1960s and 1970s, suburban voters had created a line of demarcation in trans-metropolitan transit that made automobiles the only viable means of traveling from the region's outer rings to its inner ring. Any desire residents of Cobb, Clayton, and Gwinnett Counties may have had to use mass transit to access the amenities of downtown Atlanta were overshadowed by a broad political consensus in each county shaped by the fear that MARTA would spread crime and foster racial integration in their communities.[23] The provocative "Share Crime: Support MARTA" yard signs and bumper stickers that appeared during the 1970s and 1980s in jurisdictions considering joining the rapid rail system were the most evident popular manifestation of the suburban racial and class anxieties that surrounded the issue.[24]

The vigorous opposition to MARTA in suburban Atlanta, though, was not simply a matter of racial politics but also an expression of a lifestyle preference. The residents of suburban Atlanta demonstrated an individualist ethos which was quickly becoming the common sense of suburban America. They simply preferred driving over making use of mass transit. Paul Becker, a resident of Douglasville, Georgia who was a Falcons season-ticket holder during their tenure at Atlanta Stadium, succinctly summed up the preference of suburban Atlantans for driving in a 2000 letter to the *Journal-Constitution*. He explained that he stopped renewing his Falcons season ticket when the team moved to the Georgia Dome in 1992 because he was not granted one of the assigned parking spots in the dome lot. "I don't like MARTA; I don't want to be forced to ride MARTA. I like to leave when I want to leave, not when MARTA is ready to leave," he wrote.[25] Becker's views represented a demonstrable consensus in the region. In 1980 the 2.3 million residents of metropolitan Atlanta registered more than 1.5 million cars while fewer than 1 million residents even had direct access to MARTA. In 1970 around 5 percent of the region's residents used mass transit to commute. Twenty-five years and billions of dollars later, the percentage of commuters who used mass transit remained roughly the same.[26]

Those inclined to use MARTA's rail service had to wait years for the long-proposed system to open even in Fulton and DeKalb Counties, the two that had approved the measure. Rail lines that offered commuters access to downtown Atlanta did not open until 1979, more than a decade after the Braves and Falcons arrived in the city. The first MARTA rapid rail line was, in fact, an east-west line that served primarily inner-city residents, which offered little service to suburban riders. When a north-south line opened in 1984, the trip from a MARTA station to Atlanta Stadium required either a shuttle bus ride from the Five Points or a twenty-minute walk from the stop at Georgia State University. Suburbanites predisposed to dislike the system decided quickly that MARTA trains were not only inconvenient but also unsafe. MARTA's leadership used the media to try to persuade residents of Fulton and Dekalb Counties to use their trains to patronize the city's amenities by showing off the cleanliness of the cars and the rapid rail line's closed-circuit television security system. But media coverage of a series of high-profile assaults and robberies in and around trains and stations in the mid-1980s, including a 1986 near-fatal random stabbing outside the Omni, resonated more loudly in the suburbs.[27]

Beginning in 1965, the Falcons and Braves offered a dedicated shuttle bus service that dropped fans off directly in front of the stadium. It made seven (eventually, nine) stops on its route, which included both downtown parking garages as well as a number of suburban shopping centers with large parking lots. All but one of the shopping centers was located on the city's affluent northside, demonstrating the two teams' focus on white and suburban fans as the core of their support. Collectively, Braves and Falcons shuttles stopped at parking areas with upwards of twenty-five thousand spaces. Initially, the shuttle services were administered by the ATC. MARTA took over the operation of the shuttle services in 1973 when it purchased the private bus company.[28]

The Braves shuttle was widely promoted by the franchise and the ATC in advance of the club's debut in the city. Radio and newspaper advertisements and a mass mailing of 250,000 copies of the stadium shuttle bus route ensured that the vast majority of metropolitan area residents had been made aware of the service. The advertising campaign certainly worked on opening night in April 1965, when the lame duck Milwaukee Braves played their first of seven exhibition games in Atlanta that season. More than fifteen thousand fans took advantage of the Braves shuttle service, which began two hours before the pregame festivities and ran for an hour after the conclusion of the game.[29]

The willingness of large numbers of Atlantans to use mass transit to attend a special event like opening night was one thing. Getting them to become regular patrons of mass transit was quite another. A survey conducted by the Georgia Tech School of Management after the 1966 season found that 81 percent of Braves spectators drove to the ballpark, a figure that remained steady for the next decade. In a possible chicken-and-egg scenario, Atlanta Stadium's notably small four-thousand-space parking lot proved large enough to handle most of the baseball crowds the team drew during its first decade in the city.[30]

While Atlanta Stadium's parking lot was large enough to handle the turnout at most of the Braves' eighty-one regular-season home dates each season, it was never adequate for the Falcons' regular and exhibition home dates. A 1970 Model Cities survey suggested that an additional seven thousand parking spots were needed each Sunday to accommodate Falcons game attendees. As a result, the Falcons proved far more successful at convincing their fans to patronize the ATC- and, later, MARTA-operated shuttle. The Falcons Flyer charged fans 75 cents each way to travel to and from the stadium, beginning ninety minutes before and ending ninety minutes after each game.[31]

A 1966 survey conducted for the Falcons by researchers at Georgia Tech indicated that just 16 percent of game attendees used the club's shuttle service to get to the stadium. Sixty percent of fans had either parked in the stadium lot or in a private lot in the surrounding neighborhoods. Another 10 percent had taken a charter bus to the game, which had long been a favorite mode of transportation to Georgia Tech football games among the Atlanta-area country-club set. By 1972 the same researchers found that the percentage of fans who used the Flyer to get to the stadium had nearly doubled to 31 percent. The percentage of fans who parked in the stadium lot or in the nearby neighborhoods had fallen to 50 percent, a slight majority of whom parked in "wildcat" lots, creating an estimated $38,000 in revenue that season for stadium-area residents. The percentage of fans who arrived on charter buses stayed roughly the same, at 9 percent.[32] The crowd that took the Falcons Flyer to the game tended to be shuttle regulars but not regular riders of public transportation. A 1968 survey commissioned by the Falcons found that three-quarters of Flyer patrons rode the shuttle frequently to games, while a mere 16 percent of riders used public transportation for their daily commutes.[33]

The opening of several mixed-use developments with large parking garages in downtown Atlanta during the 1970s and the opening of the initial MARTA rapid rail lines in 1979 and 1984 cut into the business of the Falcons Flyer considerably. By 1984, just 5 percent of game attendees used the suburban-oriented shuttle bus service. Approximately 30 percent of fans parked downtown, the majority of whom took a new direct shuttle from the CBD parking lots to the stadium. Another 10 percent of fans used MARTA trains, while roughly half of Falcons game attendees still parked at the stadium lot or in a nearby private spot. Still, an estimated 85 percent of Falcons fans used their automobile for at least part of their trip to the stadium.[34]

A 1968 UPI REPORT SUGGESTED THAT THE OWNERS OF Atlanta's professional sports teams were "finding out there isn't as much spectator gold in these hills as they had hoped." The arrival of new franchise after new franchise had diminished the novelty of professional sports in the city, leading to "waning enthusiasm in the face of a play for pay onslaught that included baseball, football, soccer, and basketball."[35] Not only did Atlanta's professional teams have to compete for attention with the city's existing sporting culture, which included such popular regional spectacles as college football, golf, auto racing, and professional wrestling, but also they had to compete with one another for the discretionary dollars of the region's consumers.

The Braves' April 1965 opening weekend at Atlanta Stadium offered a preview of the consistent competition that Atlanta's professional teams faced from the region's traditional sporting culture. While the three-game Braves-Tigers exhibition series drew an average of more than thirty-five thousand spectators per game, big league baseball was only the third best-attended sporting event in Georgia that weekend. On Sunday, sixty thousand spectators watched Jack Nicklaus pull away from Gary Player and Arnold Palmer for a nine-stroke victory in the final round of the Masters Tournament in Augusta. A total of 150,000 fans attended the Masters over the course of the four-day tournament. Twenty miles south of the Atlanta city limits in Hampton, Georgia, 50,700 stock-car racing fans watched IndyCar legend A. J. Foyt take over for an ill Marvin Panch at lap 212 of the 334 laps of the Atlanta 500. Foyt drove Panch's 1965 Ford to victory and the $76,000 in prize money, more than three times the payday Nicklaus received for winning the Masters.[36] Atlanta's support for the Braves in their first home weekend series demonstrated the capacity for Major League sports to serve at least momentarily as a source of metropolitan cohesion but not a unique ability among the region's leisure activities to bring people together. That weekend, larger crowds at the Masters and the Atlanta 500 demonstrated the hold that each of those events had over its respective enclaves of support.

"Our plate was too full all of a sudden," *Constitution* editor Jim Minter said of the glut of professional sports teams that were jerry-rigged onto the city's already robust sporting culture in the late 1960s and early 1970s.[37] The greatest competitor for suburbanites' attention to Atlanta's full plate of professional sports may have been the region's frequently balmy weather. Outdoor leisure activities won a far greater share of suburban Atlantans' discretionary dollars than any of the city's professional sports teams. Although Metropolitan Atlantans' embrace of outdoor leisure mirrored national trends, Georgia's climate enabled them to embrace such activities for a longer period each year than residents of most other states. Unlike residents of northern cities with established professional sports franchises, few Atlantans had a commitment to their new teams that competed with their desire for outdoor recreation. As early as September 1967, *Constitution* sports editor Jesse Outlar cited outdoor activities as a reason for the Braves' sagging attendance. Outlar explained that most suburban families would rather partake in relaxing activities like picnicking, boating, or golfing than commute back into the city on a weekend to watch a mediocre baseball team.[38] *Sports Illustrated*'s Roy M. Blount, a Georgia native himself, later referred to this phenomenon as Atlanta's "blue collar gap." "Atlanta," he wrote, "is a town of executives and poor people . . . many of its citizens can afford to boat or hunt or play golf or tennis, rather than go into town and sit among a lot of sweaty hollering fans."[39]

An explosion of family-oriented leisure infrastructure in suburban Atlanta in the 1960s and 1970s, both public and private, paralleled the emergence of Atlanta as a Major League City. Boating and golf, which appealed to both natives and newcomers, thrived as upscale leisure activities in metropolitan Atlanta. Each of the suburban counties made generous municipal investments in parks and recreation, providing their citizens with numerous well-maintained public facilities that skewed toward the upscale. It is unlikely that any previous population in human history had access to as many publicly supported golf courses, tennis courts, horse stables, or boathouses as suburban Atlantans in the 1970s. Dekalb County's Stone Mountain Park and Cobb County's Six Flags over Georgia amusement park both drew far more visitors annually than any of the city's professional sports teams. During the 1970s, Stone Mountain drew more than three million visitors each year. Six Flags over Georgia, which opened ten miles west of downtown Atlanta in 1964, drew more than two million visitors annually in the 1970s while charging customers three times as much for a day of amusement as the most expensive ticket to an Atlanta Braves game.[40]

LOCAL RADIO AND TELEVISION COVERAGE OF THE BRAVES and Falcons made it possible for fans to follow both teams without the hassle of going to Atlanta Stadium. During the late 1960s the Braves had one of the largest radio and television networks in baseball. Atlanta's wsb, the largest station in Cox Communications' media empire, served as the flagship for a six-state, thirty-nine-affiliate radio-broadcast network that brought all 162 Braves games to homes across the Southeast. Cox's wsb-tv televised twenty Braves games annually to twenty-one television affiliates across the same six Southeastern states. To avoid hurting the gate at Atlanta Stadium, all Braves television broadcasts on WSB were road games. Team management asserted that the Braves' modest television broadcast schedule would increase the novelty of attending a game at Atlanta Stadium. The Braves earned $2.5 million over four years from its initial radio and television contract with WSB. Two-thirds of the money WSB paid to the Braves went toward their radio broadcasting rights, which, due to the limits then placed on televising games, was a more lucrative revenue stream for Major League franchises.[41]

Braves broadcasts, particularly the more novel televised games, received excellent ratings across the region. In 1971 Cox asserted that Braves games had been the best-rated television program each of the previous six summers in the southeastern United States. Braves baseball drew an average of 56 percent of the region's television viewers during their summer evening telecasts. Although that figure seems impressive, the Braves' early televised games faced little competition from other stations during the year's most lightly watched and programmed broadcasting season.[42]

WTCG (later, WTBS), Ted Turner's local UHF channel turned cable-television superstation, outbid WSB for the Braves' television rights for the 1973 season, offering the club $600,000 per year for five years to broadcast 60 Braves games, both home and away. The Braves' contract with WTCG tripled the number of Braves television broadcasts as well as their annual television revenue. The WTCG deal, which increased the Braves' annual local broadcast media contract to $1,000,000, brought the club's television and radio revenue back up into the middle of the pack in MLB. During the early 1970s, the Braves' media contract lagged behind the increasingly lucrative television and radio deals being signed by most other franchises.

WTCG's innovative use of new satellite-transmission technology expanded the television reach of the Braves to cable subscribers across the South and, eventually, the United States.

By the end of 1976, WTCG could be seen in 2 million homes. Within five years, its successor station, WTBS, could be seen in more than 40 million homes. The reach of Braves baseball, though, far exceeded the grip of the team on local fans. Braves attendance continued its nosedive in the mid-1970s, corresponding with the far-broader exposure it received on local television. Following the 1975 season, Turner purchased the cash-strapped Braves and began broadcasting all 162 of their games on WTCG. The Braves continued to draw strong regional television ratings while attendance at the stadium failed to reach the modest annual threshold of one million spectators again until 1980.[43]

WAGA, Atlanta's CBS affiliate, broadcast Falcons games locally as part of CBS's share of the lucrative national television contract with the NFL, which earned each of the league's twenty-six franchises $7.7 million annually, starting in 1974. Until 1973, only the Falcons' road games were broadcast on CBS. Previously, the NFL required networks to black out games in a seventy-five-mile radius of their city of origin, whether or not the game had sold out. In response to a threatened federal antitrust intervention, the league agreed to broadcast games in and around the city of origin if the game had sold out seventy-two hours in advance of kickoff.[44] Falcons games in the early 1970s averaged a local Nielsen rating of 20, meaning that roughly one-half of television viewers in Metropolitan Atlanta during their Sunday afternoon broadcasts were tuned to their games.[45] Atlanta radio station WQXI served as the flagship of the Falcons radio network, which consisted of forty stations across five southeastern states and averaged approximately two hundred thousand listeners per game in the late 1960s.[46]

HOWEVER ONE GOT TO ATLANTA STADIUM, THE ACTUAL experience of attending a game there discouraged many potential spectators from patronizing it with any frequency. Fans and players alike complained about its steamy conditions during the summer. "It was so hot and humid that a player could wear himself down by the Fourth of July," Hank Aaron said of playing a season's worth of home dates at Atlanta Stadium.[47] Baseball and football players complained that the efforts of the multipurpose stadium's management to accommodate both franchises as well as special events ensured that the playing surface and amenities at the stadium deteriorated quickly into one of the worst in each of their respective leagues.[48]

Many baseball players complained about the quality of the playing surface at Atlanta Stadium, both its turf, which was torn up every August and September by Falcons football, and the red-clay dirt of its infield, which was notoriously uneven. "The playing surface was one of the worst in the National League and you could bank on getting at least one bad hop during a series," former big league infielder Vance Law said of Atlanta Stadium.[49] Braves Manager Bobby Cox said that when he arrived in Atlanta in 1978 "the playing field was the worst in baseball. Opposing teams wouldn't even take ground balls on it."[50] Braves pitcher Ron Reed recalled returning to Atlanta one spring in the early 1970s when "the outfield was bare dirt, spray painted green . . . two or three weeks before we returned from spring training, they had motor-cross in that stadium. And they had piles of dirt everywhere and when they removed the dirt the grass was dead."[51]

Like many multipurpose municipal stadiums built during the 1960s, Atlanta Stadium aged quickly. In an unflattering 1984 *Journal-Constitution* feature on the facility entitled "The Dinosaur on Capitol Avenue," longtime stadium manager T. Herman Graves described how the fifty-one-week "hurry up construction" on Atlanta Stadium, as well as Georgia's hot and humid climate, had made its interior prematurely grimy. "Concrete concourses that might have been sealed were not," Graves said, and "thus all kinds of gum and ground in dirt" from years earlier caked the walkways of the stadium.[52] In a 1996 letter to the editor of the *Journal-Constitution*, former stadium concessions worker Bob Hunt painted a vivid picture of the stadium's rapid deterioration in the 1970s and 1980s. "I remember the TVs never worked," he said, "I remember the patrons could not watch the game while waiting in line. I remember the rats in the tunnels where we had to go get supplies. I remember the smell—yuck."[53]

Fans who had been awed by Atlanta Stadium's modern design in the mid-1960s described it as lacking in personality, intimacy, and amenities by the early 1970s.[54] Baseball fans sitting in high-priced box seats complained frequently about their distance from the diamond, but their gripes were minor when compared to those of football fans at Atlanta Stadium, virtually none of whom had a great view of the action. When reconfigured for football, the seats at the 50-yard line, traditionally the premier seats at a football game, were further from the field than any other ground-level seats. Moreover, they were situated so close to the ground that the players standing on either sideline blocked these fans' view of the game. Sold as "partially obstructed," the seats were the cheapest in the stadium. The seats closest to the action at a Falcons game were those that encircled the end zone, which were traditionally among the lowest-priced tickets at football stadiums.[55]

At the time of the stadium's opening, most fans expressed awe over the brightly lit new ballpark, its novel baby-blue seats, and its streamlined, space-age design, which bore more than a passing resemblance to the critically acclaimed architecture of Los Angeles's recently erected Dodger Stadium (1962).[56] "Most fans' impressions of Atlanta Stadium were in comparison to Ponce De Leon Park," longtime Braves fan Karl Green said. "The intimacy everyone craves today wasn't considered desirable in 1966. Atlanta Stadium was new. It was clean. It looked modern. There were large parking lots, and it was easy to get to from the mostly new interstates."[57]

"Sure, we were impressed with a brand-new ballpark," Braves announcer Milo Hamilton said, remembering the first time he saw Atlanta Stadium in 1965. At the time, Hamilton said, "people didn't realize that multipurpose stadiums would become cookie cutters," across the urban landscape of North America.[58] "No one seemed to particularly mind the distance from the field," Karl Green recalled, citing a frequent fan complaint about the stadium in later years. If anything, the standardization of urban-renewal-era, multipurpose facilities like Atlanta Stadium and the distance they created between spectators and performers seemed modern, while the proximity of the players to the fans at a brick-and-mortar ballpark like Poncey seemed like a crass relic from a more informal, less sophisticated era.[59] As the public started to recoil from the scale and approach of many urban-renewal projects, a broad and similar contempt emerged across the country for many of the features of larger-than-life multipurpose stadiums, particularly the physical distance they so often established between fans and the on-field action. The Braves responded to this emerging desire for ballpark intimacy in 1972 by moving box seats twelve feet closer to the field. The Falcons had no leeway to alter the field configuration, forcing their paying fans to endure some of the worst vantage points in major professional sports.[60]

Taken together, all of the misgivings fans had about Atlanta Stadium make it no wonder that its revenues fell far short of initial projections. Financially, the stadium proved to be an almost immediate tax burden on the city. In seven of its first eight years of operation, the city of Atlanta was required to pay at least a half-million dollars toward the stadium's annual debt, as receipts from baseball, football, and special events were insufficient to cover the financial requirements of the initial municipal bond. In 1975 alone, the city and county had to pay $955,000 of the $1 million in annual debt service due to the lack of revenue generated by stadium events.[61]

10

Outside the Stadium It's the City

....

VISITORS TO ATLANTA STADIUM FOUND FEW AMENITIES in its immediate environs. Most of downtown Atlanta's restaurants, shops, and hotels were located more than a mile north of the stadium, clustered around the Five Points district. "When will the physical needs of stadium visitors be accounted for?" Charles E. Zink of Atlanta wrote to the *Constitution* in March 1967. He feared that the absence of nearby eateries and lodging would deter visitors from making return visits to the stadium. "When visitors come to see a ball game in our beautiful stadium from other sections of our state or from sister states, North and South Carolina, Florida, Alabama, and other states and see the condition of the few remaining stores on Georgia Avenue right next to our beautiful stadium what do you think is their reaction?" he wrote.[1]

By the late 1960s, the southern sections of the CBD that bordered the stadium had deteriorated from the bustling Whiteboard-Hall shopping district of a decade earlier into a languishing, largely abandoned commercial zone patronized primarily by the impoverished African American residents of the nearby neighborhoods. Rich's, the city's most glamorous department store, hung on in the neighborhood, but virtually every other major retailer in the southern CBD had disappeared.

Atlanta Stadium's proximity to some of the city's most impoverished and high-crime neighborhoods deterred many potential suburban patrons from attending events at the facility. In a general sense, the demographic transformation of

Atlanta in the 1960s and 1970s, particularly its CBD and the residential neighborhoods that surrounded it, deterred white suburbanites from patronizing public spaces that required social encounters with large numbers of African Americans. Between 1960 and 1980, Atlanta was transformed from a city whose population was slightly less than two-fifths African American to one that was two-thirds African American.[2]

More specifically, the proximity of Atlanta Stadium to the volatile Summerhill neighborhood stoked suburban fears about the safety of attending a Braves or a Falcons game. Located just southwest of the CBD, Summerhill transitioned from a working-class residential area to a crime-ridden, predominately poor and African American neighborhood in the decades after World War II. Urban renewal had displaced 10,000 of the neighborhood's 12,500 residents during the 1950s. City leaders had promised to construct affordable housing in the area but instead transferred 47 acres of the 354-acre district from the AHA to the Stadium Authority, which paved the land into a four-thousand-space parking lot, all in a neighborhood without a public park. By the time Atlanta Stadium opened in April 1965, an estimated ten thousand people, many of whom were unemployed and low-skilled recent arrivals from rural Georgia, had crammed into the area's remaining housing stock. Houses intended as single-family dwellings often had as many as a dozen families living in them. In 1965 the mayor's Atlanta Crime Commission declared Summerhill the Atlanta neighborhood most vulnerable to racial unrest.[3]

Five days before the Falcons played their first regular-season home game, a civil disturbance erupted in Summerhill. Though minor in comparison to the urban insurrections that engulfed other American cities the previous three summers, the Summerhill Riot accentuated existing fears about the stadium's environs. On September 6, 1966, residents of the Summerhill neighborhood protested the police shooting of a robbery suspect in the area. The demonstration escalated into a riot, as many of the estimated one thousand protestors began overturning cars and hurling rocks as the number of Atlanta police officers and Georgia state troopers on the scene swelled into the hundreds.[4]

Allen and two dozen allies from the Black clergy waded into the middle of the crowd and tried to defuse the situation. Allen and Ralph Abernathy took to a loudspeaker and encouraged the protestors to clear the usually busy Capitol Avenue thoroughfare and follow them to the nearby stadium parking lot for a grievance meeting. Moving the protestors to the stadium lot would have also helped Allen assert greater control over the crowd, as one hundred additional shotgun-bearing state patrolmen and dozens of off-duty Atlanta police officers were hidden from view inside the stadium and awaiting the mayor's orders. The crowd, which had been aroused by Stokely Carmichael and the local SNCC leadership, shouted down the idea and began jeering the mayor and the ministers. The demonstrators surged forward and rocked back and forth the police car on which Allen stood, knocking him to the ground. When Allen regained composure, he ordered the reagitated crowd dispersed. Police fired warning shotgun blasts and deployed canisters of tear gas, breaking up the unruly gathering. While SNCC claimed widespread police brutality during the riot, Allen complimented his police force for their restraint in Summerhill.[5]

The dispersal of the crowd from Capitol Avenue did not mean the end of the urban unrest in Summerhill. Despite the presence of hundreds of Atlanta police and state troopers for the next two nights, looters devastated many of the remaining businesses in the Summerhill area while motorists on nearby roadways faced a barrage of bricks and stones. A group of young men viciously beat a WSB reporter and camera operator covering an Allen-organized grievance meeting at Calvary Baptist Church the evening of the riot. The Summerhill Riot was the most destructive incident of racial violence in Atlanta in sixty years, leading to seventy-three arrests and more than two-dozen injuries.[6]

Several days after the Summerhill Riot, another civil disturbance took place just to the east of the stadium in the Bedford Pine neighborhood. Provoked by the murder of a Black teenager by a middle-aged white man, two weekend nights of rioting led to ninety arrests. Mayor Allen, whose family had personally consoled the murdered teenager's mother and offered a $10,000 reward in the case, tried to talk down the crowd from violence both evenings while angry protesters screamed in his face. The disturbance in Bedford Pine ended as quickly as it started when police arrested the assailant, who was later convicted of first-degree murder.[7]

The Summerhill Riot and its aftermath had a clear political beneficiary—Ivan Allen's old political rival, Lester Maddox. The segregationist was seeking the Democratic Party's nomination for governor that fall and running a distant fourth in every statewide poll. Maddox accused progressive politicians like Allen and former Georgia governor Ellis Arnall, the frontrunner in the 1966 Democratic field, of creating social chaos by weakening the region's longstanding institutions and hierarchies. "Riots," Maddox asserted in the days leading up to the September 13 primary, "occur only where we're ready to surrender, appease, and compromise."[8] Maddox's new focus on civil disorder catapulted him into second place in the Democratic primary behind Arnall, who had been endorsed by virtually all of Georgia's major daily newspapers and was arguably the most progressive governor in the state's history. Before the Summerhill Riot, Arnall had regarded State Senator Jimmy Carter, who was wildly popular among rural white and Black voters, as his most serious challenger.[9]

Following Maddox's surprise finish, Arnall characterized his opponent as a "preacher of fear, distrust, and radical extremism" who would turn Georgia into the "laughingstock of the nation" with his "ax-handle lawlessness."[10] The mainstream press joined Arnall in cajoling the electorate into voting against Maddox, but to no avail.[11] On September 28, 1966, Maddox shocked national observers by garnering 55 percent of the runoff vote, defeating Arnall by more than seventy thousand votes.[12] Maddox went on to win the general election against Bo Callaway, the state's first Republican congressman since Reconstruction. Despite being a Goldwater conservative who voted against the Civil Rights Act, most progressive white voters and virtually all of the state's African American voters supported Callaway, helping him win a narrow plurality of the statewide vote on Election Day 1966. Nevertheless, a 140-year-old provision in the Georgia State Constitution sent the election to the state General Assembly, since neither candidate won a majority. The heavily Democratic legislature voted by a margin of 182–66 to make Maddox the state's next governor and had him sworn in behind closed doors in January 1967.[13]

The disturbances of 1966, which helped make Lester Maddox the governor of Georgia, were not an end to the flare-ups in the neighborhoods surrounding Atlanta Stadium. The following summer, another uprising in southwest Atlanta, this time in the Dixie Hills neighborhood, emerged just blocks from the ballpark. On the afternoon of June 19, 1967, a white shopkeeper shot and killed a Black man he accused of trying to rob his store. That evening, bricks, bottles, and Molotov cocktails rained down on the police who remained on the scene after the shopkeeper was arrested. The rioters were soon dispersed with tear gas, and eight people were arrested. Concerns about the safety of Atlanta Chiefs soccer fans leaving a game at the stadium led police to detour traffic away from the four-block area at the core of the disturbance, which was a common route to the South Expressway from the stadium parking lot.[14]

All these events were uncomfortably close to the stadium for many suburbanites. They stoked existing fears in the outlying counties that Atlanta was not only unsafe but also lawless. The events also led many white suburbanites to conflate urban unrest with the city's rising crime rate, transforming two of the era's urban concerns into a pathologized and racialized leviathan. In the years following the Summerhill Riot, numerous incidents in the neighborhoods surrounding Atlanta Stadium contributed to the widespread unease about the venue's surroundings. As War on Poverty spending in the adjoining Model Cities area failed to meet the needs of its predominately poor and African American residents, crime rose dramatically in neighborhoods that had been fractured by slum clearance and stadium development in the 1950s and 1960s. Car break-ins and muggings were well-known potential hazards for visitors to the stadium, particularly for those motorists who parked on the surrounding streets rather than paying for a spot in the stadium lot.[15]

At an Atlanta Chamber breakfast in early 1976, a Chamber member asked new Braves owner Ted Turner what he planned to do about the frequent break-ins and muggings in the stadium parking lot. Turner deflected the question with humor, stating that he would run shuttle buses during games for criminals from the stadium parking lot up to the affluent neighborhoods of the city's northside. Then, the criminals could burglarize the rich people's homes in peace while the rich people enjoyed the baseball game in safety.[16]

An August 1979 *Journal* report on security at Atlanta Stadium tried to reassure fans that they were safe attending games, despite the stadium's proximity to some of the city's most dangerous neighborhoods amidst a record crime wave in the city. Atlanta tallied the nation's highest per-capita homicide rate for the fifth time in eight years in 1979, with a record 368 unlawful killings (51.0 per 100,000 citizens). During every game, the article assured fans, twenty-five Atlanta police officers patrolled the stadium itself while thirty Georgia state troopers, thirty-five armed private security guards, and a team of plainclothes Atlanta police officers patrolled the stadium's environs. Not coincidentally, the story was published soon after a rash of car break-ins and muggings of Braves fans, most of which took place in private parking areas outside the stadium lot.[17]

The dangers of parking outside the stadium lot were made

evident years earlier on one of the most high-profile nights in Falcons' history: November 30, 1970, the first time that Atlanta hosted ABC's *Monday Night Football*. Just like on Sunday afternoons, the stadium lot was filled to capacity for a Falcons home game, leading many of the remaining fans who traveled by car to seek out parking on a nearby street or in one of the many informal lots in the adjacent neighborhoods. Rarely did Falcons fans park in these high-crime areas at night, though, leading the club to more than double the size of its stadium-area security detail for the game. While the Miami Dolphins defeated the Falcons 20–7 on national television, looters broke into dozens of automobiles parked outside the stadium lot. Two cars parked on streets adjacent to the stadium were set on fire. Fans reported two armed robberies and five separate assaults that took place as they returned to their cars after the game's midnight conclusion.[18]

When reflecting on safety at the stadium, many diehard Braves and Falcons fans insist that they personally were not intimidated by the area but that many other potential patrons were. Former Braves beat writer Wayne Minshew emphasized the significant police and private security presence both inside and outside the stadium during games.[19] Beginning on the stadium's opening night in 1965, Atlanta police patrolled the stadium parking lot on foot to "prevent car looting," while officers on motorcycle trolled the surrounding neighborhoods on the lookout for trouble.[20] Minshew stressed that most crimes committed against fans in the vicinity of Atlanta Stadium happened to "people who parked away from the stadium, where they did not have to pay and where security did not exist," noting that "it takes only one incident to create a feeling of fear or dread."[21]

Alan Morris stated that he had "no safety concerns about attending games at the stadium during the 60s and 70s." Like many other stadium regulars, though, Morris admitted that his views were far from the norm. "There is a significant suburban population in Metro Atlanta who live 'outside the perimeter' who often complain in loud voices about 'crime in Atlanta' [and] who largely avoided events in downtown Atlanta, including sporting events." Morris noted the high incidence of panhandlers in downtown Atlanta during this era but said that a large police presence downtown during sporting events helped to maintain order.[22] "Safety was mostly a perception issue," Braves fan Karl Green recalled, "but with small crowds, and large parking lots on the edge of a down-at-the-heels section of town, folks just felt insecure." He too stressed that most personal and property crimes committed against Braves fans involved those who parked outside the stadium lot in the surrounding neighborhoods.[23]

The most infamous violent crime in the environs of Atlanta Stadium did in fact happen in the stadium parking lot: the October 1973 armed robbery and shooting of *Constitution* sports editor Jesse Outlar as he returned to his car following a Falcons game.[24] Outlar, the *Constitution*'s sports editor since 1957, was attacked as he left the stadium around two hours after a Falcons defeat. He had just finished filing his column on the game by phone from the press box.[25] A young Black male approached Outlar and asked him for a ride as he walked to his car in the deserted stadium parking lot. When Outlar refused, the young man pulled a pistol out of a paper bag and shot the sportswriter twice in the torso. The assailant took Outlar's briefcase, which was later found a few blocks south of the stadium, and ran toward the Summerhill neighborhood.[26] The Outlar shooting was the third high-profile assault in the stadium area in less than two months. Three nights earlier, Braves assistant public relations director Jim Schultz had been mugged in the stadium lot. In mid-August, a fan sitting in the stands during a Falcons preseason football game was struck in the leg by a stray bullet. Investigators determined that the shot had been fired from outside of the stadium.[27]

Atlanta police arrested a DeKalb County teenager named Carl Henry for the Outlar shooting. Henry was already in custody on an aggravated assault charge, the victim of which was the primary witness against him in the Outlar case. Minutes after the Outlar shooting, Henry had allegedly pointed a gun at the middle-aged man as he stood on the porch of his Capitol Avenue home. The Summerhill resident had gone outside after hearing the gunshots and saw Henry, who had once dated his daughter, running from the direction of the stadium while trying to eject the cartridge from his pistol.[28] Nine days after the incident, the sixteen-year-old was indicted for armed robbery and aggravated assault in the Outlar case as the *Constitution* sports editor lay in critical condition at Piedmont Hospital. Henry's legal defense, engineered by city councilor Marvin Arrington, one of the city's most prominent Black attorneys, focused on Outlar's failure to pick Henry's mugshot out of a lineup. Outlar's inability to identify Henry led to a hung jury and the declaration of a mistrial in the case, despite his conviction for the other aggravated-assault charge.[29] Outlar recovered from the incident, returning to work in early 1974, but suffered from nerve damage, bowel perforations, and recurrent internal hemorrhaging as a result of his wounds. One of the bullets remained lodged in his back for the rest of his life.[30]

"The first responsibility of government is public safety," the *Journal* editorialized the day after the shooting. "The city of Atlanta is not doing its job as long as the stadium area is unsafe even two hours after a major event there."[31] Outlar's own paper, the *Constitution*, noted that the shooting was "by no means the first assault in the stadium parking lot" and reflected broader pathologies in a city where "random assaults have become a common practice."[32] "There is an awful irony in the fact that Jesse Outlar was shot just outside the stadium," Outlar's colleague Reg Murphy wrote, since "a hundred times he talked and wrote about the stadium and how it promoted racial integration. It was the only place where the races got together and had fun."[33]

Mayoral candidate Maynard Jackson latched onto the Outlar shooting as an issue during the 1973 runoff election, as it provided him with a high-profile example of the crime epidemic that he accused incumbent mayor Sam Massell of allowing to fester in Black neighborhoods, particularly in the Model Cities neighborhoods that surrounded Atlanta Stadium. Jackson, who went on to win in a landslide and become the city's first African American mayor, said that incidents like the Outlar shooting were products of the "$36 million heroin industry" that was thriving in predominately Black neighborhoods like Summerhill. Citing the Outlar case, Jackson said inaction on street crime was greatly accentuating the flight of white residents from the city.[34]

Stadium Authority officials responded by adding more lighting to the parking lots. The Falcons doubled the size of their security force inside and outside the stadium to nearly three hundred, approximately seventy-five of whom were Atlanta police officers. Additionally, the Falcons extended the hours of their security forces until all team representatives, journalists, and automobiles left the lot. City police responded by making Atlanta Stadium its own precinct and designating its environs as a permanent walking beat. Talk of building a fence around the stadium parking lot was quickly shelved after the Stadium Authority decided it would lead to severe traffic bottlenecks before and after games.[35]

Despite these measures, fans remained skeptical of the stadium's security. The *Constitution*'s Tom Henderson and Art Harris reported on the fear of Falcons fans leaving the stadium after the Falcons' next home game. They overheard one woman saying to another woman, "Let's see if we can get up enough guts to walk out in the parking lot." Falcons season ticket holder Wayne Elliott told the reporters that he only felt safe walking back to his car "if I stay with a group." An unnamed fan they spoke with told the reporters that he was "mad as hell" about Outlar, "but after they catch the guy they'll let him go. So what difference does it make any way?" expressing a sentiment demonstrative of many suburbanites view of crime in Atlanta.[36]

The Outlar shooting, *Constitution* editor Jim Minter recalled, was not a turning point in the public perception of the stadium since "everybody knew that the stadium was not adjacent to a really great neighborhood." Instead, it highlighted the hazards that came with attending a game at Atlanta Stadium. Incidents like the 1973 Outlar shooting, though, "tended to make suburban people think twice," he said.[37] Braves Vice President Dick Cecil admitted to reporters that there was only so much the teams could do to protect their fans because "outside the Stadium, it's the city," a place that many metropolitan-area residents preferred to avoid.[38]

While many suburban Atlantans questioned the safety of the stadium's environs, the men of color who played professional sports in Atlanta were frequently given good reason to question their own safety in a city whose police department had come to be seen by many Black residents as a draconian, occupying force in their neighborhoods. The brutal August 1971 beating of Atlanta Braves' Black Dominican star Rico Carty by three Atlanta police officers demonstrated to the city's professional athletes that even wealthy and famous people of color were subject to such atrocities in the City Too Busy to Hate. Carty, who had spent more than a decade with the Braves' organization, was part of a cadre of Latino standouts on Atlanta's roster during the late 1960s and early 1970s that also included Orlando Cepeda and Felipe Alou.[39] Carty was one of the era's best hitters, earning the NL's batting championship in 1970. He was also a fan favorite in Atlanta, beloved both for his on-the-field theatrics and the many hours he spent with fans signing autographs, taking pictures, and chatting about the game. The local press nicknamed him "Beeg Boy," an exaggeration of the way he said "big boy," the sobriquet with which he addressed almost everyone he met.[40]

Carty and his brother-in-law, Carlos Ramirez, were beaten by three Atlanta police officers, two of whom were off-duty at the time, in the early morning hours of August 24, 1971. The Braves outfielder was returning home from the barbeque restaurant he had recently opened near Oglethorpe University,

northeast of downtown Atlanta. The assault took place after
Carty and Ramirez got into a traffic dispute with two intoxi-
cated off-duty Atlanta police officers near the North Avenue–
Georgia Tech exit on the city's North Expressway. A patrolling
police officer pulled up to the simmering altercation, recognized the two officers, and proceeded to join them in assaulting Carty and Ramirez. Carty, incidentally, was an ex-boxer
who had famously punched out Hank Aaron, with whom he
shared a mutual enmity, on a cross-country flight four years
earlier. The on-duty officer pummeled Carty repeatedly with
a slapjack, resulting in permanent damage to his right eye.[41]

Carty and Ramirez were arrested on the scene, but the truth
of the matter soon became evident. More than a dozen wit-
nesses interviewed by investigators stated that the officers
had been the aggressors in the incident. The on-duty officer
had lied to investigators, telling them he did not know the two
off-duty men when in fact they had been longtime acquain-
tances. Charges against Carty and Ramirez were quickly dismissed. The focus of the investigation turned to what Mayor
Sam Massell described as the "blatant brutality" of the three
officers. Massell called for the officers not only to be fired but
also held criminally liable for their actions.[42] Police Chief Her-
bert Jenkins referred to the incident as the "worst case of mis-
conduct of a police officer I've ever seen."[43] The three officers
were all fired from their jobs and later pled guilty to charges
ranging from public intoxication to assault. Such incidents
served, more broadly, to increase distrust of the Atlanta police
in Black neighborhoods even as those communities called for
better police protection amid rising crime.[44]

11

Atlanta Stadium, a Meeting Place

....

ATLANTA STADIUM'S FAILURES EXTENDED BEYOND THE
Braves and Falcons. From the outset, Atlanta Stadium failed
to consistently draw large enough crowds to its special events
to be considered a regional "meeting place" or "center of gravity," as its boosters had envisioned.[1]

In late 1965, the Stadium Authority tried to convince the
AFL and the NFL to host their first Super Bowl in Atlanta,
but the stadium's relatively limited seating capacity of fifty-
seven thousand prevented it from receiving serious consideration for the January 1967 game. Other warm-weather cities,
such as Los Angeles, New Orleans, and Miami, became frequent Super Bowl sites. The first nine Super Bowls were held
in those three cities, each of which had a stadium that could
accommodate more than seventy-five thousand spectators.
Despite its mild winters, Atlanta never hosted a Super Bowl
at its "miracle" stadium.[2]

Similarly, the Stadium Authority tried to organize a Christmas Day bowl game. Southern cities had hosted major college
football postseason bowl games for decades, most notably Dallas's Cotton Bowl, Miami's Orange Bowl, and New Orleans's
Sugar Bowl. In its aspiration to host both a professional football team and a major bowl game, Atlanta's civic leadership
exhibited its perpetual desire to possess the signature amenities of both the North and the South. The Stadium Authority worked closely with CBS to arrange the details of the game.
In exchange for a late afternoon Christmas time slot, the network insisted that Atlanta organizers call the game the "Santa

Claus Bowl." The SEC made a conditional arrangement with bowl organizers to send one of its top teams annually to play a nationally ranked, at-large opponent in exchange for a $200,000 payout, which would have made the game one of college football's most lucrative postseason contests. ABC offered the Stadium Authority a rival plan for a December college bowl game, which ABC officials said would feature two teams ranked in the Associated Press's final Top Ten College Football regular-season poll. The Stadium Authority decided to stick with CBS and the SEC, both of which had strong historical ties to Atlanta. In January 1965, CBS, the SEC, and the Stadium Authority brought their proposal for the game to the NCAA.[3]

The NCAA deferred their application to create the Santa Claus Bowl, citing a hesitance among committee members to sponsor a game on Christmas.[4] Additionally, the NCAA disapproved of the central role that CBS played in concocting the new game. If approved, the NCAA feared, quiet presciently, that other networks would campaign for their own made-for-television bowl games, threatening the amateur status of college football by injecting more money into the sport while lowering the quality of competition in bowl games.[5]

While the Stadium Authority awaited final word on the Santa Claus Bowl, it convinced the organizing committee of the Coaches' All-America East-West Football Game to relocate their event to Atlanta Stadium in 1966. A summer showcase for incoming AFL and NFL talent, the Coaches' All-America Game had been played previously at Buffalo's War Memorial Stadium. The American Football Coaches Association (AFCA), the game's sponsor, believed that Atlanta's larger metropolitan population, modern stadium, and traditional support for college football would increase attendance significantly. Instead, the Coaches' All-America Game flopped in Atlanta, drawing significantly smaller crowds than they had in Buffalo. Every year, the game was played on an unbearably hot and sticky June night in Georgia. After four seasons, the AFCA moved the game to Lubbock, Texas, a metropolitan area one-quarter the size of Greater Atlanta.[6]

Following a review process that lasted several years, the NCAA approved a college bowl game for Atlanta, albeit with a much different plan than the original Santa Claus proposal. The NCAA approved the creation of the Peach Bowl, a game that was to serve as a fundraiser for the Georgia Lions Club's Lighthouse Foundation, which conducted charitable work on behalf of the state's deaf and blind populations.[7] First played in December 1968, the Peach Bowl was strictly a second-tier bowl game, pitting also-rans from the ACC and the SEC against one another in contests that typically drew small crowds and were played, more often than not, in drizzly, near freezing conditions. Initially, the Peach Bowl was not even played at Atlanta Stadium. The first three Peach Bowl games were played at Georgia Tech's Grant Field due to conflicts between the Bowl's schedule and the final stretches of the Atlanta Falcons' seasons. The regionally based broadcasts of the early Peach Bowls on the Mizlou Television Network reached few homes outside of the Southeast, while the payouts the schools received for participating barely covered their travel expenses. The game teetered on the brink of bankruptcy for much of the 1970s and 1980s.[8]

ATLANTA STADIUM HOSTED A NUMBER OF NONSPORTING events during its lame-duck year, most of which failed to meet their organizers' expectations for attendance. None of the events cemented for Atlanta Stadium a status as the region's leading venue for large gatherings, calling into question almost immediately the stadium boosters' belief that the facility would serve as a social and cultural center of gravity for the metropolitan area. Grace Methodist Church, one of the area's largest congregations, rented Atlanta Stadium for a sunrise Easter 1966 service, which was cosponsored by 150 churches from throughout the metropolitan area. The April 10 event, which took place two days before the Braves' home opener, featured testimonials by New York Yankees star Bobby Richardson and Minnesota Vikings quarterback Fran Tarkenton. Despite calls by local clergymen to "fill the Stadium for Christ," the event drew eighteen thousand worshippers, far short of the organizers' goal of twenty-five thousand.[9]

The most successful nonsporting event held at Atlanta Stadium during the lame-duck season was August 18, 1965, when the Beatles played for thirty-four minutes to a crowd of thirty-six thousand screaming fans on a soupy late summer night. The band stayed in Atlanta for less than eight hours, arriving in the mid-afternoon on a chartered jet from Toronto. The Beatles left immediately after their ten o'clock performance, heading directly to the airport for another chartered flight, this time to Houston. Fans from across the Southeast who paid $5.50 each for general-admission tickets began lining up outside the stadium 4:30 a.m. on Wednesday for a show that began at 8:15 p.m. on Thursday. Beatles manager Brian Epstein told local reporters that the Beatles enjoyed their Atlanta performance more than any other show on the tour. To protect the grass playing surface, stadium officials sold tickets only in the stands. The distance between the audience and the stage enabled the Beatles to hear themselves play for the first time in months. While pleasing to the performers, this decision cut significantly into Braves, Inc.'s revenue for the evening, which only counted after the Beatles' $200,000 show guarantee.[10]

Stadium Authority–imposed restrictions on seating spectators on the playing field discouraged future concert promoters from renting out the venue. Aside from a Barbara Streisand concert in August 1966, the stadium did not host another concert for the next five years. In June 1970, the stadium hosted Cosmic Carnival, a music festival that featured performances by such rock luminaries as the Allman Brothers Band, Mountain, and Traffic. Regulations on the event, which included volume restrictions, a midnight curfew, and a requirement that fans remain in their assigned seats, convinced the concert's promoters to seek out a different venue for future Atlanta rock festivals. For the remainder of the 1970s, Atlanta Stadium occasionally hosted festivals or major drawing acts, such as Elton John and Led Zeppelin, but it never became a regular part of the era's stadium rock-touring circuit.[11]

The most heavily promoted event at Atlanta Stadium during its lame-duck year also drew its most disappointing crowd. An Emory undergraduate student named Remar Sutton decided in November 1965 that he wanted "to do something to show the world how most Americans feel" about the Vietnam War.[12] Working with a group of like-minded Emory students, Sutton organized an event called "Affirmation Vietnam," a pro-war rally at Atlanta Stadium scheduled for Saturday, February 13, 1966. Organizers said the event would demonstrate that Georgians "cast an affirmative vote for the United States' commitment in Viet Nam."[13] In the lead-up to the event, the Affirmation Vietnam organization on the Emory campus, which by the time of the rally numbered in the hundreds, gathered signatures from Georgians expressing their support for American policy in Southeast Asia. Branches of Affirmation Vietnam sprung up on fifty-two other campuses across Georgia and commenced with their own signature-gathering campaigns. By the time of the rally, 2-s college students had collected the signatures of more than two hundred thousand Georgians in support of the Vietnam War.

The local media promoted the Affirmation Vietnam event extensively and enthusiastically. Atlanta corporate sponsors provided the student organization with generous contributions, enabling it to saturate radio and television with advertisements for weeks in advance of the rally. Bob Hope filmed a television special to promote the event, which was shown on stations across Georgia.[14] Atlanta newspapers provided Affirmation Vietnam with days of front-page coverage. The papers emphasized that the event was free, that free downtown parking and shuttle buses would ferry people to the stadium, and that Affirmation organizers had put together an inspiring and entertaining program. Headliners included Hope, Anita Bryant, Georgia native and Secretary of State Dean Rusk, and Staff Sergeant Barry Sadler, fresh off the debut of his new single, "The Ballad of the Green Berets," Billboard's number one song of 1966, on *The Ed Sullivan Show*.[15]

Affirmation Vietnam organizers anticipated fifty thousand attendees at the rally, but fewer than fifteen thousand supporters actually showed up on the rainy February morning. The two-hour event included brief speeches by virtually every major elected official in the state, abbreviated performances by the assembled celebrities, and the presentation of the two hundred thousand rain-soaked signatures to South Vietnamese Ambassador Nguyen Duy Lien. Forty protestors from Atlanta's nascent antiwar movement, representing nearly as many groups as there were demonstrators, marched the mile and a half from Atlanta University, a hotbed of civil rights activism, to Atlanta Stadium and picketed against the rally. The only person arrested at the event was an Affirmation Vietnam supporter who assaulted an antiwar demonstrator outside the Stadium.[16]

The most high-profile nonsporting event hosted by Atlanta Stadium during its first decade in operation was a June 1973 Billy Graham crusade. Although the local elites who organized the crusade envisioned it as a socially unifying event, instead it laid bare mounting divisions in the region. The six-night revival proved to be one of the most politically contentious in Graham's seven-decade-long ministry. The tensions that surrounded the event were a product not only of the era's contentious national political culture but also of a metropolitan political culture in which every public matter renewed the local discourse on race.

Local developer and sportsman Tom Cousins served as chairman of the Atlanta Crusade, which he proposed that Graham hold at his newly opened Omni Coliseum. While most corporate leaders that chaired Graham's crusades served primarily in a titular capacity, Cousins insisted on spending a significant amount of time and money boosting the event. He believed that the crusade would foster a community-wide spiritual awakening, one that would ameliorate the tensions that had become evident in Metropolitan Atlanta's corridors of power, its public spaces, and its resegregated neighborhoods and communities. In March 1972, Cousins spearheaded the formation of a biracial, denominationally diverse crusade organizing committee that included representatives from African American, Evangelical, and mainline Protestant churches as well as Jewish synagogues. The organizing committee named newly elected Congressman and civil rights leader Rev. Andrew Young its co-chair to demonstrate its commitment to making the crusade a biracial gathering. The *Journal, Constitution,* and *Daily World* heaped praise on Cousins for his work on the crusade, while the Atlanta Chamber and Governor Jimmy Carter expended considerable resources helping him plan and promote the event. The outpouring of institutional support for the event convinced organizers to move the crusade from the sixteen-thousand-seat Omni to the fifty-seven-thousand seat Atlanta Stadium.[17]

In the weeks before the crusade, Graham's steadfast support for President Nixon galvanized opposition to the event from civil rights activists, including many leaders in the SCLC. Hundreds of predominately African American activists protested the crusades, holding signs that accused Graham of shirking his responsibilities to the urban poor, criticizing his support for the death penalty, and challenging him to speak out against Nixon for the Watergate scandal. The crusade's supporters portrayed their event as being above earthly politics. They defended Graham's record on civil rights, citing the desegregated gatherings he had been holding in the South since 1953 and his early support for Martin Luther King Jr. They pointed out that many Black ministers endorsed the event, including Martin Luther King Sr., who appeared onstage at the crusade.

Graham's six-night event drew approximately 228,000 people, with African Americans forming a conspicuously small minority on every evening. Graham estimated that Blacks accounted for 5 percent of attendance, a much smaller percentage of the crowd than at every other crusade he held in the South during the late 1960s and early 1970s. Cousins blamed an ongoing strike by ATC bus drivers for the small number of African Americans in attendance. Some Black pastors told Graham that many of their congregants did not attend the crusade because they were fearful of being robbed if they left their homes at night.[18] Regardless of the reasons for the small African American turnout at the 1973 crusade, the event failed to serve as a regionally unifying event and instead made the racial and cultural divisions in Metro Atlanta more evident.

BY THE MID-1970S, THE COLLECTIVE SHRUG WITH WHICH most metropolitan area residents had responded to both sporting and nonsporting events at Atlanta Stadium made it clear that the municipally financed facility had not become a regional center of gravity. The response of Atlantans to their new stadium and their new home teams proved to be archetypal for the metropolitan Sunbelt. By putting professional sports in the service of lofty civic goals, elites in Atlanta and numerous other Sunbelt cities set themselves up for disappointments as grand as the enterprises they undertook on behalf of their communities.

1. Aerial view of the metropolitan area's new "center of gravity," Atlanta Stadium circa 1968, situated south of downtown's expanding skyline and surrounded by the city's maze of expressways. Postcard. Courtesy of the author.

2. (*above*) Opening Night, 1965. Mayor Ivan Allen readies for some pregame hijinks with "umpire" and Fulton County Commissioner Jim Aldredge. The Braves would play the first of nine 1965 exhibition games at Atlanta Stadium that evening. A legal injunction kept the Braves in Milwaukee for a lame-duck 1965 season. *Atlanta Journal-Constitution* via AP.

3. (*opposite top*) After months of tense negotiations, Tom Cousins (*left*) and Sam Massell (*right*) break ground on what would become the Omni Coliseum, March 31, 1971. Charles R. Pugh/*Atlanta Journal-Constitution* via AP.

4. (*opposite bottom*) The Omni Coliseum and Omni International Complex, 1975. Tom Cousins envisioned this massive mixed-use development as the key to revitalizing Atlanta's central business district. Postcard. Courtesy of the author.

5. (*above*) Ivan Allen congratulating Hank Aaron on the Braves' 1969 NL West Division Championship, the franchise's top performance during its first decade in Atlanta. *Atlanta Journal-Constitution* via AP.

6. (*opposite top*) Atlanta Hawks rookie Pete Maravich consults with head coach Richie Guerin in his Atlanta debut, October 20, 1970, at the Alexander Memorial Coliseum. Maravich clashed frequently with head coaches Guerin and, later, Cotton Fitzsimmons during his four years with the Hawks.
AP Photo/Toby Massey.

7. (*opposite bottom*) The Atlanta Flames battle it out with the Philadelphia Flyers during the 1973 NHL Playoffs. For several seasons in the early 1970s, the Flames were the hottest ticket in town. AP photo.

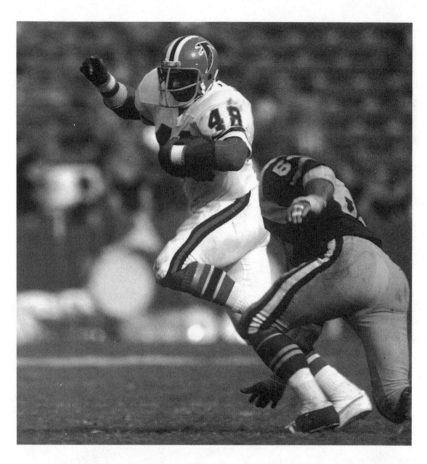

8. (*above*) Falcons running back Woody Thompson evades a Los Angeles Rams defender on October 19, 1975. The sparse crowd in evidence that afternoon exemplified the no-show problem the perennially underachieving Falcons faced throughout the mid-1970s. Peter ReadMiller via AP.

9. (*opposite top*) Before a home crowd of just 4,743, Braves third baseman Darrell Evans congratulates Hank Aaron on his 710th career homerun, September 11, 1973. While fans packed virtually every NL park in 1973 and 1974 to witness Aaron's pursuit of Babe Ruth's home run record, Atlanta Stadium remained virtually empty for all but a handful of home dates during these seasons. AP photo.

10. (*opposite bottom*) New Atlanta Braves and Atlanta Hawks owner Ted Turner celebrates a basket by his new professional basketball team at a sparsely attended January 1977 game at the Omni. Despite years of poor attendance, Turner kept Atlanta Major League. His two franchises provided a quarter-century's worth of inexpensive programming on his TBS Superstation. AP photo/Charles E. Knoblock.

11. SunTrust Park, May 2017. The Braves' new Cobb County home, paid for by the self-taxing Cumberland Community Improvement District. Thomson200, CC-0, via Wikimedia Commons.

12. The Atlanta Falcons' third home (Mercedes Benz Stadium, 2017–present), surrounded by the rubble of their second home (the Georgia Dome, 1992–2016). elisfkc from Orlando FL, CC BY-SA 2.0 https://commons.wikimedia.org/wiki /File:Mercedes-Benz_Stadium_with_the_Georgia_Dome_remains _(38732365704).jpg, via Wikimedia Commons.

12

Madison Square Garden of the Southeast

··

IN 1958 TWENTY-SIX-YEAR-OLD TOM COUSINS GOT INTO the real estate business. Cousins had graduated from the University of Georgia six years earlier, where he had been a highly decorated member of the swimming and diving teams. After a stint in the Air Force, Cousins tried his hand at several businesses before forming a real estate company with his father, which focused on the emerging suburban housing market outside of Atlanta. By the early 1960s Cousins Properties was Georgia's largest homebuilder. The younger Cousins soon diversified his business by taking on large-scale office developments, the first of which was the Piedmont-Cain Building in downtown Atlanta, which opened in 1965. Cousins, then in his early thirties, became the "token youth," as he later put it, among Atlanta's Big Mules. Like his peers in the city's establishment, Cousins was preoccupied with the revitalization of downtown Atlanta.[1]

In 1966 Cousins acquired land on the west side of downtown in an area known as "the Gulch," a dilapidated old train depot, as a prospective site for MXD.[2] Cousins wanted to build a sports arena on the site, which he regarded as a beachhead from which a much larger development would spring. He envisioned an adjoining mixed-usage complex that would combine luxury accommodations, upscale shopping, hundreds of thousands of square feet of corporate office space, and a number of unique entertainment opportunities.[3] As a suburban homebuilder turned urban developer, Cousins was simultaneously one of the primary beneficiaries of the decentralization of Atlanta and one of the foremost champions of saving downtown from becoming the hole in the center of a sprawling suburban doughnut.

Tom Cousins convinced Atlanta's civic elite of the virtues of building a downtown arena by creating an immediate need for it. He bought a professional basketball team. On May 3, 1968, Cousins and former Georgia Governor Carl Sanders held a press conference in Atlanta to announce that they had purchased the NBA's St. Louis Hawks basketball team. Cousins and Sanders said that they planned to relocate the franchise to Atlanta for the 1968–69 season, pending league approval. Mayor Allen joined them behind the microphones at the press conference, sitting beside the pair at a folding table, obscured by a basketball that had been stenciled "ATLANTA HAWKS" in all capital letters. Like the Falcons and the Braves before them, the Hawks were the first Major League team in its sport to set up shop in the South. Initially, the Atlanta papers reported the purchase price as $2 million, but several weeks later Ben Kerner, the St. Louis Hawks' longtime owner, told reporters that he had sold the franchise to Cousins and Sanders for $3.5 million, then a record for an NBA franchise. Cousins paid the vast majority of the purchase price. Sanders was largely a symbolic partner that lent more prestige and political clout to the venture than he did capital.[4] The news of the developer Cousins and ex-Governor Sanders' buying the Hawks came as a shock even to Atlanta insiders. Kerner described the sale as "the best kept secret I've ever known in sports."[5]

"Carl Sanders and I got into this simply because we thought Atlanta deserved a professional basketball team, and especially a winning team," Cousins said at the press conference announcing the move, "and I felt if we got the team, the city would get the coliseum, which it also deserves."[6] Cousins described his plans to build a "Madison Square Garden type" arena at the press conference.[7] Before pursuing the Hawks, Cousins met with Allen to tell him of his interest in financing and building a

coliseum in downtown Atlanta and buying a professional basketball team to play in the new facility. Allen advised Cousins
to acquire a franchise, find a short-term home for the team in
Atlanta, and then build a coliseum.[8] At the introductory press
conference, the Hawks new owners announced that they had
made a temporary arrangement with Georgia Tech President
Edwin Harrison to play at the Alexander Memorial Coliseum,
the seven-thousand-seat basketball arena on the Tech campus,
until they completed the proposed downtown arena, pending
approval from the University's Board of Regents.[9]

Sanders and Cousins told reporters that they planned to hire
experts to run the franchise. They did not want to manage a
basketball team. They were merely acting as civically minded
capitalists.[10] Cousins and Sanders had commissioned a private
study that they said showed strong local interest in professional basketball. Buying the Hawks, Cousins said, speaking
on behalf of both of them, was "repaying a debt to the city and
state. Atlanta and Georgia have been good to us," presenting
their business venture as purely altruistic.[11]

Sanders doubled down on Cousins' description of the project, stating, "We definitely feel there is a need for a facility similar to Madison Square Garden in the Southeast and we saw an
opportunity to bring it here through the purchase of this franchise. Atlanta deserves this . . . and we hope the community
will bring this facility into being."[12] Without going into detail,
Cousins said he was willing to build an arena, provided he had
the backing of the Stadium Authority or received some other
form of "tax considerations" from the city.[13] Allen endorsed
the idea of the Stadium Authority facilitating Cousins' work
on a downtown arena, but, he said, "it's almost impossible to
do it through general obligation bond issues. These are subject to public whims and negative votes and do not generally
reflect the will of the people," he said, referring to his own
failed efforts in 1962 to win public support for an $80 million
initiative that would have financed a Civic Center capable of
hosting professional basketball.[14]

AT THE TIME HE SOLD THE HAWKS, BEN KERNER WAS THE
NBA's longest-tenured owner and the only owner in the league
who controlled 100 percent of his team's stock. Kerner was
the lone surviving owner from the early days of the NBA in
the immediate aftermath of World War II. The history of the
Hawks franchise epitomized the NBA's instability in its early
years. Before settling in St. Louis, Kerner's club leapfrogged
around the Midwest throughout the late 1940s and early 1950s,
always earning enough money to keep the franchise going for
another season. Unlike the hobbyists and gentleman sportsmen who owned many of the other clubs, the Hawks were
Kerner's primary source of income.[15]

Thirty-two-year-old Ben Kerner paid $1,500 in 1946 for the
rights to place a National Basketball League expansion franchise in his hometown of Buffalo. Founded in 1937, the NBL
merged with the Basketball Association of America to form
the NBA in 1949. The expansion Buffalo Bisons lasted thirteen games in western New York, receiving almost no support from local fans. Kerner moved his team in the middle of
the 1946–47 season to Moline, Illinois, where he rechristened
it the Blackhawks in reference to the locally significant 1832
Black Hawk War. The Tri-Cities Blackhawks, as the team was
known in subsequent years, represented Moline and Rock
Island, Illinois, and Davenport, Iowa, just across the Mississippi River, in the NBA. The Blackhawks played at Wharton
Field House, a six-thousand seat arena in Moline, drawing
strong-enough crowds for Kerner to turn a profit every year
his team played in the Tri-Cities. Despite Kerner's box-office
success in western Illinois, NBA owners pressured him to move
his franchise into a larger market. They aspired for the NBA
to be counted among the Major Leagues, a status it was hard
for them to claim when Fort Wayne, Providence, and Moline
had franchises but many of the country's largest cities did not.
Kerner refused to stand in the way of the league's ambitions
for Major League status. He accepted an offer from Milwaukee in 1951 to move his franchise to its new city arena. Kerner

abbreviated his team's name to Hawks when he shifted his franchise to Milwaukee, removing the local specificity of the Blackhawks moniker.[16]

Greater Milwaukee's population of nearly 1.1 million was three times larger than that of the Tri-Cities region in 1950, but Wisconsin proved a far less hospitable home for Kerner's franchise. The Milwaukee Hawks struggled on the court and drew poorly for four straight seasons. Their average attendance never surpassed two thousand fans per game. Kerner tried unsuccessfully to find a local buyer and had to sell off his best players to keep the franchise from folding.[17] In 1955 he accepted an offer to move the Hawks to St. Louis, then the nation's ninth-largest metropolitan area and home to seven hundred thousand more people than Greater Milwaukee. St. Louis, though, was just as devoid as Milwaukee of professional basketball tradition.[18]

The prospects of the Hawks flourishing in St. Louis seemed remote. The city's previous entry in the NBA, the St. Louis Bombers, folded in 1950. St. Louis proper was in the midst of a white-flight-driven population decline, which reduced the city's overall population from greater than 850,000 in 1950 to just over 450,000 in 1980 and cut significantly into the working-class urban white population that made up much of the early NBA's spectatorship. The Hawks' home court in St. Louis was the Kiel Auditorium, an aging municipally owned facility that combined a nine-thousand-seat sports arena with an opera house. The arena and the opera house were separated by a far-too-thin wall. If the opera house and the arena hosted events on the same evening, cheering from the arena's balcony bled into the concert hall, while the orchestra provided background music for the action on the basketball court.

Despite these obstacles, the Hawks became the NBA's second-most popular and successful franchise of the late 1950s and early 1960s, dominating play in the league's Western Division while coming up short in the NBA Finals on three out of four occasions against the dynastic Boston Celtics of the Eastern

Division. The St. Louis Hawks won five consecutive Western Division regular-season championships (1957–61), reached the NBA Finals four times (1958, 1959, 1960, 1961), and won the NBA Championship in 1958, defeating their perennial nemesis Boston in a six-game series.

The Hawks were led by their Big Three of Cliff "Lil' Abner" Hagan, an undersized forward from Owensboro, Kentucky, who used his masterful hook shot to become one of the league's leading scorers; Slater Martin, a veteran point guard from Texas with exceptional ball-handling and playmaking skills who played on all five of the Minneapolis Lakers championship teams in the late 1940s and early 1950s; and Bob Pettit, a 6-foot-9 Baton Rouge native who was the premier scoring and rebounding forward of his generation. The darling of the St. Louis fans, Robert E. Lee Pettit Jr. garnered All-NBA honors in ten of his eleven seasons and retired in 1965 as the NBA's all-time leading scorer. The Hawks built their Western Division dynasty around Pettit, whom they drafted out of LSU in 1954, the year before the franchise moved to St. Louis. Pettit was arguably the most popular professional athlete in St. Louis history who did not play for the Cardinals baseball team.[19]

Throughout the Hawks' run as the NBA's top Western Division franchise, they enjoyed outstanding local support. Boisterous crowds that averaged well over eight thousand per night at Kiel in the late 1950s and early 1960s gave the Hawks a decided home-court advantage. On a number of occasions, the Hawks predominately blue-collar fans displayed a willingness to intervene in the action, getting into fistfights with opposing fans and players, egging the benches of visiting teams, and shouting often racially charged invective at opposing players.[20] "It was always a packed house at Kiel . . . and it was smoke-filled up to the ceiling," Cliff Hagan recalled for a 1998 *St. Louis Post-Dispatch* retrospective on the team.[21] "We had the noisiest, most hard-core fans in the league," Bob Pettit said of the Hawks' supporters at Kiel.[22] The box-office success of the Hawks in St. Louis helped make Kerner a very wealthy man and the toast of the city. For several consecutive seasons during the team's late 1950s and early 1960s heyday, the Hawks ran the most profitable organization in the NBA.[23]

The Hawks' preeminence ended in the early 1960s when the recently relocated Los Angeles Lakers superseded the aging St. Louis team in the standings. The addition of the Wilt Chamberlain–led San Francisco Warriors franchise following its 1962 relocation from Philadelphia made it even more difficult for the Hawks to compete. The Hawks' declining fortunes on the basketball court coincided to a great extent with their waning local support, which dropped to an average of 6,641 attendees per game in the 1964–65 season.[24] Kerner responded to the Hawks' diminishing attendance by scheduling several games each season in cities without NBA franchises, primarily Memphis and Miami.[25]

Falling out of the first tier of the Western Division was not the only reason attendance declined at Kiel Auditorium. Several other factors played into the lack of local interest in the latter-day St. Louis Hawks. All of a sudden, St. Louis sports fans had a number of appealing new options competing for their discretionary income. The opening of state-of-the-art Busch Stadium in 1966 made attending a Cardinals baseball game or Big Red football game a novel and likely far more comfortable experience than attending a Hawks game. The Depression-era amenities of Kiel could not compete with the comforts of the city's new stadium.[26]

For years, the Hawks had been the only winning team in town, garnering division championship after division championship while the baseball and football Cardinals posted consistently mediocre records. As the Hawks of the mid 1960s faded in the standings, the city's oldest and most popular team returned to its traditional position as a perennial pennant contender. The reemergence of the St. Louis Cardinals baseball team as an NL power after more than a decade as an also-ran proved a further obstacle to maintaining public interest in the Hawks. The Cardinals won the World Series in

1964 and 1967, the latter season drawing a franchise record 2,090,145 fans to Busch Stadium. The football Cardinals, who had yet to move to St. Louis when the Hawks won their only championship in 1958, fielded increasingly competitive football teams during the mid-1960s as well. The Big Red's success in the standings and the lure of watching the team play at the new Busch Stadium helped the team expand its season-ticket-holding base from twelve thousand to more than thirty thousand for the 1966 season.[27] Additionally, the success of the football and baseball Cardinals in the mid-1960s shifted local media coverage away from the Hawks. By the 1967–68 season, the Hawks' radio and television ratings sank to the point that Kerner's friend Gussie Busch started quietly underwriting the poorly rated broadcasts simply to keep them on the air.[28]

The arrival of the St. Louis Blues, one of six expansion franchises that formed a new Western Division in the NHL for the 1967–68 season, made the Hawks' position even more precarious. The Blues competed directly with the Hawks, playing an October through April schedule just like the incumbent basketball franchise. Blues owner Sid Salomon III invested $1.5 million in the revitalization of his team's rink, the St. Louis Arena, a long-decrepit facility that was built during the 1920s to host regional agricultural fairs. Salomon purchased the St. Louis Arena soon after the NHL granted him an expansion franchise. He made attending a Blues game a markedly more fan-friendly experience than attending a Hawks game by upgrading the lighting, restrooms, and concessions at the arena to contemporary standards. Kerner and the city of St. Louis failed to make any similar improvements to the municipally owned Kiel Auditorium during the Hawks' decade in residence. Salomon installed plush, movie theater–style chairs in the arena's box seats. Conversely, most of the seats at Kiel had been in place since the 1930s.[29]

Attending a Blues game became the city's most fashionable evening out almost immediately. Women in furs and their finest jewelry accompanied men in suits and Stetson hats to Blues games at the frequently sold out fourteen-thousand-seat St. Louis Arena.[30] The allure of professional hockey to St. Louisans in the late 1960s was not simply a matter of the game's novelty or the comfortable environs in which it was played. The Blues' immediate success on the ice contributed greatly to the team's box-office appeal. Guided by their thirty-seven-year-old goaltender Glenn Hall, the Blues made a run through the 1968 Western Division playoffs to the Stanley Cup, where they lost to the Montreal Canadiens in four games. The Blues' success in their inaugural season overshadowed the upstart 1967–68 Hawks, who won their division and posted their best regular-season record in franchise history. Despite their reemergence as one of professional basketball's best teams, the Hawks made a surprisingly early playoff exit in May 1968, playing in front of crowds of fewer than three thousand at Kiel Auditorium, less than a quarter of the number of people who paid to watch the Blues during the Stanley Cup Playoffs.[31]

Notwithstanding the variety of new distractions available to St. Louis sports fans, the renaissance of the Hawks' fortunes during the 1967–68 season seemed like the perfect thing to renew local interest in the club. But as it turned out, the Western Division champion Hawks of 1967–68 drew the smallest crowds in the franchise's history in St. Louis. The Hawks sold out one game at Kiel that season, a doubleheader with the Harlem Globetrotters, who drew remarkably well in St. Louis considering the striking racial animosity Hawks fans displayed toward Black opponents.[32]

Persistent rumors that Kerner wanted to sell the Hawks and that he could not find a local buyer for the club did considerable damage to already weakened fan morale. In January 1967, Kerner announced he was putting the team up for sale because of his declining health. Rheumatoid arthritis limited Kerner's mobility to the point that he could no longer be the hands-on operator of his club. Rather than maintain mere titular control of the franchise, he wanted to sell the team to an energetic local buyer who would restore the Hawks to their past glory. Kerner said that despite the recent down-turn in fan support and the team's less-than-ideal arena, he had made money all twelve of his years in St. Louis. Kerner received offers in excess of $3 million from potential buyers in New York, Chicago, Houston, and New Orleans, all of whom wanted to move the team to their cities, but none from inves-tors in St. Louis. Rather than sell the Hawks to owners who would surely move the team, Kerner announced that he was going to hang on to the team indefinitely, until he could find an appropriate local buyer for the club.[33]

Months before Kerner announced his plans to sell the team, he told local reporters that the city needed to build a new arena or significantly upgrade Kiel if it wanted his Hawks to stay in St. Louis permanently. In August 1966 Kerner said that Kiel Auditorium, with its lack of easily accessible park-ing lots, well-worn amenities, and small seating capacity, was preventing the Hawks from generating enough revenue to compete financially against larger-market teams playing in new arenas with twice the seating capacity of St. Louis's decrepit facility.[34] When the Hawks moved into Kiel in 1955, it had the NBA's third-largest seating capacity and was in no worse shape than at least half of the arenas in the league. By 1967 the Hawks were playing in the league's smallest arena and undoubtedly its most poorly maintained.[35] Soon after the Blues' arrival in St. Louis, Salomon offered Kerner a lease at the newly upgraded St. Louis Arena. City leaders pressed Kerner to accept Salomon's proposal, but the Hawks owner, fearing scheduling conflicts and the loss of face that becom-ing his direct competitor's tenant entailed, refused the offer.[36] The city's unwillingness to help the Hawks build a new arena frustrated Kerner tremendously, especially since the city had just shown such largesse toward the baseball Cardinals and the Big Red, approving a municipal bond that subsidized the construction of Busch Stadium.[37]

When Bob Burnes of the *St. Louis Globe-Democrat* offered up his postmortem of the Hawks' move to Atlanta, he cited three primary factors for the team's decline in local popularity: competition from other sports, the Hawks' archaic arena, and what he euphemistically called "the racial factor."[38] Retrospectives on the Hawks tend to either lean heavily on the issue of race in the team's departure or, conversely, protest too much against it being a factor in its declining popularity. Wherever the truth of the matter actually lies, "the racial factor," as Burnes described it, reshaped the relationship between the Hawks and their fans during their last years in St. Louis. The racial transformation of the Hawks' roster undoubtedly contributed to the declining local support for the team. Even as the team returned to the top of the standings in the 1967–68 season, St. Louis's predominately white basketball fans proved unwilling to support a team that no longer looked like they did. Relatively few African Americans from the city's still-small Black middle class attended Hawks games.[39]

No longer were the Hawks a team led by white southerners. Pettit, Martin, and Hagan had all retired. By the time of the 1967–68 season, all five of the team's starters and all of their regularly playing backups were Black. Several of the Hawks Black players were southerners, including center Zelmo Beaty and small forward Joe Caldwell, both of whom were Texans, but their southern heritage was clearly insufficient for many previous Hawks fans.[40] "I vividly recall people saying to me that if 'I want to go see the Harlem Globetrotters, I will go see the Globetrotters,'" longtime St. Louis sports broadcaster Ron Jacober said of the attitudes of the city's sports fans toward the 1967–68 Hawks.[41] Fans who had heckled the Celtics' Bill Russell with shouts of "go back to Africa" and "watch out, Pettit, you'll get covered with chocolate," were, not surprisingly, disinclined to embrace the transformation of their own team's roster into a predominately African American one.[42]

Reinforcing the evident racial divide between the Hawks' players and their fan base was the depiction of the team in the press. The local and national media described the Hawks' play with language steeped in racial meaning, as being built around aggressiveness and athleticism more than ball-playing skill. "Their players are heavy in muscle and quickness. They are below average by NBA standards in height and out-court shooting skill," John J. Archibald of the *Constitution* wrote of the Hawks after Cousins and Sanders announced the franchise's move to Atlanta, reflecting the consensus view of the team in the national media.[43]

The idea that the St. Louis Hawks of the late 1960s played a different style of basketball than the Hawks of the late 1950s was grounded in reality. Their starting front-court of Zelmo Beaty, Bill Bridges, and Paul Silas were all highly athletic players who displayed more lateral and vertical mobility than their predecessors Cliff Hagan and Bob Pettit. The 1967–68 Hawks starting backcourt of Lenny Wilkens and Lou Hudson certainly displayed greater agility and quickness than Slater Martin. Hawks coach Richie Guerin built his team's strategy around their superior athleticism and toughness compared to most of their opponents. "They win with hustle, cunning and brawn and are rewarded with anonymity . . . it's a running and pressing team," Guerin told *Sports Illustrated*'s Frank Deford in late 1967, begrudging the lack of stardom his outstanding cast of players enjoyed locally and nationally.[44] It was impossible not to notice the striking athleticism of Richie Guerin's Hawks teams of the late 1960s, but the idea that his Hawks were somehow lacking in manual skill relative to their predecessors was the problematic part of the media narrative surrounding the team.[45] The pigeonholing of the Hawks as an athletically superior but skill-deficient team reflected a broader anxiety in the sports media about the transformation of professional basketball into a majority-Black league.[46]

The strongest argument against the "racial factor" being the major reason for the Hawks' declining popularity in St. Louis was the enthusiastic support for the baseball Cardinals' strikingly diverse teams of the mid-to-late 1960s. The team underwent a similar demographic transformation to the Hawks during the 1960s, going from a roster that had, for decades, consisted primarily of white southerners recruited from the team's extensive southern scouting network to one whose standout players were primarily Black. Rather than shunning the increasingly diverse Cardinals, their predominately white fan base broke franchise attendance records to watch their World Series winning teams in 1964 and 1967. Most of the star players on both of those Cardinals' championship teams were Black players, including Bob Gibson, Lou Brock, Orlando Cepeda, and Curt Flood. Just like the Hawks, the Cardinals developed a reputation for aggressive play: their speed on the bases, their spectacular defensive plays, and the pitching of Bob Gibson, baseball's most intimidating pitcher of the era. Evidently, the enduring popularity of baseball in St. Louis transcended racial and socioeconomic differences in the city more easily than professional basketball, which appealed at the time primarily to the city's shrinking urban white working class.[47]

Whether racial issues, competition from other professional sports franchises, or the poor conditions at the Kiel Auditorium constituted the most significant reason for the Hawks' departure from St. Louis, it was clear by the spring of 1968 that Ben Kerner was no longer just toying with the idea of selling his team. He was now willing to sell the franchise to investors that wanted to move the team, so long as they provided the Hawks with a suitable venue.[48]

KERNER, COUSINS, AND SANDERS HAD BEEN NEGOTIATING the sale of the Hawks in secret for several weeks, shuttling back and forth between St. Louis and Atlanta in April 1968. The cloak-and-dagger character of negotiations suited both sides. The Atlantans wanted to keep negotiations private because they knew that investors from New Orleans and Memphis were also trying to buy the Hawks. Cousins and Sanders wanted to keep the story from becoming a front-page bidding war in which the honor of three of the South's most prestigious cities came into question. Kerner wanted to keep negotiations out of the St. Louis papers to avoid a box-office backlash as his excellent 1967–68 Hawks team competed in the NBA play-offs. Moreover, St. Louis fans had been largely supportive of the Hawks franchise during their thirteen-year tenure in the city (1955–68). Kerner wanted to make the team's relocation as painless as possible for St. Louis fans and himself.[49]

When Cousins and Sanders first approached Ben Kerner in early 1968 about selling the team, the Hawks owner expressed his reluctance because of their lack of a suitable arena in Atlanta. Kerner was eager to sell the team, but he did not want the Hawks to settle for a subpar building. Such a move would have tainted his legacy as owner. It would have demonstrated Kerner's lack of concern about the franchise's future stability and his unwillingness to help the NBA meet its goal of placing its franchises in North America's premier playing facilities.

When Kerner consulted with NBA Commissioner Walter Kennedy about the possibility of moving the Hawks to Atlanta, the commissioner expressed strong reservations. Kennedy said that he doubted the Atlanta group would gain league approval for a relocation unless they secured a permanent playing facility for the 1968–69 season, reiterating the league's standing concern about placing a team in the city. Several years earlier, the NBA commissioned a survey that analyzed the potential success of professional basketball in a number of North American cities. The survey concluded that Atlanta's lack of a suitable playing facility made it an unfeasible choice for expansion. The city's largest available public or private auditorium for professional basketball was the five-thousand-seat City Armory, which would have been the smallest in the league. Georgia Tech's 7,200-seat Alexander Memorial Coliseum was the city's largest basketball arena, but the University had made it clear to professional sports leagues for many years that it would not consider renting out its facilities for anything but amateur athletics.[50]

Following his meeting with Kennedy, Kerner asked Cousins and Sanders to come back to St. Louis for further discussions on the Hawks sale. Kerner suggested that if they still wanted to buy the team, they should leave the franchise in St. Louis temporarily while Cousins built his proposed downtown coliseum in Atlanta.[51] Cousins and Sanders were familiar with the unpleasantness of a lame-duck season from Atlanta's recent struggle with Milwaukee for the Braves. They were also familiar with Atlanta's courting of the St. Louis Cardinals' football team and the bidding war that ensued between the two cities while the Bidwills weighed their options.[52] To "avoid a Bidwill reenactment," as Furman Bisher later put it, Cousins contacted Georgia Tech president Edwin Harrison to see if he could rent out the Alexander Memorial Coliseum temporarily while he built the new arena.[53]

For years, Georgia Tech had been unwilling to cooperate with civic efforts to bring professional sports to the city, particularly professional football. It refused to allow prospective AFL or NFL franchises to use Grant Field as a temporary home while the city built Atlanta Stadium. Georgia Tech refused to allow even one-off exhibition football games to be held at Grant Field.[54] Tech's "resolute aloofness to such coarse and unwashed games," as Furman Bisher described it, was a product of several circumstances.[55] Most important, Georgia Tech's institutional identity was inextricably intertwined with the history and tradition of Grant Field. Fall Saturdays at Grant Field made visible not only Georgia Tech's status as a national football power but also the school's position as a pillar of Atlanta's social and cultural life. Tech administrators and alumni feared that professional sports would taint the prestige of their hallowed field, especially if, as Mayor Hartsfield had suggested, the baggage of the big leagues included bookmaking and organized crime. Allowing professional teams to play at Grant Field would also have encouraged new and direct competition with Tech for the discretionary dollars of local football fans. Conversely, Tech alumni endowed the Alexander Memorial Coliseum, a domed, indoor arena that opened in 1956 and housed Georgia Tech's far less prestigious basketball program, with none of the reverence they did for their half-century-old football field. The ambiguity of integration in Atlanta during the early 1960s also played into the unwillingness of Georgia Tech to rent out its facilities. By 1968 public facilities in Atlanta had been integrated for several years, but when the AFL and NFL asked Georgia Tech if they could rent Grant Field, the law and the local political consensus on desegregation were far murkier.

Partnering with Carl Sanders helped Cousins immensely when it came to negotiating with Harrison for use of Alexander Memorial Coliseum. Former Governor Sanders, who was prohibited by state law from running for a second consecutive term in 1966, was the presumptive favorite in the 1970 Georgia governor's race. Harrison found himself in a difficult bargaining position relative to Sanders. The college president's institution was dependent on state money. Sanders downplayed the extent to which his political status influenced Harrison's decision. Instead, the former Governor told reporters that Georgia Tech's primary motivation for allowing the Hawks to play at Alexander was that the school liked the idea of being associated with a winner. The defending Western Division champion Hawks, Sanders said, speaking reverently of his own alma mater's arch rival, merited a place on the campus of an esteemed university like Georgia Tech far more than its previous professional sports suitors, which had all been expansion football teams. In addition to Sanders' powers of persuasion and flattery, Cousins asked a number of Big Mules to contact Harrison privately, asking him to allow the Hawks to use Georgia Tech's arena. Atlanta would have to wait indefinitely for professional basketball unless Georgia Tech allowed the Hawks to play on its campus, they emphasized in their messages to Harrison, who bowed to civic pressure. On April 30, he called Tom Cousins to assure him that he would convince the Georgia Tech Board of Regents to let the Hawks use the arena on a temporary basis. Harrison agreed to rent Alexander for $1,000 per game until Cousins completed construction on his downtown arena. The arrangement with Georgia Tech enabled Cousins and Sanders to finalize their deal with Kerner. One week after Cousins and Sanders announced their purchase of the Hawks, the Georgia Tech Board of Regents voted unanimously to approve the lease that Harrison had negotiated with Cousins.[56] The NBA was coming to Atlanta.

13

The Developer Is Boss

....

WHILE NEGOTIATING IN SECRET WITH BEN KERNER, TOM Cousins commissioned a survey from the Marketing Information Service of Atlanta asking area residents if they thought the city needed a large indoor coliseum for sporting events. Three-quarters of the people surveyed agreed with the statement that Atlanta needed an arena suitable for indoor sports. Forty-five percent said they would attend professional basketball games at such a facility. Forty-three percent said they would come to the coliseum to watch professional hockey games, which made their first regular appearance on Atlanta television that fall. Many respondents to the survey told their questioners that the city needed a large indoor arena capable of hosting large concerts, performing arts events, and religious revivals.[1]

Six years earlier, the same citizenry who now felt deprived by their lack of a large coliseum had voted down financing for a municipal civic center that would have supported many of the same kinds of events. The results of the 1968 survey commissioned by Cousins confirmed his belief that Atlantans wanted an arena, but he doubted that they had changed their mind about paying for it. Cousins made it clear to everyone when he purchased the Hawks that he planned to build them an arena, preferably with the backing of the Stadium Authority. "That's the reason I bought the Hawks," Cousins told Bisher decades later. "I needed them to get the development going," to create momentum for another large-scale civic building project that would require concerted effort by the municipal government and the city's corporate elite.[2] "I was concerned with developing 60 acres of downtown Atlanta," Cousins said. "A coliseum was the key to the whole thing, some focal point to build around."[3] In the end, Cousins planned to pay for the building through the revenue it generated. The Stadium Authority's involvement in the financing would help him secure government-backed bonds, which would make for significantly lower interest rates on his repayments, potentially saving Cousins and his investment group millions of dollars. Initial public support for his downtown development project would help him jumpstart a much larger, privately financed downtown complex.[4]

Civic boosters backed Cousins's plan to build a downtown coliseum, just like they had supported Ivan Allen's efforts to build a municipal stadium once the possibility of luring an MLB team to Atlanta seemed like a sure thing. The Atlanta Chamber of Commerce and Central Atlanta Progress, a consortium of downtown business interests who made a refrain of the phrase *favorable business climate*, enthusiastically supported Cousins's plans to build an arena on the Gulch property west of downtown.[5] They lobbied the Stadium Authority to work out a financing plan with Cousins to support the construction of the facility. In the meantime, Cousins assembled local investors into an entity he later incorporated as the Omni Group, which was the ownership group of the Hawks and, eventually, the Flames. Later, the Omni Group added a third leg, the Coliseum Management Corporation (CMC), which oversaw operations at the new arena. Most of the investors were in the real estate business, either as developers or contractors. Many of them, like Cousins, were newcomers to large-scale downtown real estate and redevelopment projects. Among the investors in the Omni Group was Herman Russell, Georgia's wealthiest Black contractor, who became the first African American co-owner of a Major League sports franchise.[6]

Local politics intervened before Cousins and his associates finalized plans with the city for the arena. In January 1969

Ivan Allen announced that he would not seek a third term as mayor, citing his family and friends' advice "to not stretch myself out too far" after eight trying years in office.[7] The fall 1969 mayoral runoff pitted Vice Mayor Sam Massell, a liberal Democrat, against State Representative and City Alderman Rodney Cook, a moderate Republican. Both candidates had close ties to the city's business community. Massell was an attorney who became wealthy in the commercial real estate business, specializing in the development of professional buildings. His uncle, Ben Massell, was Atlanta's foremost real estate developer of the mid-twentieth century. William Hartsfield referred to Ben Massell as a "one-man boom" for the role he played in the formation of Atlanta's skyline. Rodney Cook came from one of Atlanta's leading commercial families. His father owned haberdasheries across the Southeast. The younger Cook created his own fortune in the insurance business.[8]

The vast majority of leaders in Atlanta's business community as well as Allen supported Cook in the election. They regarded Cook as more in line with Atlanta's incumbent governing coalition that allowed the Big Mules to maintain a civic trusteeship over political decision-making in the city. Massell, despite his strong ties to the business community, was regarded as too liberal. He had been an activist vice mayor, unlike any of his predecessors in the post, pushing the Allen administration to demand greater racial equity in the administering of city programs and, more broadly, advocating greater economic equality in Metropolitan Atlanta. Massell questioned the degree to which Atlanta's corporate elite dictated public policy, which won him strong support from the city's predominately African American municipal employees unions. In addition, Massell's progressive politics helped him earn the endorsement and aid of a number of the city's most prominent Black leaders, including Jesse Hill, Ralph Abernathy, Leroy Johnson, and Martin Luther King Sr.[9] Massell said during the campaign that civic elites, including his two-term partner at City Hall, Ivan

Allen; bank executive Mills Lane; and new Atlanta Chamber President Frank Carter, were campaigning against him because they knew "they couldn't control him and thus opposed him."[10]

Cook himself was a racially progressive politician, taking unpopular pro–civil rights stances while a member of the Georgia legislature, but Massell's combined appeal to the political empowerment of the city's Black population and his willingness to criticize the influence of Atlanta's boardrooms on its public policies turned many Big Mules into Cook supporters. The 1969 Atlanta mayoral campaign proved one of the city's most contentious. Proxies of the Cook campaign, including Allen, accused Massell of misusing his powers as vice mayor to secure campaign contributions. Massell denied the charges and accused the "downtown power structure" of blackballing him because he was Jewish. A number of Big Mules, including Allen, denied the charge vehemently. Massell won the closely contested election with a coalition built around his strong support from the Black community, which by the time of the election constituted nearly half of Atlanta's population.[11] For the first time since the formation of the city's post–World War II, biracial governing coalition, the city's Black voters split from the white corporate elite in a mayoral election. In doing so, they demonstrated that the demographic transformation of the city had reconfigured the terms of future coalitions between the city's corporate elite and its Black community.

During the campaign, Massell expressed his support for Cousins's plan to build a coliseum in downtown Atlanta, but the soon-to-be mayor demanded contractual assurances from the developer that the municipality would not end up paying for the project. Massell held firmly to both pledges when he became mayor. "I feel a city and its people are entitled to luxuries. But there is a limit," Massell said, reflecting on his role in the coliseum deal forty years later. The new mayor's expertise in commercial real estate, his familiarity with the city's political realities, and his commitment to limiting Atlanta's financial exposure in the deal made him a formidable and hands-on negotiator. "I had a foundation from which I could take a sharp pencil and paper and do something that another person could or might not have been able to," Massell said of the project.[12]

Throughout 1970, the new mayor negotiated the terms of the city's involvement in the coliseum project with Cousins. Under pressure from the NBA to break ground on an arena, Cousins conceded to many of the terms proposed by the mayor. Massell and Cousins worked out a plan whereby the Stadium Authority agreed to sell $17 million in revenue bonds to finance the construction. Cousins's Coliseum Management Corporation agreed to lease the arena for the twenty-five-year life of the bond from the City of Atlanta and Fulton County. When the CMC finished paying off the bond, Cousins agreed to let the city and county retain ownership of the facility. Since the coliseum would be municipally owned and the bonds issued to pay for it would be government bonds, both would be tax-exempt.[13]

In return, the CMC agreed to pay the principal and interest annually for the life of the bond and cover the entire cost of operating and maintaining the facility. As part of their lease arrangements with the building, Cousins's Hawks and, later, Flames agreed to contribute fifteen percent of their total gate revenues toward the annual repayment of the bond and the maintenance and operations of the coliseum. In addition, CMC had to contribute fifteen percent of the gate from all other events held at the new facility toward annual repayments, coliseum operations, and maintenance. Cousins Properties, the developer's primary corporate entity, agreed that all revenue over $225,000 per year generated by its 1,950-space, privately financed parking garage known as The Decks would be made available to pay off the principal and interest from the bonds and pay for the maintenance of the facility if revenue from the events at the coliseum proved insufficient to cover the entirety of CMC's annual bill. Revenue from The Decks, which was being built to support a Cousins-developed luxury hotel next door, cushioned against fan apathy at the new coliseum.[14] "We created an arrangement where if they never sold a single ticket there would be no bill for the taxpayer . . . it was just purely a real estate deal," Massell said of the city's pact with Cousins.[15]

Atlanta's corporate leadership backed the plan with predictable enthusiasm. During the public-comment period, the Atlanta Chamber issued a statement that said building an arena "has been one of the principal objectives of the Chamber since 1960," a reference to Allen's unsuccessful effort to build an "auditorium-coliseum." "Such a coliseum," the statement on behalf of the Chamber continued, "will help to further cement Atlanta's position as a major league city, not only in sports but in other areas which add to the life quality of a city." The Chamber applauded Massell's negotiation of a contract "which appears to reduce the exposure of tax demands on the taxpayers of the city and county to a minimum."[16]

As far as grand civic enterprises go, Cousins's vision for the Omni was more in line with the direction that the city's corporate leadership took during the 1970s as it planned and executed a series of redevelopment projects in downtown Atlanta. Unlike Allen's pursuit of a purely publicly financed stadium, Cousins rooted his plan for a coliseum in the private sector. This decision, which was shaped in large part by Massell's decisive action on behalf of Atlanta taxpayers, both alleviated taxpayer concerns about paying for nonessential civic functions and directed investment in the CBD toward privatized, secure, and enclosed spaces.

Atlanta's Black leadership expressed their strong support for the coliseum plan as well. The project received the wholehearted backing of Vice Mayor Maynard Jackson, who was elected along with Massell in 1969 and was the first African American in the city's history to hold that position. Jackson endorsed the arena financing plan and expressed particular enthusiasm about the prospective site of the arena in the commercial desert near the Techwood viaduct on the west side

of downtown Atlanta. He said the arena and future developments on Cousins's sixty-acre property would serve as a hub
of employment opportunities for Black residents in the surrounding neighborhoods. Hank Aaron and African American State Senator Leroy Johnson both served on the Stadium
Authority and supported the coliseum financing proposal.[17]

Little opposition to the arena financing plan emerged from
the public or members of either the city's or county's governing bodies. The most vocal opponent of the plan was Fulton
County Commissioner and former Atlanta Alderman Milton
Farris, who said that the $17 million figure cited for the cost
of the coliseum was deceptive. With interest, the total repayment of the revenue bonds would come to an estimated $33
million. Farris feared that the revenue sources from Cousins's enterprises that were obligated to repay the debt and
maintain the facility were not as failsafe as presented. If the
arena and the accompanying downtown development projects planned by Cousins failed to materialize or failed to draw
sufficiently large crowds, then the City of Atlanta and Fulton
County would be responsible for two-thirds and one-third of
the bill respectively.[18]

In December 1970 the Atlanta Board of Alderman and the
Fulton County Board of Commissioners approved the Coliseum deal at separate meetings. In January 1971 the Stadium
Authority sold nearly $17 million in revenue bonds at a 5.0365
percent interest rate, a far lower rate than Cousins could have
secured privately.[19] For the first five years, the Coliseum Management Corporation was obligated to pay $1.1 million per
year. For the next twenty years, it was obliged to pay $1.4 mil-
lion annually, bringing the total cost of repaying the bonds
to $33.5 million.[20] Massell and Cousins broke ground for the
Omni Coliseum on March 31, 1971. Twenty months later, the
Ira Hardin Construction Company finished the 16,500-seat
arena, just in time for the beginning of the professional basketball and hockey seasons in October 1972.[21]

An advertising agency hired by arena GM Bill Putnam suggested the grandiose "Omni" moniker for the building. Omni, Latin for "all," was meant to evoke the inclusive vision the arena's creators had for the venue as a regional entertainment center. The new arena sought out a wide range of mass-interest events besides basketball and hockey. The Omni would be the Southeast's leading indoor venue for circuses, national conventions, ice-skating shows, rock concerts, religious revivals, and professional wrestling. Splashy names were a Bill Putnam trademark. He had overseen the construction of the Forum in Los Angeles and the Spectrum in Philadelphia. Initially, the Stadium Authority, which had final say on naming the facility, resisted the flamboyant name but a 4–3 majority eventually acquiesced to the moniker, which appealed to the deep-seated civic-boosting instincts of the municipal leadership and had already been embraced by the Atlanta press corps. Calling the new arena the Omni transformed it into a signature building for downtown Atlanta, a civic asset and new point of prestige at the center of the sprawling metropolitan area.[22]

The recently incorporated architectural firm of Thompson, Ventulett, Stainback & Associates (TVS) designed the Omni Coliseum, which stood more than eleven stories high. More than 6,200 parking spaces sat less than two blocks from the arena, including 1,950 spaces in Cousins's Decks, which were connected to the arena by a dedicated, underground walkway.[23] Advertisements for events emphasized that the walkway to The Decks was "well-lit and patrolled," in an effort to assuage suburbanites' concerns about safety.[24] For events that required little floor space, like religious revivals or rock concerts, the Omni could hold as many as eighteen thousand spectators. The arena booked Disney on Ice, the Ringling Bros. and Barnum & Bailey Circus, the Harlem Globetrotters, Ice Capades, and a number of rock, jazz, and soul music concerts in the twelve months after it opened. The Omni could accommodate just over fifteen thousand for hockey, the event which required the greatest amount of floor space. TVS emphasized the Omni's superior sight lines to those of Madison Square Garden. No spectator would be more than 150 feet from the playing surface, while many seats at Madison Square Garden were more than 200 feet from the action.[25] The Omni's design won acclaim from architectural critics for its innovative use of materials and avant-garde design. Diagonal rows of reddish-brown pyramids, each the size of a three-story house, covered the arena's rooftop. TVS used rust-colored Cor-Ten weathering steel on the roof, pioneering a short-lived architectural trend in the United States.

U.S. Steel patented Cor-Ten steel alloys during the 1930s. The new technology, they believed, would cut down on the need for seasonal maintenance on steel structures. Researchers at U.S. Steel found that, over the course of several years of exposure to weather, Cor-Ten formed a solid, rust coating that kept moisture out of steel structures. Cor-Ten not only prevented steel corrosion, it strengthened with age. The technology was little used until Japanese steelmakers began using it beginning in the late 1950s. U.S. Steel tried unsuccessfully for years to persuade American entrepreneurs and planners to use Cor-Ten to avoid the costs of regularly repainting steel structures by virtually eliminating corrosion. The steelmaker failed at first to convince many investors to embrace the bizarre-looking steel that changed color from a goldenrod yellow to a deep brown rust within a couple of years. Eventually, U.S. Steel persuaded skeptical North American architectural firms in the early 1970s to use it in large-scale projects. The Omni was one of the first high-profile projects in the United States to make use of Cor-Ten technology.[26] Within seven years, TVS said, the Omni's 160,000-square-foot roof would form a permanent coating. Instead, the humid climate of the Southeast prevented the Cor-Ten steel from forming a permanent bond as it had in Japan's four-season climate. Atlanta's heat and humidity ate through the Cor-Ten roof over the course of two decades, which contributed to the Omni's rapid deterioration. During construction of the facility, TVS said the roof would eventually turn purple. Instead, the rusty pyramids matured into a darker brown.[27]

Fans and sports media gave the Omni generally good reviews, except for the Cor-Ten roof, which became an immediate subject of local ridicule. Furman Bisher called the Omni the "rusty egg carton" because of its roof. Bisher's nickname caught on among Atlantans and "the rusty egg carton" became the arena's unofficial moniker.[28] The interior of the Omni drew near-universal praise from fans and local media outlets. The new arena provided spectators with excellent sight lines for hockey and basketball. The proximity of every seat to the on-court or on-ice action made for an intimate spectator experience. The arena's red, cushioned seats were far more comfortable than the wooden bleachers at the Alexander Memorial Coliseum.[29] Attending a game at the Omni was an experience in a "total environment," Ron Taylor and Maurice Fliess, writing for the *Sunday Journal-Constitution*, said of the facility after attending an early Flames game. "Inside this environment, the developer is boss," they wrote, describing the controlled, enclosed space Cousins had created amid the unpredictable, open urban environment surrounding them.[30] Taylor and Fliess's comments anticipate Cousins' larger Omni Complex project, which aimed to create an enclave of inward-oriented predictability within a center city that seemed increasingly unfamiliar and unwelcoming to suburbanites.

Cousins Properties unveiled plans for the broader Omni International Complex on October 10, 1972, two days before the opening of the Omni Coliseum. It announced that the Omni Complex would include a luxury hotel, an entertainment complex, and hundreds of thousands of square feet in office space.[31] Entirely separate from the existing retail in downtown Atlanta, namely Rich's and Famous department stores, the Omni Complex was intended to serve as a new focal point for retail, business, and entertainment in the center of the city.[32] Building substantially onto his original group of backers, Cousins brought together a high-profile group of investors for the project that included David Rockefeller, ship-ping tycoon Stavros Niarchos, and the Ford Foundation.[33] The announcement of the $100 million mixed-use project rein-forced Cousins's frequently repeated statement that the col-iseum was just the first section of a much larger campus he planned to build in downtown Atlanta.

The October 10 announcement of the Omni Complex served another purpose. It upstaged the announcement the previous day by John Portman, Cousins's primary rival among Atlanta developers, that he planned to build a seventy-story luxury hotel at Peachtree Center, the city's original MXD. Peachtree Center is located just north of the Five Points, the historic hub of downtown Atlanta's CBD. Cousins's Omni Complex would soon stand just across the Five Points from Portman's Peachtree Center: twin behemoths that would frame the rede-velopment of downtown Atlanta.[34] Portman's vision for down-town Atlanta mirrored and, evidently, inspired that of Cousins. In an August 1966 interview with the *Chicago Tribune*, Portman described his efforts to ensure downtown Atlanta's future as a commercial, residential, and entertainment center in a rapidly decentralizing city. "A downtown cannot be a 'day time only' place and live," Portman said. "To get people to want to be in the core city, we've got to plan the city to the human scale," he said, before describing his "coordinated unit" vision for downtown redevelopment, a proposal for ensuring the human scale in urban planning through the intense management of urban space. Portman, like Cousins, wanted people living or working in downtown Atlanta to be able to access all the ame-nities they could in a suburban environment plus the signa-ture amenities of a center city within a safe, controlled, and enclosed atmosphere.

WHEN THE OMNI OPENED, EVERYONE IN THE REGION AND in the nation knew that Atlanta was Major League. The ground-breaking at the Gulch some eighteen months earlier was just another variant on a coronation that started when Atlanta lured the Braves from Milwaukee. The story of the city's mayor and its best-known developer shoveling red dirt into ceremonial souvenir jars for the one hundred children selected to be the feel-good dignitaries for the day did not even make it above the fold in any of Atlanta's daily newspapers.

More interesting than anything that happened at the Gulch that afternoon were the negotiations between Cousins and Massell over the groundbreaking event. Cousins wanted to hold a formal blue-ribbon ceremony that amounted to a cocktail party for the Big Mules. Massell protested Cousins's plan, insisting that the public be invited and allowed to participate in the groundbreaking of a building they were helping to finance and that would eventually become their property. Moreover, the mayor believed that a building being christened the Omni should welcome the public it purported to serve. Following a private negotiating session with Cousins's representative and a week's worth of public negotiations through the city's newspapers, Massell convinced Cousins to hold a public ceremony, offering free hot dogs and soft drinks to all who attended.

This trivial dispute between Massell and Cousins was hardly a decisive moment in the history of Metropolitan Atlanta, but it was emblematic of the problems Major League Atlanta would face in the coming years as it struggled to live up to its cultural aspirations. The civic elite's 1960s dream of using professional sports as a metropolitan center of gravity failed in the 1970s as the city struggled to live up to these lofty goals. In a seven-year period between 1965 and 1972, Atlanta had opened two state-of-the-art playing facilities for professional sports and had lured four Major League franchises to the city. The city's political and corporate leadership, the people who managed the concerted civic effort to acquire these amenities, made it clear that the primary social and cultural purposes for the acquisition of professional sports franchises were increasing the city's national prestige and serving as a unifying force in the region. Once these amenities were in place, though, it became increasingly unclear just who would be supporting Atlanta's teams and how they would do so. Massell's inclusive vision and Cousins's exclusive vision of who should have been the focus of the Omni's groundbreaking ceremony evoked the political and cultural divides that shaped the remaking of Metropolitan Atlanta in the late twentieth century. In particular, they display the two primary visions of Metropolitan Atlanta's future articulated by the civic elite during the 1960s and 1970s.

Despite his conflicts with his predecessor, Massell represented a continuation of the post–World War II Atlanta ethos of inclusive, negotiated settlement and coalition building. From Massell's perspective, Atlanta's significant municipal investments in mass leisure were aimed at providing all of Metropolitan Atlanta with a broadly beneficial civic luxury. Cousins, by contrast, wanted to reinvigorate the center city by satisfying the desires of the affluent suburbanites who had either abandoned the city or, as newcomers, avoided it altogether. Neither appeals to metropolitan unity or efforts to appeal to the variety of consumers across Metro Atlanta won a lasting core of patrons back to the amenities of the center city, despite the presumed appeal of professional sports.

14

The Politics of Metropolitan Divergence

....

"WHAT FOLKS WILL DO TO AVOID HAVING TO LIVE IN THE city is amazing," Steve Suitts of the Southern Regional Council, an Atlanta-based civil rights organization, told the *Boston Globe*'s Robert Scheer in 1979. "All you have to do is sit on the rail of one of those super highway bridges and look down at the cars that come in at 7:30 in the morning and you'll see just one white face after another," Suitts said, attributing the extraordinary efforts made by Atlanta commuters to avoid living in the city to two factors. He explained that white residents in suburban Atlanta shared a nearly universal desire to avoid living in integrated neighborhoods and sending their children to integrated schools, a fact that was as widely known as it was practiced but rarely stated publicly in such explicit terms, especially by its practitioners.[1]

The phenomenon Suitts described, the hasty back and forth of commuters between Atlanta's ever-expanding suburban frontiers and the city's CBD, was a product of choices made over the previous half century by both civic elites and ordinary citizens, more than 2.5 million of whom lived in the metropolitan region by the end of the 1970s. Those choices remade Metro Atlanta into a highly decentralized, politically and culturally fractured region whose denizens resisted the kind of mass cultural forces that frequently foster a sense of civic unity, including professional sports franchises.[2]

A series of contentious regional policy disputes in the 1960s and 1970s, specifically conflicts between the core city and its surrounding counties on the issues of housing development, school desegregation, annexation, and rapid transit, played a decisive role in the formulation of distinct and divergent urban and suburban political cultures in Metropolitan Atlanta. As Atlanta became a Major League City, the biracial political coalition that facilitated its economic and cultural ascension was unraveling. Institutions that sought out cross-metropolitan fealty failed to unify the region. This applied at least as much for transmetropolitan public authorities, specifically those charged with managing the region's mass transit, schools, and housing, as it did to the city's professional sports franchises, which struggled to build durable or diverse bases of support.

Foremost among these destabilizing forces was the unraveling of the Hartsfield-Allen coalition, which had won consistent support from Black voters and a clear majority of white voters in Atlanta since the 1940s. During the 1960s and 1970s, however, Atlanta's biracial electoral coalition succumbed to the demographic transformation of the city and its suburbs. At the end of Ivan Allen's two terms as mayor, sixty thousand fewer whites and seventy thousand more Blacks lived in the city of Atlanta than did at the time of his inauguration, transforming Atlanta into a majority Black city by the time of the 1970 census. By 1980, African Americans constituted more than two-thirds of Atlanta's 425,000 residents, while whites constituted more than eighty percent of the two million people living in Atlanta's suburbs.[3]

In place of the consensus-building Hartsfield-Allen regime emerged a fragmented regional political culture built around two distinct power bases: Black political leadership in the majority African American city of Atlanta and a predominately white suburban politics that asserted its civic autonomy from Atlanta. Race proved to be the most significant of prisms through which metropolitan-area residents gave meaning to the social, political, and spatial transformation of their region during the 1960s and 1970s. Undoubtedly, race has always played a major role in Atlanta politics. Its tangible impact on electoral politics became more evident following the 1946 *Chapman v. King* decision that declared Georgia's white-only primary unconstitutional. Subsequent registration drives orchestrated by the Atlanta Negro Voters' League made African Americans a force in city politics. When African Americans became an electoral majority in Atlanta during the early 1970s, race played just as profound a role in reshaping local political coalitions. The emergence of a Black electoral supermajority in Atlanta and a suburban white electoral supermajority set the parameters for the region's political culture, creating a recurring set of coalitions, norms, and taboos that privileged group or local interests over transmetropolitan cooperation.

DESEGREGATION IN ATLANTA, WROTE MATTHEW LASSITER, consisted of a labyrinth of avoidance, "a sophisticated combination of socioeconomic and geographic barriers designed to accommodate the class prejudices of the northside and to manage the racial anxieties of the southside."[4] Lassiter's description is a starting point for understanding the residential divergence of Metro Atlanta during the 1960s and 1970s. Collectively, urban renewal, housing desegregation, and the economic growth of the region prompted responses by citizens from varying social backgrounds that contributed to the decentralization of Metropolitan Atlanta into spatially discreet socioeconomic, racial, and lifestyle clusters.

The implementation of policies aimed at residential and school desegregation provoked broader opposition among white Atlanta residents than any of the other progressive reforms enacted during the 1960s and 1970s. Many white residents who tolerated life in a municipality where African Americans could eat at a downtown lunch counter could not countenance life in a city where frequent racial mixing occurred in one's own section of town. The social intimacy involved in sharing a neighborhood or a classroom with Blacks had a significantly greater impact on the practices of their everyday life than the desegregation of the CBD. A broad consensus of white residents in Atlanta and its environs came to see the extension of the rights of citizenship to African Americans as threatening their own freedoms. Specifically, many white Atlantans regarded desegregation as an affront to their freedom to associate with people of their choosing and to govern their community's affairs without government interference.[5]

Once federal courts compelled city administrators to remove all remaining legal barriers to neighborhood or school desegregation, the white residents of the Atlanta wards most affected by the changes voted with their feet. The end of legally sanctioned residential and school segregation in Atlanta proved to be the primary catalyst for white abandonment of the city, resulting in a net loss of 164,000 white residents between 1960 and 1980, a 55 percent decline in the city's white population.[6]

Middle- and working-class white Atlantans bore the social brunt of desegregation. Theirs were the neighborhoods that became destabilized as a result of court mandates, not the tony northside neighborhoods in which progressives like Ivan Allen resided. Predatory realtors helped to accelerate the white abandonment of South, East, and West Atlanta through a multifaceted campaign of harassment. White homeowners living in transitional neighborhoods received dozens of phone calls and mail solicitations from real estate brokers each week, often offering them as much as one and a half times the recently prevailing market values of their homes. Some realtors played up racial fears among children, approaching them as they walked home from school and telling them that they would be unwelcome in their soon-to-be all-Black neighborhoods.[7] Whether provoked by predatory realtors or not, white residents of transitional neighborhoods left Atlanta so quickly that the Board of Aldermen briefly considered banning the placement of for-sale signs on residential properties.[8]

The decline in Atlanta's white population during the 1960s was directly related to the simultaneous growth of Atlanta's Black population, which expanded to more than a quarter-million during the decade. Black residential expansion in

Southwest Atlanta was the primary engine of the city's demographic transformation. In 1960 Southwest Atlanta was a virtually all-white community. By 1970, African Americans constituted a supermajority of its residents. More than half of Southwest Atlanta's new African American residents had migrated there from the city's traditional Black enclaves that formed a *U* around the CBD. As Black Atlantans took advantage of the legal desegregation of housing in the city, white borrowers found it increasingly difficult to secure home loans in Southwest Atlanta, making it economically unfeasible for white residents of modest means to stay. Southwest Atlanta was soon followed by expansions onto the city's west and east sides and, eventually, into Southeast Atlanta, the urban core of "Maddox Country." With the end of legal segregation, whites abandoned each of these areas, rendering virtually every Atlanta census tract south of I-20 more than 75 percent Black by 1970.[9]

White enclaves of privilege on Atlanta's northside avoided the most tangible aspects of desegregation while accruing the economic benefits and cultural prestige that outsiders afforded to the ruling class of the region's most enlightened city. The Forward Atlanta promotional campaign, which transformed Atlanta's corporate class into one of the nation's most powerful by luring hundreds of millions of dollars in outside investment, would not have been possible without the continued cultivation of the city's reputation as a progressive oasis in the segregated South. The greatest beneficiaries of the inflow of capital investment to the City Too Busy to Hate proved to be the people who sacrificed the least to maintain this reputation. As a result, Atlanta became a city whose population consisted primarily of a socioeconomically diverse Black population and an affluent white population whose daily lives were increasingly distant from those of the city's racial majority.[10]

The residential instability of Atlanta during the 1960s and 1970s was, to a great extent, a product of the residential disruptions that began during the city's urban renewal campaign in the 1950s. Between 1956 and 1966, federally subsidized slum clearance and expressway-building programs as well as locally initiated downtown redevelopment efforts led to the destruction of twenty-one thousand predominately low-income housing units and the displacement of sixty-seven thousand predominately African American residents from the neighborhoods immediately to the east, west, and south of the CBD. Whether intended as barriers or not, Atlanta Stadium on the Washington-Rawson site, the Atlanta Civic Center on the Bedford Pine site, and the Downtown Connector (1964), a north-south expressway that cut Sweet Auburn in half, all destroyed significant portions of the city's traditional Black neighborhoods while reconfiguring the boundaries of white and Black Atlanta.[11]

The destruction of many traditionally Black neighborhoods by urban renewal and the subsequent loosening of tacit and explicit municipal restrictions on Black residential expansion led to a profound reconfiguration of the city's residential life during the 1960s. Black middle-class residents in search of quality housing began purchasing homes across Southwest and Southeast Atlanta, leading to the virtual abandonment of both sections of the city by white residents. Civic-minded progressives lamented the unwillingness of Blacks and whites to share South Atlanta's neighborhoods. Black newcomers to South Atlanta proved as indifferent as the whites who abandoned these neighborhoods to the harangues of social commentators who decried the resegregation of the area. Atlanta's Black middle class was focused on taking advantage of the end of legal segregation, not ensuring the lasting integration of their new neighborhoods, an issue over which they had almost no control. The area's new residents were motivated primarily by a desire to secure the individual, familial, and communal comforts of middle-class citizenship. African Americans cultivated a civil society of their choosing in the numerous stable neighborhoods they recreated in Southwest Atlanta.[12]

Many African Americans who could not find affordable housing in Atlanta during the 1960s moved eastward into DeKalb County or southwest of the city limits into Fulton County in the region's first wave of Black suburbanization. One in five of the region's more than half-million Black residents lived in the suburbs by 1970, a proportion twice as high as in 1960. The growth of DeKalb's Black population during the 1960s was particularly pronounced, increasing by more than 250 percent from 22,171 to 57,869. Black newcomers clustered in Dekalb's westernmost sections, which included a small portion of the city of Atlanta.[13]

Amid the residential transformation of Atlanta and its inner-ring suburbs, the quality of life in the city's poorest neighborhoods deteriorated further. The density of population in Atlanta's traditionally Black neighborhoods continued to grow as tens of thousands of African American migrants from rural Georgia moved to the city during the 1960s, adding further stress to the city's housing crisis.[14] Atlanta's civic leadership proved unwilling and unable to meet the demands for publicly subsidized housing from its new or old residents, building a total of five thousand units between 1957 and 1967, less than a quarter of the number required to provide housing for just those residents displaced by urban renewal. White residents fought the placement of public housing in their neighborhoods as vociferously as they had the integration of the private housing market. In particular, residents of still predominately white neighborhoods on Atlanta's affluent northside, Allen's white political base, proved adept at fighting the issuance of building permits for low-income housing.[15]

The Allen administration married its plans to expand Atlanta's affordable housing stock to the city's participation in the Model Cities program, a Great Society housing and antipoverty initiative administered by the Department of Housing and Urban Development (HUD). Model Cities sought to upgrade the total environment of blighted inner-city neighborhoods by focusing intense investment on relatively small sections of cities while purporting to seek out the input of area residents to help plan their neighborhood's revitalization. Allen ordered AHA to submit a Model Cities application as soon as the program became law in March 1967. AHA's decisive action earned Atlanta the first spot in the program. Model Cities focused more than $30 million in federal spending, channeled through twenty-eight different public and private agencies, on the revitalization of six adjoining, impoverished neighborhoods east, west, and south of I-20 and the CBD: Mechanicsville, Pittsburgh, Summerhill, Vine City, Peoplestown, and Grant Park. Atlanta's Model Cities site covered three thousand acres of inner-city land and contained fifty thousand people, 95 percent of whom lived below the poverty line.[16]

In Atlanta's Model Cities application, AHA explained that 71.8 percent of the 13,609 housing units in the six neighborhoods had been deemed substandard by the city. Atlanta officials said that the proposed Model Cities site required a minimum of six thousand new units to alleviate its housing crisis.[17] Beyond the mere construction of new housing, Atlanta officials envisioned a cluster of social improvements that the federally subsidized revitalization effort would bring to the community, including the remaking of the area into "a satisfying living environment," an effort to "improve and encourage development of stores, theaters, and other commercial facilities," a desire to "achieve harmonious, stable neighborhoods attractive to family groups," and an imperative to "prevent and control the outbreak of crime."[18]

Virtually none of the aspirations for the Model Cities area materialized. Fewer than 350 new homes were built in the Model Cities area between 1968 and 1973. Approximately one thousand homes received grants from Model Cities for rehabilitation or repairs, but many of these homes showed little in the way of improvement. The population in the Model Cities area actually declined by about 5,500 during the five-year program. Bureaucratic inefficiency and infighting among different factions inside and outside the Model Cities community prevented significant progress on any of the program's goals.[19]

Homeowners in the Model Cities area frequently clashed with the area's highly transient population of renters, whom the homeowners regarded as the primary source of social ills in the neighborhoods, particularly the area's escalating crime rate. Violent crime in the six Model Cities neighborhoods increased by a third during the program's five years. Forty percent of the city's staggeringly high number of homicides during this period took place in the Model Cities area.[20]

The expansion of Atlanta's low-income housing stock took place primarily outside of the Model Cities area. The city's public housing system grew from eight thousand units in 1965 to nearly fourteen thousand units in 1973.[21] Most of the new housing units were placed on Atlanta's then sparsely developed far west and south sides, miles from the employment centers of the CBD. Federal regulations adopted during the Johnson administration limited the amount of public housing that could be built in census tracts with large existing concentrations of minority populations. These rules prevented new affordable housing from being built in the historically Black neighborhoods that ringed Atlanta's CBD.[22]

Atlanta remained a highly segregated city throughout the 1960s despite the expansion of residential opportunities for Black Atlantans. A 1969 AHA survey revealed that Atlanta's near-majority Black population lived on just twenty percent of the city's land, only slightly more than it had in 1950.[23] In a 1970 study, Douglas Massey and Nancy Denton argued that Atlanta was more segregated at the end of the 1960s than it was at the end of the 1930s. White flight may have opened more neighborhoods to Black residents, but it also heightened the concentration of Blacks and whites in discreet sections of the city and the suburbs, parallel communities with little cultural or spatial common ground.[24]

While Atlanta's affordable housing stock expanded slowly, the suburban home market boomed as the metropolitan area's five suburban counties added 360,000 residents during the 1960s. Roughly half of these people settled north of the city in Fulton, Cobb, and Gwinnett Counties, including more than two-thirds of the sixty-seven thousand new residents who came from outside Metropolitan Atlanta. Whites constituted more than 98 percent of the newcomers to northern Fulton, Cobb, and Gwinnett Counties. Metropolitan Atlanta's residential patterns diverged even more strikingly over the next twenty years. The population of Atlanta shrunk from nearly a half-million in 1970 to 394,017 in 1990, paralleling its transformation from a city with a slight Black majority to a city that was more than two-thirds African American. As Atlanta shrunk, its suburban population doubled in the same twenty-year period. The metropolitan area's population grew from 1.56 million in 1970 to nearly three million in 1990. More than 60 percent of the region's population growth during the 1970s and 1980s took place in its northern suburbs as newcomers followed I-75 northward into Cobb, Clayton, northern Dekalb, and Gwinnett counties beyond the I-285 perimeter road, which locals, at the time of its 1969 opening, regarded as the outer limits of the metropolitan area.[25]

As Atlanta's center of gravity shifted away from its urban core, its suburban residents inhabited a cultural orbit that shared ever less with the residents of the center city. Most white suburbanites sent their children to almost exclusively white schools. They did most of their shopping far from the center city. They spent their leisure time within the confines of their own residential and lifestyle cluster. Those who commuted regularly into Atlanta traveled along interstates that rendered the city invisible, obscuring with concrete barriers the neighborhoods they sought to avoid.[26] Suburban Atlantans found few reasons to patronize the services offered in the center city once these services were duplicated in nearby retail centers. The merits of more convenient alternatives made even native-born suburban consumers infrequent patrons of the goods and services offered in the CBD.[27] The "Golden Crescent" at the northern end of the I-285 perimeter became the first of many upscale retail development areas in suburban

Atlanta. Located in northern Fulton County, the Golden Crescent began with a relatively modest shopping center (Phipps
Plaza, 1969) and enclosed shopping mall (Northlake Mall, 1971).
More ambitious suburban shopping developments, including
the Cumberland/Galleria (1975), which was placed strategically
at the intersection of I-75 and I-285, and the Perimeter Center Mall (1971), located at the intersection of I-285 and Georgia 400, soon followed.[28]

SCHOOL DESEGREGATION IN METRO ATLANTA FOLLOWED
a similar pattern to that of housing desegregation in the region.
City leaders tried to manage a gradual desegregation of Atlanta
schools, but continued agitation by civil rights activists led to
a series of court decisions that forced the Board of Education
to proceed more quickly than it desired. Most white Atlanta
residents proved unwilling to send their children to integrated
public schools. Some parents sent their children to one of the
proliferating private schools in the region. Far more families
relocated to the suburbs and sent their children to nearby
public schools. By the time Atlanta school leaders came to a
final desegregation settlement in 1973 with local civil rights
groups, white residents had enacted a de facto resegregation
of the region's schools by moving beyond the boundaries of
Atlanta and its busing program.

Atlanta Public Schools (APS) followed the lead of Hartsfield
and Allen on desegregation, proceeding slowly for fear that any
rapid transformations within the school system would cause
whites to abandon it immediately. Atlanta's school desegregation program began in August 1961 with the highly orchestrated enrollment of nine Black students in four city high
schools. Once token school desegregation had taken place, the
white establishment, including Allen, declared victory on the
issue. School desegregation, like housing desegregation, had
a more direct, day-to-day impact on the lives of citizens than
the mere desegregation of public accommodations, which
one could choose to avoid. Allen viewed the further desegre-

gation of APS as an administrative process to be undertaken carefully by the school system itself.[29]

APS proceeded with its desegregation plan slowly. After several school years' worth of small upticks in the number of desegregated APS classrooms, the Justice Department filed suit against APS, accusing the school system of maintaining separate white and Black school systems while engaging in token desegregation.[30] In May 1964, the U.S. Supreme Court found on behalf of the Justice Department and required Atlanta to expand its desegregation plan under the federal agency's supervision.[31]

Following the Court's decision, APS officials worked quickly to rectify the situation, fearing that the unfavorable ruling would harm the city's progressive image. They set up an expedited school desegregation plan based on the recommendations of federal officials. By January 1966, 8,831 of the 61,344 Black APS students attended desegregated institutions, nearly five times as many as during the previous academic year. Civil rights activists remained critical of APS's desegregation efforts, characterizing the reforms as more tokenism on the district's part. Conversely, many white Atlanta parents regarded the pace of school desegregation as too rapid. In August 1961, whites constituted 56 percent of APS students, a proportion comparable to the city's white population. By August 1965, whites, who remained a majority of the city's population, accounted for only 40 percent of APS students, demonstrating the unwillingness of many white parents to send their children to even marginally desegregated schools.[32]

Atlanta's court-ordered 1965 desegregation plan was far from the endpoint of legal challenges to the racial composition of APS. In October 1969 the US Supreme Court ruled in *Alexander v. Holmes County (MS) Board of Education* that "all deliberate speed" was no longer an applicable standard for school desegregation. The court's decision led to new rounds of litigation challenging desegregation programs in hundreds of southern school districts, including Atlanta's. The Atlanta

NAACP filed suit once again, seeking complete desegregation of all city schools through a busing program that would ensure the racial makeup in all public schools reflected the racial makeup of the entire city's student population.[33]

While the courts worked through a new round of litigation, school desegregation remained a catalyst for metropolitan divergence. Suburban Atlanta school districts struggled to build and staff enough facilities to keep up with the influx of new students. Clayton County's school enrollment more than doubled during the 1960s to twenty-seven thousand, while Gwinnett County's enrollment nearly doubled to nineteen thousand. The growth rates of schools in DeKalb and Cobb Counties was even more drastic. Between 1950 and 1970, DeKalb's school enrollment increased by more than 800 percent, while Cobb County Public Schools grew by more than 500 percent. By 1970, three-quarters of APS students were Black, while public schools in Cobb, Gwinnett, Clayton, DeKalb, and suburban Fulton County were all more than 90 percent white. By near necessity, voters across suburban Atlanta approved generous new bonds almost every year in the 1960s and 1970s to finance the construction of additional schools in their districts, demonstrating their willingness to support public spending if they saw it as directly beneficial or regarded its beneficiaries as deserving of largesse.[34]

The peak years for white abandonment of city schools corresponded with the final stages of the legal desegregation of APS. After a half-decade of negotiation, the Atlanta NAACP and the APS Board of Education reached a settlement. Dubbed the "Second Atlanta Compromise," the February 1973 agreement brokered by Atlanta NAACP President Lonnie King and APS chief negotiators William Van Landingham and Frank Smith gave Atlanta's Black leadership decisive control over the school system but compromised on the demand for genuine school integration. The Atlanta NAACP, the institutional force behind the litigation since the 1950s, negotiated a quintessentially Atlanta-style deal with the Board of Education. White and Black corporate, governmental, and community leaders hashed out the details of the covenant in a series of behind-the-scenes negotiations. The Second Atlanta Compromise guaranteed that African Americans would hold a majority of executive positions in the school system, including superintendent. The plan further integrated school staffing to bring the composition of each school in line with the demographics of the entire system. Additionally, the compromise created a system of biracial magnet schools designed to attract talented Black and white students from across the city. In return, the NAACP dropped its demand for a broader cross-district busing program.[35]

The national NAACP regarded the Second Atlanta Compromise as a sellout—a retreat from the organization's policy of seeking the greatest degree of integration possible in all public institutions. The national NAACP threatened to suspend the Atlanta branch from the organization but instead fired King as branch president.[36] Most Black residents of the city's poorest neighborhoods, those whose children attended the city's worst schools, shared the national NAACP's hostile reaction to the "Settlement of 1973." They wanted their children to have the opportunity to attend the city's best schools. The settlement foreclosed on that opportunity for all but the most gifted students in the city's most impoverished neighborhoods. Instead, underprivileged children in Atlanta remained primarily in the city's worst schools, far from whites and far from the children of the city's Black professional classes. The merit-based, magnet school system created by the settlement served primarily academically well-prepared children from the city's Black middle class. The Settlement of 1973 had, in effect, consolidated the Black professional class's control over one of Atlanta's foremost public institutions and distributed its benefits disproportionately to Black middle-class families.[37] The 1973 compromise ended the legal struggle over school desegregation in Atlanta, but it failed to stem white flight from the city's schools. In a 1975 survey, Atlanta realtors cited the unwillingness of whites to send their children to city schools as the primary obstacle they faced in selling homes. By the mid-1980s, whites constituted just 6 percent of the students in APS.[38]

THE METROPOLITAN-WIDE POLITICAL STRUGGLES OVER annexation and the extension of public transit were pivotal moments in the remaking of Atlanta's political culture during the 1960s and 1970s. In both instances, the efforts of civic elites to steward through solutions to these issues met the opposition of the region's two politically ascendant constituencies: Atlanta's emerging Black electoral majority and the region's predominately white and numerically larger suburban majority. In the case of annexation, city leaders who tried to manage Atlanta's racial transformation during the 1960s and 1970s fostered widespread mistrust among both white and Black voters toward transmetropolitan political reforms. In their failed efforts to manage the demographics of Atlanta's electorate and tax base, civic elites convinced an enduring supermajority of the metropolitan area's residents that plans for regional policy management would have an adverse impact on their lives.

The demographic transformation of Atlanta during World War II made the targeted annexation of populated sections of Fulton County, particularly the white and affluent settlements north of the city limits, a newly pressing priority for the city's political and business establishment. Even before America entered the war in December 1941, a new wave of tens of thousands of job-seeking African Americans began migrating to Atlanta from rural Georgia. This wave of migration did not end with the war. Atlanta's postwar economic boom and the coinciding mechanization of rural agriculture convinced even more Black Georgians to migrate to the city. Atlanta's already congested Black enclaves became even more overcrowded. By 1950, almost 40 percent of the city's Black residents lived in homes that averaged more than one resident per room, three times the rate of white residents. The 1950 census indicated that African Americans constituted nearly 40 percent of the city's population, ten percent more than in 1930. The Census Bureau projected that Atlanta would become a majority African American city by the mid-1960s if the city's demographic trends continued.[39]

"Our Negro population is growing by leaps and bounds. They stay right in the city limits and grow by taking more white territory inside Atlanta," Mayor Hartsfield wrote in a race-baiting, private note to a number of Big Mules in 1950, explaining the necessity of annexation. Atlanta, he believed, needed an influx of affluent, white residents to ensure that the city's tax base could withstand the strains being placed on municipal agencies by the migration of tens of thousands of impoverished, low-skilled, and poorly educated African Americans into the city.[40]

Hartsfield addressed the annexation issue in a manner that maintained the stability and racial status quo of Atlanta while simultaneously helping him consolidate his support among the city's white and Black leadership. He pushed for the annexation of the affluent northside Buckhead and Druid Hills suburbs, which residents of both communities approved by referendum in 1951. The annexation increased the size of Atlanta proper from 37 to 118 square miles and boosted its population by close to one hundred thousand residents, more than 95 percent of whom were white. Hartsfield sold leaders in Druid Hills and Buckhead on the plan by arguing that the execution of parallel services in the city and new suburban communities was financially burdensome to both parties. Merger, he argued persuasively, would benefit everyone in terms of taxes and water rates. Hartsfield made sure to keep his primary motivation for pursuing annexation out of the public eye, fearing that the electorate's input would enflame racial tensions or compromise his negotiations with urban Black or suburban white leaders.[41]

Hartsfield won the support of the city's African American leadership for annexation by helping Black entrepreneurs secure zoning clearances to build dozens of racially "self-contained" subdivisions and apartment complexes on the city's western periphery. The mayor's support for Black residential expansion in the 1940s and 1950s improved the quality of housing stock available to middle-income African Americans considerably. Simultaneously, it served the civic elite's goal of preventing the creation of even more densely packed Black neighborhoods around the CBD, which, city leaders feared, would discourage whites from patronizing downtown businesses.[42]

By the early 1960s, city leaders realized that the white electoral majority was again imperiled. Atlanta was once again 40 percent African American. The city's Black population had grown from 121,146 in 1950 to 186,820 in 1960, an increase of 54.2 percent. As the city's demographics became a popular preoccupation, Ivan Allen championed a new round of annexations late in his first term. Even progressives like Allen made it clear that they wanted to maintain the city's white majority. Despite his poor showings among nonelite white voters both in 1961 and 1965, Allen regarded the preservation of a white electoral majority as essential to maintaining social peace in Atlanta and preventing further erosion of its tax base.

Allen and the Atlanta Chamber backed a plan to annex the unincorporated northern Fulton County suburb of Sandy Springs, home to thirty-eight thousand predominately affluent, almost exclusively white residents. In the annexation debate, Allen, most of his allies in the Atlanta Chamber, and the editorialists of the *Journal* and *Constitution* shied away from the racial politics of annexation. Instead, they campaigned on behalf of the Sandy Springs plan by arguing that unification would reduce everyone's taxes by streamlining municipal services. In May 1966, Sandy Springs voted against annexation by a margin of more than two to one. Many voters in Sandy Springs regarded annexation as primarily a racial issue, fearing that it would lead to the busing of African American students into their community.[43]

The issue of annexation remained dormant until Allen's successor, Sam Massell, proposed an annexation of then almost entirely white northern Fulton County, including Sandy Springs. In December 1971 Massell and his allies in the Georgia General Assembly pursued annexation through the legislature rather than a referendum to circumvent the consistently fervent opposition to any such measure in the city's northern suburbs. Massell had opposed annexation during his 1969 mayoral run, describing it as a plan aimed at weakening the power of the city's Black voters, the bloc whose support was the base of his electoral coalition. Less than two years into his term, Massell came to the same conclusion that Hartsfield and Allen had years earlier. Atlanta would face economic peril if it did not annex outlying afflu-ent areas of Fulton County.[44]

In his annexation proposal, Massell called for the consolida-tion of Fulton County into two large cities: Atlanta and South Fulton City. The proposal would have more than doubled the size of Atlanta from 137 square miles to 310 square miles and increased its population from 496,000 to just under 550,000. Simultaneously, it called for the consolidation of southern Fulton County into a 134-square-mile, sixty-thousand-person municipality. Southern Fulton County had been the site of sig-nificant Black suburban settlement, and the area projected to have an African American majority by 1980. The 1970 census recorded Atlanta's population as 50.2 percent African Amer-ican. Massell's plan would have boosted the percentage of whites in the city to 53 percent and increased the proportion of white students in APS to 35 percent.[45]

Massell tried to negotiate the contentious politics of annex-ation by appealing to economic pragmatism. Channeling Harts-field, Massell said that his plan would not prevent an eventual Black electoral majority in Atlanta but would instead help white residents adjust to the city's new governing regime. To avoid the fate of "all poor" cities like Newark and Detroit, Massell said that the temporary maintenance of biracial governance through annexation would prevent even larger numbers of white taxpayers from relocating.[46]

In some respects, elite and popular responses to Massell's plan were predictable. Opposition was vociferous in the sections of northern Fulton County slated for incorporation into Atlanta as well as the communities placed within the new South Fulton City. Mayors in southern Fulton County demanded that each community be able to decide by referendum whether it wanted to join the new city individually.[47] In other respects, the response to Massell's annexation plan was exactly the inverse of his electoral coalition two years earlier. Atlanta's business establishment, which bitterly opposed the proudly liberal Massell in 1969, supported his efforts at legislative annexation. Black Atlantans, more than 90 percent of whom had supported Massell in the runoff, strongly opposed the proposal to make them once again an electoral minority without even the courtesy of a public referendum. Many Black political leaders in Atlanta saw the plan as a means of limiting Black political power more than an effort to expand the city's tax base. Without a clear base of support, Massell's annexation plan failed during the 1972 Georgia state legislative session.[48]

Changing political circumstances in Atlanta brought the legislative momentum for annexation to a halt. The assertion of Black political power in Atlanta with the 1973 election of Maynard Jackson, who had opposed all annexation proposals, combined with the continued white flight from and Black migration to the city during the 1970s, made the possibility of a large-scale annexation of populated sections of Fulton County increasingly politically unfeasible. Neither white suburban political leadership nor the city's Black political leadership saw sacrificing power as in its interest. Suburban legislators who had been willing to cede control of sparsely populated sections of Fulton County to a white-led administration were suddenly unwilling to do so to a Black-led administration, fearing that Jackson would subject businesses in the newly annexed territories to burdensome taxes and racial hiring quotas. In subsequent decades, urban and suburban opposition has stymied any serious discussion of expanding the size of Atlanta proper. Annexation has proven a racially charged issue that offers neither Black nor white politicians any benefit to pursue. Their respective constituencies prefer to preserve their power bases through local control than pursue any plan for annexation.[49]

THE DEBATE OVER RAPID TRANSIT IN METROPOLITAN Atlanta further enshrined the region's fault lines for trans-municipal political cooperation. The region's unwillingness to support comprehensive rapid transit was a product of the fragmentation of Atlanta's postwar governing consensus into distinctly urban and suburban power bases. The political fragmentation of Metro Atlanta provided numerous demographic enclaves within the region with a virtual veto over new plans for political cooperation. Atlanta's lack of regional rapid transit and unwillingness to support the rapid transit system put in place after the 1971 referendum are a product of the political culture forged during this debate.

Elite opinion in Atlanta long favored metropolitan-wide solutions to mass transit. Years before the 1962 creation of the Metropolitan Atlanta Rapid Transit Authority (MARTA), Atlanta's leadership endorsed the idea of making substantial municipal investments in public transportation. An Atlanta Chamber–laden commission created a regional transportation plan in 1946 that called for the development of a public system of buses and passenger rail lines.[50] Atlanta's political leadership conceived of rapid transit as a status symbol for the growing city. Unlike more commonplace bus systems, rapid rail transit was a signature amenity, a municipal investment that Atlanta's leaders believed would cement the city's national stature as a modern and urbane community. More importantly, the Big Mules believed that efficient transit in and out of the CBD would help downtown retain its traditional commercial role in the regional economy as suburban business recreated those offered in the center city. Civic elites envisioned a commuter-oriented system that would serve as connective tissue between the CBD and the suburbs, bringing high-income earners and consumers to nodal points within downtown Atlanta.[51]

Moreover, city leaders realized that simply building more roads would not solve Atlanta's transportation woes. Despite recent expansions of I-20, I-75, and I-85 and the 1964 opening of the Downtown Connector, intense suburban growth had led to incredible congestion on every major road leading into the city. A 1968 traffic survey found that more than 550,000 cars either entered or exited Atlanta each weekday, twice as many as in 1960.[52]

Creating a metropolitan-wide transit system proved a highly contentious, drawn out process that lasted far beyond Ivan Allen's two terms as mayor. The planning, approval, and execution of a mass-transit system anchored by a rapid railway involved numerous legislative, bureaucratic, and voter approvals that were frequently disrupted by the disapproval of both urban and suburban constituencies. The creation of a regional rapid-transit system required support across municipalities. In the end, the rapid-transit debate created a system that almost no one liked. MARTA proved neither wide enough in scope nor a source of civic mutuality. It was neither the suburban commuter rail its original proponents envisioned nor the inclusive transmetropolitan circulator into which many progressive critics had hoped to reform it.

The creation of a metro-wide transit system required action by state voters and legislative approval from the Georgia General Assembly. These two prerequisites were the first of more than a decades' worth of requirements the system had to fulfill before construction began on the project. The creation of a metropolitan transit authority required voter approval of an amendment to the state constitution. Completing even this preplanning stage took several years. Statewide voters turned down the rapid-transit amendment by a wide margin in November 1962 before approving a modified regional transit authority amendment in 1964.[53]

On June 16, 1965, the city of Atlanta and the five suburban counties all voted separately on whether they wished to join MARTA. The referendum passed by large margins in the city of Atlanta and four of the five suburban counties. The measure failed in Cobb County, despite support for the measure by area political and business leaders. Many residents told pollsters that they balked at the system's anticipated $300 million price tag, fearing that a yes vote would force the county to assume a heavy public debt load.[54]

Following the June 1965 referendum, Atlanta and the four participating metropolitan counties appointed representatives to the ten-member MARTA board of directors. The MARTA board aimed for a blue-ribbon-panel image. Corporate officials dominated the board of directors, as they had every significant municipal body during the Hartsfield-Allen era.[55] The composition of the board made it clear that the corporate commuter class was the intended ridership for the rail system, not the potentially massive Black customer base for rapid transit.[56] Critics and supporters of rapid transit alike criticized the MARTA board for its secrecy and lack of interest in public input. Tunnel vision and aloofness did not endear voters to the MARTA board's plans for a rapid-transit system. When the board submitted its three-years-in-the-making referendum proposal, a diverse group of constituencies refused to support a plan into which they had virtually no input.[57]

MARTA's proposal called for the construction of a commuter-oriented forty-one-mile, thirty-two-station rapid rail line extending from the city of Atlanta into Fulton and DeKalb Counties. Expansion into outlying Gwinnett and Clayton Counties would soon follow. In addition to the rapid rail line, MARTA would manage an expanded system of feeder bus lines that built onto the service already offered by the ATC. MARTA had worked out an agreement with ATC to purchase the private system for $15 million. The referendum employed the only constitutionally acceptable local funding mechanism for the system: a property tax. Almost all proponents of the plan would have preferred using a sales tax to finance the system, but, after years of delays, the MARTA board wanted to proceed as quickly as possible.[58] The civic establishment, particularly the region's corporate leadership, backed the proposal with great vigor. The Atlanta, Fulton, and DeKalb Chambers invested heavily in the 1968 referendum, filling the local media with advertisements sponsored by the Committee for Rapid Transit Now. Executives at Coca-Cola, Delta Airlines, and Gulf Oil wrote open letters to their employees, asking them to vote yes.[59]

City Alderman and Gulf Oil executive Everett Millican headed a very short list of white leaders in Metropolitan Atlanta who expressed their opposition to the referendum. It was Millican who, through self-financed anti-referendum advertisements, galvanized nascent public opposition to the MARTA plan. MARTA supporters accused Millican of opposing the rapid rail system because of the threat it posed to his financial interests in the oil industry. Whatever his motivations, Millican made an outstanding foil to the triumphalist Committee for Rapid Transit Now. Millican helped to focus existing displeasure with the plan by providing its opponents with a core of dispassionate policy objections to the referendum. His arguments resonated in suburban areas where the home-owning supermajority all faced a property-tax increase if the referendum passed. Many homeowners, large numbers of whom had no intention of using the system, regarded the property tax as unfairly burdensome.[60] Millican also made a strong case that many of MARTA's most enthusiastic supporters did not understand the future financial obligations totaling more than a half billion dollars to which they were committing the region's residents. He charged that not one government official in Metropolitan Atlanta had read the entire 116-page MARTA proposal, a claim that referendum supporters left largely unrebuked.[61]

Anger with the rapid-transit system's proposed funding

mechanism and the appeal of Millican's critiques of the MARTA proposal were not the only reason that the majority of white, particularly suburban, voters opposed the referendum. Locally and nationally, the cultural politics of 1968 were quite different from those of 1965, the year that voters agreed to form MARTA. In the context of Metropolitan Atlanta, the divide between the city's increasingly politically assertive near-majority Black population and the regional suburban white supermajority had become far more pronounced. A cluster of events and policy controversies with local and national consequences, including urban riots, the white voter backlash of 1966, the death of Martin Luther King Jr., the enactment of new federal housing legislation, and the prospect of court-mandated busing all made the issue of race a more conspicuous concern in the debates over many public policies, including the MARTA referendum. By the time of the November 1968 vote, a significant percentage of suburban residents regarded institutional associations between their community and Atlanta proper as a threat to their wellbeing. Rather than a means of commuting downtown, the rail system came to be seen by a majority of suburban residents as a conduit for crime, school desegregation, and housing integration.[62]

While the opposition of many suburban voters and the elements of the Maddox coalition that remained in Atlanta imperiled the MARTA referendum, it was the significant Black opposition to the proposal that doomed the November 1968 vote. Atlanta's Black voters and leadership saw the proposed rail system for what it was: a rapid-transit system designed to accommodate white commuters. Atlanta Life Insurance Company CEO Jesse Hill Jr., then the most prominent Black member of the Atlanta Chamber, predicted in 1966 that most Black voters would oppose the measure due to the lack of input that prospective Black riders had been given in planning a system that excluded significant sections of the city.

Widespread Black institutional and popular opposition to the proposed rapid-transit system became evident in late 1966 when the typically pro-Allen ASLC came out against the plan. It demanded an extension of the service into more Black neighborhoods, specifically the city's entirely unserved westside and the Model Cities neighborhoods in Southeast Atlanta. The ASLC demanded guarantees not only of nondiscrimination in employment but also that Blacks would receive a demographically proportional number of new MARTA jobs, as civil rights groups in other cities had started seeking.[63]

MARTA tried to negotiate a settlement with the ASLC to ensure Black support for the referendum. MARTA officials promised African American leaders they would enact an affirmative action program for recruiting and job training but refused to extend the western or southern terminus of its rapid-rail plans, arguing that such an expansion would lead to hundreds of millions of dollars in additional expenses.[64] MARTA's unwillingness to provide more African Americans with access to the service led the ASLC to continue to withhold its endorsement. The Black leadership's new willingness to challenge the white leadership's plans for the city was a product not only of increasing Black electoral power but also a skepticism that grew out of their experiences with urban renewal, a similarly comprehensive civic program pushed by the white establishment.

On November 6, 1968, Atlanta, Fulton County, and DeKalb County voted decisively against the rapid-transit referendum, serving up a stunning political blow to the civic establishment.[65] Through the 1968 MARTA vote, the suburban electoral majority demonstrated that it was in no way beholden to the aspirations of Atlanta's governing elite. Simultaneously, the defeat demonstrated the political strength of Atlanta's emerging Black electoral majority. No longer conjoined to the white leadership for political advancement, Black leaders and their constituents showed a new willingness to break their coalition with the city's business elite.

The results of the 1968 referendum convinced Atlanta's civic elites that they could no longer expect Black voters to simply rubber-stamp their prescriptions on major civic projects. The emerging Black electoral majority provided the city's newly assertive Black political leadership with unprecedented leverage to negotiate the terms of major civic projects in ways that offered greater benefits to their constituents. In the case of MARTA, the city's Black leadership leveraged the board's need for Black votes in a subsequent referendum into concessions that included expanded access to the service in predominately African American neighborhoods, guarantees of fixed-affordable fares, and the implementation of hiring quotas that required MARTA to provide African Americans with a representative proportion of the temporary and permanent jobs created by the construction and execution of the system.[66]

While the Allen Administration made significant progress during its final years in reformulating MARTA's mission into an electorally feasible program, it was the work of his successor Sam Massell that secured the passage of the second MARTA rapid-transit referendum in November 1971. Massell took the lead in shaping a new rapid-transit financing plan and played a highly visible role in promoting the second referendum's passage.[67] He brokered a deal between the city's white and Black leadership on the funding mechanism for the second rapid-transit referendum. The deal was predicated on the new legislative support that rapid transit enjoyed in the State House. In March 1971, new Governor Jimmy Carter signed a bill authorizing a new funding mechanism for MARTA: a ten-year, 1 percent local sales tax in the counties that voted to join the system. Pro-MARTA legislators approved the new funding mechanism in an effort to win over property-tax-leery homeowners. Instead, the new law threatened to turn still-skeptical Black leaders against the 1971 referendum. Black state legislators favored a local income tax to fund rapid transit instead of the sales-tax proposal, which they regarded as regressive. Massell responded to the legislation by working with MARTA officials to revise their proposal once again to win Black support. He convinced the board to offer patrons on city buses a fare reduction from forty cents to fifteen cents for the first seven years after it purchased the ATC. This trade-off would guarantee Atlanta bus riders the nation's lowest fare, winning over virtually all of the city's Black leadership for the 1971 referendum. Before the sales-tax controversy, most Black leaders had already been inclined to support the 1971 referendum, which provided much greater access to their constituents on the east and west sides than the 1968 proposal.[68]

ASLC sponsored a get-out-the-vote campaign among its member organizations on behalf of the referendum. The *Daily World*, which opposed the 1968 plan, endorsed the 1971 proposal because of the cheaper fare and the institutional power newly asserted by Black leaders in MARTA. Atlanta's two largest Black denominational organizations, the African Methodist-Episcopal (AME) Ministers Union and the Baptist Ministers Union, charged their members with cultivating support for the referendum. Citing their opposition to the sales tax, the SCLC's Operation Breadbasket was the only major Black Atlanta institution to oppose the referendum.[69] Massell, too, put on the hard sell in the weeks before the referendum, cajoling commuters from a loudspeaker on a hovering helicopter to support MARTA: "If you want to get out of this mess, vote yes!" he yelled from on high. He rode ATC buses around the city each morning to encourage the existing patrons of mass transit to get out to vote for its extension.[70]

The Committee for Sensible Rapid Transit, the rechristened Atlanta Chamber–backed "yes" organization, commissioned a far more visceral collection of advertisements than its 1968 predecessor. Its full-page "Will Atlanta Be the Next Traffic Fatality?" advertisement highlighted its print campaign. Featuring an image of rush-hour traffic on the Downtown Connector, the advertisement combined striking statistics with clear, concise arguments for the system. "Last year 271 residents of the Metro area died in traffic accidents," one version of the advertisement read, roughly as many people as had died in homicides in 1971 in the city of Atlanta. This irony was not lost on the pro-referendum committee, which realized that suburbanites who avoided the city out of a fear of crime were subjecting themselves to comparable dangers every day on the region's roadways.[71]

Just like in 1968, pro-referendum groups heavily outspent the plan's opponents.[72] Few elected officials in any of the affected jurisdictions expressed opposition to the proposal. All but three Atlanta City councilors and majorities on all four county commissions endorsed the plan.[73] Everett Millican again figured prominently in the debate, covering similar terrain in the anti-referendum advertisements he once again bankrolled.[74] Superseding Millican on the "no" side was attorney and businessman Moreton Rolleston Jr., a staunch segregationist who joined Lester Maddox in challenging the legality of the 1964 Civil Rights Act. Rolleston published his own series of far more racially pointed anti-referendum advertisements. He feared that a large metropolitan transit system would spread the inner-city's pathologies throughout the region, turning Atlanta into "another city like New York," a massive, interconnected metropolis that decanted its problems over a vast territory. Rolleston questioned the safety of the system, considering inner-city Atlanta's exploding violent crime rate. Rolleston focused heavily on the temporarily reduced bus fare in his advertisements. "Who will pay for MARTA? Certainly not the passengers who use it at a $.15 fare. Practically all of the expenses will be paid by those who do not use the system," one of Rolleston's advertisements read. Rolleston characterized the fifteen-cent fare as "another free ride on your tax dollars."[75]

For many voters, whether suburban or urban, race served as the prism through which they viewed the 1971 referendum vote, arguably to a greater extent than even in 1968. Polls conducted in the weeks before the vote indicated that a fear of crime spreading from the inner city and fears that MARTA would be used to facilitate residential and school integration were the most important factors determining suburban white voters' views on the referendum. Moreover, many suburban voters expressed anger that they were being asked to pay for a system they had no intention of using. Conversely, Black voters who continued to oppose the rapid-transit plan believed that the system, even in its reformed version, was designed primarily for white patrons. Many Black opponents of MAR-TA's plan feared that they would be displaced by rapid transit construction, just as tens of thousands of African Americans had been as a result of urban renewal.[76]

The 1971 rapid-transit referendum passed narrowly in Fulton (including Atlanta) and DeKalb Counties, which was legally sufficient for MARTA to begin construction. Voters in Gwinnett and Clayton Counties both rejected the referendum by margins of more than four to one. In Fulton County, the referendum passed by a mere 461 of the 110,000 votes cast, while 52 percent of DeKalb County voters supported the referendum. Black and white residents of the city of Atlanta supported the referendum at nearly equal percentages: 54.8 and 54.7 percent, respectively, just enough to overcome strong suburban opposition. Demonstrating their traditional sense of civic trusteeship, Atlanta's affluent northside voted heavily for the measure. Conversely, the most impoverished, predominately Black sections of the city opposed the referendum, confirming their continued mistrust of the plan and its proponents. Fearing an influx of underclass Black residents from the inner city, a majority of white and Black middle-class homeowners in southern DeKalb County voted against the referendum. Strong support for the measure in affluent, predominately white sections of northern DeKalb ensured the referendum's passage in the county.[77]

The passage of the 1971 referendum proved an immediate boon to Black employment and affordable transportation in the metropolitan area. MARTA's minority job training, affirmative action, and construction-contract-preference programs ensured that nearly 88 percent of the new employees hired by the authority in the year after the referendum were

African American. Most new employees became bus drivers once MARTA completed its voter-approved purchase of ATC in early 1972. By the end of 1973, the percentage of Black bus drivers in Atlanta doubled to nearly 40 percent.[78] New MARTA express bus routes provided residents of Black neighborhoods with expanded access to jobs in outlying industrial parks, hospitals, and shopping centers.[79] Even as cost overruns forced MARTA to increase the project's estimated price from $1.32 billion to $1.8 billion, the board refused to consider ending the cheapest-in-the-nation fifteen-cent fare, knowing that the core constituency of the project supported it in large part because of the fare.[80]

Construction began on the MARTA rapid transit rail in 1975 with service commencing on June 30, 1979. The Jackson administration used its clout in MARTA to push successfully for the opening of the east-west line that served primarily Black neighborhoods before the opening of the commuter-oriented north-south line, which had been the system planner's original purpose for proposing metropolitan rail transit. Although the north-south line opened less than two years after the east-west line, the prioritization of the east-west line reinforced the idea among suburban whites that MARTA rail service was a Black space no different from the city buses that white commuters had all but abandoned. Many suburban residents pointed to MARTA's failure to expand to the airport, one of the primary potential uses of the system by commuters, until 1988, as further proof of the system's focus on its Black ridership. The adoption by many metropolitan-area residents of the racially charged MARTA sobriquet "Moving Africans Rapidly Through Atlanta" most clearly expressed this sentiment.[81]

Ever so briefly, a wide swath of the region's residents regarded MARTA as a source of pride and prestige. Its sleek, clean cars, closed-circuit monitored stations, and upholstered seats counted as a luxurious urban amenity in the minds of many citizens who never used the system. In their early years, MARTA's trains remained vandalism-free relative to their competitors in other cities.[82] By the mid-1980s, a noticeable increase in vandalism and a series of high-profile violent crimes in and around MARTA trains and stations further unnerved a suburban public already inclined to regard the system as unsafe. MARTA leaders disputed claims that their system was unsafe, pointing out that the vast majority of patrons on the fifty-five million annual trips taken on its rails each year were not subjected to violent crime. In 1985, for example, MARTA police statistics cited forty-three armed robberies and thirty-three aggravated assaults within the confines of the system, a number that many in the public did not regard nearly as offhandedly as the authority's leadership. Critics said the statistics were misleading, since people spent so little of their day on the trains. Moreover, they accused MARTA police of manipulating their crime statistics, reclassifying violent offenses to make them seem either less serious or erasing the crime entirely by deeming it as off MARTA property.[83]

MARTA failed to alleviate sprawl in the Atlanta area or to become a comprehensive, metropolitan-wide system.[84] Moreover, it has spent much of the last thirty years on the verge of financial collapse. Deep cutbacks in federal support beginning in the late 1980s placed the system in a state of perpetual financial peril.[85] Suburbanites who asserted their political autonomy in voting against the MARTA referendums continued to vote with their feet against the transit system. Metropolitan Atlanta continued to sprawl outward even after MARTA rail service commenced in 1979. By the mid-1980s, commuters in the region averaged more than thirty miles driven each workday, more than any city in the United States. Atlanta-area drivers in the early 1980s traversed a highway system that had more than quadrupled its capacity since the end of World War II and was more crowded than ever, with morning and afternoon commutes that vacillated between standstills and breakneck jockeying for position well above the speed limit.[86]

During the 1970s and 1980s, corporate transplants from across the country filled Cobb, Gwinnett, and northern DeKalb counties with more than a half-million new residents, creating a housing boom of unprecedented scale in the region. The new residents of these counties were resolutely automobile commuters. They resisted any proposed expansion of MARTA with equal vociferousness as their predecessors in the suburbs.[87] Cobb County Commissioner Emmett Burton promised to "stock the Chatahoochee with piranha" if that were necessary to keep MARTA away.[88] On several occasions during the 1980s, blue-ribbon panels proposed the expansion of MARTA into Clayton, Gwinnett, and Cobb Counties, but the residents of these jurisdictions voted heavily against any proposal to expand the service into their communities.[89]

Since the passage of the 1971 referendum, downtown developers, most notably Tom Cousins and John Portman, thought that the rail system would help Atlanta create clusters of high-rise development and vitality around the stations, luring upscale residents and consumers back into the center city.[90] Certainly, some MARTA stations became hubs for burgeoning, high-density development, most notably the corporate-headquarters boom near the Midtown station and the emergence of Buckhead as an upscale commercial center around the Lenox Square station. The vast majority of development in Metropolitan Atlanta, though, continued to take place in its ever-expanding suburbs, far beyond the reach of public-transit-dependent job seekers in the center city. MARTA had been envisioned as a means of moving commuters efficiently in and out of downtown Atlanta. By the late 1980s, it had become primarily the domain of out-of-town conventioneers and the urban poor.[91]

15

Probably Room for Basketball

....

"WE WERE A CLOSE-KNIT TEAM, WHICH MADE US A TOUGH team," Coach Richie Guerin said of his Hawks club that arrived in Atlanta in 1968.[1] The Atlanta Hawks took the floor in October 1968 as the defending NBA Western Division champions. During their first two years in Atlanta, they performed like defending champions. In 1968–69 and 1969–70, they posted consecutive 48–34 seasons, finishing second in the division to Los Angeles the first year and finishing first in their second, just beating out the Lakers. Despite the trade of team captain Lenny Wilkens days before their October 1968 home opener, the core of the latter-day St. Louis roster remained in place: quick, physical forwards Bill Bridges, Joe Caldwell, and Paul Silas; offensive-minded center Zelmo Beaty; and twenty-four-year-old guard "Sweet Lou" Hudson, who was emerging as one of the league's top scorers.

The Hawks wore out opponents with their trademark aggressive, up-tempo style of basketball that carried over from St. Louis. They were among the league leaders in assists and points in the paint. Hudson, Caldwell, and Bridges were each named to the All-Star Team. Caldwell and Bridges also earned NBA All-Defensive Team nods, while Hudson finished in the top fifteen in scoring both seasons. The Hawks reached the Western Division finals in 1968–69 and 1969–70, losing both times to the Lakers. Atlanta just could not get past a Los Angeles team that included three of the greatest players in NBA history: Elgin Baylor, Jerry West, and Wilt Chamberlain.[2]

Some sportswriters attributed the Hawks' playoff failure to its predominately African American roster. In columns laden with garden-variety racial stereotypes, a number of basketball writers characterized the Hawks as uniquely unable to deliver in high-pressure situations. If the Hawks wanted to win a championship, the logic went, they needed to rebuild their roster, presumably around a white star and on-court leader. The emergence of this idea among basketball authorities dovetailed with the sentiments of the Hawks new ownership, which had sought from day one to acquire a prominent white and preferably southern player to foster local interest in the team.[3]

Despite their championship-caliber performance, the Hawks barely drew the public's notice during their inaugural seasons in Atlanta. Postseason attendance at Georgia Tech's Alexander Memorial Coliseum topped five thousand just once during the Hawks' consecutive runs to the Western Division Finals. It hadn't been any better in the regular season. Low attendance at Alexander was an immediate and consistent problem. The Hawks drew a mere 4,474 spectators per game in 1968–69, 30 percent fewer fans than their worst season in St. Louis. In 1969–70 the Hawks again failed to match their lowest St. Louis attendance figure, drawing an average attendance of 5,210. Only two of the NBA's fourteen teams drew fewer fans than the Hawks that season. Even as attendance waned in their later seasons in St. Louis, the Hawks drew, at their worst, an average of 6,288 spectators per game. The franchise had enjoyed boisterous support in St. Louis from a largely urban, blue-collar, white, and male fanbase, demographics that characterized most early NBA spectators. The crowds at Kiel Auditorium were always loud and often rough-and-tumble. No comparable fanbase emerged for the Atlanta Hawks: Black or white, blue collar or white collar, urban or suburban. It was not until the Atlanta Hawks moved into the Omni for the 1972–73 season that their average game attendance finally surpassed the franchise's worst figure in Missouri.[4]

"In general, I thought the fans in Atlanta were a lot more blasé about basketball. I grew up in the Midwest, and I was used to basketball being number one," former Hawks guard Tom Van Arsdale said of the team's local support. "I just felt like Atlanta's priorities were football, especially college football, baseball, and then basketball. There wasn't nearly as much enthusiasm for the sport there as I was used to." Van Arsdale, who played for five NBA teams, said Atlanta was the least favorite stop in his career. "I never felt like I was a part of the city."[5]

Atlanta's blasé attitude toward basketball started at the top. "I'd never even seen a pro basketball game myself. The only guy I'd ever heard of was Wilt Chamberlain," Tom Cousins said in 1977 when discussing his decade of involvement in the NBA in a *Sports Illustrated* interview.[6] Despite his lack of knowledge of professional basketball, Cousins paid Ben Kerner $3.5 million to become the majority owner of the Hawks in May 1968. Cousins had been a lifelong participant and spectator of sports, but he was not a typical gentleman-sportsman like the Falcons' owner Rankin Smith or the Rover Boys, the Braves' ownership group. Buying a professional sports franchise was not an extravagant diversion or a pleasurable side business for him. Instead, Cousins was a real estate developer who got involved with sports because he wanted to build a "Madison Square Garden type arena" in downtown Atlanta.[7] In the late 1960s, Cousins left the day-to-day operation of the club to GM Marty Blake and Coach Richie Guerin. The developer's primary concern was that the Hawks' stay at Georgia Tech be short-lived.[8]

The day after the Georgia Tech Board of Regents approved a temporary lease for the Hawks at Alexander, NBA owners met in New York to ratify the sale and relocation of the franchise. They voted unanimously on May 7, 1968, to approve the sale of the team to Cousins and Sanders and endorsed the Hawks' transfer to Atlanta.[9] Even with an agreement in place, NBA owners had their misgivings about Alexander, which many basketball insiders regarded as the league's worst building. Longtime GM Marty Blake suggested in an interview two decades after the Hawks' move to Atlanta that the NBA's approval of the franchise's relocation was more an expression of their loyalty to Kerner than an endorsement of Alexander Memorial Coliseum. "There was no way the NBA should have approved the Hawks playing at Georgia Tech," Blake said. "The Tech people were great to us and very gracious. But it was a bad building. It had terrible locker rooms and only seated about 7,200. The league wouldn't have approved it, but Benny Kerner was one of the pioneers of pro basketball, and the league people wanted to see him get out of the business with some money."[10]

The Hawks ended up playing at Alexander for their first four seasons in the NBA (1968–72), far longer than Cousins had anticipated. Alexander's seating capacity was the smallest in the NBA, even smaller than the Hawks' home court in St. Louis, the Kiel Auditorium. The poor conditions and small seating capacity at Alexander proved to be a major impediment to the Hawks' financial success in Atlanta. Fans and players alike found Alexander dark and dingy. Spectators complained that an evening spent on Alexander's wooden slat bleachers left them sore for days. Players said the floor was covered in dead spots and griped that their dressing room was more suitable for a junior varsity basketball team. Though located on the Northside, affluent consumers who might have found the arena's location more enticing than a downtown venue were deterred from attending by Alexander's dearth of convenient parking spaces. Those in search of nearby public transportation were similarly out of luck.[11]

Alexander's deficiencies were evident immediately. During the Hawks' home debut on October 16, 1968, rainwater dripped from the ceiling into the stands and, more dangerously, onto the floor. Officials stopped play more than a dozen times to mop up the slippery playing surface. The conditions at Alexander on opening night did little to encourage the 5,606 attendees to become regulars. The sparse attendance that evening was at least as embarrassing to the Hawks leadership as the dripping ceiling. Nearly two thousand seats remained empty for the team's Atlanta debut. As humiliating as the team's leadership found the opening-night box office, the crowd proved to be one of the largest of the season.[12]

The Hawks' inability to draw stemmed from more than just the uninviting environs of Alexander. The franchise's failure in its early years to find an audience in Atlanta was in no small part a product of the sudden glut in the city's sports market. The Hawks were the third Major League team to arrive in the city in three years. They played a sport that was familiar to the locals but was hardly a widespread passion. To their chagrin, the term *oversportsed*, a descriptor for the region's sudden saturation with professional teams, emerged in the local parlance soon after the Hawks' arrival.[13] The sudden arrival of the Hawks had astonished Atlanta sports fans. After two seasons of futility by the Falcons and underachievement by the Braves, Atlanta was home to a winning team, a defending divisional champion, all thanks to the clandestine efforts of two of its leading citizens. Talk of a new downtown arena added another layer of suspense to the unexpected revelation. Sports fans interviewed by *Constitution* reporters near the paper's downtown office on the day of the announcement expressed a mix of surprise and near pessimism about the Hawks' prospects in Atlanta.

Judging from their occupations as well as their perceptions of the team and its chances for success in Atlanta, the interviewees were most likely suburbanites who commuted into the city for work, just the people the Hawks regarded as their potential ticket buyers. Joe Patrick, a sales representative at a bank supply company, said "I think Atlanta is a football town, but there's probably room for basketball too and I believe it will do alright here whether or not I go." Insurance agency president John Maher said that most of his friends preferred participatory outdoor sports, but "the fishermen, gardeners, automobile and boat enthusiasts will have time on their hands in the cold winter and pro basketball should pull some of them in."

Fellow insurance man William C. Fox questioned whether or not Atlantans would support the Hawks. "I don't think basketball would go well at all except with a first class team," he said. "I think too, that they will need to acquire Southern ball players. They'll have to have a local image," Fox said, mirroring the attitudes of St. Louis basketball fans who shunned the Hawks when their roster ceased to look like their spectators. Moreover, Fox said, "They'll have to be in a first class location with first class parking," unlike, by inference, Atlanta Stadium, which stood in close proximity to some of the city's poorest and most high-crime neighborhoods and lacked sufficient on-site parking to host all of its customers for well-attended events. Alexander, with its lack of parking, would also not meet Mr. Fox's requirements.[14]

The Hawks' owners viewed the team's prospects in Atlanta far more optimistically. They believed a championship-caliber team would garner a substantial share of Atlanta sports fans' discretionary income. "I don't believe the Atlanta sports dollar is being stretched too thin," Carl Sanders said at the team's introductory press conference. Nor did he think there would be any problems "promoting a sport dominated by Negroes" in the Deep South. "I don't think color will make a difference to fans. That time is past in the South. As long as they're good, clean athletes and play a good brand of ball, the fans will support them," he said.[15]

In an interview with the *Constitution*'s Pat Zier, Sanders said the Hawks would try to acquire local and regional players whenever possible. The former governor made it clear that *regional players* was a euphemism for *white players* when he made specific reference to pursuing Pete Maravich, LSU's standout shooting guard who had just broken national scoring records as a sophomore, two basketball seasons before NBA rules allowed him to declare for the league's annual draft. The southern bona fides of Maravich, the grandson of Serbian immigrants who spent much of his childhood in Aliquippa, Pennsylvania, were questionable. He moved to the South as a nine-year-old when his father Petar "Press" Maravich became the head basketball coach at Clemson University. By comparison, current Atlanta Hawks Zelmo Beaty and Paul Silas, natives of Texas and Arkansas respectively, fit the bill of regional players far more than Maravich, but the LSU guard's status as the nation's best-known white collegiate player made him the ideal target for a southern team in search of a face for its franchise.[16]

Fear that white southerners would not embrace a predominately Black team were common among the Hawks roster. Several players expressed their reticence about playing in Georgia. Team captain Lenny Wilkens, who was traded before playing a game in Atlanta, doubted he would be able to secure a good off-season job like he had in St. Louis. Bill Bridges expressed similar economic fears and predicted that the Hawks' all-Black starting lineup would not draw well in Dixie. Prairie View, Texas, native Zelmo Beaty demonstrated his nuanced understanding of the region's racial dynamics when he stated that the intimacy of live basketball would transgress southern cultural taboos. "I never had any doubt that the south was ready for professional football. I just hope it's ready for basketball. This racial thing, of course, is what I refer to. People are up so close to the court that they get to know the players almost, every little mannerism," he said, describing the proximity of the game's predominately Black performers to its predominately white audience.[17]

"This racial thing" that Beaty referred to, namely a discomfort among whites toward social intimacy with African American athletes, was the core of the Hawks' main public-relations problem—the team's lack of a marketable face. Despite their on-court success, the Hawks' all-Black starting five was a difficult lineup to promote to the white, suburban fans the team's owners expected to patronize their games. As a result, the Hawks organization did little to present the players on their predominately Black roster as the face of their franchise.

Hawks' coach Richie Guerin, a mid-century, Bronx wiseguy straight from central casting, was himself a less-than-ideal ambassador to the Atlanta public, far more foreign to the sensibilities of Georgians than the Hawks' African American players. Paterson, New Jersey–born GM Marty Blake was cut from the same cloth as Guerin. Both Guerin and Blake were simply too blunt and confrontational to function as ambassadors for their game in the Southeast. The Atlanta papers spent the spring and summer of 1968 touting the city's new NBA team, but early ticket sales were slow, and local broadcast media made only a modest commitment to the team. WSB agreed to televise an eight-game slate for the 1968–69 season while broadcasting the full schedule on its radio station.[18]

Many contemporary observers attributed the Hawks' poor attendance to an unwillingness among the region's white majority to embrace the team's predominately Black roster. At the time the Hawks debuted in Atlanta, approximately half of the NBA's players were African American, while every noteworthy player on the Hawks roster was Black.[19] Comments by local sports fans suggesting that the team needed to acquire southern players or a local image are certainly indicative of this. Yet Atlantans' unwillingness to embrace their city's predominately Black NBA team was not unique. The entire league struggled with attendance throughout the late 1960s and 1970s in part because many white fans responded negatively to the NBA's demographic transformation. The growing aversion of white fans to the predominately Black NBA by the mid-1970s proved more debilitating to Atlanta's franchise than to clubs in most other NBA cities, many of which were located in regions with long histories as basketball hotbeds. Moreover, as the NBA's first southern outpost, Atlanta was the only league city that had recently enforced legally mandated segregation.[20]

Rarely did Atlantans acknowledge publicly that their lack of interest in the Hawks had a racial component. *Daily World* columnist James Heath overheard a man at an early Hawks game saying, "I'm going to tell Governor Lester Maddox about this and see if he can't get some white boys on the team," but the Black sportswriter said that he rarely heard people expressing such ideas within his earshot. Nevertheless, the perception that Atlanta needed a prominent white, preferably southern player to draw large crowds quickly became the common sense both inside and outside the Hawks' organization.[21]

In their early years, the Hawks tried to sell Atlantans on professional basketball by contrasting the team with the poor performing Braves and Falcons. The franchise presented itself, quite legitimately, as an immediate contender for the NBA championship, but this failed to sell many advance season tickets.[22] When the opportunity to see a winner failed to fill up Alexander, the team started focusing its promotional campaigns on the Hawks' opponents, presenting their game as an opportunity to see NBA superstars such as Oscar Robertson and Wilt Chamberlain. Implicit in this strategy was the understanding that Atlantans were not inclined to become consistent patrons of their product but might go out of their way to witness a novel entertainment experience. The Hawks organization, therefore, was expecting a predominately white consumer base (that was unwilling to support its own team's Black stars) to buy tickets to see the better-known Black stars on other clubs. Not surprisingly, this strategy failed.[23]

The Hawks entered their first season in Atlanta in an already precarious financial position. The club had an extremely wealthy owner in Tom Cousins, but his plans to invest in a downtown arena, which would be the starting point for a much larger mixed-usage complex, left him with limited resources to invest in the basketball franchise. Simultaneously, the Hawks' local media revenue and prospective gate revenue from Alexander were well below the league average. Television money from the league's national broadcasting contract with ABC hardly made up for the Hawks' deficiencies in its other revenue streams. In the late 1960s NBA franchises received modest national television revenues of less than $100,000 each from ABC, hardly enough money to pay the average annual salary of even one of the league's elite players.[24]

The demolition of the Hawks' championship-caliber team began amid its triumphs of the late 1960s. By the summer of 1970, Atlanta's roster was significantly different and weaker than it had been when the team arrived in Georgia two years earlier. Contract disputes that pitted Blake and Guerin against Lenny Wilkens, Zelmo Beaty, and Joe Caldwell led to the departure of three of the team's most prominent players in less than twenty months. St. Louis team leader Lenny Wilkens, a thirty-three-year-old point guard who had finished second in MVP balloting in 1967–68, refused to report to the club's 1968 training camp unless he received a pay increase. Wilkens sought out an annual raise from $30,000 to $60,000, which would have made him the team's highest paid player but still would have reaped him less than one-quarter as much as league MVP Wilt Chamberlain. Team management balked at signing an aging player to so lucrative a contract and instead traded him to Seattle. Similar contract disputes led to the departures of All-Stars Beaty and Caldwell after the 1969 and 1970 seasons, respectively. Both players accepted offers from the rival ABA, which more than doubled their salaries.[25]

The Hawks would soon choose to rebuild around a white star with regional appeal, Pete Maravich, whom they acquired by trading up in the 1970 NBA Draft. Atlanta made him the highest-paid player in the history of professional basketball. In the short term, it increased the Hawks' local and national profile considerably. In the long run, the move would prove disastrous for the fortunes of the franchise, both on the court and at the box office.

16

The Logical Choice

....

AN ARTICLE PUBLISHED IN THE *JOURNAL* THE WEEK AFTER the announcement of the Hawks' relocation ruminated on the possibility of Tom Cousins acquiring a hockey franchise. This prospective hockey team would join his basketball team in his yet-to-be planned, financed, approved, or built coliseum. Cousins helped create the story. Frequently, he mentioned the possibility of bringing professional hockey to Atlanta when discussing his plans for an arena.[1] Cousins later said that he considered a hockey team essential to the success of the downtown venue because he needed to "keep the Coliseum busy practically every day to make a financially sound venture."[2]

Investment in an arena created an incentive for Cousins to bring another sports franchise to Atlanta. Whereas Cousins believed that the acquisition of an NHL team would contribute to the financial stability of his planned arena, adding another professional franchise to the city's roster so quickly threatened to further saturate Atlanta's suddenly crowded sports market. In May 1965 Atlanta had no major professional sports franchises. By May 1968, one of Atlanta's leading entrepreneurs was trying to land the city its fourth franchise.

As the prospective proprietor of a downtown arena, Cousins found himself in an odd position. Historically, most North American arena operators adding a second franchise to their lineup acquired a professional basketball team to support their already established hockey club. The desire of northeastern and midwestern arena operators, many of whom owned NHL or profitable minor league hockey franchises, to lock up additional dates on their winter calendars played an important role in the formation of the NBA in the late 1940s. Cousins was one of a number of arena operators in nontraditional hockey markets during the late 1960s and early 1970s who found themselves in the inverse position.

Beyond the financial requirements of owning a club, Cousins had the problem of finding an NHL team to acquire. The *Journal*'s Bob Hertzel had looked into the realities of obtaining a hockey franchise and concluded in May 1968 that "the only way Atlanta can obtain a National Hockey League team in less than five years—indoor arena or not—is to purchase an established franchise." "We've just had a big expansion," NHL Commissioner Clarence Campbell told Hertzel, referring to the league's six-team expansion in 1967, which doubled the number of franchises in hockey's top professional league to twelve. "We have to give ourselves a chance to digest that expansion before we consider expanding again," Campbell said.[3]

The NHL commissioner estimated that it would be at least five years before the league considered adding any more franchises. Less than a year after Campbell made his prediction, the league's Board of Governors voted again to expand. NHL owners who had profited from the $2 million in expansion fees paid by each of the 1967 expansion teams lobbied successfully for another influx of capital. The NHL approved expansion franchises for the 1970–71 seasons in the hockey-mad markets of Vancouver and Buffalo, where ownership groups each paid $6 million to join the league. Investors in more than two dozen cities had sought out a franchise, including Cousins in Atlanta. Bob Hertzel of the *Journal*, reacting to the NHL's decision to pass over Atlanta for more traditional hockey towns in its 1970 expansion, assured readers that the "absence of a coliseum appeared the only detour in professional hockey's cruise onto the bustling Atlanta sports scene."[4]

Hertzel's assertion that Atlanta was one detour away from being an ideal market for hockey expansion sounded as unbelievable then as it does now. Beyond its lack of a playing facility and the NHL's proclaimed hesitance to expand any further, the Atlanta of 1968 seemed about as unsuitable a home for professional hockey as one could imagine in the continental United States. Atlanta did not have a permanent ice rink, let alone a hockey arena. The state of Georgia had never been home to a high school or college hockey team. The closest city to ever host a professional hockey team was two hundred miles away in Knoxville, Tennessee. Formed in 1961, the Knoxville Knights of the Eastern Hockey League were in the process of disbanding in the spring of 1968. Hockey did not make regular appearances on any Georgia television stations until late in 1969 when WAGA-TV, Atlanta's CBS affiliate, started showing an NHL game of the week.[5]

The plausibility of Atlanta adding a professional hockey franchise increased considerably in September 1971 with the launching of the World Hockey Association (WHA), a well-financed rival professional hockey league scheduled to begin play the following autumn. At their inaugural press conference, WHA founders Dennis Murphy and Gary Davidson, the pair who four years earlier had created the ABA, announced that they were seeking out investors to form a ten-team North American hockey league. The WHA considered both traditional and nontraditional hockey markets as locations for its franchises, including Atlanta. In the lead-up to the November 1971 announcement of the ten original WHA cities, sportswriters in Atlanta and hockey writers across the nation speculated that Cousins would receive one of the bids. The WHA surprised many hockey insiders by passing over Atlanta, its well-heeled owner, and the new coliseum that Atlanta broke ground on seven months earlier.

Instead, the WHA awarded its first southern franchise to Miami on the assumption that its large population of retired snowbirds from the Northeast and Canada would support the team. This proved to be the first of numerous failed attempts by investors to establish the sport in Florida. Many fortunes have been lost in the Sunshine State based on the belief that a rabid core of seasonally residing hockey aficionados wants to spend their discretionary income on sitting inside a cold arena. Professional hockey's first pass in Florida did not even get to the cold arena part. The fundamental problem faced by the Miami WHA franchise was its lack of a playing facility. Like Atlanta, the Florida city lacked a permanent ice rink. Unlike Atlanta, Miami had yet to break ground on a hockey arena. Unable to win local approval for a privately financed arena, the Miami WHA franchise relocated to Philadelphia in 1972 before ever playing a game.[6]

WHA founder Dennis Murphy said after the announcement of the league's first ten franchises that Atlanta's standing bid would receive strong consideration for one of the two additional spots in the WHA the league planned to announce in early 1972. Bob Cousins, Tom's brother, the president of the Atlanta Hawks, and a major player in all his downtown ventures, expressed his preference for a WHA club to an NHL one the day after the new league announced its charter members. "We are a bit uneasy as to what our chances for a winner would be in that league," Cousins said of the NHL. "Expansion clubs don't do very well. In the WHA, all the teams would be starting out on the same footing and our chances of a championship the very first season would be as good as anyone's," he said.[7] Moreover, any potential NHL expansion team in the coming seasons would be forced to build its roster from a far more diluted talent pool. Competition from the WHA's twelve franchises for available professional players would make it even harder for an NHL expansion team to produce a competitive club. Despite Bob Cousins's protestations, the NHL and the Cousins group came to an agreement to place a franchise in Atlanta for the 1972–73 season, less than ten days after the WHA passed on the city.

The advent of professional hockey in Atlanta was a marriage of convenience between the NHL and Cousins. The developer wanted a hockey team to fill up dates on the winter calendar of his new arena. The NHL wanted to keep the WHA out of large, affluent North American markets like Atlanta. Non-traditional hockey markets from Los Angeles to Phoenix to Houston to Atlanta landed franchises in either the WHA or the NHL during the 1970s as a result of the game of Risk the competing leagues played across the North American continent, seizing territory for the sake of seizing territory with little concern for the prospective city's history, culture, or climate. The fifty-five-year-old NHL, which had grown from six to fourteen members in less than five years, tried to maintain its preeminence in professional hockey by "squash[ing] the bugs scurrying along the tidy floor," in the words of WHA historian Ed Willes.[8] More specifically, granting Atlanta a franchise blocked the WHA from access to Cousins' money and his state-of-the-art arena.

In May 1968, the NHL's leadership told Atlanta it would be years before they would consider another expansion, especially to a non-hockey-playing market. Less than three years later in January 1971, NHL Finance Committee chairman William M. Jennings said Atlanta was the "logical choice" among several southern cities seeking out a franchise, a statement that seemed equally unbelievable for its perspective on Atlanta as a hockey market and the statement that a handful of cities in Dixie wanted hockey teams. Cousins's continued eagerness to procure a hockey franchise and the impending groundbreaking for the Omni Coliseum counted foremost among a number of promising signs from the Atlanta market, Jennings said.[9] Moreover, Cousins was a known commodity to many NHL owners. The half-dozen NBA franchise owners who also owned NHL clubs got to know Tom Cousins as the owner of the Hawks and found him to be an understated, steady, consensus-building presence in the league.[10]

Weekly broadcasts of NHL games that began late in 1969 on WAGA-TV had been drawing increasingly impressive ratings, demonstrating a new local interest in the sport. WAGA Station Manager Jim Ferguson said that during the 1970–71 season as many as seventy thousand Atlanta-area households watched their winter afternoon hockey broadcasts.[11] Jennings went on to cite a study commissioned by Cousins that found that as many Atlantans wanted to watch professional hockey as wanted to watch professional basketball. "The people there are very cosmopolitan. It's not a sleepy city of the old South," he said of Atlanta and its residents.[12]

Additionally, the NHL coveted Atlanta's television market, which was the gateway to the broader southeastern United States television market. A foothold in the Southeast would help the NHL achieve two of its broader goals: getting more Americans access to its product on television and, by extension, increasing the amount of money the league could negotiate for its American teams in television money when its American national contract with CBS ended after the 1971–72 season. In the 1970–71 season, the eleven U.S.-based NHL teams received only $70,000 per franchise from CBS to broadcast its games. By comparison, NFL teams received $1.4 million each from their network-television contract partners to broadcast league games.[13] The high ratings that WAGA had been drawing in Atlanta the previous two winters showing NHL games encouraged the league to take seriously the idea of bringing its game to the South and selling it to the region's local television affiliates, especially with the region's influx of northern transplants.[14]

Before the WHA announced the cities in which it would place its first ten franchises, the NHL made an impromptu decision to expand to sixteen teams for the 1972–73 season. The NHL's decision to add two new franchises was in large part an effort to inoculate its member clubs from the financial strain that their turf war with the WHA would inevitably cause them. The emergence of rival professional football and basketball leagues had forced the NFL and NBA into costly bidding wars for the services of their players. The NHL would certainly face a similar challenge from the WHA. The NHL told potential bidders in early November 1971 that it expected the two successful franchisees to pay an expansion fee of $6 million, which would be distributed evenly among the league's fourteen existing teams. Including Atlanta, applicants from five locations made serious bids for the two expansion franchises: Kansas City, Cleveland, San Diego, and Nassau County, New York. Nassau County, like Atlanta, had recently begun construction on a coliseum, a $35 million structure in Hempstead whose builders aspired to turn their facility into a new focal point for Long Island. Nassau County's prospective coliseum would sit less than fifty miles from Madison Square Garden, the home of the New York Rangers, triggering a provision in league bylaws that would require the Nassau County franchise owners to pay a $5 million indemnity to the Rangers owner for impinging on the Rangers' market, if those owners were granted a franchise.[15] None of Atlanta's other competitors had a modern facility suitable for an NHL franchise. Less than two weeks after the WHA left Cousins's bid for an expansion franchise on its waiting list, Atlanta was, all of a sudden, the most desirable open hockey market in North America.

The NHL selected Atlanta and Nassau County, New York, as its two newest expansion sites on November 9, 1971, favoring the bids that placed the league in two brand new coliseums and kept the WHA out of these prestigious and potentially lucrative venues.[16] Atlanta's old suitor Charlie Finley, owner of the floundering California Golden Seals franchise, which he clad in the same green and gold as his Oakland A's baseball team, nearly derailed the expansion process while the league negotiated with the Atlanta and Nassau County ownership groups. League rules mandated a unanimous vote by club owners on behalf of all expansion bids. While every other NHL owner favored both expansion sites, Finley opposed the idea altogether. He questioned the wisdom of the NHL expanding further while some franchises, notably his own, were in financial trouble. Finley opposed a planned redistributive expansion draft which would stock the two new teams with players from the rosters of the league's existing franchises.[17] Expansion and an expansion draft would "further dilute the already weak club," Finley said of his Golden Seals.[18] The league's other owners circumvented Finley's definite no vote by voting to lower the number of required yes votes for expansion to twelve of the NHL's fourteen franchises, stripping Finley of his veto powers.[19]

FOR WEEKS FOLLOWING THE INAUGURATION OF "ATLANTA'S Ice Age," as the advertisements for Cousins's expansion hockey franchise described it, the sports pages of the Atlanta papers commenced with an educational campaign, explaining the rules and culture of hockey to Georgians. The Atlanta papers taught its readers about the history of the NHL and ran feature stories about the league's biggest stars. They touted the wonders that awaited fans next fall at the Omni and kept Atlantans up to date on the staffing of the team's front office.[20] Team officials tried to get Atlantans excited about watching hockey while simultaneously managing their expectations for the team. Atlanta GM Cliff Fletcher, formerly the GM of the St. Louis Blues team that pushed the Hawks out of town, warned curious fans across the Southeast that they "will have to accept the fact that all we'll get in next summer's expansion draft will be a few fringe players and some aging veterans."[21] Furthermore, as Fletcher failed to mention, the most talented hockey players previously not under contract in North America and Europe had virtually all been recruited to play in the WHA.

Working with the *Constitution* and the *Journal*, the management of the expansion Atlanta hockey team promoted a "Name the Team" contest that received more than ten thousand entries. Popular entries included the Thrashers, a name used decades later by Atlanta's second NHL franchise, and the Phoenix, a tribute to Atlanta's rising from the ashes after the Civil War. A nineteen-year-old college student named Mickey Goodman, thinking in a similar vein to those who advocated the name Phoenix, suggested Flames as a moniker for the team, which was also suggestive of the city's destruction a century earlier at the hands of Sherman's army and its subsequent resurgence. Team management liked the juxtaposition of heat and Flames with hockey's ice playing surface, which it thought emphasized the team's southern identity. The expansion franchise announced that its team would be known as the Atlanta Flames at a March 1972 press conference with an extravagant ice sculpture of the team's flaming A logo as a backdrop.[22] The Flames' extensive promotional efforts in the eleven months between the franchise's establishment in November 1971 and the team's first game in October 1972 were only partially successful in the *Sporting News'* tongue-in-cheek estimation. Only four of the ten Atlantans one of their writers called at random two weeks before the hockey club's debut at the Omni knew that the team was named the Flames.[23]

17

How the Falcons Lost Atlanta

IN THE *SPORTING NEWS*'S 1976 PREVIEW OF THE NFC WEST, *Atlanta Journal* sports editor Furman Bisher described the Falcons, who were then preparing for their eleventh season in the National Football League, as a franchise that "still hasn't been able to get out of the starting gate."[1] Between 1966 and 1975, the Falcons had lost more games than any team in the league. Through ten seasons, Atlanta had posted winning records on two occasions and had yet to reach the postseason, a feat they would not achieve until 1978, their thirteenth year in the league. Another losing season loomed for Atlanta in 1976. Head Coach Francis Marion "Swamp Fox" Campbell, the third in franchise history, was fired in early October. Campbell was also the third Falcons head coach to be fired in the middle of a season.

The "Swamp Fox" spent eight seasons in Atlanta, serving as defensive coordinator under Norm Van Brocklin for five years before taking over from his stern predecessor eight games into the 1974 campaign. Campbell won just six times in his twenty-five-game tenure as Atlanta's coach, finishing off the Falcons' first decade in professional football back where the team started—as the doormat of the league. His dismissal bookended a decade of Falcons football that began with Norb Hecker's thirty-one games as Falcons head coach. After two seasons and three games' worth of "losing but improving," in Hecker's frequently used words, owner Rankin Smith replaced the former Lombardi assistant with Norm Van Brocklin, who gutted the Falcons' pedestrian roster and soon took over management of the team's player personnel.

"Coach Van Brocklin was the most intimidating coach, or person, I have ever known," Falcons placekicker Bob Etter recalled. Etter spent the 1968 and 1969 seasons with the Falcons and witnessed the transition from Hecker to Van Brocklin firsthand. In his second week as head coach, Van Brocklin cut seven of the team's starters whose performance he regarded as lackluster. "I felt intense pressure playing for Atlanta the rest of that year. Most of our players were borderline, just hoping to remain on the team," Etter said, who was himself released by Atlanta after the 1969 season.[2]

Van Brocklin had a notably poor rapport with his players, particularly with numerous Black players who accused Van Brocklin of being a racist, not only in the manner that he addressed them but also in his roster and playing-time decisions. Other Black players disagreed with the assessment, noting that their highly unpopular, self-described curmudgeon of a coach was mean-spirited and crass in all of his player dealings.[3] The mutual hostility that developed between Van Brocklin and the team's Black players was one of several instances of strained race relations during the early history of the Atlanta Falcons. Black players complained to management that they received fewer off-season speaking engagements from nonprofits and endorsement offers from local businesses than their white teammates. Falcons' management deflected the issue, characterizing it as beyond the control of the organization.[4]

In 1968 the Atlanta NAACP accused the Falcons of having a racial policy that led to the trade of several African American players. The organization said the Falcons had one of the league's whitest rosters and complained that the team had allowed "Dixie" to be played at a 1967 game. Smith denied the accusations adamantly, noting that the Falcons were one of the few Atlanta institutions that had a policy against the playing of "Dixie" at its events, which one marching band had violated

the previous season. Additionally, Smith said that the Falcons
had the league's only full-time African American scout. At the
time of the accusation, the Falcons had seven African American
players (four of whom were starters) on their roster, including running back Junior Coffey, the team's 1967 Most Valuable Player. Despite Smith's protestations, the team's earliest
signings included few Black players, but the demographics of
the Falcons' roster had changed considerably by the time the
NAACP filed its complaint.[5]

Slowly but surely, Van Brocklin built the Falcons into a competitive football team, surrounding All-Pro linebacker Tommy
Nobis with better defensive players while trying to foster something of an offensive identity for the Atlanta team. Under the
guidance of "Swamp Fox" Campbell, the Falcons developed
into an above-average defense in the early 1970s, with defensive end Claude Humphrey, linebacker Greg Brezina, and safety
Ray Brown emerging as some of the top talents at their positions. When all was said and done, Humphrey, who had earned
the NFL's 1968 Defensive Rookie of the Year award, became the
most decorated player in Atlanta Falcons history, earning six
trips to the Pro Bowl and a spot in the Pro Football Hall of Fame.

Offensively, the Falcons found a workhorse in halfback Dave
Hampton, who narrowly missed 1,000 yards rushing in both
the 1972 and 1973 seasons before finally reaching the mark in
1975. Hampton became a top-tier rusher behind an offensive
line that included standout players like center Jeff Van Note
and tackle George Kunz. Finding a steady solution at quarterback was the bane of Van Brocklin's tenure with Atlanta, as
he cycled through a half-dozen signal callers (Randy Johnson,
Bob Berry, Bruce Lemmerman, Dick Shiner, Bob Lee, and Pat
Sullivan) between 1968 and 1974. Berry, who began his career
under Van Brocklin in Minnesota, proved to be the most successful of the lot. After a breakout 1969 season in which he
tossed 10 touchdown passes and just 2 interceptions over
seven starts, Berry performed unevenly throughout the early
1970s and was traded before the 1973 season.

Van Brocklin's Falcons were a genuinely losing but improving team in the late 1960s and early 1970s. They played tough defense, finishing each season in the top half of the league in most statistical categories. Eventually, the Falcons mustered enough offense to win some games. In 1971 Atlanta posted its first winning season (7-6-1), which it followed up in 1972 with a similarly respectable 7-7 campaign. In 1973 the Falcons remained in playoff contention until the final week of the season, posting a franchise-best 9-5 record and falling one game short of the wild card to the Washington Redskins.

The football cognoscenti thought the Falcons were on the fast track to becoming a contender, but the progress of the early 1970s was soon forgotten. Injuries to halfback Hampton sidelined him for much of the 1974 season, reducing the Falcons' already tenuous offense to the rubble it had been in the late 1960s. The Falcons' vaunted defense, too, took a step back in 1974, continually backed up to their own goal line or forced back onto the field immediately after making a stand by their historically ineffective offense. Atlanta finished at or near the bottom of every offensive category in the league and scored just 111 points in fourteen games, the second-worst offensive performance during the NFL's fourteen-game era.

A coach who courted as much controversy as Van Brocklin was not the kind who got cut much slack. Fans, players, and media alike clamored successfully for the unpopular coach's firing when the team's fortunes faded during the last-place 1974 campaign. After a 2-6 start, Smith relieved Van Brocklin of his duties and let his assistant Campbell guide the team for the remainder of the season.[6]

"The Falcons learned that losing can be an extremely lonely business," Pat Summerall intoned over footage of the Falcons playing to a nearly empty Atlanta Stadium in the NFL *Films* 1974 Falcons team yearbook video.[7] Falcons fatigue became endemic in the 1974 season even among their most loyal supporters. The collapse of Van Brocklin's Falcons into a last-place team in 1974 revealed a larger problem for the organization:

a failure to win the durable allegiance of their season-ticket-holding base, which had grown frustrated with the direction of the perpetually flagging organization and broke an NFL record for no-shows. Approximately 35.1 percent (143,488) of the tickets purchased to Falcons games at Atlanta Stadium that season went unused, more than four times the league's average no-show rate that season.[8]

The Falcons secured their place in no-show infamy thanks to the unprecedentedly bad crowds they drew down the stretch. More than forty thousand purchased tickets to each of the Falcons' final two home dates went unused. On December 1, 1974, 40,302 ticket holders passed up the Falcons' four o'clock Sunday divisional matchup against the Los Angeles Rams, breaking the league's previous record for no-shows by more than seven thousand. Most of those who bothered attending left by halftime. Those who stayed did so "mainly to practice their booing," according to the *Journal*'s Furman Bisher. The *Journal* and the *Constitution* blamed the crowd of 18,648, the smallest in Falcons history, on the 36-degree game-time temperature and the availability of the game on local television. The Atlanta Braves organization, which got a cut of stadium concessions revenue, made their unhappiness with the poor turnout known to Falcons management, further straining the already less-than-cordial relationship between the co-tenants. On December 15, 1974, the Falcons hosted the Packers for their home finale on a similarly brisk Sunday afternoon. This time, 48,830 ticket buyers passed up the game, enabling the Falcons to break their own NFL single-game no-show record by more than eight thousand.[9]

The lack of local interest in the Falcons, even among their season-ticket holders, by the mid-1970s was remarkable, considering that Atlanta was arguably the most football-mad market in the country. Initially, the arrival of professional football in Atlanta in the mid-1960s seemed to add a new layer to the region's decades-long love affair with the college and high school game. When the NFL granted Atlanta an expansion franchise in June 1965, fans swamped new owner Rankin Smith's business office with ticket requests. Within three months of going on sale, the Falcons cut off 1966 season-ticket sales at forty-five thousand, a record for an expansion franchise.[10]

In their early years, Falcons season-ticket holders were widely perceived to be a white-collar set that largely overlapped with the Georgia Tech crowd. A 1968 market-research study of the Falcons shuttle-bus ridership confirmed that the Sunday-afternoon crowd at Atlanta Stadium consisted primarily of the well-to-do. Pollsters surveyed 205 patrons from all eight shuttle-bus stops on a gorgeous Sunday afternoon without any other major conflicting events in the city. All 205 patrons surveyed were white, while three-quarters of them were male. Sixty percent of adult riders were college-educated, and 77 percent of them earned more than $10,000 annually, which was approximately one and one-third times the nation's median household income in 1968.[11]

As the novelty of professional football in Atlanta faded, the Falcons' fanbase became more broadly suburban but not more broadly regional. Simultaneously, the presence of the metropolitan area's traditional elite became less pronounced as Sunday afternoons at Atlanta Stadium grew unfashionable. A 1973 market-research study commissioned by the Falcons estimated that 71.3 percent of game attendees between 1966 and 1972 came from the five-county metropolitan area. Nearly three-quarters of game attendees from the metro area came from either northeast or northwest Atlanta and its adjoining suburbs. A mere 7 percent of attendees came from out of state, dispelling the idea that the team would become a major regional draw.[12]

As Falcons tickets became less desirable among more affluent consumers, there was good reason for a broader range of fans to purchase season tickets. For middle-class families, they were a relatively affordable form of entertainment. Falcons tickets remained among the league's least expensive throughout their tenure at Atlanta Stadium. In 1966 fans paid

$6 per game for all non-obstructed-view seats in the lower and upper decks. Single-game passes were also $6. The Falcons raised their ticket prices in 1972 to $7.50, where they remained through the 1975 season. At $7.50 per game, Falcons tickets were 20 percent below the league's average ticket price in 1975 and much cheaper than a $6 ticket in 1966, which would have been nearly $10 in 1975 dollars, when accounting for inflation. Parking in the stadium lot cost just $1 through the 1978 season. A 1977 NFL study found that the average cost for a family of four to attend a Falcons game, including tickets, parking, and concessions, was $40.80, the least expensive in the league.[13]

Despite the broadening of the Falcons' fanbase in the early 1970s, relatively few African Americans attended their games. James Heath of the *Daily World* attributed to this to the economics of season-ticket sales. "Because of many factors, mainly money, whites buy up the majority of the season tickets which again give them the majority of the fans at the games. Not too many Blacks can buy two and three season tickets. They have a hard time trying to get a portion of the 5,000 seats left to sell at the gate," Heath wrote in 1975, looking back on the Falcons' first decade in Atlanta.[14]

While the Falcons' season-ticket base broadened demographically in the 1970s, the appeal of the team failed to deepen. No longer a novelty, Falcons tickets, which entitled a customer to watch the frequently atrocious team, got lost in the shuffle of the abounding leisure options available in Metropolitan Atlanta. The football-crazy Metropolitan Atlanta area supported a season-ticket base of nearly forty thousand through many lean years of Falcons football, but as the 1960s turned into the 1970s, fan patience wore out.[15] Overall ticket sales between 1966 and 1971 always averaged at least fifty thousand per game, although Falcons ownership was disturbed by the growing number of Atlanta Stadium no-shows. In 1968 approximately 17 percent of Falcons tickets purchased went unused, depriving the team of the additional in-stadium revenue their presence would have generated. Moreover, the empty patches that no-shows created in the stadium made the team's product look undesirable to television viewers. The team found it increasingly difficult to sell out its stock of individual-game tickets, leaving thousands of seats unsold for each of their 1970 home dates.[16]

To shore up the team's ticket revenue, the Falcons tried to eliminate the problem of selling seats to individual games in 1971 by increasing the number of season tickets offered for sale. Between 1971 and 1974, the franchise increased the number of season passes it offered fans from forty-five thousand to fifty-five thousand, turning virtually every seat in the stadium into the domain of a season-ticket holder. The decision corresponded with an uptick in the team's performance under Van Brocklin, enabling the franchise to meet a resurgent local demand while inoculating itself against dips in revenue and, starting in 1973, league-mandated local television blackouts if home games did not sell out seventy-two hours in advance of kickoff. The expansion of season-ticket sales backfired during the Falcons' disappointing 1974 season, as average attendance fell below thirty-eight thousand and the spectacle of no-shows at Atlanta Stadium made the team a national laughingstock. Falcons season-ticket sales fell off by more than 12,500 seats that off-season, leading the team to stop providing the press with firm sales figures for several seasons. In the late 1970s, the Falcons started making their season-ticket sales numbers public again once the total surpassed forty thousand, corresponding to an uptick in the team's performance.[17]

While Metropolitan Atlanta was one of the most football-crazy markets in the country, the intense local and regional passion for the high school and college games and the expansion of the NFL into New Orleans circumscribed the Falcons' appeal. Sunday afternoon NFL football was, chronologically, the third game day of the weekend. Often, it was also the third most important game day of the weekend for southern fans who had spent Friday night cheering on their high school team and Saturday supporting their college team. Locally, the Falcons lagged in popularity behind the state's two traditional college football powers: Georgia Tech and the University of Georgia.

The arrival of the Atlanta Falcons corresponded with the reemergence of the Georgia Bulldogs as an SEC power under Vince Dooley. In 1966 and 1968, the Bulldogs won the SEC Championship, challenging Bear Bryant's Alabama Crimson Tide for preeminence in the conference. "From the time we exited the bus above Sanford Stadium and walked down those steps until the scoreboard clock showed all zeroes, they were constantly in their fervor," Bob Etter, who played on the Bulldogs' 1966 SEC Championship team, said of the crowds "Between the Hedges" in the 1960s. During the 1970s, Georgia was the only thing preventing Alabama from winning the SEC every single season. The Bulldogs took home the 1976 SEC Championship and began the 1980s with a string of three consecutive conference titles (1980–82). This stretch of success included a National Championship in 1980, the Bulldogs' first since 1942, and running back Herschel Walker's winning of the Heisman Trophy in 1982. Walker, who remains the SEC's all-time leading rusher, was the first Bulldog to win the Heisman since Frank Sinkwich in UGA's 1942 National Championship season. In the midst of all this success, UGA expanded Sanford Stadium by more than twenty thousand seats, unveiling a new eighty-two-thousand-seat configuration in 1981, making it one of the nation's ten largest stadiums.[18]

Back in Atlanta, the Yellow Jackets were having a tougher time of it. Longtime Tech coach Bobby Dodd had said in 1966 that he was not concerned about the Falcons cutting into their popularity. Instead, he feared that the Braves, who played continuously from April through September, would cut into the local sports media's twelve-month coverage of Yellow Jacket football. Dodd's fear proved out, as coverage of Tech football, more often than not, moved to the back of the sports section during the off-season.[19] Moreover, Georgia Tech football floundered in the years after Dodd's 1966 retirement, fading from a perennially ranked national power into an also-ran that lost almost as many games as it won. Despite the Yellow Jackets' futility on the field, Tech continued to draw capacity or near-capacity crowds to Grant Field for almost every home game in the late 1960s and early 1970s, though the waiting list for season tickets diminished considerably.[20]

Interest in Tech football surged again during the coaching tenure of Franklin "Pepper" Rodgers (1974–79), whose colorful persona proved highly marketable in the swinging Atlanta of the 1970s. The virtual opposite of the Falcons' Van Brocklin, Rodgers commuted to campus on a motorcycle, wore a sailors' cap on the sideline, and kept his hair longer than many of his players. Whereas Van Brocklin told a player who wore a headband to practice to quit football and "get a job as an Indian in a cowboy movie," Rodgers encouraged his players to embrace the youth culture of the moment by wearing their hair and clothing as they liked. Tech made Rodgers the center of its marketing campaign, helping the school's sports brand stand out in the Major League City. Funky "Pepper Power" stickers adorned the bumpers of cars across the five-county area. Rodgers hosted a popular weekly television program that focused less on football and more on celebrity guests, many of whom he had become acquainted with while coaching at UCLA. The *Pepper Rodgers Show*, whose guests included the likes of Burt Reynolds, Julia Child, and Evel Knievel, drew an average local Nielsen rating of 11 in 1975, more than 500 percent higher than the ratings for the Falcons' weekly highlight show that season.[21]

Competition from more than just the pulpit soon threatened the Falcons' domain over even Sunday afternoons. Atlanta's monopoly on professional football in the Southeast proved short-lived. A confluence of events in the fall of 1966 hastened the arrival of the NFL in New Orleans, Atlanta's oldest civic rival. Atlanta had long outpaced New Orleans as an economic center, but Atlanta's civic leaders remained envious of the Crescent City's cultural import. Conversely, New Orleans's city fathers envied Atlanta's status as the New South's economic fulcrum. Leaders in both cities had been competing to become the region's hub for major professional sports since the late 1950s.[22]

In October 1966 the NFL and AFL went to the House Judiciary Committee, seeking out an antitrust exemption that would allow them to merge. House Judiciary Committee chairman Rep. Emanuel Celler (D-NY), who regarded the proposed merger as monopolistic, blocked the antitrust exemption bill from receiving a vote in his committee. Louisiana's two most powerful members of Congress, Senator Russell Long and Representative Hale Boggs, intervened in the matter, promising to use their legislative clout to push through the antitrust exemption if the league agreed to give New Orleans an expansion franchise immediately. Long, the chairman of the Senate Finance Committee, and Boggs, the House Majority Whip, evaded Celler by attaching the exempting legislation to a budget bill, earning it a successful floor vote in both houses. Weeks later, the NFL announced a 1967 expansion franchise for New Orleans, which would play temporarily at Tulane Stadium.[23]

Once New Orleans had its expansion franchise, city leaders commissioned local architectural firm Curtis and Davis to design them a signature stadium. Curtis and Davis presented city leaders with a plan for a ninety-million-cubic-foot, domed facility that would be the world's largest indoor stadium. City and state officials endorsed the plans for the Louisiana Superdome, as the facility came to be known, which would supplant Houston's Astrodome, Miami's Orange Bowl, and Atlanta Stadium as the South's most prestigious stadium. In 1969 Louisiana's legislature approved a lodging and amusement tax to secure $129 million in state-issued bonds to finance the stadium's construction. In August 1975, nearly four years after breaking ground, the seventy-five-thousand-seat dome opened for business.[24] Less than five months after opening, the Superdome hosted Super Bowl IX, the first of seven held at the world-famous venue. Atlanta Stadium, conversely, never hosted a Super Bowl.[25]

THE SPECTACLE OF NO-SHOWS AT ATLANTA STADIUM during the 1974 season was one of the few times that the national sports media paid much attention to the Falcons. Otherwise, the team remained virtually invisible on the national stage. During the 1970s the Falcons made the fewest appearances (three) of any NFL team on ABC's *Monday Night Football*.[26] In 1974 CBS made the fateful decision to feature the promising, young Falcons team on seven of its national broadcasts, offering the club more national appearances in one season than in its previous four years combined. The 1974 Falcons proved to be a ratings debacle for the network. The three-win team drew the league's lowest national television ratings. That season, the Falcons also endured their worst local television ratings in franchise history.[27]

The local media, too, proved notably unsympathetic to the Falcons, often with good reason. Before the Falcons even played a regular season game, the team had developed a contentious relationship with the Atlanta press. Coach Norb Hecker accused the media of leaking information to opposing teams prior to Atlanta's September 1966 home opener, setting the tone for his rapport with local sportswriters.[28] "Mr. Falcon" Tommy Nobis had numerous run-ins with the Atlanta media. While the All-Pro linebacker won the universal respect of teammates, coaches, and opponents, his intense and brooding personality clashed with a local press that often went straight to him for answers on the Falcons' shortcomings.[29]

The hostility between the press and Hecker's successor, Norm Van Brocklin, reached the point of physical violence. During the Falcons' 1971 training camp in Greenville, South Carolina, Van Brocklin choked the *Journal*'s Frank Hyland by his necktie for "smart-alecking" during a welcome dinner the team held for its traveling press corps. Assistant coaches restrained Van Brocklin, who, remarkably, kept his job after the physical confrontation, which was far from the first of his career.[30]

For a franchise that gave its head coach enough leeway to keep his job after assaulting a reporter, the Falcons proved awfully sensitive to press criticism. In 1976 the Falcons pulled their advertising from the *Journal* for the season after two columnists wrote unfavorably about the way the club was being managed. The Falcons tried to alleviate all of their bad publicity by continuing to do extensive charitable work across the state. Despite the best efforts of Falcons players, the franchise had the least favorable public image among Atlanta's franchises.[31]

The Falcons organization blamed many of its problems on its status as tenants at Atlanta Stadium, which forced the team to share gameday revenue with the Braves as well as the Stadium Authority. Rankin Smith and the Falcons found themselves in frequent turf battles over the placement of amenities and the decor of the stadium, demanding that Braves iconography be covered up during Falcons' games. Despite the large number of empty seats that greeted the Falcons most Sundays at Atlanta Stadium, Smith complained that the stadium had one of the league's smallest seating capacities. His players regarded it as having one of the league's worst grass playing surfaces.

"I'm not sure if the Falcons were the number one priority for the stadium at the time," said Falcons linebacker Tommy Nobis, who notes that the stadium itself was state-of-the-art at the time of its construction. "It seemed like the Braves were the priority, and we were secondary. . . . We would use their locker room. We would come out of their dugout. There were so many things we were using that were the Braves. It was basically their field, and it was just a little second class because of that situation," especially when compared to the top-notch amenities that Nobis had grown used to as an athlete at the University of Texas.[32] Falcons kicker and offensive guard Lou

Kirouac described Atlanta Stadium as "very adequate for the '60s" but noted that the dirt baseball infield "got real muddy and real slippery" if it got the least bit wet, the corollary to the Braves' complaint that the Falcons tore up the turf starting every August.[33] "Whenever they painted the grass and I fell on it," Falcons center Jeff Van Note remembered, "it used to slice my arm open. The paint was actually sharp. Then if it rained, it all ran like a woman's mascara."[34]

In 1971 Smith threatened to move the team's preseason games permanently to Georgia Tech's Grant Field but failed to reach a revenue agreement with the school. In 1973 he responded to a proposal by Fulton County to impose a new excise tax on tickets by threatening to move the Falcons games and operations to a neighboring county when his initial ten-year lease ended in 1975. Smith ended up renewing his lease at the stadium for an additional fifteen years when the tax proposal foundered. Moreover, he could not find a suburban government interested in helping him finance a new playing facility.[35]

Rumors persisted throughout the 1970s that the Falcons owner was hurting financially and looking to sell the franchise. Smith got into a 1974 dispute with the IRS over the amount of depreciation from player salaries he claimed on his income taxes. Smith won his suit with the IRS, but whispers continued about his intentions for the franchise. In 1978 Smith cut the club's operational expenses considerably by moving the team's headquarters out of Atlanta Stadium and into an office complex in Gwinnett County. Relocating thirty miles northeast of downtown slashed the club's rent by more than half and offered it greater autonomy as it planned for a future at a new playing facility.[36] By the time the Falcons moved their headquarters out to Suwanee, Smith made it clear that he was tired of the "football in the round" configuration at Atlanta Stadium and longed for a new playing facility, either in metropolitan Atlanta or elsewhere, at the end of his stadium lease in 1990.[37]

18

Atlanta's Ice Society

....

LESS THAN THREE YEARS AFTER WAGA-TV PRESENTED Georgians with their first televised hockey game, the NHL's Atlanta Flames skated onto the ice at the Omni in October 1972. The addition of professional hockey to Atlanta's sports marketplace served many masters. It fulfilled the Big Mules' desire to adorn their city with yet another Major League amenity. It helped arena operator Tom Cousins secure more than forty revenue-generating dates each year on the Omni's calendar. It enabled the NHL to keep the upstart WHA out of a state-of-the-art arena as well as a large, rapidly growing television market. It made sense in every respect but the most obvious ones: few Atlantans had ever seen hockey in person, let alone played it themselves. Until the opening of the Omni, there was nowhere to host a hockey game in Atlanta. In the words of the *Journal*'s Frank Hyland, the Flames were "lobsters in a catfish town."[1]

The sheer strangeness of placing a professional hockey team in Georgia in the early 1970s colors the largely inaccurate public memory of the Atlanta Flames' eight-year history. The dismissive standard narrative surrounding the franchise can be encapsulated in the *Sporting News*'s Al Morganti's characterization of the Flames' tenure in Atlanta as a "seven year [sic] exercise in futility."[2] Writing in the early 1990s as the NHL once again placed franchises in Dixie, Morganti's statement was demonstrative of a broad and understandable ethos among hockey purists who believed that the league's expansion into the Sunbelt was economically unwise and a destabilizing force in the sport's culture. The specific characterization of professional hockey's first gambit in Atlanta as an "exercise in futility," though, was simply not true. The Flames were a continuously competitive team, and they enjoyed the most consistent and enthusiastic support of Atlanta's four major professional sports franchises during the 1970s.

"We went to the playoffs, we had some good teams. And the city supported them," Flames forward Tim Ecclestone said, assessing the team's legacy concisely in 2008.[3] "The misconception is that hockey failed in Atlanta, but the truth is the owner of the team saw a chance to capitalize on the big profits of the sale of the team," Flames center Bill Clement said of the team's departure from Georgia.[4] The apologias offered by these former Flames are entirely accurate. The Flames performed well during their eight years in Atlanta, earning playoff bids on six occasions. The franchise's first two seasons were their only losing years in Atlanta. In addition, the Flames proved an excellent gate attraction for the vast majority of their tenure in the city. The team's departure from the city was due in large part to owner Tom Cousins's financial struggles but also to the waning of hockey as a novel attraction in the city, the franchise's lack of broadcast-media revenue, and the inability of the team to broaden its appeal beyond well-to-do northsiders and northern transplants.

The Flames' on-ice success was built from the top down. Unlike the Falcons, Atlanta's other expansion franchise, the Flames' ownership hired experienced sports executives to run their organization. Flames GM Cliff Fletcher, who worked closely with head coaches Bernie "Boom Boom" Geoffrion (1972–75) and Fred Creighton (1975–79), oversaw the creation of a consistently competitive on-ice product in Atlanta. The decision in January 1972 to hire Fletcher, a thirty-eight-year-old player-personnel expert, was arguably the shrewdest in the franchise's history. A protégé of Montreal Canadiens GM Sam Pollock, Fletcher developed great expertise in talent assessment during his time with the league's winningest franchise.

He assisted Pollock in the construction of Montreal's 1965 and 1966 championship clubs before moving on to St. Louis, where he built the expansion Blues into three-time defending Western Division champions (1968–70).[5]

Following the approach he took in St. Louis, Fletcher built the Atlanta club around strong defense. He used his first two expansion draft picks to select the talented young goalies Dan Bouchard and Phil Myre, a tandem which became the cornerstone of the club's early success. Atlanta's games were frequently low-scoring affairs, as the team employed a defense-first strategy to accentuate its strength in net. The Flames became an immediate playoff contender through their grit and goaltending more than their speed and scoring. Opposing teams complained that warm-weather Atlanta's notoriously soft home ice further augmented the Flames' defensive strength by slowing down teams with superior athletes.[6]

Fletcher did more than just play the angles to build a successful team. His skill at assessing young talent enabled him to sign a number of future NHL stars before other franchises recognized their potential. Credits to Fletcher's eye for talent included relentless two-way players like Tom Lysiak and Eric Vail as well as the brawny Willi Plett, who became one of the prototypes for the modern NHL's power forward. Fletcher's achievements look all the more remarkable when one considers that his competition for talent in the early 1970s consisted not only of other NHL clubs but also of the well-financed franchises in the rival WHA. By contrast, the New York Islanders, the NHL's other 1972–73 expansion club, spent their early years at the bottom of the standings, far out of contention. Rivals referred to the Flames as "Montreal South," as Fletcher acquired a half-dozen players who had been groomed in the Canadiens' farm system, including Myre and Lysiak. Unlike many expansion franchises, which acquire well-known players to draw in fans, Fletcher felt no pressure to sign up any aging stars. Atlanta fans, he understood, would not have known who they were anyway. Fletcher managed expectations for the team in the local press while he built a young, competitive, and compatible club, one whose striking and immediate success confounded even their staunchest boosters.[7]

Just as essential as Fletcher to the Flames' early success was the head coach that he hired: Hockey Hall of Famer Bernie "Boom Boom" Geoffrion. Accentuating the franchise's reputation as Montreal South, Canadiens legend Geoffrion inspired fierce loyalty from his players while he won over Atlantans with his jaunty personal charisma.[8] "You have to give Cliff Fletcher a lot of credit," Flames announcer Jiggs McDonald said of the GM's selection of Geoffrion. "He hired a salesman, he hired a motivator . . . the outpouring of love and support for Boom was incredible."[9] "I thought it was of paramount importance to bring in a coach with a good personality," Fletcher said in 2008. "He [Geoffrion] captured the imagination of the sporting public in Atlanta. He was one of, if not the most important, reasons hockey was able to make such an impact."[10]

"Boom Boom" came off simultaneously as a profane tough guy and a slick showman. His Quebecois accent was equal parts enchanting and amusing to southern ears. Geoffrion made hundreds of personal appearances on behalf of the team, convincing many metropolitan-area residents to give hockey a try. As a result, Geoffrion became the face of the franchise. "The Boomer," as the gregarious Geoffrion came to be known locally, was the Atlanta-area's most in-demand pitchman, after-dinner speaker, and media personality for much of the 1970s. Fans chanted "Boom! Boom!" nearly incessantly at home games.[11] Nagging health problems and a deteriorating relationship with Fletcher caused Geoffrion to resign as coach in February 1975. "Boom" accepted a front-office position with the Flames that consisted mostly of making public appearances. Later, he worked alongside Jiggs McDonald as the color commentator on Flames' broadcasts. Nevertheless, the loss of Geoffrion as coach deprived the franchise of its best promotional tool, creating a public-relations void from which it never recovered.[12]

The Flames promotional department, which was overseen by Fletcher and team President Bill Putnam, did an excellent job at presenting hockey tickets as a scarce, prestigious, and valuable commodity. At press conferences and in their promotional materials, the Flames invited area residents to join Atlanta's Ice Society, portraying hockey night at the Omni as the new glamorous evening out for the region's upper crust.[13] Advertisements presented Flames tickets as the cover charge to an exclusive club, imploring prospective members of the Ice Society to "get your tickets before the freeze." "Radio commercials done by a guy who sounds like he's depicting a recreation of Pearl Harbor tell us to rush and buy those tickets or there won't be any left," the *Journal*'s Ron Hudspeth wrote of the Flames' promotional campaign. Conversely, Geoffrion and Fletcher, who made dozens of personal appearances during the summer of 1972, adopted a softer sales approach. They presented themselves more as representatives of the sport than pitchmen for the franchise. Both methods clearly worked. The Flames sold more than 7,150 season tickets in advance of their first home game, more than the Braves and the Hawks sold combined for any one season during the 1960s or 1970s.[14]

The success the Flames showed at selling advance season tickets was a textbook example of targeted marketing. Despite a substantial advertising budget of $300,000, a team-commissioned survey found that only four in ten area residents recognized the Flames moniker just one week before their home opener. Just one-third of respondents had ever seen hockey on television and less than three percent had ever attended a game. More than 60 percent of interviewees expressed interest in learning more about hockey, but the franchise decided to seek out the devotion of a more exclusive audience. They sought out customers who might buy a season ticket as they would an annual subscription to the theater rather than a more inclusive audience, which could have provided them with a more substantial television viewership.

The Flames' very name evoked a purposeful and playful

cultural distance. Almost certainly, more fans would have recognized the team's name if it had adopted the more populist moniker favored by Fletcher, the "Rebels." The GM envisioned the Atlanta Rebels, cloaked in grey and red, skating on to the ice to the strains of "Dixie" as played by a corps of buglers in the stands. The franchise's local ownership vetoed the Canadian GM's vision, believing it would damage Atlanta's reputation as the City Too Busy to Hate. Instead, Fletcher and Putnam went with their second choice, "Flames," which evoked the city's Civil War past and juxtaposed nicely with the game's ice playing surface.[15]

Their October 14, 1972, home debut was the first event ever held at the Omni Coliseum. Less than an hour before the 8:00 p.m. opening faceoff, laborers were still bolting in five hundred seats that they failed to complete in time. A sellout crowd of 14,568 watched the Flames and Buffalo Sabres skate to a 1–1 tie in what was likely the first hockey game that most attendees had ever seen in person.[16] Like every opening night in Atlanta, fans came dressed to the nines. "It looked like you were going to a ball," Geoffrion recalled, noting that most fans showed up at every game thereafter dressed in similarly formal clothing.[17] It was "a very social crowd doing the in-thing to do," the Journal's Jim Huber and Tom Saladino wrote of the attendees that evening, "bejeweled and spit polished to perfection."[18] Atlanta fans bundled up for their night on the town, many in brand-new winter coats and furs, unaware that the arena was climate controlled to keep the seating areas warmer than the ice.[19]

Newly inducted Flames fans displayed a predictable lack of hockey knowledge. "The game began and people jumped out of their seats to watch a couple of players battling for the puck at center. 'Sit down, sit down,' I told them, 'nothing has happened yet,'" Warren Argy, an Upstate New York transplant in attendance said of the crowd.[20] Spectators cheered on all movement of the puck, responding to any progress by the rubber disc as if they were the strides of a thoroughbred hitting the home stretch of the Belmont Stakes. They honored the most pedestrian of Flames goaltender Phil Myre's saves with standing ovations. The scoreboard read, "Myre-Aculous" when the goalie made his first save of the game, stopping a slow-rolling puck that dribbled down the ice into his glove.[21] "I didn't know what the hell happened," Myre said. "I almost got caught looking up in the stands to see what was going on. I kinda thought somebody started a fight or something."[22]

The hockey cognoscenti found great humor in Atlantans' simultaneous enthusiasm for the game and ignorance of it during the Flames' first seasons.[23] Players, too, recognized that Atlanta fans were far from hockey experts, but they sure had a great time at the games. "The fans loved us in Atlanta, but it almost just seemed like they were there for a festival on a lot of nights, as opposed to caring whether the team won or lost. . . . With hockey fans in Atlanta, it was more 'let's have a party and cheer our rear ends off, and then let's have a party after the game,'" Flames center Bill Clement said.[24] "You can go to the Omni, which is the new home of indoor sports culture in Atlanta, and feel at ease," the *Journal*'s Furman Bisher explained in February 1973. "That's because you figure everybody's on the same ground. Nobody knows any more hockey than you do." While Bisher aimed to make light of the situation, he illuminated an important truth about the Flames' fanbase. Unfamiliarity with the sport was not a taboo among Flames spectators. Part of the appeal of going was that virtually everyone in attendance was learning the game together and at the same time.[25]

. The full house that watched the Flames' October 1972 debut was not a fluke. Few expansion franchises in the history of professional sports have proven as big an immediate box-office success. The team's on-ice success played no small part in this. Midway through their first season, the Flames had a winning record and were drawing frequent sellout crowds to the Omni. While the Braves, Falcons, and, eventually, the Hawks struggled, Atlantans could cheer on an instantly competitive hockey team. The franchise averaged better than 12,500 spectators per game during their first season, providing largely young and well-heeled audiences with a novel entertainment experience. Whether hockey novices or connoisseurs, Atlanta fans were also lucky enough to get an NHL team at one of the most colorful moments in the league's history. The NHL of the 1970s was animated by wild brawls, a newly wide-open style of play, rapid expansion, cartoonish goons, and helmetless players who looked like rock stars on ice. Partial Flames season tickets proved a popular holiday gift among affluent Atlantans in 1972. The club sold four thousand of them as part of a Christmas sales campaign.[26]

The Flames ended up falling short of the playoffs in their first season, but this did nothing to dampen local enthusiasm. The club's popularity at the gate peaked during their second and third seasons when they averaged more than fourteen thousand per game. The Flames made their first playoff appearance in year two, falling in the quarterfinals to the Philadelphia Flyers, who went on to win their first Stanley Cup. Atlanta's full-season ticket sales grew to approximately 8,300 in 1973–74 before reaching an all-time high of more than 9,800 in 1974–75.[27] "The one game that's still playing to full houses is the one the Flames brought to town," Bisher wrote in February 1975, as the city found itself in full "Loserville, USA" mode.[28]

"It's been amazing the way hockey has been accepted here," Fletcher said of the franchise's immediate fan support. "We know the fans were not bred on it as they were in the upper United States and Canada, but they're catching on quickly and they seem to like it."[29] On April 7, 1974, thousands of fans lined up at the Omni's box office to purchase Flames playoff tickets. At the time, several thousand tickets remained unsold for the Braves' April 8 home opener, which proved to be the night that Hank Aaron broke baseball's all-time career home run record.[30] "I was kinda scared at first," Geoffrion said about Flames' attendance, "because you were down south. Our games were on Friday. You had to fight high school football. But we conquered them. We outdrew high school football. And the Hawks and Braves were terrible."[31]

The Flames drew a largely young, professional, and affluent crowd to the Omni. "There were quite a few young kids going who took on hockey pretty well," *Constitution* editor Jim Minter recalled. "You could call it a social thing. It was real trendy at the time."[32] "It used to be the cool, charming suave sophisticated fellow about town was the one who had two tickets to a Falcons game," the *Journal*'s Ron Hudspeth wrote in January 1973, "but now, it's hockey." He described Flames games as the new evening haunt of Atlanta's fashionable set, "an Omni full of suave, sophisticated Joes and little blondes."[33]

The *Journal*'s Alex Truex described the Flames as having a "narrow base of support, mostly upper-crust north-siders," an assessment that many of their fans would have embraced, particularly in the team's early years.[34] "Hockey fans are far above the average sports fan," Flames Fan Club founder Howard Zinsenhelm explained in 1973. "They're more loyal and they're from a higher income level," he said, describing the appeal of the game to Atlanta's upscale consumers, who had previously proved unwilling to sweat in the stands alongside people of more modest means.[35] Like Zinsenhelm, a transplanted New York insurance executive, many early Flames supporters were relocated northerners. "But the natives caught on quickly," current Fan Club Copresident Joe Watkins recalled. Joe and his wife, Betsy Watkins, joined the group in 1976 and have kept it going for the more than forty years since the team left Atlanta.[36]

As natives caught on, the demographics of the fanbase changed to some extent. The official Flames Fan Club that Zinsenhelm had formed peaked in membership at around eight hundred in 1973, when it consisted primarily of the well-to-do transplants who made up much of the Flames' early, business-class crowd. The organization held monthly luncheons and dinners that featured talks by Flames players or those from opposing teams. The club often met at Dante's Down the Hatch, famed man-about-town Dante Stephensen's popular fondue restaurant in Underground Atlanta. Fan-club members formed many friendships with Flames players, especially in the group's later years as its membership waned to a more heavily native and more committed base. It was not uncommon for several Flames players to meet up for beers after the game with the friends they had made in the group. The fan club also followed the team on the road, making well-planned excursions for out-of-town games or to attend the NHL All-Star Game, as the group did on five occasions. Long before wearing sports apparel became so widespread, club members purchased red Flames jackets, which made for a striking display when they sat as a group at the Omni.[37]

Flames fans were loud and enthusiastic throughout the team's eight-year run in Atlanta. At every game, they lined the rafters with homemade banners in support of the team. "It was always a great atmosphere. Flames fans were pretty positive," Jamie Taylor recalled. Taylor's family relocated to Atlanta from Minneapolis in 1974 and embraced the Flames immediately, easing their transition to life in the South.[38] The 1974–75 Flames may be the only team in NHL history that left the ice to a standing ovation after losing a regular season game that knocked them out of playoff contention.[39]

"Till the last season, it was pretty rocking," Fan Club co-president Betsy Watkins said of the atmosphere at the Omni during a hockey game.[40] "They would blow the roof off," Flames center Bill Clement said of the noise at the Omni. [41] The Omni's organist, who made "Happy Days Are Here Again" a team anthem, would whip the crowd up into a screaming and singing assemblage, cultivating an atmosphere at the arena similar to that of the cabarets across the street at Underground Atlanta.[42] Atlanta fans showed great enthusiasm for the spectacle of hockey fights, reserving some of their loudest cheers every evening for Flames brawlers Bob Paradise and Willi Plett.[43]

Young women formed a significant portion of the Flames' following. Certainly, "little blonde secretaries," in the words of the *Journal*'s Ron Hudspeth, went on many dates at Flames games, but the hockey team also drew consistent and durable support from young women who attended the games in groups.[44] "Hockey is drawing more women's support than any sport in this town," Flames public relations director Ed Thilenius told the *Constitution* in 1975.[45] That October, the club held a free hockey clinic for female fans that drew more than 1,500 attendees. Flames players found it amusing that the women at the clinic hooted, hollered, and catcalled them as they demonstrated different aspects of the game. Flames goalie Dan Bouchard said the clamorous response they received from the female fans was typical. "When they come to a hockey game, they leave their manners in the powder room or someplace," he said. Kay Davis, an Atlanta secretary who attended, said she loved hockey because she "loves the fights." Davis also cited an intimacy she felt with the helmetless skaters in hockey that she did not in other sports. "There aren't so many players that you can't have a rapport with them," she said, "like football, I mean, which is so mechanical."[46]

Part of the appeal of hockey to young white female fans was almost certainly that the sport's participants were young, wealthy, fashionably dressed and coiffed white men. Moreover, the French names and accents of many of the players made them seem exotic. Young white women cheering on the likes of Jacques Richard and Leon Rochefort would not have been perceived by most white Atlantans as socially transgressive. If these same women had whooped it up for anyone but Pete Maravich in the Hawks' predominately African American lineup, they would have been crossing a cultural taboo, even though the Hawks' players were just as wealthy and well-dressed as the Flames players.[47]

"Atlantans would rather watch a Canadian do something they only vaguely comprehend than watch a Black American do something they used to try to do through hoops nailed to their garages," *Sports Illustrated*'s Roy Blount wrote in 1977.[48] Blount's characterization was entirely accurate. Atlantans in the 1970s demonstrated a clear preference for attending the games of the Flames, who played a foreign but almost exclusively white professional sport, rather than the Hawks, who played a familiar but predominately Black one. The Flames outdrew the Hawks in all eight of the seasons that they shared the Omni. The most dramatic difference in attendance came during the 1973–74 season, when the Flames averaged 14,162 spectators per game, nearly twice as many as the Pete Maravich–led Hawks, who averaged 7,612. The Omni's co-tenants charged roughly the same amount for tickets and played roughly the same number of games. Hawks and Flames tickets topped out at $7 and $7.50 respectively. The lowest-priced Hawks tickets were $3, while the cheapest passes to Flames games were $3.50.[49]

In the mid-1970s, one franchise seemed to rise above Atlanta's seemingly saturated sports market. Against all expectations, the Flames were the toast of town. A combination of slick promotion aimed at upscale consumers and prudent personnel management remade the fashionable set on the northside into the heart of Atlanta's Ice Society. As the decade progressed and the novelty of professional hockey wore thin, setbacks in Tom Cousins's real estate empire imperiled professional hockey's future in Atlanta.

19

Just What Atlanta Needs

....

TOM COUSINS'S LUCK COULDN'T HAVE BEEN BETTER. FROM the moment he purchased the Hawks, the real estate developer turned sportsman had coveted LSU's Pete Maravich. Coming off a sophomore campaign when he broke the NCAA's single-season scoring record, "Pistol Pete" was already college basketball's top gate attraction when Cousins, Sanders, and Allen sat behind a basketball with the words *Atlanta Hawks* stenciled on it in May 1968. By the spring of 1970, Cousins's desire to acquire the LSU star had only grown. After two seasons of lackluster fan support, the acquisition of a white star from a southern school seemed all the more imperative for the lightly drawing Hawks.

Meeting Atlanta's demographic demands proved to be just part of the Pistol's appeal. In March 1970 Maravich's college career came to an end in the consolation game of the National Invitational Tournament, as LSU fell to Bobby Knight's Army team at Madison Square Garden. By that time, Maravich had become a genuine cultural phenomenon, the author of a one-man basketball show of madcap dribbling, trick passes, and shots hit from every angle. During his senior season, national television audiences as well as standing-room-only crowds on both coasts joined spectators in SEC country in "Maravich Mania." Millions followed Maravich's pursuit and eventual obliteration of Oscar Robertson's all-time NCAA scoring record. Pistol Pete was America's most famous basketball player and he was about to fall into Tom Cousins's lap.

The implosion of the Hawks' championship-contending

roster put Atlanta in position to draft Maravich. The Hawks acquired the third pick in the 1970 NBA Draft from the San Francisco Warriors in exchange for the future NBA rights to Zelmo Beaty, who had jumped to the ABA the previous season. Detroit and San Diego held the top two picks, and both sought out frontcourt help. With the Pistons selecting St. Bonaventure center Bob Lainer and Rockets choosing Michigan forward Rudy Tomjanovich, Atlanta was free to take the guard from LSU.

The de facto swap of the established Beaty for the unproven Maravich made evident the racial motivations for the Hawks' roster overhaul, particularly once details of the rookie's first contract became public knowledge. The pennywise Hawks suddenly got generous, signing Maravich to the largest contract in the history of professional basketball, a five-year deal worth $1.9 million. Cousins had selected Maravich without consulting coach Guerin or GM Blake. Further circumventing his coach and GM, Cousins used Omni Manager Bob Kent, an acquaintance of Press Maravich, the star's father and college coach, to convince the LSU guard to sign with Atlanta rather than the Carolina Cougars, the ABA team that drafted him. Both Guerin and Blake were furious that they had been kept out of the loop. While Guerin believed the Hawks should have used the pick to select a frontcourt replacement for Beaty, Blake was enthusiastic about Maravich's potential contribution to the team. Nevertheless, Blake thought intolerable the idea of signing a rookie to a multimillion-dollar contract after being forced to turn down immensely more modest salary demands by established stars like Beaty, Wilkens, and Caldwell. Blake resigned after sixteen years on the job, setting in motion a parade of front-office shakeups that rendered the Hawks' management unstable for the remainder of the 1970s.[1]

Initially, Hawks players were enthusiastic about the decision to draft Maravich. Despite the team's consecutive trips to the Western Division Finals in 1969 and 1970, few Atlantans seemed to have taken notice of the team. Moreover, anyone who saw Maravich play knew he was a transcendent talent.

Point guard Walt Hazzard said it was proof that they were "in the process of building a dynasty."[2] Forward Bill Bridges hailed the signing of a "great white hope," believing it would increase ticket sales at Alexander considerably. "Let's face it," Bridges said, "a white player of his ability is what Atlanta and the NBA need. He may be the greatest gate attraction to come in the league, and that doesn't hurt. It could mean a couple of hundred thousand dollars to all of us Hawks."[3] Hawks management tried to rebrand the franchise around Maravich, dressing the new-look Hawks in fluorescent blue and green uniforms, ditching the blue and red regalia they brought with them from St. Louis. Two years later, the Hawks adopted similarly funky red and gold uniforms for their move to the Omni.[4]

Excitement about the Maravich acquisition soon dissipated in the Hawks locker room. Shortly after he arrived, Maravich, in the words of his biographer Mark Kriegel, became a "collecting vessel for the team's resentments."[5] Racially fueled divisions emerged within the organization once Maravich signed his contract. A consensus developed on the Hawks' predominately Black roster that Maravich and Cousins constituted one faction and the rest of the organization constituted another. The Maravich acquisition was the culmination of the dismantling of the Hawks' highly successful roster. Hawks players had remained relatively anonymous and poorly paid while performing at an elite level during the late 1960s. Maravich, on arrival, was far better paid and far more well-known than all of his teammates combined.[6]

Socially, the aloof Maravich did himself no favors by rarely engaging his teammates either in the locker room or outside of basketball. When he did socialize with other players, he annoyed many of them by talking primarily about retiring early from basketball or his preoccupation with extraterrestrials. When he went out to eat with teammates, he tried to win them over by picking up the check. This only served to remind them of how much money he was making. In addition to his larger paycheck, Maravich's instant celebrity proved a further irritant to his teammates. He was suddenly Madison Avenue's favored NBA pitchman, hocking Keds sneakers, a "Pistol Pete" basketball, and, most notably, Vitalis Dry Control hair spray, which kept those shaggy locks of his in place on the court. Maravich was slated to costar with Karen Black in a Jack Nicholson–directed film about a college basketball star, called *Drive, He Said*, but backed out due to a scheduling conflict.[7]

On the court, Maravich's teammates resented his flamboyant style of play. They felt he monopolized the ball, expended little effort on defense, and made his teammates look bad by whizzing no-look passes in their direction, which sometimes flew past them unexpectedly or bounced off their foreheads. At one point during Maravich's rookie season, teammates Walt Hazzard and Bill Bridges grew tired of his play and refused to pass him the ball. In 1970–71 Atlanta faded from the 48-win team of the previous season into a 36–46 club that barely reached the playoffs. No longer were the Hawks the athletic, hardnosed club of the late 1960s. Maravich dominated the team's pace of play. Every evening, Atlanta's fortunes went the way of the rookie's shooting performance. Maravich made matters worse by quickly developing a strained relationship with the local press, which blamed the rookie for the team's declining fortunes.[8] At one point, Maravich told the *Journal*'s truculent Frank Hyland, "If I had a gun, I'd shoot you."[9] Coach Richie Guerin had the unenviable task of trying to keep the peace on the team.

Expecting Guerin to mediate between Maravich and his teammates was a difficult task for the veteran coach. As bad as Maravich's relations with his fellow Hawks were, they were arguably worse with his coaches. Maravich had contentious relationships with his two coaches in Atlanta, Richie Guerin (1970–72) and Cotton Fitzsimmons (1972–74), both of whom tried unsuccessfully to alter his approach to the game. "Pete's style of play offended me as a coach and our players," Guerin recalled twenty years later.[10] Guerin, whose coaching philosophy focused on vigorous defensive effort and unselfishness with the ball, clashed with Maravich over his shot selection, his reliance on fancy ball-handling to create shots, and his defensive indifference.[11]

After two seasons, the Hawks replaced Guerin with the offensive-minded Fitzsimmons, whose approach to the game appeared to be more in line with Pistol's. In the short term, longtime Hawk "Sweet Lou" Hudson starred along Maravich in Fitzsimmons' offensive-friendly system, leading the Hawks to a brief resurgence in 1972–73, when the team posted a 46–36 record but made a quick playoff exit. Hudson and Maravich finished fourth and fifth in the league in scoring that season while Pistol posted a career high in assists. In the long run, though, Fitzsimmons proved no more successful than Guerin at harnessing Maravich's talents. The young star proved unwilling to accommodate Fitzsimmons's vision for him as a distributor of the ball and not simply a scorer. Fitzsimmons suspended Pistol for two games for insubordination during the Hawks' dreadful 1973–74 season, the first time the franchise missed the playoffs in twelve years.[12]

As much as anything, teammates' resentment of Maravich stemmed from the Hawks' decline in the early 1970s. While the club's roster had been severely compromised by the time of Maravich's arrival, the decision by management to invest in the rookie rather than the Hawks' veterans stung ever more as they faded from a contender into an also-ran. The Hawks went 153–175 during Maravich's four years in Atlanta, posting losing records on three occasions. Maravich played hard and played well for the Hawks, emerging quickly as one of the league's top scorers. He displayed genuine grit as he played through a series of injuries and illnesses, including a bout of mono in his second season. Maravich, though, failed to lead his team to the championships that had been expected of him when he arrived in Atlanta.[13]

The suspension signaled the beginning of the end of Maravich's time in Atlanta. The Hawks traded Maravich in May 1974 to the expansion New Orleans Jazz in his adopted home state of Louisiana for two players and four draft picks.[14] "'Showtime' with the Pistol has not been a guarantee of success, however satisfying it may have been aesthetically," the *Constitution*'s Chris Cobbs wrote on the day of Maravich's departure.[15] Cobbs anticipated the narrative that emerged quickly in the Atlanta sports media surrounding Maravich, opining the loss of one of the city's great entertainers, even though many of those same sports writers pilloried him for years for his fancy, fast, and loose style of play.[16]

Like the Hawks, the Jazz tried to create overnight enthusiasm for their team by bringing the white superstar to their southern city. Like sports fans in Atlanta, New Orleans fans did not give their professional basketball team long-term support. Maravich and the Jazz spent five frustrating years in New Orleans before the Pistol moved on to Boston and the franchise relocated to Salt Lake City. The Maravich trade proved just as frustrating for the Hawks. Neither of the players Atlanta acquired made significant on-court contributions. More discouragingly, the two most prominent players they selected with their compensatory draft picks signed on instead with the rival ABA.[17]

Fans did not share in the animosity that Maravich's teammates, coaches, or the media felt toward him. Ever so briefly, Pistol Pete's flashy ball handling, offensive prowess, and national notoriety brought in many spectators who were not basketball devotees but instead were seeking out a novel entertainment experience. Most notably, Maravich's arrival in Atlanta caused an uptick in female attendance. Professional basketball games in Atlanta, as in most other NBA cities, had largely been a male domain.[18] The *Constitution*'s Richard Hyatt described a groundswell of "long-stemmed miniskirted chicks" attending Hawks games, sitting in a sweaty gymnasium alongside the regulars.[19] Maravich's female devotees whistled at his every move on the court. A dedicated group of female followers pursued the notably shy Maravich off the court as well. Whether at home or on the road, Maravich snuck out the back entrance to avoid the admirers who stalked him before and after games.[20]

"Personally, I would trade any number of wins for the thrill of having seen Pete Maravich a few more times at his very best. That incredible pass between his legs while in midair is simply unforgettable. I couldn't care less whether they won or lost the game," Keith Coulborn of Atlanta wrote to the *Constitution* soon after his trade, describing Maravich's appeal to the casual fan.[21] "He was what basketball has become, which is a game that is as much entertainment as it is sport. And he was the ultimate entertainer," current Hawks CEO Steve Koonin, an Atlanta native who grew up idolizing Pistol Pete, said of Maravich.[22]

"I played for the fans. There's no doubt about that, but sometimes my teammates didn't appreciate that," Maravich admitted in 1987, weeks before succumbing to a heart attack at age 40.[23] In his interactions with fans, Maravich couldn't have been a better ambassador for the Hawks or the NBA. When fans approached him, he took the time to inscribe "Pistol Pete" on every item they handed him to sign. High school basketball players across Dixie adopted Maravich's look and style, sporting his shaggy haircut and experimenting with his no-look passes, much to the chagrin of their coaches. Maravich's proclivity to indulge in fancy ball handling and take the majority of shots every game was, in part, a product of his desire to please fans who chanted, "Shoot, shoot, shoot" whenever he touched the ball.[24]

Few of the fans who went to Hawks games to see Maravich the attraction became sustained patrons of the team. Hawks season ticket sales hovered around two thousand during their first two years in Atlanta. Considering all the publicity the team received, Maravich's signing did surprisingly little to improve these numbers. Season-long sales grew to just 2,400 during his first winter in Atlanta. Hawks attendance as a whole improved considerably after Maravich's arrival, but remained well below the league average. Atlanta averaged nearly six thousand fans per night during Maravich's first season, almost eight hundred more than the previous year but well under the league's average crowd of 7,648 during the 1970–71 season.

When the Hawks moved to the Omni in 1972, season-ticket sales jumped to nearly 3,200 while average attendance increased to nearly 7,500, demonstrating that the addition of Maravich to the team's roster had less of an impact on the nightly gate than relocating to a better building. Many of the new 1972–73 season-ticket holders were professionals or corporations that added the bill to their expense accounts. Even so, the Omni remained half-empty for most Hawks games, and the team's nightly attendance remained more than one thousand off the league average. Moreover, the Hawks' season-ticket base paled in comparison to that of their co-tenant, the Atlanta Flames, which sold nearly 7,200 advanced season tickets in 1972–73.[25]

Even worse for the Hawks was that they were rarely the region's feature attraction on a Friday night. In the fall, a number of high school football games outdrew the Hawks each Friday. In the winter, Friday-night professional wrestling at the City Armory usually outdrew the Hawks at Alexander. The Armory's standing-room-only crowds of five thousand continued to outnumber Hawks spectators on Friday nights even after Maravich's arrival and the team's move to the Omni. The phenomenon of a regional wrestling promotion outdrawing a major professional sports franchise only ended when the Hawks moved most weekend dates to Saturday nights in the 1975–76 season.[26]

While the Hawks drew disappointing home crowds even with Maravich in the lineup, Pistol Pete was considered a major attraction both by fans in other NBA cities as well as by network television. The Hawks were the league's second-best-drawing road team behind the Boston Celtics in three of Maravich's four seasons in Atlanta.[27] ABC was so excited by the arrival of Maravich that the network paid the NBA an extra $75,000 simply to purchase the broadcasting rights to his professional debut. The network had yet to cover an Atlanta Hawks home game and was forced to equip the poorly illuminated Alexander Memorial Coliseum with extra lighting for its telecast. The once-anonymous Hawks made five more appearances on national television that season, tying for the league high.[28]

Maravich's arrival in Atlanta had led to a brief surge in attendance and a tremendous increase in the franchise's media visibility, but local affection for the Pistol proved short-lived. His presence did not translate into durable public support or continued on-court success for the Hawks. By the end of Maravich's four year run with the team (1970–74), the Hawks had become a losing club with a depleted roster. Though Maravich and the Hawks moved to the Omni for the 1972–73 season, the crowds they drew toward the end of the former LSU star's stay in Atlanta were just as small as those that had turned out to see the team during its residency at Alexander.

The seasons the Hawks experienced following Maravich's departure were some of the dreariest ever endured by a major professional sports franchise. The club struggled to its third, fourth, and fifth consecutive losing seasons between 1974 and 1977, leading to the dismissal of Fitzsimmons. Despite their lack of success, the Hawks played exciting, up-tempo basketball under Fitzsimmons, featuring veteran guard Lou Hudson, athletic power forward John Drew, and veteran swingman Tom Van Arsdale. Unable to draw even when the team was good, the club's poor performance exacerbated its attendance struggles. The Hawks finished last in attendance for three consecutive seasons (1974–77), drawing fewer than 5,600 spectators per game each year. At the time, the league's average attendance was more than 10,000 per game.[29] Many of the fans whom Maravich had drawn to the Omni simply tuned the team out after his departure. Hudson, who remembered the sparse crowds that came to see them play at Alexander in the late 1960s, described the post-Maravich era as "the worst time I've ever had in basketball."[30]

To bolster attendance, the Hawks relied heavily on promotions, giveaways, and contests. The most outrageous of
their promotion men was Pat Williams, who took over as GM
in 1973. The thirty-three-year-old executive, who went on to
great success in NBA front offices during the 1980s and 1990s,
had already developed a reputation for staging wild halftime
promotions during brief tenures as an executive for the Philadelphia 76ers and Chicago Bulls. "Atlanta is a live-wire city
and I'm confident that pro basketball can be merchandized,
hustled, and sold to the public," Williams told reporters at
the time of his hiring.[31] Williams brought his halftime sta-
ples down to Atlanta with him, including Victor the Wrestling
Bear and Little Arlene, the era's most famous competitive
eater. Interspecies wrestling matches and hot dog eating contests became the midgame norm during the 1973–74 season.
On other occasions that winter, the Hawks gave away prizes
for the fan with the largest feet in the arena and for fans that
weighed in at more than 250 pounds. Williams also added
Easter Egg Hunt, Secret Santa, and Trick or Treat nights to
the Hawks' promotional slate. Despite the Hawks' exciting
program of off-court features, attendance remained flat as
the club struggled to a 35–47 record, and Williams left after
one season. His successor, Bud Seretean, tried to improve the
Hawks' gate by making their schedule more family friendly.
He negotiated an in-house deal with the Omni Group that
moved twenty-four of the Hawks' forty-one home dates to
Saturday or Sunday evenings at 7:00 p.m., virtually eliminating Friday nights from the schedule. The Hawks hoped the
earlier weekend start time would enable suburban families
to make it home at a more reasonable hour. Instead, the shift
to an earlier start time corresponded with a slight decline in
their weekend attendance.[32]

As Hawks' attendance fell to new depths, fans from Atlanta's Black middle class emerged as a significant portion of the
team's live audience. Despite the franchise's evident unwillingness to market itself to African Americans, Black spec-

tators embraced the flagging franchise as ever more white spectators lost interest. The desire of the Hawks ownership to make its product appealing to white customers was evident from the player-personnel decisions it made during the club's early years in Atlanta. This strategy failed to earn the franchise steady support from local customers and transformed the team into perennial also-rans. Simultaneously, the club expended minimal effort promoting their product to African Americans, who constituted a majority of Atlanta's population and were becoming increasingly enthusiastic basketball fans. This missed opportunity by the Hawks to earn steady support from Black patrons exemplified the franchise's tone-deafness to issues related to race.

During the Hawks' early years in Atlanta, African Americans constituted a tiny presence in the crowds at Alexander. The club put little effort into attracting Black patrons and it showed. A survey commissioned by the NBA during the 1971–72 season found that African Americans made up only 8 percent of the spectatorship at Atlanta Hawks games. Just 9 of the Hawks' 2,398 season ticket holders that year were Black. In cities with similar demographics to Atlanta, such as Baltimore and Detroit, African Americans made up nearly one-third of the live audience for professional basketball. African Americans, in fact, made up a larger percentage of the NBA crowds in both Portland and Seattle, where Blacks made up two and seven percent of the population, respectively, than they did in majority-Black Atlanta.[33]

The lack of Black spectators at Hawks games during the late 1960s and early 1970s was in no way reflective of the game's popularity among the region's African American population. Over the course of the 1960s, African Americans in Atlanta, like those in cities across the United States, embraced basketball to an unprecedented extent, both as a form of recreation and as a spectator sport. By the end of the decade, national surveys indicated that basketball had overtaken baseball in popularity among Black fans, challenging football for the designation as African Americans' favorite sport. While football had long been a pastime in Atlanta's Black belt, basketball became a playground fixture in the neighborhoods to the south, west, and east of downtown during the 1960s. Highly competitive summer recreational leagues and winter high school basketball games drew large crowds in predominately Black Atlanta neighborhoods. Largely African American schools such as Carver, Southwest, and West Fulton became major powers in the state high school basketball tournament during the late 1960s and early 1970s.[34]

"That's appalling for a city with Atlanta's reputation as a sports center and where there are more prosperous Blacks than any other city in the National Basketball Association," African American insurance executive Jesse Hill Jr. said of the league-commissioned report on Black spectatorship. Hill organized a 1972 meeting with Hawks management aimed at increasing the number of Black season-ticket holders. He attributed the dearth of Black attendance at Hawks games to the northside location of their home court. He believed that the opening of the Omni in the southern CBD that fall would prove a more welcoming setting for Black fans than Alexander. Construction magnate and Hawks stockholder Herman Russell, the first African American to own a percentage of a major professional sports franchise, worked with Hill to organize gatherings in the homes of prominent Black Atlantans, which amounted to season-ticket sales pitches for their friends and business associates. There is no indication that these gatherings did much to increase season-ticket sales among the city's Black professional class.[35]

While Hill's season-ticket drive proved ineffective, his prediction that African Americans would constitute a larger percentage of the crowd at the Omni came to fruition. A notable uptick in Black attendance at Hawks games during the mid-to-late 1970s correlated with the team's move to the southern CBD. The increasing number of Black spectators at Hawks games also corresponded with a broader socioeconomic change in the region, namely the expansion of Metropolitan Atlanta's Black middle class. Affirmative Action programs put in place during the 1970s by the Massell and Jackson administrations for municipal jobs and contracts contributed to a substantial increase in the number of African American residents with sufficient disposable income to attend professional sporting events. While relatively few of Atlanta's Black elites had embraced mass spectator sports outside of those being played at historically Black colleges, the cultural preferences of the city's expanding Black middle class corresponded closely with those of Atlanta's Black proletariat, leading to an increase in the number of African Americans who attended professional sporting events in the city.[36]

Hawks officials estimated in the mid-1970s that African Americans constituted between 15 and 25 percent of their live audience on most evenings, a fact that team officials feared was discouraging attendance by white customers who would have regarded any discernable presence of Black fans at the games as unacceptable. "White Atlantans who stay away from Hawks games are likely to tell you that the percentage is as high as 60," Roy Blount quipped in a 1977 profile of the Atlanta sports scene for *Sports Illustrated*.[37] Visits to Atlanta by prominent African American stars such as Kareem Abdul-Jabbar, Walt Frazier, and, especially, Julius Erving, drew far larger contingents of Black fans to the Omni, suggesting that many of these patrons were fans more generally of professional basketball and the individual, stylized prowess of its top Black performers than of the Hawks in particular. Appearances by Erving, "Dr. J," who joined the NBA's Philadelphia 76ers in 1976 after six seasons as the rival ABA's top player, drew large crowds in every NBA city during the late 1970s, including Atlanta. Sportswriters in many cities noted that the crowds that came out to see "Dr. J," who helped popularize the slam dunk, included an unprecedentedly large percentage of Black spectators. Erving made his first professional appearance in Atlanta on November 20, 1976, drawing a sellout crowd to the

Omni for the first time in three seasons. The majority-Black crowd that evening cheered on Erving every time he touched the ball. The next night, the Hawks drew just 1,076 fans for a home date against the Kansas City Kings, the franchise's smallest crowd since moving to Atlanta in 1968.[38] Despite the increase in Black attendance, finding an audience proved a multidecade struggle for the Hawks. The franchise finished below the league average in attendance in each of its first eighteen years in Atlanta (1968–86).

As the Hawks' on-court fortunes faded, the franchise's owner was dealing with the deterioration of his own fortune. On paper, Tom Cousins appeared to be one of the NBA's wealthiest owners, but the failure of the Omni International Complex to become an instant commercial hub cost him tens of millions of dollars during the mid-to-late 1970s. Cousins's flagging investment in the twin Omnis left him with few resources to invest in his basketball team. Exaggerating Cousins' financial troubles was the tendency of his organizations—sports, real estate, or otherwise—to rely on interlocking directorates. Many of the investors he assembled into the Omni Group played prominent roles in the Hawks and Flames organizations, the management of the arena, and even the Omni International Complex simultaneously. Omni Coliseum President Bill Putnam, for example, served at different times as the general manager of the Hawks and the Flames. Unlike Putnam, who had extensive experience in sports and entertainment, many of the investors in Cousins's developments came out of the real estate business and had no experience in professional sports or arena operation and had little background in downtown property management. Since Cousins's core group of investors held stakes in several of his ventures simultaneously, the financial troubles of any one arm of the organization ended up causing the entire entity to struggle. Weaker parts of the business sopped up the money and momentum of the stronger parts of the organization.[39]

The Hawks' precarious financial situation was amplified

further by the lack of broadcast-media revenue they had generated since their arrival in 1968. WSB held on to the local broadcasting rights for Atlanta Hawks basketball during their first six seasons, televising just eight games each year. The Hawks never earned more than $250,000 per season from WSB for broadcasting rights. Interest in newcomer Pete Maravich enabled WSB to expand its Hawks radio network, which broadcast all eighty-two games, to eighteen stations and its television network into four states for the 1970–71 season, but this did little to improve the club's broadcast revenue. The team was in the midst of a long-term contract with the flagship Atlanta station. The tepid Nielsen numbers the Hawks continued to draw that winter stymied whatever leverage they had to negotiate a new deal.[40]

Broadcasts of nationally televised NBA games were also consistent ratings losers on Atlanta television during the 1970s, despite frequent appearances by the Pete Maravich–era Hawks. In each of Maravich's four seasons with the Hawks, the team appeared an additional six to twelve times on Atlanta television, either on WQXI, the city's ABC affiliate, or WAGA, its CBS affiliate. On several occasions, ABC blacked out early 1970s Hawks home playoff games in the Atlanta area because of poor advance ticket sales. WQXI was forced to telecast playoff games from another part of the country while the hometown team was competing in the same playoffs just a few blocks from their studio. Consistently poor ratings caused WQXI (1973) and WAGA (1974) to cancel their Sunday afternoon "NBA Game of the Week" in the midst of successive seasons. During the 1974–75 season, Atlanta was the only NBA market without access to national broadcasts of professional basketball.[41] "Sports other than football do not really please a majority of your viewers," WQXI general manager John Tyler told the *Constitution* in 1973. Tyler replaced WQXI's basketball doubleheaders with double features of Westerns from the 1950s, which drew nearly twice as many viewers each Sunday.[42]

Poor ratings aside, national television revenue did little to boost the Hawks' bottom line. During their first five seasons in Atlanta, the team received approximately $100,000 per year from ABC as part of the NBA's long-term deal with the network. The NBA, which drew poor ratings, had little leverage to negotiate a better television deal at the time. Outside of a few traditionally passionate blue collar fanbases in the urban north, professional basketball drew atrocious ratings in the 1970s. Television revenue jumped to more than $500,000 per year for all NBA teams in 1973–74 as CBS decided to take a chance at basketball with a lucrative, but short-term, package. Continued poor ratings led CBS to negotiate a much smaller contract in 1976 that provided each team with just over $300,000 annually. It was not until the 1980s that the NBA became a ratings winner on network television.[43]

Ted Turner's WTCG came to an agreement with the Hawks to broadcast their games during the 1974–75 season after WSB refused to renew their contract. WTCG paid the Hawks a mere $100,000 for the season, but agreed to carry a slate of twenty-five road games. The Hawks were willing to accept a 20 percent cut in their meagre television revenue for an expanded schedule of televised games that would not compete directly with their gate at the Omni. The following year, WTCG expanded its coverage of professional basketball beyond the Hawks, convincing the NBA to allow it to take on an additional syndicated package of regular-season games from across the country. Despite the league's reticence to sell its product to a UHF station, the deal with WTCG provided the NBA with unprecedented access to the southeastern market.[44] WTCG's ratings for NBA games, Hawks or otherwise, proved low, but the addition of another major professional league to the station's programming further enhanced its prestige as a broadcaster. "Our profit will be minimal at best from the games," WTCG Station Manager Sid Pike told *Sports Illustrated*. "If we ran movies instead we could make much more money," he said, referring to the kind of programming that had previously been the station's bread and butter.[45]

By 1975, Cousins was looking to shed the Hawks from his portfolio. For the next two years, he entered into negotiations with several interested parties, but each one balked when they learned that purchasing the team would make them responsible for the franchise's estimated $10 million in debt. In January 1977 Ted Turner, whose WTCG had been broadcasting Hawks games for three seasons, purchased a majority stake in the team for a mere $1.5 million while assuming the lion's share of its debts. Turner, who had purchased the Braves on a ten-year, $1-million-per-year installment plan just twelve months earlier, had quickly become the primary trustee of Atlanta's moribund professional sports scene.[46]

"It was only after all other avenues failed that Ted finally got into the deal," Hawks executive Mike Gearon said of the negotiations. Much of Atlanta's civic elite viewed Turner skeptically, for both his renegade persona and their belief that his television fortune existed merely on paper. Cousins and, in turn, the NBA acquiesced to Turner because they had no clear alternatives if they wished to keep professional basketball in the Southeast.[47] Turner ran the Hawks on a shoestring budget in the late 1970s, leaving the operation of the franchise almost entirely to his associates as he insinuated himself into the cable-television business. Turner ran the team's promotional department out of the Braves' offices. He hired longtime business associate Stan Kasten as general manager and Mike Gearon, a casual friend who Turner knew often attended Hawks games, as team president. The Turner-owned Hawks dumped all of the team's large contracts and tried to rebuild the organization as if it were an expansion franchise.[48]

20

I Think the Fans Showed Poor Taste

THE YEAR 1969 WASN'T REAL—AT LEAST NOT FOR THE
Atlanta Braves. The heady September surge that helped Atlanta
leap from fourth place to first in the National League West
in 1969 was not real. This was not the team that Braves fans
watched in the late 1960s and it was not the team they saw in
the early 1970s. As the club went back to its old ways, the fans
that filled Atlanta Stadium for the Braves' run to the NLCS were
similarly absent. Following their 1969 turnaround, the Braves
spent the early 1970s mired in a mediocrity that resembled
their early years in Atlanta. They were never terrible, but they
were always disappointing. Atlanta remained one of the NL's
fiercest hitting teams but simply could not muster enough
pitching to get past the titans of the new NL West: Cincinnati,
San Francisco, and Los Angeles.

Between 1970 and 1973, the Braves never finished better
than third but also never finished in the cellar. They were
never a boring team either. Their roster still featured future
Hall of Famers Phil Niekro and Orlando Cepeda and 1970
NL batting champion Rico Carty, but their notoriety paled in
comparison to that of Hank Aaron, who was in the process
of making history. Aaron's rapid ascension on the all-time
home run list punctuated each of the Braves' early 1970s campaigns. While most sluggers slow their pace rapidly once they
reach the 500–home run plateau, Aaron accelerated his. In
less than five seasons (1968–73), Aaron went from 500 home
runs to 700, a mark he reached just before the 1973 All-Star
Game. Aaron was also part of an unprecedented 1973 power

surge on the Braves. The 1973 Braves became the only team in MLB history to feature three different players that hit at least 40 home runs: Aaron (40), third baseman Darrell Evans (41), and second baseman Davey Johnson (43).

Braves attendance fell much more precipitously than the team did in the standings. After drawing 1,458,320 fans in 1969, Atlanta's attendance fell to 1,078,848 in 1970. In 1971 the Braves hosted their one millionth fan of the season in their next-to-last home game. In the strike-shortened 1972 season, the Braves drew slightly more than 750,000 fans, beginning a streak of eight consecutive seasons when the Braves failed to draw one million spectators (1972–79). The Braves drew an average of 798,448 fans per season during the 1970s, the lowest average attendance in MLB.

It wasn't for a lack of trying by the team's promotional department that the Braves drew so poorly. The Braves boasted frequently in their advertisements that their tickets were among the most affordable in MLB. While the $5.00 dugout-level seats offered at Atlanta Stadium were among the NL's most expensive in 1970, the majority of seats were priced below the league average of $2.50. Season-ticket packages for 1975 ranged in price from $250 to $375 for eighty-one dates, the same prices charged for 1966 season tickets. In an effort to create a family-friendly environment, the Braves offered fifty-cent general-admission passes for children well into the 1970s, the cheapest ticket of any kind in MLB. A 1971 internal study indicated that few families took advantage of these inexpensive general-admission passes. Fifty-cent passes constituted a mere 6 percent of Braves ticket sales that season.[1] Despite the team's best efforts, the audience at most games at Atlanta Stadium consisted largely of chain smoking, middle-aged males. "To this day, that mix of cigarette and pipe odor takes me straight back to the Launching Pad," longtime Braves fan Mike Holcomb said of Braves crowds in the 1970s.[2]

The Atlanta Braves were among the first franchises to present professional baseball games explicitly as a family-

friendly environment. Their efforts to expand their spectatorship beyond the majority adult and male constituency that
inhabited most ballparks made sense in profoundly suburban metropolitan Atlanta. Moreover, the club's cultivation of
a family-friendly stadium environment helped the franchise
fulfill its often-stated goal of becoming a regional draw. Families from across the Southeast planned summer trips around
a visit to the ballpark. The cultivation of a family-friendly ballpark environment by MLB teams proved a broadly and highly
successful strategy, helping professional teams double their
average attendance between the mid-1970s and the early 1990s.
In Atlanta, though, the approach had mixed results.[3]

Clearly, the Braves understood that many suburbanites did
not want to venture in or out of Atlanta after dark. To this end,
the team tried to accommodate fans with earlier start times. In
1971 the Braves added a number of weekday afternoon games
to their summer months' schedules. The team's intent was
to entice suburban parents to bring their children to Atlanta
Stadium, but the Braves drew even sparser crowds for these
earlier games than they had on weeknights. The team also
moved weekend start times up an hour to 7:00 p.m. on Saturdays and 1:00 p.m. on Sundays, but this had no discernable
impact on attendance.[4]

During the early 1970s the Braves embraced nightly promotions and contests, particularly ones aimed at children, as
thoroughly as any team in the Major Leagues. They hosted several picture days each season with players and celebrity guests.
Weekend home games concluded with fireworks displays. They
gave away jackets, pennants, hats, balls, and miniature bats to
children while featuring season-long contests that gave away
automobiles to adults. Virtually every home game served as a
discount night tailored to the residents of specific neighborhoods, towns, counties, and states. In 1972 the Braves adopted
a crowd-pleasing "mod new look," adorning players and team
representatives in garish, fashion-forward regalia. The team
donned bright blue and red uniforms that would not have been

out of place in a recreational softball league. Relief pitchers commuted to the mound in a bullpen cart that resembled the Apollo moon buggy and bore the team's new, lower-case red cursive 'a' logo. The suddenly mod Braves also embraced the recent revolution in mores by hiring a new, largely blonde troop of usherettes, whom they clad in hot pants and revealing blue and red tops.[5]

The Braves added a live mascot named Chief Noc-A-Homa in 1969 as an off-the-field, in-game entertainment. He replaced a twenty-two-foot-tall Styrofoam statue of a Mohawk-wearing, tomahawk-wielding American Indian named Big Victor, which stood in right field in 1967 and 1968. The character of Chief Noc-A-Homa was portrayed by a fully enrolled member of the Chippewa Tribe named Levi Walker. The chief spent most of the game horsing around with children or attempting to rile up the crowd with antics that would draw cringes from many twenty-first-century observers. Adorned in moccasins, buckskins, and a headdress, Walker would breathe fire, war whoop, and partake in rain dances. He raided the opposing dugout on horseback and blew smoke signals from his teepee behind the left-field wall. The chief remained a genuinely popular attraction at the ballpark until the club phased him out of its in-game entertainments during the mid-1980s.[6]

The Braves attracted a local fanbase during the 1960s and 1970s that was largely white and middle class, skewing toward the white collar.[7] When the Braves arrived in Atlanta, Georgia Senator Richard Russell said, "Your Braves fans will come not only from the city, but from the forks of the creeks and the boondocks."[8] Russell was correct when he asserted that many of the Braves' most fervent fans would come from outside Metropolitan Atlanta. A Georgia Tech School of Industrial Management study suggested that the Braves' appeal in the "boondocks" extended out from rural Georgia across the Southeast. The study found that 41 percent of Braves spectators in 1966 came from outside Metropolitan Atlanta. Forty-three percent of out-of-towners came from elsewhere in Georgia, while significant numbers of out-of-town fans came from other southeastern states, including 13 percent from Alabama, 11 percent from Tennessee, 9 percent from each of the Carolinas, and 5 percent from Florida.[9]

"Once school was out, a significant amount of the attendance came from this regional base," Karl Green recalled.[10] Frequently, these fans came in large groups from out of state, often organized through Little League teams, Boy Scout troops, and church groups. Many families across the Southeast made a trip to Atlanta Stadium the centerpiece of their summer vacations, witnessing in person the players they followed through the team's regional radio and television networks. Out-of-town visitors traveled an average of 146 miles in 1966 to attend Braves games, making use of the thirty-two lanes of interstate traffic that converged on Atlanta Stadium, as city boosters often pointed to with pride. But they overestimated the extravagance of the fans who traveled to Atlanta to see the Braves, many of whom stayed with relatives who lived in the area or returned home immediately after the game on tour buses. Either way, one of the reasons that attendance dropped so dramatically at late-season Braves games was the lack of large groups from out of town.[11]

Many baseball enthusiasts in Metro Atlanta were already the fans of other teams when the Braves arrived, making it difficult for the city's new MLB franchise to win their affection. The influx of more than one hundred thousand non-Georgians to the area during the 1960s, many of whom hailed from the urban North, ensured that significant portions of the crowd during visits to Atlanta Stadium by the New York Mets, Chicago Cubs, and St. Louis Cardinals would be cheering for the opposing team. The net migration of nearly 1.1 million people to the state of Georgia between 1970 and 1990 exaggerated this phenomenon at Atlanta Stadium considerably. Many transplanted baseball fans went to Atlanta Stadium to cheer on their visiting hometown team but did not otherwise patronize Braves games.[12]

"THE PERCENTAGE OF BLACK FANS AT THE BALLPARK—
like all the ballparks in the major leagues—was very low,"
Hank Aaron said in his memoir.[13] Despite the emergence of
a Black majority in the city of Atlanta during the 1960s, few
African Americans attended Braves games.[14] During Aaron's
home run chase, a number of sportswriters expressed their
surprise at the dearth of Black fans in the stands supporting
Aaron at Atlanta Stadium. The *New York Times*' Dave Anderson attributed the lack of Black spectators at Braves games
to high ticket prices, which kept many out of the ballpark.[15]

Undoubtedly, many Black residents could not afford to
attend a game at Atlanta Stadium, despite the relative afford-
ability of Braves tickets when compared to the rest of MLB.
Twenty-nine percent of Blacks in Atlanta lived below the poverty line in 1970, more than two-and-a-half times the national
average and four times the rate of their white neighbors in the
city. At the same time, though, Atlanta had the nation's largest
and most economically diverse Black middle class, one that
included both an established urban professional and commercial class and a class of middle-income suburban homeowners centered in Fulton and Dekalb Counties. For the most
part, though, African Americans in Atlanta who could afford
to attend professional baseball games chose to spend their
discretionary dollars elsewhere.[16]

The dearth of Black fans in attendance at Braves games
reflected the well-documented decline in interest in baseball
among African Americans as both a participatory and spectator sport during the 1960s and 1970s, particularly among the
young and those that lived in cities. In a 1960 Gallup poll, 43
percent of African Americans named baseball as their favorite sport, twice as many as football and basketball combined.
By 1981, just 17 percent of Black respondents told Gallup that
baseball was their favorite sport, roughly the same number
that selected basketball and roughly one-half as many as preferred football.[17] The shifting preferences of Atlanta's Black
sports fans reflected these broader national trends. In the late

1940s and 1950s, African American spectators filled the segregated sections of Poncey to watch the Minor League Atlanta Crackers. Despite inconsistent fan support, the Atlanta Black Crackers played organized Black professional baseball at Poncey from 1920 until 1952. By the late 1970s, African American fans became a notable presence at Falcons and Hawks games, particularly when a major Black star, such as the NBA's Julius Erving or the NFL's O. J. Simpson, was playing on the visiting team.[18]

Beyond their specific feelings toward baseball, many Black Atlantans' relationship to the Braves was profoundly shaped by their relationship to the development of Atlanta Stadium. The decision to build on urban renewal property originally designated for affordable housing initiated an often-conflictual relationship between African American residents of nearby neighborhoods and the Braves, the stadium's primary tenant and a looming institutional force in Summerhill for most of the year. A place that had once been a predominately Black neighborhood had been privatized into a leisure space that accommodated primarily white patrons. Despite the broad support among Atlanta's Black leadership for the stadium project, the "Miracle in Atlanta" demonstrated to many Black residents the civic establishment's prioritization of professional sports over the housing needs of genuinely destitute people. The thousands of Summerhill residents displaced by urban renewal in the 1950s were led to believe that they would be able to return to their neighborhood once affordable housing was built in the area. Instead, the stadium made a permanent intrusion on the neighborhood, one that brought with it impositions on their community by thousands of outsiders all spring and summer.[19]

Residents of the neighborhoods surrounding Atlanta Stadium found their streets clogged with visitors' cars during games. Noise and light pollution intruded on their homes for much of the year. Moreover, the presence of predominately white and suburban visitors in Summerhill for sporting events formed a continuum with the assertion of state power over the area through urban renewal in the 1950s and 1960s as well as the ongoing conflicts between area residents and the Atlanta police. On game days, residents found many ways to reassert control over their neighborhood, primarily through the individual financial and material benefits they acquired as a result of their visitors' presence. Many Summerhill homeowners and renters alike transformed their properties into informal game-day parking lots. Other neighborhood residents convinced visitors to pay them to watch their cars, which the visitors had parked on side streets or in alleys while they attended the game. Still other neighborhood residents took advantage of the parked cars by engaging in petty acts of larceny.[20]

The Braves made noteworthy efforts to cultivate a friendly relationship with the residents of the predominately African American neighborhoods surrounding the stadium. The franchise created a Good Neighbor Program that sponsored the construction and maintenance of a local recreational center. Players held frequent baseball clinics at the center, which included ticket and equipment giveaways. Additionally, the Braves organization participated in or sponsored many community events in the surrounding neighborhoods. These programs may have smoothed over some of the rough edges in the Braves' relationship with their neighbors, but it hardly turned the predominately underprivileged residents of the Model Cities neighborhoods into enthusiastic supporters of the franchise, let alone regular ballpark patrons.[21]

For many residents of the neighborhoods surrounding the stadium, their most tangible relationship to the Braves was as an employee rather than as a fan. Atlanta Stadium offered much needed employment opportunities to residents of southeast Atlanta, though most jobs at the ballpark were low-waged, seasonal positions as ushers, security guards, ticket-takers, or concessioners. From the time of the stadium's opening, most stadium employees were African American, a proportion that grew as Atlanta itself became a supermajority Black city. As a result, Atlanta Stadium became a workplace with a predominately Black labor force that was managed by the Braves' largely white corporate leadership. Although scant evidence exists for sustained conflict between labor and management regarding stadium operations, tensions clearly emerged during the 1960s and 1970s between the predominately white attendees of Braves games and Atlanta Stadium's predominately Black workforce.[22]

The adoption of the rhetoric of color blindness by middle-class white southerners in the 1960s and 1970s transformed open expressions of racial animus into cultural taboos. But a careful reading of contemporary fan accounts of the staff at Atlanta Stadium suggests that numerous interactions between the customers and employees at Braves games took on an evident racial meaning. The Braves' stadium workforce became the de facto around-the-field face of the organization, resulting in these low-waged workers drawing much of the ire of fans who were unhappy with the management of the franchise.

"I don't feel like a welcome customer any time I have attended Atlanta Stadium. Everyone I had contact with made me feel as if they were doing me a favor to allow me to watch the game," C.N. DeCourcy wrote in response to an April 1968 column by the *Constitution*'s Furman Bisher, asking why so few fans had attended the Braves' home opener.[23] "The Atlanta Braves management should write a book on how not to run a baseball team or how to discourage attendance from games," Steve Carrington of Atlanta wrote to the *Journal-Constitution* in 1971. Carrington focused on his experiences at Atlanta Stadium's ticket office, where "the agents could care less about helping the fans and they make no effort to be friendly. I have waited for over 40 minutes for one girl to count money and chat with her co-worker while the line grew."[24] "Stadium ushers are uncooperative," an anonymous man from the Atlanta area wrote to the *Sporting News* in 1975. In the same letter, the writer noted that nearly all game attendees were white while most stadium employees were Black. To illustrate his point, he related a recent incident at a nearly empty Atlanta Stadium in which "I tried after the fifth inning to move several rows down from my ticketed seat in the upper deck. An usher stopped me and that has to take the cake for high-handed pettiness." Collectively, these interactions suggest that both racial and class dynamics exaggerated the complaints that some of the Braves' predominately white fan base had with the execution of the stadium's operations by its predominately Black and low-waged workforce.[25]

ATLANTA'S ATTENDANCE PROBLEMS REMAINED A LOCAL news item until Hank Aaron's pursuit of Babe Ruth's all-time career homerun record during the 1973 and 1974 seasons made every Braves game a national news story. The small crowds that turned out at Atlanta Stadium to see Aaron chase the most revered record in American sports shocked the national press corps. "Atlanta is the disgrace of baseball," the New York Times' Dave Anderson wrote. "Atlanta doesn't deserve Henry Aaron's drama. He'd be better off on a barnstorming tour."[26] The Braves finished next-to-last in attendance in the NL in both 1973 and 1974. Large crowds turned out in every other NL city to see Aaron and honor his every at bat with a standing ovation. In 1973 more than 2.4 million fans watched Aaron and the Braves play on the road, three times as many as saw him at home. In 1974 nearly 1.7 million fans watched the Braves play away games, almost twice as many as the 981,085 who saw them play in Atlanta that season.[27]

The poor home attendance during the 1973 season, the entirety of which Aaron spent in pursuit of Ruth's record, was particularly striking. The team drew just 800,655 despite the intense local and national media attention focused on the home run chase. Though not a winning team (76–85), the 1973 Braves were one of the greatest power-hitting teams in baseball history, making their poor attendance figures all the more noteworthy. A team with three of the NL's four leading homerun hitters, all 40–home run men, would be an attendance-boosting attraction in any city.[28] "All year long, Atlanta overwhelmed me with indifference," Aaron recalled. "I would get standing ovations in New York and Los Angeles and Chicago and St. Louis . . . but it seemed like Atlanta frankly didn't give a damn. Our crowds were so pitiful you could practically hear someone crack open a peanut. . . . The way I saw it, the only thing Atlanta was too busy for was baseball."[29]

Braves management assumed that the home run chase would bolster home attendance, but, outside of the nights when Aaron was pursuing a particular milestone, this did not happen. Fewer than ten thousand spectators witnessed several of Aaron's home runs between 700 and 712. Many of the fans that bothered to attend crammed into the left field bleachers, hoping to catch one of the right-handed-hitting Aaron's home run balls, while the rest of the stadium remained largely empty. A mere 1,362 fans witnessed Aaron's 711th home run on a Monday night in September 1973, fewer people than had attended several dozen different high school football games in metropolitan Atlanta the previous weekend.[30]

Longtime Braves fans and the media that covered the team attributed the apathetic response to the home run chase to the blasé attitudes that locals had already developed toward their professional teams. Atlanta fans proved unwilling to turn out in large numbers for a big league game unless it promised to be an event. "The city loved Hank and supported him. Everyone knew he would eventually break the record. The team did not perform well enough to generate fan interest," Alan Morris recalled.[31] Karl Green remembered that "Aaron's personality, low-key and reserved, didn't generate excitement among the fan base."[32] Aaron had been a steady home run hitter throughout his career but never threatened to break the single-season home run mark. Steady success on a frequently underachieving team had not made Aaron a transcendent figure in the city or one that cultivated deep bonds of affection among the fan base. "It was as if they knew he could not hit five or ten in one game to break the record, and that's what they seemed to be waiting for," Wayne Minshew recalled.[33]

Despite the recollection of Braves fans, the evidence suggests that race played a role in engendering local apathy toward Aaron. Undoubtedly, the national media narrative surrounding Aaron's home run chase focused far more explicitly on race than it did in the Atlanta market, where discussions of race already permeated every public issue of the day. In 1973 Aaron received 930,000 pieces of mail, fifteen times more than the next closest American celebrity, Dinah Shore. A clear majority offered words of encouragement, especially after he told reporters that he was receiving thousands of hateful letters as he pursued Ruth's record.[34] In May 1973 Aaron informed a group of sportswriters in Philadelphia that he had directed his secretary to save all the abusive mail he had received that season. When the story broke nationally, "I guess people were stunned by what they read," Aaron said, "because thousands and thousands of them started writing me positive letters."[35]

The public responded to the news of Aaron's hate mail with simultaneous revulsion and collective protestations of white racial innocence. Sixty-eight percent of fans told a 1973 Harris survey that they were cheering for Aaron to break Ruth's record. Another 62 percent expressed shock that Aaron was attracting hate mail as a result of the chase.[36] Braves fans recall that open expressions of racial hostility toward Aaron were rare in Atlanta at the time of the home run chase. "I am sure there were some who held prejudice against a Black man eclipsing a white baseball legend but I never personally heard any of this," Alan Morris said.[37]

Receiving vicious letters was nothing new for Aaron. He'd received a steady stream of them since 1968, when *Jet* magazine published an interview in which he complained about the outsized scrutiny that Black athletes received when they earned large salaries. Prior to the home run chase, most of this hate mail originated in the Southeast, where Braves baseball was followed most closely. As Aaron approached Ruth's

record, the amount of hate mail he received increased exponentially and came from across the country, but much of it
focused on the same themes.[38] The amount of money that
Aaron made preoccupied the writers of the abusive letters
he received both before and during the home run chase. In
1972 Aaron had signed a three-year deal worth a then-record
$600,000.[39] During the home run chase, many letter writ-
ers told Aaron that he was an unworthy heir to Ruth. Sometimes, the writers cited statistical reasons for their views,
but more often they relied on vulgarity and racial epithets.
Hundreds of letters directed specific threats at Aaron, which
included times, dates, and locations where the slugger would
be harmed. For the rest of the home run chase, Atlanta police
regarded many of the threats as credible and assigned an officer to serve as Aaron's personal security.[40] Braves teammate
Ron Reed, who was the starting pitcher the night that Aaron
broke Ruth's record, said that the 1973–74 season was one of
the few times that he remembers race being discussed openly
in the team's locker room. The unprecedented amount of hate
mail that Aaron received was "the only way that a lot of us had
any contact with any racial problems."[41]

In addition to the bags of hate mail, Aaron and his family
faced two direct, high-profile physical threats during the season. An Aaron hater stalked his eighteen-year-old daughter
Gaile during her freshman year at Fisk University in Nash-
ville, Tennessee.[42] In May 1973 Aaron nearly came to blows
with a group of straight-out-of-central-casting bigots in Atlanta
Stadium's right-field stands. The incident received extensive
coverage in the national sporting press, calling into question
Atlanta's reputation as a progressive oasis. The group of men
had been harassing Aaron from the nearly empty section for
several consecutive nights. Their caterwauling taunts echoed
throughout the largely vacant stadium. Such back-and-forth
between fans in the usually empty bleachers and the outfield-
ers had been common for years at Atlanta Stadium. In the past,
fans complained that it was the players directing foul language

toward them, but, in this instance, it was fans hurling abusive language at the players.[43] "At first, it was the same stuff I was used to hearing, mostly about all the money I was making for striking out and hitting into double plays, but as they became drunker and louder they became more obscene and personal," Aaron recalled.[44] He confronted the men directly before the ninth inning of a May 8 game against the Mets. Stadium security intervened before a fight broke out, escorting the men out of the stadium. After the confrontation, the Braves banned the group from the ballpark and assigned a full-time security detail to Aaron.[45]

Aaron spent much of his career as an under-the-radar superstar, but the reticent celebrity became the focus of extensive national media coverage as he approached the record. *Time* and *Newsweek* profiled him during the 1973 season. During the 1973–74 off-season, he appeared on the television programs of Merv Griffin, Dean Martin, and Dinah Shore. Aaron had been largely ignored by Madison Avenue for the first two decades of his career, but in 1973 Aaron signed an exclusive five-year, $1 million endorsement deal with Magnavox. The local media's focus on Aaron proved just as intense. Around the city, the Braves posted twenty billboards bearing his image. They issued an average of four hundred press credentials per game. The *Constitution* and *Journal* published separate special sections on Aaron, while the Atlanta Chamber established a college scholarship fund in his name. Autograph seekers hounded Aaron everywhere he traveled.[46]

All the attention did not suit the aloof Aaron. Teammates, Braves employees, and members of the local media remember Aaron as a distant and brooding figure. Aaron socialized rarely with his typically much younger Atlanta teammates, whether white or Black.[47] Aaron mistrusted the media, which he believed undervalued him relative to fellow NL stars Willie Mays and Roberto Clemente, both of whom he developed public rivalries with during the late 1960s. In 1969 Aaron threatened to quit baseball when he came to believe that Braves announcer Milo Hamilton had suggested that Clemente was the NL's top right fielder.[48]

Ten years before the home run chase, Aaron had expressed serious reservations about the Braves' relocation to Atlanta. A 1965 visit to Atlanta orchestrated by Atlanta's Black leadership assuaged enough of Aaron's fears to convince him to endorse the move, but his then-wife Barbara remained hesitant to move the family to Georgia. Her concerns were not alleviated by her earliest experiences in the city. In the stands she heard fans referring to her husband casually as a "jigaboo" and a "nigger." Once, she smushed a mustard-covered hamburger in the face of a particularly odious bigot seated behind her. In July 1966 she was refused entry to the player's parking lot by an Atlanta police officer who said he did not recognize her. She was temporarily placed under arrest after she drove through the gate against his order. Charges were never filed and the officer was reprimanded for the incident.[49] By the early 1970s racially tinged criticism of Aaron came in a more nuanced form. Aaron's second wife, Atlanta morning television host Billye Williams, the widow of civil rights activist Dr. Sam Williams, was accused by some in the Atlanta press of trying to politicize the Braves right fielder. Aaron responded to a column by the *Journal*'s Frank Hyland that suggested as much by smashing a container of strawberries into his face during the Braves' 1974 Farmer's Night.[50]

A full house of 53,775 turned out for Atlanta's April 8, 1974, home opener, the night Hank Aaron hit his record-breaking 715th home run. "It seemed like the only people not there were the President of the United States and the commissioner of baseball," Aaron recalled.[51] While President Nixon was embroiled in the Watergate scandal, MLB Commissioner Bowie Kuhn bowed out of the event to attend to a scheduled speaking engagement in Cleveland. Previously, Kuhn had not bothered to contact Aaron to congratulate him on his 700th home run. During the off-season, Kuhn entangled himself in a several-month-long conflict with the Braves over whether

Atlanta could sit Aaron during their opening series of the season in Cincinnati. The Braves organization wanted Aaron to hit both the record-tying and record-breaking home runs at home to help boost ticket sales early in the season. Atlanta had drawn just seventy-eight thousand fans to its eleven-date opening homestand in 1973. Citing "the best interests of baseball," Kuhn ordered the Braves to play Aaron in Cincinnati, where he hit his record-tying 714th home run. The national press pilloried both Kuhn and the Braves for the fracas, finding fault with Kuhn for his meddling and Atlanta for its inability to draw fans even with a marquee attraction like Aaron.[52]

The nationally televised game was nearly blacked out locally because the Braves failed to sell out the stadium seventy-two hours in advance of the first pitch. In a rare moment of leniency, NBC waived its blackout rule and allowed Atlantans to watch the game along with the 35 million other television viewers. The drizzly and cold evening commenced with pregame pomp and circumstance that included a performance of the national anthem by Pearl Bailey, the release of one thousand doves, and a "This is Your Life, Hank Aaron" segment featuring reunions with old coaches, friends, and teammates. Braves Public Relations Director Bob Hope spent the off-season planning out the event, a responsibility he regarded as deeply socially significant. Hope grew up an hour north of Atlanta in Forsyth County, which prohibited African American residents until the mid-1960s. Less than a generation later, he honored a Black man in Georgia for his contributions to professional sports.[53]

Aaron's fourth inning, two-run homer off the Dodgers' Al Downing and the subsequent ten-minute in-game ceremony to commemorate the record proved to be the end of the evening for the vast majority of those in attendance. Large numbers of fans began leaving the chilly Monday-evening, work-night, school-night game. The bleachers and the designated VIP section emptied out with comparable speed. By the time Dodgers' outfielder Manny Mota lined out to Braves' right-fielder

Dusty Baker to end the game, *Journal* reporter Frank Hyland estimated that fewer than ten thousand fans remained in the stadium. Hyland quoted a pair of "press box veterans" who said that Atlanta Stadium look liked "a Falcon game in the fourth quarter" by the time of Aaron's next at bat in the fifth inning.[54] "It seemed more like a Braves game," Aaron wrote of the sparse remaining crowd he witnessed in his next trip to the plate. "It was drizzling earlier, but you'd have thought there was a flash flood in the grandstand."[55]

"I think the fans showed poor taste. . . . I think they should have stayed for the game," Braves Manager Eddie Mathews told reporters.[56] "It was cold. People in Atlanta don't like cold all that much. . . . Everybody there just expected him to hit it and when he did, that was it," game attendee Joel Gross, who stayed for all nine innings, recalled.[57] "They came to see a home run by Hank and the game second," Braves pitcher Buzz Capra said, evoking Atlantans' persistent desire to be a part of an event.[58] Few fans proved interested in taking an after-the-fact victory lap with Aaron and the Braves. Atlanta's attendance returned to the mean in the aftermath of 715. The night after Aaron broke Ruth's record, the Braves drew 10,648. Then in six of the Braves' next twelve home dates, attendance fell below 3,500.[59] Despite fielding a competitive 88-74 team, Braves attendance fell below one million for the third straight season in 1974. A mere 11,081 turned out for the Braves' 1974 home finale, a game that many fans and media insiders believed correctly would be Aaron's last in Atlanta. "It hurt me to know that so few cared enough to buy a ticket for my last of 3076 games as a Brave," Aaron wrote in his memoir. That November, the Braves traded Aaron to the Milwaukee Brewers after the new home run king balked at the ceremonial front-office position Atlanta offered him if he retired.[60]

Unbeknownst to all but the upper echelons of the team's management, Aaron told Braves officials that, unless he was offered the team's vacant manager's position or a role in player-personnel, he preferred to play out the two remaining years

on his contract. The rift between Aaron and team management brought about his trade to the Brewers, enabling him
to finish his career as a designated hitter in the city where
he spent the first twelve years of his career. As a result of
the deal, the Braves and Brewers agreed to play a July 1975
interleague exhibition game at Atlanta Stadium. The Braves
planned to honor Aaron with a pregame ceremony and donate
proceeds from the game to his preferred charitable causes.
Less than a month before the game, a mere two hundred
advanced tickets had been sold, leading to the event's cancellation and the hardening of a rift between the Braves' ownership and Aaron.[61]

The departure of Hank Aaron rubbed away what remained
of Atlanta's romance with the Braves. The following season,
the franchise's tenth in the Southeast, was almost certainly
its least pleasant. Contrary to local mythology, the Braves
did not become a genuinely awful team until the summer
of 1975, when the team fell out of the pennant race well in
advance of Memorial Day. It was the long Braves summer of
'75 that prompted the *Constitution* to publish its "Loserville,
USA" series. "The media, generally, did not want to be associated with losing teams, especially columnists and broadcast media, as if the association made them losers," Wayne
Minshew recalled. During the 1975 season, the *Constitution*
stopped sending a beat writer on the road with the Braves,
characterizing it as a cutback brought on by the energy crisis.
Constitution writers covered road games by simply listening to
the radio broadcasts on wsb, a practice that the *Journal*, too,
soon adopted.[62] Atlanta's press corps had ceaselessly boosted
its professional sports teams in the mid-1960s. By the mid-
1970s, most of the local media had adopted an aloof, conde-
scending posture toward the city's franchises, particularly the
Braves, whom they were expected to cover day-in and day-
out for eight months each year. The Braves' history as Atlanta's first Major League team, their membership in the nation's
oldest professional sports league, and their participation in

the national pastime made them the city's most visible franchise. As a result, the Braves bore the heaviest burden from Atlanta's "Loserville, USA" reputation.

"You could hear the echoes in a mostly empty stadium, especially in '75, which was by far the worst year ever," said Wayne Minshew.[63] The 1975 Braves were a genuinely horrendous team, winning just 67 games and finishing 40 games out of first place. Lacking even the attraction of Aaron, Braves attendance dwindled to 534,672, the second worst total in baseball. The 1975 Braves threatened to draw fewer than one thousand fans on several muggy August weeknights. Finally, the Braves reached that dubious distinction on Monday, September 8, against the Houston Astros, when a mere 737 fans made it out to the ballpark, despite the fantastic Phil Niekro vs. J.R. Richard pitching matchup. Braves officials blamed the especially tiny crowd on the Alabama-Missouri college football matchup being broadcast on ABC that same evening.[64]

"There was a change in the attitude," Braves announcer Milo Hamilton said of Atlanta fans in the early 1970s, "because they felt that the ballclub just wasn't winning."[65] The highly opinionated Hamilton presented himself as a Braves partisan, leading to criticism from fans and media alike that he spent too much time "cheerleading and ticket selling" during telecasts.[66] Despite consistent radio and television ratings, Braves management fired Hamilton after the 1975 season.[67] A widely publicized on-air rant following a Fourth of July weekend home game that drew 3,728 fans likely sealed Hamilton's fate. "All I hear around town is negativism about the Braves' management, managers, and players," Hamilton said. "But it is time somebody stood up and said something positive about this ball club. And if you take a little stock in this town, it wasn't built to bring a Major League Baseball team here." Atlanta fans proved immune to Hamilton's efforts to cajole them into the ballpark. He could not call upon some collectively ingrained loyalty to the old-town team but instead had to convince consumers to buy a product that required their presence and participation, two things that relatively few of them proved willing to give.[68]

"You could buy a general admission ticket, walk in, and go sit behind home plate because the team wanted the TV cameras to see people at the game," longtime Braves fan David Hewes said, describing the atmosphere at Atlanta Stadium during the mid-1970s.[69] "It's hard to describe," Braves outfielder Dale Murphy said of his first experience playing at home in September 1976, "because no one draws crowds like that now. I was playing in front of more people in Triple-A."[70] "There were always plenty of hecklers. Because the crowds were so small, a leather-lunged guy could really get heard by his target," Braves fan Mike Holcomb recalled.[71]

"The joke around town," Alan Morris said, "was that if you called the stadium to ask what time the game started they asked you, 'When can you get here?'"[72] This joke was also one of those used by Wayne Minshew—who left the *Constitution* to become Braves public relations director—to warm up crowds at civic club speeches. "I tried self-deprecating stuff," Minshew said. Once, he asked "a club's members if they wanted to see our highlights film from the previous season, whereupon I held up a slide," drawing hearty laughs from the crowd. "A sort of sports political correctness" emerged in Atlanta in the mid-1970s, Minshew said. People who bothered to attend Braves games would try to display a studied indifference to the team, saying they were only in attendance because "somebody gave me tickets."[73] Alan Morris recalls a radio show had a giveaway in which first prize was a ticket to the Braves' next home game while second prize was two tickets to the game. He remembers Atlantans laughing over the story of a fan who parked in downtown Atlanta and left his tickets under his windshield wiper with a note that said "Free Tickets." When he returned to his car, someone had added a second pair of tickets under his windshield.[74]

During the Braves' atrocious 1975 campaign, the *Sporting News* asked Atlanta readers to write in with explanations of what was wrong with their franchise. Many fans cited the team's inept, absentee ownership, the high prices for field-level seats, parking, poor concessions, and, above all else, "the novelty of defeat wore off," as an anonymous Atlanta reader wrote. W. E. Parker, an Atlanta reader who attended fifty games in 1966 but had not attended one in 1975, wrote that he would pay to see a "professional-looking team" but not the "sand-lot players" that had been taking the field recently. "Atlanta," he explained, "is sophisticated enough to exclude medioc-rity from its entertainment list." "There are plenty of better ways to spend an evening in Atlanta than by sitting through an embarrassing ball game," furniture salesman C. T. Mont-gomery wrote, echoing Parker's sentiments. Attorney Steven Kit wrote that the "Braves have the burden of persuading fans that they are worth watching, rather than the fans having to prove to the team that they are 'good' fans." In an eight-page letter, attorney James Eichelberger argued that the popular-ity of Aaron had masked years of mounting fan disenchant-ment. In 1975 "with Aaron gone, the second bananas had it all to themselves this year, passing themselves off as major leaguers. . . . But there are better things to do than watching high-priced athletes perform as though they were condescend-ing to do you a favor."[75]

The Braves' box-office struggles proved costly for Atlanta taxpayers, who were obligated to pay two-thirds of the annual balance toward stadium bond retirement not covered by ticket sales at the facility. As revenue from ticket sales dwindled, the city of Atlanta was forced to contribute increasing amounts of money toward the retirement of the $18 million in municipal bonds issued to finance the stadium. In 1971, the first year that the Braves were contractually obligated to contribute to the debt repayment, the Stadium Authority assumed that excises on Braves' tickets would contribute approximately $500,000 toward the bond's retirement, but declining attendance lim-ited the Braves' contribution to $313,531. The city delved into its parks-improvement fund to make up the difference. The following year, the Braves contributed a mere $163,000 toward bond retirement, forcing the city to once again dip into its discretionary funds.[76]

Debt from Atlanta Stadium, which was rechristened into the more inclusive Atlanta–Fulton County Stadium in 1976, proved to be a quarter-century-long drain on the city's recreation budget and the county's general fund, costing local taxpayers more than $30 million between 1965 and 1991, more than the original cost of building the facility. Roughly $16 million of the cost came from debt service for the original stadium bonds while an additional $14 million in taxes accrued from a 1985 bond issued to pay for improvements to the decaying facility. In 1993 the privately financed Atlanta Olympic Committee, which brought the summer games to the city three years later, earmarked $11 million in its $1.7 billion budget to retire the stadium's remaining debt.[77]

Moreover, the team's declining box-office appeal turned once profitable Atlanta Braves Inc. into a drain on the ownership group's resources. Atlanta Braves Inc. turned a profit in each of its first five seasons (1966–70). All told, the Braves organization earned $3,950,276 between 1966 and 1970, more than half of which came from the $2 million in NL expansion fees it received from the fledgling Montreal and San Diego franchises in 1968. Atlanta Braves Inc. benefitted further from a series of corporate tax credits. In 1966 a corporate relocation credit enabled Atlanta Braves Inc. to avoid paying any federal taxes that year. In 1968 the organization was allowed to write off $492,000 in operating losses. Additionally, Atlanta Braves Inc. could deduct 68 percent of its players' salaries, which totaled nearly $7 million between 1966 and 1975, as depreciating assets for their first ten years as a corporation. Without the 1968 NL expansion fee and significant federal tax benefits, the Braves organization would have either lost money or barely broken even in each of its first five seasons.[78]

In spite of continued depreciation write-offs, Atlanta Braves Inc. lost money in four out of five years between 1971 and

1975. In 1971 and 1972, the Atlanta-LaSalle Corporation sub-sidiary lost more than $375,000 as revenue from ticket sales declined.[79] Atlanta Braves Inc. showed a profit of $345,865 in 1973. The Braves' uptick in 1973 came not from a major jump in ticket sales but from the club shedding its most toxic asset, the Atlanta Chiefs of the NASL. In six seasons (1967–72), Atlanta Braves Inc. lost $1.5 million on the club. Tom Cous-ins's Omni Group purchased the Chiefs in 1973 but ended up disbanding the team after one highly unprofitable season. By that time, twelve of the NASL's seventeen teams had folded, making Atlanta one of its longest holdouts.[80]

In 1974 Atlanta Braves Inc. fell just short of breaking even, despite the publicity from Hank Aaron's home run chase.[81] The club lost nearly a half-million dollars in 1975, its least suc-cessful year of operation. Within days of the season's conclu-sion, Atlanta Braves Inc. was in talks with interested buyers in Toronto, Seattle, and New Orleans. In the end, the Braves' owners ensured the franchise's future in Atlanta by selling to a familiar local face. In January 1976, the Atlanta-LaSalle Corporation sold the Braves to emerging media magnate Ted Turner for $10 million. Turner's WTCG, soon to be rechris-tened WTBS, had been televising Braves games since 1973 to consistently high ratings across the Southeast. The Atlanta-LaSalle Corporation made an unconventional deal with Turner, allowing him to pay off the $10 million over a ten-year period. Company leaders agreed to the liberal terms to get out from under a holding company that was bound to lose even more money now that its depreciation allowance had ended.

21

Instant City

....

"I HAVE NO PARTICULAR FEELING ABOUT IT BEING TAKEN down," developer Tom Cousins said in July 1997, days before the Omni Coliseum was imploded to make way for a new arena.[1] The Omni had hosted Cousins's professional sports empire, which he believed would anchor a broader revitalization of downtown Atlanta. Cousins's building had not evolved into the dynamo of commercial vitality that he envisioned, but it served admirably as Atlanta's indoor home for professional sports. The Omni housed the Atlanta Hawks for twenty-five years (1972–97) and the NHL's Atlanta Flames for eight years (1972–80) until Cousins sold the team to investors in Calgary, Alberta. By comparison, the Omni International Complex, the MXD that Cousins opened in 1975 as an extension of the coliseum, could not even be characterized as marginally successful. It failed to revive its commercially barren environs in the southern CBD. By the end of the 1970s, Cousins's sprawling, insular Omni campus was a white elephant, contributing to the CBD's reputation as a ghost town.[2]

At the time of the Omni Coliseum's opening in October 1972, Atlanta's civic leadership thought that the building would become much more than just an indoor venue for hockey and basketball. They believed that they had heralded into existence "the most magnificent sports arena in the world," in the words of Omni Group President Bill Putnam.[3] City leaders in the early 1970s foresaw the $17 million Omni jumpstarting the revitalization of a section of downtown that had been home to a derelict train yard. As the Omni Coliseum was set for demolition in 1997, Cousins asserted that the coliseum had served its primary purposes. It had housed two professional sports franchises and served as a venue for concerts, performances, and large gatherings. The developer spoke of the utility of the Omni, as if it were just another one of the more than seventy commercial and residential developments he completed over the course of his half-century career.

Twenty-five years before Tom Cousins expressed no particular feelings at the Omni's destruction, he had expressed far grander aspirations for the building. He envisioned the arena as the starting point for a broader remaking of Metropolitan Atlanta. In less than a decade, Cousins had transformed the Gulch, an abandoned train yard he purchased in 1966, into the municipally owned Omni Coliseum and the surrounding, privately held Omni International Complex. He tried to lure suburban consumers back to a center city they had come to find unpredictable, unwelcoming, and unfamiliar by offering them signature urban amenities within a controlled, enclosed space. Cousins reasoned that his arena and MXD would become the spaces where suburban Atlantans met their desires for leisure, shopping, and entertainment.[4]

The efforts of Cousins and like-minded developers to rebuild downtown Atlanta around grand and insular structures instead hardened the divide between the center city and the decentralizing region. Rather than winning steady suburban business back to the CBD, Atlanta's developer class created massive, inward-oriented campuses in the 1960s and 1970s that reinforced anxieties about the safety of the center city, precluding any genuine street-level vibrancy from developing downtown. The failure to revitalize Atlanta's CBD in the 1970s was certainly not Cousins's alone, but his notoriety, due in large part to his ownership of the Hawks and Flames, made him the public face of the downtown real estate bust.

The Omni Coliseum opened in October 1972, eighteen months after Cousins broke ground in the Gulch. The coliseum had two primary tenants in place well in advance of its opening. The arena's management had also scheduled a full slate of concerts and special events for the next twelve months. Arena project General Manager Bill Putnam had lobbied successfully for the Omni moniker, believing the grandiosity of its name would define it as having a purpose beyond hosting the aforementioned events. The name, Putnam argued, would ensure its national notoriety and articulate its creators' sense of civic purpose and aspirations for the building. Omni architects Thompson, Ventulett, Stainback & Associates (TVS) ensured that the arena would make a unique contribution to Atlanta's skyline. They won acclaim within their industry for the building's avant-garde design and use of the briefly trendy Cor-Ten weathering steel on the Omni's roof. While some fans defended the arena's modern exterior architecture, a larger share mocked the "rusty egg crate." Conversely, few fans mocked the Omni name. Atlantans' embrace of the arena's grandiose moniker was demonstrative of a sensibility that had emerged years earlier among many of the region's residents. Plenty of people who embraced the praise Atlanta received for its progressive reputation showed no interest in participating in the events or institutions that had earned the city that reputation. In a related sense, many suburban Atlantans praised the civic achievement of the Omni complexes while demonstrating little interest in frequenting them.[5]

Regulars at the Omni found it a pleasant place to watch a sporting event. "I really liked the Omni. The sight lines and the seats were better for me," Flames Fan Club co-president Joe Watkins said, noting that the Omni's slightly smaller-than-NHL-average seating capacity of 15,078 enabled its operators to install slightly larger seats. The extra leg room made watching a game at the arena a significantly more comfortable experience for Watkins, a 6-foot-4 former Marine.[6] TVS promised and delivered unobstructed sight lines from all seats in the Omni. The installation of a state-of-the-art lighting system made the arena's playing surface look like a car showroom, both in person and on television. Moreover, no spectator at the Omni sat more than 150 feet from the floor, though some fans complained that the sharp ascent of the upper-deck sections forced them to look straight down on the action.[7] "You were closer to the ice instead of being stacked on top of each other," Flames Fan Club co-president Betsy Watkins recalled, comparing it to older NHL arenas where fans sat cheek-by-jowl.[8] Hawks fans who endured the wooden bleachers at Alexander, the team's original Atlanta home, found the Omni's plush, movie theater–style seats to be a significant upgrade.[9]

Unlike Atlanta Stadium, the Omni had ample and secure public parking in close proximity to its entrances. According to Omni promotional materials, fans could choose from 6,200 spaces within two blocks of the arena or more than 10,000 public parking spots within a five-block radius. The two well-lit and heavily patrolled lots closest to the Omni were connected to the building by special aboveground and underground walkways. Print and radio advertisements in 1972 boasted that the Omni had more public parking spaces within a five-block radius than any other arena in the NBA or NHL.

Nevertheless, many suburban patrons found working their way through freeway traffic and then navigating downtown streets sufficiently unpleasant to dissuade them from taking advantage of the Omni's excellent parking facilities.[10] "It's a tremendous hassle to have to stick a half-hour into your travel itinerary for wiggle room in case you get stuck in traffic. And you will get stuck in traffic, especially if you're coming in from the north," Mike Holcomb, a Buford, Georgia, native who frequently attended professional wrestling at the Omni during the 1970s, said of the commute into the arena.[11] Arena-bound commuters had few public-transit options until MARTA rapid rail service commenced in 1979. Despite the Flames and Hawks' efforts to encourage their fans to patronize MARTA, relatively few made their way to the arena by rail, which many potential suburban customers found inconvenient or considered unsafe.[12]

Professional athletes, too, spoke highly of the Omni Coliseum and, later, the adjoining Omni International Complex.[13] "It was so convenient. I loved the venue," Flames center Bill Clement recalled. "It was connected to the hotel complex where there were bars and restaurants, and we could walk out of our locker room after a game and walk right into the complex and have a beer and a bite to eat."[14] "This is a beautiful place to play," Hawks coach Cotton Fitzsimmons said of the Omni after the team's first home game in the new venue. "The floor is excellent and the lighting is much better than at Tech," he said, comparing it to the team's previous home, Alexander Memorial Coliseum.[15] Fans and athletes alike marveled at the ability of the staff to change the arena over from hockey to basketball or another iceless event in less than two hours. Some players complained that the Omni smelled like manure for days after traveling circuses performed in the building.[16]

When the Omni opened, its assortment of amenities catered to upscale consumers more than virtually any existing NBA or NHL venue. The building offered VIP parking, a full-service restaurant inside the arena, and two separate private clubs for season-ticket holders. In little more than a decade, though, the Omni's extravagances seemed pedestrian when compared to those offered in newer facilities. Every NBA or NHL arena built after the Omni included luxury suites or club-level seating, both of which drew significant corporate patronage in most league cities. Luxury suites also served as an important source of revenue for NBA and NHL franchises. According to the statutes of both leagues, the earnings that franchises generated from such specialty seating did not have to be shared with the visiting team, as did traditional gate receipts. By the late 1980s, most NBA franchises earned between $5 million and $10 million annually from luxury seating. As much as anything, the lack of corporate-oriented luxury seating led to the Omni's early demise.[17]

Once the arena's novelty wore off, fans with more modest budgets, too, found some of the amenities at the Omni lacking, particularly its dining options. Even in its early years, the

the rooting dynamics of Atlanta wrestling. Fans continued to cheer on the faces and boo the heels, regardless of their race. Some of GCW's most popular stars of the 1970s were African Americans, including Tony Atlas, Thunderbolt Patterson, and Bobo Brazil. At the same time, Black GCW fans embraced a white superstar named Dusty Rhodes more enthusiastically than any other performer in the territory. Rhodes, whose persona was that of a perpetual underdog, lacked the bodybuilder's physique of other performers but won fans over with his unique charisma. Rhodes donned ostentatious clothing and jewelry and entertained in the ring with a funk-inspired swagger. He spoke frequently of his humble origins and appealed explicitly to "all my soul brothers and sisters out there" in televised and in-ring interviews. In July 1980 Rhodes's fans nearly started a riot at the Omni, as dozens tried to scale a steel cage to save their hero from a gang of heels that double-crossed him in the ring. Wrestlers and Atlanta police officers had to fight with the spectators to keep them from pummeling the heels. Few athletes have ever been as beloved by their fans as Dusty Rhodes was by his admirers in Georgia during the 1970s and early 1980s.[29]

Besides professional wrestling, the Omni booked a wide range of other spectacles to fill the calendar when the Hawks and Flames were not in action. GM Bob Kent worked aggressively to book major acts and events for the arena. Initially, he focused his booking efforts on entertainers that had never before performed in Atlanta. Throughout the 1970s, the Omni hosted between 100 and 150 events each year, including the approximately 80 combined home dates of the Hawks and Flames.

The Omni Coliseum became one of the region's leading venues for live events and performances. If floor space was available, the building could accommodate up to eighteen thousand spectators for staged shows, nearly four times as many people as Atlanta's traditional concert venue, the City Auditorium. It hosted many of the country's most popular entertainers, some of whom had never before played in Atlanta. Elvis Presley, Bob Hope, and Frank Sinatra all performed at the Omni on a number of occasions during the 1970s, as did major country acts such as Willie Nelson and Dolly Parton. Family-friendly events, including the Ice Capades, Ringling Bros. and Barnum & Bailey Circus, and Disney on Parade, performed for the first time in Atlanta at the new arena.[30] During the late 1970s and early 1980s, the Omni became the local venue of choice for major rock concerts, including KISS, Van Halen, and Styx.

Considering Atlanta's demographics, namely the city's majority African American population and the presence of a large Black middle class in Fulton and DeKalb Counties, surprisingly few major Black performers or events aimed at predominately African American audiences were held at the Omni during the 1970s. The ten most frequently featured entertainers at the Omni during the 1970s were all white. Certainly, some major events, particularly in its first year, featured Black performers or were marketed explicitly to Black audiences. Local civil rights groups sponsored a Martin Luther King Day benefit in January 1973 featuring Wilson Pickett. Later that year, a gospel music festival headlined by the Soul Stirrers drew a predominately Black audience. Other notable Black musicians to perform at the Omni during its first calendar year included the Temptations, the Spinners, and Atlanta natives Gladys Knight and the Pips.[31]

Several factors contributed to the dearth of Black entertainers who performed at the Omni. Certainly, the income disparity between white and Black consumers in Metropolitan Atlanta left African Americans with less disposable income to spend on concert tickets. For many African American residents of Atlanta, merely leaving their homes at night was a dangerous proposition, considering the high crime rates in so many inner-city neighborhoods. The city's inefficient mass-transit system likely discouraged attendance as well, since many inner-city Black patrons had to rely on infrequent late-night buses for their return home. The dynamics of the music business may have also contributed to the dearth of Black artists who performed at the Omni in this period. During the early 1970s, many well-known African American musicians worked for subsidiary or independent record labels, which lacked the financial wherewithal to support even their most prominent artists on extensive national arena tours. Moreover, few of the era's African American concert promoters had enough liquid capital to market arena-sized shows properly. In general, African Americans proved to be a small percentage of attendees at most events at the Omni, with the exception of professional wrestling and professional basketball games.[32]

Beyond these broader contextual explanations, there is another possible reason for the relative dearth of Black artists booked at the Omni during the 1970s. Black artists had good reason to fear boycotts by local civil rights groups if they did not have Black management. In November 1973, SCLC leader Hosea Williams, by then the city's most influential civil rights activist, led a boycott of Al Green's Thanksgiving weekend concert, his second at the Omni that year. Fresh off a run for vice mayor, Williams had turned his attention from electoral politics toward direct issues of economic empowerment in Atlanta's Black community. Williams called for a boycott of Green's return date at the Omni because of the soul singer's alleged history of "consistently selling himself exclusively to lily-white concert promoters and foreign record companies."[33]

Days before the show, thousands of tickets remained unsold, just five months after Green had drawn a sold-out crowd to the venue. Williams announced plans to organize protests against Green not only in Atlanta but also in the remaining cities on the soul singer's tour. Green's management company avoided Williams-led pickets at his concerts by making a "substantial contribution" to the SCLC. After performing to a half-filled arena, the singer never returned to the Omni and has only made rare concert appearances in Atlanta ever since. Whether coincidental or not, few African American artists performed at the Omni in the aftermath of the Al Green boycott from the mid-to-late 1970s. Among the few events targeted at African American audiences held at the Omni during the mid-1970s was a 1976 Black gospel music festival, which drew protests from civil rights groups because of its reliance on white promoters, though Williams did not personally endorse this round of protests.[34]

THE OMNI COLISEUM MAY NOT HAVE TRANSFORMED DOWNtown Atlanta into a vibrant commercial district, but it had served its most basic purposes as a venue for games and performances. Moreover, its construction costs, operating expenses, and debt service were covered entirely by its tenants, insulating taxpayers from any financial responsibility for the municipally owned facility. Conversely, the Omni International Complex was a once-in-a-generation real estate boondoggle. Cousins presented the Omni International Complex as the second step in an even larger, interrelated group of developments he planned to build in the southern CBD. He planned to open a wholesale retail market called "The Atlanta World Trade Center." In addition, Cousins envisioned a second, more residentially oriented multiuse complex by the end of the 1970s, called "OmniSouth." Cousins wanted his developments to serve every need of Atlanta's consumers. He wanted the Omni to be the place where they were entertained, where they shopped, where they dined, and, eventually, where they called home.[35]

The Omni International Complex finally opened in late 1975, three years after the arena. The $100 million, 5.5-acre space was just as grandiose and impressive as its boosters had predicted. Its twin fourteen-story office towers framed a development that included an Olympic regulation skating rink, an amusement park, ten restaurants, two discotheques, and a half-dozen movie theaters. The complex included the luxurious five-hundred-room Omni International Hotel. It featured both a shopping mall and an International Bazaar that included the likes of Gucci, Givenchy, and Hermes.[36]

The question that plagued the Omni International Complex from the outset was who exactly would be the target audience for all of its offerings. Some of the amenities available at the complex were also available in suburban locations around the metropolitan area. Others, notably the specialty shops, appealed only to a narrow, upscale clientele. Hawks and Flames fans did not flock to the complex either. There is little evidence to suggest that events at the coliseum did much to help business at the Omni International Complex, or vice versa. Between 1976 and 1978, more than three-quarters of the hotel guests at the Omni International were conventioneers, typically at the nearby Georgia World Congress Center (GWCC). Relatively few people stayed overnight at the Omni's hotel to watch the Hawks, the Flames, or any of the special events. Instead, most spectators were locals who drove in and drove out of one of the nearby parking lots, soon before and soon after their event. Most customers at the Omni complex proved to be conventioneers in search of souvenirs or supper, not locals lingering after a game or on the lookout for the latest in haute couture at the International Bazaar.[37]

Throughout its history, the Omni struggled with high vacancy rates and low sales. In January 1985, as the Omni was going through a second debt reorganization in less than ten years, the complex had a 40 percent vacancy rate, more than twice as high as the rest of downtown, which itself had the highest vacancy rate of any major American city. "The Omni," Jim Auchmutey of the *Journal-Constitution* wrote, "is a place of bored clerks, dark windows, and a few dozen people milling about looking for something."[38]

The most high-profile amenity at the complex was the World of Sid and Marty Krofft, the first indoor amusement park ever constructed. It featured the famed puppeteers' signature characters, most notably Saturday-morning television stalwart H. R. Pufnstuf. The $14 million amusement park drew huzzahs from virtually everyone who journeyed up and down its 205-foot escalator, the mechanism by which guests moved from one attraction to the next. Spread over eight stories, the park invited families into a day-long fantasyland that included not only performances by the Krofft's well known puppets but also a wide range of unique shows, exhibits, and rides. Visitors wandered through a village of giant, talking hats called Lidsville. They rode around on a three-tiered, mirrored carousel adorned with mythological beasts. The best-known ride at the World of Sid and Marty Krofft was a human pinball machine, which placed riders inside plastic-domed pinballs that were then batted around by flippers and bumpers amid a brightly colored platform. Like the complex itself, the park impressed people conceptually but did not earn the mass patronage necessary to sustain its operations. Park leadership tried to undercut their outdoor suburban competitor, Six Flags over Georgia, by charging one-third as much for admission. This strategy failed to jumpstart Krofft's gate or lure business away from their well-established competitor. Ten times as many people visited Six Flags as the Krofft's attraction during the 1976 season, the one year that the parks were in competition. The decision to keep admission prices low expedited the World of Sid and Marty Krofft's demise by cutting it off from the revenue it needed to sustain its expensive operations. The park closed in November 1976, six months after it opened.[39]

The Omni International Complex opened into an already dramatically overbuilt downtown Atlanta real estate market. The CBD was already full of brand new commercial and retail properties, office space, condominiums, and hotel rooms, all in search of occupants. The entry of the Omni into the marketplace made the already cutthroat competition for business among downtown realtors all the fiercer.[40] In March 1978, less than thirty months after the Omni opened, lender Morgan Guaranty Trust announced plans to foreclose on the property. At the time, the foreclosure on the Omni was the largest in the history of American real estate. The Omni's investors had defaulted on their loans, failing to service the $91 million in debt remaining on the MXD. In May 1978 a consortium of banks orchestrated a debt restructuring plan that enabled the Omni to remain open. A similar debt reorganization deal in 1985 kept the MXD going amid renewed foreclosure threats by creditors. The financial failure of the Omni International Complex brought Cousins himself to the brink of bankruptcy. Between 1974 and 1977, he lost \$33 million as a result of his MXD.[41]

The near-bankruptcy of the Omni International Complex forced Cousins to scrap his proposed twenty-two-acre Omni-South. The new development would have linked the Omni's campus directly to Rich's Department Store, Atlanta's most famous retailer, which was planning to make a significant investment in the project. Like the Omni, Rich's was struggling to keep open the doors of its southern CBD location. Omni-South would have created a nodal point in the southern CBD linking downtown's newest developments to the city's most historically revered retailer. Considering the track record of the Omni International Complex and the estimated \$265 million price of the OmniSouth extension, few investors showed interest in the project.[42]

The catastrophic economic failure of the Omni International Complex and the disappointing, if not altogether unsuccessful, track record of the Omni Coliseum were a product in large part of the broader phenomena which prevented Atlanta's Major League downtown of the 1960s and 1970s from drawing steady patronage from suburban consumers. Moreover, the proximity of three other recently constructed, multimillion-square-foot developments created a great deal of competition for customers around the Five Points, the historic core of Atlanta's CBD. Cousins's campus was erected during a downtown building boom that also included the construction of the Peachtree Center (1967), Colony Square (1973), and the Georgia World Congress Center (1976). In each instance, these MXDS proved to be discreet campuses that added little to the vitality of the center city. The inward orientation of each downtown campus stifled the potential flow of customers from one development to another. The successes these developments enjoyed were narrowly focused around their roles as convention hotels and hosts, not as magnets for the discretionary dollars of metropolitan-area residents.[43]

In addition, competition from rapidly expanding retail and commercial options in suburban Atlanta, particularly in and around the affluent northside neighborhood of Buckhead, further dissuaded metropolitan-area residents from returning to the center city to go shopping, have dinner, or seek out after-hours entertainment. By the time Tom Cousins announced his plans to build an MXD in the Gulch, the core of the region's retail business had already been unmoored from Atlanta's CBD. By 1975 just 7 percent of the region's retail business took place in Atlanta's CBD, one-third as much as in 1960. A mere 12 percent of the jobs in metropolitan Atlanta were then located downtown, two-fifths fewer than in 1960.[44]

Thirty-four major shopping centers were operating in suburban Atlanta by the time Cousins unveiled plans for the Omni International Complex in October 1972. The success of the Lenox Square Mall (1959) in the affluent North Atlanta neighborhood of Buckhead, located four miles north of the CBD, encouraged developers to open new and larger complexes further outside the center city. Just as the downtown MXD boom was gearing up, massive shopping centers, including Phipps Plaza (1969), the Northlake Mall (1971), and the Perimeter Center Mall (1971), expanded the retail options on Atlanta's northside considerably. They catered to an ever-expanding suburban customer base that was happy to shop closer to home in spaces they found convenient and safe.[45]

The opening of the Lenox Square Mall created a new commercial center of gravity in Metropolitan Atlanta. In the wake of the shopping center's success, a number of other commercial developments emerged in Buckhead. A series of mid-rise commercial buildings went up in Buckhead during the 1960s as did a second major shopping mall, Phipps Plaza. The 1974 opening of Tower Place, Buckhead's first skyscraper, inaugurated an office-building boom in the neighborhood that lured many potential corporate patrons away from the CBD, exacerbating downtown's already mounting real estate bubble. Between 1974 and 1985, more than six million square feet of office space were built in Buckhead, along with three luxury high-rise hotels.[46]

Finally, a fear of crime in the Omni's southern CBD environs, which was exaggerated by the demographic transformation of downtown Atlanta during the 1960s and 1970s, contributed significantly to the unwillingness of many suburban customers to patronize the Omni regularly. Though many Atlantans had long been leery of the high-crime neighborhoods adjacent to the CBD, the perception that downtown itself was dangerous became broadly shared in the metropolitan area during the 1970s. "Only the young, and the unfortunate, without better transportation, except those who still work in the area, shop downtown regularly," wrote the *Daily World*'s George Coleman in a 1971 editorial that described the deterioration of the southern CBD into a high-crime neighborhood that consisted largely of vacant store fronts and marginal businesses.[47]

Coleman traced the early 1970s surge in crime in the Southern CBD and the surrounding neighborhoods to "the uprooting of the old 'Buttermilk Bottom' people, who were chased out of the neighborhoods near Peachtree Street to make room for luxury hotels, sports stadiums, and state office buildings."[48] The social disorder that suburbanites feared in the Southern CBD was in no small part produced by the efforts of civic leaders to make Atlanta a Major League City. Rather than investing in affordable housing, city leaders made use of public lands to build Atlanta Stadium, cramping impoverished residents of the city's historic Black neighborhoods into smaller enclaves around the CBD.[49]

The hesitance of white customers to patronize businesses in the southern CBD was, in fact, just a more exaggerated version of the broader discomfort many white Atlantans felt about the demographic transformation of downtown during the 1970s.

For much of the twentieth century, the blocks surrounding the Five Points district had been the domain of white office workers. The social complexion of downtown Atlanta became steadily more diverse beginning in the 1960s as a result of several related trends. First, urban renewal pushed the residents of a number of predominately Black neighborhoods in the center city into a series of ever-smaller enclaves to the south, west, and east of the CBD. Slum clearance had exacerbated an already mounting housing crisis in Atlanta's Black Belt.[50]

Second, the affirmative action program put in place for municipal employment by the Massell administration led to a considerable increase in the number of Black office workers downtown during the early 1970s, further diminishing white hegemony in Atlanta's CBD. Third, the election of an African American mayor in 1973 and his hiring of a socially progressive Black police chief named Reginald Eaves improved the perception of law enforcement among many Black residents. The Eaves-era Atlanta Police Department (APD) seemed less aggressive and intimidating to many African American residents, who felt more comfortable spending time downtown without fear of continual harassment from law enforcement. Conversely, many Atlanta residents, both white and Black, complained that, under Eaves's leadership, the APD became too permissive of petty offenses being committed downtown. White and Black residents alike complained during the late 1960s and 1970s about the significant increase in incidences of aggressive panhandling and threatening behavior, particularly toward women, by the CBD's growing population of street dwellers, who were predominately African American.[51]

"You walk down the streets and you hear some of the most vile epithets that human mouths can utter," George Coleman of the *Atlanta Daily World* wrote in November 1971, describing the increasingly threatening atmosphere he found on downtown Atlanta streets.[52] Five months later, Coleman wrote of the fear that most residents felt when they had to interact with "the men who curse and threaten those who pass by" and who were increasingly populating the streets of the CBD. Many of "the men" described by Coleman were recently deinstitutionalized patients from the state's mental health hospitals.[53] In its 1981 annual report, Central Atlanta Progress (CAP) noted that "behavioral signs of disorder" in downtown Atlanta had grown rapidly over the previous decade. The downtown booster organization called for strict enforcement of quality-of-life codes.[54]

"Whites don't like to be outnumbered by Blacks. Even well-to-do Blacks don't like to be surrounded by low-class Blacks," Underground Atlanta restauranteur Dante Stephensen told the *Wall Street Journal*'s Janet Guyon in 1980 for a feature story focused on downtown Atlanta's struggles. The proprietor of Dante's Down the Hatch said openly and crassly what many others said in private. Moreover, he described accurately the attitudes of a clear majority of the region's middle-class residents, both white and Black, toward Atlanta's CBD, which was viewed by the suburban majority through the combined lenses of race and class.[55] Long before Stephensen made this pronouncement, the metropolitan area's middle classes left the streets of the center city, particularly at night, to conventioneers and the predominately impoverished African American residents of the surrounding neighborhoods.[56] Even downtown booster CAP said as much in its 1979–80 annual report: "Atlanta has made great strides in race relations, but it's a sad fact that many people won't come downtown because they don't like rubbing shoulders with Black people," the report stated, conceding that "our city is becoming more and more segregated, both economically and socially."[57]

Mere racism does not entirely explain the fears that many metropolitan-area residents felt toward downtown Atlanta. By the early 1970s, the city of Atlanta, including its CBD, had become a genuinely dangerous place. For most suburban residents, trips downtown for work, shopping, or leisure were their primary reasons to enter the city limits, thus situating their anxieties about Atlanta proper primarily within the CBD.

Violent crime grew exponentially across the United States during the period in question, increasing 135 percent nationally between 1960 and 1975. The crime rate in Atlanta, which had ranked as one of America's most violent cities for as long as the Justice Department had maintained national crime statistics, accelerated even more dramatically than the country as a whole in every major category of offense. Between 1960 and 1975, Atlanta's homicide rate increased 270 percent, while reported aggravated assaults (625 percent), armed robberies (1,314 percent), and sexual assaults (900 percent) grew at even more staggering paces. For four years during the 1970s, Atlanta had the highest homicide rate of any major city. In all four of those years, more than 90 percent of the perpetrators and victims had been African American. A 1974 survey commissioned by CAP found that the perception that downtown was dangerous was the top reason why suburban consumers did not frequent the area. An October 1975 *Journal-Constitution* survey indicated that nearly one-half of Atlanta residents, including a majority of Black residents, regarded crime as the city's greatest problem.[58]

The Massell administration responded to the explosion in crime, especially in downtown Atlanta, by pursuing federal War on Crime money in the early 1970s as vigorously as Allen had pursued War on Poverty money in the mid-1960s. Atlanta was one of eight cities to secure federal funding from the Department of Justice's High Impact Crime Control Program, giving the city access to $20 million for law enforcement. Federal anticrime money enabled Atlanta to hire several hundred more police officers. The force grew from 950 in 1970 to 1,415 in 1975. Massell instructed the APD to expand foot patrols in high-crime areas, including several sections of the CBD. Despite the expanded presence of law enforcement in Atlanta generally and downtown specifically, violent crime remained a major problem, though the rates for major offenses remained relatively stable, though still atrocious, in the mid-1970s.[59]

Among the victims of downtown Atlanta's declining reputation was Underground Atlanta, a gas-lit, subterranean festival marketplace and entertainment district that was Atlanta's
hottest nightspot ever so briefly in the late 1960s and early
1970s. Situated across the Five Points from the Omni Complex, Underground Atlanta opened in May 1969, two years after
businessmen Jack Paterson and Steven Fuller purchased an
abandoned, four-block section of storefronts located beneath
the city's primary railroad viaduct. The pair soon formed
Underground Atlanta Inc. and invested $10 million in the
project. The streets that became Underground Atlanta had
been the city's commercial and entertainment hub in the
late nineteenth century but had been uninhabited since the
1920s, when merchants moved their stores to street level to
appeal to automobile traffic. Inspired by historically restored
commercial districts in St. Louis (Gaslight Square) and San
Francisco (Ghirardelli Square), Paterson and Fuller sought
to transform their site into a Gay Nineties–themed nightspot, juxtaposing a romanticized recreation of Jim Crow–era
Atlanta with the massive glass skyscrapers that had emerged
around the city's former merchant's row. Underground Atlanta
was famous from the day it opened, as Paterson and Fuller
had promoted the venue's launch heavily in both local and
national publications.[60]

In the demimonde days of Underground Atlanta, young
adults, nightlife-seeking suburbanites, and conventioneers
crowded in among the district's gaslit street lamps, masonry
archways, and colored-glass windows on both weekends
and weeknights. The Underground became Atlanta's closest
cousin to New Orleans's French Quarter, with its assortment
of antiquarian-themed cabarets, cocktail lounges, boutiques,
and offbeat restaurants. The shambolic atmosphere of the
Underground established the city's 1970s reputation as "Hot-
lanta." At its early 1970s peak, the adult-oriented attraction
averaged nearly three million visitors per year, roughly as
many visitors as Dekalb County's family-friendly Stone Moun-

tain Park, a remarkable feat in a region whose entertainment
choices had skewed in recent years toward the suburban and
family oriented.[61]

In early 1974, business at the Underground began a noticeable and steep decline. Total receipts dropped by at least 10 percent each year for the rest of the 1970s. Between 1973 and 1980,
the number of businesses in the festival marketplace declined
from sixty-eight to twenty. The rapid decline of the Underground can be attributed to many factors. Almost certainly, the
novelty of Underground Atlanta wore thin for many residents
as new entertainment options, including those at the Omni
and Colony Square, and, especially, the emerging nightlife in
Buckhead Village, competed for their business. The recession
of the mid-1970s cut into the disposable income of the Underground's local and out-of-town patrons. Moreover, the abolition
of blue laws prohibiting sales of mixed drinks in several suburban counties eliminated the primary incentive for many local
customers to venture into the city for a night on the town.[62]

As great a deterrent to Underground Atlanta's continued
success as any economic matter was the perception among
locals and visitors alike that the entertainment district and its
environs had become unsafe. In part, this perception emerged
among white patrons as a result of the racial, socioeconomic,
and gender makeup of much of the Underground's clientele.
The proximity of the district to several impoverished and predominately African American neighborhoods ensured that
many groups of young, Black males made the Underground a
regular hangout. Additionally, aggressive, primarily Black solic-
itors offering either marginally legal or illegal products both
inside and outside the Underground deterred many potential
customers from visiting the area.[63] "There are five elements
that scare people," the ever-outspoken Dante Stephenson,
proprietor of Dante's Down the Hatch, one of Underground
Atlanta's most popular restaurants, told the *New York Times*
in 1975, "the beggars, the winos, the pimps, the panhandlers,
and imposing religious fanatics."[64]

Crimes against people and property were genuine problems in and around Underground Atlanta. Muggings, particularly on the Park Plaza side of the Underground, were a regular late-night occurrence, even when the district was at its early 1970s peak.[65] In February 1982, Underground Atlanta closed its doors, a year and a half after a destructive fire that spread from an adjacent abandoned hotel forced most of the remaining operators out of business. Less than a decade removed from its early 1970s heyday, Underground Atlanta ceased operations, having failed to earn the durable patronage of locals or visitors.[66]

DESPITE THEIR ASPIRATIONS AND SUCCESS AT WINNING over investors, Tom Cousins and the rest of Atlanta's developer class failed to revitalize its downtown by filling it with massive, insular MXDS. By the late 1970s, metropolitan-area consumers made clear their unwillingness to regularly patronize the center city's new retail and entertainment options. The major commercial developments in the southern CBD, in particular, struggled to stay open. Over the course of the next decade, the Omni International Complex (1987), Underground Atlanta (1982), and Rich's flagship store (1991) would either close or be radically reorganized and used for another purpose. "Most natives seek their nightlife in the suburbs. Without conventions, downtown would be totally dead," Donald Ratajczak, an economist at Georgia State University, told the *Wall Street Journal* in 1980.[67] Evie Wolfe of the Atlanta Convention Planners bureau admitted to a reporter from the *Boston Globe* in 1976 that "local business downtown isn't very good. People who work there eat lunch downtown but people just don't go downtown after dark."[68]

In the midst of the fortification of the CBD, Atlanta had become the nation's third-largest convention city as a result of its outstanding combination of facilities: its busiest-in-the-nation airport, its four thousand downtown hotel rooms, and its millions of square feet of nearby exhibition space. It was the convention business, not local patronage, that kept the establishments in the CBD open. Downtown had come to serve a much narrower purpose, both economically and socially, within the metropolitan area than its developer boosters had envisioned a decade earlier.[69] By the end of the 1970s, the CBD was no longer the retail, leisure, or commercial center of metropolitan Atlanta. When Tom Cousins decided to turn the land in the Gulch into an arena and a multifaceted urban development, this was not the downtown he thought he was making.[70]

The Omni Coliseum met its fate in the 1990s when a new generation of Atlanta leaders followed in the footsteps of their predecessors, mooring downtown revitalization to professional sports. In many respects, the demise of the Omni Coliseum began in 1977 when a debt-ridden Tom Cousins sold the Hawks to Ted Turner for $1.5 million, less than half of what he paid for the team in 1968. Turner assumed the franchise's $10 million in debt as well as the lease on the Coliseum. This proved to be the first of many retreats by Cousins from his original vision. Turner proved to be the perpetual savior of Cousins's downtown empire. He purchased the entire Omni International Complex from Cousins in 1986. Turner paid Cousins Properties a mere $21.8 million for the white elephant and agreed to assume its remaining $45 million in debt. The cable-television entrepreneur remade the complex into the CNN Center, the headquarters for his television operations.[71]

Several years after Turner finished paying off the Omni Coliseum in the early 1990s, he worked out a deal with Atlanta officials to build a new downtown arena. The building would house the Hawks and be used to lure the NHL back to Georgia. To procure an expansion hockey team, he needed a state-of-the-art facility laden with luxury boxes, which were suddenly generating millions of dollars annually for professional sports franchises. Just as they did in the 1960s, Atlanta's leadership rose to a self-imposed challenge to prove its Major League status. This time it took place in the afterglow of the city's successful

bid to host the 1996 Summer Olympics. While the replacement arena opened several years after the Atlanta games, it
was a product of the civic boosterism that enabled the city to
raise $1.8 billion, public and private money, to host the event.
Turner contributed $20 million toward arena construction
while the Atlanta–Fulton County Recreation Authority sold
$130.75 million in revenue bonds and excised $62.5 million
in car-rental fees to pay for the Omni's successor. The Recreation Authority also employed a newly fashionable financing mechanism, covering most of its bond- and debt-service
responsibilities by selling the building's naming rights to elec-
tronics giant Philips for $180 million. Philips Arena became
the home of the Hawks and the expansion Atlanta Thrashers
hockey team, which spent twelve years in the city (1999–2011)
before following the Flames to Canada, relocating to Winnipeg, Manitoba.[72]

22

Keep Hockey a Southern Sport

....

DESPITE ITS STRONG DEBUT, "ATLANTA'S ICE SOCIETY" shrank precipitously during the mid-1970s. The Flames remained a contender, reaching the Stanley Cup playoffs almost every season. They still appealed to a devoted base of northsiders, transplants, and newly converted diehards, but the size of the team's constituency shrank steadily. Flames season-ticket sales fell nearly 40 percent between 1974–75 and 1977–78, from an all-time high of more than 9,800 to fewer than 5,700. Average game attendance during the same three-year period declined from better than 14,000 to just over 10,500. An aggressive season-ticket campaign engineered by Flames President Bob Kent helped the club improve season ticket sales to 6,400 for the 1978–79 season, but sales plunged to an all-time low of 5,400 in 1979–80. Average game attendance fell below 10,000 for the first time in 1979–80 as rumors of the team's departure, which began several seasons earlier, grew to a roar.[1]

The sudden decline of the Flames' box-office appeal is a product of several factors. Some of these factors were related to playing in downtown Atlanta at the Omni and impacted the Hawks just as strongly. Most suburban patrons regarded downtown Atlanta as increasingly uninviting, inconvenient, and unsafe during the 1970s. As suburban retail and leisure opportunities expanded, their impetus for a day or a night in the center city declined. Several other factors specific to the Flames' relationship with their fans also contributed to the decline. As hockey's novelty waned in Atlanta, the Flames were in the process of gaining a reputation for playoff futility. Despite consistently strong regular-season performances, the club failed to advance beyond the opening round of the Stanley Cup playoffs on all six occasions. "We never won a playoff round when we were there, and I think that ultimately was the greatest thing that led to our demise," Bill Clement said. Playoff failures cultivated fan frustration and, eventually, apathy toward the team.[2]

The national economic downturn of the mid-1970s, even in perpetually booming Atlanta, contributed to the tightening of discretionary budgets, including those of the professionals and corporations which had, collectively, purchased many Flames season tickets each season. Additionally, the Omni Group's doomed effort to boost the poor-drawing Hawks' attendance by poaching many of the Flames' Saturday-evening dates cut into the hockey team's best night of business. Moreover, the 1975 resignation of the Flames' wildly popular coach, "Boom Boom" Geoffrion, left the franchise without a genuine public face. The loss of Geoffrion as coach corresponded to significant cuts in the team's marketing budget, lowering the public profile of the franchise just as it started to struggle at the gate.[3]

In a more general sense, media visibility emerged quickly as one of the franchise's major weaknesses. While the Flames became disinclined to invest in self-promotion, the Atlanta media, too, lost interest in serving as a public-relations arm of the franchise. Like the Hawks, the Flames received decidedly less press coverage than their baseball and football counterparts. After an initial burst of publicity, the local media relegated the Flames to the inside pages of the sports section and to infrequent television coverage. "After the first couple of years," Joe Watkins recalls, "the media was nice to them, but did as little as possible for hockey coverage. . . . They went back to high school football or college football."[4]

Bill Clement characterized the local media coverage of the team as "friendly" and "never challenging" but noted that they were mainly "reporting the facts" rather than boosting the franchise.[5] In the Flames' early years, the *Journal* and the *Constitution* did an excellent job explaining the rules and terminology of hockey as well as the history of the sport in frequent sidebars, augmenting the education being done in team promotional materials as well as by the Omni's public address announcer, who explained the rule being enforced each time the whistle was blown during a game. Nonetheless, the Flames were never the primary or even secondary focus of the Atlanta sports media.[6]

"I've always felt that between 1974 and 1976, there should have been a strong marketing program," Cliff Fletcher said in 1980. "But because of the success of the team the first two seasons, I guess they thought that they could get by without it."[7] Fletcher spoke openly during the late 1970s about the necessity of averaging thirteen thousand fans per home date and ten thousand season-ticket sales simply for the club to break even. Unlike many other franchises, the team could not rely on luxury or club seating as an additional revenue source, as the Omni contained no such sections. Nor could the Flames fall back on a robust broadcast-media contract to support their operations.[8]

One of the Flames' weaknesses as a franchise was the instability and size of their broadcast-media contracts. During the Flames' first three years in Atlanta, WSB televised twenty games each season, while WGST carried all seventy-eight games on the radio. In year one, the club drew excellent television ratings—the third largest per capita local viewership in the NHL. While radio drew a steady but small audience, television ratings declined precipitously in subsequent years, along with the novelty of televised hockey in the region. The Flames television numbers dropped in years two and three into the lower echelon of the league's local ratings despite their presence on a powerful NBC affiliate. WSB, which also carried NBC's national coverage of the NHL, dropped both the Flames and its syndication of the *Game of the Week* after the 1974–75 season. As a regional flagship station, WSB served as the epicenter of NBC's efforts to build a television audience for hockey in the South. In spite of several rounds of regional advertising campaigns, southern stations, including WSB, considered the ratings for hockey too dreadful to continue broadcasting games. Nielsen numbers for both the Flames and the *Game of the Week* on WSB fell below a 5 in the 1974–75 season, half as many viewers as NHL games drew in most northern markets.[9]

"We get fives on this station for test patterns," WSB-TV Program Director August Van Cantfort told *Sports Illustrated's* William Leggett in 1975, explaining that almost any movie shown on the station on a Saturday or Sunday afternoon would draw a better rating than any hockey game. For the duration of the Flames' stay in Georgia, the team played in the only NHL market without regular national broadcasts of league games or television coverage of the Stanley Cup finals.[10]

Atlanta's largely upscale hockey spectators demonstrated a clear preference for the live product. Many fans found hockey much easier to follow in person and believed that there was a more significant drop-off in their enjoyment of the televised game relative to other sports. In the long run, hockey proved popular in Atlanta with affluent, nightlife-seeking young people, as well as a loyal core of diehards, but not a mass television audience. In certain respects, Atlanta's consumers had a similar, if more exaggerated, response to nationally televised hockey as other viewers across the country. NBC affiliates' ratings for regular-season hockey even in northern states lagged behind the numbers other stations in their markets drew for their competing programming. In 1976 NBC decided not to renew its contract with the NHL, leaving the league without a national regular-season broadcasting contract. The end of the NHL's national television deal forced franchises to fend largely for themselves for broadcasting revenue.[11]

Ted Turner's media enterprises preserved Flames hockey on television for Atlantans, just as they had several years earlier with Braves baseball. Knowing that televised hockey would draw only modest ratings, WTCG Channel 17 offered the Flames only a modest television contract. The station agreed to broadcast twenty-two Flames games during the 1975–76 season for a mere $125,000, the smallest television package in the league. By comparison, broadcasters in established NHL markets, such as Boston and Montreal, paid more than $2 million that season for the local television rights to their hometown teams. The Flames' television revenue gap widened by the year. While other clubs negotiated new and larger broadcast packages, they sold their television rights to WTCG in each of the next five seasons for the same $125,000. During the same five-year stretch, a succession of radio stations paid $130,000 annually for the right to broadcast all Flames games not televised on WTCG.[12]

As much as any financial struggle the Flames faced during the late 1970s, the franchise's 1980 departure from Atlanta was a product of the declining fortunes of Tom Cousins's real estate empire. The persistently high vacancy rate at the Omni International Complex and its adjoining developments made Cousins's ambitious plans for downtown Atlanta economically unsustainable. He lost an estimated $33 million on the Omni International Complex between 1975 and 1978, diminishing his ability to support the franchise, especially after a series of early investors sold their stakes in the Flames as the organization started losing money.[13]

Originally, Cousins owned a mere 20 percent of the team. Six other businessmen, including team president Bill Putnam, each owned 10 percent of the Flames while four additional investors each held a 5 percent stake. All ten of Cousins' co-owners were, in addition, investors in the Omni Group, which owned the Hawks and managed the arena. Despite the big splash the Flames made in 1972–73, the majority of co-owners believed that Putnam had jeopardized their investments by spending too much money marketing the team. In July 1973, a majority of Flames stakeholders overruled Cousins and fired Putnam as team president, replacing him with co-owner John Wilcox, an attorney with no previous experience in the sports business. Wilcox channeled much of the Flames advertising budget into the Hawks' coffers, using it to promote the struggling basketball franchise in which most Flames co-owners had also invested. In the long run, this decision sank both ships.[14]

A decline in attendance during the mid-1970s turned the briefly profitable Flames into a financial burden for its penny-pinching owners. The club lost more than $1 million during the 1974–75 season, a descent into the red that got worse by the year. Flames ownership responded to the shrinking box office by freezing ticket prices at their 1974–75 level, hoping to win back wayward customers. The price freeze primarily cut the franchise off from much-needed revenue. The combination of declining ticket revenue and a measly broadcast-media contract put the Flames in a terrible financial position as they tried to keep up with rapidly increasing player salaries. The NHL's personnel-war with the WHA caused professional hockey salaries to increase by an average of 15 percent each season during the 1970s. By the time of Wilcox's departure as team president in late 1975, several co-owners had dropped out of the organization, leaving Cousins the club's majority owner. For the remainder of the Flames' tenure in Atlanta, Cousins turned day-to-day control of the organization over to Fletcher and Omni manager Bob Kent.[15]

By December 1976 Cousins and his suddenly small ownership group were having trouble making weekly payroll. Rumors that the Flames would be relocating the next spring were followed by reports that Cousins had sought out financial assistance from Georgia Governor George Busbee, who was a fervent supporter of the franchise. The governor responded by spearheading a corporate fundraising campaign. He convinced thirteen large Georgia-based companies to purchase $750,000 in tickets on expense account to help steady the franchise's finances for the remainder of the season. Against the advice of their union, Flames players demonstrated their desire to stay in Atlanta by purchasing $25,000 in tickets for local charities and offering to accept salary reductions in their off-season negotiations. In an effort to stabilize Cousins's franchise, his fellow NHL owners agreed to forgo the $2 million in expansion fees that Cousins had yet to pay them, revealing how invested the entire league was in the success of the fledgling southern franchise.[16]

Cousins spent the late 1970s looking for a buyer for his hockey team. In January 1977 the *Journal* and the *Constitution* reported that Cousins was considering selling the Flames to Miami businessman Earl Thomas for $5.2 million. Cousins pulled out of the deal when the news broke, fearing that Busbee would end his ongoing season-ticket drive if he got the impression that Thomas intended to move the team to Florida. In July 1978 Ted Turner considered buying the Flames but balked at the additional debt Cousins expected him to take on with the purchase. Later that year, actor Glenn Ford made his first of several offers for the team, which he stated publicly he would keep in Atlanta. Nothing ever materialized from the *Blackboard Jungle* star's bids. Cousins regarded Ford's offers as less serious than those that corporate and municipally backed organizations in other cities were starting to make for the franchise. By the time the Flames began what proved to be their final season in Atlanta, ownership groups in northern New Jersey, Dallas, and Calgary were vying publicly for Cousins's attention, leading even casual observers to believe that the club would relocate after the 1979–80 campaign.[17]

Even as Cousins was shopping around the franchise, the Flames tried to boost their home attendance to attract a local buyer. To this end, the Flames signed U.S. Olympic hockey team goalie Jim Craig, whom the club had drafted three years earlier while he starred at Boston University. Craig was one of the marquee names on the "Miracle on Ice" team that had upset the Soviet Union en route to the gold medal at the February 1980 winter games in Lake Placid. Craig made his NHL debut at the Omni on March 1, 1980, just one week after ascending the medal stand in upstate New York. Craig's presence in net helped the club draw its first sellout crowd of the season. Members of the Flames Fan Club handed out eight thousand miniature American flags to spectators. Chants of "U.S.A.! U.S.A.! U.S.A.!" reverberated throughout the Omni from the moment Craig came on the ice until the conclusion of the Flames' 4–1 victory over the Colorado Rockies. ABC, the network that carried the Miracle on Ice, bought the television rights to Craig's Atlanta debut and showed the game nationally.[18]

"The team handed out little posters of Jim in goal that said, 'Atlanta's Olympic Flame,'" Jamie Taylor, who attended Craig's debut, recalled. "Not an empty seat in the house. I remember it was a zoo that night. Lots of cheering. And thunderous applause when he was introduced. Lots of women crying."[19] Though Craig struggled for the remainder of the season, his presence helped the Flames increase their average home attendance from just over nine thousand to just under ten thousand per game. The Olympic hero never won another game for Atlanta and finished with a 1-1-2 record in four starts. Craig spent a sleepless month with the Flames: responding to constant media requests, receiving honors from civic groups in Atlanta and back home in Massachusetts, and jetting around the country to appear on morning programs or in advertisements. All of this left him little time to prepare to play goalie in the NHL. When he did appear with the Flames, he engendered resentment from many teammates, who felt he was displacing the team's standout goalie, Dan Bouchard. After the season, the Calgary-bound Flames honored Craig's request for a trade to an American team, where his value as a box-office attraction would be significantly higher. Craig was sent to his hometown Boston Bruins, where he failed to develop into an effective NHL goaltender.[20]

At the end of the 1979–80 regular season, Fletcher told his players and the local media that if the Flames drew sellout crowds and won their opening round playoff series against the New York Rangers, the team's ownership group would give them a one-year reprieve from moving. Fans and athletes alike came to regard Fletcher's talk as a cynical motivational and marketing ploy, especially after the franchise announced a 25 percent hike in ticket prices for the playoffs. The Flames drew large though not capacity crowds to both of their home playoff games. Homemade banners reading "Keep the Flames Burning" and "Keep Hockey a Southern Sport" hung throughout the arena. After the Rangers eliminated the Flames, Fletcher changed his tune and said he had no idea whether or not the team would stay in Atlanta.[21]

On April 15, 1980, three days after the Flames' elimination from the playoffs, Tom Cousins announced that he was "actively discussing offers involving relocation and sale of the team." Cousins said he had lost $12 million on the Flames during their eight years in Atlanta, including a record $2.8 million in the 1979–80 season. Cousins blamed the franchise's financial woes primarily on its inability to secure a lucrative broadcast-media contract. Alberta oil speculators Daryl and Byron Seaman emerged quickly as the front-runners to buy the franchise. The Seaman brothers were working closely with the city of Calgary, which had already won municipal approval to build an $80 million, twenty-thousand-seat hockey arena as part of its bid for the 1988 Winter Olympics. While negotiating with officials in Calgary, Cousins and team president Bob Kent pursued local buyers, as they had for several years, but to no avail.[22]

A "Save the Flames" campaign sprung up in response to Cousins's announcement. The organization tried in vain to put together a group of local investors to purchase a portion of the team. They also held a rally at the club's practice rink in Marietta.[23] As much as anything, the organization demonstrated that the Flames had a corps of devoted fans who were tired of being a "convenient target for everyone's slings and arrows," as Peter Wilson, a member of Save the Flames, explained in a June 1980 letter to the *Sporting News*.[24]

On May 21, 1980, Cousins announced the sale of the Flames for a league record $16 million to Vancouver real estate mogul

Nelson Skalbania, who was heading an ad hoc investment group that planned to move the club to Calgary. Initially a rival bidder to the Seamans, Skalbania merged his offer with the brothers' as well as bids by other Calgary-based investors, helping the out-of-towner win the endorsement of the city's municipal leadership. The NHL approved the move quickly, paving the way for the Calgary Flames to begin play in the fall of 1980. Ironically, one week before the announcement, the New York Islanders, the NHL's other 1972 expansion franchise, which had struggled as the early Flames flourished, claimed their first of four consecutive Stanley Cup championships.[25]

The Flames proved an immediate success in hockey-mad Calgary, drawing some of the league's largest crowds for decades to come at the Saddledome, as the arena was christened. Skalbania retained Cliff Fletcher as general manager, who continued to build consistently winning teams. The steady success cultivated by Fletcher culminated in a Stanley Cup championship for the franchise in 1989, three years after the departure of the last player who skated in Atlanta. The Flames' success in Calgary was, in certain respects, a defeat for the NHL. The relocation of the Flames to Calgary further concentrated the league in Canada and the northern United States, stymieing, for the first of many times, the NHL's aspirations to be a genuinely continental league.

Flames players appreciated the enthusiastic support they received in Calgary, but many of them missed Atlanta. "It was very close to perfection for me there in the '70s," Bill Clement said of his time in the city. Clement, who resided near the team's practice rink in Marietta, found the people friendly, appreciated the low cost of living, and took to Georgia's warm weather climate.[26] Calgary, by comparison, lacked many of the big-city amenities that players like Clement had grown used to in Atlanta, including a hopping nightlife, upscale shopping, and fancy restaurants. The significantly higher taxes that greeted players in Canada also left many of them yearning for Georgia. Many former Flames retained a home in the area or moved back to Georgia when their careers ended, often trading in on their fame to jumpstart small businesses. Former Flames Tim Ecclestone, Eric Vail, and Dan Bouchard all became successful restauranteurs in suburban Atlanta, while Willi Plett ran a popular sports-centered theme park in Cherokee County. "Boom Boom" Geoffrion resettled much of his extended family in Atlanta, where he remained a fixture at numerous charity events well into the twenty-first century.[27]

Despite the Flames' short tenure in Atlanta, the club's status as the NHL's first expansion into the South give it a unique place in the history of the sport. For a brief moment, the franchise proved that a large audience for professional hockey could be found outside of its traditional bases in the northern United States and Canada. In many respects, Atlanta's Ice Society was a forerunner to the diehard though narrow fan bases that many Sunbelt teams in the NHL have cultivated in the twenty-first century, including Georgia's second and now departed entry into the league, the Atlanta Thrashers (1999–2011).

23

Loserville No More

....

"I DON'T WANNA SEE ANY MORE HEADLINES IN THE
Atlanta *Journal-Constitution*, bless their souls, that call Atlanta,
'Losersville, U.S.A.,'" Ted Turner said at the January 1976 press
conference he called to announce his purchase of the Braves.[1]
Turner implored the local press to start referring to Atlanta
as "Winnersville." None of the city's teams resided in "Winnersville" at the time, particularly the Braves, which were in
fact in the process of getting worse. Turner promised fans
across the Southeast that the Braves would win the World
Series within five years. Instead, they finished in last place
in eight of the next fifteen seasons, further cementing Atlanta's reputation for on-field ineptitude. But Turner kept them
in Atlanta. And he kept Atlanta Major League. And, eventually, the Braves became not only winners but the envy of MLB.

Turner's purchase of the Braves in 1976 and subsequent
acquisition of the Hawks in 1977 initiated his quarter-century-
long trusteeship over Atlanta's Major League status. While
Atlantans remained mercurial consumers of the city's professional franchises, the cable-television pioneer turned
yachtsman turned professional-sports-franchise owner was
the primary reason that the city remained in the big leagues.
Pragmatically, the two franchises stocked Turner's TBS and,
later, TNT cable networks with dependable and inexpensive
programming. At the same time, Turner lost millions of dollars annually on the Braves and Hawks through many lean
years in the 1970s and 1980s, demonstrating his civic com-

mitment to a pair of institutions he clearly regarded as more important to the region than did the region's residents.

When Ted Turner purchased the Atlanta Braves in 1976, he was making a long-term investment in his television station. Three years earlier, WTCG bought the rights to broadcast Braves baseball for $600,000 per season, by then one of the lowest rates in MLB. Braves games drew steady ratings for his UHF station, which made hefty profits by broadcasting family-friendly, low-cost programming to viewers across the Southeast. NL owners regarded Turner as a fly-by-night operator, one who had purchased the Braves on the installment plan ($1 million per year for ten years) from a cash-strapped ownership. They found Turner insolent and unpredictable, better suited for adventures with his America's Cup racing team than life as a Major League mandarin. The NL wanted the Braves to accept a standing offer from Canadian investors and relocate to Toronto. NL officials acceded to a Turner ownership only when the cable operator agreed to make former Braves executive Bill Bartholomay the team's chairman.[2]

As it turned out, Turner was just the kind of stabilizing force the NL wanted at the helm of the Braves. Despite his often-contentious relationship with baseball's establishment, Turner ensured both the MLB's and NBA's future in one of the nation's largest media markets. In hindsight, Turner's tenure as Braves (1976–97) and Hawks (1977–97) owner amounted to a trusteeship over Major League Atlanta that ended just as civic boosters embraced another sports-related grand municipal enterprise. The city's bid for the 1996 Summer Olympics galvanized a new round of local investments in sports facilities, which guaranteed Atlanta's Major League future but failed to transform the city into the durable professional sports hotbed long envisioned by civic leaders.

"Ted's enthusiasm was contagious," Wayne Minshew recalled, "Ted was a great, great salesman and a visionary."[3] Such enthusiasm was necessary to keep baseball in Atlanta. The team had finished 40 games out of first place in 1975, drawing barely 534,000 fans to Atlanta Stadium, one of MLB's smallest draws of the past half-century. "No one much cared if the Braves left town," Braves public-relations official Bob Hope said. "Baseball was not really ingrained in the culture down here."[4]

For the remainder of the 1970s, the Braves performed poorly on the field, worse than they ever had under their previous ownership. Atlanta finished in last place for four consecutive seasons (1976–79). Despite the Braves' unprecedentedly poor performance, the promotional guile of Turner and his associates helped the club inch up in attendance over the latter half of the decade, finally reaching the modestly respectable one million fan threshold in the 1980 season. Turner's Braves sponsored countless promotions, the most popular of which featured the owner himself. Turner joined in mattress stacking competitions, cash grabs, and wet T-shirt contests. The Braves hosted an evening of pregame home-plate weddings and postgame professional wrestling called "Headlock and Wedlock Night." One evening, Turner bloodied his face, nudging a peanut down the third base line with his nose as part of a Georgia produce-themed race. Turner also purchased one of the league's first video-animation scoreboards.[5] "There were also a lot of college students from Tech and Agnes Scott and Atlanta University who attended the games because the beer vendors did not check IDs regularly," Alan Morris recalled.[6]

As the Braves' live audience inched toward respectability, its television viewership expanded exponentially. In 1976 WTCG began its ascent from a regional phenomenon to a national one, as Turner invested in satellite technology to beam his network, which was soon rechristened TBS, to cable subscribers across the country. Braves games in 1976 reached 695,000 homes across the Southeast. By the end of 1978, satellites brought TBS's nightly telecasts of Braves baseball to all fifty states. By the early 1980s TBS carried Braves baseball to more than twenty million homes. MLB challenged the legality of TBS's distribution of Braves games into other team's markets, but the FCC ruled that as long as the station's signal was distributed by a commonly available carrier, it could continue to broadcast as many games as it chose on cable television.[7]

"When we would go to the other cities to play exhibition games during spring training, we would have people coming up to us all the time saying they were Braves fans: 'We watch you on Turner all the time,'" Milo Hamilton said, recalling the team's earliest days on WTCG.[8] "TBS made the Braves and its players nationally known. I know my parents couldn't wait for the teams that I was on to go to Atlanta so they could see me play. I think a lot of players were a little jealous not having a national TV audience," former MLB third baseman Vance Law recalled.[9]

The convergence of the Braves' appeal on cable television, ability to draw a live crowd, and win baseball games came during the 1982 season, when Atlanta captured its first division title in thirteen years. The Braves began the 1982 season with an MLB record thirteen consecutive wins, leading fans to storm the field at Atlanta–Fulton County Stadium in celebration after the team broke the all-time record with its twelfth-straight victory to start the year. With as many as seven million people watching each night on cable television and packed houses attending games at the stadium, the likes of outfielder Dale Murphy, third baseman Bob Horner, and veteran knuckleballer Phil Niekro became household names far beyond the confines of the Southeast. The voices of announcers Ernie Johnson, Skip Caray, and Pete Van Wieren also became some of the best known in television broadcasting.

TBS branded the 1982 club "America's Team," a moniker that befit the genuinely national audience that watched its every game on the Superstation. The Braves developed a national bandwagon that *Sports Illustrated* described in a profile that season as stretching to as far-flung places as Bismarck, North Dakota; Reno, Nevada; and Juneau, Alaska. Team publications touted the large number of cable fans who made cross-country trips to see their new favorite MLB team. National television

exposure transformed the Braves' amiable, clean-living superstar slugger Dale Murphy, the NL's Most Valuable Player in 1982
and 1983, into one of the sport's most beloved figures. Even
though the 1982 Braves struggled down the stretch and were
quickly dispatched by St. Louis in the NLCS, the team drew
well all season, pulling in 1.8 million spectators at Atlanta–
Fulton County Stadium, the franchise's best figure since it
played in Wisconsin.[10]

The Braves' early-1980s moment as local and national
favorites proved short-lived. The team faded quickly from
the top of the standings, retreating back to last place in 1986,
a position the team held in four of the next five seasons. Pre-
dictably, Braves attendance collapsed during the mid-to-late
1980s, dropping from a franchise record of 2,119,935 in 1983 to
less than one million in 1988, a dubious distinction the team
reached in each of the next three seasons.

Several Minor League teams outdrew the Braves during
this period. Those fans who did attend games returned home
with stories of rat infestations and filthy bathrooms in the
near-empty stadium. "Fulton County Stadium was always
leaking water and had an unusual odor; I can still conjure up
that smell," veteran Atlanta sportscaster Jeff Hullinger said
of the atmosphere at a Braves game during the 1980s.[11] By
decade's end, Braves baseball on TBS drew less than half as
many viewers as it did in 1982. Certainly, the team's poor
performance figured prominently in the ratings drop, but
the expanding cable distribution of Chicago's WGN and New
York's WOR brought new competition to TBS, as tens of millions of viewers could now choose among daily broadcasts of
Cubs, Mets, and Braves games. As MLB expanded its reach
on cable television, Turner considered selling the Braves and
buying into a new, league-wide baseball television package.[12]

During the 1980s Turner played an ever-smaller role in the
day-to-day operations of the Braves. Instead, he turned his
attention to the expansion of his cable-television empire, pioneering twenty-four-hours-a-day news with CNN (1980) and

Headline News (1982). Additionally, Turner created a second cable network, TNT (1988), which developed far more original programming and competed with the major television networks and ESPN for the broadcasting rights to nearly every major American sport. Beyond their coverage of the Hawks and the Braves, Turner's networks began carrying packages of regional favorites like NASCAR (1983) and World Championship Wrestling (1988), as well as World Cup Soccer (1990), the Winter Olympics (1992), *Sunday Night Football* (1990), and the Goodwill Games (1986), a made-for-television, money-pit of an international athletic competition that aimed to improve Soviet-American relations in the aftermath of their reciprocal Summer Olympic boycotts.[13]

Just as Turner considered selling the Braves, the team's new GM, John Schuerholz, the first Turner hire from outside the TBS orbit, was in the process of remaking the Braves into once-in-a-generation winners. In 1991 the Braves won their first NL pennant since the franchise played in Milwaukee, achieving the greatest single-season turnaround in baseball history. Just as in 1982, the stadium became the place to be. The Braves' quickly reasserted their identity as America's Team, drawing huge television audiences on TBS and excellent home crowds. Spectators adopted the controversial tomahawk chop and chant as the team's signature cheer, which for the first time, for better or worse, gave Atlanta fans a national identity based on something other than their collective apathy. The 1991 season proved to be the starting point of a Braves dynasty that included fourteen consecutive division titles, five NL Pennants, and a World Series championship in 1995.[14]

THE BREAKTHROUGH OF THE ATLANTA BRAVES IN THE 1990s contrasted with the continued futility and frustration of their stadium co-tenants. The perennially weak Falcons made just four playoff appearances during their quarter century at Atlanta Stadium (1966–91). Their local television numbers were consistently among the NFL's lowest, and they finished below the league average in attendance in twenty-three of their first twenty-five seasons. "I remember a sparse crowd for a Falcons-Rams game in the '80s when a moribund crowd slowly began cheering, rising to their feet, cheering wildly— the great James Brown was walking toward the sidelines," Jeff Hullinger recalled. "He did a dance move in appreciation, and the crowd went crazy. Then it was back to silence as the Falcons were getting toasted."[15]

The Falcons looked to have turned a corner in the late 1970s. Under the leadership of new General Manager Eddie LeBaron, the diminutive quarterback who parlayed his guts and on-field smarts into four Pro Bowl appearances, and Head Coach Leeman Bennett, who served as offensive coordinator under Chuck Knox with the Rams, the Falcons emerged as one of the NFC's top teams in the late 1970s and early 1980s. Quarterback Steve Bartkowski, the Falcons' number one pick in the 1975 NFL Draft, became one of the league's leading passers, tossing more than 30 touchdown passes in consecutive seasons (1980, 1981). Atlanta's ferocious offensive line, which included perennial Pro Bowlers Jeff Van Note and Mike Kenn, gave Bartkowski ample time to choose his target and enabled bruising fullback William Andrews to rush for 1,000 yards on four occasions. Atlanta's heralded "Grits Blitz" defenses of the late 1970s, which were engineered by defensive coordinator Jerry Glanville, were the forerunners of the all-out pass rushes that the Super Bowl champion Chicago Bears and New York Giants teams employed in the 1980s. In the age of LeBaron and Bennett, the Falcons made the playoffs three times (1978, 1980, 1982) and won their first NFC West title (1980). The success of the Falcons rejuvenated local interest in the club, helping the team rebuild its season ticket base to nearly fifty thousand.

Following a disappointing early exit from the 1982 NFL Playoffs, Rankin Smith dismissed both Bennett and LeBaron, which led to a rapid reversal of the club's fortunes. "The franchise changed after Eddie LeBaron left. He had, as a former player, an affinity for the game that only former players have. When they moved from a football guy running everything to a non-football guy, it changed, and so did our record," Falcons standout Mike Kenn said of the change in leadership.[16] The Falcons' new regime, led by longtime Falcons personnel man Tom Braatz, proved unable to replenish the talent on the team's aging roster. The Falcons regressed to their old ways, struggling through eight consecutive losing seasons to close out the 1980s. Not surprisingly, local interest plummeted.

During the late 1980s the Falcons finished last in average attendance on four occasions, playing to "bipartisan crowds," as Falcons offensive tackle Mike Kenn referred to the audience at a 1988 home game where boisterous Saints fans drowned out Atlanta supporters at the stadium. Team owner Rankin Smith's family came to be known locally as "the Clampetts." Like the leading family on the *Beverly Hillbillies*, their critics regarded them as wealthy, genial rubes. Rankin's reliance on sons Rankin Jr. and Taylor, neither of whom displayed a particular aptitude for professional football, to run the perpetually dreadful franchise during the 1980s and 1990s encouraged this comparison.[17] Despite the team's struggles, the Smiths were highly respected by their players. "I knew Rankin Sr. well, and I really appreciated his understanding of the business role and relationship the NFL players union had with the NFL. He never held my union involvement against me personally like many other NFL owners," Mike Kenn said.[18] In 1989 Kenn became president of the NFL Players Association (NFLPA), a position he held for eight years.

Amid the Falcons' 1980s doldrums, Smith considered moving the club out of its tenancy at Atlanta–Fulton County Stadium. Smith's most serious suitors came from Jacksonville, Florida, equipped with an existing, NFL-style stadium in the Gator Bowl. Public and private boosters in Jacksonville offered Smith guarantees of nearly $19 million in annual stadium revenue, more than twice as much as the club was generating each season at Atlanta Stadium. Smith's public dalliances with

Jacksonville provided him with enough local leverage to convince the civic leadership that losing the Falcons would tarnish Atlanta's Major League image. Furthermore, the Falcons persuaded city and Fulton County officials that their football-mad constituents would finally embrace the team once it had a high-quality stadium of its own.[19] In 1989 the Fulton County Commission and Atlanta City Council approved 1 percent hotel tax increases to finance the $210 million Georgia Dome. The fourteen-acre complex was built adjacent to the Omni and the GWCC, which owned and operated the stadium. The Falcons signed a twenty-year deal to play at the seventy-two-thousand-seat Dome, which, supporters asserted, was being paid for primarily by visitors. Showing more concern for the surrounding neighborhood than the previous generation of civic boosters, Atlanta officials stipulated that the Falcons pay for the relocation of two Black churches and set up a $10 million housing trust for area residents displaced by construction. Additionally, minority-owned firms were guaranteed 35 percent of stadium contracts, and the city of Atlanta gained permanent representation on the state-run GWCC board.[20]

"The Georgia Dome is a wonder, a marvel, a sensory delight. It will be a source of pride for this city for the next 30, 40, 50 years," wrote the *Journal-Constitution*'s Mark Bradley in August 1992, weeks before its grand opening. Bradley raved over the stadium's 150 gaudy luxury boxes, maze of food courts, and excellent sight lines from every seat. A quarter-century later, it was imploded to provide parking for another new Falcons stadium.[21] The opening of the Georgia Dome produced an expected honeymoon effect, increasing Falcons' season-ticket sales from just over thirty-six thousand in 1991 to just over fifty-seven thousand in 1992.[22]

The arrival of the Georgia Dome also played no small role in upgrading the profile of Atlanta's college bowl game. The Peach Bowl's fortunes began to turn around in 1985 when the Atlanta Chamber took control of the game's management, stabilizing its shaky finances and securing the game a spot in the newly constructed Georgia Dome in 1992. In 1993 Atlanta-based Chick-fil-A became the game's title sponsor, providing it with the financial clout to offer multimillion-dollar payouts to participating schools.[23] In short order, the Chick-fil-A Peach Bowl secured a plum New Year's Eve night television spot on ESPN and exclusive agreements with the region's two premiere collegiate athletic conferences, the SEC and the ACC, to each send a high-caliber team to play in the game. During the late 1990s and 2000s, the Peach Bowl became one of college football's best-attended bowl games (seventeen consecutive sellouts) and highest-rated televised bowl games, frequently earning the most viewers for a non–Bowl Championship Series game. The success of the Peach Bowl was so great that the game earned a spot in college football's Bowl Championship Series starting in 2014.[24]

Nevertheless, initial enthusiasm for the dome proved short-lived. Complaints about the Georgia Dome sounded a lot like those fans had expressed about Atlanta Stadium. Fans griped about the lack of parking at the Georgia Dome, which included just 3,600 spaces in its adjoining garage. Commuters fresh off a drive into the city dreaded maneuvering through the narrow, labyrinthine tailgating lots that had been cobbled together in the neighborhoods around the stadium. Some fans parked at a MARTA stop and took the train into the game, but not enough to prevent pregame entrances and postgame exits from the exterior lots from turning into multihour events. Complaints by patrons about the staff at the Georgia Dome, often steeped in racial meaning, sounded similar to gripes about the employees at Atlanta Stadium.[25] Many fans regarded the downtown Atlanta environs of the Georgia Dome unsafe, as they had Atlanta Stadium and the Omni. Security on game days was always tight, but that did little to dispel broadly held perceptions of the area or the alarming crime statistics in the adjoining neighborhoods. A 2001 study by security firm CAP Index found that the neighborhood around the Georgia Dome had the highest rates of both violent and property crime of any zip code that included an NFL stadium.[26]

The Falcons' move into the Georgia Dome also corresponded with a demographic shift in the team's live audience—a notable upswing in attendance by African American fans. This likely had less to do with the dome itself than with the growth of the city's Black middle class, which also helped improve the Hawks' attendance during the 1980s. Additionally, the emergence of a pair of African Americans as the team's most high-profile players also contributed to the Falcons' appeal to Black spectators. In the early 1990s the franchise enjoyed a vogue that corresponded with the emergence of Deion "Prime Time" Sanders and Andre "Bad Moon" Rison as two of the league's most popular players. Sanders and Rison became the NFL's first two players strongly associated with hip-hop culture. The Falcons' all-Black jerseys, reintroduced in 1991 as a tribute to the team's original uniforms, soon became a youth fashion staple, due in large part to the throwback uniforms' association with the Falcons' stars. It also helped that the Jerry Glanville–coached, Black-clad Falcons of the early 1990s were winners, earning a wild-card spot in 1991. The Falcons' fortunes reversed shortly thereafter, but the team retained its foothold among African American fans.[27]

WELL IN ADVANCE OF THE FALCONS' MOVE TO THE GEORGIA Dome, the Braves had been looking into an upgrade or a replacement for rapidly aging Atlanta Stadium. Initially, the Braves considered several suburban sites for a new stadium, but Atlanta's successful bid for the 1996 Summer Olympics altered these plans. Doing what Atlanta has always done best, the city's civic elite engaged in a multifaceted promotional campaign, convincing the International Olympic Committee (IOC) to award Atlanta the games in September 1990. The city's corporate leadership, most notably Coca-Cola, CNN, and Delta, financed the local Olympic organizing committee while providing Atlanta with continuous visibility as the voters made up their minds. Former Atlanta Mayor and UN Ambassador Andrew Young made use of his enduring global popularity to stress Atlanta's legacy in the civil rights movement. He swayed many African IOC representatives by emphasizing the opportunity they had to place the games in a majority Black city for the first time.[28]

The Atlanta Organizing Committee spent $1.8 billion ($500 million of U.S. taxpayer dollars and $1.3 billion in privately raised funds) to prepare for the games, building twelve new playing facilities in which to host Olympic events. The largest of these venues was an eighty-thousand-seat, $209 million Olympic Stadium, which hosted the opening ceremony as well as track and field events. Following the Summer Olympics, the stadium was reconfigured into a fifty-thousand-seat baseball park, the cost of which was incorporated into the original construction budget. The remaking of Olympic Stadium into Turner Field, the Braves' new home, transformed the venue into a quintessential 1990s ballpark. Architects from Heery International, Rosser International, and Ellerbe Becket created a stadium that juxtaposed nostalgic homages to the game's past with posh amenities aimed at upscale consumers, including a pair of tony steakhouses and a veritable shopping mall of a team store. Many of these niceties were named in honor of Hank Aaron, who had developed a close relationship with Ted Turner and worked for the Braves in scouting for a number of years. Atlanta fans had long since reversed their indifference toward the slugger, embracing his legacy as the singular moment in the team's history. At Turner Field, Aaron's legacy became ever present and consumable.[29]

Atlanta's successful 1996 Olympic bid also facilitated the construction of a new basketball arena for the Turner-owned Atlanta Hawks. Despite frequent national-television coverage on TBS, the Hawks had struggled on the court and at the box office for much of Turner's tenure as owner. By the mid-1990s, the Hawks were in the middle of a forty-five-year sabbatical between Conference Finals appearances (1970–2015). The franchise had enjoyed two genuine eras of on-court and box-office success during Turner's ownership: the late 1970s and the late 1980s. Under the direction of Head Coach Hubie Brown, the Hawks became a hardnosed, defensively minded team, reminiscent of Richie Guerin's clubs of the late 1960s. Like Guerin, Brown was a no-nonsense city guy (Brown hailed from Elizabeth, New Jersey) who cultivated basketball toughness and smarts on a team with a largely unheralded roster. Atlanta's backcourt of Eddie Johnson, Armond Hill, and Charlie Criss was arguably the best in the league, while Tree Rollins and Dan Roundfield were a rugged duo in the low post. The Hawks turned the Omni into a boisterous home venue during the 1979–80 season, winning fifty games and taking home the NBA Central Division championship. Decimated by injuries, the Hawks fell apart the following season, leading to Brown's departure and a rapid decline in local interest.[30]

It took several years of rebuilding, but the Hawks were once again winners in the late 1980s. Led by former Hubie Brown assistant Mike Fratello, the Hawks began an almost immediate turnaround after the acquisition of University of Georgia star Dominique Wilkins, whose athleticism and scoring prowess earned him the nickname the "Human Highlight Reel." Between 1985 and 1989, the Hawks posted four consecutive 50-win seasons. Nicknamed "Air Force One" for their awe-inspiring slam dunks, the Hawks clubs of the late 1980s were one of the league's most exciting teams. Wilkins rivaled Michael Jordan as the league's most dynamic player, besting the Bulls star in the 1985 Slam Dunk Contest and winning the 1985–86 NBA scoring title. Like Jordan, Wilkins was a highly marketable star, serving as a pitchman for Coke, Minute Maid, and Reebok. Hawks guard Anthony Jerome "Spud" Webb, who won the 1986 NBA Slam Dunk contest despite his 5-foot-7 frame, also became one of the league's most recognizable players. Turner placed the wildly popular Hawks on the global stage, sending them on a two-week 1988 tour of exhibition games in the Soviet Union. The Hawks enjoyed significant box-office success during this period as well, drawing nearly 13,400 spectators per game in 1986–87, the first time the franchise finished above the league average in attendance since moving to Atlanta. African American fans, who had started attending Hawks games in notably larger numbers beginning in the mid-1970s, figured prominently in the Hawks' expanding audience. The city's growing Black middle class embraced the finally winning team and its exciting, locally grown superstar.[31]

By the mid-1990s, though, the franchise had faded back into mediocrity, and its attendance figures were again among the NBA's lowest. The Hawks sought out a replacement for the rapidly aging Omni in the midst of the Olympic building boom, enabling the franchise to benefit from the surge in civic vitality that accompanied the 1996 summer games. Turner contributed $20 million toward arena construction, while the Atlanta–Fulton County Recreation Authority sold $130.75 million in revenue bonds and excised $62.5 million in car-rental taxes to pay for Philips Arena, a building whose corporate naming-rights fee covered the vast majority of the bond's repayment. Replete with state-of-the-art, upscale amenities, Philips Arena was intended to revitalize local support for the Hawks and help the city reestablish itself as an NHL market. On both accounts, the founders' intentions went largely unmet. By the time Philips Arena opened in 1999, the Hawks had been sold to Time Warner as part of its multibillion-dollar deal with the Turner organization. The NHL returned to Atlanta that same year in the form of the Time Warner–owned Thrashers, which played twelve seasons (1999–2011) in Georgia before relocating to Winnipeg, Manitoba. Like the Flames, the Thrashers appealed to a core of season-ticket-holding diehards but lacked broad popular support.

Both the Hawks and Thrashers were purchased in 2004 by a consortium of East Coast business leaders called Atlanta Spirit LLC. The most prominent figures in Atlanta Spirit were self-professed basketball enthusiasts, but their ownership of the Hawks proved just as frustrating as Turner's or Cousins's and ended in far more troubling fashion. In September

2014 Atlanta Spirit majority owner Barry Levenson admitted to sending a 2012 email to team GM Danny Ferry that argued that the Hawks' consistently poor ticket sales were due to the large number of African American fans who attended the team's games. In January 2015 the entire Atlanta Spirit ownership group agreed to put the team up for sale following the public and media backlash in response to Levenson's email. Private equity billionaire Tony Ressler purchased the team from Atlanta Spirit in June 2015.[32]

THE 1997 DEBUT OF TURNER FIELD FOR THE NOW PERENnially contending Braves led to a short-lived explosion in the team's season ticket base from five thousand to better than thirty thousand. Despite the Braves' continued success on the diamond, the novelty of Turner Field soon faded. The team's consistent regular-season success and postseason futility soon fostered apathy among its new fanbase. Braves attendance had peaked at more than 3.8 million in 1993 but fell steadily in subsequent years. By the early 2000s, the Braves had faded to the middle of the pack in attendance, despite their ongoing streak of divisional titles. The inability of the Braves to sell out even during the playoffs renewed old taunts about the fickleness of Atlanta sports fans. Between 1997 and 2005, the Braves failed to sell out more than three-quarters of their home playoff games at Turner Field, displaying a fan apathy unrivaled among the era's contending franchises. While virtually every other club's postseason games drew at or near capacity crowds, the Braves often had more than ten thousand empty seats for playoff games.

Turner had long since sold the team as part of his media empire's 1996 merger with Time Warner. In 2007, Time Warner sold the team to another corporate behemoth, Liberty Media, a telecommunications company that held a large minority share in the Braves' parent company.[33]

Soon after ownership of the Braves passed into Liberty Media's hands, team executives announced that Turner Field would require $150 million in infrastructural upgrades if the franchise was going to stay in the stadium beyond the end of its lease in 2016. The administration of Atlanta Mayor Kasim Reed showed little interest in making a new round of investments in a stadium that was barely a decade old. Reed, a product of the Black governing coalition that had dominated Atlanta electoral politics since the 1970s, was willing to accommodate the development priorities of the city's corporate establishment but not without substantial material concessions in the form of employment guarantees or municipal investments. There was no indication that the Braves' new ownership was willing to make such a deal. Instead, the new owners levied complaints about Turner Field's center-city surroundings that sounded a lot like the complaints that had emerged among the franchise's original owners about Atlanta Stadium's environs. The new owners complained that a lack of parking, traffic congestion, and a dearth of amenities in the surrounding neighborhoods discouraged suburbanites from attending Braves games. They also complained that attending games at Turner Field was inconvenient for their predominately suburban fan base. In 2012 the club released a map displaying the distribution of their season-ticket holders across the metropolitan area. The vast majority of red dots on the map were located in the predominately white and affluent northern suburbs of Fulton and Cobb Counties.[34]

In late 2013 Braves officials acted upon their threats, announcing that they had negotiated a stadium deal in secret with Cobb County officials. The plan called for a $392 million public contribution toward the construction of a $622 million stadium, which would be owned by the Cobb-Marietta Coliseum and Exhibit Hall Authority. The Braves agreed to a thirty-year lease at the facility, which would pay for the balance. The county planned to pay back the stadium revenue bonds by channeling money from existing room and car-rental taxes. Additionally, a special, self-taxing zone known as the Cumberland Community Improvement District (CCID), a local business association created in the early 1990s to encourage investments in municipal infrastructure, imposed a series of new fees and a property-tax increase to help pay back the bonds. Since the stadium deal imposed no new countywide taxes, it required only a simple majority yes vote from the five-person Cobb County Board of Commissioners. Despite vigorous opposition by the county's powerful Tea Party organization, the measure passed 5–0 in November 2013. Construction on the stadium began in September 2014 on a sixty-acre piece of land within the CCID. The stadium was built between I-285 and I-75 near the upscale Cumberland Mall, an office park, and a convention center. It was eight miles from the closest MARTA stop. Despite the Braves' protests about the gridlock surrounding Turner Field, nearly as much daily traffic passed by their new ballpark as their previous one in the southern CBD. Apparently, getting out of traffic was much less of a concern to the Braves than getting out of the center city. The Braves took up permanent residence at SunTrust Park in April 2017.[35]

JUST AS THE BRAVES WERE PREPARING TO LEAVE TURNER Field, the Falcons, their former Atlanta Stadium co-tenants, were getting ready to move out of the Georgia Dome, which the team's new owner, Home Depot cofounder Arthur Blank, regarded as anachronistic and in need of significant repairs. Blank had purchased the Falcons from the Smith family in 2001 for $545 million. Beginning in the late 2000s, Blank expressed his desire to build a new, state-of-the-art facility for the Falcons and his expansion Major League Soccer franchise. Initially, Blank stated that he wanted an outdoor arena for the Falcons but ended up pushing for a downtown domed stadium with a retractable roof. Unlike previous owners, Blank was willing to pay for the lion's share of the new stadium. Blank's willingness to foot most of the bill was, in large part, a product of the skepticism that Atlanta officials, particularly Kasim Reed, expressed in response to the Falcons' claims that the stadium needed replacing. As a result, the public contribution to Atlanta's most recent downtown stadium project proved significantly more modest than in previous agreements. When accounting for inflation, the municipal investment in what came to be known as Mercedes-Benz Stadium was comparable to the $18 million one the city made in Atlanta Stadium back in the mid-1960s. In exchange for ownership of the stadium, the GWCC Authority agreed in 2013 to issue $200 million in municipal bonds to support the project. The city agreed to direct money from an existing room tax toward the repayment of the bond. AMB Group, the Blank-owned parent company of the Falcons and the Atlanta United soccer team, signed a thirty-year lease at the facility and agreed to cover the remainder of construction costs, which totaled a record $1.6 billion. In a deal similar to their Georgia Dome agreement, the Falcons agreed to invest $30 million into housing redevelopment in the surrounding Vine City neighborhood and to secure at least 31 percent participation by female and minority contractors.[36]

By the time Mercedes-Benz Stadium opened in August 2017, Atlanta's municipal leadership had made evident its new approach to negotiating with professional sports franchises. City leaders would only agree to municipal subsidies of stadiums and arenas insofar as these facilities offered tangible economic benefits to their core constituents—including Atlanta's Black residents. This new, pragmatic approach adopted during the Reed administration in its negotiations with the Braves, Thrashers, and Falcons mirrored the attitude that metropolitan-area residents had always taken toward professional sports. Civic leaders in Atlanta proper had ceased to be devotees of professional sports, enabling them to display unprecedented agency in their dealings with the franchises. Atlanta fans had always acted this way, perceiving of the teams as they would any other consumer product. The civic establishment has finally adopted this tactic, learning from the experiences not only of previous generations of Atlanta leaders but also municipal leaders in other Sunbelt cities that sought out Major League status. Atlanta's leadership has decided to leave grand municipal investments in professional sports to suburban municipalities and the private sector. This lesson may have dawned on civic elites in Atlanta, but it appears to be years away from becoming the common sense among big-city leaders, particularly those in communities still looking for tangible and obvious ways to assert their Major League status.

24

How the Sunbelt Became Loserville, U.S.A.

....

ATLANTA'S EXPERIENCE AS A MAJOR LEAGUE CITY WAS far from anomalous. As Ted Turner initiated his efforts to rejuvenate Atlanta's stagnant sports scene, the municipal and corporate leaders in a number of other Sunbelt cities were embarking on quests to become Major League, just as Atlanta had a decade earlier. Civic elites in rapidly growing cities such as Phoenix, San Diego, and Tampa believed, like their predecessors in Atlanta, that by making municipal investments in professional sports they would provide their communities with a wellspring of unity and prestige. Residents of these metropolitan areas responded to their new stadiums and teams in the 1980s and 1990s much like Atlantans did to theirs during the 1960s and 1970s. Few of the franchises established in Sunbelt cities during the last quarter of the century became objects of civic devotion. In most instances, they drew collective shrugs that calcified quickly into permanent postures, except when these teams were competing for a league championship.

The failures of Tampa, San Diego, and Phoenix to become hotbeds of support for their new professional sports franchises stem from many of the same reasons that the teams in Metropolitan Atlanta failed to ignite durable local passions. In each instance, civic boosters engaged in an unsuccessful, top-down effort to construct a sense of community through professional sports. Much like Atlanta, population growth in these emerging metropolises skewed heavily toward the suburbs, which circumscribed the appeal of live events held primarily in the center city. Moreover, much of the population growth in Sunbelt cities came as a result of the migration of people from other parts of the country. Newcomers who were inclined to follow spectator sports brought with them loyalties to far-away professional franchises that did not translate into consistent support for the teams representing their new cities.

At the same time, locals in each of these regions had developed distinct spectator and participatory sporting cultures in the absence of the big leagues. The pre–Major League sporting culture in each of these Sunbelt cities remained popular long after the arrival of the big leagues. Furthermore, many of the activities that appealed to locals, particularly outdoor activities that took advantage of the Sunbelt's balmy weather, proved popular among newcomers as well, pulling even more potential discretionary dollars away from the new professional sports franchises. Even the residents of newly Major League cities that were inclined to support their new franchises were frequently frustrated by their team's poor performance. In most instances, the owners of new Sunbelt teams were well heeled but inexperienced at managing professional franchises. Their managerial ineptitude ensured that most new Sunbelt sports franchises developed reputations for on-the-field futility that exaggerated the social and cultural factors already limiting their local appeal.

THE MAKING OF MAJOR LEAGUE SAN DIEGO HAS TWO corresponding creation stories: one that involves its civic elites and one that involves a single-minded but cash-poor sports enthusiast. Neither quest to make San Diego a city with a vibrant professional sporting scene succeeded. In the early 1960s, San Diego, like Atlanta, seemed readymade for professional sports expansion. Buoyed by a booming aerospace industry and the steady presence of the U.S. Navy, San Diego County's 1.1 million residents enjoyed a high per capita income, and the purchasing power of their dollars was among the best in the nation. Despite the significant amount of discretionary income available in the region, professional sports proved no match for San Diego's robust leisure culture, which was built around its gorgeous weather and seventy miles of beaches. Boating, surfing, and golf were yearlong pastimes for San Diego's middle- and upper-income residents. For those inclined toward spectator sports, the region's athletics calendar included professional golf tournaments, Minor League Baseball, and San Diego State football, which ranked among the nation's top small college programs. Nevertheless, a number of municipal elites wanted San Diego to possess leisure amenities like those available in Los Angeles and San Francisco. Civic boosters' efforts to make San Diego Major League followed closely on the heels of Atlanta's and met with similar results.

Much like in Atlanta, a prominent sportswriter helped kickstart San Diego's push for professional sports. *San Diego Union* Sports Editor Jack Murphy played a decisive role in organizing the civic elite's efforts to make theirs a Major League City. In 1961 he persuaded hotelier Barron Hilton to move his AFL Chargers south after one season in Los Angeles, which had been an NFL stronghold since the 1940s. Initially, the San Diego Chargers played in Balboa Stadium, a World War I–era municipal park that they shared with San Diego State. Murphy convinced the dormant San Diego County Stadium Authority to seek public financing for a multipurpose facility capable of hosting not only professional football but also MLB, which city leaders had already started pursuing. The Stadium Authority put a $27.75 million bond initiative before county taxpayers in November 1965. Stadium boosters, which included virtually all of the city's business, corporate, and media establishment, mounted a well-financed campaign on behalf of the plan, which passed with 72 percent of the vote. In August 1967, San Diego Stadium, soon to be renamed Jack Murphy Stadium, debuted as the home of the NFL Chargers.[1]

The Chargers proved to be a well-run but only occasionally well-loved organization. They have had three owners: Barron Hilton (1961–66), insurance executive Gene Klein

(1966–84), and construction magnate Alex Spanos and family (1984–present). The team enjoyed several periods of great success, including the 1960s, early 1980s, mid 1990s, and mid-2000s, which brought about upswings in local support. In general, though, San Diegans proved fickle in their affections for the Chargers, leading to several stretches in the 1970s and late 1980s when many home games were blacked out on local television because they failed to sell out in advance. Alex Spanos blamed aging Jack Murphy Stadium for his team's lack of support. He threatened to move the team on several occasions beginning in the late 1980s. The generation of San Diegans succeeding the ones that made their city Major League refused to make a similar investment in a modern football stadium. In November 2016, San Diego County voters turned down a ballot initiative that would have financed a new Chargers stadium, setting in motion the relocation of the franchise to Los Angeles for the 2017 season.[2]

San Diego's path to MLB proved swift, but local support for the team has been tenuous from the start. With a modern stadium in place, San Diego was in an excellent position to secure an MLB team. Banker Arnholt Smith, the owner of San Diego's Minor League baseball club, paid a $10.2 million expansion fee for an NL franchise, which began play in 1969. Smith's San Diego Padres proved to be an unmitigated disaster. From the outset, the Padres played as poorly as they drew. The notoriously stingy Smith maintained one of the league's smallest payrolls as well as its worst record, finishing in last place in each of the five seasons that he owned the club (1969–73). During that same stretch, the Padres finished last in attendance each season, never drawing more than 644,273 fans annually to Jack Murphy Stadium.[3] By 1972 Smith was weighing offers for the club from investors in a half dozen North American cities. At the time, Smith's United States National Bank was under investigation by the Securities and Exchange Commission and Internal Revenue Service for embezzlement and tax evasion. In 1979 Smith was convicted and sentenced to three years in prison for tax fraud, six years after United States National Bank became the largest bank failure in American history.[4]

The Padres nearly moved to Washington DC in 1974 after Smith agreed to a $12 million deal with mid-Atlantic grocer Joseph Danzansky. A last-minute matching offer by McDonalds' executive Ray Kroc kept the Padres in San Diego. Kroc's family strove to turn around the franchise's fortunes on the field and at the box office for the next sixteen years, with some success. Under Kroc's ownership, the Padres fielded an often-respectable team, even winning an NL Pennant in 1984. The Padres' attendance improved briefly, ascending to the middle of the pack in the NL before cycling back toward the bottom even when the team played well.

In 1990 the Kroc family sold the Padres to a group of fourteen investors headed by television executive and future Boston Red Sox owner Tom Werner. The stability created in the organization by the Kroc family eroded soon thereafter. The product on the field deteriorated as did fan support, leading majority owner Werner and his partners to make drastic cost-cutting measures. In 1992 and 1993 the Padres engaged in a notorious fire sale of their roster, trading off virtually all of their marquee players. Season-ticket holders filed a class-action lawsuit against the team, claiming that the Padres had deceived them in an off-season letter asserting that the team was going to make every effort to keep its remaining high-caliber players. The parties settled out of court, resulting in a partial refund for season-ticket holders. In 1994 Werner sold his majority stake in the Padres, capping off the frustrating first quarter century of MLB in San Diego.[5]

A sports enthusiast and laundromat owner named Bob Breitbard engaged in his own quixotic effort to make San Diego Major League. Working outside the civic elite, Breitbard brought professional basketball and hockey to San Diego, neither of which gained a foothold in the city. In 1965 Breitbard paid $25,000 for a franchise in the Western Hockey League.

Unable to convince municipal leaders to build him a hockey rink, Breitbard erected the $6 million, fourteen-thousand-seat San Diego Sports Arena with bonds backed privately by the Union Oil Company. The Minor League San Diego Gulls hockey team began play at the new building in 1966, making the Gulls the first professional hockey team in Southern California. In 1967 Breitbard borrowed an additional $1.75 million to purchase an NBA expansion franchise to join the Gulls at the new arena. Just like the Gulls, the San Diego Rockets basketball team proved short-lived in the city. The shockingly overextended Breitbard could not convince enough San Diegans to patronize games at the Sports Arena to make either club financially viable. In 1971 Breitbard sought tax relief from the city, which had not only built the Padres and Chargers a stadium but was providing them with money to spend on advertising. When the city refused to subsidize Breitbard's teams, he sold the Rockets for $5.6 million to a group of investors who moved the team to Houston. The Gulls simply went out of business.[6]

Subsequent investors have tried unsuccessfully to make a go of it with both professional hockey and basketball in San Diego. A Canadian entrepreneur named Peter Graham brought ABA and WHA franchises to the city briefly during the mid-1970s. The NBA returned to San Diego in the late 1970s in the form of the Clippers, which had relocated from Buffalo in 1978. The Clippers lasted six unsuccessful and unprofitable seasons at the San Diego Sports Arena before moving to Los Angeles in 1984. Neither the NBA nor the NHL has since placed a franchise in San Diego. With the loss of the NFL Chargers in 2017, San Diego stands as the largest market in the United States with just one major professional sports franchise.[7]

THE TAMPA BAY REGION, WITH ITS MASSIVE POPULATION of northern transplants, agreeable climate, and ambitious civic leadership, has succeeded in luring the NFL, MLB, and NHL to the cities of Tampa and St. Petersburg. Yet none of Tampa

Bay's franchises have won over a sizeable or resilient enough audience to be characterized as a treasured local institution.

Investors in the Tampa Bay region began actively pursuing an NFL franchise in 1970, when a group of Hillsborough County business leaders met with New England Patriots owner Billy Sullivan to discuss purchasing his struggling franchise. In 1972 a similar group met with NFL commissioner Pete Rozelle to campaign for an expansion franchise in Tampa. That same year, Baltimore Colts owner Carroll Rosenbloom played three of his team's exhibition games at Tampa Stadium, a no-frills, forty-six-thousand-seat facility that the city had built in the mid-1960s as a home for the University of Tampa's football team. Rosenbloom sought unsuccessfully to win league approval to relocate the Colts to Hillsborough County. Tampa's aggressive pursuit of professional football paid off soon thereafter, when the NFL decided to place a new franchise in the rapidly growing metropolitan area for the 1976 season, precluding the expansion of the short-lived but well-financed World Football League (WFL) into the region. Tax attorney Hugh Culverhouse, one of the region's early pro football boosters, paid a $16 million expansion fee for the franchise that became the Tampa Bay Buccaneers. In preparation for the Buccaneers, the City of Tampa spent $13 million renovating its municipal stadium, more than three times the original cost of the facility, expanding its capacity by more than twenty-seven thousand seats.[8]

Culverhouse, who represented the likes of Richard Nixon and Bebe Robozo in his law practice, made an extensive survey of the NFL's recent expansion into Atlanta, hoping to avoid the pitfalls of the Buccaneers' poorly performing and drawing predecessor in the Southeast. Rather than relying on friends and family to run the team, Culverhouse worked closely with NFL commissioner Rozelle to find suitable candidates to fill his front office. He interviewed dozens of coaches, players, and general managers to gain an understanding of the league's inner workings. He hired an up-and-coming league insider named Ron Wolf to run the team's personnel department and the University of Southern California's legendary John McKay to coach the team.

Additionally, Culverhouse built the Buccaneers an office complex and training center to ensure that they did not have to struggle for space and practice time at a shared, publicly owned facility like the Falcons had at Atlanta Stadium. Culverhouse's assumption that the Falcons' problems were primarily managerial rather than a product of both the team's leadership and the particulars of the Atlanta marketplace proved incorrect. In spite of his best efforts, the Buccaneers proved to be one of the NFL's worst drawing and worst performing teams during the last quarter of the twentieth century. Mirroring the situation in Georgia, college football proved to be a greater beneficiary of Florida's population explosion than the professional game. While Floridians flocked northward on fall Saturdays to watch the emerging national powers at the University of Florida in Gainesville and Florida State University in Tallahassee, Tampa Stadium remained largely vacant on Sundays, leading to local television blackouts of dozens of Buccaneers home games during the 1980s and 1990s.[9]

In 1989 Culverhouse met with government officials from Sacramento, Baltimore, and St. Louis to discuss moving his team to their cities. In addition, the Buccaneers owner spoke with officials in Orlando about hosting three of his team's eight annual home games in Orlando's municipally owned stadium, the Citrus Bowl. Health problems prevented Culverhouse from proceeding with any relocation plans. In 1992 he turned control of the team over to a group of trustees as he sought cancer treatment. When Culverhouse died in 1994, his estate put the franchise up for sale and talk of the Buccaneers' relocation commenced immediately. Eventual buyer Malcolm Glazer, a shopping-mall baron who resided seasonally in Tampa, seemed an unlikely candidate to move the team, but he held out the possibility of relocating the Buccaneers if local taxpayers refused to approve funding for a new football stadium. In 1996 Tampa voters narrowly approved a half-cent, thirty-year "community investment tax," a Trojan horse sales tax that paid for the $168.5 million in bonds required for stadium construction as well as a range of other municipal projects totaling up to $2.7 billion. Polling in the weeks leading up to the vote indicated that Tampa voters would have turned down the ballot initiative if it had been focused exclusively on the football stadium.[10]

Tampa Bay's aspirations for MLB have proven similarly expensive and no more successful upon its eventual arrival. In an effort to lure an MLB team, the city of St. Petersburg built the $130 million Florida Suncoast Dome, which opened in 1990 without a tenant. Civic leaders in the Tampa Bay region came close to convincing both the San Francisco Giants and Chicago White Sox to take up residency at the dome, but a largely privately financed stadium deal in San Francisco and a largely publicly financed one in Chicago convinced the owners of both MLB clubs to stay in their home markets. Eight years after its opening, the Florida Suncoast Dome (by then, Tropicana Field) became home to an MLB club, the expansion Tampa Bay Devil Rays. The Tampa Bay MLB club has long proven to be a box-office loser, drawing some of the league's most meagre crowds and television deals even when the team performs well. The Rays' transplant-filled market ensures that when clubs from New York, Boston, or Chicago come to town, fans of the visiting team almost always outnumber those cheering for the hometown Rays. Rumors of the Rays leaving town have existed for nearly as long as the franchise.[11]

The NHL, too, has tried to crack the Tampa Bay market but with limited success. The league renewed its ambitions to expand across the Sunbelt in 1990 when it voted to award a franchise to Tampa-St. Petersburg. Expanding into Florida proved an immediate boondoggle. The NHL nearly pulled Tampa's bid when the new franchisees fell four months behind on the first of two $22.5 million expansion-fee payments. Absentee majority owner Takashi Okubo, a Japanese resort baron who never saw the team play in person, promised the league that his franchise would sell ten thousand advanced season tickets and put together a public and private deal to build a hockey arena in the region. In fact, the Tampa Bay Lightning, as the team was named, sold barely 3,500 season tickets for its first campaign, which the team played at the Florida State Fairgrounds Exposition Hall, a converted livestock exhibition barn. The team spent the next three seasons (1993–96) at the Suncoast Dome, which had yet to acquire an MLB team. Okubo refused to invest in a scouting department for the Lightning, making it the only team in major professional sports without one. Not surprisingly, the team performed terribly, missing the playoffs in nine of its first ten seasons.[12]

The Tampa Stadium Authority, in the meantime, had floated $86 million in municipal bonds to help pay for a hockey arena. The omnibus sales tax that funded the Buccaneers' new stadium also provided the public financing for the downtown hockey arena, the Ice Palace. In spite of Okubo's frugality and the public support it received for its arena, the Lightning managed to lose $102 million between 1992 and 1999, making it professional sports's most indebted franchise. The Lightning had only a modest television deal and were one of the few teams in the league that regularly drew fewer than ten thousand spectators during the 1990s. Okubo sold the team in 1998 to a South Florida businessman named Art Williams for $130 million. Williams, who tried to introduce Floridians to live hockey by simply giving away one hundred thousand tickets, proved to be the first of a succession of new owners or ownership groups that have possessed the Lightning since the late 1990s. Despite frequent ownership changes, the Lightning has stabilized into a common market position for Sunbelt NHL teams. The club's continued existence is supported by a rabid, affluent season-ticket-holding base that numbers about ten thousand. Much like in Atlanta in the 1970s, few locals outside its zealous base pay much attention to the team.[13]

WELL AHEAD OF PHOENIX'S CONCERTED CIVIC EFFORTS in the 1980s and 1990s to become Major League, the city secured a professional basketball team. In 1968 a dozen-headed local investment group paid $2 million for an NBA franchise. Many league observers questioned the move, regarding Metropolitan Phoenix, which had just cracked the one-million-resident plateau, as too small, remote, and insufficiently urban to support major professional sports. These observers were soon proven wrong, as Maricopa County became an NBA hotbed. Unlike many Sunbelt expansion teams, the Suns proved to be a well-run organization. In 1968 the franchise hired twenty-nine-year-old Chicago Bulls junior executive Jerry Colangelo as GM. Colangelo spent the next thirty-five years in the position, transforming the Suns into a fixture in the Western Conference playoffs and the Suns' perpetually filled arena, the Arizona Veterans Memorial Coliseum, into one of the loudest buildings in professional sports. Colangelo ended up leading an investment group that purchased the team in 1987, ensuring its stability into the next century. Beyond their exemplary leadership, the Suns benefitted greatly from a lack of local competition. Whereas the Atlanta and San Diego markets crowded rapidly, the Suns had two decades to establish themselves in the local marketplace before they faced competition from other big league teams in the 1980s and 1990s. The Suns' strong management and ability to build a robust fanbase over many years in a one-professional-sport market account in large part for the success of professional basketball in Phoenix relative to Atlanta and San Diego.[14]

Nevertheless, the steady success of the Suns franchise has proven anomalous in the Metropolitan Phoenix professional sports market. For the most part, the "Valley of the Sun" has struggled as an MLB, NHL, and NFL market in the decades since their arrival in the 1980s and 1990s. Like many other Sunbelt cities, Phoenix's disappointing career as a pro sports town followed decades of determined effort by civic boosters to make their city Major League. Public officials and private boosters in Maricopa County started cooperating in the early 1970s to bring professional football to the Valley. Phoenix made a serious bid for a 1976 NFL expansion team, but league insiders regarded Arizona State's then fifty-thousand-seat Sun Devil Stadium, the prospective home of a Phoenix-area team, as less NFL ready than either Seattle's new taxpayer-financed Kingdome or Tampa's recently expanded municipal stadium. The apparent inadequacy of Sun Devil Stadium nudged forward a proposed twenty-thousand-seat expansion, which was already in the works to accommodate emerging football power Arizona State's growing fanbase. Arizona State's newly attractive stadium brought a series of professional football suitors to the region during the 1980s. Between 1983 and 1985, Sun Devil Stadium served as the home field of Phoenix's first professional football team, the Arizona Wranglers of the short-lived United States Football League (USFL). With no forthcoming plans for NFL expansion, civic boosters in the valley courted several franchises that were then considering relocating. In January 1984 Phoenix businessman Anthony Nicoli came to an agreement with Baltimore Colts owner Robert Irsay to buy the team for $50 million, but a public-relations backlash caused Irsay to back out of the deal. Two months later, Irsay moved his team to Indianapolis instead, sneaking out of Maryland in the middle of the night with a fleet of out-of-state Mayflower moving vans. In 1985 Phoenix went through another very public franchise-relocation drama, as Philadelphia Eagles owner Leonard Tose failed to win league approval to move his team to Arizona.[15]

The NFL finally came to Maricopa County in 1988 when St. Louis Cardinals owner Bill Bidwill convinced his fellow executives to support his bid to relocate to Sun Devil Stadium, three years after he first announced his attentions to move his franchise to Arizona. Bidwill, who had long clashed with St. Louis officials over his shared municipal stadium, soon became disenchanted with Sun Devil Stadium, which he shared with Arizona State. The Cardinals drew poorly from the start, leading to local television blackouts of their almost never sold out games. Arizonans, who were used to low-cost amenities and entertainments, balked at paying an average of $45 per ticket, nearly one-third higher than the league's average, during the Cardinals' first season in the desert. Locals accustomed to attending Arizona State's night games at Sun Devil Stadium were hesitant to attend the day games that the NFL required for the majority of the Cardinals' home schedule. Those inclined to spend an afternoon at Sun Devil Stadium frequently left early to avoid the scorching sun that enveloped the field's largely exposed seating. When the Cardinals did draw well, it was often the result of visiting fans. Large numbers of transplants who lived in the area showed up to Cardinals games to cheer on their hometown teams from Chicago, New York, and Philadelphia. Additionally, inexpensive flights from Dallas, Denver, and San Francisco ensured that the crowds at Sun Devil Stadium were often the domain of the visiting team.[16]

Bidwill threatened to move the Cardinals out of Arizona on several occasions. He finally earned public support for a new, football-only stadium in November 2000 in a referendum put forth by the newly created, state-run Arizona Sports and Tourism Authority. Fifty-two percent of Maricopa County voters approved a rental-car tax to support construction of a $455 million domed stadium in Glendale, a bedroom community in Phoenix's West Valley. A $154.5 million portion of the price tag was paid for by the for-profit University of Phoenix, which purchased the naming rights for the building that opened in 2006.[17]

Jerry Colangelo proved to be the driving force behind the arrival of both MLB and the NHL in Arizona, bringing organizational experience and stability to both franchises, baseball's Arizona Diamondbacks and hockey's Phoenix Coyotes. Colangelo, who had long cultivated a reputation as an above-the-fray force for continuity within Arizona's often-transient business community, took on a trusteeship over both projects,

ensuring the support of Maricopa County's municipal leadership for both ventures. Despite the prominent role that Colangelo and his associates played in bringing both franchises
to the region, neither team has proven a durable local draw.

Colangelo was far from the first person to bring high-level
baseball to Arizona. Baseball had long been a popular spectator
sport in the region. Since 1947, a number of MLB teams have
held their spring-training exercises in Arizona, forming the
preseason Cactus League in 1952. At the time that Colangelo's
group started seeking an MLB franchise, the Cactus League
hosted fourteen of MLB's twenty-eight teams each February
and March. Arizona State has been a national college baseball
power since the mid-1960s, appearing in twenty-two College
World Series and winning five national championships. Considering its baseball pedigree, Phoenix seemed like a surefire
site for the MLB expansions being proposed in the late 1980s,
just as the metropolitan area's population reached two million.[18]

Martin Stone, the owner of the San Francisco Giants' Minor
League affiliate in Phoenix, began a public pursuit of an MLB
franchise in 1987, seeking out municipal financing for a downtown stadium to lure a team to Arizona. Initially, Stone tried to
make a deal with Phoenix Cardinals owner Bill Bidwill to join
forces in pursuit of a multipurpose dome, but Bidwill chose
instead to sign a lease at Sun Devil Stadium. Phoenix Mayor
Terry Goddard continued to support Stone's domed-stadium
plan and helped bring a bond initiative on its behalf before city
voters in October 1989. More than 60 percent of Phoenicians
voted against the plan, which would have used a property-tax
increase, a highly unpopular funding mechanism in any situation, to finance a $100 million dome for a team that did not
yet exist. The vote prevented Phoenix from making a serious
bid for the round of MLB expansion that granted Denver and
Miami franchises for the 1993 season. In 1990 the Arizona
State Legislature made any future attempt to finance a stadium significantly easier by granting the five-member Maricopa County Board of Supervisors the right to raise sales

taxes 0.25 percent without a referendum if any municipality in the county acquired an MLB team. At the time, this statute received little attention, but in a few years it became wildly controversial.[19]

When word spread that MLB planned another round of expansion for the late 1990s, a group of baseball boosters, including Phoenix sports attorney Joe Garagiola Jr. and Maricopa County Supervisor Jim Bruner, coalesced around Colangelo. In 1993 the Suns owner proceeded to create Arizona Baseball Inc., an organization created to submit an expansion proposal to MLB and raise $125 million for the anticipated expansion-franchise fee. As president of Arizona Baseball Inc., Colangelo took on the responsibility of negotiating any future stadium deals with local municipalities. Arizona Baseball Inc.'s proposal was received enthusiastically by MLB in 1995. The organization's bid was buoyed by strong endorsements from the well-connected Colangelo's close friends: league commissioner Bud Selig and Chicago White Sox owner Jerry Reinsdorf. In March 1995 MLB awarded Arizona Baseball Inc. an expansion franchise, which would be named the Arizona Diamondbacks and would begin play in 1998.[20]

The greatest drama related to Arizona Baseball Inc.'s efforts to lure MLB came in early 1994 when the contentious debate surrounding the stadium sales tax reached the Maricopa County Board of Supervisors. Approval of the 0.25 percent sales tax to raise $238 million for stadium construction required only a simple majority of the five-member board, leading to a contentious debate over the measure, which won a 3–1 majority with one recusal. In 1995 Maricopa County broke ground on a domed baseball stadium that came to be known as Bank One Ballpark. Bank One paid $140 million for the naming rights to the Diamondbacks' stadium, following a pattern Colangelo helped initiate in 1989 by orchestrating the sale of the Suns' arena's naming rights to America West Airlines. Support for the measure had severe consequences for all three yes voters. Sales-tax supporter Ed King lost his reelection bid to an anti-

tax candidate, while an affirmative vote derailed a nascent congressional bid by Jim Bruner, who had in fact driven a hard
bargain with Colangelo on the terms of stadium financing.
Sales-tax supporter Mary Rose Wilcox suffered, by far, the
most serious consequences. More than three years after the
vote, a mentally ill man who opposed the tax shot and wounded
Wilcox in the back as she left an August 1997 Board of Supervisors meeting. The assailant, Larry Naman, had been preoccupied with the stadium tax issue for years, an obsession
stoked by several venomous local talk-radio programs that
had lambasted all three yes-voting supervisors since the day
they supported the measure.[21]

With a franchise and a stadium deal in place, the Colangelo
organization proceeded to build a top-notch player-personnel
and marketing organization for the Diamondbacks. As a result,
the franchise enjoyed a great deal of success in their early
seasons, finishing in the top half in NL attendance in each
of their first five campaigns (1998–2002), which also corresponded with its greatest period of success. The franchise
secured a great deal of early fan interest by cultivating a family-
friendly stadium environment, keeping ticket prices below the
league average and allowing fans to pack lunches to bring to
the ballpark. Just as important, the team invested heavily in
free agents, building a highly competitive team that culminated in a 2001 World Series championship. The Diamondbacks' win-now approach faltered soon after 2001. As the more
expensive back ends of free-agent contracts approached, the
team traded away many of its best players, claiming that it
was unable to afford the payments because of its small television contract and affordable ticket prices relative to major-
market teams. In the years since their lone championship,
the Diamondbacks have yet to reach the heights of their early
years but have often fielded a competitive team, earning four
additional postseason appearances. Despite this success, the
Diamondbacks have not retained their strong local support in
a market that shares many similarities to Atlanta, including

its high percentage of transplants, warm climate, and highly decentralized population. Both the Atlanta and Arizona franchises have long promoted their family-friendly stadium environments, but, in both cases, this seems to have done little to ensure steady attendance figures. Since 2004 the Diamondbacks have failed to finish in the top half in NL attendance and maintain one of MLB's smallest local television deals despite Phoenix's status as the nation's eleventh largest metropolitan area.[22]

Jerry Colangelo also played a prominent role in bringing the NHL to Arizona but soon receded to the background of the franchise, which has teetered on the brink of bankruptcy since its arrival in the valley. Whether it was a product of his hubris or his widely publicized sense of noblesse oblige for his adopted hometown, Colangelo regarded himself as the connective tissue between Metropolitan Phoenix—whose full potential as a professional sports marketplace, he believed, remained unexploited—and the corridors of power in the Major Leagues. In December 1995 the Suns owner took the lead in a group of local investors who purchased the NHL's Winnipeg Jets, sparking an outcry among hockey fans across North America who decried the movement of professional hockey away from its traditional Canadian hotbeds in favor of potentially lucrative but hockey-illiterate markets. Conversely, many NHL officials, including Commissioner Gary Bettman, were enthusiastic supporters of the move, which they believed would help the league further establish itself in the Sunbelt. The Phoenix Coyotes, as the franchise was rechristened, took up residency initially in America West Arena, the home of the Phoenix Suns, before moving in 2003 to the $220 million Glendale Arena, which was financed by the residents of the West Valley city. The Coyotes failed to turn a profit in each of their first ten seasons, leading Colangelo's group to sell the team in 2006 to Phoenix-area trucking magnate Jerry Moyes. After three years of financial losses, Moyes tried to sell the team to Blackberry executive Jim Balsillie, who intended to move the

Coyotes to his hometown of Hamilton, Ontario. NHL owners voted 26–0 against the move, fearing that a departure from Phoenix would once again signal the league's retreat from its aspirations for continent-wide appeal. Instead, the NHL itself purchased the team from Moyes, who had declared bankruptcy. For four seasons, the NHL ran the Coyotes franchise before finally selling the team to a consortium of Phoenix-area business leaders, called IceArizona, in 2013.[23]

The experiences of San Diego, Tampa, and Phoenix as they pursued professional sports franchises in the late twentieth century differed in substantial ways from Atlanta's quest for Major League status in the 1960s and 1970s. Although San Diego, Tampa, and Phoenix all, to a greater or lesser extent, tied their push for big league teams to broader efforts at downtown redevelopment, none of these Sunbelt cities connected its urban-renewal plans as explicitly or thoroughly to stadium construction as the civic leadership in Atlanta. The racial politics of Metropolitan Atlanta also differed significantly from those found in the aforementioned Sunbelt cities. The emergence of a Black political leadership class in Atlanta that won municipal power away from the city's hegemonic white leadership, the Big Mules who pushed for significant public investments to make Atlanta Major League, has no parallel in Phoenix, Tampa, or San Diego, where the city's traditional white business classes remain ensconced in city hall.

Despite these differences, the Sunbelt cities that have joined Atlanta in major professional sports share a common set of market dynamics and a common set of outcomes in their respective quests to become big league. In each instance, the corporate and political classes in a Sunbelt boomtown made a top-down push to acquire major professional sports teams. A combination of desires among civic elites, namely a yearning for big-city amenities, novel attractions in the center city, and a wellspring of regional unity, led them to push for substantial municipal investments in the form of stadiums for professional sports teams just as the national marketplace for such franchises became increasingly flexible. In each instance, the cluster of professional sports franchises that settled in a Sunbelt city failed to live up to the local elite's expectations. The tendency of cities to acquire several teams in succession left markets oversaturated long before any one of the teams developed a steady fan base. Often, the owners of Sunbelt franchises were new to the sports business and mismanaged their franchises into the bottom rungs of their respective leagues. Most significantly, professional sports franchises in Sunbelt cities often failed to connect with the constituent populations in these new metropolises. Many locals held firm to the recreational and spectator pastimes they enjoyed in the absence of the Major Leagues. Most newcomers did not become stalwart supporters of the new, unfamiliar teams and, sometimes, unfamiliar sports being marketed to them in the local media. Sunbelt newcomers proved more likely to take up the warm weather recreational pursuits of their new neighbors than to become diehards of the new local professional sports franchises, a passion that proved more contingent on a set of experiences common to the urban North than many Sunbelt investors had anticipated. The durable support that many franchises in the urban North enjoyed amid franchise free agency proved to be as much a product of tradition and familiarity as it did success on the field.

Notes

. . . .

Introduction

1. Lewis Grizzard, "Loserville, U.S.A.," *Atlanta Constitution*, July 11, 1975, 1A, 14A; Lewis Grizzard, "Loserville, U.S.A.: The Sahara of Pro Sports," *Atlanta Constitution*, July 12, 1975, 1A, 16A.

2. Grizzard, "Loserville, U.S.A.," 1A, 16A.

3. Jim Minter, in phone discussion with the author, July 9, 2013.

4. William Leggett, "Decline of a Brave New World," *Sports Illustrated*, May 5, 1975; Fields, *Take Me Out to the Crowd*, 22.

5. Schaffer and Davidson, *Economic Impact of Falcons, 1984*, 8.

6. Anthony Monahan, "A Disappointing Success," *Chicago Tribune*, August 21, 1966, 133.

7. Rob Parker, "The City of Atlanta Doesn't Deserve to Win," ESPN.com, January 6, 2012.

8. Allen and Hemphill, *Mayor*, 152–64; Jim Minter, "The Mayor Surrenders Atlanta," *Sports Illustrated*, July 12, 1965, 14–17.

9. Vrooman, "Franchise Free Agency," 191–219; Leone, "No Team, No Peace," 473–523.

10. Rosentraub, "Are Public Policies Needed?," 377; Shropshire, *Sports Franchise Game*, 13–19.

11. See Sugrue, *Origins of the Urban Crisis*; Self, *American Babylon*; Schulman, *From Cotton Belt to Sunbelt*; Wiley and Gottlieb, *Empires in the Sun*; Rosentraub, "Are Public Policies Needed?," 377–78.

12. Josza, *Big Sports, Big Business*, 53–54.

13. Vrooman, "Franchise Free Agency," 191–219; Leone, "No Team, No Peace," 473–523.

14. Danielson, *Home Team*, 140–43, 225; Josza, *Big Sports, Big Business*, 106–7.

15. Schulman, *The Seventies*, xii.

16. Lassiter, *Silent Majority*, 276.

17. J. E. Miller, *Baseball Business*, 297.

18. Kruse, *White Flight*, 13; Danielson, *Home Team*, 65.

19. Danielson, *Home Team*, 7, 254–65.

20. "A Spectacular Weekend," *Atlanta Journal*, April 9, 1965, 18.

1. Forward Atlanta

1. "Our Big Decision: Allen or Maddox?" *Atlanta Sunday Journal-Constitution*, September 17, 1961, 6B; "Atlanta's Call to Greatness," *Atlanta Constitution*, Sep-

tember 6, 1961, 4; "Allen, Maddox Grimly Attack," *Atlanta Journal*, September 21, 1961, 1, 13; WSB-TV, "C. A. Alexander Endorsement of Ivan Allen," August 19, 1961, AFP, box 1, folder 8, Kenan Library.

2. Gene Patterson, "A Letter to the New Mayor," *Atlanta Constitution*, September 23, 1961, 1. The letter is also found in Patterson, "1961: The Rock and the Anchor," 81–82.

3. "Allen, Maddox Rip into Each Other," *Atlanta Journal*, September 19, 1961, 1; Maddox, *Speaking Out*, 42–44.

4. Kruse, *White Flight*, 26–27.

5. Walker, "Protest and Negotiation," 111; Stone, *Regime Politics*, 27–28.

6. Bayor, *Race and Shaping of Twentieth-Century Atlanta*, 26; Stone, *Regime Politics*, 27–28; Kruse, *White Flight*, 35.

7. Bayor, *Race and Shaping of Twentieth-Century Atlanta*, 31–32; Stone, *Regime Politics*, 36–37; Kruse, *White Flight*, 78–79; Bayor, "Civil Rights Movement," 289–92.

8. Weise, *Places of Their Own*, 188.

9. Nagin, *Courage to Dissent*, 2–7, 17–58; Pomerantz, *Where Peachtree Meets Sweet Auburn*, 14–20, 123–27, 146–48, 180–86.

10. Weise, *Places of Their Own*, 30; Emmett John Hughes, "The Negro's New Economic Life," *Fortune*, September 1956, 248.

11. Hughes, "Negro's New Economic Life," 248.

12. Martha Ezzard, "The Way We Are," *Atlanta Journal*, July 29, 1996, 6A; John Huey, "The Atlanta Game," *Fortune*, July 22, 1996, 42–57.

13. H. Martin, *William Berry Hartsfield*, 47–52.

14. Pomerantz, *Where Peachtree Meets Sweet Auburn*, 13; Kuhn, Joye, and West, *Living Atlanta*, 90–93.

15. H. Martin, *William Berry Hartsfield*, 39–41, 138–39; "Atlanta Awaits Millionth Citizen," *New York Times*, September 27, 1959, 58; Claude Sitton, "Atlanta: Southern Air Hub," *New York Times*, February 1, 1959, x31; "Half Million at Work in Metro Atlanta," *Atlanta Constitution*, August 28, 1964, 54; US Census Bureau, "Cities: Table C"; Walter McQuade, "Atlanta: The Hopeful City," *Fortune*, August 1966, 156; Whitlegg, "A Battle on Two Fronts," 128–38.

16. Stone, *Regime Politics*, 55–56; Allen and Hemphill, *Mayor*, 30–33; Seymour Freedgood, "Life in Buckhead," *Fortune*, September 1961, 8–12; Claude Sitton, "Personality: Banker Has Good Luck Charm," *New York Times*, March 19, 1961, F3; Lassiter, *Silent Majority*, 100–104.

17. *Measure the Job—Measure the Man*, Allen campaign pamphlet, 1961, AFP, box 1, folder 8, Kenan Library; Bayor, *Race and Shaping of Twentieth-Century Atlanta*, 35–38; Stone, *Regime Politics*, 52–55; Allen and Hemphill, *Mayor*, 35–39; Pomerantz, *Where Peachtree Meets Sweet Auburn*, 268.

18. "Ivan Allen for Mayor Schedule, Week of August 28, 1961," 1961, AFP, box 1, folder 8, Kenan Library; "Our Big Decision: Allen or Maddox," *Atlanta Sunday Journal-Constitution*, September 17, 1961, 6B; Bayor, *Race and Shaping of Twentieth-Century Atlanta*, 35–38; Allen and Hemphill, *Mayor*, 52–63; Pomerantz, *Where Peachtree Meets Sweet Auburn*, 292–96; Allen for Mayor confidential memorandum no. 6, 1961, AFP, box 1, folder 8, Kenan Library; *Measure the Job— Measure the Man*, Kenan Library.

19. Pomerantz, *Where Peachtree Meets Sweet Auburn*, 299.

20. Raleigh Bryans, "Allen Pledges 'Forward City,'" *Atlanta Journal*, September 23, 1961, 1, 3; "Our Big Decision: Allen or Maddox," 6B; Short, *Everything Is Pickrick*, 42–48; Maddox, *Speaking Out*, 41–44; Rice, "Urbanization, 'Atlanta-ization,' and Suburbanization," 45–46.

21. "Lester Maddox Says: It's Your Decision!": advertisement, *Atlanta Journal*, September 19, 1961, 8B.

22. Pomerantz, *Where Peachtree Meets Sweet Auburn*, 287–88; Kazin, *Populist Persuasion*, 1–8, 9–24.

23. Short, *Everything Is Pickrick*, 34–36; Maddox, *Speaking Out*, 31–35.

24. Pomerantz, *Where Peachtree Meets Sweet Auburn*, 299.

25. H. Martin, *William Berry Hartsfield*, 129; Kruse, *White Flight*, 198; Short, *Everything Is Pickrick*, 36–41; Maddox, *Speaking Out*, 41–42.

26. "Atlanta Voted for Peace and Progress," *Atlanta Journal*, September 23, 1961, 2.

27. Bryans, "Allen Pledges 'Forward City,'" 1.

28. "Atlanta Voted for Peace and Progress," 2.

29. "Results of the Mayor's Race," *Atlanta Journal*, September 23, 1961, 3; Bayor, *Race and Shaping of Twentieth-Century Atlanta*, 36–38; Allen and Hemphill, *Mayor*, 58–63; Pomerantz, *Where Peachtree Meets Sweet Auburn*, 299–300.

30. Raleigh Bryans, "Mayor Bows Out," *Atlanta Journal*, June 7, 1961, 1; Allen and Hemphill, *Mayor*, 30–34, 43–51; Stone, *Regime Politics*, 55–56.

31. Rutheiser, *Imagineering Atlanta*, 153.

32. Allen and Hemphill, *Mayor*, 32–34.

33. Lassiter, *Silent Majority*, 109–11; Allen and Hemphill, *Mayor*, 30–34; "Forward Atlanta": promotional pamphlet, 1963, FASF, Kenan Library.

34. Herman Hancock, "Ivan Allen Sworn In, Calls for Bond Issue; Plan Means Tax," *Atlanta Constitution*, January 3, 1962, 27.

35. William Emerson, "When the Paper Clips Jump," *Newsweek*, October 19, 1959, 94–96.

36. Rutheiser, *Imagineering Atlanta*, 157–59; Bayor, *Race and Shaping of Twentieth-Century Atlanta*, 188–96.

37. Allen and Hemphill, *Mayor*, 32–34; Hancock, "Ivan Allen Sworn In," 27; Rutheiser, *Imagineering Atlanta*, 157–59; Julie B. Hairston, "MARTA Marks 25 Years of Trains," *Atlanta Journal-Constitution*, June 30, 2004, 1B.

38. Rutheiser, *Imagineering Atlanta*, 61–63, 153–55; Bayor, *Race and Shaping of Twentieth-Century Atlanta*, 41; "It's a Long Term Problem," *Atlanta Journal*, December 27, 1962, 16; Weise, *Places of Their Own*, 170–71, 191–96.

39. Lassiter, *Silent Majority*, 94–97; Stone, *Regime Politics*, 46–48; Hein, "Image of a 'City Too Busy to Hate,'" 205–6; Pomerantz, *Where Peachtree Meets Sweet Auburn*, 259.

40. Margaret Shannon, "Atlanta Desegregation Begins at 4 Schools," *Atlanta Journal*, August 30, 1961, 1, 8, 12; "Peace Means Progress," *Atlanta Sunday Journal-Constitution*, August 27, 1961, 6B; "High Schools' Desegregation Begins Here Wednesday," *Atlanta Sunday Journal-Constitution*, August 27, 1961, 1, 20; Margaret Shannon, "Serenity Cloaks Atlanta Schools," *Atlanta Constitution*, September 5, 1961, 1; "School Guard Kept Up Here," *Atlanta Journal*, August 31, 1961, 1, 12; Hornsby, "Black Public Education in Atlanta," 21–27.

41. Allen and Hemphill, *Mayor*, 30–34.

42. Gendzel, "Competitive Boosterism," 551–52; Ambrose, *Atlanta*, 177–80; Lassiter, *Silent Majority*, 100–111.

43. Allen and Hemphill, *Mayor*, 32–34; Gendzel, "Competitive Boosterism," 553; Hancock, "Ivan Allen Sworn In," 27.

44. "Profile of Atlanta Stadium," *Braves Banner*, June 1983, ABF, Baseball HOF; "Atlanta Stadium Program: Special Dedication Edition" 1965, AFCSSF, folder 1, Kenan Library; Bisher, *Miracle in Atlanta*, 28–29, 45–50; Allen and Hemphill, *Mayor*, 152–54; Charles Haddad, "A Major League Dream," *Atlanta Journal-Constitution*, October 19, 1991, 1G.

45. Sam Massell, in phone discussion with the author, July 2, 2013; "Atlanta Stadium Program: Special Dedication Edition," 1965, AFCSSF, folder 1, Kenan Library; Jesse Outlar, "Stadium Group Calls on Mayor Today," *Atlanta Constitution*, May 5, 1960, 16; Bisher, *Miracle in Atlanta*, 6–8; H. Martin, *William Berry Hartsfield*, 164.

46. Rutheiser, *Imagineering Atlanta*, 78–81; Bill Torpy, "Atlanta's Visionary," *Atlanta Journal-Constitution*, July 13, 2003, 1C; H. Martin, *William Berry Hartsfield*, 39–41, 61–72, 86–93, 139.

47. "Copy of Statement by Ivan Allen, Jr., Mayor of Atlanta, before Committee on Commerce, Regarding S. 1732," July 26, 1963, IAMP, box 1, folder 9, Kenan Library.

48. "Statement by Ivan Allen Jr., City Wide Meeting," January 29, 1964, IAMP, box 1, folder 9, Kenan Library.

49. "Copy of Statement by Ivan Allen, Jr., Mayor of Atlanta," Kenan Library.

50. "Atlanta Stadium Program: Special Dedication Edition," 1965, AFCSSF, folder 1, Kenan Library.

2. America's Virgin Sports Territory

1. Jim Auchmety, "Mayor Kept City Too Busy to Hate," *Atlanta Journal-Constitution*, July 6, 2003, 1A; Fred Russell, "Southern Stumbled on Color Line," *Sporting News*, April 4, 1962, 13.

2. Furman Bisher, "The Stadium Call to Arms," *Atlanta Journal*, March 5, 1964, 62, 66.

3. John McGourty, "Former Flames Recall Hot Times in Atlanta," NHL.com, January 24, 2008.

4. Ambrose, *Atlanta*, 116–18; Bisher, *Miracle in Atlanta*, 41.

5. Jim Minter, in phone discussion with the author, August 16, 2013.

6. "Georgia Tech Media Guides 1981 and 1982," SPP, box 1, folder 10, Kenan Library; Jesse Outlar, "Ticket Boom at Tech," *Atlanta Constitution*, August 21, 1965, 10; Seymour Freedgood, "Life in Buckhead," *Fortune*, September 1961, 11–12; Georgia Institute of Technology, *Engineering for Success*, 9–10, 140–65, 184; C. Martin, "Racial Change," 532–34, 551–61; Jack Thompson, email message to author, August 16, 2013; "Pros No Worry to Bobby Dodd," *Washington Post*, January 22, 1966, D2.

7. "University of Georgia Football Media Guides, 1952–1966," SPP, Kenan Library; "The Fan Explosion," *Atlanta Journal*, October 16, 1968, 16; University of Georgia, "Home Football Attendance"; "Georgia's Crowned," *Atlanta Constitution*, November 30, 1966, 1D.

8. Tygiel, *Baseball's Great Experiment*, 278; Bellamy and Walker, "Did Televised Baseball Kill the 'Golden Age'?," 59–68; Bob Burnes, "Shaky Southern Teetering Toward Extinction," *Sporting News*, September 20, 1961, 5.

9. Tim Darnell, "The Atlanta Crackers," New Georgia Encyclopedia, October 19, 2006, https://www.georgiaencyclopedia.org/articles/sports-outdoor-recreation /atlanta-crackers.

10. Bisher, *Miracle in Atlanta*, 33–38; Jesse Outlar, "Braves Settle for Crackers," *Atlanta Constitution*, November 30, 1964, 12; Karl Green, in phone discussion with the author, August 16, 2013.

11. Kuhn, Joye, and West, *Living Atlanta*, 266–68; Tim Darnell, "The Atlanta Black Crackers," New Georgia Encyclopedia, November 3, 2006, https://www .georgiaencyclopedia.org/articles/sports-outdoor-recreation/atlanta-black -crackers; Leslie Heaphy, "The Atlanta Black Crackers," Society for American Baseball Research, 2010, https://sabr.org/journal/article/the-atlanta-black -crackers/.

12. Bisher, *Miracle in Atlanta*, 34.

13. Bisher, *Miracle in Atlanta*, 34–38, 56; Jesse Outlar, "Requiem for Poncey," *Atlanta Constitution*, May 24, 1965, 16; Green, in phone discussion with the author; Tim Darnell, "Ponce de Leon Ballpark," New Georgia Encyclopedia, January 22, 2004, https://www.georgiaencyclopedia.org/articles/sports-outdoor-recreation /ponce-de-leon-ballpark.

14. Joel Gross, email message to author, August 15, 2013.

15. Bob Burnes, "Shaky Southern Teetering Toward Extinction," *Sporting News*, September 20, 1961, 5; Fred Russell, "Why Did Southern Go Under?," *Sporting News*, March 28, 1962, 11; Russell, "Southern Stumbled on Color Line," 13.

16. Bisher, *Miracle in Atlanta*, 34–40; Tygiel, *Baseball's Great Experiment*, 265–67, 276.

17. Russell, "Southern Stumbled on Color Line," 13; Tygiel, *Baseball's Great Experiment*, 265–67, 276; Auchmety, "Mayor Kept City Too Busy to Hate," 1A.

18. Bob Harig, "Unlike Most Practice Rounds, the Masters' Brings Plenty of Passion," ESPN.com, April 7, 2008; Jesse Outlar, "Big League Audition," *Atlanta Constitution*, April 12, 1962, 12; Bisher, *Miracle in Atlanta*, 40; Furman Bisher, "Masters Opens with Jacks," *Atlanta Journal*, April 8, 1966, 47; Steven R. Lowe, "Bobby Jones (1902–1971)," New Georgia Encyclopedia, June 18, 2002, https:// www.georgiaencyclopedia.org/articles/sports-outdoor-recreation/bobby-jones -1902-1971.

19. Jack McCallum, "Crossing the Line," *Sports Illustrated*, April 3, 2000.

20. "Atlanta International Raceway: Race Information," ARSF, Kenan Library; Bill Blodgett, "Lorenzen Sweeps Third 500 in Row," *Atlanta Constitution*, April 6, 1964, 19; Hal Hayes, "Hurtubise Hurries to '500' Win as 70,000 Fans Watch AIR Classic," *Atlanta Constitution*, March 28, 1966, 33; "Roberts Fireballs His Way to Torrid Dixie 300 Win," *Atlanta Constitution*, August 1, 1960, 13; Bisher, *Miracle in Atlanta*, 40–41; "1967 Season Ticket Renewal Brochure," ABSF, Kenan Library.

21. "Lakewood Races Should Be Stopped," June 13, 1950, ARSF, Kenan Library.

22. Marion E. Jackson, "Sports of the World," *Atlanta Daily World*, April 7, 1964, 7.

23. Beekman, *Ringside*, 114–23; *Ringsider*, Atlanta Wrestling Program, September 23, 1969, WSF, Kenan Library; Hornbaker, *National Wrestling Alliance*, 294–95; Pedicino, *History of Professional Wrestling in Atlanta*; Bisher, *Miracle in Atlanta*, 41.

3. Franchise Free Agency

1. Vrooman, "Franchise Free Agency," 209.

2. Jozsa, *Big Sports, Big Business*, 71, 88, 93, 106–7.

3. Danielson, *Home Team*, 140–43, 169, 179, 225; Josza, *Big Sports, Big Business*, 106–7.

4. Abbott and Nicolaides, "Professional Sports and Sunbelt Cities," 27–28.

5. Danielson, *Home Team*, 169, 179.

6. Riess, *City Games*, 237.

7. Cave and Crandall, "Sports Rights and the Broadcast Industry," 3–5.

8. Jozsa, *Big Sports, Big Business*, 65–71.

9. US Census Bureau, "Historical Income Tables: Household"; Bernard and Rice, *Sunbelt Cities*, 18; Bernat, "Convergence in State Per Capita Personal Income," 36–44.

10. Johnson, "Municipal Administration and Sports Relocation," 519.

11. Rosentraub, "Are Public Policies Needed?," 378; Beisner, "Sports Franchise Relocation," 448.

12. Zimbalist, *May the Best Team Win*, 123, 129–30.

13. Rosentraub, "Are Public Policies Needed?," 391; Beisner, "Sports Franchise Relocation," 448; Johnson, "Municipal Administration and Sports Relocation," 527.

14. Beisner, "Sports Franchise Relocation," 448.

15. Rosentraub, "Are Public Policies Needed?," 381.

16. Zimbalist, *May the Best Team Win*, 2, 16–17.

17. Zimbalist, *May the Best Team Win*, 2, 16–17.

18. Jozsa, *Big Sports, Big Business*, 49–51, 53–54.

19. Johnson, "Municipal Administration and Sports Relocation," 520–21; Davidson, *Breaking the Game Wide Open*, 249; Kevin Baumer, "What Every NFL Owner Paid for Their Team," *Business Insider*, November 16, 2010.

20. Riess, *City Games*, 239; Coates and Humphreys, "Stadium Gambit," 16.

21. Long, "Public Funding for Major League Sports"; Abbott and Nicolaides, "Professional Sports and Sunbelt Cities," 27–28; Greenberg, *Stadium Game*, 113–14; Santo, "Beyond Economic Catalyst Debate," 457.

22. Riess, *City Games*, 239; Coates and Humphreys, "Stadium Gambit," 16.

23. Danielson, *Home Team*, 225, 235–36.

24. Greenberg, *Stadium Game*, 113–14; Santo, "Beyond Economic Catalyst Debate," 457; Long, "Public Funding for Major League Sports."

25. Danielson, *Home Team*, 238; Riess, *City Games*, 241–42.

26. Danielson, *Home Team*, 225, 235–36.

27. Greenberg, *Stadium Game*, 113–14.

28. Noll and Zimbalist, "Build the Stadium—Create the Jobs," 2; Euchner, *Playing the Field*, 10–11.

29. Riess, *City Games*; Noll and Zimbalist, "Build the Stadium—Create the Jobs," 29; Shropshire, *Sports Franchise Game*; Baade and Sanderson, "Employment Effect of Teams and Sports Facilities," 112–13; Rosentraub, *Major League Losers*.

30. Baim, "Sports Stadiums as 'Wise Investments'"; Noll and Zimbalist, *Sports, Jobs, and Taxes*; Riess, *City Games*; Danielson, *Home Team*; Santo, "Beyond Economic Catalyst Debate," 455–79; Rosentraub, *Major League Losers*, 448–51.

31. Danielson, *Home Team*, 5; Gendzel, "Competitive Boosterism," 530–32; Shropshire, *Sports Franchise Game*; Euchner, *Playing the Field*, 185; Trumpbour, *New Cathedrals*, 1–2; Santo, "Beyond Economic Catalyst Debate," 455–79.

32. Vrooman, "Franchise Free Agency," 203.

33. Cave and Crandall, "Sports Rights and the Broadcast Industry," 3–5.

34. Stuart, *Twilight Teams*, 5.

35. Riess, *City Games*, 236; Abbott and Nicolaides, "Professional Sports and Sunbelt Cities," 27–28.

36. Vrooman, "Franchise Free Agency," 203; Andrea Woo, Brian Cazenevue, Daniel G. Habib, Gene Menez, and Bill Syken, "Teams on the Move," *Sports Illustrated*, December 27, 2004, 27.

37. Coates and Humphreys, "Stadium Gambit," 16; Vrooman, "Franchise Free Agency," 203; Cave and Crandall, "Sports Rights and the Broadcast Industry," 3–5; Danielson, *Home Team*, 140–42.

38. Zimbalist, *May the Best Team Win*, 123, 129–130.

39. Danielson, *Home Team*, 169, 179; Cave and Crandall, "Sports Rights and the Broadcast Industry," 3–5; Woo et al., "Teams on the Move," 27.

40. Willes, *Rebel League*, 6–7; Danielson, *Home Team*, 169, 179; Cave and Crandall, "Sports Rights and the Broadcast Industry," 3–5; Woo et al., "Teams on the Move," 27.

41. Jozsa, *Big Sports, Big Business*, 65–71, 88, 93, 106–7; Riess, *City Games*, 232; Danielson, *Home Team*, 140–42.

42. Danielson, *Home Team*, 140–47; Euchner, *Playing the Field*, 89–92; Ribowsky, *Slick*, 306–9; Jozsa, *Football Fortunes*, 60; Woo et al., "Teams on the Move," 27.

4. Greatest Location in the World

1. *Atlanta Stadium Program: Special Dedication Edition*, 1965, AFCSSF, folder 1, Kenan Library.

2. Sally Sanford, "Plan Offered for Coliseum," *Atlanta Journal*, February 19, 1962, 1; Allen and Hemphill, *Mayor*, 69, 152–54; "Copy of Statement by Ivan Allen, Jr., Mayor of Atlanta, before Committee on Commerce, Regarding S. 1732," July 26, 1963, IAMP, box 1, folder 9, Kenan Library; "Bond Issue Voting Heavy," *Atlanta Daily World*, August 3, 1962, 1, 5.

3. Sanford, "Plan Offered for Coliseum," 1; Raleigh Bryans, "All Bond Issues Approved in Vote," *Atlanta Journal*, May 16, 1963, 1, 12; Raleigh Bryans, "Final Debates Offered Here on Bonds," *Atlanta Journal*, May 14, 1963, 1, 12; Jesse Outlar, "Letter to the Mayor," *Atlanta Sunday Journal-Constitution*, May 12, 1963, 46; John H. Britton, "Voters Get the Bond Issue at Polls Today," *Atlanta Daily World*, August 2, 1962, 1, 5.

4. Allen and Hemphill, *Mayor*, 69, 152–154; Bob Spicer, "Stadium Next, Mayor Says," *Atlanta Constitution*, May 17, 1963, 45; Stone, *Regime Politics*, 60–65.

5. Bisher, *Miracle in Atlanta*, 11–14, 51; "Lawyers Title News: Atlanta Stadium," August 1966, AFCSSF, folder 1, Kenan Library; Furman Bisher, "Allen Got the Ball Rolling Here," *Atlanta Journal-Constitution*, July 3, 2003, 2D; John Logue, "Stadium by 1964 in the Works Here," *Atlanta Journal*, June 6, 1963, 1; Ernest Mehl, "'Build Park or Lose Franchise,' Finley Tells Kaycee City Council," *Sporting News*, September 29, 1962, 16; Ernest Mehl, "A's Shift More Plausible," *Sporting News*, July

27, 1963, 4; *Atlanta Stadium Program: Special Dedication Edition*, 1965, AFCSSF, folder 1, Kenan Library.

6. "Profile of Atlanta Stadium," *Braves Banner*, June 1983, ABF, Baseball HOF; Jim Minter, "Southside: How Big League Baseball Came to Atlanta," *Atlanta Journal-Constitution*, November 9, 1995, 2M; Allen and Hemphill, *Mayor*, 152–55; Bisher, *Miracle in Atlanta*, 15–18; "Atlanta Stadium Zooms Off Ground, Heads for Reality," *Sporting News*, June 22, 1963, 15; Jim Minter, "The Mayor Surrenders Atlanta," *Sports Illustrated*, July 12, 1965, 14–17; *Atlanta Stadium Program: Special Dedication Edition*, 1965, AFCSSF, folder 1, Kenan Library.

7. Allen and Hemphill, *Mayor*, 154.

8. Keating, "Atlanta: Peoplestown," 35–39; Allen and Hemphill, *Mayor*, 152–57; Bisher, *Miracle in Atlanta*, 15–18, 52–53; Logue, "Stadium by 1964," 1; Marion Gaines, "Stadium Near Reality after Citizens Back It," *Atlanta Constitution*, March 7, 1964, 1, 9; Jesse Outlar, "Stadium Kickoff," *Atlanta Constitution*, June 7, 1963, 49.

9. Bisher, *Miracle in Atlanta*, 15–18; Allen and Hemphill, *Mayor*, 152–59; "Super Stadium, Super Market," AFCSSF, folder 1, Kenan Library; *Atlanta Stadium Program: Special Dedication Edition*, 1965, AFCSSF, folder 1, Kenan Library.

10. Allen and Hemphill, *Mayor*, 156.

11. Allen and Hemphill, *Mayor*, 152–61; Bisher, *Miracle in Atlanta*, 15–29; Bisher, "Allen Got the Ball Rolling," 2D.

12. Bisher, "Allen Got the Ball Rolling," 2D.

13. Bisher, *Miracle in Atlanta*, 28–29, 45–50; Minter, "Mayor Surrenders Atlanta," 14–17; *Atlanta Stadium Program: Special Dedication Edition*, 1965, AFCSSF, folder 1, Kenan Library; "Profile of Atlanta Stadium," *Braves Banner*, June 1983, ABF, Baseball HOF.

14. Bisher, *Miracle in Atlanta*, 27–29, 42–50; "Lawyers Title News," Kenan Library; Allen and Hemphill, *Mayor*, 157–61; Gendzel, "Competitive Boosterism," 553; Minter, "Mayor Surrenders Atlanta," 14–17.

15. Logue, "Stadium by 1964," 1; Bisher, *Miracle in Atlanta*, 30–32, 46–47; "Atlanta Whiffs, Renews Big Time Club," *Sporting News*, July 20, 1963, 3; Ernest Mehl, "Kaycee City Council Trying to Hand Me Rotten Deal, Finley Claims," *Sporting News*, January 18, 1964, 4.

16. Jim Minter, "Sanders, Allen Go to Bat in Cleveland," *Atlanta Sunday Journal-Constitution*, July 7, 1963, 43; Furman Bisher, "NL Club to Hear Atlanta's Pitch," *Atlanta Journal*, July 8, 1963, 18; Furman Bisher, "The Foot Is in the Door," *Atlanta Journal*, July 9, 1963, 14; "Atlanta Dispatches Envoy to Majors," *Atlanta Constitution*, June 27, 1963, 1; Bisher, *Miracle in Atlanta*, 54–57; Jesse Outlar, "An Official Pitch," *Atlanta Constitution*, July 6, 1963, 24.

17. *Atlanta Stadium Program: Special Dedication Edition*, 1965, AFCSSF, folder 1, Kenan Library.

18. "Lawyers Title News," Kenan Library.

19. Bisher, "NL Club to Hear Atlanta's Pitch," 18; Povletich, *Braves New World*; Gendzel, "Competitive Boosterism," 553–55; Tim Tucker, "Q&A with Bill Bartholomay," *Atlanta Journal-Constitution*, April 12, 2006, 1D; Bisher, *Miracle in Atlanta*, 27–28, 54–57.

20. Gendzel, "Competitive Boosterism," 539; Veeck, *Hustler's Handbook*, 265; Bisher, *Miracle in Atlanta*, 25, 144–45; "Braves Honeymoon Over at Milwaukee,"

Washington Post, February 3, 1962, C7; Veeck and Linn, "Another Gone with the Wind," *Sports Illustrated*, June 7, 1965, 32–54.

21. Gendzel, "Competitive Boosterism," 546; Povletich, *Braves New World*; "The Team That Made Milwaukee Furious," *Boston Globe*, June 13, 1965, A7; "'61 Worst Nosedive Since Move in '53," *Sporting News*, October 18, 1961, 1, 2; "Braves Honeymoon Over," C7; "Braves Fans Win Battle of Six Packs," *Chicago Tribune*, June 6, 1962, C2; "Brewtown Broods," *Sporting News*, June 2, 1962, 1.

22. Veeck, *Hustler's Handbook*, 266–72; Gendzel, "Competitive Boosterism," 539–41; "Syndicate Buys Perini's Braves," *Boston Globe*, November 17, 1962, 1; Bob Wolf, "Last Li'l Steamshovel Chugs into Barn," *Sporting News*, December 1, 1962, 11.

23. Gendzel, "Competitive Boosterism," 541; Bisher, *Miracle in Atlanta*, 25; Veeck, *Hustler's Handbook*, 272; Davidson and Outlar, *Caught Short*, 89–90.

24. Shropshire, *Sports Franchise Game*, 28; Kahn, *Boys of Summer*, 428; Gendzel, "Competitive Boosterism," 535–36.

25. "Big Milwaukee Red Carpet to Greet Braves," *Chicago Tribune*, April 5, 1953, C1; Van Wieren and Klapisch, *Braves*, 87–88; Davidson and Outlar, *Caught Short*, 55–56.

26. Povletich, *Braves New World*.

27. Bragan and Guinn, *You Can't Hit the Ball*, 274.

28. Buege, *Milwaukee Braves*, 3–22, 175–82; Gendzel, "Competitive Boosterism," 536–37; "Why Should Taxpayers Foot Bill for the Stadium?" *Boston Globe*, September 30, 1963, 7; William Povletich, "When the Braves of Bushville Ruled Baseball," *Wisconsin Magazine of History*, Summer 2007, 5–6.

29. Quirk, "Economic Analysis of Team Movements," 53; Veeck, *Hustler's Handbook*, 280–83; Gendzel, "Competitive Boosterism," 547–48; "Milwaukee Braves Offered Fat TV and Radio Contract," *Atlanta Constitution*, September 12, 1964, 42; Veeck and Linn, "Another Gone with the Wind," 32–54.

30. "Milwaukee Braves Offered Fat TV and Radio Contract," 42; Veeck and Linn, "Another Gone with the Wind," 32–54; Quirk, "Economic Analysis of Team Movements," 53.

31. John Logue, "Plans Told for Stadium," *Atlanta Journal*, August 6, 1963, 14; "Profile of Atlanta Stadium," *Braves Banner*, June 1983, ABF, Baseball HOF; Bisher, *Miracle in Atlanta*, 48–50, 165–67; "Atlanta Stadium Zooms Off Ground," 15; John Logue, "Dome Included in Stadium Plan," *Atlanta Journal*, October, 22, 1963, 1; *Atlanta Falcons 1974 Fact Book*, SPP, box 2, folder 11, Kenan Library.

32. Bisher, *Miracle in Atlanta*, 73–76; Rutheiser, *Imagineering Atlanta*, 153–55; Logue, "Stadium by 1964," 1.

33. Marion Gaines, "Major League Team Accepts 15 Year Lease," *Atlanta Constitution*, April 9, 1964, 1, 16; "Atlanta Votes Speedy Okay on Park," *Sporting News*, March 21, 1964, 4; "Two Bills Propose Stadium Financing," *Atlanta Journal*, March 4, 1964, 1; Raleigh Bryans, "Aldermen Caught in Crush of Atlanta Stadium," *Atlanta Journal*, March 7, 1964, 4; Furman Bisher, "Atlanta Launches Crash Program: Stadium by '65," *Sporting News*, April 18, 1964, 34; Gaines, "Stadium Nears Reality," 1, 9.

34. Bryans, "Alderman Caught in Crush," 4.

35. Bisher, *Miracle in Atlanta*, 50.

36. Furman Bisher, "A Happy Probability," *Atlanta Sunday Journal-Constitution*, July 7, 1963, 43.

37. Stanley Scott, "Aldermen Reject Non-Racial Clause for Atlanta Stadium," *Atlanta Daily World*, April 14, 1964, 1; Stanley Scott, "Stadium Plan Is Sent to Finance Committee," *Atlanta Daily World*, April 7, 1964, 1, 7.

38. Reece Cleghorn, "Allen of Atlanta Collides with Black Power and White Racism," *New York Times*, October 16, 1966, 32–33, 134–40.

39. Bryans, "Alderman Caught in Crush," 4; Scott, "Aldermen Reject Non-Racial Clause," 1; Scott, "Stadium Plan Is Sent," 1, 7; Gaines, "Stadium Near Reality," 1, 9.

40. Scott, "Aldermen Reject Non-Racial Clause," 1.

41. Marion Gaines, "City Panel Okays Stadium Financing," *Atlanta Constitution*, April 10, 1964, 1; Marion Gaines, "Big Leaguers Accept Lease," *Atlanta Constitution*, April 9, 1964, 16; Scott, "Stadium Plan Is Sent," 1, 7.

42. Marion Gaines, "Stadium a Good Buy, Mayor Says," *Atlanta Constitution*, November 21, 1964, 3; Gaines, "City Panel Okays Stadium Financing," 1.

43. "Two Bills Propose Stadium Financing," *Atlanta Journal*, March 4, 1964, 1; Sally Rugaber, "Ground Breaking Set on New City Stadium," *Atlanta Journal*, April 13, 1964, 2; Bisher, *Miracle in Atlanta*, 73–76; Gaines, "Stadium Near Reality," 1, 9.

44. *Braves Banner*, June 1983, ABF, Baseball HOF; *Atlanta Stadium Program: Special Dedication Edition*, 1965, AFCSSF, folder 1, Kenan Library; Sally Rugaber, "Empty Steps Lead to Stadium," *Atlanta Journal*, April 16, 1964, 34; Bisher, *Miracle in Atlanta*, 42–43; Bisher, "Atlanta Launches Crash Program," 34; Sally Rugaber, "Ground Broken for Stadium Here," *Atlanta Journal*, April 15, 1964, 1; Allen and Hemphill, *Mayor*, 160–61.

45. "Lawyers Title News," August 1966, AFCSSF, folder 1, Kenan Library; Minter, "Mayor Surrenders Atlanta," 14–17; *Atlanta Falcons 1972 Fact Book*, SPP, box 2, folder 10, Kenan Library.

46. Gaines, "City Panel Okays Stadium Financing," 1; Allen and Hemphill, *Mayor*, 160–61; *Atlanta Falcons 1972 Fact Book*, SPP, box 2, folder 10, Kenan Library; *Atlanta Stadium Program: Special Dedication Edition* 1965, AFCSSF, folder 1, Kenan Library.

47. Allen and Hemphill, *Mayor*, 152–53.

5. *Wisconsin v. Milwaukee Braves*

1. C. C. Johnson Spink, "Braves' Shift Needs Only Okay by NL," *Sporting News*, July 11, 1964, 1; John Logue, "Braves Won't Deny Move Here," *Atlanta Journal*, July 3, 1964, 12; Bill Veeck and Ed Linn, "Another Gone with the Wind," *Sports Illustrated*, June 7, 1965, 32–54; Huston Horn, "Bravura Battle for the Braves," *Sports Illustrated*, November 2, 1964, 32–33; Furman Bisher, "Everybody Talks Except the Braves," *Atlanta Journal*, July 8, 1964, 30; Jesse Outlar, "Braves Play Silent Game," *Atlanta Constitution*, August 11, 1964, 29.

2. Buege, *Milwaukee Braves*, 369–70; Gendzel, "Competitive Boosterism," 543; Bisher, *Miracle in Atlanta*, 91–96, 102–5; Jack Williams, "Braves' Move Here Gets OK Wednesday," *Atlanta Constitution*, October 20, 1964, 1, 32; Marion Gaines, "Milwaukee Braves Make It Official as Directors Vote to Move Here," *Atlanta Constitution*, October 22, 1964, 1, 8; Jack Nelson and Marion Gaines, "Braves Sign Contract to Play Here 25 Years," *Atlanta Constitution*, November 11, 1964, 1, 16; "Braves Will Ask League Today for Permission to Shift to Atlanta," *New York Times*, October 22, 1964, 28; Marion Gaines, "League Delays Transfer of Braves until Court Removes Injunction," *Atlanta Constitution*, October 23, 1964, 1.

3. Nelson and Gaines, "Braves Sign Contract," 1, 16; Furman Bisher, "Braves Slated to Sign 25-Year Atlanta Lease," *Atlanta Journal*, November 9, 1964, 1, 10; Jim Minter, "A Happy Homecoming for the Braves," *Atlanta Journal*, October 22, 1964, 34.

4. Bud Shaw, "The Dinosaur on Capitol Avenue," *Atlanta Journal-Constitution*, May 26, 1984, 1C.

5. Alex Coffin, "Massell, Cousins Get Together on Coliseum Event," *Atlanta Constitution*, March 30, 1971, 2A; Alex Coffin, "Coliseum Deal's 'Pluses' Outlined," *Atlanta Constitution*, December 15, 1970, 2; *Omni Souvenir Dedication Book*, OSF, Kenan Library.

6. Gendzel, "Competitive Boosterism," 542–43; "Milwaukee Fans React: Let B's Suffer," *Boston Globe*, June 6, 1965, 57; Bisher, *Miracle in Atlanta*, 152–54; Jack Williams, "Allen Confab Gets Nowhere," *Atlanta Constitution*, November 16, 1964, 11; Bill Blodgett, "Allen Heads to Chicago for Grobschmidt Talk," *Atlanta Constitution*, November 14, 1964, 11.

7. Aaron and Wheeler, *I Had a Hammer*, 174.

8. Buege, *Milwaukee Braves*, 397; Bragan and Guinn, *You Can't Hit the Ball*, 291–311; Bisher, *Miracle in Atlanta*, 77–82, 159–64; William Leggett, "Atlanta You Can Have the Rest, Leave Us Eddie Mathews Our Hero," *Sports Illustrated*, April 26, 1965, 24–25.

9. Bragan and Guinn, *You Can't Hit the Ball*, 305.

10. Veeck and Linn, "Another Gone with the Wind," 38; "Braves Take Atlanta Tag," *Chicago Tribune*, August 10, 1965, C1; "Braves Boom . . . But Gate Is Poorest Ever," *Atlanta Constitution*, April 28, 1965, 35; "Braves High, Aaron Rips 2; But Crowd Low: 913 Paid," *Atlanta Constitution* May 5, 1965, 43; "B's Acquire Worst Image of All Clubs," *Boston Globe*, June 23, 1965, 43.

11. Aaron and Wheeler, *I Had a Hammer*, 175; Bisher, *Miracle in Atlanta*, 159–64; "Bragan Replies to Grobschmidt Blast at Braves," *Sporting News*, July 24, 1965, 7; "Bragan Blasts Fans," *Atlanta Journal*, June 13, 1965, 53; "US Judge Orders Braves Here in '66," *Atlanta Journal*, February 24, 1966, 1, 4.

12. Minter, "Happy Homecoming for the Braves," 34; Bragan and Guinn, *You Can't Hit the Ball*, 291–311.

13. James Enright, "Players All Packed and Ready to Hop First Plane for Atlanta," *Sporting News*, July 18, 1964, 10; Torre and Verducci, *Chasing the Dream*, 96.

14. "Maye Fears Negro Players Will Face Jim Crow in Atlanta," *Chicago Defender*, October 22, 1964, 38; "Dixie Bias the Real Issue in Braves' Atlanta Move," *Chicago Defender*, July 23, 1964, 38.

15. "Braves to Atlanta? Aaron Unhappy," *Chicago Defender*, October, 20, 1964, 22; "Milwaukee or Atlanta: Braves Talk Up," *Atlanta Constitution*, July 7, 1964, 31; Bragan and Guinn, *You Can't Hit the Ball*, 311; Bryant, *Last Hero*, 305–12; "Dixie Bias the Real Issue," 38.

16. Bragan and Guinn, *You Can't Hit the Ball*, 311; Bryant, *Last Hero*, 305–12.

17. Bragan and Guinn, *You Can't Hit the Ball*, 305–6; "To Be Equal," *Chicago Defender*, November 7, 1964, 9; Howard Bryant, "Atlanta Pro Sports and Integration," espn.com, January 12, 2011.

18. Bryant, *Last Hero*, 310–11.

19. "Braves' Players Assured Atlanta Fully Integrated," *Boston Globe*, October 22, 1964, 45.

20. Bisher, *Miracle in Atlanta*, 170–71; "Aaron, Mathews Pay Visit to Atlanta Stadium," *Washington Post*, January 31, 1965, C3; Jesse Outlar, "Atlanta Wins Hank," *Atlanta Constitution*, February 1, 1965, 10; Jesse Outlar, "Hank, Eddie Here, Aaron Denies Fear," *Atlanta Constitution*, January 29, 1965, 39.

21. Bryant, *Last Hero*, 312–13.

22. Gendzel, "Competitive Boosterism," 544–50; Povletich, *Braves New World*; "Wisconsin Sues Braves, Cites State Trust Law," *Washington Post*, August 7, 1965, D2; "Milwaukee County Sues Braves, Seeks Triple Damages for Club Move," *Sporting News*, August 14, 1965, 12.

23. Gendzel, "Competitive Boosterism," 544–50; Bob Wolf, "Wisconsin Carries Trust Case to Highest Court," *Sporting News*, October 23, 1966, 16; Wayne Minshew, "No Support Caused Move—Bartholomay," *Atlanta Constitution*, January 14, 1966, 51; "Wisconsin Court Rules against Braves' Shift," *Washington Post*, April 14, 1966, C1; "Baseball Called Legal Monopoly," *New York Times*, July 28, 1966, 1; "Braves Heading for Higher Court," *Atlanta Journal*, April 14, 1966, 1; "Braves Drop 2 Verdicts," *Atlanta Constitution*, April 14, 1966, 1.

24. "A Plague on Both Their Houses," *Sports Illustrated*, April 25, 1966.

25. Karl Green, in phone discussion with the author, August 16, 2013.

6. Gravitating toward Atlanta

1. Bisher, *Atlanta Falcons*, 18–24; Bisher, *Miracle in Atlanta*, 9–11; Bill Clark, "Atlanta Set for AFL Bid," *Atlanta Constitution*, March 19, 1964, 47; Jesse Outlar, "NFL Picks Atlanta for '66," *Atlanta Constitution*, June 22, 1965, 1.

2. Coates and Humphreys, "Stadium Gambit," 15–17.

3. Howard Tuckner, "Atlanta Favored for Last Berth in AFL," *New York Times*, January 15, 1960, 15; Jesse Outlar, "Pro Goal in Sight," *Atlanta Constitution*, January 30, 1960, 19; Jesse Outlar, "Sports Action, Inc." *Atlanta Constitution*, January 20, 1960, 24; Bob Christian, "Major Sports Inc. Casts Lot with AFL," *Atlanta Journal*, January 14, 1960, 12; "Atlanta Grid Group Aligns Ponce de Leon," *Atlanta Constitution*, January 13, 1960, 14; Jesse Outlar, "Oakland Applicants," *Atlanta Constitution*, January 27, 1960, 14; Jesse Outlar, "Dodgers and Chargers," *Atlanta Constitution*, February 5, 1960, 14.

4. Tuckner, "Atlanta Favored for Last Berth," 15; Outlar, "Sports Action, Inc.," 24; Christian, "Major Sports Inc. Casts Lot," 12; Jesse Outlar, "Atlanta Presents Case to Late Arriving Hunt," *Atlanta Constitution*, January 16, 1960, 8; Bob Christian, "Geography Favors Atlanta in AFL Bid," *Atlanta Journal*, January 16, 1960, 6; Outlar, "Dodgers and Chargers," 14; Jesse Outlar, "AFL Now or NFL Later," *Atlanta Constitution*, June 27, 1962, 37.

5. Furman Bisher, "Atlanta Enters Pro Football Loop," *Atlanta Journal*, May 3, 1960, 1, 19; Furman Bisher, "Atlanta in Pro Football," *Atlanta Journal*, May 4, 1960, 32; Al Thomy, "Atlanta Gets Pro Football: AFL Coming '61 or '62," *Atlanta Constitution*, May 4, 1960, 41.

6. MacCambridge, *America's Game*, 129–34, 157–59, 172–74.

7. J. Miller, *Going Long*, 17–18.

8. Bisher, *Atlanta Falcons*, 18–24; Jim Minter, "Two NFL Exhibition Games Slated for City for Next Season," *Atlanta Journal*, January 18, 1962, 14; "Halas Favors Atlanta in an Expansion of NFL," *Atlanta Constitution*, August 11, 1962, 11.

9. Bisher, *Atlanta Falcons*, 18–24; Bisher, *Miracle in Atlanta*, 9–10; Jesse Outlar, "McCane Promises Atlanta Stadium," *Atlanta Constitution*, June 26, 1962, 18; Jim Minter, "AFL's City Courtship May Be Real Thing," *Atlanta Journal*, January 20, 1962, 4; "Atlanta Interest in AFL Shown in Exhibitions—Foss," *Atlanta Constitution*, May 25, 1962, 49; "Bus Service Available for Game Tonight," *Atlanta Daily World*, August 4, 1962, 5.

10. Bisher, *Miracle in Atlanta*, 9–10.

11. Al Thomy, "American Field Death Sighted," *Atlanta Constitution*, August 11, 1962, 12; Bisher, *Atlanta Falcons*, 18–24; Bisher, *Miracle in Atlanta*, 9–10.

12. "Go South, Young Ballplayer," *Sports Illustrated*, April 20, 1964; Jim Minter and Raleigh Bryans, "NFL Football Team to Move Here in '65," *Atlanta Journal*, April 10, 1964, 1, 27.

13. "Bidwill's Aids Will Carry on Sports Empire," *Chicago Tribune*, April 20, 1947, A1; Burnes, *Big Red*, 1–30; Rosentraub, *Major League Losers*, 293; Maracek, *St. Louis Football Cardinals*, 3–15.

14. MacCambridge, *America's Game*, 116–21; Burnes, *Big Red*, 31–35; Maracek, *St. Louis Football Cardinals*, 16–30; Lipsitz, "Sports Stadia and Urban Development," 1–7.

15. Rich Koster, "Stadium Is St. Louis' Passport to Big League Professional Football," *St. Louis Globe-Democrat*, May 8, 1966, 16H; Burnes, *Big Red*, 31–35, 42–49, 89–92.

16. Burnes, *Big Red*, 31–35, 42–49, 89–92; Bisher, *Miracle in Atlanta*, 89–91; Jim Minter, "St. Louis Fighting to Keep Cardinals," *Atlanta Journal-Constitution*, May 31, 1964, 54; "Cards Brass Meets to Discuss Stadium," *Atlanta Constitution*, May 25, 1964, 13.

17. Tom Banks, in phone discussion with the author, July 9, 2013.

18. Bob Broeg, "No Decision by Big Red," *St. Louis Post-Dispatch*, June 9, 1964, 17; John Logue, "Bidwill Brothers Talk Atlanta," *Atlanta Constitution*, May 27, 1964, 31; Jesse Outlar, "The Card Deal," *Atlanta Constitution*, July 2, 1964, 12; Minter, "St. Louis Fighting," 54; "Football Cards Ponder Future—With Atlanta in It as Well as St. Louis," *Chicago Tribune*, May 26, 1964, C4.

19. Wayne Thompson, "Card Owners Visit, Talk of Transfer," *Atlanta Constitution*, May 22, 1964, 12; "Cards Brass Meets to Discuss Stadium," *Atlanta Constitution*, May 25, 1964, 13; Ted Schafers, "Many People Contributed Much to Success of New Stadium," *St. Louis Globe-Democrat*, May 7–8, 1966, 2H–12H; "Cards Break Sod, but May Not Stay," *Atlanta Constitution*, May 26, 1964, 35.

20. Jesse Outlar, "Bidding on the Bidwills," *Atlanta Constitution*, May 23, 1964, 18; Outlar, "Card Deal," 12; Jesse Outlar, "Pro Football Cardinals Moving Here," *Atlanta Constitution*, July 11, 1964, 1, 10; Bisher, *Miracle in Atlanta*, 89–91; Ed Wilks, "Big Red Status Is Unchanged," *St. Louis Post-Dispatch*, July 1, 1964, 4C; "Big Red Agree to Stay after Rent Is Cut," *St. Louis Post-Dispatch*, July 27, 1964, 1, 5.

21. Ed Wilks, "Segregation Could Be Problem for Atlanta Professional Sports," *St. Louis Post-Dispatch*, June 18, 1964, 4E.

22. Ed Wilks, "Segregation Could Be Problem," 4E.

23. Outlar, "Pro Football Cardinals Moving Here," 1, 10; Tom McCollister, "Cards Move Only a Word Away," *Atlanta Journal*, July 11, 1964, 4; Jesse Outlar, "Cards Owners Face Heavy Pressure," *Atlanta Constitution*, July 11, 1964, 10.

24. Outlar, "Pro Football Cardinals Moving Here," 1.

25. "Big Red Going to Atlanta: To Play Vikings," *St Louis Post-Dispatch*, August 5, 1964, 1.

26. "Football Cards Don't Relish Idea of Move," *Philadelphia Inquirer*, July 20, 1964, 17; Robert Morrison, "Griesedieck May Be Key to Keeping Big Red," *St. Louis Post-Dispatch*, July 19, 1964, 1E.

27. Jan Van Duser, "Baseball Cards Urging Football Cards to Stay," *Atlanta Constitution*, July 15, 1964, 35; Jan Van Duser, "Cards Face 11th Hour Pressure," *Atlanta Constitution*, July 25, 1964, 10; Olson, *Stuart Symington*, 408–11.

28. "Busch Urges Cardinals to Remain in St. Louis," *Washington Post*, July 15, 1964, C2; "St. Louis Fighting to Keep Cardinals," *Atlanta Sunday Journal-Constitution*, May 31, 1964, 54; Jan Van Duser, "'It's Official' Cards Not Coming," *Atlanta Constitution*, July 27, 1964, 11.

29. Van Duser, "'It's Official,'" 11; Burnes, *Big Red*, 89–92; Bill Kerch, "Mayor, Civic Groups Pledge Aid to Big Red," *St. Louis Globe-Democrat*, July 27, 1964, 1C, 6C; Bob Burnes, "The Battle Has Only Started," *St. Louis Globe-Democrat*, July 28, 1964, 12.

30. Van Duser, "'It's Official,'" 11; Bill Clark, "No NFL Expansion Seen," Atlanta Constitution, July 28, 1964, 27; "Grid Cardinals Decide to Stay in St. Louis," *Boston Globe*, July 25, 1964, 13.

31. Bisher, *Atlanta Falcons*, 18–24; Allen and Hemphill, *Mayor*, 162–64; "Ex-Cox Executive Leonard Reinsch Dies," *Atlanta Journal-Constitution*, May 10, 1991, 1F.

32. Bisher, *Atlanta Falcons*, 18–24; "Two Bids for Denver Broncos," *Washington Post*, February 16, 1965, C2; "Broncs Stay in Denver, Atlanta's Bid Rejected," *Atlanta Constitution*, February 16, 1965, 29; J. Miller, *Going Long*, 207.

33. Bisher, *Atlanta Falcons*, 18–24; Jesse Outlar, "AFL May Beckon, But City to Wait," *Atlanta Constitution*, June 7, 1965, 12; "Atlanta Gets AFL Franchise for '66," *Washington Post*, June 9, 1965, D1; Furman Bisher, "AFL Is Ours, but Is NFL Playing Bluff?," *Atlanta Journal*, June 8, 1965, 12.

34. Jack Williams, "Rozelle Hails Atlanta's Pro Look," *Atlanta Constitution*, June 9, 1965, 37.

35. Outlar, "AFL May Beckon," 12; Allen and Hemphill, *Mayor*, 162–64; Cook, *Carl Sanders*, 270–71.

36. Bisher, *Atlanta Falcons*, 18–24; Jim Minter, "Smith Enters NFL Bid," *Atlanta Sunday Journal-Constitution*, June 13, 1965, 13; "Halas Fears NFL Atlanta Move May Mean AFL Invasion Here," *Chicago Defender*, June 22, 1965, 28.

37. "Lou Harris and Associates, Inc. Survey on Professional Football Preferences in Atlanta," AFF, Football HOF; "Poll Says Atlanta 5 to 1 for NFL," *Atlanta Constitution*, June 24, 1965, 19; Jesse Outlar, "The Harris Report," *Atlanta Constitution*, June 24, 1965, 39.

38. "Statement from Commissioner Rozelle: 6/23/65," AFF, Football HOF.

39. "Atlanta to Join AFL in '66," *Atlanta Constitution*, June 5, 1965, 16.

40. "Cox Group in Atlanta Pays Record 7.5 Million for Franchise in AFL," *New York Times*, June 9, 1965, 55; Jesse Outlar, "Rozelle's Choice," *Atlanta Constitution*, June 30, 1965, 31.

41. Jim Minter, "AFL Escalates Franchise War," *Atlanta Journal*, June 29, 1965, 1.

42. Jan Van Duser, "Atlanta Selects NFL after Rankin Smith Is Awarded Franchise," *Atlanta Constitution*, July 1, 1965, 1, 48.

43. Allen and Hemphill, *Mayor*, 164.

44. Bisher, *Atlanta Falcons*, 23–24.

45. MacCambridge, *America's Game*, 219–33.

7. Not Catching On around Town

1. Jim Minter "Braves Among Favorites," *Atlanta Journal and Constitution Magazine*, April 10, 1966, 9; Bragan and Guinn, *You Can't Hit the Ball*, 317–26; Walt Browning, "Bragan Waves '66 Flag," *Atlanta Journal*, April 9, 1966, 47; Wayne Minshew, "Joe Torre Signs, Sees Braves Flag," *Atlanta Constitution*, February 19, 1966, 41.

2. Thomas Stinson, "'66 Braves Just a Start for Some," *Atlanta Journal-Constitution*, April 13, 2016, 3D.

3. "Stars Agree—Stadium Tops," *Atlanta Journal*, April 9, 1965, 1; Torre and Verducci, *Chasing the Dream*, 97; Ron Reed, in phone discussion with the author, July 8, 2013; Wayne Minshew, in phone discussion with the author, July 1, 2013.

4. Minshew, in phone discussion with the author.

5. Aaron and Wheeler, *I Had a Hammer*, 181–86; *Braves Banner*, August 1984, ABF, Baseball HOF.

6. "Atlanta Greets Braves with Downtown Parade," *Washington Post*, April 13, 1966, D3.

7. "The Score in Atlanta: Football 45,000, Baseball 3,000," *New York Times*, April 24, 1966, 53.

8. Barney Kremenko, "Show Me," *Sporting News*, May 14, 1966, 13.

9. Wayne Minshew, "54,000 See L.A. Edge Braves, 2–1," *Atlanta Constitution*, June 27, 1966, 1; "Traffic Police to Be Doubled in Stadium Area Tomorrow," *Atlanta Constitution*, June 25, 1966, 1.

10. "50,671 Fill Stadium, Usher City into Majors," *Atlanta Constitution*, April 13, 1966, 1; Wayne Minshew, "Braves Fall to Pirates 3–2 in 13," *Atlanta Constitution*, April 13, 1966, 1; "City Going All Out Today as Its Braves 'Play Ball,'" *Atlanta Constitution*, April 12, 1966, 1; "Atlanta Prepares for Big 'World Premier,'" *Atlanta Sunday Journal-Constitution*, April 3, 1966, 61.

11. Tim Tucker, "Q&A/Bill Bartholomay," *Atlanta Journal-Constitution*, April 12, 2006, 1D.

12. Tom McCollister, "Atlanta Fans Lashed by Pirates' Walker," *Atlanta Journal*, April 14, 1966, 45.

13. Furman Bisher, "The Law Hath No Mercy," *Atlanta Journal*, April 14, 1966, 45.

14. "Yankees Rebel Nip Braves, 5–4," *Atlanta Constitution*, April 9, 1966, 13; "Go Braves!" *Atlanta Constitution*, April 8, 1966, 4; Walt Browning, "Yanks Edge Braves 2–1," *Atlanta Journal*, April 10, 1966, 10; Tom McCollister, "The Yankees Are Coming," *Atlanta Journal*, April 7, 1966, 7; "An Analysis of Local Attitudes Toward the Atlanta Baseball Club," ACF, Baseball HOF.

15. Anthony Monahan, "Atlanta: The Southern City That Isn't," *Chicago Tribune*, August 21, 1966, 133.

16. Hope, *We Could've Finished Last without You*, 8.

17. Furman Bisher, "Behold, the Enlightenment," *Atlanta Journal*, April 30, 1968, 1D.

18. "Braves 1975 Season Ticket Fact Sheet," ABSF, Kenan Library; "1967 Season Ticket Renewal Brochure," ABSF, Kenan Library; "Eight Clubs in Majors

Boosting Ticket Prices," *Sporting News*, April 6, 1968, 23; "Baseball Ticket Sales and Concessions Information, 1971–1972," AFP, box 2, folder 10, Kenan Library.

19. Jesse Outlar, "The TV Game," *Atlanta Constitution*, May 25, 1966, 41.

20. Jesse Outlar, "Braves on Parade," *Atlanta Constitution*, February 12, 1966, 19; "Braves Go Visiting on Caravan," *Atlanta Journal*, April 10, 1967, 11B.

21. Wayne Minshew, "Hospitals, Schools Prime Stops for Braves' Caravan," *Sporting News*, February 25, 1967, 17.

22. *Braves Banner*, September 1984, ABF, Baseball HOF; Wayne Minshew, "Even the Mayor Doused in Atlanta Celebration," *Sporting News*, October 18, 1969, 22; Jim Minter, "Braves Bubble Home in West," *Atlanta Journal*, October 1, 1969, 1A; "Cheers! Braves Knock Off Redlegs to Take Western Division Pennant," *Atlanta Constitution*, October 1, 1969, 1D.

23. Howard Bryant, *Last Hero*, 346–49; Minshew, in phone discussion with the author; Charlie Roberts, "This One 'Biggest,'" *Atlanta Constitution*, October 1, 1969, 3D.

24. Roberts, "This One 'Biggest,'" 3D.

25. Wayne Minshew, "Let's Have 4-Club Playoff to Hike Gate," *Sporting News*, December 9, 1972, 46.

26. Teague Jackson, "Braves Try Again after Wipe Out," *Atlanta Journal*, October 6, 1969, 1D; "Playoffs Give Atlanta a $7.5 Million Boost," *New York Times*, October 7, 1969, 54; Sam Hopkins, "Wild Weekend Here for Fun and Games," *Atlanta Constitution*, October 4, 1969, 1D.

27. "Atlanta Braves, Inc.: Consolidated Statement of Earnings, 1971–1972," AFP, box 2, folder 10, Kenan Library; Lester Smith, "Braves' Gate, Operating Income Improved in '69," *Sporting News*, January 31, 1970, 47; Lester Smith, "Tax Losses Aid Braves' Banner Profits for '66," *Sporting News*, January 14, 1967, 28'; "Braves Report 1969 Profit of $347,000," *Washington Post*, January 1, 1970, E2; Lester Smith, "Expansion Inflates Braves' Income," *Sporting News*, March 29, 1969, 27; Lester Smith, "1972 Braves Lost 333,327—Even with Benefit of Tax Credit," *Sporting News*, January 27, 1972, 50.

28. Furman Bisher, "Will Soccer Become Our Cup of Tea?" *Atlanta Journal*, April 21, 1967, 51; *Atlanta Chiefs Official Tara Stadium Program*, AHSF, Kenan Library.

29. Martin Kane, "The True Football Gets Its Big Chance," *Sports Illustrated*, March 27, 1967, 16; Dave Brady, "TV Loot Is Newest Soccer Goal," *Washington Post*, October 2, 1966, C4.

30. Tom Dial, "Chiefs Anxious to Get Rolling," *Atlanta Constitution*, March 27, 1969, 60.

31. Furman Bisher, "Chiefs Cannot Continue as Charity Case," *Atlanta Journal*, September 25, 1968, 1D; Norman Abey, "Atlanta May Lose Chiefs," *Atlanta Journal*, September 12, 1971, 1D.

32. *Atlanta Chiefs Official Tara Stadium Program*, ACSF, Kenan Library; Jeff Myers, "Woosnam of Atlanta Voted Top Coach in Pro Soccer," *Sporting News*, September 28, 1968, 46; Jesse Outlar, "Welcome Champs," *Atlanta Constitution*, May 25, 1968, 8.

33. *Atlanta Chiefs Official 1967 Program*, ACSF, Kenan Library; "Soccer Gets Solid Round of Applause," *Atlanta Constitution*, April 8, 1967, 8; Jim Minter, "Love

Affair Born as Soccer Debuts," *Atlanta Journal*, April 23, 1967, 53; Tom Dial, "Mayor Allen Kicks Off Youth Soccer Program," *Atlanta Constitution*, June 21, 1968, 17.

8. Losing but Improving

1. *Game Day Spotlight: Falcons 1966 Fact Book*, AFF, Football HOF; Bisher, *Atlanta Falcons*, 30; Jim Minter, "Falcons Win Name Game for Atlanta's NFL Entry," *Atlanta Sunday Journal-Constitution*, August 29, 1965, 1.

2. "Atlanta Tickets Buyers Learn Location Facts," *Kansas City Times*, March 23, 1966, 15; "Falcon Fans Unhappy," *Chicago Tribune*, March 23, 1966, C2; "Atlanta to Stop Ticket Drive, 40K Sold," *Washington Post*, December 23, 1965, B5; Bill Clark, "Falcons Set to Launch Ticket Drive," *Atlanta Constitution*, October 29, 1965, 53.

3. Bill Clark, "Falcons Slate Prices; Choose Team Emblem," *Atlanta Constitution*, October 5, 1965, 17.

4. Roy M. Blount, "Losersville U.S.A.," *Sports Illustrated*, March 21, 1977, 80.

5. Al Thomy, "Nobis, NFL Rookie of Year, Bargain at Any Price—Hecker," *Sporting News*, January 7, 1967, 5; "Atlanta Falcons 1967 Preview," AFF, Football HOF; "Falcon Facts: February 1967," AFF, Football HOF; Jesse Outlar, "Mr. Nobis Makes His Point(s)," *Atlanta Constitution*, October 30, 1967, 37; "Hard Nosed Nobis Learns to Hit First and Think about It Later," *Sporting News*, December 3, 1966.

6. John Logue, "Smith Begins Life at 40 Certain of Grid Success," *Atlanta Journal*, July 1, 1965, 1; "Owner Rankin Smith Will Let Football Men Run Atlanta Team," *Washington Post*, July 25, 1965, C3.

7. Lou Kirouac, in phone discussion with the author, August 13, 2013; "The Falcons of '66," *Atlanta Sunday Journal-Constitution*, September 4, 1966, 1–2.

8. "Where Are They Now?," *Atlanta Journal-Constitution*, November 17, 1996, 2E.

9. Lucy Soto and Doug Payne, "Rankin Smith, 1924–1997," *Atlanta Journal-Constitution*, October 27, 1997, 1; "Fans' Patience with Falcons Has Flown the Coop," *Atlanta Journal-Constitution*, December 8, 1996, 13J; "Falcon Owner Turns on His Critics," *Pro Football Weekly*, September 1, 1968.

10. "Falcon Facts: February 1967," AFF, Football HOF.

11. "Paul Brown Talks NFL Atlanta Post," *Washington Post*, August 6, 1965. 14; "Lombardi, Atlanta Had 'Serious' Talks" *Atlanta Journal*, December 23, 1965, 1.

12. Bisher, *Atlanta Falcons*, 29; "Where Are They Now?," 2E; Jesse Outlar, "Falcons Hire Norb Hecker," *Atlanta Constitution*, January 27, 1966, 47.

13. *1966 Atlanta Falcons Fact Book*, AFF, Football HOF; "Falcons Await NFL 'Freeze,'" *Chicago Defender*, February 10, 1966, 40; Jim Minter, "Rozelle: Atlanta Gets 1965 Break," *Atlanta Journal*, July 1, 1965, 70; "Falcons to Get Choice of 8 or 10," *Atlanta Constitution*, February 14, 1966, 1D.

14. "Where Are They Now?," 2E.

15. Bisher, *Atlanta Falcons*, 29; "Where Are They Now?," 2E; Outlar, "Falcons Hire Norb Hecker," 47.

16. "Where Are They Now?," 2E.

17. Jim Minter, "Falcons Pull It Off Big," *Atlanta Journal*, December 12, 1966, 53.

18. "Where Are They Now?," 2E

19. "Falcons Follow Form, 'Losing and Improving,'" *Atlanta Journal*, October 31, 1966, 10; Jim Minter, "Falcon 'Moral Victory' an Affair to Remember," *Atlanta*

Journal, November 14, 1966, 1D; Jim Minter, "Should Have Won, Will Win, Vow Mad Falcons," *Atlanta Journal*, September 12, 1966, 47.

20. Jim Minter, "Lombardi: Falcons Not 'Tough' Team," *Atlanta Journal*, October 24, 1966, 54; Al Thomy, "Packers 'Can' Falcons, 56–3," *Atlanta Constitution*, October 24, 1966, 39.

21. Jim Minter, "NFL 'Leaks' Burn Hecker," *Atlanta Journal*, September 10, 1966, 10.

22. Tommy Nobis, in phone discussion with the author, July 22, 2013; "Unitas Pulls the Trigger—Falcons Surrender, 49–7," *Atlanta Constitution*, November 13, 1967.

23. "Falcon Facts: July 1967," AFF, Football HOF; "Falcon Facts: June 1969," AFF, Football HOF; "Falcon Facts: June 1972," AFF, Football HOF; Schaeffer and Davidson, *Economic Impact of Falcons, 1984*, 1.

24. Bisher, *Atlanta Falcons*, 46–52; "Falcons Fire Brocklin," *Chicago Defender*, November 6, 1974, 35; Al Thomy, "I'm Glad It's Over," *Atlanta Constitution*, October 2, 1968, 25; Steve Hummer, "NFL: Is This the Worst Falcons Season Ever? The Five Most Miserable Years," *Atlanta Journal-Constitution*, November 4, 2007, 6E.

25. Darrell Simmons, "Falcons Miss Chances During Frozen Finale," *Atlanta Journal*, December 16, 1968, 1D; Bisher, *Atlanta Falcons*, 46, 51–52, 75; Schaeffer and Davidson, *Economic Impact of Falcons, 1973*, 6; "Atlanta Falcons, Pre-Season Prospectus 1969," AFF, Football HOF; "1972 Atlanta Falcons, Pre-Season Prospectus," AFF, Football HOF.

26. Roy Blount, "A New Slant on an Old Game in ATL," *Sports Illustrated*, September 1, 1969, 34.

9. Atlanta Stadium, Center of Gravity

1. "A Spectacular Weekend," *Atlanta Journal*, April 9, 1965, 18.

2. William Leggett, "Atlanta You Can Have the Rest, Leave Us Eddie Mathews Our Hero," *Sports Illustrated*, April 26, 1965, 24–25.

3. Hal Hayes, "It's Play Ball in New Stadium," *Atlanta Constitution*, April 9, 1965, 1, 17; Hal Hayes, "Sanders on Mound, Mayor 1st Hitter for Opening," *Atlanta Constitution*, April 9, 1965, 53; "Braves Win in Atlanta's New Stadium," *Chicago Tribune*, April 10, 1965, C3; Joel Gross, email message to author, August 15, 2013.

4. John Pennington, "Happy Atlantans Welcome Braves," *Atlanta Journal*, April 9, 1965, 1, 6; Leggett, "Atlanta You Can Have the Rest," 24–25.

5. Leggett, "Atlanta You Can Have the Rest," 24–25; "60,000 Fans Greet Braves in Atlanta," *Washington Post*, April 10, 1965, 43.

6. Furman Bisher, "A Snow Job, or, It Was Love at First Sight," *Atlanta Journal*, April 10, 1965, 6.

7. Jesse Outlar, "This Is Atlanta Stadium's Debut," *Atlanta Constitution*, April 10, 1965, 15; John Pennington, "Happy Atlantans Welcome Braves," *Atlanta Journal*, April 9, 1965, 1, 6.

8. Lee Walburn, "'Atlanta' Braves Due for Stadium Inaugural," *Atlanta Journal*, April 8, 1965, 1.

9. Jesse Outlar, "Braves, Stadium: Plenty to Cheer About," *Atlanta Constitution*, April 13, 1965, 12; Harry Murphy, "Victory Christens Atlanta's Stadium," *Atlanta Journal*, April 10, 1965, 1.

10. Pennington, "Happy Atlantans Welcome Braves," 1, 6; Bisher, *Miracle in Atlanta*, 2; Joe Strauss, "Braves and Stadium Starred 25 Years Ago," *Atlanta Journal-Constitution*, April 13, 1991, 8.

11. Murphy, "Victory Christens Atlanta's Stadium," 1.

12. "37,232 Watch Braves Cage Tigers, 6–3, in Rousing Debut of Stadium," *Atlanta Constitution*, April 10, 1965, 1, 16; "Braves Win in Atlanta's New Stadium," *Chicago Tribune*, April 10, 1965, C3.

13. Huber and Saladino, *Babes of Winter*, 21.

14. Stone, *Regime Politics*, 67–75.

15. Pomerantz, *Where Peachtree Meets Sweet Auburn*, 340.

16. Donald Sabath, "Atlanta: City Renaissance at Its Best," *Cleveland Plain Dealer*, May 15, 1966, 32.

17. Jay Jenkins, "And Everybody Was Having a Ball," *Atlanta Constitution*, April 10, 1965, 16; Robert E. Baker, "Atlanta Busy Polishing Blurred Racial Image," *Washington Post*, March 1, 1964, E3.

18. Furman Bisher, "Great Night, Weak Plot," *Atlanta Sunday Journal-Constitution*, April 11, 1965, 51.

19. Leggett, "Atlanta You Can Have the Rest," 24; Bisher, *Miracle in Atlanta*, 3.

20. Bill Clark, "Cline's 9th Inning Dash Gives Braves the Sweep," *Atlanta Constitution*, April 12, 1965, 16; Leggett, "Atlanta You Can Have the Rest," April 26, 1965, 24–26; "Braves Sweep Series in Atlanta," *Atlanta Journal*, April 11, 1965, 14; Jesse Outlar, "Team Scores a Victory," *Atlanta Constitution*, April 16, 1965, 16; "Braves Boom . . . But Gate is Poorest Ever," *Atlanta Constitution*, April 28, 1965, 35; Jesse Outlar, "No Boos, No Pickets . . . Just a Rebel Flag, Cheers," *Atlanta Constitution*, April 16, 1965, 16.

21. Bragan and Guinn, *You Can't Hit the Ball*, 316.

22. Jim Minter, in phone discussion with the author, July 9, 2013.

23. Rutheiser, *Imagineering Atlanta*, 156.

24. Kruse, *White Flight*, 248; Whitelegg, "Battle on Two Fronts," 129–32; "Racial Roadblock Seen in Atlanta Transit System," *New York Times*, July 22, 1987, 48; Ken Wills, "Cobb is Debating MARTA Proposal," *Atlanta Constitution*, June 27, 1980, 1C.

25. "Sound Off: Falcons Attendance," *Atlanta Journal-Constitution*, October 1, 2000, 4D.

26. David Pendered, "Plans to Nowhere," *Atlanta Journal-Constitution*, May 24, 2004, 1E; Whitelegg, "Battle on Two Fronts," 130–31.

27. John Brady, "MARTA's Drive to Cut Parking Lot Vandalism Paying Off," *Atlanta Constitution*, July 5, 1984, 23A; Sharon Bailey, "MARTA Keeps TV 'Eyes' Open for Crime in the Station," *Atlanta Constitution*, March 27, 1980, 1C; "Graffiti and Vandals' Attacks Rub Gloss off Atlanta Transit," *New York Times*, November 8, 1985, 22; "Crime Reports Spoil Atlanta's Pride in Rapid Transit System," *New York Times*, May 22, 1986, 8.

28. "Baseball 1967," *Atlanta Journal*, April 10, 1967, 4B; "What the Braves Fans Spent," *Atlanta Constitution*, November 14, 1966, 4; Wilt Browning, "Braves Pad Atlanta's Purse with $30 Million," *Atlanta Journal*, November 8, 1966, 44; Jim Minter, "America Watches Atlanta in Its Moment of Glory," *Atlanta Journal*, April 13, 1966, 74.

29. Murphy, "Victory Christens Atlanta's Stadium," 1; Bisher, *Miracle in Atlanta*, 2; Strauss, "Braves and Stadium Starred," 8; "37,232 Watch Braves Cage Tigers, 6–3," 1, 16.

30. "What the Braves Fans Spent," *Atlanta Constitution*, November 14, 1966, 4; Carole Ashkinaze, "The State of the Stadium," *Atlanta Journal*, August 13, 1978. 1.

31. "Atlanta Falcons Pre-Season Prospectus 1969," AFF, Football HOF; "Falcon Facts: January 1971," AFF, Football HOF.

32. Schaeffer and Davidson, *Economic Impact of Falcons, 1973*, 7.

33. "Market Operations Research: The Demographic Characteristics of People Who Ride Buses to Atlanta Falcons Games," 1968, AFF, Football HOF.

34. Schaeffer and Davidson, *Economic Impact of Falcons, 1973*, 7–10; Schaeffer and Davidson, *Economic Impact of Falcons, 1984*, 1–6, 9–12; "Sound Off: Falcons Attendance," 4D.

35. "Atlanta No Windfall for Sports Ventures," UPI *Report*, June 7, 1968, AFCSSF, folder 1, Kenan Library.

36. Bill Blodgett, "Panch, Foyt Share 'Wheels' in Speeding to '500' Victory," *Atlanta Constitution*, April 12, 1965, 11; Bisher, *Miracle in Atlanta*, 4; Furman Bisher, "Love at First Sight for Braves in Dixie," *Sporting News*, April 24, 1965, 7; Jesse Outlar, "The Sport State," *Atlanta Constitution*, April 13, 1965, 18.

37. Jim Minter, in phone discussion with the author, July 9, 2013.

38. Jesse Outlar, "Lost Tribe," *Atlanta Constitution*, September, 15, 1967, 1D.

39. Roy M. Blount, "Losersville, U.S.A.," *Sports Illustrated*, March 21, 1977, 85.

40. Beau Cutts, "The Grass Is Greener in the Suburbs," *Atlanta Constitution*, April 29, 1980, 1B; B. Drummond Ayres, "What's Doing in Atlanta," *New York Times*, July 24, 1977, 27; "Atlanta: More than a City to Just Pass Through," *Washington Post*, February 6, 1972, H8.

41. Dick Grey, "Forget the Tube, Braves Are Here," *Atlanta Journal*, April 12, 1966, 56; "Braves to Get $2.5 Million," *Atlanta Constitution*, February 4, 1966, 14; *Pow-Wow*, October 1971, ABF, Baseball HOF; Charlie Roberts, "Image Boost Aim— McHale," *Atlanta Constitution*, December 2, 1965, 53.

42. Wayne Minshew, "Braves' Telecasts Earn No. 1 Rating in Southeast," *Sporting News*, February 5, 1972, 45.

43. "Club by Club Air Income," *Sporting News*, March 24, 1973, 42; Kinlaw, "Franchise Transfer."

44. Johnson, "Congress and Professional Sports," 113–14.

45. Minshew, "Braves' Telecasts Earn No. 1," 45.

46. Schaeffer and Davidson, *Economic Impact of Falcons, 1973*, 4, 15; "Falcons 1972 Media Guide," AFF, Football HOF; "Atlanta Falcons Pre-Season Prospectus 1969," AFF, Football HOF.

47. Aaron and Wheeler, *I Had a Hammer*, 186.

48. Tommy Nobis, in phone discussion with the author, July 22, 2013; Jack Wilkinson, "Goodbye Atlanta–Fulton County Stadium," *Atlanta Journal-Constitution*, September 15, 1996, 13E; Ron Reed, in phone discussion with the author, July 8, 2013; Lou Kirouac, in phone discussion with the author, August 13, 2013; Jeff Schulz, "Final Home Opener at Stadium Brings Falcons Memories," *Atlanta Journal-Constitution*, September 7, 1991, D3.

49. Vance Law, email message to author, March 10, 2019.

50. Wilkinson, "Goodbye Atlanta–Fulton County Stadium," 13E.

51. Reed, in phone discussion with the author.

52. Bud Shaw, "The Dinosaur on Capitol Avenue," *Atlanta Journal-Constitution*, May 26, 1984, 1C.

53. "The Fans Remember," *Atlanta Journal-Constitution*, September 16, 1996, 1D.

54. Ashkinaze, "State of the Stadium," B1; Karl Green, in phone conversation with the author, August 16, 2013.

55. John Logue, "Football in the Round," *Atlanta Sunday Journal-Constitution*, September 4, 1966, 16; "Falcon Facts: January 1971," AFF, Football HOF.

56. "Bright, Colorful Ballpark," *Sporting News*, April 3, 1965, 44; Johnny Tallant, in phone conversation with the author, August 18, 2013.

57. Green, in phone discussion with the author.

58. Milo Hamilton, in phone discussion with the author, July 11, 2013.

59. Green, in phone discussion with the author.

60. Frank Hyland, "It's a Whole New Ball Game," *Atlanta Journal*, March 28, 1972, 2D.

61. Ashkinaze, "State of the Stadium," B1.

10. Outside the Stadium It's the City

1. "Hotels Near Stadium," *Atlanta Constitution*, March 18, 1967, 4.

2. Rutheiser, *Imagineering Atlanta*, 160.

3. Rutheiser, *Imagineering Atlanta*, 153–54; Bayor, "Civil Rights Movement," 301; Wayne Kelley, "Summerhill Was Likely Spot for Trouble When It Came," *Atlanta Journal*, September 7, 1966, 18; Pomerantz, *Where Peachtree Meets Sweet Auburn*, 344–50.

4. "15 Injured as Hundreds of Negroes Riot, Toss Rocks at Police, Smash Cars Here," *Atlanta Constitution*, September 7, 1966, 1, 12; Tom Dunkin, "Allen and Jenkins Blame SNCC," *Atlanta Journal*, September 7, 1966, 1, 16; Orville Gaines and Raleigh Bryans, "2 Officials Pledge to Take Firm Action," *Atlanta Journal*, September 7, 1966, 1, 16; Paul Hemphill, "Pop Bottles, Bricks Fly in Troubled Area Here," *Atlanta Journal*, September 7, 1966, 1, 16; Pomerantz, *Where Peachtree Meets Sweet Auburn*, 344–50; Stone, *Regime Politics*, 61–73.

5. "15 Injured as Hundreds of Negroes Riot," 1, 12; "Atlanta Arrest Sets Off Riot," *Boston Globe*, September 7, 1966, 1; Pomerantz, *Where Peachtree Meets Sweet Auburn*, 344–50; Hemphill, "Pop Bottles, Bricks Fly," 1, 16; Reese Cleghorn, "Allen of Atlanta Collides with Black Power and White Racism," *New York Times*, October 16, 1966, 251; Dick Hebert, "In the Middle of Mob—The Mayor," *Atlanta Constitution*, September 7, 1966, 1.

6. Bill Winn, "'You Should've Seen It, Man . . . It Was a Bad Scene,'" *Atlanta Journal*, September 7, 1966, 13; "15 Injured as Hundreds of Negroes Riot," 1, 12; Dick Hebert, "In the Middle of Mob," 1; "Defendants in Riot Cases Fined in Municipal Court," *Atlanta Journal*, September 7, 1966, 1; Pomerantz, *Where Peachtree Meets Sweet Auburn*, 344–50; Stone, *Regime Politics*, 61–73; "Carmichael May Face Insurrection Charge," *Atlanta Journal*, September 8, 1966, 1, 8; Keeler McCartney, "Carmichael Arrested on Riot Charges in Raid on Snick Office," *Atlanta Constitution*, September 9, 1966, 1.

7. Don Winter, "Boulevard Riot Area Opened for Traffic," *Atlanta Journal*, September 12, 1966, 1, 10; Orville Gaines, "Gunshot Survivor Picks Out Photo," *Atlanta Journal*, September 14, 1966, 1; Orville Gaines, "Couple Held Here in Boulevard Death," *Atlanta Journal*, September 13, 1966, 1; "Fire Bombs Exploded in Boulevard Violence," *Atlanta Constitution*, September 12, 1966, 1, 7; Stone, *Regime Politics*, 61–73.

8. Duane Riner, "Would Have Prevented Riots Here, Maddox Says," *Atlanta Constitution*, September 23, 1966, 1, 14.

9. Pomerantz, *Where Peachtree Meets Sweet Auburn*, 350; Bill Winn, "Profiles of Top Democratic Candidates," *Atlanta Sunday Journal-Constitution*, September 18, 1966, 6; Ann Carter, "Arnall at Shopping Center for Round of Handshakes," *Atlanta Journal*, September 2, 1966, 1.

10. Sam Hopkins, "Maddox Preaching Fear, Extremism, Arnall Says," *Atlanta Constitution*, September 22, 1966, 1; William O. Smith, "Arnall Labels Foe Radical Extremist," *Atlanta Journal*, September 20, 1966, 1.

11. "Arnall: Could Lose if Turnout's Small," *Atlanta Constitution*, September 23, 1966, 1.

12. Charles Pou, "Callaway Opens Drive to Be GOP Governor," *Atlanta Journal*, September 30, 1966, 1; William O. Smith, "Maddox Vows to Ax Guides," *Atlanta Journal*, September 30, 1966, 1; Charles Pou, "Runoff Winner Maddox," *Atlanta Journal*, September 29, 1966, 1; William O. Smith, "Arnall, Maddox Both Predict Runoff Victory," September 16, 1966, 1; William O. Smith, "Callaway to Start with Parade Here," *Atlanta Journal*, September 17, 1966, 1; Charles Pou, "Maddox Asks Arnall to Quit for Party Unity," *Atlanta Constitution*, September 18, 1966, 1.

13. Jack Bell, "Record Vote Is Indicated with Early Turnout Here," *Atlanta Journal*, November 8, 1966, 1; Wayne Kelley, "Supreme Court Upholds Right of Assembly to Elect Governor," *Atlanta Journal*, December 12, 1966, 1; "Assembly Can't Pick Governor, U.S. Court Opens Way to Runoff," *Atlanta Constitution*, November 12, 1966, 1; Charles Pou, "Maddox Officially Takes Office; Vows No Place for Extremism," *Atlanta Journal*, January 11, 1967, 1; Kruse, *White Flight*, 251–52; Sam Hopkins, "City Vote Piles Up for GOP," *Atlanta Constitution*, November 9, 1966, 1.

14. Joe Brown and Duane Riner, "Negro Killed, 3 Shot in Dixie Hills; Mayor Declares Emergency," *Atlanta Constitution*, June 21, 1967, 1, 8; Joe Brown and Duane Riner, "Dixie Hills Quiet under Late Curfew," *Atlanta Constitution*, June 22, 1967, 1, 17; "Mob in Atlanta Stone Police after Speech by Carmichael," *Cleveland Press*, June 20, 1967, 1; Don Winter and David Nordan, "Rocks, Bottles Fly at Policemen Here," *Atlanta Journal*, June 22, 1967, 1; Stone, *Regime Politics*, 61–73.

15. Keeler McCartney, "Violence at Stadium Brings Warnings," *Atlanta Constitution*, December 2, 1970, 6A; Bill Montgomery, "Police Step Up Stadium Force," *Atlanta Journal*, August 22, 1979, C1, C6; Sam Hopkins and Barry Henderson, "Foot Patrol at Stadium Is Ordered," *Atlanta Constitution*, October 9, 1973, 1A, 15A; Tom Henderson and Art Harris, "Fence Studied for Stadium Parking Lots," *Atlanta Constitution*, October 15, 1973, 1A, 2A; Headley, *Atlanta Youth Murders*, 59.

16. Hope, *We Could've Finished Last without You*, 82.

17. Bill Montgomery, "Police Step Up Stadium Force," *Atlanta Journal*, August 22, 1979, C1, C6; "Metropolitan Atlanta Crime Commission: 1975–1979," MACCP, Kenan Library.

18. Keeler McCartney, "Violence at Stadium Brings Warnings," *Atlanta Constitution*, December 2, 1970, 6A.

19. Wayne Minshew, in phone discussion with the author, July 1, 2013.

20. "37,232 Watch Braves Cage Tigers, 6–3," *Atlanta Constitution*, April 10, 1965, 1, 16.

21. Minshew, in phone discussion with the author.

22. Alan Morris, email message to author, August 13, 2013.

23. Karl Green, in phone discussion with the author, August 13, 2013.

24. Jim Minter, in phone discussion with the author, July 9, 2013.

25. Jesse Outlar, "The Non-Spectaculars," *Atlanta Constitution*, October 8, 1973, 1D.

26. Jim Gray, "Jury Deadlock Brings Outlar Case Mistrial," *Atlanta Constitution*, March 15, 1974, 6A; "Youth Is Suspected in Atlanta in Sports Editor's Shooting," *New York Times*, October 9, 1973, 34.

27. Barry Henderson, "Jesse Outlar Wounded by Gunman at Stadium," *Atlanta Constitution*, October 8, 1973, 1A, 12A.

28. Sam Hopkins and Barry Henderson, "Foot Patrol at Stadium Is Ordered," *Atlanta Constitution*, October 9, 1973, 1A, 15A; "Youth Charged with Shooting Sports Editor," *Atlanta Daily World*, October 17, 1973, 1; Orville Gaines, "Outlar Wounded, Gunman Hunted," *Atlanta Journal*, October 8, 1973, 1A, 6A; Jim Gray, "I Cannot Identify Suspect, Outlar Says," *Atlanta Constitution*, March 15, 1974, 6A.

29. Gray, "I Cannot Identify Suspect," 6A; Jim Gray, "Jury Deadlock," 6A; "Outlar Rules Out Youth as Suspect," *Atlanta Journal*, October 9, 1973, 1A.

30. Gray, "I Cannot Identify Suspect," 6A; Gray, "Jury Deadlock," 6A.

31. "A Brutal Assault," *Atlanta Journal*, October 9, 1973, 14A.

32. "Stadium Violence," *Atlanta Constitution*, October 9, 1973, 4.

33. Reg Murphy, "Who's Ready to Stop the Violence?" *Atlanta Constitution*, October 9, 1973, 4A.

34. Joe Ledlie, "Jackson Says Massell Allowed Outlar Attack," *Atlanta Journal*, October 8, 1973, 1; "Stadium Crime," *Atlanta Journal*, October 10, 1973, 4A.

35. Gaines, "Outlar Wounded, Gunman Hunted," 1A, 6A; Hopkins and Henderson, "Foot Patrol at Stadium Is Ordered," 1A, 15A; Sam Hopkins, "Stadium Crime Curbs Expected," *Atlanta Constitution*, October 12, 1973, 8A; Tom Henderson and Art Harris, "Fence Studied for Stadium Parking Lots," *Atlanta Constitution*, October 15, 1973, 1A, 2A.

36. Henderson and Harris, "Fence Studied," 1A, 2A.

37. Minter, in phone discussion with the author.

38. Henderson, "Jesse Outlar Wounded," 1A, 12A.

39. Charlie Roberts, "Braves Have the Latin Look," *Atlanta Journal-Constitution*, April 6, 1969, 1D.

40. Wayne Minshew, "Atlantans Up in Arms at Carty Snub," *Sporting News*, May 30, 1970, 12; Aaron and Bisher, *Aaron*, 199; Wayne Minshew, "Carty Buys 25 Pairs at a Clip," *Sporting News*, July 22, 1967, 20.

41. "Carty: Beating Caused Eye Damage," *Chicago Tribune*, August 27, 1971, c6; Hugh Nations, "Jury to Hear Carty Affair," *Atlanta Journal*, August 28, 1971, 1; Aaron and Bisher, *Aaron*, 199, 210–11; "Highlight," *Sports Illustrated*, July 3,

1967, 12; Hamilton, *Making Airwaves*, 142–43; Aaron and Wheeler, *I Had a Hammer*, 185, 215.

42. Alex Coffin and Sam Hopkins, "3 Policemen Suspended in Carty Fight," *Atlanta Constitution*, August 26, 1971, 1; "Free Rico in Assault," *Chicago Defender*, September 25, 1971, 41; "Atlanta Suspends Police in Carty Case," *Boston Globe*, August 26, 1971, 40; Nations, "Jury to Hear Carty Affair," 1; Alex Coffin, "Chief Raps 3 Policemen," *Atlanta Constitution*, August 27, 1971, 1.

43. Coffin, "Chief Raps 3 Policemen," 1.

44. "3 Cops Fired in Beating of Carty," *Chicago Defender*, September 4, 1971, 1.

11. Atlanta Stadium, a Meeting Place

1. "A Spectacular Weekend," *Atlanta Journal*, April 9, 1965, 18.

2. "Atlanta Asks for Superbowl," *Washington Post*, November 24, 1966, M4.

3. "Peach Bowl for Atlanta?" *Atlanta Constitution*, December 11, 1966, 4; Jack Williams, "Stadium Sure to Get '65 Exhibition Games; Football Bowl Studied," *Atlanta Constitution*, November 10, 1964, 1; Gordon S. White, "Network Urges Atlanta Contest," *New York Times*, January 12, 1965, 43; Bill Clark, "ABC Network Enters Atlanta Bowl Picture," *Atlanta Constitution*, January 13, 1965, 32; Mickey McCarthy, "CBS Eyes Atlanta Stadium for Santa Claus Bowl Site," *Atlanta Constitution*, January 11, 1965, 11.

4. White, "Network Urges Atlanta Contest," 43.

5. McCarthy, "CBS Eyes Atlanta Stadium," 11; "Proposed Santa Claus Bowl Faces Lengthy NCAA Study," *Atlanta Constitution*, January 12, 1965, 12; Cooper Rollow, "NCAA Defers Bowl Application by CBS," *Chicago Tribune*, January 12, 1965, B1.

6. "All-American Football Game Shifts to Atlanta in 1966," *New York Times*, September 2, 1965, 26; Ford, "Coaches' All-America Game," 15–18.

7. "Lions Approve Bowl Project," *Atlanta Journal*, June 14, 1965, 18; Wayne Minshew, "No Ruling on Atlanta Bowl Expected until Next Year," *Atlanta Constitution*, January 6, 1966, 43.

8. David Davidson, "The State of the Peach," *Atlanta Sunday Journal-Constitution*, January 2, 1977, 2D; Gary Stokan, in phone discussion with the author, July 10, 2013; Jim Minter, in phone discussion with the author, July 9, 2013; "Lions Approve Bowl Project," 18; "New Yorker Reveals Plans for Bowl Game in Atlanta," *Atlanta Journal*, June 8, 1965, 20; Minshew, "No Ruling on Atlanta Bowl Expected," 43.

9. "Sports Stars, Pastor Speak Easter at Atlanta Stadium," *Atlanta Constitution*, February 12, 1966, 6; Margaret Hurst, "18,000 at Stadium Hail Resurrection," *Atlanta Constitution*, April 11, 1966, 1, 9.

10. "Beatles Perform in Atlanta," *New York Times*, August 19, 1965, 36; Dick Gray, "The Scream—One Gigantic Shriek," *Atlanta Journal*, August 19, 1965, 1, 12, 19; Walker Lundy, "1st Beatle Fans Arrive at 4 a.m.," *Atlanta Journal*, August 18, 1965, 1, 12; "Memories Are Safe at Home in the Heart," *Atlanta Journal-Constitution*, October 27, 1996, 9J; Dick Bowman, "Congratulations Atlanta!" *San Diego Union*, October 10, 1965, 1C.

11. Setlist, s.v. "Atlanta Stadium," last modified March 17, 2013, https://www.setlist.fm/search?query=atlanta+stadium; Patrick Edmondson, "Cosmic Carnival 1970," The Strip Project, February 13, 2014, http://www.thestripproject.com/cosmic-carnival-1970/.

12. Wayne Kelley, "Thousands Gather for Viet Rally Here," *Atlanta Journal*, February 12, 1966, 1, 8.

13. John Askins, "50,000 Seen Backing War," *Atlanta Journal*, February 11, 1966, 1, 8.

14. Kelley, "Thousands Gather," 1, 8; "50,000 Expected in Atlanta to Back War Policy Today," *New York Times*, February 12, 1966, 10; Gene Roberts, "10,000 Rally in Atlanta to Back Vietnam Policy," *New York Times*, February 13, 1966, 2.

15. Askins, "50,000 Seen Backing War," 1, 8; Kelley, "Thousands Gather," 1, 8; "Viet Nam Rally to Pack City's Stadium Today," *Atlanta Constitution*, February 12, 1966, 1; "Plan 'Affirmation: Viet Nam' Rally in Atlanta," *Chicago Tribune*, January 30, 1966, 2.

16. Askins, "50,000 Seen Backing War," 1, 8; Kelley, "Thousands Gather," 1, 8; John Askins, "15,000 Wet Georgians Affirm Viet Nam Policy," *Atlanta Journal*, February 13, 1966, 1, 18, 24.

17. S. Miller, *Billy Graham and Rise*, 167–73; "Atlanta '73," BGSF, Kenan Library; Gayle C. White, "Billy Graham Crusades," New Georgia Encyclopedia, October 4, 2013, https://www.georgiaencyclopedia.org/articles/arts-culture/billy-graham-crusades.

18. S. Miller, *Billy Graham and Rise*, 172–73.

12. Madison Square Garden of the Southeast

1. Walter Woods, "Tom Cousins: Atlanta Power Player Retires," *Atlanta Journal-Constitution*, December 7, 2006, 1B.

2. Huber and Saladino, *Babes of Winter*, 13.

3. Rutheiser, *Imagineering Atlanta*, 164; Tom Walker, "Omni Complex to Help City's Global Look," *Atlanta Journal*, October 11, 1972, 1A, 9A; Bob Hertzel, "Study Shows Atlanta Wants Arena," *Atlanta Journal*, May 7, 1968, 4D.

4. "Atlanta Hawks Give City Third Big-Time Sport," *Sporting News*, May 18, 1968, 42; "St. Louis Hawks Sold to a Group in Atlanta," *New York Times*, May 4, 1968, 52; Mickey McCarthy, "Hawk Sale Approved," *Atlanta Constitution*, May 8, 1968, 51; *Omni Souvenir Dedication Book*, OSF, Kenan Library.

5. Furman Bisher, "Hawks: 'Stolen' from Milwaukee," *Atlanta Journal*, May 7, 1968, 1D.

6. Jim Minter, "NBA Expected to Approve Hawks' Move," *Atlanta Sunday Journal-Constitution*, May 5, 1968, 1H; Digital Library of Georgia, *Interview with Hawks Coach*.

7. Jim Minter, "Tommy Cousins Plans New Roost for Hawks," *Atlanta Journal*, May 4, 1968, 1B.

8. Denberg, Lazenby, and Stinson, *From Sweet Lou to 'Nique*, 31; "Atlanta's Hawks Covet New Coliseum," *Washington Post*, May 7, 1968, D5.

9. Bill Clark, "Atlanta Gets Profesional Basketball," *Atlanta Constitution*, May 4, 1968, 1, 16; Furman Bisher, "Atlanta Hawks for Sale to Right Party," *Atlanta Journal*, May 6, 1968, 1C; "Atlanta's Hawks Covet New Coliseum," D5.

10. Minter, "NBA Expected to Approve Hawks' Move," 1H.

11. Bill Clark, "'Tech Gave Us Chance to Land a Winner'—Cousins," *Atlanta Constitution*, May 4, 1968, 17.

12. "Atlanta's Hawks Covet New Coliseum," D5.

13. Minter, "NBA Expected to Approve Hawks' Move," 1H; Al Thomy, "Young Lions Bought Hawks Because City Deserved 'Em," *Sporting News*, June 1, 1968, 46.

14. WSB-TV, *Interview with Hawks Coach*.

15. Rosen, *First Tip-Off*, 11–36; Denberg, Lazenby, and Stinson, *From Sweet Lou to 'Nique*, 17–19; "Pro Basketball Era Ends with Kerner," *Sporting News*, January 21, 1967, 12.

16. Denberg, Lazenby, and Stinson, *From Sweet Lou to 'Nique*, 17–19.

17. "Milwaukee's Pro Basket Club for Sale," *Chicago Tribune*, February 21, 1954, A2.

18. Denberg, Lazenby, and Stinson, *From Sweet Lou to 'Nique*, 17–19.

19. Bob Burnes, "Bob Pettit: NBA Answer to Musial," *Sporting News*, February 15, 1964, 31; "Pettit Leaving Super-Star Imprint on NBA," *Sporting News*, March 13, 1965, 32; Denberg, Lezenby, and Stinson, *From Sweet Lou to 'Nique*, 22–26; Bernie Miklasz, "Pettit Is One of St. Louis' Biggest Sports Stars," *St. Louis Post-Dispatch*, May 22, 2004, 3.

20. Maracek, *Full Court*, 59–61, 194–195; "Pro Basketball Era Ends with Kerner," 12; Keith Schildroth, "Friends Remember Kerner as a 'Pioneer,'" *St. Louis Post-Dispatch*, November 26, 2000, F7; "Celtics Pelted with Eggs in Loss to Hawks," *Washington Post*, December 29, 1960, D2; "Fans Listen to Auerbach, Throw Eggs," *Washington Post*, January 29, 1959, D3; Milton Gross, "Bigots Insulted Russell's Kids," *Boston Globe*, February 24, 1966, 51.

21. Tom Wheatley, "Hawks Recall Their Big Championship Moment," *St. Louis Post-Dispatch*, January 19, 1998, C5.

22. Bernie Miklasz, "NBA's Boom Still a Bust in St. Louis," *St. Louis Post-Dispatch*, July 1, 1990, 1F.

23. Lowell Reidenbaugh, "Kerner Cashing In as Promotion King," *Sporting News*, March 23, 1960, 1, 2.

24. Denberg, Lazemby, and Stinson, *From Sweet Lou to 'Nique*, 24–26; Kriegel, *Pistol*, 185–89.

25. Darrell Simmons, "Fan Interest Makes Hawks Fly," *Atlanta Journal*, May 17, 1968, 4D; Denberg, Lazemby, and Stinson, *From Sweet Lou to 'Nique*, 24–26; "Hawks Dropping Memphis Games," *St. Louis Post-Dispatch*, April 24, 1967, 3C.

26. Simmons, "Fan Interest Makes Hawks Fly," 4D; Kriegel, *Pistol*, 185–89.

27. Maracek, *Full Court*, 152–53; Simmons, "Fan Interest Makes Hawks Fly," 4D; Kriegel, *Pistol*, 185–89.

28. Maracek, *Full Court*, 152–53; Bob Broeg, "Hawks' Bubble Burst in Inflated Sports Market Here," *St. Louis Post-Dispatch*, May 5, 1968, 2C.

29. Wally Cross, "The Bashing Sport," *St. Louis Post-Dispatch*, October 8, 1967, 3; Dan O'Neill, "Years of Change: Colorful History: Stillman's Group Will Be Eighth to Own the Blues," *St. Louis Post-Dispatch*, May 10, 2012, C1; Bob Burnes, "In Brighter Days, Blues Hockey Was a Social Symbol," *St. Louis Globe-Democrat*, January 13, 1983, 6B; Simmons, "Fan Interest Makes Hawks Fly," 4D.

30. Burnes, "In Brighter Days," 6B; Maracek, *Full Court*, 199–200; Richard Caldwell, email message to author, October 27, 2011.

31. Burnes, "In Brighter Days," 6B; Archibald, "Guerin's Always the Boss," 4H; Simmons, "Fan Interest Makes Hawks Fly," 4D; Kriegel, *Pistol*, 185–89.

32. Simmons, "Fan Interest Makes Hawks Fly," 4D; Reidenbaugh, "Kerner Cashing In," 1, 2; "Pro Basketball Era Ends with Kerner," 12.

33. "Hawks Not for Sale, Kerner Says," *Chicago Tribune*, February 2, 1967, E5; "Put Hawks Up for Sale in St. Louis," *Chicago Tribune*, January 4, 1967, C3; "3 Groups Bidding for NBA Club," *Chicago Tribune*, January 5, 1967, E4; "Schoenwald Group May Go After Hawks," *Chicago Tribune*, January 6, 1967, C6; "Hawk Flip-Flop Takes Heavy Toll on Ben's Health," *Sporting News*, February 21, 1962, 2; Maracek, *Full Court*, 207–13; Broeg, "Hawks' Bubble Burst," 2C; "Pro Basketball Era Ends with Kerner," 12.

34. "Hawks Need New Arena, Owner Says," *Washington Post*, August 18, 1966, C2; "Ben Kerner Hopeful of New Arena," *Washington Post*, February 9, 1968, D3.

35. Frank Deford, "Fast Start for Ben's Hawks," *Sports Illustrated*, November 13, 1967, 24.

36. "Ben Kerner Hopeful of New Arena," D3.

37. Broeg, "Hawks' Bubble Burst," 2C.

38. Bob Burnes, "Hawks Sold, Will Move to Atlanta," pts. 1 and 2, *St. Louis Globe-Democrat*, May 4, 1968, 1G; May 5, 1968, 7G.

39. Jeremy Rutherford, "Departure of Hawks Still Is Bittersweet Affair," *St. Louis Post-Dispatch*, September 26, 1999, D16.

40. Kriegel, *Pistol*, 185–89; Archibald, "Guerin's Always the Boss," 4H.

41. Ron Jacober, in phone discussion with the author, June 13, 2013.

42. Gross, "Bigots Insulted Russell's Kids," 51.

43. John J. Archibald, "Hawks Play 'Inside' Game to Earn Aggressive Label," *Atlanta Sunday Journal-Constitution*, May 5, 1968, 3H.

44. Frank Deford, "Fast Start for Ben's Hawks," *Sports Illustrated*, November 13, 1967, 24.

45. Maracek, *Full Court*, 204–6; Archibald, "Guerin's Always the Boss," 4H.

46. Halberstam, *Breaks of the Game*, 35–36.

47. Golenbock, *Spirit of St. Louis*, 464–502; William Leggett, "Speed Won the Series," *Sports Illustrated*, October 26, 1964, 10. "Story of 1967 Cardinal Pennant in a Word: Balance," *St. Louis Post-Dispatch*, October 1, 1967, 12J.

48. Maracek, *Full Court*, 214; Bob Hertzel, "Hawks Purchase: 'Now or Never,'" *Atlanta Journal*, May 6, 1968, 1C.

49. Hertzel, "Hawks Purchase," 1C; WSB-TV, *Interview with Hawks Coach*.

50. Hertzel, "Hawks Purchase," 1C; Bill Clark, "Will NBA Come Here?" *Atlanta Constitution*, March 9, 1967, 33.

51. WSB-TV, *Interview with Hawks Coach*; Bill Clark, "Will NBA Come Here?" *The Atlanta Constitution*, March 9, 1967, 33.

52. Furman Bisher, "Hawks: 'Stolen' from Milwaukee," *Atlanta Journal*, May 7, 1968, 1D.

53. Bisher, "Hawks: 'Stolen' from Milwaukee," 1D.

54. Minter, "NBA Expected to Approve Hawks' Move," 1H.

55. Bisher, "Atlanta Hawks for Sale," 1C.

56. Minter, "NBA Expected to Approve Hawks' Move," 1H; Bill Clark, "Atlanta Gets Professional Basketball," *Atlanta Constitution*, May 4, 1968, 1, 16; Furman Bisher, "Hawks Approval Certain," *Atlanta Journal*, May 7, 1968, 1D; Bob Hertzel, "Regents Approve Hawks Use of Tech," *Atlanta Journal*, May 8, 1968, 1D.

13. The Developer Is Boss

1. Bob Hertzel, "Study Shows Atlanta Wants Arena," *Atlanta Journal*, May 7, 1968, 4D.

2. Denberg, Lazenby, and Stinson, *From Sweet Lou to 'Nique*, 31.

3. Denberg, Lazenby, and Stinson, *From Sweet Lou to 'Nique*, 30.

4. "Atlanta Aims for Arena, Pro Hockey," *Washington Post*, May 14, 1968, D2; Alex Coffin, "Coliseum Deal's 'Pluses' Outlined," *Atlanta Constitution*, December 15, 1970, 2.

5. Sam Hopkins and Alex Coffin, "Top Atlanta Leaders Urge Coliseum Okay," *Atlanta Constitution*, December 15, 1970, 1.

6. Huber and Saladino, *Babes of Winter*, 16.

7. Digital Library of Georgia, WSB-TV *News Clip of Mayor Allen*.

8. "Chronological History: Sam Massell," SMPF, Kenan Library; "Sam Massell 1969 Campaign Ephemera," SMPF, Kenan Library; "Massell 6th Man in Mayoralty Race," *Atlanta Journal*, June 17, 1969, 1; Jon Nordheimer, "Massell Elected Atlanta Mayor," *New York Times*, October 22, 1969, 1.

9. Bill Shipp, "Cook, Massell Head for Runoff," *Atlanta Constitution*, October 8, 1969, 1; Alex Coffin, "Massell Charges Plot to 5," *Atlanta Constitution*, October 21, 1969, 1A, 8A; Bob Hurt, "Abernathy Assails Allen's Call for Massell Withdrawal," *Atlanta Constitution*, October 21, 1969, 12A; Bruce Galphin, "Mayoral Race Is Splitting Atlanta's Ruling Coalition," *Washington Post*, September 7, 1969, 6; Alex Coffin, "Massell Tangles with Militants," *Atlanta Constitution*, September 15, 1969, 12A.

10. Coffin, "Massell Charges Plot," 1A.

11. Alex Coffin, "Massell Winner with 61,558," *Atlanta Constitution*, October 22, 1969, 1; Bill Shipp, "Reported to Chief—Massell," *Atlanta Constitution*, October 21, 1969, 1.

12. Sam Massell, in phone discussion with the author, July 2, 2013.

13. Coffin, "Coliseum Deal's 'Pluses' Outlined," 2; Massell, in phone discussion with the author; "State of the City Annual Message, January 4, 1971," SMPF, Kenan Library; *Omni Souvenir Dedication Book*, OSF, Kenan Library.

14. Walker, "Omni Complex to Help City's Global Look," 1A, 9A; Richard Miles, "Plan for Coliseum to Face City and County Opposition," *Atlanta Constitution*, December 14, 1970, 1; Massell, in phone discussion with the author.

15. Massell, in phone discussion with the author.

16. Hopkins and Coffin, "Top Atlanta Leaders Urge Coliseum Okay," 1.

17. Hopkins and Coffin, "Top Atlanta Leaders Urge Coliseum Okay," 1; *Omni Souvenir Dedication Book*, OSF, Kenan Library.

18. Miles, "Plan for Coliseum," 1.

19. Ron Taylor and Maurice Fliess, "'Beautifuls' Hail Sold-Out Omni," *Atlanta Sunday Journal-Constitution*, October 15, 1972, 1, 12; Margaret Hurst, "Coliseum Wins County Okay," *Atlanta Constitution*, January 21, 1971, 1A; "State of the City Annual Message, January 4, 1971," SMPF, Kenan Library.

20. Coffin, "Coliseum Deal's 'Pluses' Outlined," 2.

21. Jesse Outlar, "A Timely Social," *Atlanta Constitution*, March 31, 1971, 1D; Alex Coffin, "Massell, Cousins Get Together on Coliseum Event," *Atlanta Constitution*, March 30, 1971, 2A; Alex Coffin, "Massell Plays Ball at Coliseum Site,"

Atlanta Constitution, April 1, 1971, 1A; Jim Stewart, "Omni Doors Open to Atlanta Tonight," *Atlanta Constitution*, October 14, 1972, 1, 12.

22. *Omni Souvenir Dedication Book*, OSF, Kenan Library; Huber and Saladino, *Babes of Winter*, 16–17, 22–23; Frank Wells, "Coliseum Adds to City's Big League Image," *Atlanta Constitution*, January 19, 1973, 12C; Tom Linthicum, "Omni Is Out, It's Atlanta Coliseum," *Atlanta Constitution*, June 9, 1972, 8A.

23. Huber and Saladino, *Babes of Winter*, 24; Robert M. Craig, "Thompson, Ventulett, Stainback, and Associates," New Georgia Encyclopedia, September 19, 2013, https://www.georgiaencyclopedia.org/articles/arts-culture/thompson-ventulett-stainback-and-associates-tvs.

24. "Getting to the Omni is a Lot Easier Done than Said": advertisement, *Atlanta Journal*, October 13, 1972, 10C; *Omni Souvenir Dedication Book*, OSF, Kenan Library.

25. Frank Hyland, "Coliseum Ready in '72?" *Atlanta Sunday Journal-Constitution*, December 13, 1970, 1H; Huber and Saladino, *Babes of Winter*, 24; *Omni Souvenir Dedication Book*, OSF, Kenan Library.

26. Robert M. Craig, "Thompson, Ventulett, Stainback, and Associates" *The New Georgia Encyclopedia*, September 19, 2013; Elizabeth A. Harris, "Constructing a Façade Both Rugged and Rusty," *New York Times*, August 27, 2012; "COR-TEN: Making Its 50th Anniversary on the Market," *Nippon Steel News* 377, March 2010, 1–2.

27. Huber and Saladino, *Babes of Winter*, 25; Taylor and Fliess, "'Beautifuls' Hail Sold-Out Omni," 1, 12; *Omni Souvenir Dedication Book*, OSF, Kenan Library.

28. Huber and Saladino, *Babes of Winter*, 23.

29. *Omni Souvenir Dedication Book*, OSF, Kenan Library.

30. Taylor and Fliess, "'Beautifuls' Hail Sold-Out Omni," 1, 12.

31. Tom Walker, "Omni Complex to Help City's Global Look," *Atlanta Journal*, October 11, 1972, 1A, 9A.

32. Massell, in phone discussion with the author.

33. Rutheiser, *Imagineering Atlanta*, 165.

34. Rutheiser, *Imagineering Atlanta*, 161–62; Alfred Borcover, "Fantasy in Atlanta's Omni," *Chicago Tribune*, June 13, 1976, C1.

14. Politics of Metropolitan Divergence

1. Robert Scheer, "Tourists Seldom See the Real Face of Atlanta," *Boston Globe*, February 18, 1979, A3.

2. Euchner, *Playing the Field*, 3–22; Danielson, *Home Team*, 102–16; Riess, *City Games*, 240–45; Rosentraub, *Major League Losers*, 33–72.

3. University of Virginia Census Database, *County and City Data Book*, 1980; Jeffrey Scott, "Barricade Was Turning Point for Allen," *Atlanta Journal-Constitution*, July 4, 2003, 1D; Stone, *Regime Politics*, 77.

4. Lassiter, *Silent Majority*, 106–7.

5. Kruse, *White Flight*, 1–12.

6. University of Virginia Census Database, *City and County Data Book*, 1980.

7. "An Answer to Block-Busting," *Atlanta Constitution*, May 16, 1967, 4; George M. Coleman, "Scare Tactics Have Failed to Create All Black City," *Atlanta Daily World*, November 5, 1971, 1, 4.

8. Alex Coffin, "City Asked to Ban Home 'Sale' Signs," *Atlanta Constitution*, May 19, 1967, 1.

9. Kruse, *White Flight*, 234–45; Bayor, *Race and Shaping of Twentieth-Century Atlanta*, 62; University of Virginia Census Database, *City and County Data Book*, 1980; Ambrose, *Atlanta*, 187.

10. University of Virginia Census Database, *City and County Data Book*, 1980; University of Virginia Census Database, *City and County Data Book*, 1970; Kruse, *White Flight*, 234–45; Hartshorn, *Metropolis in Georgia*, 45–6.

11. Rutheiser, *Imagineering Atlanta*, 61–62, 153–55; Hartshorn, *Metropolis in Georgia*, 41–48.

12. "A City Responds to the Crisis," *Atlanta Sunday Journal-Constitution*, May 26, 1968, 9A; Rutheiser, *Imagineering Atlanta*, 61–62; Hartshorn, *Metropolis in Georgia*, 41–48.

13. Laub, *Single Family Residential Development*.

14. Rutheiser, *Imagineering Atlanta*, 61–62; Hartshorn, *Metropolis in Georgia*, 41–48; "City Responds to Crisis," 9A.

15. Lorraine Bennett, "Housing Needs Attention," *Atlanta Journal*, September 8, 1969, 1A, 4A; Hartshorn, *Metropolis in Georgia*, 43–48; Rutheiser, *Imagineering Atlanta*, 154–55.

16. Sam Hopkins, "Model Cities Didn't Solve Crime, Housing," *Atlanta Constitution*, October 12, 1973, 1; Rutheiser, *Imagineering Atlanta*, 119–20, 154; "Model Cities," *Atlanta Constitution*, April 9, 1969, 4; Duane Riner, "$14 Million Spent; No New Homes Yet," *Atlanta Sunday Journal-Constitution*, May 30, 1971, 2A.

17. Thompson, *Review of Certain Aspects*, 1–6; Hopkins, "Model Cities Didn't Solve Crime, Housing," 1.

18. Hopkins, "Model Cities Didn't Solve Crime, Housing," 1.

19. Hopkins, "Model Cities Didn't Solve Crime, Housing," 1; Riner, "$14 Million Spent," 2A; Thompson, *Review of Certain Aspects*, 1–6.

20. Rutheiser, *Imagineering Atlanta*, 119–20; Hopkins, "Model Cities Didn't Solve Crime, Housing," 1.

21. Research Atlanta, *Public Housing in Atlanta*, RAP, Kenan Library; Glover, "Atlanta Blueprint," 8.

22. Bennett, "Housing Needs Attention," 1A, 4A; Hartshorn, *Metropolis in Georgia*, 43–48; Rutheiser, *Imagineering Atlanta*, 154–55; Stone, *Regime Politics*, 61–73.

23. Bennett, "Housing Needs Attention," 1A, 4A.

24. Kruse, *White Flight*, 237.

25. Jaret, Ruddiman, and Phillips, "Legacy of Residential Segregation," 122–29; Allen, *Atlanta Rising*, 197–99; Hartshorn, *Metropolis in Georgia*, 45–46; University of Virginia Library Census Data Base, *City and County Data Book*, 1980; Rutheiser, *Imagineering Atlanta*, 101–7; "The Ghetto Spreads," *Atlanta Constitution*, May 28, 1968, 4.

26. Lassiter, *Silent Majority*, 328; Allen, *Atlanta Rising*, 199.

27. Kruse, *White Flight*, 245–51.

28. Brian O'Shea, "Perimeter Mall Turns 35," *Atlanta Journal-Constitution*, August 17, 2006; B. Drummond Ayres, "What's Doing in Atlanta," *New York Times*, July 24, 1977, xx7; Leon Lindsay, "Atlanta: More Than a City to Just Pass Through," *Washington Post*, February 6, 1972, H8.

29. Stone, *Regime Politics*, 48; Jim Auchmutey, "Mayors Kept City Too Busy to Hate," *Atlanta Journal-Constitution*, July 6, 2003, 1A; Alton Hornsby, "Black Public Education in Atlanta, Georgia, 1954–1973," 30–31.

30. Hal Gulliver, "Supreme Court Restudying Grade-a-Year Desegregation," *Atlanta Constitution*, March 30, 1964, 7; Anthony Lewis, "Court Asks for Faster Integration," *New York Times*, May 31, 1964, E5; Hornsby, "Black Public Education in Atlanta, Georgia, 1954–1973," 30–31; Hein, "Image of 'City Too Busy to Hate,'" 206.

31. Lewis, "Court Asks for Faster Integration," E5.

32. Stone, *Regime Politics*, 48, 77, 103–6; Lewis, "Court Asks for Faster Integration," E5; "Atlanta Prodded in Integration," *New York Times*, March 7, 1964, 52; Hornsby, "Black Public Education in Atlanta, Georgia, 1954–1973," 30–31. All twenty Catholic schools in Georgia desegregated for the 1962–63 school year, just as white parents in Atlanta began seeking them out as an alternative to integrated public schools.

33. Kruse, *White Flight*, 237–38; Stone, *Regime Politics*, 103–6; Steve Stewart, "'Majority Black' Plan Is Urged for Schools," *Atlanta Constitution*, March 20, 1973, 6A.

34. Tom Linthicum, "Where Do the Whites Go?" *Atlanta Constitution*, November 4, 1971, 1A, 20A.

35. Steve Stewart, "School Plan Approved; 4 Appeals Are Expected," *Atlanta Constitution*, April 5, 1973, 1; "City School Agreement Assailed," *Atlanta Constitution*, May 3, 1973, 22A; Stone, *Regime Politics*, 103–6; Nagin, *Courage to Dissent*, 393–402, 436.

36. "City School Agreement Assailed," 22A; Stone, *Regime Politics*, 103–6; Pomerantz, *Where Peachtree Meets Sweet Auburn*, 395.

37. Nagin, *Courage to Dissent*, 385–406; Stone, *Regime Politics*, 103–6.

38. Kruse, *White Flight*, 239; "Atlanta: A City in Crisis," *Atlanta Sunday Journal-Constitution*, March 23, 1975, 1A, 16A.

39. Keating, *Atlanta: Race, Class, and Urban Expansion*, 64.

40. Bayor, *Race and Shaping of Twentieth-Century Atlanta*, 88.

41. Bayor, *Race and Shaping of Twentieth-Century Atlanta*, 85–92.

42. Weise, *Places of Their Own*, 188; Kruse, *White Flight*, 35–38.

43. Bayor, *Race and Shaping of Twentieth-Century Atlanta*, 85–92; Lassiter, *Silent Majority*, 3–5, 10–12; Kruse, *White Flight*, 1–12, 247–48.

44. "Mayor of Atlanta Urges Annexation," *New York Times*, December 29, 1971, 19; "'Abolish Atlanta' Gains in Georgia," *New York Times*, November 9, 1969, 65; "Plan to Expand Atlanta Encounters Opposition," *Boston Globe*, December 29, 1971, 8; Bill Seddon, "Sorry, Annex-Backers—It Wasn't Horseshoes," *Atlanta Sunday Journal-Constitution*, March 12, 1972, 14A.

45. "Mayor of Atlanta Urges Annexation," 19; "'Abolish Atlanta' Gains in Georgia," 65; "Plan to Expand Atlanta Encounters Opposition," 8; Bayor, *Race and Shaping of Twentieth-Century Atlanta*, 85–92.

46. Lassiter, *Silent Majority*, 112–13.

47. Bayor, *Race and Shaping of Twentieth-Century Atlanta*, 85–92; "'Abolish Atlanta' Gains in Georgia," 65; "Seeks to Double Size of Atlanta," *Chicago Tribune*, December 29, 1971, B11.

48. Bayor, *Race and Shaping of Twentieth-Century Atlanta*, 85–92; "'Abolish Atlanta' Gains in Georgia," 65; "Plan to Expand Atlanta Encounters Opposition," 8.

49. Allen, *Atlanta Rising*, 191–93; Bayor, *Race and Shaping of Twentieth-Century Atlanta*, 85–92.

50. Lochner & Company and De Leuw, Cather & Company, *Highway and Transportation Plan*; David Pendered, "Plans to Nowhere," *Atlanta Journal-Constitution*, May 24, 2004, 1E.

51. Allen, *Atlanta Rising*, 198.

52. Marion Gaines, "Freeway Link-Up Expected to Be Ready by Oct. 1," *Atlanta Journal*, June 8, 1964, 2A; "Atlanta Flow Compared to Other Cities," *Atlanta Journal*, September 21, 1969, 10.

53. U.S. Congress Office of Technology Assessment. *Assessment of Community Planning*, 1–11; Ambrose, *Atlanta*, 183.

54. Dick Hebert, "Rich Bids for Bus Company and Merged Transit Accord," *Atlanta Constitution*, December 13, 1967, 1, 14; "If Suburbs Cannot Agree on Transit Now, Let's Begin on Smaller Scale," *Atlanta Constitution*, January 23, 1965, 4; "Rapid Transit: Who Will Be Taking Part?" *Atlanta Sunday Journal-Constitution*, June 6, 1965, 6B.

55. Stone, *Regime Politics*, 98–102.

56. Walker Lundy, "MARTA Friend, Foe Collide," *Atlanta Journal*, October 31, 1968, 2A.

57. Pomerantz, *Where Peachtree Meets Sweet Auburn*, 378–79; Stone, *Regime Politics*, 98–102; Schroeder and Sjoquist, "Rational Voter," 27–28; Lundy, "MARTA Friend, Foe Collide," 2A.

58. Schroeder and Sjoquist, "Rational Voter," 27–31; Walker Lundy, "Rapid Transit Fails by Heavy Margin," *Atlanta Journal*, November 6, 1968, 2A; "A Landmark Decision on Rapid Transit," *Atlanta Sunday Journal-Constitution*, October 13, 1968, 22A; Pomerantz, *Where Peachtree Meets Sweet Auburn*, 378; "Rapid Transit Question Box," *Atlanta Journal*, October 31, 1968, 2A.

59. "Transit Urged in DeKalb," *Atlanta Constitution*, October 25, 1968, 1; "Farris Endorses Rapid Transit Plan," *Atlanta Journal*, November 2, 1968, 10; Stone, *Regime Politics*, 98–102.

60. Lundy, "MARTA Friend, Foe Collide," 2A; "To the Voters of Atlanta, Fulton and DeKalb," *Atlanta Journal*, November 4, 1968, 32; Duane Riner, "Maddox Asks Free TV Time to Air Rapid Transit Debate," *Atlanta Constitution*, March 27, 1968, 2; "'Phooey' on Rapid Transit," *Atlanta Constitution*, April 13, 1968, 4; "Approval of Rapid Transit Means 'Go,'" *Atlanta Journal*, November 4, 1968, 4A.

61. "Vote 'No' on 228 Advertisement," *Atlanta Journal*, November 4, 1968, 11; Lundy, "Rapid Transit Fails by Heavy Margin," 2A; Schroeder and Sjoquist, "Rational Voter," 27–28; "Atlanta's Hopes for Rapid Transit Rise," *New York Times*, March 14, 1971, 72; Kruse, *White Flight*, 248–49.

62. Kruse, *White Flight*, 248–49; Rutheiser, *Imagineering Atlanta*, 156.

63. Bayor, *Race and Shaping of Twentieth-Century Atlanta*, 188–96; Pomerantz, *Where Peachtree Meets Sweet Auburn*, 378; Stone, *Regime Politics*, 98–102; Rutheiser, *Imagineering Atlanta*, 156.

64. "MARTA Meets the Public," *Atlanta Constitution*, May 18, 1968, 4; "Open Season on Rapid Transit," *Atlanta Constitution*, October 25, 1968, 4; Bayor, *Race and Shaping of Twentieth-Century Atlanta*, 188–96.

65. Lundy, "Rapid Transit Fails by Heavy Margin," *Atlanta Journal*, November 6, 1968, 2A; "A Landmark Decision on Rapid Transit," *Atlanta Sunday Journal-Constitution*, October 13, 1968, 22A; Pomerantz, *Where Peachtree Meets Sweet Auburn*, 378; Schroeder and Sjoquist, "Rational Voter," 27–28.

66. Stone, *Regime Politics*, 78–79, 98–102.

67. Alex Coffin, "Blacks Withhold MARTA Support," *Atlanta Constitution*, August 26, 1971, 8A; Bayor, *Race and Shaping of Twentieth-Century Atlanta*, 188–96; Stone, *Regime Politics* 98–102; Pomerantz, *Where Peachtree Meets Sweet Auburn*, 395.

68. "Massell for Mayor 1973 Campaign Materials," SMPF. Kenan Library; Hugh Nations, "Shift in the Balance of Power," *Atlanta Journal*, November 5, 1971, 1A, 10A; Schroeder and Sjoquist, "Rational Voter," 27–31; "Atlanta's Hopes for Rapid Transit Rise," *New York Times*, March 14, 1971, 72; Stone, *Regime Politics*, 98–102; "Here's How Proposed Transit System Works," *Atlanta Constitution*, November 8, 1971, 6A; Coffin, "Blacks Withhold MARTA Support," 8A.

69. R. S. Allison, "MARTA a Must for Metro-Atlanta Poor," *Atlanta Daily World*, October 31, 1971, 1, 4; "Rapid Transit Gets $30 Million Boost," *Atlanta Daily World*, November 7, 1971, 1; "Clergymen Here Urge 'Yes' Vote for Rapid Transit," *Atlanta Daily World*, November 9, 1971, 1; Philip D. Carter, "Vote Mass Transit, Atlantans Urged, to Miss the Crunch," *Washington Post*, November 8, 1971, A2; "MARTA Foe Calls Timing of Grant Influence Tactic," *Atlanta Journal*, November 6, 1971, 1A, 4A.

70. Bill Seddon, "Massell Shows City to 12 Other Mayors," *Atlanta Constitution*, November 4, 1971, 16A; Maurice Fliess, "Mayors Issue Transit Alert," *Atlanta Journal*, November 4, 1971, 1; Maurice Fliess, "Mayor Rides for MARTA," *Atlanta Journal*, November 3, 1971, 2A.

71. "Committee for Sensible Rapid Transit," *Atlanta Journal*, November 2, 1971, 9A.

72. "High Cost of Selling Rapid Transit," *Atlanta Constitution*, November 11, 1971, 4A.

73. Alex Coffin, "Transit Road Rocky, Uphill," *Atlanta Constitution*, March 29, 1971, 7A; Maurice Fliess, "MARTA Foe Maps City Transit Buy," *Atlanta Journal*, November 2, 1971, 8A; Raleigh Bryans, "Transit Vote Result Cloudy," *Atlanta Sunday Journal-Constitution*, November 7, 1971, 1A, 21A; "The MARTA Vote," *Atlanta Constitution*, November 8, 1971, 4A.

74. "Rapid Transit: Two Views," *Atlanta Constitution*, November 8, 1971, 1A, 6A.

75. "Questions about MARTA's Rapid Transit Advertisement," *Atlanta Journal*, November 3, 1971, 12.

76. Bayor, *Race and Shaping of Twentieth-Century Atlanta*, 188–96; Stone, *Regime Politics*, 98–102; Pomerantz, *Where Peachtree Meets Sweet Auburn*, 395; Carter, "Vote Mass Transit, Atlantans Urged," A2.

77. Schroeder and Sjoquist, "Rational Voter," 27–28; Kruse, *White Flight*, 248–49; Bayor, *Race and Shaping of Twentieth-Century Atlanta*, 188–96; "Rapid Transit Gets Green Light in Fulton-DeKalb Cliff-Hanger," *Atlanta Journal*, November 10, 1971, 1A, 8A, 20A; "Fulton, Dekalb Voters Approve MARTA Plan," *Atlanta Daily*

World, November 11, 1971, 1; "Middle, Upper Income Whites Put It Over," *Atlanta Constitution*, November 10, 1971, 10A.

78. Joseph Kraft, "Atlanta Transit Plan Boosts Black Cause," *Boston Globe*, February 25, 1973, A7; Bayor, *Race and Shaping of Twentieth-Century Atlanta*, 188–96; Stone, *Regime Politics*, 98–102.

79. Kraft, "Atlanta Transit Plan Boosts Black Cause," A7.

80. Ralph Blumenthal, "50 Cent Fare? It's 15 Cents in Salt Lake City and Atlanta," *New York Times*, August 31, 1975, 28; Sharon Bailey, "MARTA's Cost Rises $450 Million," *Atlanta Constitution*, October 9, 1973, 3.

81. Allen, *Atlanta Rising*, 198–99; William E. Schmidt, "Atlanta's Rapid Transit System to Reach Out Today for Suburban Riders," *New York Times*, December 15, 1984, 10; Rutheiser, *Imagineering Atlanta*, 157–59.

82. William E. Schmidt, "Graffiti and Vandals' Attacks Rub Gloss Off Atlanta Transit," *New York Times*, November 8, 1985, A20.

83. "Crime Reports Spoil Atlanta's Pride in Rapid Transit System," *New York Times*, May 22, 1986, A20.

84. Rutheiser, *Imagineering Atlanta*, 157–59.

85. William B. Schmidt, "Atlanta Is Finally Flowing," *New York Times*, December 8, 1985, E5; "Crime Reports Spoil Atlanta's Pride," A20; Julie B. Hairstone, "MARTA Marks 25 Years of Trains," *Atlanta Journal-Constitution*, June 30, 2004, 1B.

86. Bullard, Johnson, and Torres, "Dismantling Transportation Apartheid," 51–52; Schmidt, "Atlanta Is Finally Flowing," E5.

87. Whitelegg, "Battle on Two Fronts," 129; Bayor, *Race and Shaping of Twentieth-Century Atlanta*, 188–96; Pendered, "Plans to Nowhere," 1E; Allen, *Atlanta Rising*, 198–99.

88. Kruse, *White Flight*, 248–49.

89. "Central Area Survey II, 1980-Present (1987)," CAPP, box 54, folder 2, Kenan Library; Kruse, *White Flight*, 248.

90. Allen, *Atlanta Rising*, 198–99.

91. Sally Salter, "Atlanta: Rapid-Transit Station Is the Hub of Burgeoning Buckhead Area," *New York Times*, May 12, 1985, CR16; Kruse, *White Flight*, 248–49.

15. Probably Room for Basketball

1. Ailene Voisin, "Atlanta's First Hawks Willing to Share Place in History," *Atlanta Journal-Constitution*, December 8, 1993, E1.

2. Denberg, Lazenby, and Stinson, *From Sweet Lou to 'Nique*, 31–32.

3. Halberstam, *Breaks of the Game*, 35–36; Voisin, "Atlanta's First Hawks," E1.

4. "Pro Basketball Era Ends with Kerner," *Sporting News*, January 21, 1967, 12; Kriegel, *Pistol*, 191; Association for Professional Basketball Research, "NBA/ABA Home Attendance Totals"; "Hudson, Hawks Topple San Diego," *Atlanta Constitution*, March 28, 1969, 65; George Cunningham and Darrell Simmons, "Hawks Turn on the Heat While Mopping Up Lakers," *Atlanta Journal*, April 16, 1969, 4E.

5. Tom Van Arsdale, in phone discussion with the author, July 10, 2013.

6. Roy M. Blount, "Losersville, U.S.A.," *Sports Illustrated*, March 21, 1977, 82.

7. Jim Minter, "NBA Expected to Approve Hawks' Move," *Atlanta Sunday Journal-Constitution*, May 5, 1968, 1H; Digital Library of Georgia, *Interview with Hawks Coach*.

8. Denberg, Lazenby, and Stinson, *From Sweet Lou to 'Nique*, 31–32.

9. Bisher, "Hawks Approval Certain," *Atlanta Journal*, May 7, 1968, 1D; Bob Hertzel, "Regents Approve Hawks Use of Tech," *Atlanta Journal*, May 8, 1968, 1D.

10. Denberg, Lazenby, and Stinson, *From Sweet Lou to 'Nique*, 32.

11. *Omni Souvenir Dedication Book*, OSF, Kenan Library; Mickey McCarthy, "Hawk Sale Approved," *Atlanta Constitution*, May 8, 1968, 51; Jim Minter, "Tommy Cousins Plans New Roost for Hawks," *Atlanta Journal*, May 4, 1968, 1B; Hertzel, "Regents Approve Hawks Use of Tech," 1D.

12. Jesse Outlar, "Hawks Try 'Big O,' Get Only Zero," *Atlanta Constitution*, October 17, 1968, 47; Paul Delaney, "More Black Fans Sought by Hawks," *New York Times*, June 25, 1972, S4; "Hudson-Led Hawks Rip Milwaukee," *Atlanta Constitution*, October 20, 1968, 1D; Frank Hyland, "Hawks Can't Beat Atlanta Tradition," *Atlanta Journal*, October 17, 1968, 1D.

13. Jim Minter, in phone discussion with the author, July 9, 2013; Pat Zier, "Pros Won't Damage Tech, Say Owners," *Atlanta Constitution*, May 7, 1968, 43; Charlie Roberts, "Hawks Will Fly into Open Arms," *Atlanta Constitution*, May 4, 1968, 19.

14. Roberts, "Hawks Will Fly into Open Arms," 19.

15. Zier, "Pros Won't Damage Tech," 43.

16. Zier, "Pros Won't Damage Tech," 43.

17. Bill Clark, "Hawks' Negro Standouts Are Honestly a Bit Wary," *Atlanta Constitution*, May 17, 1968, 2B.

18. John J. Archibald, "Hawks Play 'Inside' Game to Earn Aggressive Label," *Atlanta Sunday Journal-Constitution*, May 5, 1968, 3H; John J. Archibald, "Guerin's Always the Boss," *Atlanta Sunday Journal-Constitution*, May 5, 1968, 4H; Frank Deford, "Beware of the Hawks," *Sports Illustrated*, April 13, 1970, 48.

19. "Atlanta Hawks 1968–1969 Media Guide," AHSF, Kenan Library.

20. Halberstam, *Breaks of the Game*, 15–16, 35–36; Roberts, "Hawks Will Fly into Open Arms," 19.

21. James Heath, "Sports Note Pad," *Atlanta Daily World*, July 13, 1975, 6.

22. Frank Hyland, "Hawks 'Feel' Another Title," *Atlanta Journal*, October 16, 1968, 1D; "Atlanta's Newest Pro Athletes," *Atlanta Journal*, October 15, 1968, 3C.

23. Outlar, "Hawks Try 'Big O,'" 47; Renfroe, "This and That in Sports," *Atlanta Daily World*, November 28, 1978, 7.

24. Maracek, *Full Court*, 206–8; Jeremy Rutherford, "Departure of Hawks Still Is Bittersweet Affair," *St. Louis Post-Dispatch*, September 26, 1999, D16.

25. Jeffrey Denberg, Lazenby, and Stinson, *From Sweet Lou to 'Nique*, 32–33; "Wilkens, Hawks in $$ Squabble," *Chicago Defender*, September 26, 1968, 42; Kriegel, *Pistol*, 189–90.

16. The Logical Choice

1. Bob Hertzel, "Atlanta Five Years from Professional Hockey," *Atlanta Journal*, May 7, 1968, 4D; Huber and Saladino, *Babes of Winter*, 13.

2. "Planned Sports Arena for Atlanta's Newest Pro Teams," *Chicago Defender*, May 14, 1968, 24; "Atlanta Aims for Arena, Pro Hockey," *Washington Post*, May 14, 1968, D2.

3. Hertzel, "Atlanta Five Years from Professional Hockey," 4D.

4. Hertzel, "Atlanta Five Years from Professional Hockey," 4D.

5. Steve Clark, "Atlanta Enters Hockey Arena Ice Cold," *Atlanta Constitution*, November 10, 1971, 7C.

6. Jim Huber, "New Hockey League Names Ten; Atlanta Next?" *Atlanta Journal*, November 1, 1971, 6D; Willes, *Rebel League*, 25–27.

7. Huber, "New Hockey League Names Ten," 6D.

8. Willes, *Rebel League*, 18.

9. Stan Fischler, "New NHL Expansion Seen by 1974," *Sporting News*, January 30, 1971, 27.

10. Huber and Saladino, *Babes of Winter*, 13.

11. Huber and Saladino, *Babes of Winter*, 21.

12. Fischler, "New NHL Expansion Seen by 1974," 27.

13. Jim Huber, "NHL Ready to Open in Atlanta in 1972," *Atlanta Journal*, November 8, 1971, 1D; Wayne Minshew, "Atlanta Isn't in NHL Yet," *Atlanta Constitution*, November 9, 1971, 1D.

14. Al Thomy and Wayne Minshew, "'No Problem on Owners,'" *Atlanta Constitution*, November 10, 1971, 1C, 5C.

15. Huber and Saladino, *Babes of Winter*, 11–15; Bob Verdi, "NHL Expands to 16 in '72," *Chicago Tribune*, November 10, 1971, C1; Huber, "NHL Ready to Open in Atlanta," 1D.

16. Huber and Saladino, *Babes of Winter*, 9–12; Verdi, "NHL Expands to 16," C1.

17. Huber, "NHL Ready to Open in Atlanta," 1D; Minshew, "Atlanta Isn't in NHL Yet," 1D.

18. Bob Verdi, "NHL Adding Today?" *Chicago Tribune*, November 9, 1971, D3.

19. Verdi, "NHL Expands to 16," C1.

20. Huber and Saladino, *Babes of Winter*, 15.

21. Leo Monahan, "Fletcher Warns Atlanta Fans," *Sporting News*, February 19, 1972, 11; Tony Petrella, "Fletcher Smooth Behind Scene," *Atlanta Constitution*, September 28, 1972, 1D.

22. *Omni Souvenir Dedication Book*, OSF, Kenan Library.

23. Dan Stoneking, "Will Atlanta Embrace Hockey?" *Sporting News*, October 7, 1972, 57.

17. How the Falcons Lost Atlanta

1. Furman Bisher, "NFC Western," *Sporting News*, September 11, 1976, 56.

2. Bob Etter, email message to author, March 12, 2019.

3. Lewis Grizzard, "Dutchman Blasted by Ex-Falcons," *Atlanta Journal*, October 26, 1972, 1D; Frank Hyland, "Van Brocklin," *Atlanta Journal*, October 31, 1972, 1D.

4. Jim Minter, "Let's Not Discriminate," *Atlanta Journal*, January 10, 1969, 1D.

5. "Falcons Deal Off Ron Smith, Deny Racial Discrimination," *Washington Post*, January 9, 1968, D3; "Falcons Deny Unfair Race Practices," *Chicago Defender*, January 9, 1968, 26; Bob Hertzel, "NAACP Protests Falcon 'Policy,'" *Atlanta Journal*, January 8, 1968, 1C; Bob Hertzel, "NAACP Complaints a Falcon Puzzle," *Atlanta Journal*, January 9, 1969, 1C; "White Falcons," *Atlanta Constitution*, January 22, 1966, 4.

6. Al Thomy, "Norm's Exit from Atlanta Marked by Bitter Volleys," *Sporting News*, November 23, 1974, 18.

7. NFL Films, "1974 Atlanta Falcons."

8. David Moffit, "Falcons Whip Packers in Atlanta's 'No-Show Bowl,'" *Sporting News*, December 28, 1974, 16; "48,830 Fail to Show for Falcon Game," *St. Louis Globe Democrat*, December 16, 1974, 1; Schaeffer and Davidson, *Economic Impact of the Falcons, 1984*, 3–8.

9. Ron Hudspeth, "Falcon Diary," *Atlanta Journal*, December 3, 1974, 1D; Al Thomy, "An Icy Cold Holding Ending: LA Easy Victor in Studio Game," *Atlanta Constitution*, December 2, 1974, 1D; "Bad Weather, Bad Team," *Atlanta Journal*, December 2, 1974, 1D; David Moffit, "40,000 Empty Seats at Ram Feast," *Sporting News*, December 14, 1974, 24; Furman Bisher, "Failure Over-Exercised," *Atlanta Journal*, December 3, 1974, 1D; Moffit, "Falcons Whip Packers," 16; "48,830 Fail to Show," 1.

10. "Atlanta Ticket Buyers Learn Location Facts," *Kansas City Times*, March 23, 1966, 15; "Falcon Fans Unhappy," *Chicago Tribune*, March 23, 1966, C2; "Atlanta to Stop Ticket Drive, 40K Sold," *Washington Post*, December 23, 1965, B5; Bill Clark, "Falcons Set to Launch Ticket Drive," *Atlanta Constitution*, October 29, 1965, 53.

11. "Market Operations Research: The Demographic Characteristics of People Who Ride Buses to Atlanta Falcons Games," AFF, 1968, Football HOF.

12. Schaeffer and Davidson, *Economic Impact of the Falcons, 1973*, 1, 6–8.

13. "Falcon Facts: July 1969," AFF, Football HOF; *Falcons Newsletter*, November 1991, AFF, Football HOF; "Atlanta Least Expensive, Washington Most Costly," *Sporting News*, September 17, 1977, 59; "Falcons Raise Prices, Plan More Seats in '76," *Atlanta Constitution*, January 9, 1976, 1D; Schaeffer and Davidson, *Economic Impact of the Falcons, 1973*, 5; Vicki Pearlman, "Falcons Parking Fee Has Fans Squawking," *Atlanta Journal*, August 22, 1979, C1.

14. James Heath, "Sports Note Pad," *Atlanta Daily World*, July 13, 1975, 6.

15. Darrell Simmons, "Falcons Miss Chances During Frozen Finale," *Atlanta Journal*, December 16, 1968, 1D; "Eagles Fly High Early to Rap Falcons, 38–7," Atlanta Constitution, October 9, 1967, 12; Charlie Roberts, "49ers Defend Atlanta's Defenseless Forces," *Atlanta Constitution*, October 17, 1966, 38; Bisher, *Atlanta Falcons*, 46, 51–52, 75.

16. "Atlanta Falcons Pre-Season Prospectus 1969," AFF, Football HOF; "Atlanta Falcons, Pre-Season Prospectus, 1971," AFF, Football HOF; Furman Bisher, *Atlanta Falcons*, 6–7, 75.

17. Schaeffer and Davidson, *Economic Impact of the Falcons, 1984*, 7; Al Thomy, "Falcon Ticket Figures Are Vague," *Atlanta Constitution*, March 18, 1975, 1C; "Falcons Fast Facts: 1974," AFF, Football HOF; Bisher, *Atlanta Falcons*, 15; Al Thomy, "Falcon Patrons Down 12,564," *Atlanta Journal* April 3, 1975, 1D; Al Thomy, "Falcon Sales Take Nosedive," *Atlanta Constitution*, May 3, 1968, 59.

18. University of Georgia, "Home Football Attendance."

19. "Pros No Worry to Bobby Dodd," *Washington Post*, January 22, 1966, D2; Wayne Minshew, in phone discussion with the author, July 1, 2013; Rodgers and Thomy, *Pepper!*, 165.

20. Georgia Institute of Technology, *Engineering for Success*, 160–65, 170–72.

21. Rodgers and Thomy, *Pepper!*, 6, 24–28, 164–167; Dan Jenkins, "Ever See So Many Geniuses?," *Sports Illustrated*, September 16, 1974, 34.

22. J. D. Reed, "The Louisiana Purchase," *Sports Illustrated*, July 22, 1974, 66–72; "Seven Cities Bid for 16th NFL Franchise," *Atlanta Constitution*, May 19, 1966, 1.

23. Jesse Outlar, "Welcome Saints!" *Atlanta Constitution*, November 2, 1966, 35; MacCambridge, *America's Game*, 228–30.

24. "New Orleans Sports Civic Leaders Shoot for 'Instant' Domed Stadium," *Atlanta Constitution*, February 3, 1966, 51; Reed, "Louisiana Purchase," 66–72; "Seven Cities Bid," 1.

25. "Superdome to Host Super Bowl in 1975," *Atlanta Constitution*, April 4, 1973, 6C.

26. *Falcons Newsletter*, Fall 1974, AFF, Football HOF.

27. Al Thomy, "TV Flop: Falcons a Disappointment to CBS, Too," *Atlanta Constitution*, December 9, 1974, 1D.

28. Jim Minter, "NFL 'Leaks' Burn Hecker," *Atlanta Journal*, September 10, 1966, 10.

29. Al Thomy, "Nobis, NFL Rookie of Year, Bargain at Any Price—Hecker," *Sporting News*, January 7, 1967, 5; Jesse Outlar, "Mr. Nobis Makes His Point(s), And All the Falcons Say Thanks," *Atlanta Constitution*, October 30, 1967, 37; Furman Bisher, *Atlanta Falcons*, 105–6.

30. "Dutchman, Writer Get into Scuffle," *Atlanta Constitution*, August 26, 1971, 1D; Bob Oates, "NFC Western," *Sporting News*, September 25, 1971, 46; "Van Brocklin and Writer Involved in Heated Row," *Atlanta Journal*, August 9, 1971, 1D; "Scorecard," *Sports Illustrated*, September 13, 1971, 12.

31. "Falcons, Hometown Paper Feuding," *Sporting News*, August 3, 1976, 44.

32. Tommy Nobis, in phone discussion with the author, July 22, 2013.

33. Lou Kirouac, in phone discussion with the author, August 13, 2013.

34. "Final Home Opener at Stadium Brings Falcons Memories," *Atlanta Constitution*, September 7, 1991, D3.

35. "Falcons to Tech?" *Atlanta Journal*, August 9, 1971, 1D; Bud Shaw, "The Dinosaur on Capitol Avenue," *Atlanta Journal-Constitution*, May 26, 1984, 1C.

36. Al Thomy, "Falcons for Sale? Could Be," *Atlanta Constitution*, November 25, 1974, 1C; "Owner Views Tax Plan as Threat to Falcons," *Washington Post*, January 19, 1973, D6; "Club Owners Face Bombshell in Falcon Suit," *Sporting News* November 2, 1974, 39.

37. Shaw, "Dinosaur on Capitol Avenue," 1C; Gayle White, "City Leaders Go to Bat for Intown Stadium," *Atlanta Constitution*, February 15, 1985, C1.

18. Atlanta's Ice Society

1. Frank Hyland, "The Flames' Dilemma: Lobsters in a Catfish Town," *Atlanta Journal*, April 3, 1980, 2C.

2. Al Morganti, "A Stormy Start," *Sporting News*, November 25, 1991, 38.

3. Craig Custance, "Old Flame(s)," *Atlanta Journal-Constitution*, January 23, 2008, 1D.

4. Bill Clement, in phone discussion with the author, June 26, 2013.

5. Roy M. Blount, "Losersville, U.S.A.," *Sports Illustrated*, March 21, 1977, 83; Dick Beardsley, "Five Year Plan," *Atlanta Journal*, April 1, 1974, 6D; Leo Monahan, "Atlanta Fans Warming Up to Fast-Charging Flames," *Sporting News*, December 23, 1972, 4; Mark Mulvoy, "Trouble in Paradise, but Not Very Much," *Sports Illustrated*, December 3, 1973, 28; *Atlanta Flames Fact Book 1974–1975*, AFLAMSF, Kenan Library.

6. Gary Mueller, "Flames Break Up Goalie Tandem," *Sporting News*, December 31, 1977, 38; Gary Mueller, "Low-Scoring Flames Buttress a Strong Defense," *Sporting News*, October 25, 1975, 55; *Atlanta Flames Fact Book 1974–1975*, AFLAMSF, Kenan Library.

7. *Atlanta Flames Fact Book 1974–1975*, AFLAMSF, Kenan Library; Leo Monahan, "Fletcher Warns Atlanta Fans," *Sporting News*, February 19, 1972, 11; Tony Petrella, "Fletcher Smooth Behind Scene," *Atlanta Constitution*, September 28, 1972, 1D.

8. Huber and Saladino, *Babes of Winter*, 9–10.

9. Rick Carpiniello, "An Interview with Jiggs McDonald on Boom Boom Geoffrion," Lohud.com, July 14, 2014, https://www.lohud.com/story/sports/nhl/rangers/2014/07/14/guest-blogger-george-grimm-interview-jiggs-mcdonald-boom-boom-geoffrion/12616265/.

10. John McGourty, "Former Flames Recall Hot Times in Atlanta," NHL.com, January 24, 2008, https://www.nhl.com/news/former-flames-recall-hot-times-in-atlanta/c-370370.

11. *Atlanta Flames Fact Book 1975–1976*, AFLAMSF, Kenan Library; Phil Garner, "Southern Fans Love Mayhem on Ice," *Atlanta Journal-Constitution Magazine*, January 7, 1973, 14–23; Monahan, "Atlanta Fans Warming Up," 4; Huber and Saladino, *Babes of Winter*, 30–33, 59, 154–158; Al Smith, "Boomer Leaves Flames, NHL," *Atlanta Constitution*, March 14, 1975, 1D.

12. Joe and Betsy Watkins, in phone discussion with the author, July 3, 2013; Furman Bisher, "Geoffrion Sows Well," *Atlanta Journal-Constitution*, April 29, 2001, 4D; Smith, "Boomer Leaves Flames, NHL," 1D; Huber and Saladino, *Babes of Winter*, 30–33, 154–58; Furman Bisher, "Old Flame Dies in Atlanta," *Sporting News*, February 22, 1975, 2; *Atlanta Flames Fact Book 1975–1976*, AFLAMSF, Kenan Library.

13. Huber and Saladino, *Babes of Winter*, 9–10, 21.

14. Mark Mulvoy, "A New Southern Rising," *Sports Illustrated*, December 4, 1972, 17–18; Ron Hudspeth, "For Atlanta's Suave Set, A New Love: Pro Hockey," *Atlanta Journal*, January 12, 1973, 2D.

15. *Omni Souvenir Dedication Book*, AFLAMSF, Kenan Library; *Flames Magazine* 1 (1972–73), AFLAMSF, Kenan Library; "NHL Hockey," *Sporting News*, June 3, 1972, 48; Huber and Saladino, *Babes of Winter*, 9–10, 20–21; "Will Atlanta Embrace Hockey?" *Sporting News*, October 7, 1972, 57.

16. Ron Taylor and Maurice Fliess, "'Beautifuls' Hail Sold-Out Omni," *Atlanta Sunday Journal-Constitution*, October 15, 1972, 1A; Jim Huber, "Flames Tie Christens Omni," *Atlanta Sunday Journal-Constitution*, October 15, 1972, 1D.

17. Jack Wilkinson, "An Old Flame," *Atlanta Journal-Constitution*, July 26, 1999, 4D.

18. Huber and Saladino, *Babes of Winter*, 57.

19. *Flames Magazine* 1 (1972–73), AFLAMSF, Kenan Library.

20. Mulvoy, "New Southern Rising," 17–18.

21. Wilkinson, "Old Flame," 4D; Huber and Saladino, *Babes of Winter*, 57–59.

22. Huber and Saladino, *Babes of Winter*, 58.

23. Garner, "Southern Fans Love Mayhem," 14–23; Mulvoy, "Trouble in Paradise," 28.

24. Clement, in phone discussion with the author.

25. Furman Bisher, "Hockey Madness Sweeps Atlanta," *Sporting News*, February 17, 1973, 32.

26. *Atlanta Flames Fact Book 1974–1975*, AFLAMSF, Kenan Library; Huber and Saladino, *Babes of Winter*, 51; Jim Huber, "Flames Debut: The End and the Beginning," *Atlanta Journal*, October 14, 1972, 11A; Monahan, "Atlanta Fans Warming Up," *Sporting News*, December 23, 1972, 4.

27. Al Smith and Warren Newman, "Skating on Thin Ice," *Atlanta Sunday Journal-Constitution*, March 30, 1980, 1D, 15D.

28. Bisher, "Old Flame Dies," 2.

29. Monahan, "Atlanta Fans Warming Up," 4.

30. Dick Beardsley, "Second-Year Expansion Team, Huh?" *Atlanta Journal*, April 8, 1974, 1D.

31. Wilkinson, "Old Flame," 4D.

32. Jim Minter, in phone discussion with the author, July 9, 2013.

33. Hudspeth, "For Atlanta's Suave Set," 2D.

34. Alan Truex, "The Ice Age: From Blizzard to Meltdown," *Atlanta Journal*, May 23, 1980, D1.

35. Garner, "Southern Fans Love Mayhem," 14–23.

36. Joe and Betsy Watkins, in phone discussion with the author.

37. Jim Huber, "Flames Can Smell That Playoff Loot," *Atlanta Journal*, January 13, 1973, 10A; Huber and Saladino, *Babes of Winter*, 64–65; Garner, "Southern Fans Love Mayhem," 14–23.

38. Jamie Taylor, email message to author, December 12, 2019.

39. Tony Petrella, "Fans Great, But Ice Greater," *Atlanta Sunday Journal-Constitution*, October 15, 1972, 12D; Joel Gross, email message to author, August 15, 2013; "Flames Trying for Home Ice," *Atlanta Sunday Journal-Constitution*, March 30, 1980, 6D; "Dignity in Defeat," *Atlanta Journal*, April 5, 1975, 9A; George Cunningham, "Only the Flames Flamed Out," *Atlanta Constitution*, April 5, 1975, 1C.

40. Joe and Betsy Watkins, in phone discussion with the author.

41. Clement, in phone discussion with the author.

42. Tony Petrella, "Flames, Islanders End Season with 4–4 Tie," *Atlanta Constitution*, April 3, 1973, 2C.

43. *Flames Magazine* 1 (1972–73), AFLAMSF, Kenan Library; Tony Petrella, "They Don't Look for 'The Dentist,'" *Atlanta Constitution*, October 16, 1972, 4D; Hudspeth, "For Atlanta's Suave Set," 2D.

44. Hudspeth, "For Atlanta's Suave Set," 2D; Cunningham, "Only the Flames Flamed Out," 1C.

45. Wayne Minshew, "Flames Turn On the Gals," *Atlanta Constitution*, October 7, 1975, 2D.

46. Minshew, "Flames Turn On the Gals," 2D.

47. Furman Bisher, "The Omni: A New World of Splendor," *Atlanta Sunday Journal-Constitution*, October 15, 1972, 12D; Garner, "Southern Fans Love Mayhem," 14–23.

48. Blount, "Losersville, U.S.A.," 77–84.

49. Mulvoy, "Trouble in Paradise," 28; Smith and Newman, "Skating on Thin Ice," 1D, 15D; Association for Professional Basketball Research, "NBA/ABA Home Attendance Totals"; Jim Stewart, "Omni Doors Open to Atlanta Tonight," *Atlanta*

Constitution, October 14, 1972, 1A; *Flames Magazine* 2 (1972–73), AFLAMSF, Kenan Library.

19. Just What Atlanta Needs

1. Frank Deford, "Merger, Madness and Maravich," *Sports Illustrated*, April 6, 1970, 47; "Maravich Signs with NBA Hawks," *Washington Post*, March 27, 1970, D1; Denberg, Lazenby, and Stinson, *From Sweet Lou to 'Nique*, 34; Thomas Stinson, "Pistol Pete Misfired for Hawks," *Atlanta Journal-Constitution*, June 26, 2005, 1E.

2. Stinson, "Pistol Pete Misfired for Hawks," 1E.

3. "Maravich, Hawks 'Great White Hope,'" *Chicago Defender*, March 28, 1970, 34.

4. Frank Deford, "The Hawks: Fouled Up but Flourishing," *Sports Illustrated*, March 8, 1971, 42; Peter Carry, "We Have a Slight Delay in Showtime," *Sports Illustrated*, October 26, 1970, 31; Kreigel, *Pistol*, 195–99; "Atlanta Hawks to Have 'New Look' for NBA Play," *Atlanta Daily World*, October 6, 1970, 5.

5. Kreigel, *Pistol*, 197.

6. Furman Bisher, "Omni-Potence," *Atlanta Sunday Journal-Constitution*, March 19, 1972, 4D; Furman Bisher, "One Man—But No Team," *Sporting News*, February 16, 1974, 2; George Cunningham, "Losing Hawks Talk It Over," *Atlanta Constitution*, November 5, 1971, 5D; Richard Hyatt, "Those Were the Days," *Atlanta Constitution*, April 10, 1972, 10D; Kreigel, *Pistol*, 191–95; Deford, "Hawks: Fouled Up," 42.

7. Kreigel, *Pistol*, 193–94, 204–5, 227–30; Noah Sanders, "Pistol Pete Now Is up against the Pros," *New York Times Magazine*, October 11, 1970, 32–34; Jesse Outlar, "Maravich: A Sad End," *Atlanta Constitution*, January 12, 1980, C1.

8. Bisher, "Omni-Potence," 4D; Bisher, "One Man—But No Team," 2; Cunningham, "Losing Hawks Talk It Over," 5D; Hyatt, "Those Were the Days," 10D; Kreigel, *Pistol*, 191–95; Deford, "Hawks: Fouled Up," 42.

9. Deford, "Hawks: Fouled Up," 42.

10. Roy M. Blount, "Losersville, U.S.A.," *Sports Illustrated*, March 21, 1977, 82.

11. Kreigel, *Pistol*, 194; Denberg, Lazenby, and Stinson, *From Sweet Lou to 'Nique*, 36.

12. Denberg, Lazenby, and Stinson, *From Sweet Lou to 'Nique*, 40–41; Kreigel, *Pistol*, 227–30; Chris Cobbs, "Maravich to Accept Trade," *Atlanta Constitution*, May 3, 1974, 1D.

13. *Next Season*: promotional flier for 1970–71, AHSF, Kenan Library; "That Old Gang," *Atlanta Constitution*, January 5, 1973, 1D; Peter Carry, "He's Shooting the Works," *Sports Illustrated*, November 12, 1973, 50; Frank Hyland, "The Pistol Fires a Blank,'" *Atlanta Journal*, March 16, 1972, 1E; Cunningham, "Losing Hawks Talk It Over," 5D; Hyatt, "Those Were the Days," 10D.

14. Darrell Simmons and Ron Brocato, "The Trade: It Wasn't for Pete's Sake," *Atlanta Sunday Journal-Constitution*, May 5, 1974, 10D.

15. Cobbs, "Maravich to Accept Trade," 1D.

16. "Opinion," *Atlanta Constitution*, January 4, 1977, 4D; Kreigel, *Pistol*, 227–30.

17. Kreigel, *Pistol*, 227–30; Cobbs, "Maravich to Accept Trade," 1D; Stinson, "Pistol Pete Misfired for Hawks," 1E.

18. "Pete Maravich: Problems of Adjustment Over," *New York Times*, February 28, 1971, S6; George Cunningham, "Hawks Forming Circus Act?" *Atlanta Constitution*, April 11, 1972, 1D.

19. Hyatt, "Those Were the Days," 10D.

20. Carry, "He's Shooting the Works," 27; Darrell Simmons, "Pete: Love Story," *Atlanta Journal*, October 16, 1973, 1D; Kriegel, *Pistol*, 204–5.

21. Denberg, Lazenby, and Stinson, *From Sweet Lou to 'Nique*, 42.

22. "Hawks Retire 'Pistol' Pete Maravich's No. 44," NBA.com, March 3, 2017, https://www.nba.com/news/atlanta-hawks-retire-pistol-pete-maravichs-no-44.

23. Pistol Pete Videos, "Reflections on Pistol Pete Maravich."

24. Kriegel, *Pistol*, 201; Carry, "We Have a Slight Delay in Showtime," 31.

25. *Flames Magazine* 2 (1973–73), AFLAMSF, Kenan Library; "Atlanta Hawks 1974–1975 Media Guide," AHSF, Kenan Library; Beau Cutts and Randy Donaldson, "Omni Is a Success," *Atlanta Constitution*, January 8, 1973, 6D; Jim Stewart, "Omni Doors Open to Atlanta Tonight," *Atlanta Constitution*, October 14, 1972, 1A; Carry, "He's Shooting the Works," 50; Association for Professional Basketball Research, "NBA/ABA Home Attendance Totals."

26. Association for Professional Basketball Research, "NBA/ABA Home Attendance Totals"; "Hudson, Hawks Topple San Diego," *Atlanta Constitution*, March 28, 1969, 65; George Cunningham and Darrell Simmons, "Hawks Turn on the Heat While Mopping Up Lakers," *Atlanta Journal*, April 16, 1969, 4E; "Atlanta Discovers Sub for Success," *Atlanta Journal*, March 28, 1969, 1D; James, *Wrestling Record Book*, 87–124.

27. Outlar, "Maravich: A Sad End," C1; Denberg, Lazenby, and Stinson, *From Sweet Lou to 'Nique*, 36.

28. Deford, "The Hawks: Fouled Up," 42; Carry, "We Have a Slight Delay in Showtime," 31; Kriegel, *Pistol*, 195–99; Sanders, "Pistol Pete Now," 32.

29. Malcolm Moran, "Atlanta Fans Learn to Care for Hawks," *New York Times*, April 22, 1979, S10; George Cunningham, "Hawks Lose, Drew Is Fined," *Atlanta Constitution*, March 26, 1975, 1D; Tom Van Arsdale, in phone discussion with the author, July 10, 2013.

30. Darrell Simmons, "Hawks Reach All-Time Low," *Atlanta Journal*, April 6, 1976, 1D; George Cunningham, "Hawks' Streak at 13," *Atlanta Journal-Constitution*, April 4, 1976, 3D.

31. "Williams Quits Bulls for Atlanta," *Chicago Tribune*, August 5, 1973, B2.

32. Carry, "He's Shooting the Works," 50; "Hawks Open at Home Against the Pistol," *Atlanta Constitution*, August 12, 1975, 1D; Williams and Denney, *Ahead of the Game*, 61–64; "Free Hawks Tickets by WSB," *Atlanta Daily World*, January 22, 1974, 2.

33. Paul Delaney, "More Black Fans Sought by Hawks," *New York Times*, June 25, 1972, S4.

34. Justin Felder, "Carver Celebrates Anniversary of Milestone Basketball Championship," Fox5Atlanta.com, March 20, 2017, https://www.fox5atlanta.com/sports/carver-celebrates-anniversary-of-milestone-basketball-championship; "GHSA Boys Basketball Champions," Georgia High School Association, 2017, https://www.ghsa.net/ghsa-boys-basketball-champions.

35. Delaney, "More Black Fans Sought," S4.

36. Joel Gross, email message to author, August 15, 2013; Blount, "Losersville, U.S.A.," 77–84; Stone, *Regime Politics*, 98–102.

37. Blount, "Losersville, U.S.A.," 80.

38. "Sellout Home Crowd at Hawks-76ers Game," *Atlanta Daily World*, November 23, 1976, 5; George Cunningham, "Dr. J, Erving, Talent-Laden 76ers Seek Identity before Record Crowds," *Atlanta Journal*, November 20, 1976, 1C, 5C; "NBA Central," *Sporting News*, December 11, 1976, 28; Blount, "Losersville, U.S.A.," 82; George, *Elevating the Game*, xviii.

39. Jeremy Rutherford, "Departure of Hawks Still Is Bittersweet Affair," *St. Louis Post-Dispatch*, September 26, 1999, D16; Halberstam, *Breaks of the Game*, 9–16, 34–36; Huber and Saladino, *Babes of Winter*, 16; "Omni Foreclosure Looms," *Washington Post*, March 4, 1978, 17.

40. "Guide to Georgia: Fall 1971," AHSF, Kenan Library; *Report to the Atlanta Regional Commission on Public Response and Survey Aspects of WSB TV Shows*, ARCP, 1974, Kenan Library; "25 Hawks Road Games Set for Television," *Atlanta Daily World*, September 15, 1974, 7; "Hawks on TV," *Atlanta Journal*, October 16, 1968, 2C.

41. *Report to the Atlanta Regional Commission*, ARCP, Kenan Library; George Cunningham, "NBA Games Off Atlanta TV," *Atlanta Constitution*, January 13, 1973, 4D; "Hawks and TV Vie for Fans," *Atlanta Sunday Journal-Constitution*, April 8, 1973, 1D.

42. Cunningham, "NBA Games Off Atlanta TV," 4D.

43. Halberstam, *Breaks of the Game*, 9–16, 34–36.

44. "25 Hawks Road Games Set for Television," 7; Huber and Saladino, *Babes of Winter*, 183–84.

45. William Leggett, "Decline of a Brave New World," *Sports Illustrated*, May 5, 1975, 40.

46. Moran, "Atlanta Fans Learn to Care," S10; "NBA Central," *Sporting News*, January 15, 1977, 33.

47. Jeffrey Denberg, Lazenby, and Stinson, *From Sweet Lou to 'Nique*, 46–47.

48. Blount, "Losersville, U.S.A.," 82; Furman Bisher, "Cheaper by the Dozen Hawks," *Sporting News*, November 12, 1977, 2.

20. The Fans Showed Poor Taste

1. "Season Ticket Information: 1966–1970," ABF, Baseball HOF; "Braves 1975 Season Ticket Fact Sheet," ABSF, Kenan Library; *1967 Season Ticket Renewal Brochure*, ABSF, Kenan Library; Lester Smith, "Eight Clubs in Majors Boosting Ticket Prices," *Sporting News*, April 6, 1968, 23; "Baseball Ticket Sales and Concessions Information, 1971–1972," AFP, box 2, folder 10, Kenan Library.

2. Mike Holcomb, email message to author, September 6, 2016.

3. Bill James, "The Prisoner's Dilemma," Grantland, March 21, 2012 (site discontinued).

4. Al Thomy, "Nights Made for Sleeping, Not Baseball," *Atlanta Constitution*, May 3, 1974, 2D.

5. "Promotions," ABF, 1972, Baseball HOF; *Pow-Wow*, Spring 1969, HAF, Baseball HOF; "Buckhead Community Night," ABSF, Kenan Library; Frank Hyland, "It's a Whole New Ball Game," *Atlanta Journal*, March 28, 1972, 2D.

6. "Braves 1969 Official Game Program," ABSF, Kenan Library; *Braves Banner*, May 1985 and June 1983, ABF, Baseball HOF; "Noc-A-Homa," MF, Baseball HOF; Hope, *We Could've Finished Last without You*, 36–38; "The Fans Remember," *Atlanta*

Journal-Constitution, September 16, 1996, 1E; Jane Harris, "Real Injun Is Braves' Mascot," *Sporting News*, October 11, 1969, 8. In the late 1980s, the Braves replaced Chief Nock-A-Homa with Homer, a cartoon-like American Indian mascot with a full body suit. In subsequent decades, the franchise has deemphasized performing American Indian mascots, as the practice has become more controversial.

7. Johnny Tallant, in phone discussion with the author, August 18, 2013; David Hewes, email message to author, December 19, 2011; Alan Morris, email message to author, August 19, 2013; Joel Gross, email message to author, August 15, 2013.

8. Charlie Roberts, "Braves 'Take It All' as Hoopla Climaxes," *Atlanta Constitution*, April 12, 1966, 39, 44.

9. "What the Braves Fans Spent," *Atlanta Constitution*, November 14, 1966, 4; Wilt Browning, "Braves Pad Atlanta's Purse with $30 Million," *Atlanta Journal*, November 8, 1966, 44.

10. Karl Green, in phone discussion with the author, August 16, 2013.

11. Morris, email message to author; Tallant, in phone discussion with the author; Wayne Minshew, in phone discussion with the author, July 1, 2013.

12. Green, in phone discussion with the author; James Lizon, email message to author, March 19, 2019; Minshew, in phone discussion with the author; Morris, email message to author; University of Virginia Census Database, *City and County Data Book*, 1960–80.

13. Aaron and Wheeler, *I Had a Hammer*, 184–85.

14. Hewes, email message to author; Tallant, in phone discussion with the author; Morris, email message to author; Gross, email message to author.

15. Dave Anderson, "Empty Seats for the Aaron Drama," *New York Times*, September 28, 1973, 39.

16. University of Virginia Library Census Database, *City and County Data Book*, 1960–80; "Atlanta, Mecca for Middle-Class Blacks, Also Harbors Poverty," *New York Times*, January 20, 1986, A16.

17. Jeffrey M. Jones, "The Disappearing Black Baseball Fan," Gallup.com, July 15, 2003, https://news.gallup.com/poll/8854/disappearing-black-baseball-fan.aspx.

18. Bisher, *Miracle in Atlanta*, 34–40; Fred Russell, "Southern Stumbled on Color Line," *Sporting News*, April 4, 1962, 13; George Cunningham, "Dr. J, Erving, Talent-Laden 76ers Seek Identity before Record Crowds," *Atlanta Constitution*, November 20, 1976, 1C, 5C; "Sellout Home Crowd at Hawks-76ers Game," *Atlanta Daily World*, November 23, 1976, 5; "A Depressing 49er Finish," *San Francisco Examiner*, December 17, 1979, 1, 55.

19. Keating, "Atlanta: Peoplestown," 35–39; Stone, *Regime Politics*, 60–65; Aaron and Wheeler, *I Had a Hammer*, 184–85; Rebecca Burns, "The Other 284 Days," *Atlanta Magazine*, June 21, 2013, 32–36.

20. Sam Hopkins and Barry Henderson, "Foot Patrol at Stadium Is Ordered," *Atlanta Constitution*, October 9, 1973, 1A, 15A; Tom Henderson and Art Harris, "Fence Studied for Stadium Parking Lots," *Atlanta Constitution*, October 15, 1973, 1A, 2A; Bill Montgomery, "Police Step Up Stadium Force," *Atlanta Journal*, August 22, 1979, C1, C6; John McCosh, "Out of the Ballpark," *Atlanta Journal-Constitution*, April 13, 2000, 1JD; Hope, *We Could Have Finished Last without You*, 62; Keeler McCartney, "Violence at Stadium Brings Warnings," *Atlanta Constitution*, December 2, 1970, 6A; Schaeffer and Davidson, *Economic Impact of the Falcons, 1973*, 7.

21. Aaron and Wheeler, *I Had a Hammer*, 184–85; "Promotions," ABF, 1972.

22. Aaron and Wheeler, *I Had a Hammer*, 184–85; Holcomb, email message to author; Lee Walburn, "Bill Lucas," *Atlanta Magazine*, May 1, 2011.

23. Furman Bisher, "Behold, the Enlightenment," *Atlanta Journal*, April 30, 1968, 1D.

24. "Braves Handicap," *Atlanta Sunday Journal-Constitution*, September 26, 1971.

25. Oscar Kahan, "What Ails Braves? Just Ask the Fans!" *Sporting News*, November 8, 1975, 43.

26. Anderson, "Empty Seats for Aaron Drama," 39.

27. Louis Harris, "Most Root for Aaron," *Washington Post*, September 17, 1973, D12; Aaron and Wheeler, *I Had a Hammer*, 242–49; Jesse Outlar, "A Letter to Lou," *Atlanta Constitution*, August 9, 1975, 1C.

28. Hope, *We Could Have Finished Last without You*, 43–55; Jesse Outlar, "Two More Fences," *Atlanta Constitution*, October 1, 1973, 1D.

29. Aaron and Wheeler, *I Had a Hammer*, 231–32.

30. Aaron and Bisher, *Aaron*, 215–17; "Only 1362 Fans See Aaron Clout," *New York Times*, September 18, 1973, 49; Mike McKenzie, "Just Another Memory," *Atlanta Journal*, July 21, 1973, 12A.

31. Morris, email message to author.

32. Green, in phone discussion with the author.

33. Minshew, in phone discussion with the author.

34. Preston, *Major League Baseball*, 98–100; Aaron and Wheeler, *I Had a Hammer*, 233–34, 242–49.

35. "On No. 715, Thank God It's Over," *Atlanta Journal-Constitution*, April 2, 1991, E1.

36. Harris, "Most Root for Aaron," D12; Aaron and Wheeler, *I Had a Hammer*, 242–49.

37. Morris, email message to author.

38. Aaron and Wheeler, *I Had a Hammer*, 187.

39. Al Thomy, "$600,000 Cushion to Aid Aaron's Bid for Ruth Mark," *Sporting News*, March 18, 1972, 34; Wayne Minshew, "Aaron Slurred as He Assaults Ruth's Mark," *Sporting News*, May 26, 1973, 5; "Insiders Say," *Sporting News*, May 24, 1975, 6.

40. Aaron and Wheeler, *I Had a Hammer* 236–39, 242–49.

41. Ron Reed, in phone discussion with the author, July 8, 2013.

42. "On No. 715, Thank God It's Over," E1; "Abuse by Atlanta Fans Closes in on Aaron," *Washington Post*, May 9, 1973, E1; Minshew, "Aaron Slurred," 5; Aaron and Wheeler, *I Had a Hammer*, 235; Aaron and Bisher, *Aaron*, 215–17.

43. Frank Hyland, "Trouble . . . Trouble," *Atlanta Journal*, April 4, 1974, 20S; "Abuse by Atlanta Fans," E1; Aaron and Bisher, *Aaron* 215–17.

44. Aaron and Wheeler, *I Had a Hammer*, 231–32.

45. Hyland, "Trouble . . . Trouble," 20S; "Abuse by Atlanta Fans," E1; Aaron and Bisher, *Aaron*, 215–17.

46. *Pow-Wow*, January 1974, HAF, Baseball HOF; Aaron and Wheeler, *I Had a Hammer*, 223–25, 286; Philip Dougherty, "Advertising: Aaron's Big Blast," *New York Times*, April 10, 1974, 63; Tom Buckley, "The Packaging of a Home Run" *New York Times* March 31, 1974, 262; Bryant, *Last Hero*, 362–64; Wayne Minshew, "Aaron

Giving Sherman Tips on How to Capture Atlanta," *Sporting News*, September 29, 1973, 12; Frank Hyland, "The Long Winter," *Atlanta Journal*, April 4, 1974, 4s.

47. Bryant, *Last Hero*, xii–xv, 324–26, 415; Hyland, "Trouble . . . Trouble," 20s.

48. Wilt Browning, "Aaron Target Won't Be Still," *Atlanta Journal*, April 17, 1969, 1D; William Leggett, "Hank Becomes a Hit," *Sports Illustrated*, August 18, 1969, 34; Hyland, "Trouble . . . Trouble," 20s; Aaron and Wheeler, *I Had a Hammer*, 191–92, 220–22; Milo Hamilton, in phone discussion with the author, July 11, 2013; Walt Browning, "Aaron: Get Milo off My Back," *Atlanta Journal*, September 9, 1969, 1C; Wayne Minshew, "Feud Over—Aaron, Milo Reach Truce," *Sporting News*, September 27, 1969, 13.

49. Bryant, *Last Hero*, 305–9; Aaron and Wheeler, *I Had a Hammer*, 183–84; Hyland, "Trouble . . . Trouble," 20s.

50. Aaron and Wheeler, *I Had a Hammer*, 282–83; Aaron and Bisher, *Aaron*, 207; Mike McKenzie, "Aaron's 'Secret' Official Now," *Atlanta Journal*, July 20, 1973, 1D.

51. "On No. 715, Thank God It's Over," E1.

52. "Hank Aaron is 'Man of Hour,'" *Atlanta Daily World*, April 9, 1974, 1; Bryant, *Last Hero*, 371, 380–85; Jesse Outlar, "Aaron Hits 714," *Atlanta Constitution*, April 5, 1974, 1; Frank Hyland, "Aaron to Play All Three?" *Atlanta Journal*, April 4, 1974, 1D; Wayne Minshew, "Kuhn Pressures Braves to Start Hank," *Atlanta Constitution*, April 4, 1974, 1G; Hyland, "Trouble . . . Trouble," 20s; "Teammates Defend Aaron," *Atlanta Journal*, April 8, 1974, 9D; "Hammering at Henry," *Sports Illustrated*, March 4, 1974, 27.

53. Furman Bisher, "I Just Thank God It's Over," *Atlanta Journal*, April 9, 1974, 1, 8H; Wayne Minshew, "The Hammer Hails the Big One," *Sporting News*, April 27, 1974, 7; Frank Hyland, "It's Over: Hammerin' Hank Stands All Alone at 715," *Atlanta Journal*, April 9, 1974, 1A; "Aaron Hammers No 715 and Moves Ahead of Ruth," *Atlanta Constitution* April 9, 1974, 1; Aaron and Wheeler, *I Had a Hammer*, 267, 279; "Return of Ol' 693," *Atlanta Journal*, April 9, 1974, 1D, 4D; Bryant, *Last Hero*, 365–66.

54. Frank Hyland, "Mathews Upset for Fans Leaving Early," *Atlanta Journal*, April 9, 1974, 1D, 4D; Furman Bisher, "Home Run No. 715," *Atlanta Journal*, April 9, 1974, 8H.

55. Aaron and Wheeler, *I Had a Hammer*, 272.

56. Hyland, "Mathews Upset," 1D, 4D.

57. Gross, email message to author, August 15, 2013.

58. Hyland "Mathews Upset," 1D, 4D.

59. Frank Hyland, "Aaron Takes Night Off; Braves Suffer Post-715 Blahs," *Atlanta Journal*, April 10, 1974, 1E; Ray Kennedy, "Warning: Dangerous Slurves Ahead," *Sports Illustrated*, July 8, 1974, 17; Wayne Minshew, "John Too Much for Braves, 4–0," *Atlanta Constitution*, April 11, 1974, 1E.

60. Aaron and Wheeler, *I Had a Hammer*, 288.

61. Dick Young, "Braves' Fans Snub Aaron," *Sporting News*, July 5, 1975, 12; Furman Bisher, "Hammering Hank Is Headed Home," *Atlanta Journal*, October 4, 1974. 1D; "Aaron Happy to Return Home," *Chicago Defender*, November 4, 1974; Tim Tucker, "A City's Favorite Record," *Atlanta Constitution*, July 22, 2007, 1E.

62. Minshew, in phone discussion with the author.

63. Minshew, in phone discussion with the author.

64. Fields, *Take Me Out to the Crowd*, 55–63.

65. Milo Hamilton, in phone discussion with the author, July 11, 2013.

66. Dick Gray, "Mellow Milo Hardsells the Braves," *Atlanta Journal*, June 28, 1966, 35; Morris, email message to author.

67. Jesse Outlar, "Milo Had No Inkling of Firing," *Atlanta Constitution*, October 9, 1975, 1G.

68. "Hamilton Rips Fans," *Sporting News*, July 26, 1975, 29.

69. Hewes, email message to author.

70. "Goodbye Atlanta–Fulton County Stadium," *Atlanta Journal-Constitution*, September 15, 1996, 13E.

71. Holcomb, email message to author.

72. Morris, email message to author.

73. Minshew, in phone discussion with the author.

74. Morris, email message to author.

75. Kahan, "What Ails Braves?" 43.

76. Jim Stewart, "Empty Seats Cost Us $800,000," *Atlanta Constitution*, October 3, 1972, 1A.

77. "The Stadium Deal: A Final Hurdle," *Atlanta Journal-Constitution*, March 3, 1993, D4.

78. "1967 Season Ticket Renewal Letter," ABF; "Atlanta Braves, Inc.: Consolidated Statement of Earnings, 1971–1972," AFP, box 2, folder 10, Baseball HOF; Lester Smith, "Braves' Gate, Operating Income Improved in '69," *Sporting News*, January 31, 1970, 47; Lester Smith, "Tax Losses Aid Braves' Banner Profits for '66," *Sporting News*, January 14, 1967, 28; "Braves Report 1969 Profit of $347,000," *Washington Post*, January 1, 1970, E2.

79. "Atlanta Braves, Inc.: Consolidated Statement of Earnings, 1971–1972," AFP, box 2, folder 10, Baseball HOF; Smith, "Tax Losses," 28. Lester Smith, "1972 Braves Lost 333,327—Even with Benefit of Tax Credit," *Sporting News*, January 27, 1973, 50; Lester Smith, "Braves Post First Loss Since Move to Atlanta," *Sporting News*, January 29, 1972, 39.

80. Lester Smith, "Braves Move Out of Red—Show Profit of 345,865," *Sporting News*, March 9, 1974, 28.

81. Wayne Minshew, "Channel 17 Owner Ted Turner to Buy Braves for $12 Million," *Atlanta Constitution*, January 7, 1976, 1.

21. Instant City

1. "Tom Cousins: Atlanta Power Player Retires," *Atlanta Journal-Constitution*, December 7, 2006, 1B.

2. Jim Galloway, "Turner Wants to Tack CNN onto Name of Omni Arena," *Atlanta Journal*, March 6, 1987, 1; Furman Bisher, "Omni Offered Moments of Splendor," *Atlanta Journal-Constitution*, April 20, 1997, 18E; Rutheiser, *Imagineering Atlanta*, 217–18.

3. "Omni Praised by Capacity Crowd," *Atlanta Daily World*, October 17, 1972, 1.

4. Ron Taylor, "'Beautifuls' Hail Sold-Out Omni," *Atlanta Sunday Journal-Constitution*, October 15, 1972, 1, 12.

5. Taylor, "'Beautifuls' Hail Sold-Out Omni," 1A; Jim Stewart, "Omni Doors Open to Atlanta Tonight," *Atlanta Constitution*, October 14, 1972, 1, 12; Huber and

Saladino, *Babes of Winter*, 16–17, 22–25; *Omni Souvenir Dedication Book*, OSF, Kenan Library; Frank Wells, "Coliseum Adds to City's Big League Image," *Atlanta Constitution*, January 19, 1973, 12C.

6. Joe Watkins, in phone discussion with the author, July 3, 2013.

7. *Omni Souvenir Dedication Book*, OSF, Kenan Library; Tom Van Arsdale, in phone discussion with the author, July 10, 2013; Paul Jones, "Omni Only 92 Percent Ready for Opening," *Atlanta Constitution*, October 3, 1972, 6A; Huber and Saladino, *Babes of Winter*, 24–25.

8. Betsy Watkins, in phone discussion with the author, July 3, 2013.

9. *Omni Souvenir Dedication Book*, OSF, Kenan Library; Leo Monahan, "Atlanta Fans Warming Up to Fast-Charging Flames," *Sporting News*, December 23, 1972, 4; Jim Huber, "Atlanta Inaugurates Omni as Sports Palace of South," *Sporting News*, October 28, 1972, 45.

10. Huber and Saladino, *Babes of Winter*, 24–25; David Hewes, email message to author, December 19, 2011; *Omni Souvenir Dedication Book*, OSF, Kenan Library; "Getting to the Omni Is Easier Done than Said": advertisement, *Atlanta Journal*, October 13, 1972, 4A.

11. Mike Holcomb, email message to author, September 6, 2016.

12. Huber and Saladino, *Babes of Winter*, 24–25; Hewes, email message to author; *Omni Souvenir Dedication Book*, OSF, Kenan Library.

13. Mike McKenzie, "Lucas' Magic Not Enough for the Hawks," *Atlanta Journal*, October 16, 1972, 1D; Van Arsdale, in phone discussion with the author.

14. Bill Clement, in phone discussion with the author, June 26, 2013.

15. Art Chansky, "Forwards Fight in Hawks Win," *Atlanta Constitution*, October 16, 1972, 3D.

16. Tony Petrella, "A Twinbill 'No Big Deal,'" *Atlanta Constitution*, January 15, 1973, 3D; Ron Hudspeth, "Meanwhile at the Omni," *Atlanta Journal*, January 15, 1973, 1D; *Omni Souvenir Dedication Book*, OSF, Kenan Library.

17. Shropshire, *Sports Franchise Game*, 9–10, 75.

18. "Flames Notes," *Atlanta Constitution*, January 3, 1976, 4C; Stewart, "Omni Doors Open," 1A; Bisher, "Omni Offered Moments of Splendor," 18E.

19. *Omni Souvenir Dedication Book*, OSF, Kenan Library; "All Concerned Agree: It's Good to Rid Atlanta of Omni," *Chicago Tribune*, May 12, 1997, 2D; Robert M. Craig, "Thompson, Ventulett, Stainback, and Associates (TVS)," New Georgia Encyclopedia, May 29, 2008, last updated May 9, 2019, https://www.georgiaencyclopedia.org/articles/arts-culture/thompson-ventulett-stainback-and-associates-tvs; Huber and Saladino, *Babes of Winter*, 25; Taylor, "'Beautifuls' Hail Sold-Out Omni," 1, 12; Tom Walker, "Omni Complex to Help City's Global Look," *Atlanta Journal*, October 11, 1972, 1A, 9A.

20. John McGourty, "Former Flames Recall Hot Times in Atlanta," NHL.com, January 24, 2008, https://www.nhl.com/news/former-flames-recall-hot-times-in-atlanta/c-370370.

21. Since the 1940s, Paul Jones's Atlanta-based ABC Booking, the forerunner of GCW, had been the state's top wrestling promotion. ABC Booking and, later, GCW possessed territorial rights to the region through the National Wrestling Alliance (NWA), a cartel of regional promoters who controlled virtually all of the top wrestling talent in the United States and Canada between the late-1940s and the

mid-1980s. Beekman, *Ringside*, 112–14; James, *Wrestling Record Book*, 87–124; History of the WWE, "The Omni: 1973–1979"; Shoemaker, *Squared Circle*, 8–14.

22. Solie, "Gordon Solie Interview"; Beekman, *Ringside*, 112–14; James, *Wrestling Record Book*, 87–124; History of the WWE, "The Omni: 1973–1979"; Association for Professional Basketball Research, "NBA/ABA Home Attendance Totals."

23. Beekman, *Ringside*, 112–14; Solie, "Gordon Solie Interview."

24. Scott Beekman, *Ringside*, 114–23; James, *Wrestling Record Book*, 162–63.

25. Solie, "Gordon Solie Interview"; James, *Wrestling Record Book*, 87–124; Beekman, *Ringside*, 114–23.

26. Roy M. Blount, "Losersville, U.S.A.," *Sports Illustrated*, March 21, 1977, 85.

27. Holcomb, email message to author, September 6, 2016.

28. Blount, "Losersville, U.S.A.," 85; Solie, "Gordon Solie Interview"; Holcomb, email message to author.

29. James, *Wrestling Record Book*, 87–124.

30. Setlist.fm, "The Omni Atlanta Concert Setlists"; Beau Cutts and Randy Donaldson, "Omni Is a Success," *Atlanta Constitution*, January 8, 1973, 6D; Furman Bisher, "Omni's 20 Years of Memories," *Atlanta Journal-Constitution*, February 21, 1993, G1; "Omni Planning College Basketball Program," *Atlanta Journal*, April 1, 1976, 3D; "Ice Capades Opens at Omni Thursday Night," *Atlanta Constitution*, October 14, 1972, 1A; Maurice Fliess, "Omni Unfinished but Will Open to 'All,'" *Atlanta Journal*, October 11, 1972, 18A.

31. "RCA Records King Benefit Concert for Social Center," *Chicago Defender*, January 17, 1973, 1; Setlist.fm, "The Omni Atlanta Concert Setlists."

32. Solie, "Gordon Solie Interview"; Blount, "Losersville, U.S.A.," 77–84; George, *Where Did Our Love Go?*, 140; Brown, "'And the Beat Goes On,'" 165–71.

33. "SCLC Calls Off Green Boycott," *Chicago Defender*, November 26, 1973, 4.

34. "Al Green Boycotted by SCLC," *Amsterdam News*, December 1, 1973, A1; Charlie Cherokee, "Charlie Cherokee Says," *Chicago Defender*, November 27, 1973, 8; Setlist.fm, "Al Green Concert Setlists"; "Hosea Calls Planners of Boycott Wrong," *Atlanta Daily World*, April 30, 1976, 2; "Wrester Has Hosea in Court Again," *Atlanta Daily World*, October 12, 1978, 2.

35. "OmniSouth—1979," CAPP, box 97, folder 3, Kenan Library; Sam Massell, in phone discussion with the author, July 2, 2013; Rutheiser, *Imagineering Atlanta*, 165.

36. Tom Walker, "Omni May Wind Up Close to Original Concept," *Atlanta Constitution*, December 11, 1983, OSF, Kenan Library; Mary Greenbaum, "Atlanta Sobers Up," *Fortune*, June 1978, 118; Horace Sutton, "Atlanta Grows 'Up,'" *Chicago Tribune*, August 22, 1976, C2; Alfred Borcover, "Fantasy in Atlanta's Omni," *Chicago Tribune*, June 13, 1976, C1; Rutheiser, *Imagineering Atlanta*, 161–65; Allen, *Atlanta Rising*, 200.

37. *A Preliminary Analysis of the Impact of MARTA's Omni Station on Omni International Atlanta*, ARCP, 1981, Kenan Library; Allen, *Atlanta Rising*, 200.

38. Jim Auchmutey, "The Omni: Neat, Clean, and Empty," *Atlanta Sunday Journal-Constitution*, January 6, 1985, 1.

39. Allen, *Atlanta Rising*, 196–97; Borcover, "Fantasy in Atlanta's Omni," C1; "Omni Complex to Help City's Global Look," *Atlanta Journal*, October 11, 1972, 1A, 4A; Wayne King, "Atlanta's Upward Surge Stalls as Omni Building Complex Falters," *New York Times*, February 11, 1978, 45.

40. Douglas R. Sease, "Atlanta Sobered by Real Estate Bust," *Washington Post*, March 4, 1978, E1; Beau Cutts, "Omni May Get Loan Refinancing," *Washington Post*, May 13, 1976, E12.

41. King, "Atlanta's Upward Surge Stalls," 45; Auchmutey, "Omni: Neat, Clean, and Empty," 1; Rutheiser, *Imagineering Atlanta*, 161–65.

42. Allen, *Atlanta Rising*, 200.

43. Rutheiser, *Imagineering Atlanta*, 164–65, 180–84; Walker, "Omni Complex to Help City's Global Look," 1A, 9A; Bob Hertzel, "Study Shows Atlanta Wants Arena," *Atlanta Journal*, May 7, 1968, 4D.

44. Charles Moore, "Atlanta Tops U.S. Job Gains," *Atlanta Constitution*, January 2, 1965, 6; Rutheiser, *Imagineering Atlanta*, 49; "Atlanta: City Renaissance at Its Best," *Cleveland Plain Dealer*, May 15, 1966, 32; "A City in Crisis," *Atlanta Sunday Journal-Constitution*, March 30, 1975, 1A, 12A.

45. "Perimeter Mall Turns 35," *Atlanta Journal-Constitution*, August 17, 2006, 1JH; Rutheiser, *Imagineering Atlanta*, 49; "City in Crisis," 1A, 12A; Ambrose, *Atlanta*, 183–85.

46. Rutheiser, *Imagineering Atlanta*, 63; Sallye Salter, "Atlanta: Rapid Transit Station Is the Hub of Burgeoning Buckhead Area," *New York Times*, May 12, 1985, CR16; Sam Massell, in phone discussion with the author, July 2, 2013; Booth, *Transforming Suburban Business Districts*, 169–72.

47. George M. Coleman, "One Race Downtown Section Must Be 'Impossible Dream,'" *Atlanta Daily World*, November 4, 1971, 1.

48. George M. Coleman, "All Share Guilt in Fears, Frustrations of This Area," *Atlanta Daily World*, November 2, 1971, 1.

49. "Atlanta and Crime," *Atlanta Daily World*, April 4, 1972, 6; Hinton, *From War on Poverty to War on Crime*, 1–6.

50. Bayor, *Race and Shaping of Twentieth-Century Atlanta*, 85–92; Allen, *Atlanta Rising*, 196–97, 206–8.

51. Allen, *Atlanta Rising*, 196–97, 206–8; "Downtown Issues, 1974," CAPP, box 93, folder 3, Kenan Library; Robert Scheer, "Tourists Seldom See the Real Face of Atlanta," *Boston Globe*, February 18, 1979, A3.

52. Coleman, "All Share Guilt," 1.

53. "Atlanta and Crime," *Atlanta Daily World*, April 4, 1972, 6.

54. "Central Area Survey II, 1980–Present (1987)," CAPP, box 54, folder 2, Kenan Library.

55. Janet Guyon, "Bustling Atlanta Seems Built More for Outsiders than Its Own," *Wall Street Journal*, September 23, 1980, 37.

56. Allen, *Atlanta Rising*, 206–8; Curtis Wilkie, "Atlanta—A Resilient City," *Boston Globe*, September 5, 1976, A2.

57. "Central Atlanta Progress Annual Report (1979)," CAPP, box 38, folder 3, Kenan Library.

58. Metropolitan Crime Commission, *Crime in Metropolitan Atlanta, 1975–1979*, MACCP; U.S. Department of Justice, *Crime in Eight American Cities*, 7, 24–25; "Atlanta: A City in Crisis," *Atlanta Sunday Journal-Constitution*, March 23, 1975, 16A; Frederick Allen and Jim Merriner, "Library, No; Streets, Yes, Atlantans Say," *Atlanta Journal-Constitution*, October 3, 1975, 1A; Headley, *Atlanta Youth Murders*, 28–32; University of Virginia Census Database, *City and County Data Book*, 1980.

59. University of Virginia Census Database, *City and County Data Book,* 1975; "Cutting Crime," *Atlanta Constitution,* November 3, 1971, 4A; "Massell's State of the City Address," *Atlanta Constitution,* January 3, 1973, 10A; "City Seeks to Increase Parks Police," *Atlanta Constitution,* August 5, 1971, 4A; "Massell for Mayor 1973 Campaign Materials," SMPF, Kenan Library.

60. "Visitor's Guide and Map to Underground Atlanta," UASF, Kenan Library; Jon Nordheimer, "Atlanta Brightens Its Cellar," *New York Times,* September 11, 1969, 49; Rutheiser, *Imagineering Atlanta,* 166–67; Lee Simowitz, "Underground Atlanta Finds It's 1900 Again," *Atlanta Constitution,* April 9, 1969, 1.

61. William A. Evans, "While Atlanta Grows Upward It Is Spreading Underground": promotional flier, UASF, Kenan Library; Peter Applebome, "Atlanta Places Its Bets on a New Underground," *New York Times,* June 11, 1989, 26; "Underground Atlanta to Return to Gay Nineties," *New York Times,* April 20, 1969, R8.

62. Wayne King, "Underground Atlanta Complex Is Beset by Problems," *New York Times,* February 19, 1975, 16; Rutheiser, *Imagineering Atlanta,* 166–67; "Atlanta: Another Struggle," *Boston Globe,* July 31, 1977, B18; Allen, *Atlanta Rising,* 196–97.

63. Rutheiser, *Imagineering Atlanta,* 164.

64. King, "Underground Atlanta Complex," 16.

65. David Morrison, "City Police to Fight Muggings," *Atlanta Constitution,* September 30, 1972, 1A.

66. Suzanne Dolezal, "9 Alarm Blaze Guts Unoccupied Hotel, Underground Firms," *Atlanta Sunday Journal-Constitution,* June 29, 1980, 6A; Rutheiser, *Imagineering Atlanta,* 166–67; Paul Gapp, "Atlanta: Capital of the New South," *Chicago Tribune,* March 26, 1980, 1.

67. Janet Guyon, "Bustling Atlanta Seems Built More for Outsiders than Its Own," *Wall Street Journal,* September 23, 1980, 37.

68. Wilkie, "Atlanta—A Resilient City," A2.

69. Guyon, "Bustling Atlanta," 37.

70. "Central Area Survey II, 1980–Present (1987)," CAPP, box 54, folder 2, Kenan Library; Guyon, "Bustling Atlanta," 37; Allen, *Atlanta Rising,* 206–8.

71. Jim Galloway, "Turner Wants to Tack CNN onto Name of Omni Arena," *Atlanta Journal,* March 6, 1987; Rutheiser, *Imagineering Atlanta,* 217–18.

72. Richard Sandomir, "Philips to Pay $180 Million to Name New Atlanta Arena," *New York Times,* February 3, 1999, 47; Fulton County Commission, "Minutes of Special Call Meeting."

22. Keep Hockey a Southern Sport

1. Al Smith and Warren Newman, "Skating on Thin Ice," *Atlanta Sunday Journal-Constitution,* March 30, 1980, 1D, 15D; Alan Truex, "The Ice Age: From Blizzard to Meltdown," *Atlanta Journal,* May 23, 1980, D1; Alan Truex, "Flames Won't Reveal Ticket Sales," *Atlanta Sunday Journal-Constitution,* March 23, 1975, 12D; Alan Truex, "Flames' Ticket Sales Down," *Atlanta Journal,* August 7, 1975, 4D; Huber and Saladino, *Babes of Winter,* 75.

2. Bill Clement, in phone discussion with the author, June 26, 2013.

3. Huber and Saladino, *Babes of Winter,* 75; Roy M. Blount, "Losersville, U.S.A.," *Sports Illustrated,* March 21, 1977, 83; Smith and Newman, "Skating on Thin Ice," 1D, 15D.

4. Joe Watkins, in phone discussion with the author, July 3, 2013.

5. Clement, in phone discussion with the author.

6. Leo Monahan, "Atlanta Fans Warming Up to Fast-Charging Flames," *Sporting News*, December 23, 1972, 4; *Omni Souvenir Dedication Book*, AFLAMSF, Kenan Library.

7. Smith and Newman, "Skating on Thin Ice," 1D, 15D.

8. Blount, "Losersville, U.S.A.," 83; Truex, "Flames' Ticket Sales Down," 4D; Huber and Saladino, *Babes of Winter*, 183–84; William Leggett, "Decline of a Brave New World," *Sports Illustrated*, May 5, 1975, 34.

9. *Flames Magazine* 1 (1972–73), AFLAMSF, Kenan Library; *Atlanta Flames Fact Book, 1974–1975*, AFLAMSF, Kenan Library; *Atlanta Flames Fact Book 1975–1976*, AFLAMSF, Kenan Library; Jack Craig, "NBC to Woo the South for Hockey," *Sporting News*, December 15, 1973, 26; Leggett, "Decline of Brave New World," 34; Huber and Saladino, *Babes of Winter*, 55, 87; Tony Petrella, "Flames: The Omni Welcomes Ice Age," *Atlanta Constitution*, October 14, 1972, 1D; "Flames and WSB Announce 1974–75 TV Schedule," *Atlanta Daily World*, September 19, 1974, 6.

10. Leggett, "Decline of Brave New World," 34.

11. *Atlanta Flames Fact Book 1974–1975*, AFLAMSF, Kenan Library; Jim Minter, in phone discussion with the author, July 9, 2013; Huber and Saladino, *Babes of Winter*, 87; Tony Petrella, "Flames: Omni Welcomes Ice Age," 1D.

12. *Atlanta Flames Fact Book 1975–1976*, AFLAMSF, Kenan Library; Huber and Saladino, *Babes of Winter*, 183–84; Smith and Newman, "Skating on Thin Ice," 1D, 15D.

13. Truex, "Ice Age: From Blizzard to Meltdown," D1.

14. Smith and Newman, "Skating on Thin Ice," 1D, 15D; Huber and Saladino, *Babes of Winter*, 83.

15. Bruce Baake, "Flames to Offer Number of Incentives in 1976," *Atlanta Daily World*, May 25, 1976, 2; Smith and Newman, "Skating on Thin Ice," 1D, 15D.

16. Truex, "Ice Age: From Blizzard to Meltdown," D1; mith and Newman, "Skating on Thin Ice," 1D, 15D; Blount, "Losersville, U.S.A.," 78; "Gate Slumping at Half-Million Rate," *Sporting News*, December 18, 1976, 33.

17. Vic Dorr, "Flames for Sale? Cousins Says 'No,'" *Atlanta Constitution*, January 5, 1977, 1C; Alex Truex, "Cousins Puts End to Flames Sale Rumor," *Atlanta Journal*, January 7, 1977, 1D; Alan Truex, "Cousins: Flames Not for Sale," *Atlanta Journal*, January 5, 1977, 1D; Truex, "Ice Age: From Blizzard to Meltdown," D1; Gary Mueller, "NHL Hockey," *Sporting News*, January 29, 1977, 22.

18. Tom Tucker, "Craig Debut Is Golden," *Atlanta Sunday Journal-Constitution*, March 2, 1980, D1; Kathy Blumenstock, "The Flame Is Still Burning Brightly," *Sports Illustrated*, March 10, 1980, 22; "Craig in the Nets as Flames Tackle 'Home Ice' Dilemma," *Atlanta Journal*, April 25, 1980, 1D; Jim Naughton, "Craig, Olympic Hero, Caught in Dual Role," *New York Times*, March 30, 1980, s6; "This Flame Is Red Hot," *Boston Globe*, March 3, 1980, 32.

19. Jamie Taylor, email message to author, December 12, 2019.

20. Jim Naughton, "Jim Craig: He Reinforces What's Right," *New York Times*, June 8, 1980, s1; Blumenstock, "Flame Is Still Burning," 22; Naughton, "Craig, Olympic Hero," *New York Times*, March 30, 1980, s6; Tom Tucker, "'Big Mouth' Bouchard Rips Flames Again," *Atlanta Journal*, April 4, 1980, 1D.

21. Clement, in phone discussion with the author; Al Smith, "Flames Not Dead Yet," *Atlanta Journal-Constitution*, April 12, 1980, 1C; Tom Tucker, "Mac the Knife Is Back," *Atlanta Journal*, March 21, 1980, 1D; Tom Tucker, "Flames Flicker Out, 5–2," *Atlanta Sunday Journal-Constitution*, April 13, 1980, 1D.

22. "Flames' Owner Considers Bids to Sell Hockey Team," *New York Times*, April 17, 1980, B27; Tom Tucker, "Flame Playoff Failure Fuels the Rumor Mill," *Atlanta Journal*, April 14, 1980, 7D; Smith and Newman, "Skating on Thin Ice," 1D, 15D.

23. Joe and Betsy Watkins, in phone discussion with the author, July 3, 2013; "Flames to Calgary? Fans React," *Sporting News*, May 17, 1980, 60.

24. "Voice of the Fan," *Sporting News*, June 14, 1980, 4.

25. Custance, "Old Flame(s)," 1D; "Skalbania Buys Flames," *Sporting News*, June 14, 1980, 50; Eric Duhatschek, "Skalbania's New Flame Is Calgary," *Sporting News*, October 18, 1980, 30; Tom Tucker, "Kent Denies Story of Bid for Flames," *Atlanta Journal*, April 17, 1980, 1D; Truex, "Ice Age: From Blizzard to Meltdown," D1.

26. Clement, in phone discussion with the author.

27. Parton Keese, "Flames Struggling to Thaw Out in Calgary," *New York Times*, December 14, 1980, S1; Custance, "Old Flame(s)," 1D; Tom Tucker, "Flames Put Out the 'For Sale' Sign," *Atlanta Journal*, April 16, 1980, 1D; Jack Wilkinson, "An Old Flame," *Atlanta Journal-Constitution*, July 26, 1999, 4D.

23. Loserville No More

1. Fields, *Take Me Out to the Crowd*, 34.

2. Turner and Burke, *Call Me Ted*, 109–12; Christian Boone, "A Brave(s) New World for Turner," *Atlanta Journal-Constitution*, January 1, 2009, 1E.

3. Wayne Minshew, in phone discussion with the author, July 1, 2013.

4. Boone, "A Brave(s) New World," 1E.

5. Fields, *Take Me Out to the Crowd*, 49–51; *Braves Banner*, June 1983, ABF, Baseball HOF; Roy M. Blount, "Loserville, U.S.A.," *Sports Illustrated*, March 21, 1977, 76–80; David Hewes, email message to author, December 19, 2011.

6. Alan Morris, email message to author, August 13, 2013.

7. Turner and Burke. *Call Me Ted*, 133–38; *Braves Banner*, June 1985, ABF, Baseball HOF.

8. Milo Hamilton, in phone discussion with the author, July 11, 2013.

9. Vance Law, email message to author, March 10, 2019.

10. *Braves Banner*, June 1985, ABF, Baseball HOF; *Braves Banner*, May 1984, ABF, Baseball HOF; Furman Bisher, "Van Wieren's Voice a Perfect Guide," *Atlanta Journal-Constitution*, January 25, 2009, 2C; Turner and Burke, *Call Me Ted*, 133–38.

11. Jeff Hullinger, email message to author, March 10, 2019.

12. Rick Reilly, "Peach State Lemons," *Sports Illustrated*, October 3, 1988, 44; Morris, email message to author; Bill Zack, "Last Place: Home of the Braves," *Sporting News*, October 8, 1990, 10.

13. Furman Bisher, "After Merger, Turner's Heart Still with Braves, Hawks," *Atlanta Constitution*, September 13, 1996, 1; Dave Nightengale, "Goodwill but Not Much Excitement," *Sporting News*, August 13, 1990, 45; Michael Knisley, "Mr. Universe," *Sporting News*, January 3, 1994, S2; Turner and Burke, *Call Me Ted*, 215–21.

14. Bisher, "After Merger," 1.

15. Hullinger, email message to author.

16. Mike Kenn, email message to author, March 19, 2019.

17. Reilly, "Peach State Lemons," 44; Matt Winkeljohn, "The Sale of the Falcons," *Atlanta Journal-Constitution*, December 7, 2001, 12; Schaeffer and Davidson, *Economic Impact of the Falcons, 1984*, 4–8.

18. Kenn, email message to author.

19. Peter Applebome, "Atlanta in Accord on Plans for a Domed Stadium," *New York Times*, June 7, 1989, A16; Schaeffer and Davidson, *Economic Impact of the Falcons, 1984*, 14.

20. "The Georgia Dome," *Sporting News*, June 19, 1989, 63; "Falcons '93," AFF, Football HOF; Applebome, "Atlanta in Accord," A16; "The Spectacular Georgia Dome (1994)," AFF, Football HOF; "Georgia Dome: A New Experience for Falcons Fans (1991)," AFF, Football HOF; Mark Bradley, "Dome an Apt Symbol of Vibrant Sports City," *Atlanta Journal-Constitution*, August 24, 1992, 1D.

21. Bradley, "Dome an Apt Symbol," 1D.

22. *Falcons '92*, AFF, Football HOF.

23. Jim Minter, in phone discussion with the author, July 9, 2013; Gary Stokan, in phone discussion with the author, July 10, 2013; Georgia Institute of Technology, *Engineering for Success*, 160–65.

24. Stokan, in phone discussion with the author; Mike Fish, "The Peach Bowl: Robust Peach Owes Its Rescue to Chamber," *Atlanta Journal-Constitution*, December 26, 1999, 7G.

25. Matt Winkeljohn, "Low Fan Ceiling," December 2, 2001, *Atlanta Journal-Constitution*, 1E; "Sound Off: Falcons Attendance," *Atlanta Journal-Constitution*, October 1, 2000, 2E.

26. "Georgia Dome in Most Dangerous NFL-Stadium Neighborhood, Study Says," *Atlanta Business Chronicle*, September 7, 2001; Winkeljohn, "Low Fan Ceiling," 1E.

27. "This Year the Falcons are Back in Black," *Sporting News*, September 17, 1990, 4; *Falcons Newsletter*, 1991, AFF, Football HOF; Andy Friedlander, "The Marketing of Deion Sanders," *Sporting News*, June 12, 1989, 47.

28. Russell Shaw, "Whistling Victory in Dixie," *Sporting News*, October 1, 1990, 8.

29. *Tomahawk Magazine*, April 1997, ABF, Baseball HOF; Caruso, *Turner Field*, 21–83.

30. Armond Hill, in phone discussion with the author, August 26, 2019.

31. Rembert Browne, "A Hawks Homecoming," *Grantland*, November 2, 2012; Denberg, Lazenby, and Stinson, *From Sweet Lou to 'Nique*, 63–69.

32. "Meet the Owners: Atlanta Hawks and Atlanta Thrashers," *Atlanta Journal-Constitution*, April 4, 2004, 1A; Richard Sandomir, "Philips to Pay $180 Million to Name New Atlanta Arena," February 3, 1999, *New York Times*, 47; Furman Bisher, "Omni Offered Moments of Splendor," *Atlanta Journal-Constitution*, April 20, 1997, 18E; Adi Joseph, "Barry Levenson Will Sell Atlanta Hawks after Releasing Racist Email," USA *Today*, September 7, 2014, https://www.usatoday.com/story/sports/nba/hawks/2014/09/07/bruce-levenson-racist-email-atlanta-owner-sell-team/15241591/.

33. Mark Bradley, "Does Atlanta Care about the Braves?," *Atlanta Journal-Constitution*, October 2, 2002, 1A; Caruso, *Turner Field*, 21–83; Bisher, "After Merger," 1.

34. Max Blau, "Bye-Bye, Braves," Creative Loafing, November 19, 2013, https://creativeloafing.com/content-185671-cover-story-bye-bye-braves; Walter, "Mapping Braves Country"; Charlie Harper, "Opinion—A New Cobb?," Creative Loafing, November 27, 2013, https://creativeloafing.com/content-230661-opinion---a-new-cobb.

35. Harper, "A New Cobb?"; Dan Klepal and Brad Schrade, "Cobb Commissioners Approve Braves Stadium Deal," *Atlanta Journal-Constitution*, May 28, 2014; Blau, "Bye-Bye, Braves."

36. Thomas Wheatley, "Mayor and Falcons Strike Stadium Deal," *Atlanta-Journal Constitution*, March 7, 2013, 1.

24. Loserville, U.S.A.

1. Richard W. Johnson, "A Playground Divided," *Sports Illustrated*, November 8, 1971, 32–43.

2. "The Owners," *Sports Illustrated*, September 13, 1993, 40–44; "Game Over," *San Diego Union-Tribune*, January 12, 2017, 1; MacCambridge, *America's Game*, 161; William Mack, "Another View from the Top," *Sports Illustrated*, May 9, 1988.

3. Johnson, "Playground Divided," 32–43.

4. "Owners," 40–44.

5. Ray Kennedy, "Who Are These Guys?," *Sports Illustrated*, January 31, 1977, 54.

6. Johnson, "Playground Divided," 32–43.

7. Willes, *Rebel League*, 6–7; Jerry McGee, "San Diego Sports Icon Bob Breitbard Dies at 91," *San Diego Union-Tribune*, May 17, 2010, 2.

8. Harris, *League*, 109–11, 132–35, 157–59; Morgan, *Glory for Sale*, 102; Vrooman, "Franchise Free Agency," 209.

9. Kennedy, "Who Are These Guys?," 50.

10. Vito Stellino, "NFL Owners Love the Stadium," *Sporting News*, October 9, 1989, 42; Nick Pugliese, "Mr. C," *Sporting News*, September 5, 1994, 6; Paul Attner, "Seeing Is Deceiving," *Sporting News*, September 23, 1996, 28; Spirou and Bennett, *It's Hardly Sportin'*, 20; Jeff Testerman, "We Paid for It; It Paid Off," *St. Petersburg Times*, January 25, 2001, 1.

11. Jozsa, *Major League Baseball Expansions and Relocations*, 37; "Which Expansion Team Has the Brighter Future?," *Sports Illustrated*, April 20, 1998, 28; E. M. Swift, "Hey Fans, Sit on It," *Sports Illustrated*, May 15, 2000, 38; "Baseball Panel Backs Phoenix, Tampa Bay," *Arizona Republic*, March 8, 1995, A1, A16.

12. Al Morganti, "A Stormy Start," *Sporting News*, November 15, 1991, 38; Fischler, *Cracked Ice*, 309–13.

13. Morganti, "Stormy Start," 38; Swift, "Hey Fans, Sit on It," 38.

14. Bob Logan, "Colangelo Has Suns Climbing for Summit," *Chicago Tribune*, May 23, 1976, B3; "Jerry Colangelo," *Arizona Republic*, May 12, 1995, BB2; Joe Gilmartin, "Suns' Colangelo NBA Executive of the Year," *Sporting News*, May 16, 1981, 46.

15. Harris, *League*, 132, 157, 208, 562–65; Steadman, *From Colts to Ravens*, 6–7, 217; MacCambridge, *America's Game*, 354.

16. Morgan, *Glory for Sale*, 22–23, 158; Jozsa, *Football Fortunes*, 61–62; Steadman, *From Colts to Ravens*, 24, 260; MacCambridge, *America's Game*, 354.

17. Morgan, *Glory for Sale*, 22–23, 158; Jozsa, *Football Fortunes*, 61–62.

18. Rick Thompson, "A History of the Cactus League," *Spring Training Magazine*, March 1989, 4–7; Gary Rausch, "The Cactus League Is a Major League Tourist Attraction in Arizona," *Chicago Tribune*, February 26, 1989, M23.

19. Baim, "Sports Stadiums as 'Wise Investments,'" 15–16.

20. "Baseball Panel Backs Phoenix, Tampa Bay," *Arizona Republic*, March 8, 1995, A1, A16; "DBacks Ownership a Mixed Bag," *Arizona Republic*, March 30, 1998, C33; Richard Obert, "Floating on Air, Colangelo Readies Big Party Today," *Arizona Republic*, March 11, 1995, C1.

21. "County Close to Deal on Ballpark," *Arizona Republic*, January 9, 1994, A1; David Schwartz and Eric Miller, "Negotiators Strike Deal on Big-League Ballpark," *Arizona Republic*, January 15, 1994, A1; "Supervisor Is Shot," *Arizona Republic*, August 14, 1997, A1, A12; William Hermann, "Suspect: Tax Spurred Shooting," *Arizona Republic*, August 14, 1997, A1, A12; Mike McCloy, "Wilcox Snags 50 Tickets for Opening," *Arizona Republic*, March 31, 1998, A1; Mike McCloy, "'Guy Has a Gun,'" *Arizona Republic*, August 15, 1997, A1.

22. Ken Rosenthal, "All Arizona Has to Do Now, Right Now, Is Win," *Sporting News*, March 12, 2001, 49; Nick Piecoro, "Jerry Colangelo's Shadow Remains Prominent," AZCentral.com, September 27, 2014, https://www.azcentral.com /story/sports/mlb/diamondbacks/2014/09/27/jerry-colangelos-shadow-remains -prominent-diamondbacks/16344607/.

23. Michael Farber, "Out of the Ashes," *Sports Illustrated*, September 21, 2009, 34.

Bibliography

....

Manuscripts and Archives

Digital Library of Georgia, University of Georgia Libraries, Athens, Georgia
    "Interview with Hawks Coach," WSB-TV news clip aired May 1, 1968, http://dbsmaint.galib.uga.edu/news/clips/wsbn08200.html
    "News Clip of Mayor Ivan Allen on His Decision Not to Run for Re-Election in a Speech before the Rotary Club on the Race Problems of Atlanta, Georgia," WSB-TV news clip aired January 6, 1969, https://dlg.usg.edu/record/ugabma_wsbn_wsbn44605
Fulton County Commissioner, Roswell, Georgia
    "Minutes of Special Call Meeting, November 29, 1995," FultonCountyGa.gov, November 29, 1995, accessed June 7, 2016, http://agendaminutes.fultoncountyga.gov/sirepub/cache/2/ctsjiklqskjlhdquvjh2x3z0/18363206192021083240668.PDF
Kenan Research Library at the Atlanta History Center, Atlanta, Georgia
    Allen Family Papers (AFP)
    Atlanta Braves Subject File (ABSF)
    Atlanta Chiefs Subject File (ACSF)
    Atlanta Flames Subject File (AFLAMSF)
    Atlanta Fulton-County Stadium Subject File (AFCSSF)
    Atlanta Hawks Subject File (AHSF)
    Atlanta Regional Commission Papers (ARCP)
    Auto Racing Subject File (ARSF)
    Billy Graham Subject File (BGSF)
    Central Atlanta Progress, Inc. Papers (CAPP)
    Forward Atlanta Subject File (FASF)
    Ivan Allen Mayoral Papers (IAMP)
    Omni Subject File (OSF)
    Metropolitan Atlanta Crime Commission Papers (MACCP)
    Research Atlanta Papers (RAP)
    Sam Massell Personality File (SMPF)
    Stephen Prothero Papers (SPP)
    Underground Atlanta Subject File (UASF)
    Wrestling Subject File (WSF)
National Baseball Hall of Fame and Museum Archives, Cooperstown, New York

Bibliography

Atlanta Braves Folders (ABF)
Atlanta Crackers Folder (ACF)
Hank Aaron Folders (HAF)
Mascot Folder (MF)
Professional Football Hall of Fame Museum Archives, Canton, Ohio
Atlanta Falcons Folders (AFF)
University of Georgia Athletic Department, Athens, Georgia
"University of Georgia Home Football Attendance, 1950–1980," unpublished
document provided by Michael Terry, May 15, 2012
University of Virginia Census Database
Atlanta Historical City and County Data Books, accessed June 2, 2013 (page
discontinued), http://www2.lib.virginia.edu/ccdb/
U.S. Census Bureau
"Cities: Table C." Census.gov, accessed May 21, 2021, https://www2.census.gov
/library/publications/2010/compendia/ccdb07/tabc.pdf
"Historical Income Tables: Household." Census.gov. Accessed January 7, 2015
(page discontinued), https://www.census.gov/hhes/www/income/data
/historical/household/

Published Works

Aaron, Henry, and Furman Bisher. *Aaron.* New York: Crowell, 1974.
Aaron, Henry, and Lonnie Wheeler. *I Had a Hammer: The Hank Aaron Story.* New
York: Harper Collins, 1989.
Abbott, Carl, and Becky M. Nicolaides. "Professional Sports and Sunbelt Cities."
OAH Magazine of History 18, no. 1 (October 2003): 27–28.
Allen, Frederick. *Atlanta Rising.* Atlanta: Longstreet, 1996.
Allen, Ivan, and Paul Hemphill. *Mayor: Notes on the Sixties.* New York: Simon &
Schuster, 1971.
Ambrose, Andy. *Atlanta: An Illustrated History.* Athens GA: Hill Street, 2003.
Association for Professional Basketball Research. "NBA/ABA Home Attendance
Totals." Accessed January 5, 2014. http://www.apbr.org/attendance.html.
Baade, Robert A., and Allen R. Sanderson. "Employment Effect of Teams
and Sports Facilities." In *Sports, Jobs, and Taxes: The Economic Impact
of Professional Sports Teams and Stadiums*, edited by Roger Noll and
Andrew Zimbalist, 92–118. Washington DC: Brookings Institution
Press, 1997.
Baim, Dean. "Sports Stadiums as 'Wise Investments': An Evaluation." *Heartland
Policy Study* 32 (November 1990): 591–603.
Bayor, Ronald. "The Civil Rights Movement as Urban Reform: Atlanta's Black
Neighborhoods and a New 'Progressivism.'" *Georgia Historical Quarterly* 77,
no. 2 (Summer 1993): 289–92.
———. *Race and the Shaping of Twentieth-Century Atlanta.* Chapel Hill: Univer-
sity of North Carolina Press, 1996.
Beekman, Scott. *Ringside: A History of Professional Wrestling in America.* West-
port CT: Praeger, 2006.
Beisner, John. "Sports Franchise Relocation: Competitive Markets and Taxpayer
Protection." *Yale Law and Policy Review* 6, no. 2 (1988): 429–48.

Bibliography

Bellamy, Robert V., Jr., and James R. Walker. "Did Televised Baseball Kill the 'Golden Age' of the Minor Leagues?." *NINE: A Journal of Baseball History and Culture* 13, no. 1 (2004): 59–68.

Bernat, G. Andrew. "Convergence in State Per Capita Personal Income, 1950–99." In *Survey of Current Business*, edited by US Bureau of Economic Analysis, 36–48. Washington DC: US Bureau of Economic Analysis, June 2001. https://apps.bea.gov/scb/pdf/2001/06june/0601cspi.pdf.

Bisher, Furman. *The Atlanta Falcons: Violence and Victory.* Englewood Cliffs NJ: Prentice Hall, 1973.

––––––. *Miracle in Atlanta: The Atlanta Braves Story.* Cleveland: World, 1966.

Booth, Geoffrey. *Transforming Suburban Business Districts.* Washington DC: Urban Land Institute, 2001.

Bragan, Bobby, and Jeff Guinn. *You Can't Hit the Ball with the Bat on Your Shoulder: The Baseball Life and Times of Bobby Bragan.* Fort Worth TX: Summit Group, 1992.

Brown, Scot. "'And the Beat Goes On': SOLAR—The Sound of Los Angeles Records." In *Issues in African-American Music: Power, Gender, Race, Representation,* 165–71. Edited by Portia K. Maultsby and Mellonee V. Burnim. Abington, UK: Routledge, 2016.

Bryant, Howard. *The Last Hero: A Life of Henry Aaron.* New York: Pantheon, 2010.

Buege, Bob. *The Milwaukee Braves: A Baseball Eulogy.* New York: Douglas American Sports, 1988.

Bullard, Robert D., Glen S. Johnson, and Angel O. Torres. "Dismantling Transportation Apartheid: The Quest for Equality." In *Sprawl City: Race, Politics, and Planning in Atlanta,* edited by Robert D. Bullard, Glen S. Johnson, and Angel O. Torres, 39–68. Washington DC: Island, 2000.

Burnes, Robert L. *Big Red: The Story of the Football Cardinals.* Saint Charles MO: Piraeus, 1975.

Caruso, Gary. *Turner Field: Rarest of Diamonds.* Atlanta: Longstreet, 1997.

Cave, Martin, and Robert W. Crandall. "Sports Rights and the Broadcast Industry." *Economic Journal* 111 (February 2001): 3–5.

Coates, Dennis, and Brad R. Humphreys. "The Stadium Gambit and Local Economic Development." *Regulation* 23, no. 2 (2000): 15–20.

Cook, James. *Carl Sanders: Spokesman of the New South.* Macon GA: Mercer University Press, 1993.

Danielson, Michael. *Home Team: Professional Sports and the American Metropolis.* Princeton NJ: Princeton University Press, 2001.

Davidson, Donald, and Jesse Outlar. *Caught Short.* New York: Atheneum, 1972.

Davidson, Gary. *Breaking the Game Wide Open.* New York: Atheneum, 1974.

Denberg, Jeffrey, Roland Lazenby, and Tom Stinson. *From Sweet Lou to 'Nique.* Edited by Arthur Triche. Atlanta: Longstreet, 1992.

Euchner, Charles. *Playing the Field: Why Sports Teams Move and Cities Fight to Keep Them.* Baltimore: Johns Hopkins University Press, 1993.

Fields, Robert. *Take Me Out to the Crowd: Ted Turner and the Atlanta Braves.* Huntsville AL: Strode, 1977.

Fischler, Stan. *Cracked Ice: An Insider's Look at the NHL.* Lincolnwood IL: Masters, 1999.

Ford, Mark. "The Coaches' All-America Game." *Coffin Corner* 25, no. 2 (2003): 15–18.

Gendzel, Glen. "Competitive Boosterism: How Milwaukee Lost the Braves." *Business History Review* 69, no. 4 (1995): 530–66.

George, Nelson. *Elevating the Game: Black Men and Basketball*. New York: Harper Collins, 1992.

———. *Where Did Our Love Go?: The Rise and Fall of the Motown Sound*. New York: Omnibus, 2003.

Georgia Institute of Technology Department of Athletics. *Engineering for Success: Georgia Tech Football Media Guide 2011*. Atlanta: Georgia Institute of Technology, 2011.

Glover, Renee Lewis. "The Atlanta Blueprint: Transforming Public Housing Citywide." Atlanta Housing Authority, 2012. Accessed July 2, 2015 (page discontinued). http://www.atlantahousing.org/pdfs/Chapter8_TheAtlantaBlueprint.pdf.

Golenbock, Peter. *The Spirit of St. Louis: A History of the St. Louis Cardinals and Browns*. New York: It Books, 2001.

Greenberg, Martin. *The Stadium Game*. Milwaukee WI: Marquette University Press, 2001.

Halberstam, David. *The Breaks of the Game*. New York: Ballantine, 1981.

Hamilton, Milo. *Making Airwaves: 60 Years at Milo's Microphone*. Champaign IL: Sport Publishing, 2006.

Harris, David. *The League*. New York: Bantam, 1987.

Hartshorn, Truman. *Metropolis in Georgia: Atlanta's Rise as a Major Transaction Center*. Atlanta: Ballinger, 1976.

Headley, Bernard. *The Atlanta Youth Murders and the Politics of Race*. Carbondale: Southern Illinois University Press, 1999.

Hein, Virginia. "The Image of a 'City Too Busy to Hate': Atlanta in the 1960s." *Phylon* 33, no. 3 (Fall 1972): 205–6.

Hinton, Elizabeth. *From the War on Poverty to the War on Crime: The Making of Mass Incarceration in America*. Cambridge MA: Harvard University Press, 2016.

History of the WWE. "The Omni," 2014. Accessed June 1, 2016. http://www.thehistoryofwwe.com/omni70s.htm.

Hope, Bob. *We Could've Finished Last without You: An Irreverent Look at the Atlanta Braves, the Losingest Team in Baseball for the Past 25 Years*. Atlanta: Longstreet, 1991.

Hornbaker, Tim. *National Wrestling Alliance: The Untold Story of the Monopoly that Strangled Professional Wrestling*. Toronto: ECW, 2007.

Hornsby, Alton. "Black Public Education in Atlanta, Georgia, 1954–1973: From Segregation to Segregation." *Journal of Negro History* 76, no. 1 (Winter 1991): 21–47.

Huber, Jim, and Tom Saladino. *The Babes of Winter: An Inside History of Atlanta Flames Hockey*. Huntsville AL: Strode, 1975.

James, Mark. *Wrestling Record Book: Atlanta, GA, 1960–1984*. Memphis TN: Memphis Wrestling History, 2014.

Jaret, C. L., E. P. Ruddiman, and K. Phillips. "The Legacy of Residential Segregation." In *Sprawl City: Race, Politics, and Planning in Atlanta*, edited by Robert D. Bullard, Glen S. Johnson, and Angel O. Torres, 122–29. Washington DC: Island, 2000.

Bibliography

Johnson, Arthur T. "Congress and Professional Sports: 1951–1978." *Annals of the American Academy of Political and Social Science* 445 (1979): 102–15.

———. "Municipal Administration and the Sports Franchise Relocation Issue." *Public Administration Review* 43, no. 6 (November-December, 1983): 519–28.

Josza, Frank. *Big Sports, Big Business: A Century of League Expansions, Mergers, and Reorganizations.* Westport CT: Praeger, 2006.

———. *Football Fortunes: The Business, Organization, and Strategy of the NFL.* Jefferson NC: McFarland, 2010.

———. *Major League Baseball Expansions and Relocations, 1876–2008.* Jefferson NC: McFarland, 2008.

Kahn, Roger. *The Boys of Summer.* New York: Harper Perennial, 2006.

Kazin, Michael. *The Populist Persuasion: An American History.* Ithaca NY: Cornell University Press, 1998.

Keating, Larry. "Atlanta: Peoplestown—Resilience and Tenacity versus Institutional Hostility." In *Rebuilding Urban Neighborhoods: Achievements, Opportunities, and Limits,* edited by W. Dennis Keating and Norman Krumholz, 33–40. Thousand Oaks CA: Sage, 1999.

———. *Atlanta: Race, Class, and Urban Expansion.* Philadelphia: Temple University Press, 2001.

Kinlaw, Francis. "The Franchise Transfer That Fostered a Broadcasting Revolution." Society for American Baseball Research, 2010. Accessed June 23, 2014. http://sabr.org/research/franchise-transfer-fostered-broadcasting-revolution.

Kriegel, Mark. *Pistol: The Life of Pete Maravich.* New York: Free Press, 2007.

Kruse, Kevin. *White Flight: Atlanta and the Making of Modern Conservatism.* Princeton NJ: Princeton University Press, 2005.

Kuhn, Clifford, Harlan E. Joy, and E. Bernard West. *Living Atlanta: An Oral History of the City, 1914–1948.* Athens: University of Georgia Press, 1990.

Lassiter, Matthew. *The Silent Majority: Suburban Politics in the Sunbelt South.* Princeton NJ: Princeton University Press, 2006.

Laub, Richard. *Single Family Residential Development: Dekalb County 1945–1970.* Atlanta: Georgia State University Historic Preservation Program, Spring 2010. Accessed October 1, 2014. http://www.dekalbhistory.org/documents/Single-FamilyResidentialDevinDeKalbCounty.pdf.

Leone, Katherine. "No Team, No Peace: Franchise Free Agency in the National Football League." *Columbia Law Review* 97, no. 2 (March 1997): 473–523.

Lipsitz, George. "Sports Stadia and Urban Development." *Journal of Sports and Social Issues* 8 (1984): 1–17.

H. W. Lochner & Company and De Leuw, Cather & Company. *Highway and Transportation Plan for Atlanta, Georgia.* Atlanta: Georgia Institute of Technology, January 1946. Accessed June 12, 2013. https://smartech.gatech.edu/handle/1853/36611?show=full.

Long, Judith Grant. "Public Funding for Major League Sports Facilities Data Series (5): A History of Public Funding, 1890 to 2005." Edward J. Bloustein School of Planning and Public Policy Center for Urban Research Working Paper Series, New Brunswick NJ, 2006.

MacCambridge, Michael. *America's Game: The Epic Story of How Pro Football Captured a Nation.* New York: Random House, 2004.

Maddox, Lester G. *Speaking Out: The Autobiography of Lester Garfield Maddox.* Garden City NY: Doubleday, 1975.

Maracek, Greg. *Full Court: The Untold Stories of the St. Louis Hawks.* St. Louis MO: Reedy, 2006.

————. *The St. Louis Football Cardinals: A Celebration of the Big Red.* St Louis MO: Reedy, 2009.

Martin, Charles H. "Racial Change and 'Big Time' College Football in Georgia: 1892–1957." *Georgia Historical Quarterly* 80, no. 3 (Fall 1996): 532–62.

Martin, Harold H. *William Berry Hartsfield, Mayor of Atlanta.* Athens: University of Georgia Press, 1978.

Miller, James Edward. *The Baseball Business: Pursuing Pennants and Profits in Baltimore.* Chapel Hill: University of North Carolina Press, 1990.

Miller, Jeff. *Going Long: The Wild 10-Year Saga of the Renegade American Football League in the Words of Those Who Lived It.* New York: McGraw-Hill, 2004.

Miller, Steven P. *Billy Graham and the Rise of the Republican South.* Philadelphia: University of Pennsylvania Press, 2008.

Morgan, Jon. *Glory for Sale: Fans, Dollars, and the New NFL.* Baltimore MD: Bancroft, 1997.

Nagin, Tomiko. *Courage to Dissent: Atlanta and the Long History of the Civil Rights Movement.* Oxford, UK: Oxford University Press, 2011.

NFL Films. "1974 Atlanta Falcons Team Season Highlights: 'A Fresh Start.'" YouTube video posted, May 25, 2020, by Sports Odyssey. https://www.youtube.com/watch?v=JtnXlGR3nVw.

Noll, Roger, and Andrew Zimbalist. "Build the Stadium—Create the Jobs." In *Sports, Jobs, and Taxes: The Economic Impact of Professional Sports Teams and Stadiums,* edited by Roger Noll and Andrew Zimbalist, 7–14. Washington DC: Brookings Institution Press, 1997.

————, eds. *Sports, Jobs, and Taxes: The Economic Impact of Professional Sports Teams and Stadiums.* Washington DC: Brookings Institution Press, 1997.

Olson, James. *Stuart Symington: A Life.* Columbia: University of Missouri Press, 2003.

Patterson, Eugene. "1961: The Rock and the Anchor." In *The Changing South of Gene Patterson: Journalism and Civil Rights, 1960–1968,* edited by Roy Peter Clark and Raymond Arsenault, 61–88. Gainesville: University Press of Florida, 2002.

Pedicino, Joe, dir. *The History of Professional Wrestling in Atlanta.* Aired May 19, 1986, on WATL.

Pistol Pete Videos. "Reflections on Pistol Pete Maravich" Video. April 15, 2019. https://www.pistol-pete-videos.com/reflections-on-pistol-pete-maravich/.

Pomerantz, Gary. *Where Peachtree Meets Sweet Auburn.* New York: Scribner, 1996.

Povletich, William, dir. *A Braves New World.* 1992; Milwaukee: Wisconsin Historical Society, 2009. DVD.

Preston, Joseph G. *Major League Baseball in the 1970s: A Modern Game Emerges.* Jefferson NC: McFarland, 2004.

Quirk, James P. "An Economic Analysis of Team Movements in Professional Sports," *Law and Contemporary Problems* 38, no. 1 (Spring 1973): 42–66.

Ribowsky, Mark. *Slick: The Silver-and-Black Life of Al Davis.* New York: MacMillian, 1991.

Bibliography

Rice, Bradley R. "Urbanization, 'Atlanta-ization,' and Suburbanization: Three Themes for the Urban History of Twentieth Century Georgia." *Georgia Historical Quarterly* 68, no. 1 (Spring 1984): 45–46.

Riess, Steven A. *City Games: The Evolution of Urban Society and the Rise of Sports.* Urbana: University of Illinois Press, 1991.

Rodgers, Pepper, and Al Thomy. *Pepper!: The Autobiography of an Unconventional Coach.* New York: Doubleday, 1976.

Rosen, Charlie. *The First Tip-Off: The Incredible Story of the Birth of the NBA.* New York: McGraw-Hill, 2008.

Rosentraub, Mark. "Are Public Policies Needed to Level the Playing Field Between Cities and Teams?" *Journal of Urban Affairs* 21, no. 4 (1999): 377–95.

———. *Major League Losers: The Real Cost of Sports and Who's Paying for It.* New York: Basic, 1999.

Rosenzweig, Roy. *Eight Hours for What We Will: Workers and Leisure in an Industrial City, 1870–1920.* Oxford, UK: Oxford University Press, 1983.

Rutheiser, Charles. *Imagineering Atlanta: The Politics of Place in the City of Dreams.* New York: Verso, 1996.

Santo, Charles. "Beyond the Economic Catalyst Debate: Can Public Consumption Benefits Justify a Municipal Stadium Investment?" *Journal of Urban Affairs* 29, no. 5 (2007): 455–79.

Schaeffer, William A., and Lawrence F. Davidson. *The Economic Impact of the Falcons on Atlanta, 1973.* Atlanta: Atlanta Falcons, 1973.

———. *The Economic Impact of the Falcons on Atlanta, 1984.* Atlanta: Atlanta Falcons, 1984.

Schroeder, Larry D., and David L. Sjoquist, "The Rational Voter: An Analysis of Two Atlanta Referenda on Rapid Transit." *Public Choice* 33, no. 3 (1978): 27–31.

Schulman, Bruce J. *From Cotton Belt to Sunbelt: Federal Policy, Economic Development, and the Transformation of the South, 1938–1980.* Oxford, UK: Oxford University Press, 1991.

———. *The Seventies: The Great Shift in American Culture, Politics, and Society.* New York: Free Press, 2001.

Self, Robert. *American Babylon: Race and the Struggle for Postwar Oakland.* Princeton NJ: Princeton University Press, 2004.

Setlist.fm. Al Green Concert Setlists & Tour Dates. Accessed January 17, 2015. https://www.setlist.fm/setlists/al-green-bd6b9a6.html.

———. Atlanta Stadium. Accessed June 23, 2013. http://www.setlist.fm/venue/atlanta-stadium-atlanta-ga-usa-13d6551d.html.

———. The Omni Atlanta Concert Setlists, Georgia. Accessed January 17, 2015. https://www.setlist.fm/venue/the-omni-atlanta-ga-usa-4bd637ba.html.

Shoemaker, David, *The Squared Circle: Life, Death, and Professional Wrestling.* New York: Avery, 2013.

Short, Bob. *Everything is Pickrick: The Life of Lester Maddox.* Macon GA: Mercer University Press, 1999.

Shropshire, Kenneth. *The Sports Franchise Game: Cities in Pursuit of Sport Franchises, Events, Stadiums, and Arenas.* Philadelphia: University of Pennsylvania, 1995.

Solie, Gordon. "Gordon Solie Interview." By Jeremy Hartley. Transcribed by Earl Oliver. *Solie's Vintage Wrestling*, 1998. Accessed January 17, 2014. http://www .solie.org/interviews/solie2.html.

Spirou, Costas, and Larry Bennett. *It's Hardly Sportin': Stadiums, Neighborhoods, and the New Chicago*. Dekalb: Northern Illinois University Press, 2003.

Steadman, John F. *From Colts to Ravens: A Behind the Scenes Look at Baltimore Professional Football*. Baltimore: Tidewater, 1997.

Stone, Clarence. *Regime Politics: Governing Atlanta, 1946–1988*. Lawrence: University Press of Kansas, 1989.

Stuart, Jeffrey Saint John. *Twilight Teams*. San Francisco: Sark, 2000.

Sugrue, Thomas. *The Origins of the Urban Crisis: Race and Inequality in Post-War Detroit*. Princeton NJ: Princeton University Press, 1996.

Thompson, Fletcher. *Review of Certain Aspects of the Model Cities Program in Atlanta, Georgia*. Washington DC: Department of Housing and Urban Development Publications, August 1971. Accessed June 11, 2013. https://www.gao .gov/products/b-171500-10.

Torre, Joe, and Tom Verducci. *Chasing the Dream: My Lifelong Journey to the World Series*. New York: Bantam, 1997.

Trumpbour, Robert. *The New Cathedrals: Politics and Media in the History of Stadium Construction*. Syracuse NY: Syracuse University Press, 2006.

Turner, Ted, and Bill Burke. *Call Me Ted*. New York: Grand Central, 2008.

Tygiel, Jules. *Baseball's Great Experiment: Jackie Robinson and His Legacy*. Oxford, UK: Oxford University Press, 2008.

U.S. Congress Office of Technology Assessment. *An Assessment of Community Planning for Mass Transit: Volume 2: Atlanta Case Study*. Washington DC: U.S. Government Printing Office, 1976. Accessed June 12, 2013. http://digital .library.unt.edu/ark:/67531/metadc39346/.

U.S. Department of Justice. National Criminal Justice Information and Statistics Service. *Crime in Eight American Cities: Advance Report*. Washington DC: U.S. Department of Justice, July 1974.

Van Wieren, Pete, and Bob Klapisch. *The Braves: An Illustrated History of America's Team*. Atlanta: Turner, 1995.

Veeck, Bill. *The Hustler's Handbook*. New York: Putnam, 1965.

Vrooman, John. "Franchise Free Agency in Professional Sports Leagues." *Southern Economic Journal* 64, no. 1 (1997): 191–219.

Walker, Jack L. "Protest and Negotiation: A Case Study of Negro Leadership in Atlanta." *Midwest Journal of Political Science* 7, no. 2 (May 1963): 111.

Walter, Andy. "Mapping Braves Country." *Atlanta Studies*, November 2, 2015. https://doi.org/10.18737/atls20150909.

Weise, Andrew. *Places of Their Own: African American Suburbanization in the Twentieth Century*. Chicago: University of Chicago Press, 2005.

Whitlegg, Drew, "A Battle on Two Fronts: Competitive Urges 'Inside' Atlanta." *Area*, June 2002, 128–38.

Wiley, Peter, and Robert Gottlieb. *Empires in the Sun: The Rise of the New American West*. New York: Putnam, 1982.

Bibliography

Willes, Ed. *The Rebel League: The Short and Unruly Life of the World Hockey Association.* Toronto: McClelland & Stewart, 2005.

Williams, Pat, and James Denney. *Ahead of the Game: The Pat Williams Story.* Grand Rapids MI: Baker, 1999.

Zimbalist, Andrew. *May the Best Team Win: Baseball Economics and Public Policy.* Washington DC: Brookings Institution Press, 2004.

Index

....

Index

Index

Index

Index